Wombs and Alien Spirits

New Directions in Anthropological Writing

History, Poetics, Cultural Criticism

George E. Marcus, Rice University
James Clifford, University of California, Santa Cruz
Editors

Nationalism and the Politics of Culture in Quebec
Richard Handler

The Pastoral Son and the Spirit of Patriarchy:
Religion, Society, and Person among East African Stock Keepers
Michael E. Meeker

Belonging in America: Reading Between the Lines
Constance Perin

Himalayan Dialogue:
Tibetan Lamas and Gurung Shamans in Nepal
Stan Royal Mumford

Wombs and Alien Spirits:
Women, Men, and the *Zār* Cult in Northern Sudan
Janice Boddy

People as Subject, People as Object:
Selfhood and Peoplehood in Contemporary Israel
Virginia R. Domínguez

Debating Muslims:
Cultural Dialogues in Postmodernity and Tradition
Michael M. J. Fischer and Mehdi Abedi

Sharing the Dance:
Contact Improvisation and American Culture
Cynthia J. Novack

Wombs and Alien Spirits

Women, Men, and the Zār *Cult in Northern Sudan*

Janice Boddy

The University of Wisconsin Press

The University of Wisconsin Press
114 North Murray Street
Madison, Wisconsin 53715

3 Henrietta Street
London WC2E 8LU, England

5 4 3

Printed in the United States of America

Library of Congress Cataloging-in-Publication Data
Boddy, Janice Patricia.
Wombs and alien spirits: women, men, and the Zār cult in northern Sudan/Janice Boddy.
422 pp. cm.—(New directions in anthropological writing)
Bibliography: pp. 363–383
Includes index.
1. Women, Muslim—Sudan. 2. Zār—Sudan. 3. Marriage customs and rites, Islamic—Sudan. 4. Spirit possession—Sudan. 5. Sex customs—Sudan. I. Title. II. Series.
HQ1793.5.B64 1989
305.3′09625—dc20 89-40250
ISBN 0-299-12310-3 CIP
ISBN 0-299-12314-6 (pbk.)

for the women of "Hofriyat"
from a kindred spirit

Contents

Tables and Figures

Tables

Figures

Acknowledgments

Wombs and Alien Spirits has had a long gestation, and there are many to whom I am grateful for assistance with its birth. Any list of individuals will be plagued by omissions, but in particular I would like to thank the following for their hospitalities, kindnesses, comments, and inspirations. Laurie Arnold Abi-Habib, Nadia Abu-Zahara, Julie Anderson, Pauline Aucoin, Judith Brown, Kenelm Burridge, Marcia Calkowski, Jenny Carpenter, Isobel Clark, Peter Clark, Elizabeth Coville, Carole Farber, Lina Fruzzetti, Ellen Gruenbaum, Krz Grzymski, Sondra Hale, Carol Holzberg, Hanna Kassis, John G. Kennedy, Jack Kirshbaum, Linda LaMacchia, Michael Lambek, John LeRoy, George Marcus, Gordon Lester-Massman, Tom McFeat, Shuichi Nagata, Jay O'Brien, Sarah Orel, Sandra Pady, the Pagoulatos family, Judith Pugh, Chip Reed, Debbie Reed, Pam Reed, Peter Shinnie (to whom I am deeply indebted), Jacqueline Solway, and Elvi Whittaker. I am grateful to members of the University of Calgary—University of Khartoum archaeological expedition to Meroë for much needed moral support, and to friends and family in Canada (who worried, twice). Fieldwork in Sudan was made possible by a Canada Council Doctoral Research Fellowship and travel grant, and a Social Sciences and Humanities Research Council of Canada Postdoctoral Fellowship. I was assisted in obtaining the appropriate research permissions by Dr. Abu Salim and Dr. Muhammad Ibrahim Ahmed of the National Records Office in Khartoum; and by Dr. Abdel Ghaffar Mohammed Ahmed and Dr. Atif Saghayroun of the Economic and Social Research Council of Sudan. My husband, Ronald Wright, first drew my attention to similarities between *zār* and the genre of allegory, took time from his own writing to read the manuscript in its entirety, and helped in more ways than I can say. But above all, I am profoundly grateful to the people of "Hofriyat" and its urban settlements, without whose care, cooperation, and welcome my research was sure to have failed. To them, and to their spirits, I owe a debt that I can never repay. Our dialogue, I hope, continues.

University of Toronto
April 1989

Note on Transliteration

I have tried to remain faithful to the pronunciation of colloquial Sudanese Arabic while generally following the rendition of Arabic vowel values found in Hans Wehr's *A Dictionary of Modern Written Arabic* (edited by J. Milton Cowan, 1976). The result is a compromise biased in favor of the local dialect, but one which should contain enough information to enable scholars unfamiliar with Sudanese speech to recognize Arabic roots if not actual words. Some discrepancies between colloquial and classical pronunciations are described in the appended glossary (e.g., the colloquial *tōb* is classically written and pronounced *thōb*). For colloquial usage there is no better source than Hillelson's *Sudan Arabic, English-Arabic Vocabulary* (second edition, 1930), though I have not consistently preferred his transliterations. Hillelson, for instance, transcribes the word for "house" as *bēt;* following Wehr I transcribe it as *bayt*. In this book, stressed Arabic consonants are indicated by a dot below the letter, long vowels by a line above. I have not transliterated the letter *hamza,* a glottal stop rarely pronounced in the village where I worked. (The exception to this is note 15, chapter 9.) An inverted comma (ʿ) indicates the Arabic letter *ʿayn,* which has no equivalent in English.

For the sake of readability, familiar place names (Khartoum, Mecca) and the names of individuals (Zaineb, Sadiya) are written as pronounced, not as properly transliterated. Beginning in part 2, the names of individual spirits are italicized (and, where warranted, glossed) so as to distinguish them from humans. Spirit species are distinguished from commonplace Arabic categories by an initial capital, hence *Khawājāt* are "Westerner" spirits, including Europeans, North Americans, Hindus, and Chinese, whereas *khawājāt* are human foreigners. When a spirit species and human group share a designation that is a *proper* noun, only the spirit species is italicized (e.g., Ḥalib [human "gypsy"], *Ḥalib* [spirit "gypsy"]); diacritical marks are preserved in both.

Except where noted, only Arabic singulars are used, plurals being formed by the addition of a nonitalicized *s*. Adjectival and nominal forms of Arabic place names are indicated by the addition of an *i* to the end of a word, as in Arabic. Thus, if Ḥabish refers to Ethiopia or its collective population (and *Ḥabish* refers to the Ethiopian species of spirit), Ḥabishi means an individual Ethiopian or something Ethiopian. Where specifically warranted, feminine forms are rendered by lengthening the terminal *i* and adding *ya,* so that an individual female Ethiopian is a Ḥabishīya.

Not all words in the spoken dialect are Arabic or Arabic derivations. Remnants of earlier vernaculars (whether Nubian or Bejawi) are written as spoken, following Hillelson wherever possible. See Hillelson's introduction to the 1930 edition for a fuller discussion of the colloquial language.

Glossary

Included here are words that appear more than once in the text and are not glossed within it each time, plus dialect words and those whose spoken values (as given in the text) differ from classical renditions.

ʿabīd	slaves
ʿAbīd	the "Slave" or southerner society of *zayran*
ʿādāt	customs, practices, by extension, "our culture"
ʿagl	for *ʿaql,* reason, the ability to behave properly
ʿāila	family, kin group, lineage
ʿamal	black magic; literally, "doing" or "making"
ʿamm	father's brother
ʿamma or *ʿammat*	father's sister
ʿArab	nomad or Arab
ʿArāb	plural of ʿArab
ʿArāb	the "Nomad" or "Arab" society of *zayran*
ʿarīs	bridegroom
ʿarūs	bride
ʿayāna	sick woman, one who is the focus of a *zār* rite
ʿayn ḥārra	hot eye, evil eye
abiyaḍ	white
agārib	relatives, kinsfolk; literally, "close ones" (see *garīb*)
aḥmar	red
akhwān	brothers, siblings
angarīb	Sudanese rope bed
araki	arak, a potent alcoholic beverage
aswad	black
awlād	children, sons (plural of *wad* or *walid*)
awlād ʿamm	patrilateral parallel cousins
awlād ḥarām	bastards, "forbidden children"
awlād khālāt	matrilateral parallel cousins
awlād laban	"milk children": those classed as siblings because nursed by the same woman

bāb	door
bahāim	domestic animals, herd, cattle
bahr	river, Nile
bakhūr	incense
banāt	girls, daughters, or virgins
Banāt	the "Daughters" society of *zayran* (see *Sittat*)
baraka	blessing, God's favor
Bashawāt	the "Pasha" society of *zayran*
bayt	house
bayt al-wilāda	"house of childbirth," womb
bit or *bint*	girl, daughter
bit ʿamm	father's brother's daughter
bowāb	doorman, doorkeeper, "husband" in the language of the *zār*
buṭon	stomach, inside space
dallūka	large pottery drum used in weddings and *zár* ceremonies
darāwīsh	dervishes, holy men, members of religious fraternities
Darāwīsh	the "Holy Men" society of *zayran*
Darwīsh	one member of the *Darāwīsh*; also adjectival form
dasatīr	plural of *dastūr*
dastūr	synonym for *zār* spirit; literally, "door bolt" or, in another context, "permission"
dilka	cosmetic paste made of aromatically smoked dough
dīwān	reception room, men's sitting room
dunyā	this world, earthly existence, opposed to the afterlife in the context of Islam
dura	grain, *Sorghum vulgare*
faki	for *faqi,* local religious leader, holy man, and/or Islamic doctor
fakka-t-ar-rās	pulling apart the head, part of a *zār* ritual
Fallata	West Africans or western Sudanese
Fallata	the "West African" society of *zayran*
Fallatīyat	female "West African" spirits
fataḥ-t-akh-khashm	"opening of the mouth," name of two payments in the context of a wedding
fōg	above, over (position of a *zār* relative to its host)

fugāra	for *fuqara,* plural of *faki*
fūl, fūl maṣri	fava beans, Egyptian beans
gabīla	tribe
gāḍī	for *qāḍī,* religious court judge
gadr	for *qadr,* fate, ability
garʿa	gourd
garāba	closeness, relationship, kinship
garīb	close (adjective)
garībna	our relatives
garmosīs	red and gold bridal veil used also at childbirth and male and female circumcisions
ghabīya or *ghaybūba*	trance; literally, "absence"
ghabiyāna	absent, entranced (feminine)
gūlla	pottery jar, smaller than a *zīr*
Ḥabish	Ethiopia, Ethiopians
Ḥabish	the "Ethiopian" society of *zayran*
Ḥabishī	an individual Ethiopian male, or Ethiopian (adjective)
Ḥabishīya	an individual Ethiopian female, or Ethiopian (adjective)
ḥabōba	grandmother; literally, "little darling"
ḥabōbāt	plural of *ḥabōba*
ḥafla	party, celebration
ḥaj	pilgrimage to Mecca and holy places in the Hejaz
ḥakīm	physician, doctor
ḥalāl	allowable, permissible, legitimate
ḥalāwa	candy, a sweet
Ḥalib	gypsy; collectively, people from Syria, gypsies
Ḥalib	the "Gypsy" society of *zayran*
Ḥalibīya	a female gypsy
ḥall	loosen, untie
ḥamām	pigeon, collectively, pigeons
ḥamāma	one pigeon, or one female pigeon
ḥamāmat	female pigeons
harīra	bracelet of red silk with a long tassel, part of the *jirtig*
ḥārr	hot, painful
hilāl	new moon, crescent, gold piece
ḥilū	sweet (adjective)
ḥinnā	henna

ḥōsh	house yard and/or the wall that encloses it
ḥulāla	loosening, animal sacrifice following childbirth or marriage
ḥumra	local wedding perfume; literally, "redness"
ʿīd	feast
itḥarrig	burn, inflame, said of angered *zayran*
jabūdi	Arab women's dance
jalabīya	men's garment, loose ground length shirt with wide sleeves
janā	fruit, harvest
jinn	spirit (collective)
jinni	one *jinn*
jirtig	charms, jewelry, and cosmetic preparations designed to protect those undergoing crisis rites, particularly if they implicate fertility
karrō	horse or donkey cart
khajal	propriety, shame
khajlāna	ashamed, embarrassed (feminine)
khāl	mother's brother
khālat	also *khāla, khālta,* mother's sister
khālāt	mother's sisters, female siblings in the ascendant generation
khashm	mouth, orifice
khashm al-bayt	subtribe, one man's descendants, front door
khawāja	foreigner or Westerner, "Mr."
Khawāja	the "Westerner" society of *zayran*
khawājāt	plural of *khawāja*
khawājīya	female foreigner or Westerner, "Mrs."
khudām	servants
Khudām	the "Servant" or "Slave" society of *zayran* (see *ʿAbīd*)
khuḍara	green (feminine)
kisra	unleavened waferlike bread made of sorghum flour (*dura*)
koḥl	antimony
laḥma	flesh, meat
layla	night, evening
layla-t-ad-dukhl	"night of entrance," wedding night
layla-t-ag-gayla	"night of staying," night after the wedding
layla-t-al-ḥinnā	"henna night," night before the wedding proper

mahr	bridewealth, given the bride or the bride's father, ostensibly to be kept for her in the event of divorce
marā	woman, nonvirgin
maṭlūga	for *maṭlūqa,* loose woman, woman of questionable morals
maṭlūgāt	plural of *maṭlūga*
mazūr	possessed by a *zār*
mashaṭ	thin braids, married woman's coiffure
mīdān	open area, place used for ceremonial purposes, location of a *zār* ritual
mushāhara	complex of practices, illnesses, and ideas concerning blood; specifically, genital blood associated with femininity and fertility
nafs	animal life force, self (as opposed to "reason," *ʿagl*)
nāʿim	smooth (adjective)
nās	people, folk
nās al-balad	country people, peasantry
nāshif	dry (adjective)
nazal	descend, go into trance
naẓīf	clean (adjective)
nazīf	hemorrhage, excessive blood loss, especially from the vulva
nisba	genealogy, pedigree
nizūl	descent, *zār* "dance," bobbing action attendant on entering trance
nufāsa	woman in childbirth
ragīṣ	dance
ragīṣ bi rugaba	dance of the neck, women's pigeon dance
ragīṣ bi ṣuluba	bride's dance, "dance of the buttocks"
rahaṭ	short skirt made of leather thongs and worn by maidens in the past, often decorated with beads and cowrie shells
raqūba	hut, made of mats and/or reeds
rās	head
rīḥ	wind, spirit
rīḥ al-aḥmar	"red wind," *zār* spirit
rowḥān	plural of *rīḥ*
roṭāna	foreign language; literally, "gibberish"

sadd al-māl	payment, settlement of money, with connotations of blocking up; payment of *mahr* before a wedding
ṣadīg	friend, confidant
sagīya	for *saqīya,* ox-driven irrigation wheel
sāḥar	sorcerer
Sāḥar	the "Sorcerer" society of *zayran*
saʿīd	small antelope (e.g., dik-dik), euphemism for young Hofriyati women
shabāl	woman's gesture of flicking her hair at an approaching man in the context of a wedding dance, said to confer luck
shadīd	strong, very
sharīʿa	religious (Islamic) law
sharmūṭ	air-dried meat cut in strips
sharmūṭa	prostitute
shawaṭīn	devils, evil spirits (plural of *shayṭan*)
shaykh	male leader, person of respect, head of a religious fraternity
shaykha	female curer of the *zar* cult
shaykhat	plural of *shaykha*
shayla	foodstuffs and trousseau items given by the groom to his bride and her family prior to their wedding
shayṭan	devil, evil spirit or black *jinn*
sitt	lady
sitt al-ʿilba	lady of the tin box (of *zār* incense), seer
Sittat	the "Ladies" society of *zayran*
sūq	market
ṭahir	pure
ṭahūr	circumcision; literally, "purification"
ṭallug	for *ṭalluq,* divorce, loosen, set free
ṭarīga	for *ṭarīqa,* path, way, men's religious fraternity
ṭawālī	immediately, directly, straight
ṭisht	aluminum wash tub, used also in drumming the *zār*
tōb	for *thōb,* women's modesty garment: nine meters of cloth divided in two lengths that are sewn together along the length; worn wrapped around the body and covering the head
wad or *walid*	child, son
wad ʿamm	father's brother's son

waḍʿa ash-shubka	setting of the net, or snare; initial gift from groom to bride, hence, engagement
wadī	desert watercourse, dry except during the rains
wazīr	spokesman, aide to the bridegroom
wazīra	spokeswoman, aide to the bride
wilād	children, "those born of . . ."
ẓahr	to make visible, manifest, evident; to gain or have knowledge
zār	a type of spirit, the illness it can cause, and the ritual by which the illness is assuaged; more generally, the "cult" that surrounds such spirits
zarīʿa	crop, offspring
zayran	*zār* spirits
zikr	for *dhikr,* "remembrance" ceremony of the Islamic fraternities
zīr	large water jar
zurīʿa	sprouted grain

Wombs and Alien Spirits

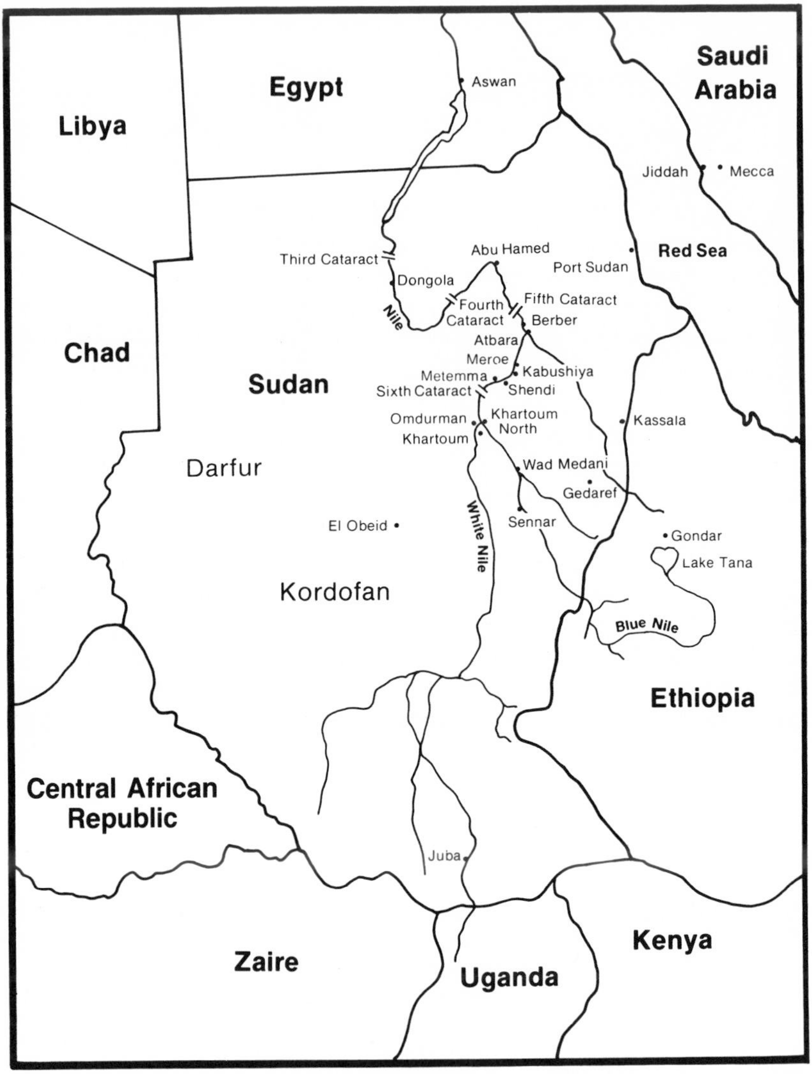
Libya
Egypt
Aswan
Saudi Arabia
Jiddah
Mecca
Red Sea
Port Sudan
Abu Hamed
Third Cataract
Dongola
Nile
Fourth Cataract
Fifth Cataract
Berber
Atbara
Meroe
Metemma
Kabushiya
Shendi
Sixth Cataract
Chad
Sudan
Omdurman
Khartoum North
Khartoum
Kassala
Darfur
Wad Medani
Gedaref
El Obeid
White Nile
Sennar
Gondar
Lake Tana
Kordofan
Blue Nile
Ethiopia
Central African Republic
Juba
Zaire
Uganda
Kenya

Map of Sudan

Prologue

No moon tonight. The courtyard, darkly lit, is fogged with smoke rising from a censer near the musicians. Drums and bell tones break the hot still air—repeating, endlessly, their harsh compulsive rhythms. I am taken up, no longer really here, no longer aware of my foreignness, no longer aware of theirs. A hand reaches down and grabs my arm. Jarred to wakefulness, I stare at a black grinning face, eyes roguish, devilish, but eyes that I know, they are Sumaya's.

She pulls me to my feet, takes my arm like a beau. Locked together we parade through the dancing ground: white woman, embarrassed; Sudanese woman not herself, inhabited by Dodomayo, a Greek zār *spirit who has chosen me for His wife. As usual Dodomayo is drunk, and I must periodically support His weight as he stumbles against me in the dust. A crowd of shrouded chanting women breaks into giggles as He grabs my waist and I react with displeasure. He laughs, leers, tries another embrace, calls out loudly for wine. It is our wedding night . . . but first, first we must dance.*

The drums abruptly stop. I am released. Sumaya's body shudders; she sinks to the ground, covers her face with her wrap. Someone offers a glass of water and she drinks. Moments later she sits upright, sighs, and rubs her legs. She looks weary but composed. The drums begin again, summoning another spirit. Sumaya is returned.

The subject of this book is spirit possession. But equally, it describes the cultural and social context that produces a particular system of possession beliefs and is, in turn, constructed by it. The system of which I write is *zār;* the context a village in northern Arabic-speaking Muslim Sudan that I have called "Hofriyat."[1]

The worlds of Hofriyati humans and *zār* spirits are parallel worlds, and they are contiguous; the latter, within the realm of nature but normally invisible to humans, overlies the former like a transparency covering a map. Just as a transparency illuminates certain characteristics of terrain not immediately apprehended by the reader of a map, so the *zār* world

1. Names of the village and individuals are pseudonyms.

illuminates the human, highlighting its contours and contrasts, casting many of its features—positive and negative—into sharp relief. For those who observe and interact with spirits, as for those who experience possession, the human world is the foundation upon which the spirit world rests; it is ultimately the latter's source of meaning.

The question of how to discover "meaning" in the course of ethnographic research haunted my initial stay in Hofriyat. It was not just that the best I might achieve would be a form of translation, a relatively faithful but nonetheless constructed interpretation of Hofriyati culture. That much was acknowledged from the start. Like most ethnographers I was plagued by the doubt that I could ever come to appreciate the world of my informants in terms which made sense to them.[2] But once in the village the problem was more acute: where to begin? My first two months seemed to be wasted sifting through sterile soil. If the world is meaningful to Hofriyati (as I clearly assumed it was), its meaning was heavily veiled. When I would ask why something was done or what something meant, the answers I received struck me as tautological and, frankly, trivial.[3] "Women undergo circumcision [*ṭahūr,* "purification"] to make their bodies pure and clean." "We marry our relatives [*agārib,* "close ones"] because they are close." No one volunteered what I would then have considered "deeper" explanations. There was surprisingly little exegesis of symbolic constructs, and few references were made to the tenets of Islam.

Since I was spending virtually all of my time with women, I wondered if my expectation as to the location of meaning for my informants had been misplaced. For example, perhaps Islam—which women refer to rarely and when they do, they use as a sort of gloss, an ultimate but unelaborated source of significance—is less directly meaningful for them than for men, who readily cite the Quran in support of their beliefs and social arrangements. There appear to be important differences between men's and women's versions or elaborations of Hofriyati culture, and this book examines some of these. Such differences are hardly surprising in the context of sexual segregation where, as explored within, social interactions between men and women, even within the household, are restricted and constrained. Similar observations have been made for Oman (Wikan 1982), Egyptian Bedouin (Abu-Lughod 1986), and Morocco (Rosen 1978; Dwyer 1978; Messick 1987).

This book speaks largely from a feminine perspective, and may be re-

2. See, for example, Fernandez (1985); Geertz (1983).

3. Audrey Richards (1982: 120–21) experienced similar frustrations when questioning Bemba men about the purposes of female initiation rites. Since her female informants offered more detail, the responses she received might have reflected gender-specific differences in the distribution of knowledge or, as discussed below, significant cultural differences between the sexes.

garded as an addition from Muslim Africa to the anthropological literature on women and gender relations. But more than this, since the *zār* cult is dominated by women—who comprise two-thirds of the permanent adult population in Hofriyat, master more than half of village ceremonies, and are often de facto heads of households—it contributes to a growing body of work in which women are accorded full status with men as culture producers and social actors.[4]

I do not, however, wish to deny the existence of gender asymmetries in Hofriyat, nor that women's cultural productions—their narratives, their implicit or "practical ideology,"[5] their rituals—may speak largely, as Ardener says, with "muted" voice. Ardener (1975 : 21 ff.) maintains that although women's constructions of reality may differ from men's, they must in some way be expressed *through* men's where, as in Hofriyat, men's comprise the dominant paradigm. The presiding discourse in the village is a localized version of Islam ostensibly controlled by men,[6] in which *zār* spirits play a legitimate though, from men's public perspective, tangential role. In this sense, women's amplification of *zār* beliefs into a possession cult can be seen as a kind of counterhegemonic process (cf. Williams 1977; Gramsci 1971; Sider 1980): a feminine response to hegemonic praxis, and the privileging of men that this ideologically entails, which ultimately escapes neither its categories nor its constraints. Thus, on the one hand, women tacitly reproduce the dominant system of meanings simply by participating in it, as they do. Yet this is only part of the story, for women's own system exists: accepted meanings reworked in the alternate discourse of possession are hardly less eloquent for being muted; they are merely inexplicit.[7] Messages communicated by women to both male and female villagers via the *zār* often have subversive overtones as well as supportive ones; gender-appropriate meanings emerge when individuals read these messages in light of their own experiences. Such communication is largely achieved through indirection: as discussed in subsequent chapters, ambiguity and ambivalence are qualities salient to expressions of women's reality in Hofriyat, allowing more to be implied than can be stated with impunity.

4. For examples, see Abu-Lughod (1986); Altorki (1986); Bell (1984); Bledsoe (1980); Dubisch, ed. (1986).

5. From Eickelman (1976 : 157, 1981 : 86 ff.).

6. However, the reality of this is complex; to a certain extent, hegemonic constructs are the product of an authoritative legitimating context (Islam, as villagers define it) and not actually "controlled" by hegemonic agents (village men). Men are equally subject to these constructs, though they may manipulate them more readily than women. The distinction between agentative and nonagentative hegemony has been suggested by John L. Comaroff (1986).

7. Apropos of this point, see Comaroff (1985) on the ambivalence of Zionist symbolism in South Africa.

I will argue at various points how my interpretation of the *zār* diverges from that of I. M. Lewis for whom the cult is properly situated as part of a subordinate "female sub-culture" which, "if only in fantasy, marches forward in pace with the dominant culture of men" (1971*a*: 99). There is considerable truth in this vision, yet it remains to be seen who, if anyone, leads the march or engages in fantasy. The assertion reflects a common but, I think, erroneous assumption that public "culture" in northern Sudan is monolithic, a masculine preserve from which women are categorically excluded and to which they can only react. The perspective locates women in the context of men, but sees men solely in the context of themselves. Despite apparent male control of Islamic discourse in Hofriyat, villagers of either sex would deny the validity of this view.

Nor, as I will show, is the *zār* in Hofriyat a truly "peripheral cult" as Lewis claims, playing no direct part in upholding the moral code of the society, as distinguished from the "main morality cult" of Islam (ibid., p. 31 ff.). Such a stance oversimplifies matters; the *zār* defies categorization, and in its multidimensional nature lies its force. Among Lewis's many insights into the phenomena of possession, his best known concern has been to demonstrate the intentional use of possession beliefs by women wishing to ameliorate their subordination. Some of my informants surely use possession thus, but one cannot explain the cult away merely by documenting its instrumental potential. An overfocus of any sort detracts from the subtlety and richness of the *zār:* its polysemy, its potential to alter women's and men's perceptions of themselves, each other, and their cultural constructs; or to effect tangible changes in their lives, while also reinforcing village morality.

I am in greater sympathy with Lewis's (1986) recently published argument that possession cults provide a foil for mainstream Islam and thereby help to define it. This accords with my own observations which point to a dynamic relationship between the two inexorably linked forms of discourse, one muted, indirect; the other not. Moreover, the dialectic between the *zār* and Islam on a religious level corresponds to that between women and men in an everyday world pervaded and informed by sexual complementarity. It is important to realize that if women are constrained by their gender from full participation in Islam, men are constrained by theirs from full participation in the *zār.*[8] The worlds of the sexes in Hofriyat are also parallel worlds: like humans and spirits, women and men occupy a single physical plane but separate though contiguous realities.

That said, I am convinced there exists a set of assumptions about the world and its appropriate order which male and female villagers tacitly share. In the field I soon appreciated that I would not discover this com-

8. See also Lambek (1981: 61–62).

mon ground by discounting my informants' mundane responses in favor of those that referred to some ultimate, sacred reality beyond. And through the process of writing it became obvious that what I sought lay not so much behind my informants' statements as in them, and not so much in Islam as, so to speak, in front of it. Assumptions informing villagers' statements reflect a fundamental, received knowledge of the world: a knowledge that both shapes and is embedded in quotidian discourse, and suffuses the local ideology of Islam but is in no way reducible to it as doctrinally defined. This is vernacular knowledge (cf. James 1988)—of personhood, morality, integrity—sufficiently implicit and grounded in experience to accommodate ideological shifts without undergoing radical reformulation.[9] In general, Hofriyati women hold Islam commensurate with vernacular knowledge, where men are more given to scrutinizing practice and the knowledge on which it is based for departures from a (locally constructed) universal ideal. But different styles of approach do not vitiate the common context.[10] And even doctrinal ideology is ambiguous enough to allow scope for interpretation by elaborating some of its potential significances rather than others (cf. Altorki 1986). On these bases women negotiate the gender asymmetries and constructs that shape their lives, claiming for them a significance not always concordant with men's but nonetheless immanent and potential within the constructs themselves.

Hence the Hofriyati world, though I conventionally describe it as "a culture," should not be thought of as an entity, or reification, so much as a heuristically bounded set of intersecting, overlapping discourses, a situation Bakhtin (1981; Todorov 1984 : 55 ff.) labels heteroglossia. It consists in a plurality of voices orchestrated by common themes, idioms, meanings, resonant with the participation of others in the past and here and now.

I was unaware of this discursive process at first, and unable to articulate it as such until I returned from the field. There, having caught glimpses of villagers' enduring assumptions in coming to terms with the practice of female circumcision[11] (which, more than anything else that I encountered, represented "otherness"), I became concerned to trace the informal logic of everyday life in Hofriyat, to find both the coherence and indeterminacy in what villagers see as commonsensical, to uncover the intrinsic and the "natural" in quotidian interactions. Such a quest scholars like Geertz (1973, 1983), Bourdieu (1977, 1979), and Schutz (1962), arguing from different epistemological positions, regard as proper concern for cultural analy-

9. Or perhaps as James (1988), following Foucault (1972), suggests for the Uduk of the Sudan-Ethiopia border zone, such understandings are "archival": historically antecedent to current ideological precepts.

10. See Holy (1988) for a discussion of similar issues with regard to the Berti of western Sudan, and Tapper and Tapper (1987) on Turkey.

11. See Boddy (1982*b*).

sis. It is the mundane environment of the *zār* which, I will argue, empowers it to convey a range of meanings. It is also this unevenly shared quotidian discourse that, in supporting and reproducing apparent gender asymmetries—in embodying power relations—fuels the counterhegemonic potential of the *zār*.

The results of this grounding enterprise are presented in the opening section of the book, portions of which were published first elsewhere (Boddy 1982*b*, 1988). In these pages, little direct discussion of spirits can be found: their concern is the human world. Although spirits are essential participants in this world, attention is first directed to the human moral codes, idioms, and ideas which give it substance. Here I owe much to Bourdieu's (1977 : 4 ff.) discussion of "practical knowledge", and Geertz's (1973 : 360 ff.) appreciation that "thinking" is a social act when informed by cultural symbols, images and objects collectively impressed with meaning. Such images are the building blocks of my approach to understanding Hofriyati women; I have sought to portray them through metaphors they predicate upon themselves and others, and through metaphors by which others—Hofriyati men and non-Hofriyati spirits—comprehend them.

It will soon become apparent that women's conceptions of themselves are as much the product of negation (they are not-male, not-*zār*) as of positive assertion; further, that the village identity they share with men is similarly forged. This is one reason the book is structured as it is, dealing first with relations between women and men in the human realm; then with relations among women, men, and spirits; and finally with the spirits as a separate domain, whose traits and characteristic behaviors are a construction on the human realm that speaks about it in a variety of subtle (and not always flattering) ways. My purpose is to view both possession and the villagers whose lives it refracts from a variety of angles, each of which instructs and illuminates its alternates.

In keeping with this aim, part 2 of the book details how the spirit world impinges on and breaks into the human. Since villagers claim that *zār* possession is an illness (basically incurable yet ameliorable through ritual observance), discussion shifts to its etiology. *Zār* affliction is thus situated within the ethnomedical context of the village; and the social, physical, and cognitive conditions under which a spirit illness might be invoked or disclosed are examined. Points raised for consideration are documented here in a series of possession incidents and case histories. Gradually, it emerges that possession constitutes a metasocial context; by implicating nonhuman beings in the afflictions of humans, it plays a role in the negotiation and renegotiation of meaning by rephrasing interpersonal conflict or, to borrow Crapanzano's (1977*b* : 169) phrase, recasting it on the "demonic" stage. Further, possession structures certain problematic experiences for Hofriyati, especially for Hofriyati women, and helps to effect emotional realignments of kin relations and social positions in ways deemed favorable to the possessed.

Not only is the *zār* metasocial, it is also, from the perspective of Hofriyati, metacultural. Early in part 2, I introduce the idea, by no means new, that possession beliefs and performances constitute a cultural text (cf. Lambek 1981) or, to be ethnographically precise, a series of texts, a virtual library of meanings available to be appropriated, referred to, and continuously reproduced by Hofriyati of either sex under certain conditions, whether or not they are possessed. But more than this, the *zār* has potential to operate at a *meta*cultural level: as an intellectual resource located at a remove from everyday meanings, an allegorical production. For those who take it up and read it in this light, it comments upon and reorders quotidian meanings, unmasking their latent indeterminacies and broadening them in light of women's particular concerns, sometimes in novel ways. All of this is made available to Hofriyati through *zār* trance rituals that are intended to cure a host of spirit-related ailments. At several levels, then, possession performs a therapeutic function.

The third and final part of the book is devoted to exploring the spirit world apart from contexts of possession in Hofriyati humans, and comparing it to the world of everyday village life.[12] Spirits, like their human counterparts, are social beings, in some respects similar to Hofriyati but in others strikingly different. Here, the *zār,* as a corpus of beliefs and their ritual dramatization, is viewed as an aesthetic form. Fully situated in its metacultural aspect, the *zār* is a story village women tell themselves about themselves and others, a portrait of village culture as it profoundly is not (Geertz 1973:443 ff.), but also, more profoundly, as it is. For in *zār* the village's historical consciousness is implicitly expressed through the bodies of its most potent moral icons, its women. I consider what messages villagers—but especially Hofriyati women—might derive from their own possession experiences and from their observation of spirits manifest in fellow humans. Possession by *zayran* (plural of *zār*), however social they may be, creates a paradox in and for those involved, as the possessed are simultaneously themselves and alien beings. Apart from their more specific potential significances, such incidents highlight villagers' cultural distinc-

12. The distinction I make between the human world and that of *zayran* is somewhat arbitrary: from an analytical perspective, they constitute a single social reality; from Hofriyati's perspective, *zayran* are very much part of their everyday lives, though the spirits' extraordinary qualities, e.g., their powers and invisibility, distinguish them from humans in significant ways. In Hofriyati thought, humans and *zayran* occupy different elements or zones of the universe, and entry of a spirit into the human realm, however common, violates the boundary between them. The distinction I make is not, I stress, between secular and sacred realms: in the *zār* world as in the human, sacred and secular contexts interpenetrate; neither is extricable from the other. Both *zayran* and humans are creatures of Allah and subject to his laws.

tiveness, both emphasizing the boundaries of village society and demonstrating its vulnerability to permeation from without. But equally, they are provocative, opening up directions of thought (cf. Ricoeur 1976) not always apparent to Hofriyati nor, indeed, willingly pursued by them. In this sense too, the *zār* makes affirmative use of potentially destructive ambiguity: it "edifies by puzzlement" (Fernandez 1980, 1982 : 22). Its pedagogical promise is as substantial as any other.

This book is a hierarchized description of Hofriyati cultural meanings seen largely through women's eyes: of vernacular logic, its negotiation through acknowledgment of possession affliction, and its secondary—metacultural, counterhegemonic—elaboration in *zār* belief and ritual. Much that the book recounts will likely pertain to northern Sudanese society in general. However, one is confronted throughout by villagers' concern for maintaining, sometimes stretching, yet always controlling the boundaries of their social world, a concern implicit in everyday practice, expressed in ritual, and echoed among other peasant groups similarly encased in ethnically complex nations troubled by a history of external domination.[13] Such local distinctiveness finds outward expression in the minutiae of dress, comportment, language, dance step, drum rhythm, and basketry design, among others—tangible features readily appreciated by other riverain Sudanese. Despite an underlying similarity, there is considerable intervillage variation along the Nile, and I can claim neither to have provided a definitive ethnography for the area, nor to have exhausted the possible interpretations of the *zār*.

A final point: although I have drawn upon the works of numerous authors for guidance, and am grateful to many others who so generously discussed and criticized my work, the view of Hofriyati culture developed in these pages is a product of interactions between me and my Hofriyati informants during two periods of fieldwork.[14] Less translated or exegetical than continuously negotiated, it is an interpretation—one opening among several into an alien world of meaning.

13. See Isbell (1985) for an interesting example from highland Peru.

14. From January 1976 through March 1977, and December 1983 through April 1984.

Part 1

The Human World

1

Departures

The solace of such work as I do with brain and heart lies in this—that only there, in the silences of the painter or the writer can reality be reordered, reworked and made to show its significant side. Our common actions in reality are simply the sackcloth covering which hides the cloth-of-gold—the meaning of the pattern.

—Lawrence Durrell, *Justine, The Alexandria Quartet*

Hofriyat, March 31, 1976. The train will be late getting in to Kabushiya. North of Shendi, dunes from last night's sandstorm block the tracks, and we are forced to wait for several hours while the route is being cleared. The sun is relentless; the air in our carriage is stifling; my clothes are soaked with perspiration. Turbaned fellow travelers, inured to discomfort and delay, converse over glasses of strong sweet tea served from floral thermos flasks—redundant, surely, in this heat. Across the aisle a child sleeps in his mother's arms oblivious to a dozen bluebottles implacably sucking moisture from the corners of his eyes. For me the wait is endless.

An hour later the train shudders along its length and comes awake. Tea washes into the aisle. We begin to move, fitfully at first, then slowly gathering speed. Gritty desert air sweeps through the carriage like the blast from a kiln; it brings but slight relief. At 2:00 P.M. we reach our destination. Ali, a young man from the area where I now live, descends from his perch atop the train. He lifts one of my cases and together we alight into the sweltering dust.

*Not far from the tracks, several donkey carts (*karrōs*) mark time before a row of whitewashed shops. After an obligatory haggle that succeeds only in establishing rapport, I hire one to take us the rest of the way to Hofriyat. Our driver is a seedy-looking older man (two gold teeth, others black or missing) who has three wives and warns me he is looking for a fourth. He is surprised to see me, he says, without the archaeologists.*

"Their work is finished," I explain, "but I've come back to study Arabic and local customs." Already the recitation is pat.

The driver's expression betrays doubts for my sanity. "Our land is poor," he says, "and summer's heat is coming. We have no electricity like you khawājas *have. Our life in the country is hard; Khartoum is the place for you foreigners.*

There you have Pepsis. Also refrigerators, and fans. Here there is nothing but dust!" He pauses. "And what will you eat?"

Wearily, I climb onto the cart and settle inelegantly on a sack of fetid onions. "Kisra," I tell him. (This is a native bread.)

He laughs, twisting to look over his shoulder. (Reins tighten, overworked donkey protests.) "Ha! Kisra is no good for the bellies of foreigners. It makes them ill!"

I smile thinly, uncertain I should prove him wrong.

The karrō turns onto a northbound trail deeply rutted by recent lorry traffic. Our path bisects hamlets strategically seated on the desert's fringe; to the west beyond, a green band of cultivation flanks the Nile. Halfway to the village we overtake the mummified carcass of a camel claimed by the sun en route to market—a poor omen. I steady the basket propped against my feet. It is loaded with the paraphernalia of fieldwork: plastic-bound notebooks, pens, aspirins in pink paper jackets (significantly preferred by Hofriyati, I had discovered, to the loosely bottled kind), and Nescafé. My research now begins in earnest. This thought, once exhilarating, turns onerous; for the remainder of the journey I am engulfed by alternate waves of panic and resolve.

My reverie breaks as we pass an enormous dōm palm, sentinel to the outskirts of Hofriyat. At once a horde of ragged children rise up out of the sand to surround the cart. Unhappily, I realize they are shouting a version of my name, heralding our approach to the rest of the village. A nervous Ali springs to his feet, totters as the karrō takes a bump, and skullcap askew, bids them let us continue. At this the driver, noting the current value of civil speech, threatens with his whip. Still chanting, the children leap aside.

A chorus of watchdogs—uniformly brown and underfed—now defy us as we near the first mud walls of Hofriyat. There are smells of acacia cooking fires and goat dung on the burning sand. Women wrapped in gaily coloured tōbs (modesty garment consisting of a long cloth that encircles a woman's body covering it from head to foot) appear in their doorways, some smiling and waving, others reserved but nonetheless observant. A few men stand to one side, aloof, curious. I feel that I have walked on stage without having read the play.

To no avail I seek a familiar face in the growing crowd. "Fi baytik," someone says, "At your house." The karrō comes to a halt outside the compound I have arranged to rent, and I am relieved to see some earlier acquaintances standing there in welcome: Nafissa, the shaykh's unmarried daughter; Samira, her cousin; Sadig, the young man I have engaged to assist with my work; and Zaineb, a married woman nine years my senior and mother of seven who would soon become my most trusted friend and informant.

Refreshed by draughts of water, Ali and the driver take their leave. Sadig departs in search of 'Asma, my landlady, who has left for her fields with my house keys in tow. Now unconstrained by masculine presence, Nafissa remarks that most villagers did not think I would return alone: surely my brothers would *have forbidden it! Only Zaineb was certain I would come. We fall to heavy silences, unsure of what should follow.*

Moments later Sadig returns followed by the irascible ʿAsma, whose image is a travesty of feminine propriety in the eyes of my companions. She approaches briskly, berating us and everything, tōb *weathered and torn, hair stuck out from her head in a fan of Medusa braids. She extracts the keys to my living quarters from a long chain of similar items—leather amulets, coin purses, and the like—slung around her neck and tucked beneath her skirts for safety.*

*The door swings open. A shaft of sun precedes us, playing on a swirl of glinting motes. Everywhere is evidence of the desert's itinerant sovereignty: tables, rope beds (*angarībs*), all are coated with a fine grey dust. Warily, I lift an* angarīb *away from the wall, and a stick-legged spider larger than an outstretched hand sidles toward us from the gloom. Sadig grabs a palm-leaf broom and quickly kills it; I am not encouraged by the thought of finding others of its kind.*

Sadig's mother Asia arrives, balancing a jerry can of water on her head. Eying the mess, she offers to help me clean the place tomorrow, at sunrise. She insists I get rid of the mats with which the archaeologists had covered the ground since these may shelter scorpions. Then we will remove any loose dirt from the earthen floors and wet them down. This, she explains, makes a hard (insect proof) surface and if repeated daily will help to cool the room. I agree to try. Already ʿAsma is bargaining for the discarded mats.

*I am invited to "lunch" (*ghadā, *a meal normally eaten in midafternoon) on pumpkin stew with the womenfolk at Nafissa's. Five of us circle the communal tray dipping wads of bitter* kisra *into a congealing mass of vegetables and goat intestine. The pumpkin is sweet and spiced with cinnamon; I avoid the meat.*

Before we have finished, a little girl bursts into the ḥōsh *(houseyard) gesturing excitedly. She speaks quickly and I cannot follow. At once the women rise and arrange their wraps preparing to depart. There is much hasty conversation; an atmosphere of merriment prevails. Nafissa motions me to come along; I grab my notebook.*

Outside in the narrow passage that separates neighboring ḥōshs, *Nafissa explains that her cousin Khadija, Samira's older sister, is about to have a baby. Several months ago Khadija returned to the village from Khartoum where she had been living with her husband. It is customary for women to give birth, says Nafissa, in their mothers' homes. Khadija's labor is advanced; the midwife has been summoned.*

We duck beneath a mud-brick arch and step into a biblical tableau. Samira's ḥōsh *seethes with commotion. Women occupy every available foothold, loudly alternating bits of gossip with religious utterances, anxious for news of delivery. Men have begun to gather outside the walls: two hands, a turban, then a pair of eyes peer briefly over top.*

Presently, Zaineb emerges from the room to my right. She tells us not to worry. The sapling uprooted and placed in Nile water during the last months of

Khadija's pregnancy has borne leaves: she will have an easy birth. Now the midwife is opening Khadija's circumcision scar and making her final examination.

I ease toward the delivery chamber; not yet daring to enter, I observe from the stoop. The room is dark and even more crowded with women than the yard. Khadija lies on an angarīb, *elevated by a roll of mattresses. The midwife stands at her feet. Kinswomen hold her knees apart, another supports her head. The air is damp, foul with yesterday's incense and the smell of blood. It resonates with invocations: "Ya Hassan! Shaykh Hamid! Ya Nabī!" Near the door an old woman on a circular mat fingers worry beads, before her a bulb of garlic and an iron nail. All at once the noise and confusion stop. An ominous silence builds—then abruptly collapses into ululations as birth is announced. The room quickly empties.*

Men have now entered the ḥōsh, *jubilant kin of the baby's parents. One leaves for Kabushiya on a borrowed donkey to telegraph Khadija's husband. A smiling Samira thrusts handfuls of dates into my pockets and makeshift pouches in the ladies'* tōbs. *The men prepare to sacrifice a goat. A few minutes later my friends and I depart assured of Khadija's health; we make our way across the square to Zaineb's house for tea.*

Once there I ask about the shouting, the silence, the nail and the garlic, all that I have witnessed. People shout the names of saints, I am told, to summon their strength and to drown the cries of the woman giving birth; they are silent during the birth itself and until the afterbirth is safely delivered unless complications arise that call for speech. The younger women know nothing of the nail and the garlic. Zaineb's mother informs us that these are present to divert the evil eye, to prevent hemorrhage and obstruction of the uterus.[1] *My notebook is fast filling up.*

We sit chatting amiably until encroaching darkness necessitates the lighting of a lamp. Zaineb's youngest have been fed and soon drop off to sleep. We leave them in the care of her mother and quietly depart the ḥōsh, *heading for a vacant house at the edge of Hofriyat. A teen-aged girl is being married this week. Over the next few nights she will be taught the bridal dance by other village women. The coaching party, called an* ʿallumīya *("teaching"), must take place in secrecy, away from the prying eyes of men and boys.*

On arriving, thirty of us press into a newly whitewashed room. We sit on the floor surrounding a multicolored mat (referred to, however, as "red," aḥmar*). A kerosene lantern suspended from the central support bathes the room in uneven yellow light; the flowing forms of women paint its walls with shadow. Windows are shuttered, the door is closed and bolted, the air grows thick with heat. Incense burning in a painted brazier clouds the atmosphere with musk. Our greetings, lengthy and ceremonious always, tonight seem strangely solemn.*

Someone drums a beat on the dallūka *(a large pottery drum), others start*

1. These practices are part of a complex known as *mushāhara,* discussed in chapter 3.

to sing and clap, hints of solemnity dissipate. The songs are love songs, highly sentimental and traditional to weddings. Throughout the evening, younger girls vie with each other in remembering the latest tunes.

The bride stands barefoot on her mat moving sensuously in time to the music but hardly changing place: the wedding dance is a "dance of the buttocks" (ragīṣ bi ṣuluba)*, not of the feet. Her friends shout encouragements and critiques of her style; some suggest points for improvement. It is important to do the step well: her dance is at once the climax of her wedding and a personal triumph. She performs it publicly only once, as a virgin.*

The rhythm shifts. Across the room a woman rises to her knees and starts bobbing up and down from the waist. Her torso moves with impossible speed. Zaineb whispers that she must be possessed by Lulīya, an Ethiopian zār *known to admire local weddings and to parody the manner of a Hofriyati bride when summoned during rituals. The drummer desists; the woman slumps to the floor. Someone speaks to the intruder, "Too bad, too bad. What do you want?" No response. "What do you want? Who are you?" Nothing. The group replays the song that elicited the episode; the woman moves as before. But now when the drumming ends, she stops and sits back on her heels, disheveled, dazed. Lulīya has gone; the party resumes with no more spirit interruptions.*

Three times in the ensuing hour an elderly woman is sent to scare away some boys who have gathered hoping to catch a glimpse of the activities inside. A shutter bangs. At first we think the boys have returned. But wind-blown sand soon chokes the room, extinguishing the lamp. A dust storm is upon us and we quickly disband. My flashlight cannot penetrate the boiling murk—useless. Those of us from the other end of the village fight our way to the path. Progress is slow; we strain into the wind, our faces flattened by its force, feeling with invisible hands along invisible outside walls. Inexplicably, it starts to rain. It stops a moment later, but not before we are thoroughly drenched.

At last I reach my house and manage to open the door. Inside there is no letup. Hot dust pours through ceiling fronds and pushes through fastened shutters, whirling round in a mad abrasive vortex. Twice I light the lamp, twice it blows out. Closing my sand encrusted eyes, I witness an explosion of tiny white sparks. There is dust between my teeth, in my ears, my nose; in every pore. Still the wind does not abate. So I sit down in the darkness on an angarīb*—my back to the wall despite monstrous spiders—and wait for dawn.*

The Village

Hofriyat is a small village of some five hundred permanent residents located on the east bank of the Nile in northern Sudan, approximately two hundred kilometers downstream of the capital, Khartoum. Administratively, it is part of a three-, and for some purposes, four-village area having its own "people's council" in the district of Shendi, Nile Province/State.[2] On weekdays[3] a converted Bedford lorry provides local bus service between the area and Shendi town, a sizable settlement roughly forty kilometers to the south. Here, there are district courts and administrative offices, a daily *sūq* (market), and a small hospital.

For everyday needs, people look to Kabushiya a few kilometers from Hofriyat. This is a town of more than three thousand inhabitants and houses the closest railway depot, post office, telephone, and police detachment. Here too are several shops carrying a miscellaneous assortment of canned goods, cloth, soap, perfume, plastic footwear, spices, grains, and dried legumes; plus a semiweekly *sūq* where fresh meat and a variety of fruits and vegetables can be bought in season. On market days the local court convenes at Kabushiya to hear both civil and criminal suits; cases of magnitude or difficulty are passed on to the district courts in Shendi, which also consider matters falling under *sharīʿa* (religious) jurisdiction.[4]

Within the three-village area there is a simple mosque; a bakery; a cooperative, diesel-generated mill where households process grain for flour; and both boys' and girls' primary schools. The closest junior secondary schools are found in Kabushiya; like the primary schools these are sexually segregated, but unlike them students are boarded during the week.

A two-room dressing station on the edge of Hofriyat serves the village area; it is staffed by a male nursing assistant trained in first aid, basic obstetric care, and commonly encountered diseases. Much of his work involves treating malaria with injections of chloroquine, scorpion bites with antidote, and a host of other ailments with tetracycline; occasionally, he is called upon to assist the government-trained midwife in diagnosing problematic pregnancies for referral to Shendi. Those with obscure or intractible illnesses are sent to one of two clinics in the vicinity of Kabushiya, thence to Shendi hospital.

Within the village are two small privately owned shops (*dukkāns*) and one cooperative store (*tʿaown*). These supply flour, sugar, tea, tomato paste, kerosene, and similar staples, though stock is variable and plagued by shortages. The shops are also the focus of men's social activities in the village, functioning much as coffee houses do in larger settlements: men congregate before them in the evenings, conversing with friends and neighbors over glasses of tea. Resident adult men constitute an informal village

2. In 1983 there occurred a reorganization of districts within Sudan; Nile Province was renamed Nile State.

3. In Sudan and the rest of the Muslim world, weekends are Fridays.

4. Shortly before my second field trip, *sharīʿa* law was extended to include all facets of life; previously, it had been concerned primarily with family matters and questions of inheritance.

assembly; a few belong to the village-area people's council, and several to the village-area improvement committee for which there exists a women's counterpart. Neither committee meets on a regular basis.

I confess to knowing little about the mandate of men's formal political organizations; here I was handicapped by my sex. They are, by informants' accounts, relatively powerless within the state apparatus and serve more to channel villagers' aspirations than to implement them. The informal assembly, however, plays an important though unofficial role in mediating internal disputes with an eye to preventing their escalation beyond village precincts. A sanction often heard in arguments between neighbors is the threat to involve the police. Such action is undesirable, as it reifies the initial breach and exposes a lack of harmony within the village. Internal harmony is something all Hofriyati are concerned to preserve, if only in facade. And no one wants, or ought to want, those who lack ties of obligation in the village and are unfamiliar with its residents to become embroiled in local issues. For when this happens, informants say, the village's interests are not served.

The *shaykh* of Hofriyat, whose daughter was introduced in the foregoing section, is a government official; he was chosen by acclamation, confirmed by the national council, and holds no hereditary title. His position is mainly that of intermediary: he is the residents' link to the national government and the government's link the village. Aside from acting as official spokesman in the village, his principal duty is tax collection. Hence his position is precarious: to retain credibility he must estimate covillagers' harvests and herds (as well as those of desert groups within his domain) in ways that neither they nor outside administrators consider inequitable. The current *shaykh* has proved himself capable of balancing conflicting interests, having occupied the post for the past seventeen years. The job carries some prestige but relatively little opportunity for material gain; its incumbent must be a man of "true words" (*kalām ṣaḥḥ*) and a permanent, full-time resident. He is thus precluded from the often lucrative though periodic labor emigration which most men undertake, and makes most of his living by farming.

Physically, the village consists of mud-brick houses that are situated within courtyards surrounded by high mud-brick walls. There is neither electricity (though one family now possesses a gasoline generator) nor running water. Water is taken from several communal wells and sometimes from the Nile; though laden with disease, the latter is considered especially beneficial to drink. Most households own transistor radios, and in the interval between my two visits, three had acquired televisions powered by automobile batteries periodically recharged in Shendi. Despite such diversions, life in Hofriyat is considered hard compared to that in Khartoum or Omdurman: the city exerts considerable pull, especially on young men.

Recently, two rickety Nissan buses have begun to ply the desert route between Kabushiya and Khartoum North on alternate days, linking villagers more directly with their relatives in the cities and bringing emigrant husbands home for an occasional weekend holiday. The trip is arduous, bumpy, dusty, and unspeakably cramped, but a comparatively quick eight hours if sufficient passengers can be found to expedite departure.

Language and Literacy

Like most riverain Sudanese, Hofriyati speak a dialect of Arabic which contains remnants of earlier vernaculars, principally Nubian and Bejawi (Gassim 1965). Because of this mix, it differs in pronunciation, structure, and semantics from other dialects of Arabic spoken in the Middle East and North Africa, though it is closest, perhaps, to Egyptian. Even within the Arabic-speaking Sudan, there is tremendous regional variation, and it is often possible to locate a stranger's village area merely by listening to his speech.

In this book, all Arabic words and phrases are reported as given. No effort has been made to "correct" word use or grammar, to make the local dialect conform to rules of the classical or modern standard language. To do so, were it possible, would mean losing the distinctive flavor of Hofriyati speech. It should be noted, however, that my most intensive contact in Sudan has been with rural women, and it is mainly from them that I have learned the language. On overhearing men's conversations, I am often struck by how these differ linguistically from women's. Men occasionally use classical pronunciation amongst themselves, and tend to be more exacting in their lexical choices, favoring abstract and unconventional words over synonyms commonly used in cross-sex parlance. Erudition provides an arena of competition for men, most of whom, unlike their wives, are literate.

Women, instead, tend to generalize, sometimes telescoping two like-sounding words into a single sememe with the result that one or both assume a wider range of significance than they would have in standardized forms of Arabic. That malapropisms of this sort occur may be due to the fact that certain words which are quite different in the written language are similarly pronounced in Hofriyati speech: classical phonemic distinctions do not correspond exactly to those of the local dialect. For example, in Hofriyat a phonemic distinction does not usually exist between sounds represented by the letters *dhal* (ذ) and *zay* (ز): *dhal,* pronounced classically as "th" in *that,* is usually pronounced as "z," though occasionally it is pronounced as "d" (*dal,* د).[5] In a language whose grammar consists

5. Similarly, the letter ʿ*ayn* (ع) is frequently pronounced as ʾ*alif* (ا) with or without *hamza* (ء); *hamza* itself may be replaced with *ya*ʾ (ى); *qaf* (guttural "k"; ق) is as elsewhere

mainly in the inflectional expansion of triliteral roots, such variation often leads to the production of homonyms, fueling the already allusive speech of village women. Whether similarities in pronunciation have led to shared meanings or shared meanings to similarities in pronunciation is a moot point. But I would suggest the widespread illiteracy of female adults to be a significant factor in this synthesizing process. Since few until lately have received any schooling, many are unaware of any distinction between *dhal* pronounced as "z" and *zay* itself. Thus, relative to men's, women's speech is more polysemic and concrete (cf. Goody 1980). Somewhat ironically, it therefore resists aspirations of hegemonic groups to contain potential polyphony by privileging certain meanings over others (cf. Bakhtin, quoted by Todorov [1984:57–58]).

The disjunction of male and female linguistic codes is symptomatic of a wider phenomenon: the division, common to Muslim cultures, between men's and women's social worlds. This rift is deepened in Hofriyat by a pattern of labor emigration that entails prolonged separations of husbands from their wives (cf. Kennedy 1978*a*: 10 for Egyptian Nubia).

Environment

The Hofriyat village area straddles two ecological zones, where true desert of rock and fine blown sand starts yielding southward to semidesert acacia scrub with an average annual rainfall in the vicinity of five centimeters. But rainfall here is unpredictable, as throughout the African Sahel: some years, about one in five, it receives considerably more than this (up to fifteen centimeters) and others far less. From early 1980 through 1984 there had been no significant precipitation; the summer of 1985 brought considerable improvement. Given these conditions, the region is marginal for cultivation undertaken at a distance from the river. More than rain, it is the annual inundation of the Nile upon which farming in the area depends.

To say that the climate is uniformly hot as well as dry would be to understate the case. Even so, villagers distinguish three seasons.[6] *Kharīf*, or the rainy season, ought to begin sometime in mid July, bringing with it occasional thunderstorms, frequent cloudy afternoons, and daytime tem-

usually pronounced as a hard English "g" though it is sometimes pronounced as *kaf* (ك , "k") occasionally as *jim* (ج , "dj") or, more rarely, as the Egyptian glottal stop. *Tha*ʾ (ث), classically pronounced as the "th" in *think*, is locally pronounced as *sin* (س , "s") or as *ta*ʾ (ت , "t"); *mim* (م , "m") is often replaced by *ba*ʾ (ب, "b"), and so on. For a thorough discussion of Sudanese variations see Hillelson (1930*a*).

6. In Buurri, adjacent to Khartoum, Barclay (1964:26–27) notes that four seasons are recognized. Between mid October and early December comes *ad-darat*, or "autumn." *Addarat* was not spoken of in Hofriyat, possibly because it is even less humid there than in the confluence area.

peratures somewhat cooler than those of summer, averaging between 40° and 44° C. In late August or early September the Nile flood is at its peak. As it recedes in mid to late September, planting commences on the fertile floodplain (sorghum, millet, legumes, some tomatoes and squash), and ploughing on the banks for irrigated grain cultivation.

Winter (*shitā*), and with it riverbank planting (sorghum, maize and clover for fodder, okra, aubergine, radishes, onions, cress, tomatoes, fava beans and other legumes),[7] gets under way in late October or early November, after the rains, when temperatures fall as much as ten degrees. In December 1976 I recorded one afternoon high of only 25°; a week-long cold snap in January 1984 saw temperatures rise to only 20° C. However, days as cool as these are exceptional, calling for sweaters, blankets, and woolen scarves to be worn at least during morning hours. Winter in Hofriyat is a seemingly endless series of perfect sunny days and spotless skies. When one day in January 1976 a single cloud appeared overhead, several archaeologists working nearby rushed for their cameras, so strange was the event. In 1984, clouds were more common owing, I was told, to the increasing effect of the Aswan High Dam on local weather patterns. Windstorms—always a possibility—become more frequent in February, when temperatures also start to climb. By the end of March they are again averaging 40° C in midafternoon, and biting sandstorms are common.

Summer (*ṣayf*) takes hold in mid April or early May. At this time the Nile is at its lowest flow, as little as a sixteenth the volume it carried at full flood.[8] Sandstorms continue, whipped by *samūm,* hot winds that blow mercilessly from the desert. Temperatures as high as 50°C are not unusual now, and old and young alike are forced to rest during the heat of the day. The clear blue skies of winter pale to white-hot skies in *ṣayf* when humans, plants, and animals need careful tending lest they succumb to dehydration. In late summer, mature onions are harvested and warehoused until early winter, when they become scarce elsewhere in Sudan and villagers can claim a higher price. Summer is the "hungry" season; there is little produce available and people subsist largely on beans (*fūl maṣri*), *kisra,* and leavened bread (when imported wheat is available), with bits of meat, some greens, and onions from time to time. During *ṣayf,* Hofriyati frequently complain of lethargy or boredom (*zihuj*): their inertia—and mine—is palpable.

The seasonal cycle is completed when *ṣayf* gives way to *kharīf* with the welcomed onset of rain. Such rains as fall are rarely gentle, often damaging fragile mud-brick walls and irrigation channels, and collecting in large

7. Most years, irrigation land produces two crops of onions and some vegetables, one harvested in winter, the other, more precarious, in summer.

8. Ministry of Information and Culture, Government of Sudan (n.d.).

stagnant pools wherever the baked earth refuses to let it drain. But for all its destruction, the rain works wonders rejuvenating a parched terrain. For a week or two, patches of bright green relieve an otherwise monotonous grey-brown landscape.

History

Sources of contemporary Hofriyati practice are heterogenous. In the last four thousand years or more, the area has been settled, invaded, or explored by several different peoples, most of them literate. All have left their mark on riverain Sudanese culture, some contributing significantly to its underlying matrix, others remaining unassimilated, but in no way forgotten. Parts 2 and 3 of the book (and especially chapter 8) demonstrate how spirit possession draws upon this past for its material and, reworking it, provides occasion for reflection and resistance. The following pages provide an outline of historical events and processes relevant to understanding Hofriyati today and, from the late eighteenth century on, specifically the *zār*.[9]

Beginning about 2000 B.C., the regions of the upper Nile were periodically conquered by Egypt and welded into a province of its empire. An important outcome of this was the growth of an Egyptianized yet, as is now accepted, wholly indigenous civilization centered at Napata near the fourth cataract. Around 750 B.C., this kingdom, known as Kush, took advantage of weaknesses in the Egyptian state and pushed north, successfully founding Egypt's twenty-fifth dynasty. A branch of the royal family was soon installed at (old) Meroë near present-day Hofriyat.

Kush's hegemony was short-lived, effectively ending in 661 B.C. Yet the kingdom flourished in the south until long after that date. Initially, its strength lay in its domination of the caravan traffic in slaves and luxury goods between Egypt and southern Sudan, and its exploitation of gold deposits in the eastern desert. But after it lost control over Egypt, trade with that area declined, and the locus of power began to drift upstream.

Now the city of Meroë, located on the edge of an ecological zone somewhat more favorable for agriculture, assumed greater importance. While Napata remained the religious center of Kush, Meroë became its administrative capital sometime in the sixth century B.C. After the third century B.C., the royal cemetery was also moved here, resulting in the eventual construction of over fifty pyramidal tombs (see Shinnie 1967).

9. I have based my account on the writings of several historians and archaeologists, omitting references wherever the authorities concur. Controversial points and facts not replicated in other works are specified by citation. Other sources are listed in the bibliography.

The remains of these structures and of the various palaces and temples of Meroë itself are within sight and walking distance of contemporary Hofriyat (see map, page 2). Insofar as most villagers are unaware of their illustrious heritage, the existence of these ruins affords fertile ground for legend and speculation about the occult.

Meroë at the height of its power between the third century B.C. and the start of the Christian era exerted suzerainty far to its south along the White Nile, probably to the region of the Sudd (Haycock 1971:35). But after this point and until its collapse in A.D. 350, when the capital was sacked by Axumite invaders, the state gradually waned. Incursions of nomadic pastoralists, always a source of harassment, became more frequent and were less readily repulsed. As would happen so often thereafter, the area now split into several small principalities.

Meroitic state religion was based on that of ancient Egypt. Over the centuries it, too, degenerated, undermined by political upheavals and the Christianization of the Lower Nile. When in mid sixth century A.D. a few monophysite priests were sent to proselytize in Nubia, they rapidly achieved success in converting the sedentary population. Thence until the establishment of Islam some eight centuries later, Nile villagers were at least nominally Christian.

During the sixth century the area known as Nubia contained three independent Christian kingdoms.[10] Between the first cataract at contemporary Aswan and the third was Nobadia; south of there and extending as far as ancient Meroë (or, according to Vantini [1981:22], Atbara) was Makuria; and beyond this, Alodia or ʿAlwah with its capital near present-day Khartoum. It would be erroneous to assume, however, that these were well-established kingdoms with permanent, defended boundaries. As Adams (1967:13) notes, the number of states likely fluctuated over the years and there were large areas "which did not acknowledge authority beyond that of a local chief, except at intervals when they were directly threatened with attack by their stronger neighbours." The Hofriyat area bridged Makuria's and ʿAlwah's former zones of influence and could well have been autonomous throughout this period.

Though Egypt fell to Muslim Arab invaders in A.D. 641, Nubia was left politically unmolested for several centuries afterward. In 651 the Nubian princes struck a treaty with Egypt providing for mutual security and

10. Emperor Justinian and his Egyptian-born wife, Theodora, dispatched rival missions to Nubia. The former sent priests of Melkite (Council of Chalcedon) persuasion, identified politically with Byzantium, while the latter sent monophysites. Monophysites came to be identified with Egypt against the emperor. Although monophysitic (Coptic, Egyptian) Christianity seems eventually to have triumphed, there is considerable dispute about its initial success. The kingdoms' official stances varied with the political climate, while proselytization among the populace was effected equally by itinerant priests and merchants of both persuasions. See Kirwin (1937) and Vantini (1981) for details of the controversy.

trade but prohibiting settlement of either group in the other's domains. Despite the pact, Arabs and Arabized Egyptians began trickling into Sudan as early as the seventh century. These migrants were mainly pastoralists seeking refuge from organized government and taxation; they gravitated to the deserts, beyond reach of Nubian administrators.

The slow penetration of Sudan from the north continued until late in the twelfth century when events in Ayyubid Egypt led to dissolution of the former peace and recision of Nubia's status as a protected zone. Half a century later, Egyptian border tribes came under increasing pressure from the newly established Mameluke regime in Cairo, and those who found it expedient now moved south virtually unimpeded. Included in this larger wave were Jaʿali and Jawabra ancestors of contemporary Hofriyati.

The states of lower Nubia gave way as the infiltration of Arabic speakers intensified. Like their predecessors, most of these were pastoralists wishing to maintain a nomadic life and seeking the fertile grasslands that flank the river's confluence to the south. Yet after the fall of Old Dongola to Muslim forces in 1317, some Arabs, marrying into the local Nubian population, began to form small tribal organizations along the main Nile (Ibn Khaldun, cited by Hasan 1967:127). Moreover, Christian Nubians had become increasingly isolated from the established Church. Under the migrants' influence—not always benign—they followed Egypt's lead and shifted religious direction, gradually adopting Islam.

In 1504, ʿAlwah, the uppermost Nubian state, was overrun by an unidentified group whose origins are much disputed. They are said by various authors to have come from the White Nile region (having either Shilluk or, as Spaulding (1972) suggests, Nubian forebears), from Bornu, or Ethiopia (see Holt and Daly 1979). Garnering support from Arab settlers, their rulers soon converted to Islam and founded the Funj Sultanate with its capital at Sennar on the Blue Nile. The Funj quickly linked together in a loose confederacy numerous petty chiefdoms that had risen in the wake of Nubia's demise, permitting regional rulers to remain as vassals of the Funj leader or his Arab viceroy. Funj dominance introduced a period of limited stability and prosperity along the reaches of the Nile. Trade was extended and intensified and the sedentary population grew. Muslim scholars were encouraged to take up residence in Sudan, the better to educate its population in the ways of their newfound faith.

Toward the end of the eighteenth century the authority of the Funj miscarried. Several kingdoms that had been vassals of the Sennar state gained virtual independence, among them Shendi, which included Hofriyat. The resultant balkanization was accompanied by local wars and internecine disputes that all but guaranteed the success of the Turko-Egyptian conquest in 1821.

Cultural Resilience

Recent archaeological evidence suggests there is far more continuity to Sudanese cultural history than previously was supposed.[11] Though migrations occurred from time to time, these are now thought unlikely to have entailed extensive displacements of populations or to have eclipsed existing traditions (Adams 1967, 1984; Haycock 1971; Shinnie 1967; Trigger 1965). Many customs and beliefs of contemporary Arab Sudanese probably predate the coming of Islam, and some may be more ancient still.

Several, such as bed burial, can be recognized in modified form today. It is known that before, during, and after the Meroitic period the dead were interred on *angarībs*, native beds. As they were in the past, *angarībs* are still the most common furnishings in Sudanese households, being manufactured of a wooden frame strung with palm-fiber rope. In Hofriyat a corpse is borne to the cemetery on an *angarīb,* though it is now removed from this prior to burial itself. Adams (1967 : 24), however, reports that until recently, beds used in funeral processions were abandoned at the grave site when mourners returned to their villages. Today, Hofriyati leave funerary *angarībs* to be purified in the sun for several weeks before restoring them to domestic use.

Facial scarification is another tradition with ancient roots which has but recently begun to fade. Most settled northern Sudanese above the age of forty-five[12] are distinguished by having three vertical cuts on each cheek,[13] a motif found also on the faces of royalty depicted in Meroitic temple reliefs.

Descent is determined patrilineally in contemporary northern Sudan, but this was not always the case. Meroë and Christian Nubia were matrilineal societies; moreover, women in both enjoyed limited access to political office.[14] Meroitic *candaces* (queens) are known to have ruled during their sons' minorities (Haycock 1971 : 36; Reisner 1922 : 193; Trimingham 1965 : 44), and in Nubia, queen mothers were customarily consulted by the king about affairs of state (Hasan 1967 : 117). Writing in the fourteenth century, the Muslim historian Ibn Khaldun remarks that succession among Nubians passed from a man to his sister or his sister's son (Area Handbook 1960 : 15; Holt and Daly 1979 : 23). Such tendencies appear

11. Until recently the early history of northern Sudan was depicted as a series of catastrophic migrations or invasions of various groups, "barbarians" from the south if their cultural remains were somewhat crude, members of more "civilized" northerly cultures if they were not. See Hillelson (1930*b*) and Arkell (1961) for examples.

12. According to my informants the practice was abandoned in their area during the 1950s.

13. These are marks of the Jaʿaliyīn confederacy; the Shayqīya, a riverain group smaller than the Jaʿaliyīn but politically opposed to them in the past, have three horizontal facial cuts.

14. See Mohammed (1987) for an exhaustive treatment of the historical sources for matrilineality and women's political roles in Meroë and Sudanese Nubia.

to have survived the adoption of Islam with its strong patrilineal and patriarchal emphasis: in 1772 the explorer James Bruce (1813, 6:448) reached Shendi and there found enthroned a woman, whom he called Sittina, "Our Lady." Burckhardt (1922:247), who spent a month in Shendi in 1814, confirmed that women typically played an important role in determining royal succession. It may not be rash to suggest that the custom finds current expression in the exhalted and often tyrannical position of the Sudanese grandmother, *ḥabōba* or "little darling," though this is not unusual in Middle Eastern societies. Intriguing, too, is the propensity for Hofriyati households to be organized around a group of related women, discussed later on.

A number of other practices betray the area's non-Arab heritage. The tradition of drawing a cross in antimony on the forehead of a newborn child, the use of fish bones and palm fronds in making ritual ornaments (*jirtig*), and the custom of bathing in the Nile on ceremonial occasions are just a few which probably date from Christian times or earlier. It is doubtful that Islamic beliefs supplanted those of Christianity so much as that the two systems, having numerous affinities, gradually coalesced, Islam gaining doctrinal ascendancy. Historians assert that the Church and Islam coexisted for centuries after the important Arab migrations of the middle ages (Hold and Daly 1979:25).[15] In fact, pockets of Christians could still be found along the upper Nile well into the eighteenth century (Haycock 1972:20).

Wherever Islam has taken root it has adapted itself to local conditions by incorporating and reworking indigenous elements. These do not simply disappear from convert's beliefs but are, instead, assimilated to Arabic categories and reinterpreted in light of the Quran and Hadith.[16] Given its Christian antecedents, it is hardly surprising that popular Islam in Sudan today evinces an elaborate hagiology and cult of saint veneration, plus a host of spirits, new and old, classified as *jinn*. Syncretism and synthesis have long been partners in the process of Hofriyati culture, and remain so to this day.

The Recent Past

The period from the nineteenth century to the present is most relevant to issues and events portrayed in the *zār,* for during the prolonged period of

15. Holt and Daly (1979:25): "Christianity lingered into the sixteenth century. . . . A Portuguese source, connected with the embassy to Ethiopia in 1520–6, speaks of the recent existence of a hundred and fifty churches in ʿAlwa, and witnessed the arrival of a delegation to ask for priests to be sent to their land."

16. *Ḥadīth,* literally, "speech," "sayings": the words and actions of the Prophet compiled and written by his followers after his death.

colonial expansion and unrest that marked the 1800s the cult became established in Sudan (Constantinides 1972).

By the late eighteenth century the *mek* (king or chief)[17] of Shendi, though tacitly subject to the Funj overlord in Sennar, was for all practical purposes independent. He and the majority of riverain inhabitants under his rule were known as the Jaᶜaliyīn, an amalgam of loosely related tribes (*gabīlas*) of Arabs and Arabized Nubians living along the Nile between Khartoum and the Atbara confluence.[18]

In addition to Jaᶜaliyīn proper there were small groups of Jawabra whose traditional Sudanese homeland is said to be near Dongola farther north. My informants maintain that Jawabra came to Hofriyat in the eighteenth century as Islamic missionaries intent on bringing enlightenment to illiterate Jaᶜali farmers. Jawabra acknowledge kinship with the Jaᶜaliyīn, however, through traditional genealogies (largely fictional; see Holt and Daly (1979:4)) showing both groups descended from the Prophet Mohammed's uncle, ᶜAbbas. At present these two major divisions are so completely intermarried that none of Hofriyat's households is distinctly one or the other.

On the eve of the nineteenth century the population on both sides of the Nile in Shendi district was about twenty-four thousand, with a further six thousand inhabiting the capital, Shendi town (Robinson 1925:108). Rural residents practiced animal husbandry and cultivation, farming much as they do today: on the floodplain after the annual inundation, in the *wadīs* (rainfall runoff courses in the desert) after a significant rainy season, and along the riverbanks by means of *sagīya* (ox-driven waterwheel) irrigation.[19] They were semisedentary at best, and remained so until the middle of the present century, establishing permanent dwellings close to the river but leaving these for extended periods to camp near their pasturelands and *wadī* plantations to the east. Barclay (1964:27) aptly refers to such practice as "transhumant" cultivation.

Townsfolk, on the other hand, were chiefly engaged in commerce. Shendi was then an important entrepôt on caravan routes between Egypt and Sennar, Kordofan, Darfur, and Bornu, and between all of these and Suakin on the Red Sea coast; it had a decidedly international flavor. Apart from *dura* (*Sorghum vulgare*), imported because the town could not supply caravaneers as well as residents, the most significant items of trade were camels and slaves. The latter, considered pagans and therefore exploitable, were captured in the south and marched north to Shendi market; while

17. According to Trimingham (1965:87, n. 4), this "is a title and not the equivalent of Arabic *malik* ('king')," though the similarity is suggestive.

18. See MacMichael (1967).

19. Since the 1960s, *sagīyas* have gradually been replaced by diesel pumps.

most were exported, a good many were kept by local families as domestic and agricultural laborers.

Although the Funj had encouraged Islamic educators to settle within their domains and a religious school had been operating successfully near Shendi since the early seventeenth century (Hasan 1967 : 77), it seems that most of Shendi's population wore their Islam lightly. Married women, who today are always closely covered when abroad, were not veiled. Maidens wore nothing but a short thong skirt called a *rahaṭ*. Virtually nonexistent were *ḥōsh*s, the high-walled enclosures surrounding houses, within which women are now expected to spend most of their time.[20] Townswomen, hardly secluded, were free to occupy themselves with brewing and marketing *marīsa,* the native beer, or serving *araki,* a potent date alcohol. Burckhardt and his contemporary Cailliaud (1826) independently report that drunkenness, thieving, and a state of general lawlessness prevailed. A few religious practitioners lived in the region, but no mosques had yet been built. Such as it was, the *mek,* not the *sharīᶜa,* was the principal source of law and order.

Shendi in the early 1800s was also constantly at war with nomadic pastoralists who lived in the surrounding deserts (Burckhardt 1922 : 248, 310; Robinson 1925). Periodically, the riverain settlements were destroyed by marauders or abandoned in the face of attack. Afterward, villagers either rebuilt or relocated with kin elsewhere along the Nile, a pattern often repeated in subsequent years.

Traveling south by caravan in 1814, Burckhardt arrived at a village near contemporary Kabushiya. Here, he writes,

> are a great number of dispersed huts and hamlets. The Arabs Djaalein [Jaᶜaliyīn] here pasture their numerous herds of cows, camels, and sheep. They have also a few water-wheels, and grow considerable quantities of onions, with which they supply the Shendy market. Their huts are made of mats . . . (Burckhardt 1922 : 245)

Seven years later, Cailliaud rode through these parts in the vanguard of Mohammed ᶜAli's invasion force and noted dwellings of more substance, an indication of peace, perhaps, or increased sedentariness. Houses today are solidly built of sunbaked brick, animal husbandry is less important than in the past, and villagers can be considered seminomadic only in the modern sense of labor migration. It is interesting, however, that onions

20. Hofriyati maintain that *ḥōsh*s (Arabic plural: *ḥayshan*) are a fairly recent innovation there. Houses and other domestic buildings were rarely enclosed until about thirty or forty years ago. Women were not as restricted then, they say, as they are today (though they *were* pharaonically circumcised), and unmarried girls still wore the *rahaṭ*. This issue is taken up later in the chapter.

are still the principal cash crop produced in the area.

In 1821 Shendi surrendered after minimal resistance to Ismaʿil Pasha, son of Mohammed ʿAli and commander of the Turkish occupation on the east bank. Hoping to tap a lucrative pipeline of wealth and slaves, Ismaʿil imposed heavy taxes on the local population which had not been closely governed for some time. His army raided the villages in search of food and booty; underground grain reservoirs were emptied of even that portion of the harvest kept for seed. Most villagers lost their slaves, jewelry, and livestock; many lost their lives, as it was Turkish custom for the army paymaster to purchase the ears of Jaʿali killed for fifty piasters a pair (Robinson 1925 : 111).[21] In 1822 the crops failed and people could not pay the tribute demanded. They revolted unsuccessfully; their leaders were decapitated. Toward the end of that year, Ismaʿil imposed a further levy on the population, and Mek Nimir was unable to raise it. Instead, in collaboration with Shendi townsfolk and refugees from the north, Ismaʿil and his entourage were assassinated.

In no time at all, the Turks descended on Shendi with the full force of their revenge. Villages were devastated, townspeople massacred. Those who had foreseen this repercussion and those who managed to survive it fled with what little they had to the Ethiopian frontier, homes and fields abandoned. The area remained a wasteland until 1829 when the Turkish governor pardoned all concerned in the rebellion except Mek Nimir and his family, members of the Saʿadab Jaʿaliyīn. The peasantry were ordered to return to their villages and many complied.

The period of Turko-Egyptian occupation was marked by successive waves of unrest and resettlement, punctuated by brief periods of prosperity. Locals were drained by heavy taxes designed in part to ensure forfeiture of their slaves to the Egyptian army. Famine was frequent since villagers were able to store little grain against crop failure or drought. Importantly, according to Constantinides' (1972) exhaustive historical inquiry, it was during the Turko-Egyptian occupation that the *zār* first appeared in Sudan: many spirit figures represent foreigners encountered by Sudanese during the Ottoman era, as well as in the more distant past.

Given their impoverishment under the Ottoman regime, it is little wonder that when messianic revolt occurred in 1881 under the leadership of Mohammed Ahmed, the declared Mahdi (deliverer or rightly guided one), Hofriyati joined enthusiastically. Many elder villagers whom I met in 1976 had lost relatives fighting for the Mahdist cause in the Battle of Metemma in 1885.

Their support waned, however, after the Mahdi's death later that year. Most riverain villagers were bitterly opposed to his successor, the Khalifa

21. Jaʿaliyīn, ostensibly because they were Muslims, were not themselves enslaved.

Abdallahi, as he was neither of the Mahdi's family nor from his homeland, the Nile valley. The Khalifa belonged, instead, to the Taʿishi, one of several Baggara (cattle keeping) tribes from Kordofan[22] whom Hofriyati consider less civilized than themselves. On assuming control of the newly independent government the Khalifa ousted incumbent Jaʿaliyīn and placed his own tribesmen and patrons in all important offices, thereby forestalling conspiracy but increasing resentment for his administration. Moreover, taxes under his rule were considered even more repressive than those demanded by the Ottomans; punishment for nonpayment was often death (Rehfisch 1967:46).

In 1889, shortly after a thwarted revolt of the northern sedentary tribes, the Khalifa sent a force of some five thousand men accompanied by almost twice as many camp followers on an expedition to Egypt that—wittingly or not—was doomed to fail. The army proceeded down the west bank of the Nile intending to levy reinforcements from the disaffected Jaʿaliyīn and, though this was a year of devastating famine, living off the land on both sides of the river during the march north. Since the Khalifa's men were not paid on a regular basis, plunder was merciless in the villages through which they passed.

Residents who had not yet evacuated now fled in terror as news of the approaching army was received. One woman's parents, alerted by the distant rumble and desperate to avoid the "bloodthirsty Baggara," hurriedly left Hofriyat taking no provisions. Somewhere they managed to steal a bit of grain but whenever they lit a fire to cook it the Khalifa's men would loom on the horizon and they were forced to move on. Everywhere it was the same: living in the open, eating whatever they could scrounge, making do with what clothing they had worn from the start. Her father used the skin of a dead donkey to fashion crude sandals for himself and other refugees; what remained of the leather was boiled for soup.

Others told me that when the "Baggara" arrived, they wantonly killed any men who had remained in the village. Moreover, they enslaved the women, including the local religious leader's unmarried daughters. In 1977 I met aged twins who were infants during the Mahdiya, whose mother had been forced to work for the Khalifa's force. The family had survived on what she could steal from the troops.

In 1898, aided by the Jaʿaliyīn, a joint British and Egyptian campaign succeeded in reconquering the Mahdi's domain. A few months later the noted Egyptologist, E. A. Wallis Budge made his way to Bejrawiya near contemporary Hofriyat. Everywhere he found desolation. Land bordering the river was densely overgrown; it had not been cultivated for several years. Gaps in the riverbank showed where waterwheels once stood, their

22. See Cunnison (1966).

wood long since ripped out and used for fuel. Here and there a few hardy souls had come back and were beginning the arduous task of clearing the ground for planting (Budge 1907, 1:261–80). Gradually, survivors returned to the river as so often they had in the past, settling in their old villages or wherever they could find some land to farm. But the population had been decimated. Shendi town, which housed six thousand people in 1800, was inhabited by fewer than five hundred a century later when external rule returned (Budge 1907, 2:402).

The Contemporary Context

Hofriyati who managed to live through the period just described had lost most of what they possessed at its conclusion. Herds were seriously reduced; land ownership was in a muddle due to the comings and goings of the last hundred years. In 1906 and again in 1927 the Anglo-Egyptian colonial government tried to sort it out by registering land in the Hofriyat region. Claims were to be proved through possession of unambiguous title (Mustafa 1971:7) or continuous occupation and use for a period not less than ten years. I was told that because this last condition was so formidable, many people no longer living in Hofriyat became registered owners of local plots, while newcomers to the village ended up with arable land elsewhere. Although Hofriyati confess to having "liked the British," they were clearly ambivalent about the imposition of such practices as registration, and even now, long after independence (1956), prefer to work out their own arrangements despite legal title; advice on land issues is sought from local savants (*arāḍis*) in cases of dispute.[23]

Given their history, villagers are understandably wary of powerful outsiders who would intervene in their affairs, and have a healthy cynicism about the benefits of a national government which, they maintain, rarely works in their interests. Although there have been obvious improvements to the area since Anglo-Egyptian Condominium rule, those I spoke to were adamant that government—regardless of regime[24]—has always been more interested in keeping townspeople happy than improving the lot of the *nās al-balad*, the countryfolk. Prices of basic foodstuffs escalate con-

23. Government registration officials from Shendi also consult these men on occasion.

24. Anglo-Egyptian rule (1899–1955) culminated with independence in 1956 and the beginning of parliamentary government. This was short-lived, ending in 1958 with a military coup by General Aboud. When parliamentary elections again were held in 1964, the result was an unstable coalition government. As new elections were being planned, the army returned to power in a coup in May 1969 under Colonel Nimeiri, whose regime lasted until its overthrow in April 1985. After a brief transitional period, elections were held in 1986 and again in 1988. The precarious parliamentary coalition that resulted was overthrown by a military coup on June 30, 1989.

tinually, shortages are common in the rural areas because transport is problematic. The erratic availability of fuel for diesel pumps makes irrigation farming a hazardous venture. Villagers do take advantage of government programs that confer an immediate benefit, such as participating in a local cooperative that from time to time distributes small quantities of fixed-price commodities, such as sugar. Yet they tend to see themselves as distinct from the *ḥakūma* (government) and relatively powerless in relation to it. Resident villagers' response to state intrusion is basically one of selective avoidance: not surprisingly, strategies such as negotiation with the *shaykh* are employed to limit the amount of annual crop tax a farmer must pay, and people who own cattle are careful to conceal their herds from inquiring eyes.

A number of recent events have affirmed villagers' scepticism and wariness of external involvement. Sometime after Sudanese independence in 1956, an eminent "son of the village" and member of government joined a plot to overthrow the existing head of state. The coup failed and, owing to the efforts of a foreign leader, the man was captured. He was publicly tried and quickly executed. His kin and their neighbors throughout the village area were disconsolate: though many had supported neither his action nor his political stance, he was nonetheless one of their own. And since that time, Hofriyati say, the village has been neglected by the government, receiving only minimal benefits compared with those of other localities.

A second issue involves the Sudan Socialist Union (SSU), the political organization founded in 1970 by then President Nimeiri after existing political parties were disbanded following the coup (May 1969) which brought him to power. Few (if any) Hofriyati joined that organization despite repeated rumors that only SSU members would have free access to medical facilities, be permitted to ride the train, or hold a government post. Many villagers, men and women, were indignant that they should be pressed into joining a "political party" (*ḥizb*) against their will, and simply refused. Then in January 1977, a zealous SSU member and district representative on the regional council took it upon himself to secure closure of the local *bayt andīya* (clubhouse), a drinking spot (and, reputedly, a brothel run by southern Sudanese) situated in the desert on the outskirts of a nearby village. Hofriyati of both sexes objected to the move, which had been undertaken in the name of religion and morality. Women were especially upset because men would now start drinking at home, and this they said would undoubtedly disrupt domestic life. As for the SSU's involvement, villagers regarded it as the thin edge of the wedge, and resented the intrusion.

During my second period of fieldwork, most villagers I spoke to expressed considerable antipathy for the government's imposition of *sharīʿa* law in the autumn of 1983. Although both women and men consider themselves pious Muslims, they objected to the corporal punishments stipulated under the law as brutal and unnecessary. *Sharīᶜa* also prohibits the consumption of alcohol; but with characteristic ingenuity a number of villagers had resisted the ban.[25] Here, and in ways less apparent than these described below, Hofriyati demonstrate concern for maintaining the integrity of their social world and policing its boundaries where they can, while yet transforming in accommodation to their external milieu: taking from the outside world what they deem beneficial and leaving behind what they do not. This orientation can be attributed neither to atavism nor xenophobia: it is a pragmatic disposition continually reinforced by their history of engagement with others, regardless of conviction.

Beginning with the Turko-Egyptian occupation in 1820, the area has been increasingly drawn into a global political economy, largely by invasive means. Paralleling these developments has been a coincidental rise in Islamic consciousness, starting with the establishment and growth of reformist religious orders in Sudan early in the nineteenth century.[26] Reformatory zeal culminated with the Mahdiya, but Islamization continued after the Anglo-Egyptian reconquest. Omdurman theological school, modeled on the al-Azhar in Egypt, graduated its first class in 1920. The Muslim Brotherhood, committed to Islamization of the state and purification of the religion itself, was founded in Egypt in 1928 and quickly attracted urban Sudanese as followers; it remains extremely active today. The revitalized concern for adherence to a proper Islamic life-style was also felt, if less dramatically, in rural areas like Hofriyat; the result was the establishment there of a *khalwa,* or religious school, where boys were encouraged to memorize the Quran and gain a degree of literacy. The trend has persisted with the development in the area of locally organized (and latterly state funded) schools for boys (late 1960s) and girls (early 1970s).

Hofriyati women assert that sometime around 1930 their menfolk began to "read the books" and, in consequence, adopted an increasingly conservative posture toward female kin. Before this, women say, they were more scantily clothed and had considerable freedom to go about the village at any hour they chose or visit neighboring villages unchaperoned. Whatever its effects on private belief, the change was publicly announced in the building of houseyard enclosures (*ḥōsh*s) and a more stringent regulation of women's behavior. Here, and perhaps elsewhere in Sudan, the stricter enforcement of women's seclusion signified a growing adherence to the practices and tenets of Islam in the face of increasing foreign influence. But for Hofriyati, "Islam" includes a range of customary practices that are not required under doctrinal Sunni Islam or even contravene its

25. As far as I know, women do not drink alcoholic beverages except in the context of a *zār,* but many male Hofriyati socially imbibe.

26. This was part of a revivalist wave that also produced the Wahhabi movement in Arabia. See Holt and Daly (1979:42–43); Trimingham (1965).

rulings.[27] It may be more accurate to suggest that cultural resistance to encroachment from without was being phrased in the idiom of Islam by circumscribing women's activities. In the process, villagers turned a reformatory trend designed to homogenize local practice into a new expression of their identity, and did so through the bodies of women.

Having glimpsed their past, it is hardly surprising to realize that for Hofriyati, a "proper Islamic life-style," however much defined in local terms, should counsel social and cultural insularity. Yet the exigencies of sedentary life in a harsh and fickle environment recommend otherwise. Coupled with a legacy of political caprice on the part of culturally foreign dominators, they suggest that villagers need to forge effective links with non-Hofriyati if they are to survive. At the very least they admonish Hofriyati to cultivate an awareness of external threats and options.

This theme, of exteriority versus interiority, of the necessity for an outward orientation as against the value of an inward focus, is prominent in Hofriyati cultural process at the present time. And as subsequent chapters suggest, it is the concept of womanhood, which, for villagers of either sex, has come to represent its dialectical tension in a number of domains.

In light of the above, it is important to recall that the *zār* became established in Sudan sometime after 1820; moreover, my companions reported that in the village, uninterruptedly occupied only from the turn of the century, the cult gained ground in virtual tandem with local Islamization. I suggest that this concurrence is not fortuitous, that the *zār* expresses women's resistance to certain aspects of "Islam," or quotidian discourse, much as "Islam" and, for that matter, the *zār,* constitute complementary forms of local resistance to the intrusion of foreign influence. These are issues explored in later chapters of the book.

Migration and the Local Economy

In the years since British registration there has been little alteration of land records, save when the Nile changed its course through the floodplain in 1966,[28] and in cases of disputed inheritance or outright sale of which there

27. See Barclay (1964: 136–210).

28. Local land specialists maintain that every hundred years or so a major change occurs in the course the Nile threads through its floodplain following the annual inundation. Reregistration is necessary because land that "belongs" to one side of the river now appears on the opposite bank. Yet this does not result in a boon for farmers on the other shore. An imaginary line (*mirin:* a boundary between plots irrigated from different sources) is drawn through the center of the floodplain: if the river covers land that an individual owned before the change, then extra land that surfaces on the opposing shore belongs to him. This may be fair to landholders, but increases the problem of fractionation. Further, land across the river is inaccessible to the majority who own no boats and do not dare swim the Nile for fear of crocodiles. Perhaps the worst effect of such a change was that which occurred just before 1966: the flow moved toward the west bank, too far for Hofriyati waterwheels to draw water

have been few. Rather than register legacies, people prefer to keep land in the name of the deceased,[29] a practice that disguises the present severity of its fractionation. Many individuals hold de jure title to minute tracts in several locations. If they wish to farm, they, along with residents possessing land far from the village, must rent out what they own in order to lease consolidated plots closer to home. So, despite the relative inelasticity of registration, there exist ways other than purchase or inheritance to gain access to productive land. But such means are costly, leaving the tenant farmer with a mere 30–40 percent of his yield after deducting for rent, water, taxes, and seed. What remains is often spoken for by local merchants who have advanced him credit throughout the year.

Since pacification, the population in Sudan has swelled, and it is improbable that the narrow strip of arable land beside the Nile could now support the village had no labor emigration taken place.[30] But with the growth of government and industry in the cities and recent increased demands for labor in Saudi Arabia and the Gulf, many Hofriyati men have abandoned farming to work outside the village; some of the younger generation have never taken it up. Most of the employed secure jobs in service occupations by activating kinship connections. Many work in shops, hotels, restaurants, and bars (before September 1983), drive taxi or *karrō,* become hospital orderlies, porters and clerks for firms and ministries in Khartoum and Omdurman, or join the army. One is a medical assistant who runs a clinic in a nearby village,[31] three are primary school teachers elsewhere in Sudan. In addition there are a few skilled mechanics and factory workers. A similar pattern of kin sponsorship[32] has more recently enabled village men to find employment in Libya, Jidda, Abu Dhabi, or Kuwait where, in addition to the service occupations above, they work on construction projects.[33]

---

for irrigation on the eastern shore. Many men were forced to abandon farming since only those with diesel pumps could continue to irrigate successfully.

29. See also Barclay (1964: 33) on similar practices near Khartoum.

30. I do not intend the impression that past practice was inflexible. Farming used to be a far more mobile occupation than it is today (cf. Barclay 1964: 27), taking families or parts of families to different locations: the riverside, or *wadīs* at various times in the year. And before Condominium rule, people apparently changed their villages of residence when land became scarce and new opportunities opened up elsewhere, through marriage or some other kinship connection. Moreover, I was told that villagers might change their occupations from farming to herding when possible and expedient, and vice versa. Finally, labor migration is an option that has ancient roots in northern Sudan and certainly may have been practiced before the Mahdiya.

31. The clinician in Hofriyat comes from a neighboring village in the area.

32. One is either recruited through the auspices of a kinsman already in the foreign country, or is sponsored by kin in Sudan who mobilize their contacts at home and abroad and sometimes pool resources to finance a work permit.

33. It is significant that in collecting occupational data, I was forced to list a fair proportion of occupations (16.5 percent) as "unknown": my informants in such cases were

A labor migrant's family—by birth or marriage—commonly remains in the village, where he supports them with periodic remittances. He visits when possible: weekly if he works in Shendi, only once a year if employed in Arabia or Libya. A few also relocate their wives and children, but such moves are rarely permanent. Those who leave generally maintain close ties in Hofriyat, returning to mourn at funerals, give birth, or attend weddings and various religious festivals. Paradoxically, perhaps, labor emigration has permitted even expatriate villagers to sustain a sense of themselves as distinct from the world around them, not only because they continually confront ethnic and political realities different from their own, but because engagement provides resources necessary to support the village's relative insularity in the context of underdevelopment.

Only two Hofriyati women work outside the village, and these are both employed as teachers in girls' primary schools. Very few women participate in farming the fields near Hofriyat. I know only of two (of some hundred and thirty women) who regularly take part in sowing and weeding, and both are seen as pariahs by other women: one is my former landlady who, thrice married, has been on her own for extended periods. Because she is without male kin in the village she has periodically had to fend for herself. The other is a spinster who refused all offers of marriage—to most, an unthinkable act—and whose parents agreed not to force a match. She occasionally works alongside her brothers on land inherited from their father, but is chiefly engaged in dairying. Other women in farming families will contribute their labor at harvest time, but only when insufficient males are available to help. Neither they nor their menfolk consider farming women's responsibility.

There are remarkably few paid male agricultural workers in Hofriyat (four out of a total of sixty-three men engaged in farming in 1977; none in 1984); on occasion, seasonal help is contracted from (male) outsiders, chiefly settled nomads living in the desert some kilometers from the village. But I was told that this is rare.[34] For most farmers, cooperation among male kin and neighbors is the way that temporary labor shortages are met.

Ideally, then, women do not cultivate, and at least on a daily basis, most appear to meet this ideal. But many do participate in other areas of agricultural production. It is mainly their duty to care for the family's sheep and goats, for example. Most, but not all, women who go to the fields to collect fodder for their animals, or fuel for their *kisra* hearths, are older women past childbearing age: those whose morals are least likely to

women who could not specify *how* their absent sons, brothers, fathers, or husbands made a living—just that they did.

34. However, I am recently informed that with the drought, many western Sudanese have drifted to the Nile and expanded the farm labor pool.

be compromised should they meet unrelated men. Of seventy-seven women who either headed households or were wives of household heads in 1977, twenty-five (32.5 percent) said they regularly went to the *jazīra* (farmland, literally, "island": land which is yearly inundated by the Nile) for this purpose. The fifty-one younger women living in these households were all relegated to work in the *bayt,* house. In addition to domestic work, women of farming families were productively engaged in tasks like cleaning grain for storage, but within the courtyard's walls.

Women can and do own arable land or lease it. In either case, a woman generally asks a kinsman to cultivate her fields along with his own in return for a portion of the crop, or designates a coresident son for this job. Six of the above twenty-five actively own land (that is, land that is not being held or used by their brothers as part of a larger legacy), a further three own a bit and rent some more, four rent fields and own none. All maintain some control over what is planted in their fields; all but three are either cowives whose husbands reside most of the time elsewhere, divorcées, or widows, and have some remittance income. The remaining twelve women are engaged on land that their husbands own or rent.

It is important to note that landholdings along the river in Hofriyat are small and very difficult to measure. Their size is expressed in *ʿūds*: the length of a man's extended arm.[35] This describes the width of a strip of land that runs from the start of the floodplain to the edge of the river. Since the river changes course periodically, the length of the field may vary, while its width remains fairly stable. At the same time, the floodplain itself meanders, making an *ʿūd* at the south end of the village somewhat longer than an *ʿūd* at the north. The largest plot (avowedly) owned by a woman in Hofriyat is 13.5 *ʿūds* or approximately 1.5 acres (0.6 of a hectare).[36] It is more than twice as large as other women's personal holdings, which range from 0.2 to 0.6 of an acre. Men's acknowledged holdings average between 0.5 and 2.0 acres, though most who cultivate lease additional plots from nonfarming families with land. Brothers often cooperate in farming, but their extended families do not form a fully corporate group: expenses, taxes, and proceeds are divided proportionately, though profits and in some cases, losses, may occasionally be pooled.

At present, as in 1977, roughly half of functioning Hofriyati households (total N = 77) are supported principally though not exclusively by farming, a further third equally by farming and employment income, the remainder solely by remittances. Yet only 34 percent of all adult males who

35. The "standard" arm generally belongs to a local land specialist or *arāḍi,* and may vary slightly from generation to generation.

36. This was granted to her and her sons from her husband's holdings when she launched an appeal to the *qāḍī* (religious judge) on the grounds that her husband, who had other wives, no longer supported her.

were born in Hofriyat or born elsewhere and married village women (N = 184) now engage in agriculture on a full- or part-time basis. While the largest proportion of men actually residing in Hofriyat are farmers, fewer than half of these exclusively work plots that they or their families own.

Today more men native to Hofriyat live outside the village for most of the year than live within it. However, adult women are far less mobile. Whereas the nonresidency rate for males between the ages of fifteen and forty-nine is 63 percent, the comparable rate for women is only 25 percent. An explanation for this can be found in the fluctuating residence pattern engendered by villagers' dependence on labor emigration. The residence cycle for a typical Hofriyati household progresses as follows. Between the ages of sixteen and twenty an unmarried man whose family does not own land in sufficient quantity or command some other resource—such as a diesel irrigation pump—that affords him full-time lucrative employment, will leave the village in search of work. With help from kin he may take a job in a government department or service industry. He works in Khartoum or, as was becoming more prevalent in 1984, in Arabia for several years, living with other village men in shared accommodation. Regularly, he sends home money to help support his parents and siblings, while setting aside as much as possible against his future wedding.

When, in his mid to late twenties he feels he has sufficient savings, he returns to the village to find a wife. His mother provides him with a list of suitable candidates whom she has scrutinized for this purpose, rating each on her charms and abilities, and the type of closeness (previous kinship) in the match. A man should marry endogamously: preferably his father's brother's daughter, but failing that another cousin. He might have a favorite, perhaps a girl he admired as she danced at another's wedding. He discreetly shops around, makes his choice, then, on his mother's advice and usually with her approval, consults the menfolk responsible for his intended bride. They, in turn, may seek the girls' consent, though this is not considered necessary.[37]

If both sides agree to the alliance, and the religious practitioner can find no astrological impediment to the match, an auspicious date is chosen for signing the marriage contract and transferring the *mahr* or *sadd-al-māl*—a dowrylike payment from the groom to the bride's father, ostensibly to be held for her in trust should she later be divorced. Sometime between that date and the wedding itself the groom presents his bride with the *shayla* (literally, the burden or "that which is carried"): a trousseau of

37. In matters of family law, most northern Sudanese follow the Maliki school of Islamic jurisprudence, which stipulates that a daughter may be married against her wishes should her morals be jeopardized. This condition is so vague that fathers rarely consult their daughters about prospective suitors; however, Hofriyati parents generally do not force a match which their daughter opposes. Here a girl's mother might act as her advocate.

clothing, cosmetics, and jewelry, plus quantities of spices, oil, and flour to be used in preparing meals for her family's expected guests. He might then return to the city to resume work until he has acquired everything else that is needed to mount the wedding feast.

The wedding itself is celebrated in the village with festivities lasting as long as seven days. Afterward the groom goes back to work, leaving behind his bride in Hofriyat. Though he regularly forwards funds for her maintenance, he himself returns only for holidays and emergencies. Following her wedding a woman may be taken to live with her husband's kin; more commonly she remains in her natal household until after the births of several children. Her husband might then build her a house in the village (often in or near his parents' compound), or one of them may have acquired a house through inheritance.

However, should a man rise in his job to a point where he can afford to support a small family in the city, he may send for his wife and children.[38] There they live in rented accommodation, shared, perhaps, with kin, until his wife again becomes pregnant. Early in her second trimester she returns to the village with her youngest offspring, remaining there until a few months after the baby's birth. Then she rejoins her husband in the city, the entire cycle being repeated with subsequent pregnancies. School-aged children either remain in the city to be cared for by relatives during their mother's absence, or accompany her to Hofriyat where they enroll in the local public school. Several may continue to reside with grandparents in the village after their mother's departure.

At some point, however, the cost of housing a burgeoning family in Khartoum or Omdurman becomes too great. A man now considers re-establishing his family in the village where it is cheaper for them to be maintained. He or his wife might hold rights to a vacant house or access to some residential land on which to build. Once settled in Hofriyat his wife is left to tend the children while he goes back to work.

As he approaches later middle age a man contemplates taking up a less taxing occupation in the village where he can be close to family and friends. Men over fifty begin trickling back to Hofriyat, content to rent a little farmland and be supported by their sons. Now as permanent residents they can actively participate in local politics, spend a day at cards or backgammon drinking endless glasses of tea, and enjoy the prestige of being household heads.

Unlike the majority of men, women spend most of their lives in their natal villages, or sometimes in their husbands' villages should they happen to have wed non-Hofriyati. The ratio of adult women to adult men in Hofriyat is understandably high: 2.2 : 1. Yet it is a situation which many

38. He might also seize this opportunity to take a second, "city" wife.

women say they prefer. While rural life is hard in comparison with that in the towns and cities of Sudan where electricity and running water are standard luxuries, women are freer here to do as they wish within the bounds of appropriate behavior. Though men are kept informed about their womenfolk's activities in letters and reports from visiting kin, husbands and fathers are not present to govern every move.

Marriages that follow the pattern I have described are fragile. They are fraught with prolonged separations during which opportunities arise for a man to take a second wife and this, for financial reason if no other, may lead to divorce for the first. Thus women in the village pay a price for their relative liberty. Husbands at large are an unceasing source of worry and frustration, a strain which the *zār,* to some extent, addresses.

In Hofriyat there exists a seemingly endless variety of living arrangements, all of which make sense in terms of the residence cycle outlined above. Many of these complex, highly fluid households are doubtless the products of financial expediency. Yet underlying this is an explicit preference for women who are near relatives to live together,[39] and if not in the same household, then at least close by. The comparative boundedness of women within the village and even within specific households is, I suggest, one expression of a prevalent theme in Hofriyati culture: the tendency toward enclosure described in earlier pages but more fully explored in chapters 2 and 3.

Women's World

A woman's day begins at dawn, with a cacophony of birdsong, rooster calls, and donkey brays that circles through the village as first light breaks on the horizon. For some the morning starts with prayer. Soon from every *ḥōsh* comes the sound of charcoal being pounded, followed by a banging of kerosene-tin stoves to loosen last night's ashes, and the sweet promising odor of burning grass as women start their cooking fires.

The kettle is put on to boil, with quantities of tea and sugar for the morning brew. School-aged children are awakened, "*Gom, ya* Mohammed." "*Gomi, ya* Hayat; *gomi, yalla!*" Then the woman, a married daughter, or one too old for school, takes a battered enamel bowl and enters the goat pen to milk the animals. The milk is boiled, added to the simmering tea, and poured into glasses. Children drift into the kitchen: a low, simple

39. Because most marriages are between close kin, even women who live with their husbands' mothers are likely to be living with a near consanguineal relative. However, women prefer to reside with their own mothers and sisters and, because they spend so much time in their mothers' homes with each pregnancy, are often able to extend such visits to quasi-permanent residence.

room at the back of the compound with a gap between walls and ceiling to allow the escape of cooking fumes. The children sit on battered *angarībs* among dishes and utensils set to dry the night before, drink their tea, and eat some bread or rice left over from yesterday's dinner. Someone takes a tray of tea and bread to the men's quarters where, if they are in the village, the woman's husband and older sons will have spent the night. Soon the children head off to school. Her husband leaves for the fields, or if he is a migrant home on vacation, he rises late, visits friends, or plays with his younger children. By 7:00 A.M., village paths are empty of men.

A woman and her daughters now tidy the house, sweep the courtyard, fetch water from the wells to fill the household's several water jars, wet down the earthen floors. If the cooperative bakery is not suffering a shortage of fuel or flour, one of them may visit to buy the day's bread. Or, if her *ḥōsh* is equipped with an outdoor clay oven and wheat flour and wood are plentiful, she may bake the round, leavened loaves herself, and sell any surplus to her neighbors. Two or three times a week, she or one of her daughters carries a load of *dura* to the local mill where it is ground into flour for *kisra*. Several women make the trip together, baskets balanced atop their heads, a dignified yet animated procession.

Breakfast (*faṭūr*) must next be prepared and served around nine o'clock, when children return briefly from school and men from their pursuits, unless they have been invited out. The meal typically consists of bread and *fūl* (stewed fava beans). If there are guests, small quantities of fried sheep's liver, chopped boiled egg, mashed eggplant and peanut salad, or raw tomatoes and onions may also be served, providing the ingredients can be obtained from neighbors or brought by men from the *sūq*. A child, usually a little boy, may now be sent to one of the local shops to buy a bit of tea or sugar if the family's stores are low, or to see if neighbors can part with a handful of rice or some lentils for the afternoon meal. Alternatively, if a dish is plentiful and no guests expected that day, a serving may be sent next door.

When breakfast is ready, bowls of food are placed in the center of an aluminum tray and surrounded by wheat bread or *kisra*. People sit on *angarībs* or chairs around a small tin table that holds the tray, or squat before it on the earthen floor. A container of water is passed, and each in turn rinses her right hand before breaking bread and using the piece to spoon some food from the bowls. In most households, men and older boys eat separately from women, at slightly different times and, if the house is commodious, in different rooms. Children eat together in the kitchen.

If the men are busy in the fields and cannot return for breakfast, canisters of food and a thermos of tea are taken to them by the woman or her daughter, who may use this opportunity to gather fodder or fuel on the way home. Dishes must next be washed, and *kisra* batter mixed and left a few hours to season. But if the day is warm, *kisra* is baked before or just after breakfast.

Women spend the time between 10:00 A.M. and 1:30 or 2:00 P.M. in various activities. Once or twice a week, the laundry must be done. If she is not tied to the house by several young children or a resident husband, a woman may take the family's clothes to a friend and kinswoman's house, where the work is performed in a genial atmosphere with others similarly engaged. Alternatively, women of adjacent households may congregate to embroider sheets, or make *ṭubugs*. These flat, circular basketry covers for food trays are bought for a few piasters (deducting for materials) by elderly grandmothers, then resold to Fallata women,[40] who market them in Kabushiya. Others might gather for a fodder-collecting trip to the *jazīra*, or meet to braid each other's hair, stain each other's hands and feet with henna (sometimes for a small fee), or take smoke baths in the kitchen (see chapter 2).

Women are also under considerable obligation to use this time to visit sick neighbors and relatives, mothers newly delivered, girls and boys recently circumcised, households in mourning. Not to do so within an day or two of the event would cause a rift in the community, significantly damaging the woman's reputation and that of her household, even her kinship group. The obligation holds for adjacent villages: most days, bands of colorfully attired women can be found along the lorry paths that link Hofriyat to neighboring hamlets, en route to kinswomen's homes.

Within the village, older women with hands too arthritic for basketry or needlework, or younger women desiring company, gather in each other's homes for coffee around 11:00 A.M. A number of women excel in making coffee, which is roasted over an open fire, pounded fine, then boiled Turkish style with a little cardamom or cinnamon, and served with sugar in tiny porcelain cups. Those who begin to drink coffee, they say, must do so every day in order to avoid the headaches that come when you stop. Men who are at home will also be served at this time, though rarely with the women.

In short, the midday hours are for socializing with other women: in leisure, obligatory visiting, or communal work. Small children accompany their mothers or are left in the care of older siblings. Until they are five or six, children of both sexes play together within or outside the courtyard walls. After that age, girls are increasingly confined to the home, unless attending school or performing chores. Younger girls discharge a good many household tasks before or after school: their work enables their mothers to socialize as much as they are obliged to do.

40. The origins of the Fallata are in West Africa or western Sudan. A handful of Fallata men and women are engaged in buying and selling in the circular market system that twice weekly includes Kabushiya.

Women with husbands and children to feed return home between 1:00 and 2:00 P.M. in order to prepare lunch (*ghadā*), the most important meal of the day. Ambulatory children, however, are fed wherever they happen to be; they eat and even sleep in the homes of neighbors and kin, who assume a generalized responsibility for their care. Women, too, will eat with their sisters or cousins if visiting in the neighborhood and no men are at home to command their presence.

If it has not been done earlier, one woman in the household now bakes sheets of wafer-thin *kisra* on the family griddle—a hot and demanding task which, like laundry, is often shared with neighbors. Vegetables must be washed and prepared for stewing, or if meat is available, it must be washed, cut, and fried or boiled. Most people eat fresh meat only once or twice a week—on market days, or when a neighbor has slaughtered a goat and divided the carcass for sale or exchange. Most subsist on various kinds of vegetable sauces, thickened with desiccated okra or powdered *sharmūṭ*, strips of air-dried meat. Farming families keep a cow or two, and use the milk to make *rōb,* a thin yoghurt eaten like sauce with *kisra.*

Lunch is served about 3:00 P.M. and followed by tea. Men and their guests, should there be any, rest in their quarters during the heat of the day before again departing the *ḥōsh*. Women return the kitchen to order, then rest or visit until just before sundown. In late afternoon they round up their goats, let loose since morning to forage, and herd them into enclosures. If necessary they are milked again: for those who have animals the evening tea is prepared with goat's milk, as at dawn. Men and older children gravitate home for tea some time between 5:00 and 6:00. Yet this is also a favorite time for visiting, by verbal invitation, and from 4:30 on the *ḥōsh* may be teaming with people or empty of all but the elderly. Evening tea is one time when men and women occasionally sit together and talk.

At nightfall, younger children are put to bed after a supper of rice and milk or leftovers from lunch. Adults and older children eat a small meal (*ʿashā,* supper) of leftovers, fine egg noodles mixed with oil and sugar, or *fūl* purchased from one of two ladies who regularly prepare it for sale from their kitchens. *ʿAshā* is taken just before retiring, at about nine o'clock; it is an informal affair and often skipped.

In clement weather the household's *angarīb*s are brought outdoors: sisters and neighbors sit talking beneath the stars until their babies drop off to sleep. One who lives alone with young children arranges for an older child to sleep with her in her *ḥōsh*.

During visits, women socialize: *itwannas,* a word that connotes both amiable conversation and exchange of information. Women in Hofriyat are by no means isolated from one another, though the fact that many men are outside the village for much of the year, or even much of the day, contributes to their relative autonomy. A number of my friends suggested that if their husbands or fathers were present they would be unable to leave the *ḥōsh* as often as they do. A man cannot deny his wife or adult daughter the opportunity to visit others in times of crisis, for that is both her duty and prerogative as a representative of the household. But he can stipulate that her visits be brief and prevent her from entertaining friends in their home. Women visit each other spontaneously when their husbands are absent from the village, for then they are not so busy (husbands are spoken of as guests whose whims, by local hospitality codes, must be catered to), and many of their tasks can be shared. But when a friend's husband is at home there is always the possibility of running into unrelated men who are his visitors. This causes a woman, married or not, considerable embarrassment, and is something she seeks to avoid.

Thus husbands and even fathers—her own and others'—are often viewed by a woman as obstacles to *wanasa,* sociability, companionship with those of her own sex. *Wanasa* has implications beyond mere conversation. For it is through her relationships with other women that a married woman, especially, gains access to an informal network of exchange in food and other staples (often in short supply), clothing, child care, advice, support, and information. News or gossip is important not only for keeping her attuned to crises in others' households which call for her attention, and not only for synchronizing the exertion of moral pressure on menfolk (to obviate a divorce or future marriage; see Constantinides [1982 : 193]), but also because it enables her to perform her role in social reproduction more effectively. She learns which women's brothers or sons are contemplating marriage, what their economic prospects are, which of the *banāt* (virgins, unmarried girls) would make suitable brides for her kinsmen. Possession of such information is particularly relevant in a community like Hofriyat, where politically and economically significant social relations are mediated by kinship and reproduced by way of marriage. Women, as managers of information and masters of reconnaissance, wield considerable local power.

Not only do women manage information, they also manage their households. The "lady of the house" (*sitt al-bayt*) keeps close control over its stores of food and other necessary supplies. When stock in any item is low, it is her responsibility to tell her husband or father of the lack, and his responsibility to replace it. Alternatively, if he is a labor migrant, he regularly sends her money, either directly or through a kinsman, with which to meet the family's expenses. She in turn requests a resident kinsman to obtain the items she needs from Kabushiya. Daily requirements are met within the village at one of the local shops; provided the mails are good and her remittance arrives on time, she uses cash; otherwise, she buys on credit. Significantly, any money a woman earns weaving *ṭubugs* or selling cooked food belongs to her alone, and need not be put toward balancing household accounts (though it often is). But a young wife without the help of a teen-aged daughter finds little time for such pursuits, let alone time to acquit her visiting obligations. This is particularly true if and when her husband is in the village; then, women say, the work is doubled. The laundry must be done more regularly, the house more scrupulously cleaned; meals should be more elaborate and prepared more closely to schedule. Having a man around the house clearly has its disadvantages.

Yet to suggest that gender relations are conflictual would be to convey a false impression. Women also socialize with men, typically their brothers and sons, with whom they may experience strong bonds of affection and trust. Sibling and maternal relations tend to be close to Hofriyat, where marital ones are often marked by wariness, at least in their earlier years, despite the fact that most people marry close kin.

Still, a woman's everyday world is peopled mainly by other women and, of course, by children. The following chapter examines how Hofriyati women and men regard each other as different kinds of human being; here I would caution that this derives as much from their distinctive and complementary social experiences—from the fact of segregation itself[41]—as from jural asymmetries or ideological precepts about the natures of females and males.

41. For an extensive discussion of this issue see Wikan (1982) on women in Oman.

2

Enclosures

Fear Allah, in whose name you plead with one another,
And honour the wombs that bear you.

—Quran 4 : 1

Throughout a turbid past and into an unsettled present, Hofriyati have shown remarkable capacity for adapting to changing circumstances. Their culture is—or historically appears to be—extremely fluid, even capricious: now absorbing, now abandoning some practice or belief. Small changes take place quickly: certain symbolic household ornaments (discussed in this chapter) that were ubiquitous in village homes in 1976 had completely disappeared from use when I visited again in 1984, replaced by painted Quranic inscriptions, glossy high-tech ads, and posters of Marlboro cowboys.[1] When asked what had become of the ornaments, women said, "We have left them. Such things are not Islam." The implication that cigarettes and automobiles *are* Islam reflects the current relevance of Arabia as a locus of material as well as spiritual power. Substantial changes—significant shifts of religious orientation or kinship reckoning—may be more gradual, accretions of minor mutations and assimilations. Hofriyati culture has responded to external threats and influences with flexibility and resilience,[2] protected, perhaps, by a dynamic syncretism and capacity for metamorphosis. Contemporary practice is informed and enriched by various religious and secular traditions, but is more than the sum of these. Embedded in its surface expressions—customs (*ʿādāt*), beliefs, ceremonial procedures—lies a network of interlocking symbols, idioms, and metaphors that provides the context in whose terms Hofriyati interact and derive meaning from their experiences of the world. This system of reference, part religious, part mundane (the two defy separation), itself drawn from several sources, may be one of the more enduring aspects of village culture.

1. These decorations reflect the increased impact of fundamentalist Islam, and Western secularism as filtered through Egyptian television dramas, which in turn results largely from men's participation in the labor force outside of Hofriyat, either within Sudan or, more frequently, abroad. See Kennedy (1978*b* : 142) on similar changes in Egyptian Nubia; this issue in Hofriyat is further discussed in chapter 9.

2. Much as Kennedy (1978*c* : 151) suggests for Nubians in Upper Egypt.

Hofriyati logic of everyday life—for that is what I am talking about: an implicit, commonsense or "natural" philosophy—is reconciled to change yet relatively stable in form. Stability, however, is not ultimation. Villagers' practical consciousness comprises a nexus of ideas and metaphors which serve as guides to experience and its interpretations, but do not wholly determine either. This feature, an essential pliancy or indeterminacy (S. F. Moore 1975 : 219 ff.) is not always a positive one, as will be seen. But coupled with a firmly moral sense of identity, it may be key to Hofriyati survival.

Village culture concedes the impossibility of standing still, of remaining untouched by historical vicissitudes or the challenges of a demanding environment. Its participants do not resist change; they embrace it and, in so doing, seek to control it. Ideas and objects originating in the outside world are often absorbed and processed in such a way that, rather than diminishing the integrity of Hofriyati culture, they actually sustain it.[3] Villagers are at once disposed to novelty and to perceive a thread of coherence, explicability, in the flux of everyday life. The political climate shifts, men working outside the village are swayed by urban ways, local styles are transformed by Egyptian soap operas avidly followed on battery-run TVs, yet Hofriyati maintain a strong image of themselves as distinct from other groups (cf. O'Brien [1986] on ethnicity as adaptation in Sudan).

In this chapter and the next I describe that image and its premises as they appear to a non-Hofriyati observer. I reiterate that this is an interpretation and not to be mistaken for exegesis. It is my understanding of informants' ideas and assumptions about the world they inhabit, my phrasing of what is implicit in Hofriyati practice. Villagers are, I submit, conscious of such concepts, since their breach occasions controversy; but they are not necessarily self-conscious of them, or conscious in an obviously articulable way.

How to proceed with such an enterprise? In writing of her discoveries in the field an ethnographer frequently feels pressed, as I have, to anticipate herself, opening with general conclusions and working backward to particulars. That, of course, is the reverse of how one actively learns an alien ideational system—to the extent that one can. The novice is first tossed about on waves of seemingly unintelligible events. Eventually, she finds a toehold. By unromantic, plodding detective work: tracing blind leads, dogging the flimsiest clues, asking frequent impertinent questions, clearly invading others' privacy, she comes to see a pattern in what earlier struck her as chaos.[4] A "plot" is pieced together from specific details. The

3. See Knight (1985 : 3–4) for a discussion of similar processes among the Tuareg.

4. Whether this derives from the ethnographer's need to impose order on her experiences, or her informants' is, of course, a central problem in anthropology. See Dwyer (1982); also, along different lines, Rosen (1982).

data presented here have been reworked considerably, but I have tried to preserve some taste of this process in describing how I made sense of my observations in Hofriyat.

To get at the underlying principles of villagers' cultural logic I investigate some of its salient expressions: pharaonic circumcision, cousin marriage, life crisis rites and prohibitions. Such issues are of particular interest to women, and the reader is reminded that an interpretation of women's reality is what is aimed for in this book. While women's cultural "competence" undoubtedly varies from men's in some respects, there is substantial overlap in others, and a basic complicity on fundamental meanings. One area of mutual concern is human fertility and reproduction; this, indisputably, is the focal value in Hofriyat.[5] Circumcision, possession, crisis rites, all speak to this crucial issue; so salient is it that most village ceremonies are modeled on the wedding and phrased in the symbolism of marriage (cf. Kennedy 1978*c*: 158; Barclay 1964: 241).

The wedding in Hofriyat is a powerful image: it crystallizes cultural meanings and provides an arena for manifesting, negotiating, and realizing village identity. The staging of one is a public concern for weeks in advance. Nonresident villagers flock home for the ceremony, whose successes and shortcomings fuel conversations for months to come. Festivities are carefully tape-recorded. Cloned cassettes quickly circulate through the village, and the thin warble of love songs from the latest nuptial dance accompanies women as they cook or wash clothes until replaced by the next. The wedding in Hofriyat is, in Singer's terms, a "cultural performance" (1955, 1958; also Geertz 1973; Ortner 1973), an encapsulated expression of villagers' central concepts and relevant concerns. But more than this, it supplies a metaphoric representation of how social relations are—or ought to be—contracted between disparate parties other than men and women in Hofriyat: spirits and humans, foreign societies and one's own. It is a key cultural construct, an exposition of which constitutes—more or less implicitly—the organizational framework for this book.

Pharaonic Circumcision

My first glimpse of the symbolic matrix informing Hofriyati life came from attempting to understand the practice of female circumcision. During the summer of 1976 I witnessed several of these operations, performed on all girls sometime between the ages of five and ten.[6] Despite my (self-confessed) reluctance, village friends made a point of my attendance, wak-

5. As it is in lower Nubia to the north (Kennedy 1978*b*: 130 ff.).

6. Circumcisions are performed on both sexes during school holidays in May and June. In 1984 I saw none because I left the village at the end of April.

ing me in the dark predawn lest I miss the surgery at daybreak. What follows is a description of one such observation.[7]

June 12, 1976. A band of pink traces the horizon as Zaineb and I thread a maze of walls into the heart of the village. We enter a houseyard washed in shadows. Miriam, the local midwife, has finished circumcising one sister and is preparing to operate on the second. (Sisters close in age are usually circumcised together; otherwise, the operation is an individual affair.) A crowd of women, many of them ḥabōbāt *(grandmothers) have gathered in the yard—not a man in sight. I find myself propelled to the center of the room; it is important, says Zaineb, to see this up close. She bids me record what I see.*

The girl lies docile on an angarīb, *beneath which smoulders incense in a cracked clay pot. Her hands and feet are stained with henna applied the night before. Several kinswomen support her torso; two others hold her legs apart. Miriam thrice injects her genitals with local anesthetic, then, in the silence of the next few moments, takes a small pair of scissors and quickly cuts away her clitoris and labia minora; the rejected tissue is caught in a bowl below the bed. Miriam tells me this is the* laḥma juwa, *or inner flesh. I am surprised there is so little blood. She says that hemorrhage is less likely to occur at sunup, before the child has fully risen.* Mushāhara *customs, too, prevent bloodloss, the henna being part of these.*[8] *Miriam staunches the flow with a white cotton cloth. She removes a surgical needle from her midwife's kit—an elaborate red tin box—and threads it with suture. She sews together the girl's outer labia leaving a small opening at the vulva. After a liberal application of antiseptic the operation is over.*

Women gently lift the sisters as their angarībs *are spread with multicolored* birishs, *"red" bridal mats. The girls seem to be experiencing more shock than pain, and I wonder if the anesthetic has finally taken effect. Amid trills of joyous ululations we adjourn to the courtyard for tea; the girls are also brought outside. There they are invested with the* jirtig*: ritual jewelry, perfumes, and cosmetic pastes worn to protect those whose reproductive ability is vulnerable to attack from malign spirits and the evil eye. The sisters wear bright new dresses, bridal shawls (called* garmosīs, *singular), and their family's gold. Relatives sprinkle guests with cologne, much as they would at a wedding; redolent incense rises on the morning air. Newly circumcised girls are referred to as little brides (*ʿarūs*); much that is done for a bride is done for them, but in a minor key. Importantly, they have now been rendered marriageable.*

Before Miriam received government training in midwifery, female circumcisions were performed differently in Hofriyat, though their ceremonial

7. Portions of the following were previously published in *American Ethnologist* 9(4): 682–98 and 15(1):4–27 (Boddy 1982*b*, 1988).

8. *Mushāhara* is discussed in chapter 3.

aspects were much as I describe. For women circumcised prior to 1969 the operation was more radical, less sterile, and in the absence of anesthetic injections, more painful than it is today. My friends recounted their own experiences: A circular palm-fiber mat with its center removed was fitted over a freshly dug hole in the ground.[9] The girl was seated on the mat at the edge of the hole. As kinswomen held her arms and legs, the midwife, with no apparent concern for sterile procedure, scraped away all of her external genitalia, including the labia majora, using a straight razor. Then she pulled together the skin that remained on either side of the wound and fastened it with thorns inserted at right angles. (Fresh acacia thorns produce a numbness when they pierce the skin and may have helped relieve the pain.) These last were held in place by thread or scraps of cloth wound around their ends. A straw or thin hollow reed was inserted posteriorly so that when the wound healed there would be an opening in the scar for elimination of urine and menstrual blood. The girl's legs were then tied together and she was made to lie on an *angarīb* for up to forty days to promote healing. When the wound was thought to have healed sufficiently the thorns were removed and the girl unbound.

Both operations described are versions of pharaonic circumcision, *ṭahūr faraownīya.*[10] According to villagers the practice is a legacy of the pharaonic past, whence its name. However, analysis of human mummies from that period fails to confirm this assertion so far as premortem vaginal closure is concerned (Ghalioungui 1963:96; Huelsman 1976:123; Barclay 1964:238). From historians' and travelers' accounts we know that the custom has long been practiced in this area. Yet its origins remain obscure (Abdalla 1982:63–72; Boddy 1982*a, b*:685–86; Cloudsley 1983:101–3; Gruenbaum 1982:5; Sanderson 1981:27–29).

Though conventionally termed "circumcision," the procedure is not physically equivalent to the like-named operation performed on boys. In Hofriyat, male circumcision entails removal of the penile prepuce, as it generally does throughout the Middle East and, indeed, the West. Pharaonic circumcision, however, is more extreme, involving excision of most external genitalia followed by infibulation: intentional occlusion of the vulva and obliteration of the vaginal meatus. It results in the formation of thick, resistant scar tissue, a formidable obstruction to penetration.

A less severe operation, structurally similar to that performed on boys,

9. This is also basic to the practice of smoke bathing (later discussed) and was used in rope delivery, an outmoded method of delivery where a woman in labor would support herself by grasping onto ropes suspended from the main ceiling beam of a room. The shallow pit was intended to receive blood and other fluids.

10. The operation post-1969 is referred to as *ṭahūr wasiṭ,* "intermediate circumcision." In Hofriyat as elsewhere in Sudan, it is often (mistakenly) referred to as "*sunna*" circumcision, discussed in note 11. See also Gruenbaum (1982:7) and Cloudsley (1983:109).

is currently gaining ground in Khartoum and Omdurman. This is referred to as *maṣri* (Egyptian) or *sunna* ("orthodox," traditional) circumcision and consists in removing only the prepuce or hood of the clitoris. It is not yet practiced in Hofriyat and is a matter of some controversy there. Men working in Saudi Arabia and the Islamic principalities of the Gulf have come under increasing influence from fundamentalist Wahhabi Islam; some now perceive infibulation as contrary to Islamic tenets and advocate the less radical operation, considering it to be religiously approved.[11] But women are skeptical of the innovated procedure. While realizing that it is less hazardous to health than pharaonic circumcision, they continue to oppose it on aesthetic and hygienic grounds and in this lies a clue to its deeper significance. Several women I questioned in 1984 made their feelings graphically clear: each depicted *sunna* circumcision by opening her mouth, and pharaonic, by clamping her lips together. "Which is better," they asked, "an ugly opening or a dignified closure?" Women avoid being photographed laughing or smiling for precisely this reason: orifices of the human body, and particularly those of women, are considered most appropriate when closed or, failing that, when minimized. This theme receives extensive treatment below.

Fertility and Sexuality

Several writers[12] have noted that one expressed purpose of pharaonic circumcision is to increase a man's sexual pleasure by diminishing the size of the vaginal opening. Yet male Hofriyati who favor the *sunna* procedure on religious grounds also say they expect it would reduce gynecological problems and improve sexual relations (see also Kennedy 1978*c*: 166). Hence, the pleasure argument might well be a rationalization for the practice that has simply outworn its effectiveness in Hofriyat.

There exists a broad range of explanations for infibulation[13] which together form a complex rationale that operates to sustain and justify the

11. This is a matter of some debate, though as El Dareer (1982:71) remarks, to say that circumcision is "*sunna*" makes it unquestionable for Muslims, for whom Islam is not merely a set of religious beliefs, but a way of life. The Hadith stipulate that whereas circumcision is required for males, *khafḍ* (reduction) is an embellishment for females. Yet few if any women in Saudi Arabia are circumcised, and even the minor operation has been outlawed in Egypt since 1967 (Cloudsley 1983:110). Hofriyati are aware that not all Muslim women are circumcised or, more radically, infibulated; they do believe, however, that Bedouin girls in Saudi Arabia undergo a "*sunna*" operation in infancy. In Sudan, "*sunna*" circumcision is often confused with what I have described as the *wasiṭ* or intermediate operation (note 10).

12. See Barclay (1964:240); Cloudsley (1983:116–17); Gruenbaum (1982:8); El Dareer (1982:74); Assaad (1980:13); Ammar (1954:120); Kennedy (1978*b*:131).

13. For examples, see Boddy (1982*b*); Sanderson (1981); El Dareer (1982); Abdalla (1982).

practice. Among them, however, those which refer to the preservation of chastity and the curbing of women's sexual desire seem most persuasive, given that in Sudan, as elsewhere in the Muslim world, the dignity and honor of a family are vested in the conduct of its womenfolk (cf. Barclay 1964; Hayes 1975; Trimingham 1965; also see Ammar 1954; Assaad 1980; El Saadawi 1977; and Kennedy 1978*c* for Egypt). Women are regarded by men as weak, morally inferior beings, oversexed and inherently inclined to wantonness, devoted to sensuality. Much as Rosen (1978: 566 ff., 1982) and Dwyer (1978: 152–53) have described for Morocco, Hofriyati stipulate that women and men differ in the amounts of *nafs:* animal life force, including lusts, emotions, and desires, and *ʿagl:* reason, rationality, ability to control one's emotions and behave in socially appropriate ways, that each sex is capable of realizing. Whereas men are thought to develop considerable *ʿagl* as they mature, the amount that women are able to develop is less. On this point, women and men concur. But men go on to propose that women are wholly governed by their carnal natures: being less intelligent than men, they are unable to exercise conscious restraint.[14] Hence the need for circumcision to curb and socialize their sexual desires, lest a woman should, even unwittingly, bring irreparable shame to her family through misbehavior.

Yet, as significant as this explanation seems, it represents, I suggest, an essentially masculine point of view. Women's acquiescence is less than complete on the issue, and from their (albeit muted) perspective, the rationale confuses causes with effects. Moreover, it places undue emphasis on women's sexuality where to them the principal concern is, and should be, their fertility. In what follows here and in subsequent sections, I substantiate this claim by drawing on information given mainly by female informants. Fertility and sexuality are, of course, two sides of the same coin, yet each sex publicly emphasizes one more than the other. Both sides point to villagers' fundamental concern with human reproduction, underscored throughout Hofriyati symbolism.

What prepubescent infibulation *does*—though this need not be its original purpose nor, perhaps, what it is intended to do in Hofriyat today—is ensure that a girl is a virgin when she marries for the first time. It does control her sexuality and makes it less likely that she will engage in extramarital affairs. A young girl both dreads and eagerly anticipates her wedding day: she welcomes the elevation in status while fearing what it implies, having to endure sexual relations with her husband. Informants told me that for women circumcised in the radical manner, it may take as

14. This conflicts, however, with local images of the sexes: metaphors for women evoke domestic animals and birds, and are mainly collective (chapter 3). And while faunal metaphors for men are rare, those that exist refer to singular, untamed, powerful animals such as leopards.

long as two years of continuous effort before penetration can occur. But for a man it is a point of honor to have a child born within a year of his marriage. Thus the midwife may be summoned in secret, under cover of darkness, to assist the couple by surgically enlarging the bride's vaginal orifice, a service for which she charges an exorbitant fee.[15]

Because they find it so painful, many of the women I spoke to said they avoid sex whenever possible, encouraging their husbands only when they wish to become pregnant. Yet pregnancy is regularly desired by both husband and wife, for having children is the hallmark of an economically productive marriage and the principal criterion of social adulthood (see also Gruenbaum 1982 : 17); it discharges the divine mandate to procreate (cf. Delaney 1988 : 77). Sexual relations do not necessarily become easier for the couple over time. When a woman gives birth the midwife must be present not only to cut through the scar tissue and release the child,[16] but also to reinfibulate her once the baby is born.

Reinfibulation guarantees that after each delivery a woman's body is restored, at least superficially, to its premarital "virginal" condition. Further, during her forty-day confinement she is again presented to her husband as a bride and given gifts of clothing and jewelry similar to those she received at her wedding, though these are diminished in scale. As is discussed later in the book, a woman's reinfibulation and her husband's repeated "bridal" prestations should be seen as exchanges that serve to reestablish the essential dynamic of the marital relationship: production and provisioning on the part of the husband, consumption and, subsequently, reproduction on the part of the wife. Thus a divorced or widowed woman might undergo reinfibulation in anticipation of remarriage—renewing, in a sense, her virginal status, and preparing herself to reengage the conjugal dialectic.

As Hayes (1975) has rightly observed, virginity assumes a special significance in northern Sudan, for here its physiological manifestations are socially controlled.[17] Its loss does not entail an absolute and irrevocable change of state, but one which is, in part, reversible. As she succinctly remarks, "In Sudan, virgins are made, not born" (p. 622). Contrary to West-

15. Lest it be thought that older women as a group therefore have a vested economic interest in seeing the custom maintained, it should be pointed out that midwives are few and in the past learned the profession from their mothers and maternal aunts. As Cloudsley (1983 : 117) notes, however, a call for the midwife may be a blow to a husband's self-esteem and reflect on his virility, "so he may insist there shall be no outside interference and use a knife, razor, fingernail or piece of glass" to open his wife.

16. For infibulated women an anterior episiotomy is usually necessary, and may be administered in addition to the more standard posterolateral incision (see Cloudsley 1983 : 117). Much depends, however, on the midwife's circumcision technique, which is not standardized.

17. See also Cloudsley (1983), whose book *Women of Omdurman* is subtitled *Life, Love, and the Cult of Virginity*.

ern assumptions, "virginity" in Hofriyat is a social construct, not a physical condition. And it has less to do with sexual innocence than a woman's dormant fertility. Here, fertility and reproduction are the salient concepts, though their practical implication in pharaonic circumcision is oblique and sometimes obscured by the explicit, and formally masculine, ideology.

Thus, while the operation restrains female sexuality, this is not the purpose avowed it by women. Informants assert that it is performed on young girls so as to make their bodies clean (*naẓīf*), smooth (*nāᶜim*), and pure (*ṭahir*), this last term furnishing the Sudanese colloquial for circumcision in general: *ṭahūr* ("cleansing" or "purification").[18] Women say a girl who has not been purified through circumcision may not marry, thus may not bear children and attain a position of respect in later years. Circumcision prepares her body for womanhood: it confers on her the right to bear children, while marriage provides her with opportunities to advance her position by giving birth, especially to sons.

The promiscuity argument earlier described apparently confuses the sexuality of women with their ability and prerogative to bear children, where these aspects of womanhood ought to be distinguished. The pleasure argument, on the other hand, overly dissociates the sexuality of males from their ability to impregnate women. The following incident demonstrates: I once overheard a man talking about his beautiful *bit ᶜamm*—father's brother's daughter and the preferred spouse—whom he wished he had wed. This woman had been married for over a year and had not yet conceived. Said the man, "By God, if I had married her, she would have had twins by now!" Despite appearances, then, fertility is of paramount concern to both sexes (cf. Kennedy 1978*b, c*).

Infibulation neither increases nor for that matter limits male sexual pleasure—this is largely irrelevant here—so much as it ensures or socializes female fertility (also Kennedy 1978*b*: 131). By removing their external genitalia, female Hofriyati seek not to diminish their own sexual pleasure—though this is an obvious effect—so much as to enhance their femininity. Pharaonic circumcision is a symbolic act which brings sharply into focus the fertility potential of women by dramatically deemphasizing their sexuality. In insisting upon circumcision for their daughters, women assert their social indispensability, an importance which is not as the sexual partners of their husbands,[19] nor—in this highly segregated, overtly male authoritative society—as their servants, sexual or otherwise, but as the mothers of men. The ultimate social goal of a woman is to become, with her husband, the cofounder of a lineage section. As a respected *ḥabōba* she

18. Ancillary notions embraced by this radical are chastity, modesty, and virtuousness. See Wehr (1976: 570–71).

19. Women I spoke to did not object to their husbands' visiting brothels, so long as they did not spend too much money in such establishments.

is "listened to," she may be sent on the *ḥaj* (pilgrimage to Mecca) by her husband or sons, and her name is remembered in village genealogies for several generations (Boddy 1985 : 103–5).

Village women do not achieve social recognition by behaving or becoming like men, but by becoming less like men, physically, sexually, and socially (see also Assaad 1980 : 6). Male as well as female rites stress this complementarity: while the salient female reproductive organ is enclosed by infibulation, that of the male is exposed or, as one Sudanese author states, "unveiled" (Al-Safi 1970 : 65) through circumcision. Only after genital surgery are people eligible to become social persons, to assume the responsibilities of life as Hofriyati women and Hofriyati men.

Creating Female Persons

The attempt to understand gender in its social and cultural contexts has unmasked and challenged our fundamental assumptions with every turn of the debate. Anthropologists have long understood that "sex roles"—the normative activities of women and men—vary considerably from culture to culture (Brown 1970; Friedl 1975). We recognize that the character and degree of social asymmetry between the sexes is highly variable, both between cultures and between different domains within a single culture (Whyte 1978; Collier and Rosaldo 1981; Leacock 1981; Rosaldo 1980; Sacks 1982). And we strive to overcome androcentric and "state" biases (Sacks 1976) in our theoretical models. Yet, as authors such as Sacks (1976), Strathern (1981), and Ortner and Whitehead (1981) have noted, we have yet to appreciate fully a bias that underlies much of the research into women's status and subordination, namely, "an assumption that we know [a priori] what 'men' and 'women' are . . . that male and female are predominantly natural objects rather than predominantly cultural constructions" (Ortner and Whitehead 1981 : 1), and as such, ideologically produced (Strathern 1985 : 194, 1987; Messick 1987). For the female ethnographer, one message rings clear: though her sex may grant her greater access to women in an alien society, it guarantees no privileged insight into what it *means* to be a woman in another cultural context; she and her informants may share a common biology:[20] they do not share a common gender.

When freed from the constraints of naturalistic assumptions, gender is properly seen as a symbolic construct, variable in constitution from one society to the next. The work of scholars such as Gilligan (1982) and

20. Yet even this is subject to debate. See Buckley and Gottlieb (1988 : 40–47) for an overview of the issue.

Chodorow (1974, 1978) suggests that early gender socialization proceeds in universally similar ways, and establishes certain basic differences in the psychological (interpersonal) orientations of male and female children. Yet, as a growing body of ethnographic literature attests, the specifics of these differences, the contents of and relations between gender categories that inform and reproduce particular gender identities, are socially and culturally relative. Gender socialization is a process whereby humans in the course of interaction are molded and continuously shaped to appropriate images of femaleness and maleness. It is with this contextual aspect of genderization that I am here concerned.

The Hofriyati world is suffused by gender: gender constructs permeate the fabric of meaning and inform the idioms of daily life. Yet to understand women's position in this world, it is not enough to discover its logic; we need also to consider how such meanings are reproduced, continually created and embodied by individual actors. In Hofriyat, I suggest, we need to contemplate the implications of pharaonic circumcision for a female child's developing self-perception. Through this operation and other procedures involving pain or trauma, appropriate feminine dispositions are being inculcated in young girls, dispositions which, following Bourdieu (1977 : 15), are inscribed in their bodies not only physically, but also cognitively and emotionally, in the form of mental inclinations, "schemes of perception and thought." But alone the trauma of pharaonic circumcision is insufficient to shape the feminine self, to propel it in culturally prescribed direcitons: such acts must also be meaningful to those who undergo and reproduce them. Here, as will be seen, meaning is carefully built up through the use of metaphors and associations which combine to establish an identification of circumcised women with morally appropriate fertility, hence to orient them toward their all-important generative and transformative roles in Hofriyat society. Paradoxically, however, to achieve this gender identity, women implicitly repudiate their sexuality.

I noted earlier that in Hofriyat, adult males and females are considered to be different kinds of person, defined by a complementarity attributed only in part to nature. When a child is born it is identified as male or female according to its genitalia. However, to villagers, genitalia are ambiguous and by themselves inadequate determinants of a child's future gender identity. Babies are considered to have the potential to develop into fully female or fully male adults, but this potential cannot be realized without ritual activation and prudent monitoring. A child is formally initiated to its gender between the ages of five and ten, when, as villagers say, he or she has developed a minimal degree of *ʿagl,* reason, self-awareness, the ability to recognize and follow Allah's laws. It is then that the child is circumcised. Apart from naming, which is sex specific, explicit socialization until this point is similar for male and female children: both are treated fondly and leniently and nursed for as long as two years, though boys, who are considered physically weaker than girls in infancy, may be less precipitately weaned. As babies they are dressed alike,[21] beginning to wear shifts of differently patterned material from about the age of three. Young boys and girls freely play together in the village streets: neither is required to do housework or help with farming. But all this changes dramatically with the child's circumcision, an event long anticipated, for threats of its imminence are often used by adults to scatter play groups too raucous for their ears.

Genital surgery accomplishes the social definition of a child's sex (see Ammar 1954: 121 ff.; Assaad 1980: 4 ff.; Kennedy 1978*c*: 158); it completes and purifies a child's natural sexual identity by removing physical traits deemed appropriate to his or her opposite: the clitoris and other external genitalia in the case of females, the prepuce or covering of the penis in the case of males. So doing, the operations implicitly identify neophytes with their gender-appropriate spheres of interaction as adults: the interiors of house yards enclosed by high mud walls in the case of females; the outside world of farmlands, markets, other villages, and cities in the case of males. Females are associated with enclosure, and enclosure ultimately with fertility; males are associated with the outside, with political and economic engagement of the world beyond the *ḥōsh*.

But more than this: among Hofriyati, women actively and ongoingly construct other women, in a sense completing Allah's original creation of woman (Hawa, or Eve in the Judeo-Christian tradition) from the body of man. By eliminating any vestiges of maleness, they constitute women as separate entities and distinct social persons, and by so doing, proclaim a triumph for *ʿagl* over *nafs*.

According to the gender socilization model proposed by Rosaldo (1974) and Chodorow (1974) to account for asymmetrical valuations of the sexes cross-culturally, a psychological orientation of females to the domestic sphere and males to the public domain arises and is reproduced largely through the (culturally guided) efforts of male children to differentiate themselves from the feminine world of early socialization. Whereas boys must actively learn to be men, girls can passively "be absorbed into womanhood without effort" (Rosaldo 1974: 25). But this model is incompletely applicable to the Hofriyati context, where a female gender identity is neither wholly ascribed nor automatically assimilated by the female child. Here children of both sexes must actively achieve their gender identities through the directed experience of trauma. Genital operations

21. However, they wear shirts which leave the genital area exposed, and diapers are not worn.

simultaneously shape a child's body to the culturally appropriate gender image and launch the child on a process of internalizing the inferences of that image, of taking up the dispositions and identifications it suggests are suitable for adult life. The surgery establishes the conditions of adult gender complementarity, and it is in the nature of this complementarity, in its implications for social interaction, that gender asymmetries arise.

Circumcision marks the start of sexual segregation for the child: after their operations, boys should no longer sleep with their mothers and sisters, but accompany their older brothers in the men's quarters. Similarly, an infibulated girl is increasingly restricted to association with womenfolk and expected to assume greater domestic responsibility. Boys and girls who once played together happily are now unseemly chums. I overheard one mother chastise her eight-year-old daughter for continuing to play with boys: "Get out of the street," she said, "Do you think your cousin will want to marry you if he sees you every day?"

Perhaps the most notable feature of village life is this polarization of the sexes, most marked between men and women of childbearing age. To an outsider it appears as if there are two virtually separate, coexisting societies that only occasionally overlap. Men and women generally do not eat together, they occupy different quarters in the family compound, and they associate with those of their own sex in segregated areas at ceremonies and religious events. Further, while men have ultimate authority over women, this is far less actual than supposed. In everyday affairs, women are more strictly governed by the *ḥabōbāt* than by their male kin, and when it comes to a matter of direct control by her husband, the Hofriyati woman is expert in the art of passive resistance.

The nature of male authority is instructive. A woman is legally under the control and care of her father and, after his death, her brothers for as long as they live. When she marries she also becomes accountable to her husband, but her immediate male kin retain moral responsibility for her welfare. Theoretically, a measure of both economic and moral responsibility passes to her adult sons, especially should she be widowed or divorced. What these men share is the right to allocate and, in the case of her husband, to use the woman's reproductive potential.

Through marriage a man acquires access to his wife's fertility and she, the means to activate it. Children are the capital on which male and female careers are built; yet, since parents have independent claims in their offspring, these careers are distinct. This is important because marriages themselves are fragile and, for men, may be polygamous.

Moreover, men's explicit emphasis on controlling women's sexuality through circumcision, and women's implicit emphasis on thus socializing and controlling their fertility are complementary expressions of the same fundamental paradigm. For the only offspring considered socially and morally viable are those born of circumcised women in arranged and lawful marriages, most appropriately contracted between close kin.[22]

The identification with morally appropriate fertility inculcated in young girls through their circumcisions is reinforced and augmented in everyday life through conversations and interactions informed by a variety of metaphoric associations. As was noted earlier, my closer female friends volunteered that the operation is intended to make women pure (*ṭahir*), clean (*naẓīf*), and smooth (*nāʿim*). As I began to learn the various implications of these qualities, gradually piecing together what I was observing with what I was being told, it became increasingly clear that there exists a certain fit between this practice and others. A wide range of activities, concepts, and what villagers refer to as their customs (*ʿādāt*) appeared to be guided by a cluster of interrelated idioms and metaphors, sometimes explicitly formulated but more often not. It is this referential substratum that I have described as constituting the informal logic of routine life in Hofriyat. Partly religious and partly secular, it underlies both ritualized and nonritualized behavior, providing a number of overlapping contexts that shape social discourse.

Thus, to determine the fuller significance of female circumcision and glean some insight into the cultural system as a whole, I will trace further applications of its essential qualities: purity, cleanliness, and smoothness. Each interpretation leads to others, the enterprise fanning out from its point of departure until one is faced with a complex of relations in which certain themes, or idioms, predominate. The process is like the weaving of a tapestry: certain threads are left hanging in places, later to be caught up again and worked into the pattern. Symbols interpenetrate, associations ramify, until gradually the images they harbor are revealed.

What follows is based primarily on my observations between 1976 and 1977. To some extent Hofriyati symbolic representations have changed since then: the house ornaments I describe as being made of ostrich eggshells and dried gourds are no longer to be found. Their disappearance could signify a weakening of the symbolic matrix supporting the central value of fertility[23]—which the suggestion that villagers are moving toward acceptance of the less drastic "*sunna*" circumcision might also sustain. However, I am not convinced this is the case. Villagers are under considerable pressure from external sources (e.g., Egyptian television, Saudi Islam,

22. I was told that if a man "only wants children" he should marry a southern Sudanese, for they are prodigiously fertile. If, on the other hand, he wants children who will respect him, support him in his old age, bring honor to the family, behave with grace and tact, exercise good judgment—in short, who are moral beings, his wife must be Hofriyati, a kinswoman, and needless to say, circumcised.

23. On this point, see also Kennedy (1978*c*: 167).

the national declaration of *sharīʿa* law in 1983) to evince a style that is at once more "modern," less "superstitious," and more fundamentally Islamic. Given villagers' history of resilience, locally relevant idioms may have become more implicit or, in assimilating the changes, be assuming other outward forms. It is, perhaps, too soon to tell.

Purity, Birds, and Fertility

The one situation other than male and female circumcision and female ritual purity in which I consistently heard people use the descriptive *ṭahir* (pure) was in reference to certain types of birds. Among domestic birds, pigeons are considered *ṭahir* while chickens are regarded as dirty (*waskhān*). The former are pure, I was told, because they splash around in water when it is set out for them (indeed, the term for pigeon, *ḥamām,* is cognate with that for bath: *ḥammām*), and they reside above the ground in large tins which people suspend from the rafters of their verandas. Pigeon meat, referred to as *laḥma naẓīfa*—"clean flesh," is a delicacy, and pigeon broth a local panacea.[24] Chickens, by contrast, are filthy creatures which scratch in the dust, eat their own excrement, and generally make a mess of people's courtyards. Their meat is almost never eaten by villagers (except when pressed for food), as it, too, is dirty; that chicken is consumed with relish by Hofriyati's seminomadic neighbors is a conscious distinction between the two groups. Nonetheless, hens are kept by villagers because they produce eggs, and these are considered "clean food" (*ākil naẓīf*). According to the local variant of Galenic-Islamic (humoral) medicine, foods that are clean "bring blood" (*byjīb ad-dum*), that is, increase the amount of blood in the body.

Unmarried women who dance at wedding parties are often referred to as "pigeons going to market" (*ḥamāmat mashīn fi sūq*). The women regard themselves as on display for prospective husbands, since it is usually at such affairs that arrangements for subsequent marriages are initiated. Women dance at these parties with a mincing, rhythmic forward step, their arms, draped with the cloth of their *tōbs*, forming winglike extensions to the sides. This, sometimes called the "pigeon dance" (see also Cloudsley 1983 : 40, 54) is described as a "dance from the neck" (*ragīṣ bi rugaba*) as it involves moving the head to and fro, chin upturned and eyes rolled back, in the controlled manner of a courting pigeon or small bird (*zarzūr*) walking along the ground.

24. So pure are pigeons that persons of limited means might substitute a pair for the obligatory sacrificial lamb at the *ʿId al-Aḍḥa* (the Muslim great feast) or, for that matter, whenever animal sacrifice is called for.

Wild water birds, the ducks, geese, and ibis that inhabit the banks of the Nile, are also considered "clean." Until recently, people had the cheekbones of their daughters incised with a small scar in the shape of a rounded *T*. This is called a "bird track" (*dārab aṭ-ṭayr*) and thought to resemble the footmarks of water birds on the beach. It is considered a mark of beauty, a feature which enhances a woman's desirability.

From all of this, one can outline a strong metaphoric connection between marriageable women and birds associated with water. Both are *naẓīf*. Both domestic water-linked birds (pigeons) and women are *ṭahir*. Young women are sometimes referred to as birds and in some cases said to act like birds. Inversely, birds of this type behave like humans since they "bathe."

More abstractly, cleanliness, purity, and femininity are identified with birds and fluids, notably water and blood. Water is associated with agricultural fertility and generativity, for Hofriyat is located on the Nile at the edge of the desert, and food production depends on the river's annual inundation. Blood, on the other hand, is linked to human fertility as expressed in the red symbolism attached to "brides," a category that includes newly circumcised girls. Her blood is the source of a woman's fecundity, and great care is taken to prevent its loss, contamination, or misappropriation. The enclosure of her womb through circumcision is but one such procedure.

An intriguing parallel to the Hofriyati bird metaphor is found farther north along the Nile, in Silwa, Upper Egypt. There, clitoral excision is practiced, and the native ethnographer Ammar (1954: 121), discussing the complementarity of male and female genital operations, writes, "In the colloquial language of the village, circumcision of the boy is sometimes referred to as 'cutting his pigeon' while in the case of the girl it is described as 'cutting her cockscomb.'" The association of "pigeon" with the "feminine" foreskin is strikingly similar to expressions of femininity in Hofriyat. Locally, the association between marriageable, circumcised women and birds is echoed by village men, who speak of having amassed sufficient funds to wed in terms of being able to "nest" (*ʿaish*) a wife: to provide on a continual basis the materials she requires to remain within the home and raise a family.

Associations like those outlined above are, it will be seen, pervasive in the everyday world of Hofriyat. They repeatedly direct villagers' attention to what are appropriate feminine characteristics. And in the process, gender images are naturalized, become taken for granted, and women's gender identities are continuously produced.

Links between femininity, blood, purity, birds, and fertility are immanent in a variety of other situations. During my first period of fieldwork, I rented a sleeping room that was decorated with painted ostrich eggshells suspended from the ceiling corners. They have since been removed from this house and from others in Hofriyat, but in 1976 my room was typical in this respect. Questions as to the significance of these objects met with suppressed giggles from my companions. They explained that these were *manāẓir,* "visions" or "views," things to look at. The concept of "seeing" is well developed in Hofriyat: someone is thought to absorb certain qualities of what is seen; correspondingly, she might effect changes in something or someone by emitting visual influences, this being the logic of the evil or "hot" eye, *ʿayn ḥārra.* Although the designs on the eggshells may have been significant, they were highly variable and, according to informants, subject only to the painter's creative impulse; they could be painted by men or by women. When prodded further as to their significance, my friends replied that ostrich eggshells and similarly shaped gourds (then more commonly used) were so placed because the woman who slept in the room wished to conceive. But these objects were permanent fixtures in the majority of homes; they were not put up and taken down at a woman's whim. They were not, in other words, signals in a sexual semaphor designed to rally a husband's consummate attentions. Rather, they were charms, fertility objects: "We look at them because we want sons," said one informant.

As symbols and harbingers of fertility these objects figured in several contexts. First of all, a man's testes are euphemistically referred to as his "eggs" of which the massive ostrich egg was considered an exaggerated model. And though villagers themselves make no such explicit connection, it is noteworthy that the object was something associated with birds. Of course, only the shell of an ostrich egg would be used for decoration; the egg itself was removed by making a small puncture in the shell and draining off the contents. Ostrich eggshells and their latter-day counterparts, gourds of similar size and form, were prized for their shape, resistance, smooth rounded surfaces, and creamy white color.

Whiteness is a quality normally associated with cleanliness, purity, and value; it is "the color preferred by the Prophet" (see El-Tayib 1987: 52). Foods that are white are generally classed as "clean" and thought to "bring blood." Since a woman's fertility is closely connected to the quantity and quality of blood she carries within her,[25] foods which "increase" the blood invigorate latent fertility or impart strength during pregnancy. These are eggs, goat's milk, goat cheese, cow's milk, fish, rice, sugar, and white flour. Of them, only goat's milk and sugar may be considered staples; all are, to some extent, scarce or limited and expensive.

There is another group of foods considered clean. Again, these are expensive, and purchased rarely: on special occasions, as treats, or for a

25. As is discussed in chapter 3, the flowing of blood from the genital region substantially increases an individual's vulnerability to spirit attack, and may result in a loss of fertility (see also Kennedy 1978*c*: 159 ff.). Menstrual blood is regarded with ambivalence as it signifies both a loss of fertility and its continuity.

pregnant woman. Some of the more common ones are tinned fish, tinned jam, oranges, bananas, guavas, watermelon, and grapefruit. Such foods are often associated with Europeans, Egyptians, and Lebanese, that is, people having light or, as villagers say, "white" complexions. The link to foreign groups is intriguing, since villagers generally see the outside world as an important locus of power.[26] Yet these foods are thought to be especially clean because they are all contained or enclosed, hence protected from dirt and dryness.

Hofriyati are especially conscious of skin color. White skin is clean, beautiful, and a mark of potential holiness. I, being Caucasian, was repeatedly told that my chances of getting into heaven—should I choose to become Muslim—were far greater than those of the average Sudani. This is because the Prophet Mohammed was white, and all white-skinned peoples are in the favored position of belonging to his tribal group. Ranked in order of desirability, the skin color of villagers ranges from "yellow" or light through increasingly darker shades called "red," "green," and "blue." The term *aswad* (black) is usually reserved for southern Sudanese or "Africans," people who in earlier times might have been enslaved.

The aforementioned concepts of cleanliness, whiteness, potency, enclosedness, and smoothness intersect in the domain of women's cosmetics. Just before her wedding a young girl undertakes an elaborate regimen of physical preparation for the first time in her life. To begin with, she removes all of her body hair using a thick, sticky concentrate of boiled sugar and lime juice (called *ḥalāwa,* candy or sweet) in the manner of depilatory wax. I am told that women cannot use razors for this purpose as do men, who remove their pubic hair. Women must experience *ḥārr,* "heat" or "pain," when they depilate, whereas men must use a "cold" (*bārid*) method, such as shaving, to remove their facial and pubic hair. Infibulation is also referred to as *ḥārr:* heat and pain are identified with acts of feminine purification.

Once her skin has been cleared of hair, the prospective bride takes a smoke bath (*dukhāna*). If such does not already exist, a hole is dug in the kitchen floor or other appropriate spot indoors and fitted with a doughnut-shaped mat.[27] Then the hole is filled with fragrant woods and lighted. The woman removes her clothing, wraps herself in a special blanket made of tightly woven goat or camel hair, and sits over the hole taking care to envelop the rising smoke. Here she may stay for several hours, adding wood from time to time and gossiping with her friends. The bath is considered a success if, when she emerges, the top layer of her skin can be sloughed off, exposing a lighter and smoother surface underneath. Her

26. This point is developed later on with reference to spirit possession. See Ohnuki-Tierney (1984) for similar observations on foods (and other imports) among the Japanese.

27. As in pharaonic circumcisions prior to 1969.

skin should also give off a powerful smoky scent for several days (see El-Tayib 1987). Note that this further act of purification is also accomplished through the application of heat and its product smoke.

To remove the dead skin, she again applies *ḥalāwa,* or massages herself with a concoction of smoked dough fragranced with aromatic woods (*dilka*). When all traces of *dilka* paste have been rubbed away, she oils herself and applies smoky smelling perfume. Then her hands and feet are stained with henna, whose purposes are to cool the body, protect against excessive blood loss (here, at consummation; see chapter 3), and ornament the extremities.

These preparations may take several days to complete and are intended to make her skin soft, smooth, clean, fragrant, and lighter in color. After treatment, performed for the first time when she becomes a bride and henceforward whenever she wants to attract the attentions of her husband, a woman's body shares several qualities with the ostrich egg fertility object. Both are clean and "white," both are pure. What is more, the shape of the ostrich egg, with its tiny orifice, corresponds to the idealized shape of the circumcised woman's womb. So, too, the cleanliness, whiteness, and enclosedness of valued edibles evoke images of the bride and of fecundity. All this is concentrated, if more crudely put, in the popular simile "a Sudanese girl is like a watermelon because there is no way in" (Cloudsley 1983: 118).

A distinctive feature of objects described as "enclosing" is their ability to retain moisture. Similarly, a bride's cosmetic routine is supposed to prevent her from perspiring. Human sweat and its odor are thought gauche in Hofriyat at all times, but at a wedding, especially despicable. Moreover, the link between pure or "purified" women and moisture retention is negatively expressed by the metaphor for prostitute: *sharmūṭa. Sharmūṭa* means, literally, "that which is shredded or in tatters." But in local parlance *sharmūṭ* (masculine) is meat that has been cut into strips and hung to dry. The relation of dry to moist sets off the distinction between prostitutes and brides and thus, between female sexuality (inappropriate fertility) and female fertility (domesticated sexuality).

That dryness should be identified with sterility (here in the social sense) is scarcely surprising given the desert climate of Hofriyat. This association has broader implications and is extended to women whose morals are not questioned. In 1984 I attended the wedding of a thirty-eight year old maiden. As usual, I was later asked by Hofriyati friends what I had thought of the bride. When I said that I thought she was pretty, one man retorted, "Oh no, not pretty . . . that bride's as dry as dust! There'll be no children in that house!"

The associations outlined thus far become more firmly established as we progress. They combine to signify that on the day of her wedding a young woman has reached a peak of appropriate, potential fertility, defined in terms of the qualities whiteness, smoothness, purity, enclosedness, moistness, and imperviousness. Indeed, she is, in a sense, objectified, transformed into a symbol, a superb condensation of her culture's salient values.[28]

Fluids, Reproduction, and Enclosure

Attention now shifts to symbolic relations devolving from the egg-shaped gourd, the alternate fertility object. Such a gourd (*garʿa*) may be used in place of an ostrich eggshell only after it has been preserved by drying in the sun. One knows that a *garʿa* is ready to be decorated and hung in a room if, when shaken, its seeds can be heard to rattle inside. Although the dryness of the gourd (or for that matter, the ostrich eggshell) appears to contradict its association with fertility as predicated on moisture, what it symbolizes, I think, is generative potential. The metaphor is an agricultural one: the vocabulary of cultivation provides a figurative lexicon for things having to do with reproduction and, to a degree, with the recreation of village social structure. For instance, the progeny of a man or woman is referred to as his or her *janā* (fruit, harvest) or *zarīʿa* (crop, that which is sown). A man's immediate descendants, the lineage section of which he is head, is also his *zarīʿa*.

In view of this, the fact that the appropriately shaped gourd contains seeds in an enclosed (womblike) space is exceedingly significant. To begin with, native theories of conception have it that the fetus is formed from the union of a man's semen, spoken of as his seed, with his wife's blood, the source of her fertility. Sexual intercourse causes the woman's blood to thicken or coagulate, and she ceases menstruation until after the baby's birth: while pregnant, a woman nourishes her husband's future "crop" within her (cf. Delaney 1988). Thus, although Hofriyati are not explicit on this point, I think it possible to suggest that pharaonic circumcision has as much to do with preventing the loss of genital blood (menstrual or otherwise) from within, as with protecting the womb from inappropriate penetration from without. Given that women bear primary responsibility for reproduction (later discussed), and men for safeguarding the family honor, the two rationales understandably represent gender-distinctive views.

Ideas about conception correlate with those concerning parents' respective contributions to the body of their child. Women told me that although young people learn differently in school these days, a child receives

28. On this point, see also La Fontaine (1985*a*: 13, 125 ff.) and Dubisch (1986*a*: 37, *b*: 211). For a provocative and controversial discussion, see Irigaray (1985: 170–97).

its bones from its father and its flesh and blood from its mother (cf. Holy 1988:474). This complementarity can be broadened to the level of social organization: just as the skeleton structures the body, so endogamous patrilineal descent groups structure the village. But endogamy, though preferred, is not always possible in practice. Moreover, adherence to the rule is not a great concern of those entering second or subsequent marriages. The upshot of this is that sisters frequently marry into lineages unrelated or only distantly related to each other. And no matter what their descent affiliations, the children of such women are considered close relatives, hence potential mates. Women therefore link together the several named descent groups in the village. People belonging to different patrilines who acknowledge close kinship say *bayn niḥna laḥma wa dum:* "between us there is flesh and blood." If it is through men that the social order receives its structure, its rigidity and permanence—its "bones"—then it is through women that it receives its fluidity and ephemeral integration—its "blood" and its "flesh."[29] Villagers' logic of procreation is fundamental to understanding both gender constructs and marital strategies, discussed below.

There are several other contexts in which fluids and moisture figure prominently as markers of femininity and potential fertility. The most obvious of these has to do with the division of labor by sex. While cultivation is thought primarily to be men's work, fetching water from the wells for household consumption is traditionally the task of women.[30] Thus through their individual labors, farming and getting water, men and women provide the household with materials for its staple food, *kisra*.

Kisra is made by mixing *dura* flour with an almost equal amount of water. A cupful of this batter is spread thinly over an extremely hot seasoned griddle and left a few moments to bake; when the edges are crisp and dry the crepelike product is removed.

Kisra batter is mixed by hand in a special container called a *gūlla*. This

29. Similar metaphors surface in other Arabic-speaking communities. Referring to his study of Arab villages in Israel along the border with Jordan, Abner Cohen (1974:76) writes, "A woman always belongs to the lineage of her father. When she is married out, her father would tell those who marry her, 'For you the womb, for us the bone.'"

30. In the absence of menfolk, some women keep kitchen gardens; as was noted in chapter 1, others work in the fields alongside male kin when extra labor is required. However, this does not alter the typification of farming as a masculine activity. That getting water was feminine work was made clear to me in the following way: I had hired Sadig, a boy of fifteen formerly employed by the Canadian archaeological team, to do a number of tasks that would free my time for research, namely, going to market and filling my water jars when needed. Since the archaeologists had hired men to do these jobs, I foresaw no difficulty. A few months into my research, however, Sadig fell ill and I was informed by his mother that she would now take over his duties of bringing water. On his recovery her son would do other odd jobs and go to market, but no water. It seems that as I learned more and more Arabic and my skin became progressively darker from the sun, I was gradually transformed from a foreigner (*khawāja*), for whom it is respectable to work in any capacity, into a woman. Men do not perform women's tasks unless there is no woman available to perform them, let alone do women's work for a "woman"!

is a rounded pottery jar about the size of an average pumpkin, with an opening at the top somewhat larger than a woman's fist. It differs from water jars (*zīrs*) which are far larger, capable of holding forty liters of water or more. *Zīrs* are made of a porous clay that permits sweating, hence cooling, of the water they contain. *Gūllas*, however, must be nonporous; they must not allow anything inside them to seep out.[31] This feature likens them to other objects here described as moisture retentive: foods that are enclosed, dried gourds and ostrich eggshells in their mundane use as water containers, the cosmetically prepared body of the infibulated bride, all evoking the further positive qualities of cleanliness, purity, femininity, and fecundity.

Significantly, besides serving as a bowl for mixing *kisra,* the *gūlla* has another function, relative to childbirth. If a woman miscarries when only a few months pregnant, the expelled matter is treated like menstrual blood (itself seen as a form of miscarriage) and put down the latrine. But should she require the services of a midwife to open her up, a different method of disposal is called for. The fetus is first wrapped in white cloth, as for a corpse, then placed in a *gūlla* and buried within the confines of the *ḥōsh.* The symbolism of this act becomes clearer when one considers what is done in the case of stillbirth. If a baby is born but fails to breathe, its body is wrapped and buried without ceremony just outside the front door (men's entrance) to the *ḥōsh,* against its outer wall. Yet should an infant expire having taken even one breath, then normal funeral procedure must be followed, and the child buried in the graveyard on the outskirts of the village.

Both the *gūlla* and the *ḥōsh* appear in this context as symbols for the womb. In the case of the *gūlla* it is an object of daily life in which the fruits of men's and women's labors are combined. The mixture when transformed by heat produces *kisra,* the staple food, that which sustains human life. It is important to note that only women mix and bake *kisra*. Similarly, in the impervious womb are mixed a man's seed and a woman's blood: substance and fluid, like grain and water. This mixture, when transformed by the generative warmth of the womb, reproduces human life, hence also sustains it. And of course, only women can gestate and give birth. Symbolically, there is no receptacle more fit to receive an aborted mixture of male and female contributions than the *gūlla,* impervious container of unbaked "life."[32]

31. With the increasing availability of cheap enamel ware, fewer *gūllas* are being made. The enamel bowls that replace them meet the condition of nonporousness and function as *gūllas* do.

32. Given the contemporary link between the *gūlla,* the ostrich egg, fertility, and the womb, it is interesting to note that in sites attributed to predynastic Nubian culture ("A" Horizon, fourth millennium B.C.; see Adams [1984, chapter 5]), ostrich eggs (plain or deco-

Here again women are associated with significant fluids, namely, water and blood, and with heat and pain, designated by a single word, *ḥārr.* Pharaonic circumcision, hair removal techniques, smoke bathing, baking *kisra,* being pregnant, giving birth, are all described as "hot" and painful. That men are not associated with these qualities is emphasized by their need to use a "cold" method of hair removal such as shaving, which involves no pain. Yet a male's experiences, too, are considered *ḥārr* when he undergoes circumcision and is thereby removed from a sexually ambiguous, partially feminine state. In preparation for the event the boy is cosmetically decorated as a bride and covered with a woman's bridal veil (*garmosīs*).[33] He now sheds genital blood (as women must frequently do) but ought never to do so again. Indeed, he now loses that part of his anatomy thought appropriate only to females, and is rendered more fully masculine.

Fluids and experienced heat are markers of fertility and femininity. They are generative, potent, transformative: they alter bodies and existing substances, activate the productive potential contained in seeds or semen. Women's culturally induced transformative and generative qualities encompass their domestic roles in the marital relationship: in the *ḥōsh* they receive raw meat, grains, and vegetables brought to them from the outside by men (who cultivate, butcher, transact in the market), and transform these into cooked food through the application of liquids and heat.[34] Moreover, it should not be surprising, given its feminine, transformative efficacy, that genital surgery is thought to induce maturation and is sometimes performed as a "cure" on an uncircumcised child who has suffered a series of illnesses (see also Kennedy 1978*c*: 158).

To return to the identification of the *gūlla* with the womb, there is a certain level of exegesis in this interpretation. One of my informants suggested that the *gūlla* may be used for this purpose because in its shape it resembles the gravid *bayt al-wilāda,* the womb, literally, the "house of childbirth." The house metaphor is important, and we return to it in a moment.

rated with human figures, birds, and other animals) have been found buried with children and, in at least one grave, a newborn infant (Nordström 1972). Of course, the significance of these objects may have been entirely different than it is in Hofriyat today.

33. He is, however, referred to as a bridegroom, *ʿarīs.* See also Kennedy (1978*c*: 154).

34. Though apparently similar to Ortner's (1974) depiction of women as those who culturalize a negatively valued nature, who are closer to that nature than men and therefore attributed lower status, I would argue that since men confront the outside world in attaining such goods in the first place, the opposite might well apply in Hofriyat. However, I do not think the nature/culture argument is helpful to understanding Hofriyati gender relations: the situation here shows more complexity than the model allows and, in some respects, turns Ortner's assessment of the domestic and public on their heads. For Hofriyati the "domestic" world—the *ḥōsh,* the family—is the more highly valued. The world outside the *ḥōsh* and the village is regarded with ambivalence. These points receive considerable attention in chapter 3, indeed throughout the book.

I stated earlier that the *ḥōsh,* the walled enclosure of a house yard, also symbolizes the womb. More accurately, it represents an initial stage in the process of becoming human. The miscarried fetus has not, strictly speaking, been born; it does not emerge with a wholly developed human body. Its progress is halted in the womb, and it must be disposed of within the *ḥōsh*. The stillborn child emerges fully developed, but it does not breathe; its progress is halted or fixed at the point of birth. As it has emerged from the womb, passing through the vaginal canal, it is buried outside the men's door of the *ḥōsh,* against the outer wall. The child who breathes but then dies is indeed fully human, for breath is the essence of life. A child who has breathed is placed with other humans who have lived, who have passed from the *ḥōsh* and the village to the grave. Significantly, women, whose bodies and persons are associated with the *ḥōsh* in this and several more contexts, and who preside over births and all other crisis rites having to do with life in this world (*dunyā*), are not permitted to be present at a burial. Such is the province of men: death represents a movement beyond the (feminine) world into the (masculine) spiritual domain. Women may later visit the grave, but only between menses, since visits during menstrual flow are thought to endanger their fertility (see also Kennedy 1978*b*: 131). That which represents the continuity of physical life should not be brought into contact with that which both denotes its end and symbolizes its incorporeal persistance.

One last point: the symbolism of village spatial organization in customs having to do with unsuccessful pregnancy not only expresses the physical relationship between mother and child. It also describes the unsuccessful emergence of an individual into society. The child who dies at birth skips over the social phase of being, going directly from the womb to the grave.

The Ḥōsh: *Physical and Social Enclosure*

Enclosed areas within the village are generally considered clean and protected places. *Ḥōsh* yards are swept daily, as are the floors of rooms and verandas within. Clean spaces, interior spaces, these are social areas. They are places of relative safety where one is least likely to be possessed by malevolent spirits ("black" *jinn*), thence driven mad. *Jinn* of all types (including *zayran*) frequent open areas such as the desert, ruined houses, and rubbish heaps. The surrounding countryside is considered dangerous (especially at night when spirits are most active), village paths less so, and the insides of *ḥōsh*s safer still. Yet social spaces are not always bounded by high walls, although these are preferable. In 1976 some homes in the village were ringed merely by thorn fences or marking stones (all of which had been replaced with mud-brick walls by 1984). However humble its borders, the ground inside such enclosures was regularly swept smooth to maintain the distinction between it and unmarked space.

The village, too, is bounded, if less obviously: to the west by farmlands and the river, to the north and south by other villages, to the east by the desert, *akh-khalā,* the emptiness. The graveyard is located on the westernmost fringe of the desert, on sterile land between the village and emptiness beyond. Moving east from the river toward the desert, conditions shift from relative fecundity and abundance to barrenness and sterility, with humans poised between the two.

This in-between space, social space, is organized concentrically. At the hub is the *ḥōsh* or *bayt* (house): an extended family and the place where life begins. Surrounding this in the village are kinsmen and neighbors, considered the same by local people: they are referred to as *nās garīb,* "those who are close" or *garībna,* "our kin." In nearby villages are more distant relations and affines and, farther still, nonkin Arab Sudanese. Soon thereafter one arrives at the periphery of the known, and readily negotiable, social world.

It is relevant to mention that social space is also bounded ideologically. People marry "close." Explicitly, one ought to marry within the patriline, preferably a father's brother's son or daughter, but given demographic limitations one is expected to wed as close a relation as possible. It is not surprising, then, that the best and most prestigious marriage is between bilateral parallel cousins whose parents are parallel cousins. Yet despite a preference for patrilateral parallel cousins, my data indicate that matrilateral parallel cousins are also highly desirable mates, followed by cross-cousins, then other kin in a declining order of preference. If for some reason an individual marries further afield, he ought still to observe an implicit rule of territorial endogamy. Neighbors are "close" by contiguity and definition: villagers acknowledge a plethora of consanguineal and affinal links to all other Hofriyati.[35] Social space as expressed through kinship and marriage thus replicates the social organization of physical space: both are based upon the idea of relative enclosure within a circumscribed area, a principle I call "interiority."

These considerations lead back to some earlier relinquished threads in the argument. Significant with regard to the relative enclosure of physical space are certain tenets concerning the human body and its openings. Established notions of aesthetic propriety depict a human face as beautiful when characterized by a small mouth and narrow nostrils. Further, body

35. This includes the families of former slaves, although they are considerably less intermarried with the families of freeborn Hofriyati than the latter are amongst themselves. The preference for marrying those who are "close" by proximity, if not consanguinity, is being maintained by migrants in Khartoum and Omdurman. Villagers who have permanently relocated their families in the city are currently pursuing a policy of intermarriage with their neighbors.

passages are attractive to potentially dangerous *jinn,* and places where they might abide. Burial customs dictate that these openings, including the spaces between fingers and toes, be washed, perfumed, and stuffed with cotton before the corpse is wrapped for subsequent transfer to the cemetery. This is to ensure the expulsion of lingering *jinn* and to prevent the soul of the deceased from reentering its mortal remains. Thus, while orifices of the body are necessary for sustaining life, they are dangerous, not aesthetically pleasing if large, and not to be left open after death. The physical enclosure of the corpse contrasts with the relative openness of a menstruating or postparturient woman, thus contributing to the logic of their separation, discussed above and in chapter 3.

The idiom of enclosure is further dramatized by certain ethnomedical practices in the village. Remedies are often based on the assumption that pain and swelling are caused by things coming apart or opening. A common cure for headache, or "open head" (*rās maftūḥ*) is to wrap a band of cloth around the crown and to tighten this by twisting the cloth with a key or a shaft of wood. Alternatively, the head may be closed by the application of hot irons to four equidistant points on the skull, starting from mid-forehead. Pulled tendons and ligaments are also treated by "fire" (*nār*): hot iron rods are placed at either end of the affected area so that what has come apart may be fused together again by heat. The associations of heat, fusing together, closing, and the aesthetic preference for small body openings again call to mind the practice of infibulation, with its attendant relations of transformativeness, femininity, and fertility.

Full Circle: Womb as Oasis

The idiom of (relative) enclosure, premised on the value of the interiority, has gradually emerged in this analysis as one which underwrites a diversity of villagers' practices and ideas. The *ḥōsh,* the womb, and many more objects of daily life (including, for that matter, women's *tōbs*, which may be thought of as portable enclosures), ideas concerning the human body, reproduction, imperviousness, and the fertility potential of brides, all that was outlined above, appear repeatedly in contexts that play upon this theme. These contexts culminate in another set of associations concerning the *ḥōsh,* the womb, and sexual complementarity.

As I noted earlier, the sexes are spatially as well as socially segregated. They occupy opposite sides of the dancing ground at ceremonies, are housed and fed in different households during communal feasts. The *ḥōsh,* too, is divided into men's and women's quarters, with separate entrances for each. The "front" door (no specified orientation) is known as the men's entrance and is used by official guests and strangers. The men's reception room (*dīwān*) is generally located in the forepart of the courtyard, near this door. The "back" door is known as the women's entrance and is for the use of women, close male kin, and neighbors. Women's quarters are situated in the rear of the compound, as is the kitchen, where *kisra* is baked. When the *ḥōsh* is considered a politicoeconomic unit, then internal or domestic affairs are overseen by women, while external affairs such as wage labor and marketing are the province of men. Though women are not, strictly speaking, secluded, there is a strong feeling that they ought to remain within the confines of the *ḥōsh* unless fetching water or visiting kin. There is thus a fairly firm association of women with internal affairs, enclosedness, and the interior of the *ḥōsh,* and of men with external affairs, nonenclosedness, and the front of the *ḥōsh*. The *ḥōsh,* remember, is symbolic of the womb—here seen as divided into male (outer, vaginal) and female (inner, uterine) domains. These relations provide further images with which Hofriyati think about social reproduction, to which we now return.

The men's entrance to the *ḥōsh* is known as the *khashm al-bayt:* the "mouth," "opening," or "orifice" of the house. This term also refers to a group of kin. Properly speaking, a *khashm al-bayt* comprises several related lineages, hence a subtribe. But in Hofriyat and elsewhere in Sudan (Barclay 1964 : 91) the term is used only in reference to people who live in or originate from a common *ḥōsh* or *bayt*. It is a lineage section.

Extension of anatomical terms to nonanatomical subjects, as described above, is common in Hofriyat. The supports of an *angarīb* are its "legs" (*kurʿayn*). Importantly, doors and orifices through which things or people pass are "mouths" or "nostrils" (*khashms*), and the insides of houses and other enclosed areas are "bellies" or "stomachs" (*buṭons*). In the case at hand, the *khashm al-bayt* is associated with males, but the *bayt* itself with females: nonanatomical terms may conversely apply to parts of the anatomy, and the word for "house" is explicitly linked with the womb.

The womb is called the *bayt al-wilāda,* the "house of childbirth," and the vaginal opening is its *khashm,* its mouth or door. There thus exists an implicit link between the *khashm al-bayt,* the men's door to the house yard and, metaphorically, one man's immediate descendants, and the *khashm* of the *bayt al-wilāda,* a woman's genital opening.[36] The men's door literally opens into an enclosed area occupied by a man's sons and daughters, his "crop." The *khashm al-bayt al-wilāda,* the "door" of the womb, also opens into an enclosed area where this crop was sown and nurtured, and which is all the more completely enclosed and purified by a woman's circumcision. Just as the *ḥōsh* protects a man's descendants, the enclosed, infibulated

36. I should point out that the term *khashm* was used only in reference to the men's door, not the women's, which was designated merely as *waraʿ*, "back." They were thus lexically differentiated.

womb protects a woman's fertility: her potential and, ultimately, that of her husband. Like the *ḥōsh* poised between the Nile and the desert, the womb of a Hofriyati woman is an oasis, the locus of human fertility, a focal social value for both women and men, hence properly safeguarded and preserved.

Thus pharaonic circumcision is for women in Hofriyat an assertive, symbolic act. Through it they emphasize and embody in their daughters what they hold to be the essence of femininity: uncontaminated, morally appropriate fertility, the right and the physical potential to reproduce the lineage or found a lineage section. In that infibulation purifies, smooths, and makes clean the outer surface of the womb, the enclosure or *ḥōsh* of the house of childbirth, it socializes or, in fact, culturalizes a woman's fertility. Through occlusion and subsequent enclosures of the vaginal meatus, her womb becomes, and is reestablished as, an ideal social space: enclosed, impervious, virtually impenetrable. Her body becomes a metonym for the resilience of village society in the face of external threat. Much as Sondra Hale (1985) describes for Nubians farther north, women in Hofriyat are truly and concretely "symbols of the homeland."

The infibulated virginal bride, enclosed, pure, ostensibly fertile, is a key symbol in the Hofriyati cultural system (cf. El-Tayib 1987:64–65). She superbly concentrates its values, figuratively representing interiority, one of its salient organizing precepts. But brides and other women are more than artifacts, symbolic expressions of their culture. They are social actors. And what I have been referring to as the "idiom of enclosure" is not an abstract principle or a set of rules but, following Bourdieu (1977: 15), a disposition "inculcated from the earliest years of life and constantly reinforced by calls to order from the group, that is to say, from the aggregate of individuals endowed with the same dispositions, to whom each is linked by [her] dispositions and interests." This disposition is a permanent one, like that of honor (*nif*) among the Kabyle (Algeria) which supplies Bourdieu's example. It is "embedded in the agents' bodies in the form of mental dispositions, schemes of perception and thought, extremely general in their application" (ibid.). Moreover, the implicit organizing precept of interiority corresponds to Bourdieu's notion of a "generative scheme" that underwrites a wide range of practice: "The 'customary rules' preserved by the group memory are themselves the product of a small batch of schemes enabling agents to generate an infinity of practices adapted to endlessly changing situations, without those schemes ever being constituted as explicit principles" (Bourdieu 1977: 16).

What I consider to be the logic of daily life in Hofriyat is thus an implicit philosophy, an organizing scheme immanent in practice. Interiority is not a reification, an explicitly formulated "rule" whose existence transcends the moment of its evocation. Rather, it is a quality or pattern intrinsic to the background of tacit assumptions in terms of which practice—with all its inevitable uncertainties, ambiguities, and strategies—unfolds. Phrased differently, interiority is the gist of a largely taken for granted world within which the apparently uncomplicated propositions of casual conversation and interaction make sense (cf. Berger and Luckmann 1966: 153). And the polysemic layout of domestic space, the transitive images of femininity and the *ḥōsh*, the signs embedded in daily activities are as much its techniques as its representations. They are, as Comaroff (1985: 54) puts it, "major media of socialization," "invisibly tuning people's minds and bodies to their inner logic."

Thus the simple, mundane acts of fetching water and baking bread, which girls begin to perform following their circumcisions, or even, perhaps, of eating an orange or opening a tin of fish—all are resonant with implicit meanings. They are metaphors both in thought and practice which, following Fernandez (1974), when predicated upon the inchoate self contribute to its identity. For in appropriating them, in enacting them, a girl becomes an object to herself (p. 122). And as Fernandez suggests, self-objectification must occur—by taking the view of the "other"—before she can become a subject to herself (p. 122). The metaphors predicated on female Hofriyati by themselves and others help to shape their dispositions, their orientations to the world, their selfhood. They are the means by which a woman's subjective reality, closely governed by the cultural construction of womanhood, is—not merely expressed—but realized and maintained. The painful and traumatic experience of circumcision first orients her toward a disposition and self-image compelled by her culture's values. And she is invited to relive that experience at various points in her life: vicariously, through participating in younger women's operations; actually, after each delivery; and metaphorically, with any procedure involving heat or pain, fluids, or other feminine qualities detailed above. Both in ritual and in many small moments throughout her working day, informative values are implicitly restated and her disposition reinforced. Hofriyati men and women, in constituting the latter as embodiments of the moral world, thereby inscribe the apparent political and economic subordination of women within their very selves. As Asad (1986: 153) suggests, it is the very coherence of such cultural concepts constructing womanhood in Hofriyat that renders them so powerful, so compulsive, so politically effective.

Marriage and the Social Order

Further consideration of the bride—through one of her legendary portrayals—enables us to get a closer look at Hofriyati notions of morality and social structure, and another context of interiority. The most popular folk hero in Hofriyat and much of northern Sudan is a young woman, Fatna (Fatima) the Beautiful. Fatna combines all the positive qualities of a bride with intelligence, wit, and a naive penchant for getting into (and out of) potentially dangerous predicaments. Intriguingly, these are all situations where her fertility is threatened with inappropriate use. The numerous tales in which she figures inevitably concern the prospect of her unorthodox marriage. In some, her betrothed turns out to be a brother from whom she has been estranged since childhood. In others she is kidnapped and eventually wed to an outsider and nonrelative, a sultan's son.[37]

At least one story shows her as unwittingly having committed incest and borne a child as a result. In her effort to conceal the birth from kin she unintentionally kills her son by hiding him in the kitchen smoke pit, where he suffocates. This episode reiterates the strong association between the floor hole and acts involving the purification and socialization of feminine fertility: smoke bathing and infibulation. It also bears a striking resemblance to practices associated with miscarriage: the disposal of incompletely formed humans within the *ḥōsh*. Such points are instructive. Fatna's baby is physically sound: he breathes. Yet, as we shall see, he is not completely human, for he is not the product of a sanctioned sexual relationship. His "burial" not only takes place inside the *ḥōsh,* but inside the kitchen, the women's domain within the *ḥōsh,* suggesting, perhaps, the child's extreme interior origin in a sexual union of siblings from the same womb.

Fatna's troubles devolve from the fact that the fertility of village women is appropriately exercised (hence that Hofriyati relationships are properly reproduced both physically and socially) only under certain conditions. First, a woman must be married: before conceiving, she must have been made the legal spouse of a man who has obtained from her father, brothers, or guardian rights of access to her reproductive potential. Should she become pregnant out of wedlock, whether before marriage or through adultery, her male kin have the right—even the duty—to kill her for so dishonoring her family.

Sometimes (though rarely, I am told) a woman shamed escapes death and survives to give birth. Yet, however healthy her child, he is always considered abnormal. Children born outside of wedlock lack an essential morality with which the legally born are innately imbued. *Awlād ḥarām,* "forbidden children," are thought to be criminals by nature. They are held incapable of socially acceptable behavior, unwilling or unable even to clean

37. F. C. T. Moore (1975), who provides a structural analysis of several Fatna tales, considers the stories to explore the difficulties of endogamous marriage. While I would agree, my analysis pursues the problem from a different angle. In a number of respects (i.e., her wit, charm, and intelligence) Fatna resembles Sheherazade of the Arabian Nights, on whom she may have been patterned. Her escapades, however, are Sudanese in context.

themselves or engage in civil communication. Illegitimate children are severely stigmatized, feared, and shunned by all; only with considerable difficulty, say villagers, might they overcome their inherent disabilities to lead upstanding lives.[38] Clearly, socialization begins in the womb, and is bound to succeed only if the womb has been impregnated by an appropriately designated sire. Law and nature are mutually influential.

But more than this, Hofriyati aver that children must be raised by natural kin if they are to fulfill their potential to become responsible, moral beings. I discovered this quite by accident when talking with a group of women shortly after a thwarted attempt to overthrow the Sudanese government in 1976: when the smoke had cleared, Radio Omdurman reported a high civilian death toll; many children had been orphaned. We switched off the news, and our conversation turned, as so often it did, to the topic of children. I was asked if on my return to Hofriyat some future year, I would bring along the children I'd likely have borne in the interim. I hedged: perhaps I could adopt one of the orphaned Sudanese children instead? My friends were horrified. Surely I would be murdered, they said, if I attempted to raise a child who was neither my own nor my spouse's, nor the child of a close relative. Such a child would have no reason to respect or obey me. Freed from the moral constraints of life with his natural family, he would certainly develop antisocial inclinations despite heroic attempts to guide him. My friends' comments point unerringly to the fact that morality inheres in kinship—indeed, *is* kinship. Social life: patterned, controlled, known human behavior, depends upon the nurturance of offspring by their natural kin.

This leads to a second condition for the appropriate exercise of fertility: not only must a couple be married, they should also be closely related. All kin, both consanguineal and affinal, are deemed "close" (*garīb*) to one or another degree. All, excluding full and half siblings, parents and their siblings, their spouses, and the siblings and children of parents' living spouses, are recognized as potential mates. The excluded kin are those between whom sexual relations are considered incestuous, with whom marriage would be "too close." Especially in the case of first marriages, people are tacitly encouraged to wed their closest available kin after these excep-

38. Here again, cultivation parallels human reproduction. When onions are grown for cash, the best of the previous year's crop are planted in autumn four or five to an irrigation plot (*ḥoḍ*) and allowed to mature. Their seeds are collected and later scattered in the parent onion's plot. The parent is referred to as the *faḥl* or "stallion"; the seedlings, when ready for market in June or July, are considered the best and sweetest onions, much desired throughout the country. However, the demand for onions is continuous, and farmers often complement their seedling crop with an earlier one, by planting the previous year's smallest reserved bulbs. By thus circumventing the prolonged process of growing an onion from seed (in the "home" of its legitimate sire, surrounded by its *akhwān*, or "siblings") farmers are able to turn a quick profit by supplying onions when seedlings everywhere are immature; however, the farmers agree that such onions, called *awlād ḥarām*, are definitely inferior in quality.

tions. Ultimately, however, they are not forced to seek such unions despite their alignment with official ideology; matrimonial strategies are practical, guided by self-interest or group concerns having political, economic, and symbolic implications (cf. Bourdieu 1977: 30 ff.). Thus it sometimes happens that nonrelatives marry. Even so, it is usual for spouses to be selected from within the four-village area, from within the range of the known and morally certain. Reciprocally, it might therefore be said that kinship inheres in morality, and morality, in propinquity. Of all first marriages involving native Hofriyati, recorded in my census of 1977 (N = 205), just sixteen (7.8 percent) were contracted between families who did not formerly acknowledge kinship, and in only four of these (2.0 percent) did a partner come from outside the vicinity.

The system of marital preference I outline below is partly implicit, partly normative and explicit. In Hofriyat, marriage is one domain in which "the dialectic between the schemes immanent in practice and the norms produced by reflection on practices" (Bourdieu 1977: 20) can best be detected. Here, then, the tendency toward interiority is most clearly formulated, apparent in relatively systematic form to Hofriyati themselves.

Marital preferences depicted by villagers can be imagined in terms of the enclosure concept outlined earlier with regard to infibulation. Marriages between siblings or other prohibited kin would effectively close, hence atomize, the *khashm al-bayt,* making the family a world unto itself—in some ways desirable—but thereby preventing it from establishing useful and potentially lifesaving relationships outside. Yet marriages with nonkin outsiders are equally ominous: they open the family and village to unfamiliar, possibly unsettling influences and make social reproduction a random affair. Should a man wed an unrelated outsider he is scorned as one whose wife is a "she-goat from the market," so uncertain is her pedigree, so greatly has he had to rely on the word of strangers to vouch for her character and that of her family. Just as the *sūq* goat which seemed a good bargain in Shendi may prove otherwise once its owner gets it home, so the alien bride who seems sweet, honest, and hardworking before her wedding may show herself to be difficult, demanding, barren, or untrustworthy shortly thereafter. He or she who does not marry "close" takes a far greater risk than one who does, despite any gain in the extension of practical relationships that might accrue if the gamble comes off. Marriages that are too distant—or, for that matter, too close—jeopardize the harmony and cooperation so highly valued in Hofriyat.

Thus, the family (and by extension the village) is like a human body whose orifices, though necesary to sustain life, are thought dangerous, hence carefully constricted (cf. Douglas 1966). The orifices or openings of the family are the marriages of its members. These openings are controlled symbolically and, in part, officially, by a graded preference for marriages between close kin, people between whom there already exists a high level of moral obligation. Affinal relationships in Hofriyat should duplicate and build on those of consanguinity and physical proximity.

Cousin Marriage

When asked whom they ought to marry and whom they actually marry, villagers' responses do not vary: "We marry close (*garīb*); we marry our *awlād ʿamm*." Strictly speaking, *awlād ʿamm* are children of a paternal uncle: patrilateral parallel cousins.[39] In Hofriyat and throughout the riverain Arab Sudan, village social organization derives, formally and ideally, from a variable number of patrilineal descent groups (rarely corporate in any material sense), the members of which trace common ancestry to a male kinsman living a minimum of four and maximum of eight generations ago. Thus one might think that when villagers say they marry *awlād ʿamm,* they are saying they marry endogamously with respect to lineage. Yet this is not actually the case.

Demographic vicissitudes make it impossible for everyone in the village to wed an actual father's brother's daughter or son, although a striking proportion of genealogically documented first marriages (48 of 205) have conformed to this type. Hofriyati I spoke to are well aware that their practice falls short of the stated preference, yet when villagers say they marry *awlād ʿamm,* they indicate that virtually all marriages (except a few considered "not close") correspond to this description. The paradox evaporates when we realize that *awlād ʿamm* has literal, classificatory, and figurative significances in Sudan. Hence its application in this context can be thought of as a kind of "officializing strategy" (after Bourdieu 1977: 38 ff.), a way to align practice with the tenets of an explicit ideology imported from the heartland of Islam (cf. also Eickelman [1976], and on a related matter Bledsoe [1980]).

Dealing with the term's figurative significances first, it can mean simply "those who are married": spouses become close (or closer) kin as a result of the nuptial tie, hence may be considered *awlād ʿamm* after the fact, if not before. The category is also a euphemism for spouses now deceased or moved away who are known to be kin, but whose precise interlinkage others have forgotten.

More substantially, northern Sudanese kin terminology classifies the

39. Numerous authors have attempted to account for the practice, preference, or ideology of patrilateral parallel cousin marriage in Middle Eastern and North African societies. See, for examples, Kronenberg and Kronenberg (1965) on the evidence from riverain Sudan; also Ayoub (1959); Barth (1954); Bourdieu (1977); Das (1973); Gilbert and Hammel (1966); Goldberg (1967); Hilal (1972); Keyser (1974); Khuri (1970); Meeker (1976); Murphy and Kasdan (1959, 1967); and Patai (1965). Full consideration of this issue in light of the Sudanese data is beyond the scope of this book.

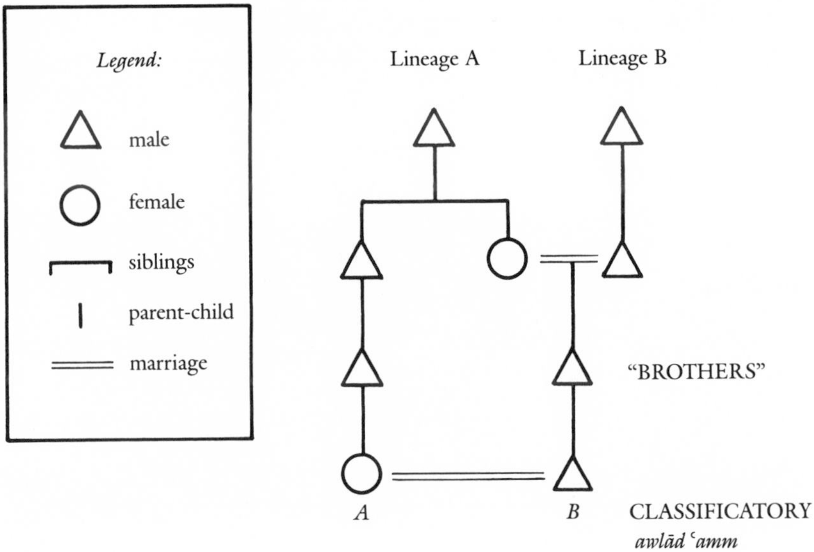

Fig. 2.1. Example of a Lineage Exogamous Marriage between Classificatory *Awlād ʿAmm*

children of actual *awlād ʿamm,* indeed of all first cousins, as "brothers" and "sisters," though conveniently *not* as prohibited spouses. Regardless of their sex, actual first cousins are "siblings" from the point of view of the next generation. And as the children of "siblings," they in turn are cousins, hence "siblings" from their children's point of view. This entire process of updating relationships regresses hypothetically to infinity, but realistically terminates in tracing to the fifth ascending generation. As figure 2.1 illustrates, marriages between classificatory *awlād ʿamm* may therefore be lineally exogamous. Such marriages are considered "close" yet not as desirably "close" as those between actual *awlād ʿamm* nor, in fact, between first cousins of any delineation.

In Hofriyat, marriages between *awlād ʿamm* are thus desirable because they are *garīb,* "close": and the concept of closeness (*garāba*)[40] at once underwrites, justifies, and ambiguates the official marriage "rule." Marriages between matrilateral parallel cousins or patrilateral and matrilateral cross-cousins—real or classificatory—are considered "close," as are those between various other kin, including affines. Salient to the definition of closeness is the demonstration and/or belief of prior kinship, the stronger and more immediate (*ṭawālī*) the link, the less ambiguous the moral obligation between families and the more desirable—ostensibly—the marriage. Closeness is a matter of degree; it is a relative value.

40. The term also means "relationship" or "kinship."

Thus marital preferences, much like village social space, are graded concentrically: defined by the degree of closeness to nonmarriageable kin. Most immediate kinship precludes marriageability; but if a marriage ideal can be formulated for Hofriyat it would have to be that closest kinship—hence prohibited marriage—in one generation breeds most preferred marriageability in the next. After this, cross-generationally prohibited marriage *or* most preferred marriageability in one generation ensures second most desirable marriageability two generations hence (among second cousins). Furthermore, the prohibition of marriage between a man and a woman creates marital potential not only among their descendants, but among their collateral and affinal kin as well. Thus, however strategic the actual choice of mate, prior kinship can usually be attested and the match deemed officially proper: Hofriyati are greatly concerned to maintain their networks of practical (i.e., practically significant) kin by repeated intermarriage (cf. Bourdieu (1977: 39).

Marriages are implicitly ranked into four distinct classes of preference according to the closeness of prior kinship between spouses; the degree of closeness constitutes a gauge of the potential usefulness each spouse's network of kin represents to the other's, as well as of the moral (symbolic) capital conserved and safeguarded by the match. The classes, as described by informants, are (1) *garīb ṭawālī* (immediately close): actual first cousins of any sort, accounting for 40 percent of first marriages (N = 205) at the time of fieldwork; (2) *garīb shadīd* (very close, strongly close): classificatory first, and cross-generational cousins (second cousins and cousins "degrees removed"), 36.2 percent of first marriages; (3) *garīb sai* (somewhat close, only close): patrilateral or matrilateral kinship believed but not immediately demonstrable, 16.0 percent of first marriages; (4) *mush garīb* (not close): no prior kinship known or believed to exist, 7.8 percent of first marriages. For classes 1 and 2, kinship is readily traceable; for class 3, the knowledge of closeness precedes its justification by reference to "one grandmother," a common "grandfather" (i.e., ancestor), membership in a single "family" (*ʿāila wāḥid*), or more specific ties that "must" perforce exist (cf. Eickelman 1976: 101–2).

Sexual Complementarity and Symmetry

Each of the above classes is also ordered internally to some extent, though I am wary of reifying what are actually very flexible distinctions. Among one's preferred spouses *garīb ṭawālī*, villagers explicitly favor marriage with a patrilateral parallel cousin, referred to as a *wad ʿamm ṭawālī* (immediate father's brother's son), or *bit ʿamm ṭawālī* (immediate father's brother's daughter). This preference is borne out statistically, comprising the largest proportion of first marriages in Hofriyat: 22.4 percent, with a further 1.0 percent involving bilateral parallel cousins. The latter are considered even closer than simple *awlād ʿamm* but are, understandably, rare. After these, villagers (both men and women) deem marriage with a direct matrilateral parallel cousin best, followed by marriage with a direct cross-cousin. While there is no expressed preference for mother's brother's daughter over father's sister's daughter, marriage with the former is more prevalent, describing 6.3 percent as opposed to 1.3 percent of first marriages.

Before proceeding further to analyze apparent and stated preferences obtaining at all degrees of closeness, I should point out that since villagers are complexly intermarried in every known generation, extant or deceased, it is common that a couple should be related in several different ways. Moreover, when discussing the consanguineality between spouses, men and women of a single household often specified different genealogical pathways. Men were generally inclined to favor linkages concordant with the official dogma of patrilineal descent, preferring to reference more distant patrilineal relationships over immediate ones traced through women.[41] Women, on the other hand favored most immediate linkages, whether through men, women, or both sexes. When discussing the relationships on which marriages are based, women, it seems, are more pragmatic, and men more ideological.[42] This is consonant with women's ideological mutedness in Hofriyat, yet it also reveals men's apparent desire to officialize political strategies, thus cloaking them in the mystique of lineage integrity.

Accepting that marriage between *awlād ʿamm* (*ṭawālī*) is the expressed ideal, why does there exist a secondary normative preference for marriage with matrilateral kin over more distant patrilateral relatives? Moreover, why the apparent preference for parallel cousins over cross-cousins? The answers, I think, lie in the direction of Hofriyati sexual complementarity and the desire for symmetry and cooperation in actual social relations. Regarding matrilaterality, it is reasonable to suppose that Hofriyati women, who are highly influential in negotiating (albeit informally) the marriages of their children, would rather that their sons marry their own siblings' daughters than those of their husbands' sisters. A woman's relationship with her husband's sister is an unequal one and may be rife with tension, for the bond between a brother and sister is exceedingly strong in Hofriyat and remains so despite their respective marriages. Thus wife and sister may be rivals for a man's regard and the moral and financial support he bestows (see also Wikan 1980), which may lead the former to

41. See also Bourdieu (1977:42) on the Kabyle of Algeria, who appear to be more adamant on this issue than Hofriyati.

42. Such gender-specific strategies appear similar to those noted by Rosen (1978) in Morocco.

avoid the latter as potential mother-in-law to her child. Moreover, the tendency toward matrilocal residence and matrifocal groupings in Hofriyat might well foster (officially) subordinate yet practically significant preferences among men for marriage with maternal kin.

Again, it may be recalled that a mother largely determines her son's prospective mates by observing young girls who are segregated from his view and advising him on his selection. She therefore exercises considerable control over the information her son and his father require in order to initiate a proposal, a step not lightly undertaken as it places the family's most significant resource, its reputation, on the line (see also Altorki 1986).[43] Men's dependence on women's intelligence of other households gives women scope to maneuver and implement their own political aspirations, to consolidate a kinship network and assure themselves of support. A girl, on the other hand, is more likely to marry a man chosen (from available suitors acting on information provided by senior women) by her father and brothers. In light of these circumstances and the intimate brother-sister tie, it is not surprising that mother's brother's daughter marriage occurs more frequently than marriage to father's sister's daughter.

This also explains, in part, why matrilateral parallel cousins are preferred in Hofriyat over patrilateral cross-cousins. But it fails to resolve the apparent general preference for parallel cousins. A potentially fruitful interpretation here might be that parallel cousin marriage is more consistent with the organizing idiom of enclosure. A marriage between parallel cousins can be considered less "open," less parlous than one between cross-cousins. The families of the former stand in a balanced relationship before their marriage: calculation of prior kinship is symmetrical, through a pair of brothers or sisters. Symmetrical, then, are the rights and obligations by which their families are bound. Moreover, same sex siblings inherit equal shares of their parents' estates, and one may replace the other in a marriage following the latter's death (via levirate or sororate). For most purposes, same sex siblings are social equivalents.

When cross-cousins marry, however, the relationship between their families is asymmetrical and unbalanced: a brother remains morally responsible for his sister after her marriage. He is her legal custodian and inherits twice as much as she on their parents' deaths. Indeed, he may hold her portion of the estate in trust throughout her life, using it as he sees fit. A woman, moreover, relies on her brother to support her in disputes with her husband and maintain her in the event of divorce. These circumstances

43. Women have a vested interest, then, in maintaining the system of sexual segregation plus the association between infibulation and the right or the ability to bear true, that is, morally sound, "Hofriyati" children. But to get to this point they themselves must have undergone manipulation by their elders. See Bledsoe (1984) for similar observations on older women's roles in the Sande secret society among the Kpelle of West Africa.

in the parental generation may make marriages between cross-cousins more problematic, more prone to disquiet than those between parallel cousins. It is interesting that the relative simplicity of expressions describing parallel cousins—*awlād ʿamm*, and *awlād khālāt* (matrilateral parallel cousins)—compared with the more cumbersome terms for various cross-cousin relationships—for example, *wad ʿammat/bit khāl* (father's sister's son/mother's brother's daughter)—underscores the symmetry of the former and the asymmetry of the latter. The concern for balance between families allied by marriage may be an expression in Hofriyat of the vague *sharīʿa*-based marriage rule called *kafāʿa* (literally, "equality"), which stipulates that spouses should be equivalent in status (see Bates and Rassam 1983 : 200).

But status of this sort need not be the only consideration: shared substance, the stuff of moral identity, may be a stronger, if equally implicit factor in the preference for parallel over cross-cousin marriages. Recall that according to the Hofriyati theory of procreation, a child receives her bones from her father and her flesh and blood from her mother. Matrilateral parallel cousins therefore share a common source of flesh and blood. Cross-cousins, though linked by flesh and blood, do not, since their mothers are not sisters of the same womb, nor their fathers brothers of the same seed. Matrilateral parallel cousins are, in this sense, closer than cross-cousins of any type. I do not think I violate Hofriyati understandings to suggest that shared substance provides an alternate criterion for marriageability to that of common patrilineal descent. In fact, the former subsumes the latter and may well predate it; as vernacular knowledge, it accords with the Quran (Sura 86 : 5–7) and Arab practice, yet it is also consonant with matrilineal ideology which informed Nubian society in the days before Islam (chapter 1). A consubstantial notion of closeness may thus form part of an invisible Hofriyati cultural archive (cf. James [1988]; see also the prologue to this book); it is fundamental to local ideas of personhood and morality (as the implications of sibling ties suggest), but can be shaped to a variety of ideological positions.

The normative preference that spouses be close kin decreases sharply when people wed for a second time. One's first marriage to a kinsman operates to maintain and intensify existing relationships, and if there are progeny or the subsequent marriage is polygynous, the initial marriage will continue to fulfill this function beyond its effective dissolution. Perhaps this is why people remarrying can be more overtly strategic or guided by personal considerations, since such unions are not often arranged and are largely matters of choice for both women and men. Whatever the reason, the field of potential spouses now widens considerably and marriages between traceable kin become less common, dropping to 32.7 percent (N = 92) from 76.2 percent for first marriages (N = 205).

Second marriages effectively and, I suggest, strategically extend the range of marriageable kin for the offspring of a sibling group, creating close relationships—hence marriage potential—in subsequent generations where none might have existed otherwise. This is true to a limited extent when a man increases his descendants by having children with more than one wife,[44] since his children by each are recognized as siblings. All bear their father's name, are readily identified as members of an extended family, and are rarely segmented in genealogies. Marriages between the children of patrilateral half siblings are equivalent to marriages between those of full siblings.

However, a woman's children by two or more husbands do not belong to one family but to the households and descent groups of their respective fathers.[45] Yet they, too, are considered siblings and their children highly appropriate mates. Here we see another way in which marriages of the first degree of closeness (*ṭawālī*) can be contracted between different patrilines. Such intermarriages link the various lineages in Hofriyat, blurring their distinctions and offsetting any tendency toward descent group atomization.

The significance of sexual complementarity in kinship reckoning and the importance of relationships traced through women are explicitly acknowledged by Hofriyati. In gathering information on family structure, I found that local (male) genealogists present their data in two distinct forms. Predictably, they begin by reciting a ***nisba awlād ʿamm,*** a line of descendants traced exclusively through males. They would state the name of a male ancestor (usually an eponym), then give a systematic listing of his descendants, eliminating or glossing over those who died without offspring or whose only progeny were female, and indicating the lines along which fissioning had occurred. Information about daughters and wives was provided in this context only after persistent request; even so, it was incomplete.

The second method stresses not divergence but interrelationship and convergence among lines of ***awlād ʿamm,*** and is referred to as a ***nisba awlād khālāt,*** a genealogy of maternal aunts. It lists for a single ascendant generation a group of sisters and their respective, usually multiple, husbands. Since it is rarely possible (nor always desirable) for sisters to marry into the same sibling group, they frequently marry quite far afield. Moreover, as noted, people contemplating second marriages are not as constrained to marry "close." Thus it often happens that the husbands of sisters are themselves nonkin or remote relatives. A ***nisba awlād khālāt*** shows how several families, perhaps distant or unrelated if patrigenealogies alone are con-

44. In Hofriyat there can be no sororal polygyny.

45. This is true regardless of whether the levirate was invoked in remarriage. Hofriyati do not practice a "true" levirate: the children of brothers always belong to their genitor's line.

sulted, are in fact closely related once uterine links in immediate ascending generations are revealed. *Awlād khālāt* genealogies are kept precisely because uterine relationships are sources of moral identity and grounds for future marriages between ostensibly discrete lines of descent. The tracing of matrilateral kinship through sisters and their descendants provides fluidity and integration to village social organization. As noted earlier, uterine relationships supply the metaphoric flesh and blood that bind together the "bones" of Hofriyat society, its various and increasing lines of *awlād ʿamm*.

Fatna's Dilemma

From all of this it is possible to conclude that despite a doctrine of patrilineality and patrilateral parallel cousin marriage, relationships in Hofriyat are traced through either parent when determining eligibility to wed. Potential mates are more likely to trace through fathers than through mothers, especially where first marriages are concerned, and this tendency was, as one might expect, slightly more marked for females (63.4 percent, N = 186 traceable first marriages of women) than it was for males (60.2 percent, N = 166 traceable first marriages of men). Yet roughly a third of all traceable first marriages were contracted with a matrilateral relative.[46]

Considering the remotest link to which prior kinship was traced, one finds, again, that calculation led most often to an ancestral pair of brothers (42.4 percent of 177 known cases). However, 27.7 percent of the time it led to a pair of sisters and 23.1 percent to a brother and sister, with some minor variations making up the rest. The frequency with which prior kinship was actually, if not always officially, traced to one or more women is striking, given the strong patrilineal emphasis in Hofriyat. Further, because of the broad classificatory nature of northern Sudanese kinship, relationship to an ancestral sibling pair might have been traced in countless ways through any combination of male and female links, bearing in mind the relative order of preference that both parents in the first ascending generation be males, then females, and so on.

We are left with the ineluctable conclusion that kinship in Hofriyat is actually reckoned cognatically. Just as villagers recognize that male and female contributions are necessary to any enterprise, be it ceremonial, eco-

46. In 35.0 percent or 58 of the 166 first marriages of men in which relationship between spouses could be traced with relative ease, a man was acknowledged to have wed a matrilateral kinswoman; in a further 5 cases (3.0 percent), his wife was related to him through both parents equally. The comparable figures for women's first marriages (N = 186) are 58 (31.2 percent) and 7 (3.8 percent). In the few cases (3 for males, 3 for females) unaccounted for by these percentages, the marriage was contracted affinally, through the prior marriage of a brother or sister.

nomic, or reproductive, so they trace kinship through both sexes when seeking prior relationships on which marriages can be built. And just as men and women complement each other physically and physioreproductively, so they provide through their marriages complementary means for organizing and reproducing society. In Hofriyat, where, as noted earlier, politically and economically significant social relations are mediated by kinship and reproduced through marriage, networks of connubial relationships—not lineages—are the focal social groups.

When Hofriyati say they marry close or when they say they marry *awlād ʿamm,* they are using conventional idioms which signify they wed cognatic kin and are biased in favor of patrilateral relatives. But it is some sort of prior kinship between spouses that is important above all else. For kinship, however traced, binds individuals in a complicated web of social and moral obligation whose intensity is maintained and verified by their marriage. It is only when biological parents are socially, morally, and legally obligated that their offspring can develop into true—that is, moral—Hofriyati. The closer the kinship between parents, the more certain will be the outcome, and the more appropriate the use of a Hofriyati woman's fertility.

Still, marital choice is strategic not only morally and symbolically, but also materially. Where extended families share corporate resources beyond those embraced by a common fund of honor and obligation, closest marriages are both economically feasible and morally sound. But given the convolutions of Hofriyati kinship produced by repeated endogamy, evaluation of closeness is ambiguous, leaving much to opportunism and the forging of individualistic networks of alliance within a group of kin.[47] Thus individuals sometimes forfeit opportunities to wed their closest available kin, if more distant matches, traceable in hundreds of different ways, appear to hold greater promise. The potential benefits to be gained from this must be weighed against the possibly pernicious effects of opening more widely the *khashm al-bayt* through marriages with remote kin or strangers.

Here, in practical terms, is Fatna's dilemma: to whom does she trust her fertility—her potential and that of society as a whole? Paradoxically, if she entrusts it to her brother, the kinsman to whom she is most morally bound, her fertility is used inappropriately: she faces social isolation, a dangerous mistake in this harsh land of limited resources. Yet to entrust her fertility to an outsider is an equally dangerous move despite the fact that her mate could turn out to be wealthy and powerful, indeed, a sultan's

47. On this and related points relative to the Middle East, but also to Botswana where similar processes have been observed, see Barth (1973); Bourdieu (1977); Comaroff and Comaroff (1981); Comaroff and Roberts (1981); Comaroff (1985); H. Geertz (1979); Peters (1972); Rosen (1982); and Solway (n.d.).

son. The perils of Fatna illustrate problems which continually confront villagers in this and other contexts: how close is too close? and more telling perhaps, how distant is too distant, how open too open? These issues, emanating from the dialectic of practice and ideology, lead to the consideration of certain ramifications of Hofriyati logic and morality in chapter 3.

3

Boundaries and Indeterminacies

This chapter probes the implications and parameters of interiority and its suggested counterpart, exteriority, which constitute major though tacit motifs in Hofriyati thought. Interiority, recall, is a relative value: human relationships, for example, are classed as to the quality of closeness that obtains between principals, the categories forming a series of ever widening concentric circles. At the center stands the immediate family, importantly, a group of siblings. In successive annulations are more distant kin and covillagers, nonkin Muslim Sudanese and, at the outer limits, strangers. Trust, commitment, even potential usefulness, diminish at points genealogically and geographically more distant from the Hofriyati individual. Yet such categories are by no means fixed. They are transient configurations, shifting in their composition as strangers become familiar, as nonkin become kin through marriage and assume reciprocal obligations that they previously did not hold. The system does have operational boundaries: Hofriyati are forbidden to marry non-Muslims; and inner extremes: siblings may not wed; yet its limits are rarely so absolute and impenetrable. If interiority be considered a cultural imperative or guide for behavior, it is by no means determinate.

Boundaries between what is compatible with villagers' implicit paradigms and what is anathema are not always apparent. Limits of acceptable behavior are inevitably obscured by pragmatics, for an act considered inappropriate in one set of circumstances may be deemed fitting in another. The legends of Fatna and the sultan's son, to which I later return, reveal that attributes like wit, wealth, and power can be valued above those of close kinship in a potential mate. No criterion is absolute or essential: a rich nonrelative may be more suitable to wed than a poor first cousin if one is penniless.

As S. F. Moore notes, social life is never without such a lack of specificity:

> Established rules, customs, and symbolic frameworks exist, but they operate in the presence of areas of indeterminacy, or ambiguity, of uncertainty and manipulability. Order never fully takes over, nor could it. The cultural,

> contractual, and technical imperatives always leave gaps, require adjustments and interpretations to be applicable to particular situations, and are themselves full of ambiguities, inconsistencies, and often contradictions. (S. F. Moore 1975:220)

In Hofriyat, I suggest, this may be especially true.[1] Here, gaps and ambiguities are built into situations by the relativity of the idiom that informs them. Further, by enjoining their minimization, villagers admit that openness and ambiguity inhere in social relations, human physical characteristics, and a host of other contexts. Interiority implies its opposite much as female implies, and is implied by, male. In this there is a partial contradiction: villagers' system of meanings both provides for ambiguity and seeks to contain it. Yet because of this orientation, they may be equipped to expect a gradual permutation of the social and physical environment; their implicit generative schemata anticipate change in furnishing a model for its negotiation and comprehension. At the most practical level, this enables Hofriyati of either sex to exploit the ambiguity of their convoluted, cognatic relationships in negotiating personal networks of affines and kin.

Still, if propriety is ambiguous and manipulable, it does have certain parameters. Its limits are best discerned when transgressed, when morality and individual integrity are threatened. Here I undertake a further exploration of villagers' world by searching for these boundaries. How do Hofriyati assert their identity, maintain their integrity, or violate that of others? What is the definition of a "person" in Hofriyat, and does this vary by sex? Finally, how does a Hofriyati woman place herself within the world, and what does this imply for her participation in the *zār*? The symbolism of food provides a point of departure.

It is another clean, cool morning, refreshingly still and cloudless. Zaineb, Samira, and I walk single file on the high firm ground of the railway track, following it toward Kabushiya and the station. A Hofriyati husband and wife are leaving today on the first leg of their pilgrimage to Mecca; we are going to see them off.

At the station pilgrims and well-wishers from several villages add knots of color to the dun terrain. The women are delighted by the outing and the chance to revive old friendships. A number of them greet me; few seem surprised by my presence.

Soon the train arrives. Travelers board, weighed down with provisions for their lengthy and arduous trip. Maᶜsallamas *are hurriedly called through coach windows, and in moments the train chugs away. The crowd begins to disperse.*

1. In societies such as those of the Middle East and North Africa, ostensibly bound by rigid sets of rules and burdened with impracticable ideologies, indeterminacy may be more obvious to the observer. Moreover, within these societies there is a well-developed appreciation for relativity and perspective. See, for examples, Altorki (1986), Bourdieu (1977), Eickelman (1976), Geertz (1983), Geertz, Geertz, and Rosen (1979), Rosen (1982).

An old man, bent and wizened, has been glaring at me throughout the pilgrims' departure. Now he approaches Samira and with a wordless gesture asks her who I am. Samira tells him I am her cousin, her bit ʿamm. *She and Zaineb struggle to keep straight faces while the old man searches a dusty memory for the name of Samira's kinsman who had fathered a light-eyed child. His distress is tangible. Yet my friends are relishing their joke and seem reluctant to end the charade.*

Moments later I relent. "I have come from Canada," I say, "and am living for a while in Hofriyat."

Disbelieving, he stares me in the eye for a second or two then turns to Samira and rasps, "Does she eat kisra*?"*

"Yes," says Samira.

"Well, then, she is Sudanese!"

Food, Identity, and Sexual Complementarity

Scenes like this were not uncommon during the months I spent in the field. Interest in my alimentary habits was patent. To some extent it was thought that being non-Sudanese, I was precluded from eating Sudanese foods on a regular basis, as if in order to preserve my Westernness I must periodically consume Western foods in a Western manner. Whenever I ate *kisra* at communal meals, villagers would boast I had become Sudani, or better, Hofriyati. I quickly came to understand that how and what one does or does not eat has symbolic import: making something originally external to oneself an integral part of one's body is a powerful metaphoric operation, at minimum signaling participation in villagers' or some other world of meaning. More tangibly, incorporation substantively maintains or alters a specific type of human being. The notion surfaces in a number of contexts, many but not all of them having to do with nutrition.

With regard to identity, reliance on *kisra* distinguishes Arab Sudanese, particularly Ja'ali and Jawabra sedentaries, from other social groups. Further, the prohibited consumption of pork, blood, or animals not ritually slaughtered in the Islamic (*ḥalāl*) way sets apart Muslim Sudanese from their non-Muslim countrymen.[2] A basic similarity of diet thus characterizes Hofriyati and is emblematic of their ethnicity (cf. Barth 1969; Cohen 1974).

Yet not all villagers eat the same foods. Dietary differences, particularly strong among women, derive not only from the personal preferences

2. I was once given some bacon by British friends in Khartoum. My friends in the village were keen to try this "new meat," but I was reluctant. When I told them it was *laḥma kanzīr* (pig meat) they were undeterred. I did not wish to seem ungenerous, even less to presume a better understanding than they of religious matters, but felt I had to ask if pork was not forbidden by Islam. They were surprised by the suggestion and went off to consult a

one expects to find in any community. Often they result from self-imposed restriction. Whenever I dined with a group of women, it was all but inevitable that one would deny herself some dish or ingredient, remarking, "*Āṣlu mā bākilo*"—"Never do I eat it." For some, prohibition undoubtedly has a practical basis: many avoid cow's milk because they cannot tolerate it. But there are idiosyncratic avoidances where instrumental benefit is less apparent. Some women do not eat one or another variety of "small meat" (*laḥma ṣaghīra*): pigeon, fish, and eggs, all prestigious foods associated with fertility. Others avoid "large meat" (*laḥma kabīra*): goat, mutton, and beef, except on ceremonial occasions, and then profess reluctance. Not only meat but all types of food—including certain *kisras*—may be subject to prohibition. Such personal food avoidances have a particularizing effect (cf. Lévi-Strauss 1966). They serve to establish the uniqueness of individuals, highlighting differences where otherwise, as between full sisters, there is social and, given local conceptions of bodily constitution, physical equivalence. In short, they are assertions of personal identity,[3] regardless of their source: whether imposed by the woman herself or, as may be the case, by a possessive *zār*.

Food is also used symbolically in Hofriyat to claim prestige, establish relative status, and impart a sense of welcome thereby upholding family honor. Serving guests scarce or expensive foods—described in chapter 2 as "white" or "enclosed," often associated with foreign cultures and the power of the outside world—is a mark of hospitality, which should be augmented when the invitation is returned. Culinary potlatching is one competitive venue in Hofriyat, though meager resources limit its amplification. On a smaller scale, women visiting other households in the village—a moral imperative whenever a crisis or ceremony occurs (cf. Eickelman 1984; Altorki 1986)—gauge the warmth of their reception by the sweetness of the tea they are given to drink. Variations from the saccharine norm may be read as status messages of one sort or another.

In a separate vein, men engage in status jockeying through the physical appearances of their wives. A corpulent wife with smooth clear skin is a

---

kinsman. It seems that since women had not been given an opportunity to eat pork before this, the question of its prohibition had never been raised. Women remain unaware of many religious tenets for similar reasons.

3. When a sheep or goat is slaughtered in the Arab Sudan, the animal's organs—liver, kidneys, stomach, lungs, and spleen—are washed, then cut up and eaten raw mixed with lime juice, salt, onions, peanut paste, and cayenne pepper. This dish, known as *murārā* ("bitterness" or "gall," possibly because the contents of the animal's gall bladder are poured into the lungs before serving), should still be warm with life when served, indicating freshness and affirming hospitality. I tried *murārā* on several occasions but, fearing parasitic infection, eventually confessed that I would prefer to have mine cooked. I worried that my request would give offense, but needn't have: at least one other woman avoided raw *murārā*, so mine was seen as a legitimate preference which in time contributed to my village identity.

mark of prosperity, an obvious sign that she is well provided for, need not work hard, and spends a great deal of time entertaining friends and being entertained in turn. Large women are deemed beautiful and healthy, living reflections of their husbands' ability and concern. The ideal Hofriyati woman is a good consumer when given opportunity; she considers this an integral privilege of marital status (see also Yousif 1987).

The cases of host and husband are instructive. Here, social position is asserted not by eating or avoiding certain foods but by providing comestibles for others. These others—guests and wives—help affirm status claims vis-à-vis themselves and villagers in general by consuming foods provided. Provision and consumption aid in the establishment of mutual but unequal relationships, and bolster complementary social identities.

Nowhere is this more obvious than in the complementary exchanges between a groom and his bride at the time of their wedding, exemplary expressions of the transactions that should inform their married life. The economic and, by extension, reproductive potential of a marriage is symbolized in the *shayla:* gifts of clothing, jewelry, perfume, and comestibles which the groom presents to the bride and her family once the *mahr* (bridewealth functionally similar in some ways to dowry) has been transacted. The main part of the *shayla* is a trousseau consisting of sets of outfits, the greater the number of sets, the higher the donor's prestige and the better his demonstration of ability to provide for a wife and future children. During my first visit to Hofriyat, a "five-five-five" *shayla* was considered extremely respectable, consisting of five pairs of shoes, five dresses, *tōbs*, slips, brassieres, panties, handbags, and nightgowns.[4] Also included are a *garmosīs*—the red and gold shawl which veils a bride during her wedding and will cover her after the birth of each child[5]—plus one or more suitcases, store-bought perfumes and cosmetics, a watch, and as much gold jewelry as the groom can afford. Moreover, he must give a *tōb* to the bride's mother and each of her unmarried sisters. In 1976 a good *tōb* purchased in Sudan cost at least US $ 100, and few men spent less than $150; prices in 1984 were every bit as steep. Besides these gifts, which are on public display in the bride's home for a week or so before the ceremony, the groom is responsible for provisioning the bride's family and guests throughout the festivities, and must stage a suitable wedding feast for some five hundred people or more. Thus even in 1976 the cost of getting married, borne almost entirely by the groom, was extremely high.

When I went back to the village in 1983, I was told that with the

4. Indeed, most marriages at that time involved *shaylas* on the order of "three-three-three."

5. Her sons and daughters will also be covered by their mother's wedding *garmosīs* (or its replacement) after their circumcisions.

return of young men from lucrative jobs in Saudi and oil-rich principalities of the Gulf, the average *shayla* had risen to the order of "twelve-twelve-twelve," the *mahr* had also escalated dramatically, and the celebrations—complete with paid musicians from Khartoum—had grown enormous. It was said that any man who had not secured employment in Arabia could not afford to marry: several farming families had gone deeply into debt to local merchants so that their sons might wed. And contrary to popular wisdom, the situation was little better for a man who married his *bit ʿamm* than for one who did not.

Faced with such crippling inflation, the village-area council imposed restrictions on the size of the *shayla* (it could no longer exceed "three-three-three"), limited the *mahr* for a virgin bride to £S 100 (then about US $55), and stipulated the amounts of spice, oil, flour, and other food-stuffs that the groom must provide. Although this now enables men who are less well-off to marry without incurring financial ruin or loss of face, few weddings remain within these bounds. While a returned migrant worker might present a three-three-three *shayla* in public, everyone knows that another nine "sets" or more will be delivered to the bride's home at night to remain hidden until after the wedding and shown only to close relatives behind closed doors.

Importantly, presentation of the *shayla* sets in motion the ideal dialectic between husband and wife, inaugurating his role as producer-provider, and her complementary one as consumer and, ultimately, reproducer. It may be recalled from chapter 2 that Hofriyati men speak of marriage as "nesting" a woman; the image is appropriate: much as a bird is left to incubate her eggs while her consort flies between the nest and the outside world to forage and provision her with food, so a wife remains (ideally) in the *ḥōsh* while her husband works outside the village, in fields or more distant locations, in order to provide for his family. Just as men bear primary responsibility for production in Hofriyat (though they hardly perform all the labor), women bear primary responsibility for nurturance and reproduction (though men's procreative role is in no way denied).[6] Gender attributions such as these contribute to the sexes' constructions of selfhood, to their respective dispositions, thus intimating suitable roles for them in other domains of life.

In the implicit ideology of the village, production and reproduction articulate and are dynamically sustained in a marriage. This ideal is both celebrated and expressed in the wedding. Hofriyati say that a bride enters her first marriage naked, as she entered the world. She must give away all

6. See also Morsy (1978: 141–42). This is not, I emphasize, a gendered division of labor, but a gendered division of responsibility. Implications of this point are considered in subsequent chapters.

of her maiden clothing,[7] henceforth to be attired by her spouse who provides even the dress she wears to perform the wedding dance. This last she dons after several days of concealment and arduous cosmetic preparation designed to enhance and protect her fertility—and its outward manifestation, her beauty—emerging at last to face the assembled village reborn, as a married woman. Moments before her debut she is visited in hiding by the groom who, in front of witnesses, breaks a few threads (said to number seven) from the *garmosīs* with which she is veiled. This substitutes, on a social level, for what in other Muslim societies may be physically proved by displaying a blood stained cloth: it marks the official activation of the bride's reproductive potential.[8] The dressing of the bride (symbolic of her spouse's future productive contributions) and the formal surrender of her virginity (establishing the allocation of her fertility) must be seen as mutual exchanges solemnized by the wedding rite. And that they should be so considered is restated with every birth: after delivery and reinfibulation—which, as Hayes (1975:622) points out, is a social renewal of virginal status—a woman's husband presents her with further gifts of clothing and jewelry, thereby reestablishing the dynamic complementarity of their relationship.[9]

Violations of "Closeness"

The Hofriyati cultural system suggests a moral-ideational continuum ranging from extreme interiority or closure to extreme exteriority or openness, along which the ideal activities and characteristics of men and women are respectively placed, and according to which their behavior is evaluated. While the exemplary self for either sex is "closed," contained, integral, the

7. The gesture carries the same meaning as when a North American bride tosses her bouquet: those who receive the girl's clothes will soon be married. When I returned to Hofriyat in 1983, friends asked why I had not brought my prenuptial clothes to distribute among them. Did I not know, they joked, that everyone wants a "rich" husband from the West? The current of truth in this jibe is patent, and concentrates my ambiguous status well—setting me off as a privileged foreigner while also implying a form of sisterhood.

8. The custom is called *guṭaʿa ar-rahaṭ:* breaking the *rahaṭ,* the short thong skirt customarily worn by maidens until a few decades ago. The groom would pull seven thongs from his bride's skirt to publicly signify what we would describe as her loss of virginity, better seen in Hofriyat as the social allocation of her fertility.

9. Yousif (1987) describes gender complementarity among the inhabitants of an Omdurman suburb in terms similar to those discussed here, stressing the role of food. The ideal husband provides what it is the wife's duty to cook. Interestingly, a man who fails to fulfill his role is referred to as a *makshoufhal* (*makshūf ḥāl*), literally, "uncovered condition" (1987:71, 89 n. 1). On the other hand, a man who protects his wife and treats her well is called a *mastourhal* (*mastūr ḥāl*), literally "protected" or "covered condition" (1987:74, 90 n. 6). Yousif suggests the condition described is that of the husband, whose irresponsibility, in the first case, is apparent to others ("uncovered"). It is relevant, however, that the husband's actions are revealed through the condition of his wife.

relationship between husband as provider/producer and wife as consumer/ reproducer shows how this continuum expresses gender interdependence: men working outside the *ḥōsh* provide food and other items for women, working within it, to allocate, transform, and ingest. Despite the inherent relativity of Hofriyati cultural precepts, certain acts are deemed morally improper under most conditions, among these, behaviors that subvert such complementarity. Interesting here are departures from the provider-consumer model of marital relations, phrased metaphorically as food violations.

In Hofriyat a woman's possessions—her land, goats, clothing, jewelry—belong to her alone. In theory her husband cannot dispose of them unilaterally; he must obtain her consent. Despite this understanding a man might sell his wife's animals and gold, neglecting to inform her until after the transaction is complete. A woman thus slighted can be heard to complain, "*Zōji ākulni*"—"My husband has eaten me." Here, consumer has become provider, the roles of man and woman are reversed. More than this, the ideal consumer (woman) metaphorically becomes that which is consumed.

Such a transgression of propriety is interpreted not only as a threat to the woman's limited autonomy in marriage, but also to personal integrity. This, in turn, may jeopardize physical well-being, since Hofriyati do not differentiate between body and person. So by violating her property, a man violates his wife's integrity, absorbs her identity, denies her independent existence, and threatens her health. He commits an antisocial act, comparable to cannibalism. Like Fatna's crime of incest, his is a violation of excess: an overdetermination of closeness, thought especially heinous by women since it springs from an underrecognition of gender distance—complementarity. By enforcing religiously sanctioned asymmetries, he denies his wife her separate worth.

A woman might also accuse her husband of wishing to devour her when she feels unjustly overworked. Here, too, the provider-consumer relationship has broken down. When a woman must cultivate in order to make ends meet—as well as perform a significant schedule of domestic tasks—because her husband has abnegated financial responsibility or is suspected of saving for another wife, she will claim he is "eating" her. He uses money freed by her labor for his own ends such that the nature of their interdependence is reversed. Her hard won self-image as complement to her mate is contradicted by the realpolitik of male privilege. And again the violation of personal integrity is depicted as a violation of bodily integrity.

An undervaluation of closeness also breaches Hofriyati norms: the recluse, the man who never marries, the woman who persistently fails to attend her neighbor's ceremonies or visit during times of crisis, all behave inappropriately. Antisocial acts like these may bring unwelcome suspicion that the offender possesses an evil eye or worse, is a sorcerer (*sāḥar*), considered literally cannibalistic.

Responses to Boundary Violation

When a villager sees himself or herself the victim of an antisocial act, of an explicit violation of the ideals of "closeness," cooperation, or gender interdependence, response tends in the direction of excessive interiority, which is equally if conversely antisocial. Here the sufferer is said to "desire death" (*dayr am-mōt*) and might well attempt to take his own life. Witness the following case:

Several years ago Jaffar, an industrious man not yet married, built himself a house with the help of his two brothers, ʿIsa and Ibrahim. When it was finished, ʿIsa and his wife moved into the house on the understanding that once Jaffar married they would have to find other accommodation.

At his wedding in 1976 Jaffar asked ʿIsa to vacate the house two months hence, after the ʿĪd aṣ-Ṣaghīr, *the "small feast" following the fasting month of Ramadan. During the interval he frequently reminded ʿIsa of his plans to take over the house, yet ʿIsa made no plans to move. The morning after the ʿId Jaffar gave his brother £S 10 (then about US $25) to help defray the cost of materials for a new house, and suggested that ʿIsa temporarily shelter his family with his wife's mother while he built his own* ḥōsh. *Still ʿIsa did not leave: he considered he had a right to Jaffar's house since he had contributed labor to its construction and occupied it continuously for close to seven years.*

At noon the next day Jaffar went to the disputed house. ʿIsa was not at home. He told ʿIsa's wife to gather her things and get out. She refused. They quarreled heatedly. In the fray he hit her with his walking stick and threatened to upset the table on which she kept her kitchen things (a serious affront). ʿIsa's wife fled screaming to her sister's ḥōsh.

With this the entire village was alerted to the argument. ʿIsa's wife's sister (a strong-willed woman) threatened to send for the police, but was prevented by the informal assembly of men that quickly convened outside her door. Moments later, everyone adjourned to Jaffar's father's ḥōsh *to talk the matter out.*

ʿIsa and Ibrahim arrived from their fields. Both claimed that Jaffar was in the wrong: the house, they said, belonged equally to all three. Hearing this, Jaffar grabbed his dagger from its cinch on his upper left arm and moved to plunge it into his chest. Immediately, his father, mother-in-law, sister, brother Ibrahim, and Ibrahim's wife rushed forward and attempted to wrest the dagger from his grasp. Jaffar's mother-in-law and sister-in-law were badly gashed as Jaffar struggled to prove the honorability of his position and expose his brothers' treach-

ery by this final act. With considerable effort his relatives forced him to drop the knife. Jaffar himself was unhurt.

The women were sent from the room. After an hour's negotiation an equitable solution was reached: Jaffar was to pay each of his brothers £S 15 for their labor in building the house which ʿIsa would vacate immediately. All three then agreed to cooperate in building a new home for ʿIsa and his wife. The bond between brothers had been reaffirmed (though ʿIsa's house had yet to be finished when I visited again in 1984).

I asked my friends why Jaffar should wish to kill himself over what seemed to me a trivial matter, a conflict of perspectives. They did not consider his response unusual: "He was angry with his brothers, they said he was wrong . . . of course he wished to die!"

I was later told that a violation of the normally supportive relationship between close kin frequently leads to threatened—or actual—suicide.[10] When a dispute of this nature erupts, violence is not directed at kinfolk straightforwardly, but obliquely, through the victim himself. In Hofriyat the "desire for death" is the idiom by which this is expressed. Here again, social violations against the person transmute into physical (and self-punitive) terms. Even if one does not actively seek death, it is feared that he or she might give up the will to live, refuse to eat, become ill, and die. I doubt it would fall short of the mark to suggest that the demise of supportive relationships between closest kin is interpreted by villagers to signal the death of the self. The self in Hofriyat comprises one's body, social dispositions, and identity, all of them unthinkable except in relation to kin.

Integrity and Violation of Body Boundaries

An individual's integrity is jeopardized not only when she falls victim to a moral breach of "closeness." Other excesses also threaten the boundaries of propriety and the physical self. Self-control and dignity are qualities highly valued by villagers. Displays of emotion are considered vulgar, but more readily tolerated in women than in men. Women's natures, Hofriyati say, their greater *nafs* (animal life force, passion) and lesser amount of *ʿagl* (reason), render them less able than men to keep their emotions in check.

When a woman experiences anger toward kinfolk, utter grief at their loss, or anxiety for their well-being, she may claim to be ill (see also Con-

10. I have no statistics on actual suicides. A year before my arrival a man from Hofriyat who was working in Khartoum immolated himself, but why he should have done so was a mystery to my informants. Villagers say that every now and then a man disappears, ostensibly into the Nile, leaving a pile of clothing on the bank. But since bodies are rarely recovered, friends suggested that such men merely feign suicide to escape intolerable constraints of village life and begin anew somewhere else.

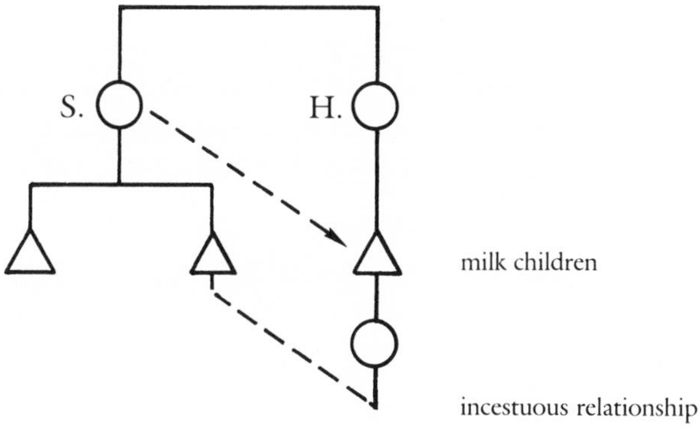

Fig. 3.1. Milk Children

stantinides 1977). She explains that she is being "eaten" by excessive emotion, consumed by something like a "fire" within. Here the metaphor of eating/consuming describes situations in which things formerly under control and regulated by concepts of harmony, balance, and closeness have gone awry. One is also said to be consumed by a fever (as in English), by pain, hunger, or a thorn that has punctured the skin. To be thus consumed is to experience a violation or breach of one's normal, ideal, physically contained and socially relational self.

Transformations effected by "consuming" or incorporating have moral and ethical ramifications. These may be negative—as when a man mistreats his wife—or benign. In what follows, the breach of a physical boundary fundamentally alters relations among kin but does not necessarily damage them. Remember that what a person actually ingests to some extent determines his or her identity. Nowhere is this more important than in the case of mother's milk.

Sometime around 1930 two sisters gave birth to sons in the same month. The women were in the habit of keeping each other company during the morning hours when their husbands were at work in the fields. One day when Howari was busy at the well her baby began to cry. Thinking he must be hungry, Saida picked him up and nursed him.

Years later Saida's youngest son asked to marry the daughter of Howari's eldest. But the match, which was close and therefore desirable, could not be sanctioned. Whether wittingly or not, Saida's action in nursing her sister's son had created a bond of actual siblinghood between her children and Howari's. It would have been incestuous for Saida's son to wed his mothers's sister's son's daughter, for she was in reality his maternal brother's child (Figure 3.1).

It makes no difference that the women in question were sisters. When unrelated children are nourished by the milk of one woman, they and all their siblings become *awlād laban,* "milk children," considered true maternal siblings with regard to mutual obligation and the purposes of marriage.[11] Here the potential violation of a kinship boundary results from an earlier breach of a physical one: the use of one's breast milk to feed another's children. Resolution of the ambiguity this entails for offspring's identities is achieved by extending the range of siblinghood. Hence, even natural kinship is indeterminate and mutable. Significantly, shared consumption of so vital a fluid as mother's milk actually creates close kinship. Note the associations of femininity, fluids, generativity, and consubstantial "closeness" reiterated here.

Mushāhara *Beliefs and Boundaries*

Ideas about incorporation are represented in practices and conditions involving another essential female fluid—blood, the source of a woman's fertility. Women are prone to illnesses involving excessive blood loss, called *nazīf* (not to be confused with *naẓīf,* meaning clean, nor as I was told, with menstrual blood despite an association with the word for "month"). Such ailments and their cures or prophylactics are collectively referred to as *mushāhara,* derived from the Arabic *shahr,* meaning "new moon" or "month" (Wehr 1976:490). As Kennedy (1978*b*:126) notes with reference to *mushāhara* among Egyptian Nubians: "The basic idea of the customs associated with the term is that if certain actions are engaged in before the appearance of the new moon (indicating the beginning of the lunar month), harm will befall an individual undergoing a 'crisis' rite."

In Hofriyat these associations of *mushāhara* are not emphasized, despite the new moon's acknowledged auspiciousness. However, the link is made implicitly, for one of the *jirtig* ornaments worn by children recuperating from circumcision and bridegrooms during their weddings is a cloth band tied around the crown of the head, to which a crescent-shaped piece of gold metal is fastened at mid forehead. This crescent is referred to as *hilāl,* or "new moon." *Mushāhara* is closely connected with the *jirtig,* as shown below; and their joint association with the moon can hardly be fortuitous: just as *mushāhara* practices are concerned to control female genital bleeding, lunar rhythms are emblematic of regularized, disciplined genital

11. The effect of this, of course, is to extend the range of marriageable kin in the following generation. Milk kinship, like multiple marriage, broadens one's network of kin, hence broadens the field of potential spouses for the children of those it renders siblings. See Altorki (1980:233–44) for a discussion of this issue among Saudi Arabian elites, also Eickelman (1984:97–98), Simoons (1976:313–29), Farb and Armelagos (1980:116–17).

flow.[12] That the link is suppressed by Hofriyati may indicate the ambivalence with which they regard women's blood loss, for despite their valiant efforts, even menstruation resists human control. I first describe the contexts of *mushāhara,* then discuss their implications.

A woman or girl is likeliest to suffer *mushāhara* hemorrhage at childbirth, circumcision, or defloration; hence as in Upper Egypt, the customs associated with such times are essential elements of life crisis rites (cf. Kennedy 1978*b*: 128; Trimingham 1965: 171).[13] A woman experiencing blood loss from the genital region is particularly at risk from spirits (*zayran* and other *jinn,* including river sprites), which might enter through the pregnable orifice and, possessing her, inflict sterility.

The causes of genital hemorrhage and its cures were related to me as follows. A female who has given birth, is newly circumcised, or has become a bride must wear a gold ring made of a coin and known as a *khatim ginay maṣri* ("seal of the Egyptian guinea"). This is one of the several *jirtig* charms that protect young people after their circumcisions, men and women at their weddings, and pregnant women especially at the time of delivery—occasions on which vulnerable individuals are exposed to female (or, in the case of circumcised boys, "feminine") genital blood. Should a woman who has given birth, a bride, or a newly circumcised girl neglect to wear such a ring, and should she then see a woman wearing gold, immediately she will start to hemorrhage. Moreover, when a woman discovers she is pregnant, any gold she is wearing at the time cannot be removed until after the birth, lest she miscarry. My friends explained that *nazīf* is often caused or exacerbated by spirits which, as Kennedy (1978*b*: 133) notes, are thought to be attracted to blood and gold; a menstruating woman who visits the graveyard therefore courts sterility, for it is known to be riddled with *jinn.* The gold a woman wears may divert the spirits' attentions from her genital region, which is rendered assailable because it has been opened, has bled, and is liable to bleed again. This condition also, of course, attends the newly deflowered bride.

Women who have recently shed blood through genital surgery and childbirth are apt to suffer uncontrollable hemorrhage if visited by people

12. Citing biological evidence, Buckley (1988: 203) suggests that the new moon—occurring twelve to fourteen days after the full moon which, it is hypothesized, can provide sufficient photic stimulation for hormone release—"comprises the naturally occurring lunar phase for the onset of menstruation." I make no claim that Hofriyati women exhibit menstrual synchrony (this is not a topic my present data can address), but the recognition of a lunar controlled menstrual cycle could well be implied in the *mushāhara* context.

13. See also Ahmed Al-Safi (1970: 20); Barclay (1964: 211–13); Crowfoot (1922: 23); Hills-Young (1940: 333); El Tayib (1955: 146–47); Trimingham (1965: 180). According to El Tayib (1955: 146), *mushāhara* "was applied to all apparently inexplicable ailments to which a pregnant woman was exposed, and which would cause miscarriage or a difficult birth, if not treated and dispelled at once." In Hofriyat, however, the customs are not confined to childbirth.

returning from a funeral, or who have seen a corpse or butchered animal and not yet erased the effects of death from their vision. To prevent such blood loss, a bowl of Nile water containing some millet and an axhead or some coins is placed outside the door to the room in which the girl or woman is confined. Her visitors must first look into the bowl, after which they may enter the room with impunity. If river water is not provided for the purpose, guests should gaze into a well and see there a reflection of the stars or moon before proceeding to their destination. Should one suffer *nazīf* as the result of a guest's omission, one might counteract the affliction by peering into a bowl of Nile water containing a gold coin, or into a well in which stars are reflected just after sundown. These practices suggest a complex structural symmetry of cosmic and earthly media in their complementary gender representations: the symmetry of the night sky with (feminine) water, of stars and the moon with coins and axheads (humanly produced, masculine objects that also reflect); more abstractly, perhaps, they suggest the complementarity between eternal life above ("masculine" transcendence for which death is birth) and carnal ("feminine") existence below. It is the fact that the objects can be seen, by looking up or down, that links them in a common context.

Another association of blood with female fertility highlights the complementarity between marriage partners and is relevant here. During his wife's pregnancy a man is forbidden to slaughter animals lest his shedding of animal blood induce miscarriage in his wife (see also Zenkovsky 1949: 40–41). The association is one between husband and wife alone, for a man can commission a neighbor or kinsman to slaughter on his behalf. As in other *mushāhara* contexts discussed below, it is the mixing of distinct experiential domains having to do with blood that must be avoided.

One of my friends recounted the following incident, a typical case of *mushāhara* and its cure:

> When I gave birth to my youngest daughter the pains came on very quickly. There was no time to prepare for the birth. My eldest daughter was pregnant at the time and she came to assist me. She was wearing her gold *khatim ginay maṣri*. I was wearing no gold and I became ill with *nazīf* immediately. I lost much blood. Then my daughter gave me her ring to wear and I began to recover. Later, my husband's brother came to visit me. He had just circumcised a young boy and had blood on his shirt. He forgot to change his clothes and I saw the blood and again began to hemorrhage. I had no milk for my baby. So my brother-in-law got some water from the river, put it in a white bowl and put a gold *khatim* on the bottom. He made me look at this and I became well.

Mushāhara hemorrhage is associated with the susceptible woman seeing gold when she is wearing none, seeing someone who has seen death, and for the newly delivered, seeing the blood of circumcision (male or female). Since the affliction is also said to cause a lack or a weakening of her milk, it can jeopardize her child even after successful delivery. In a pregnant woman not yet come to term, miscarriage or stillbirth might result.

Excessive blood loss might also occur if a vulnerable girl or woman sees a female "gypsy" or Ḥalibiya. The Ḥalib[14] are itinerant traders and blacksmiths whose abilities in salesmanship have earned the women among them a reputation for being a little too brash, too familiar, and too undignified for Hofriyati tastes. In addition to this and their unsettled lifestyle, traveling openly as they do in the company of men, Ḥalib women differ from Hofriyati because they are not infibulated. If a gypsy woman enters a courtyard (which she is wont to do uninvited) where a woman or girl is ritually confined, immediately the door to the invalid's room is shut and closely guarded so as to prevent the two from making visual contact.

Mushāhara beliefs outlined here concern the transmission of debilitating and restorative effects on fluids having to do with female fertility (blood and milk) by means of sight. Seeing, then, is another means of incorporation. The essence of what one regards is absorbed by the eyes and may be transmitted later to those whom one meets. This also supplies the basis for Hofriyati's concept of the evil or "hot" eye (*'ayn ḥārra*): that someone's appreciative (envious) look might unwittingly cast misfortune upon the person, animal, or thing admired. With respect to *mushāhara,* should a woman be brought into contact with such dangers as death at those times when she is extremely vulnerable, when her precarious gift, fertility—the ability to generate life—is made potent or somehow imperiled, then the resultant mixing of experiential domains cannot but do her harm. The activation of her fertility in marriage ought to cause a retention of blood (signifying pregnancy); but when the bleeding process normal to manifesting or protecting her fertility is damaged, the opposite—hemorrhage—results. And damage stems from ambivalence: it occurs when the essence of death is mixed with that of birth, or conversely, when the condition for immortality is combined with that for mortality. It also occurs when she who has shed residual, postpotent ("black") blood in childbirth absorbs the essence of potent ("red") circumcision blood; or when a normally reserved, dignified, and enclosed Hofriyati female weakened by childbed or circumcision is brought into ocular contact with the uninfibulated, unconfined, and by Hofriyati standards, undignified gypsy, the antithesis of ideal womanhood. Her susceptibility is less if she wears the gold ring made from an Egyptian coin (referred to as an "official seal" or

14. Some Hofriyati say the term derives from *ḥalab,* meaning animal milk, as these people are nomadic and once lived almost exclusively on the milk from their herds; others say that it comes from Ḥalib, the Arabic name for Aleppo, a town in Syria, whence the Ḥalib are thought to originate. See also Ahmed Al-Shahi (1972).

"stamp" since it bears the face of a person), because this pleases Solomon, the overlord of *jinn*. It also diverts the *jinn*'s attention, for these spirits are prepared to take advantage of a woman's physical and ritual defenselessness whenever the occasion should arise.

But if wearing gold defends her from spirit attack, neglecting to wear it may increase her vulnerability should she then see it worn by another. Now the spirits which hover about a visitor's jewelry may be drawn not to hers, but to her blood. With this she is tacitly reminded that blood and gold are close yet imprecise equivalents: the former inherently more precious, however noble or alluring the latter may be.[15] Again we are faced with complementary gender associations: between females, fluids, blood, internal space, and intrinsic worth on the one hand, and—since men provide jewelry for their wives—males, substances, gold, the outside world, and humanly attributed value on the other. Moreoever, the wearing of gold reiterates the bride, womanhood at its apex of purity and latent fertility which men array, infibulation protects, and reinfibulation is designed to reenclose. When worn by the *nufāsa*, the woman in childbirth, gold helps offset the impurity of delivery: the opening of her vaginal orifice and the consequent shedding of so-called "black" or postproductive blood.

The color black is conspicuously linked with impurity and attributed to things which have lost their generative potency. My informants noted that another *mushāhara* custom is to place an eggplant in the confinement room, either under the woman's *angarīb* or suspended on the wall. In local parlance, an eggplant is referred to as an *aswad*, a "black" (short for "black tomato"). Cloudsley (183:137) sheds some light on this practice in writing about childbirth in Omdurman: there, eggplants may be hung on the wall behind the delivered woman's head where they remain until they shrivel and fall of their own accord: "Older women told me the aubergine is used rather than any other plant because it is black and repels the evil eye . . . it also represents the placenta, so its shape may be significant. The intention is to preserve the womb which the Sudanese fear may split or be damaged in childbirth."

The shape of the eggplant recalls the eggshell/gourd fertility object in Hofriyat and the imperative that the womb be enclosed; its associations with danger and the placenta make sense, for with birth the placenta loses its nutritive potency and may imperil a woman's life if not immediately delivered.[16] The eggplant is a negative counterpart of the egg-shaped fertility object; whereas the latter is a visual distillation of fertility, the for-

15. The association of gold with noble status in this part of Sudan dates to Meroitic times. Gold jewelry that was part of the royal regalia in Christian Nubia (ʿAlwah) was appropriated by rulers during the Funj sultanate (El-Tayib 1987:43) in the sixteenth century A.D.

16. See Kennedy (1978*b*:127) on eggplant and *mushāhara* in Egyptian Nubia.

mer represents its culmination while disarming visions that threaten its continuance.

One who has absorbed a potentially dangerous sight might visually transmit its essence to a reflective object in a white bowl containing Nile water or to a reflection of the stars in a well (a spatial and, perhaps, gender inversion [see p. 102]) whereupon the negative influence is shattered, refracted, dissipated in the ritually pure fluid and rendered innocuous. Often, too, reflection and reversal are used to foil the evil eye: fragments of mirrors are typically plastered into the sides of doorways so that persons entering might at a glance divest themselves of pernicious emissions.

In the bowl of river water intended to defuse noxious visions are placed some *dura* seeds or dough plus a metal axhead, hatchet, or some coins. These items have well-known everyday significances in Hofriyat, as discussed in chapter 2: water is associated with female labor and fertility; tools, coins, and *dura* with farming and male labor; and *kisra* dough represents the combined result of women's and men's subsistence activities, metaphoric of their separate reproductive contributions to the body of a child. While this was not explicitly stated by informants, it seems reasonable to suggest that these objects provide a positive replacement for the negative visions jettisoned at the threshold of a room. The combination of elements reads as an affirmation of fertility, and its visual essence will be transmitted by visitors' eyes to the female whose reproductive function is jeopardized. Moreover, water from the Nile, associated with fertility and femininity, is used in a number of contexts involving purification and the maintenance of health: a woman completing her forty-day confinement after birth bathes in Nile water; a pregnant woman drinks it; one who is barren hopes to remedy the situation by pressing a cupful of it to her womb (Zenkovsky 1949:40).[17] Hence seeing Nile water purifies and calibrates sight for the visit to a woman's confinement chamber. Further, Kennedy (1978*b*:132) notes that in Egyptian Nubia, gold, axheads, and coins are "spirit attracting substances" and by immersing them in the purity of Nile water, one dispels the spirits infesting them. Even in their mundane reference to male labor, such items connote defense of the feminine ideal.

All of these associations build on the theme of fertility and the need to protect it from threat. The significance of genital openings and doorways as essential boundaries and transition points is reiterated in the *mushāhara* context; so too is the value of inner space: *ḥōsh*s, wombs, and rooms. The bowl of Nile water must be placed just outside the *khashm al-bāb*, the

17. Also, following his wedding the groom leads a procession to the Nile where he ritually bathes; a similar procession takes place for a woman possessed by *zayran* at the end of her curing ceremony.

room's doorway—literally, "the mouth of the door"—so as to prevent dangerous influences from penetrating the highly charged space within. Women undergoing life crisis, more so than men, are required to remain inside a room for the duration of their vulnerability, usually for forty days. And this vulnerability is linked inexorably to their fertility.

Customs which prevent or cure *mushāhara* illness prevent or cure violations of bodily integrity caused by visually mixing experiential domains and, in turn, by spirits attracted to female genital blood—exposed human fertility. *Jinn,* who are drawn to interstitial regions of the body (body passages, cavities, the spaces between digits) and impure, between-places in the social area of the village (like ruined houses), may also be summoned by paradox and the ambiguity which stems from merging categories that should be kept distinct. And they may be dispelled by reversal, inversion, or restatement of the appropriate order. All are situations involving the violation and reconstitution of significant boundaries (cf. Douglas 1966).[18] Later we will see that *jinn,* and specific among them *zayran,* are associated with thresholds, fertility, ambiguity, and paradox in a number of other contexts as well.

Breathing

People incorporate the essences of visions and may be infiltrated by spirits. But these methods, added to those of consumption and sexual intercourse, are not the only ones by which Hofriyati, willingly or not, take into their bodies what originates in the outside world. Like visions, smells may have positive or negative effects on well-being.

In Hofriyat, bad odors can cause illness.[19] A smell of sweat or of the "black blood of childbirth" conveys the essence of all that is negative ("open") in the corporal world and disposes a woman to possession by *jinn,* particularly if she is ritually susceptible. Thus the interiors of confinement chambers and bridal visiting rooms are fumigated regularly with so-called "sweet" bridal incense, considered prophylactic against lingering *jinn*.

Perfume and cologne are used copiously by both sexes in Hofriyat. Indicative of purity, cleanliness, ceremonial extravagance, and health, commercially produced ("cold") scent (*rīḥa bārda*) is showered liberally on

18. In a related vein, one reason for viewing the reflection of stars in a well after sunset may be to ensure that the visitor does not confront a vulnerable woman *during* the transition from day to night. Sunset and sunrise are considered dangerous, ambiguous times when devils and other *jinn* are about; they are referred to as the *ḥamarayn,* the "two reds." *Ḥamarayn* are discussed in chapter 9.

19. See James (1988:71–73) for similar observations on the Uduk in southeastern Sudan.

guests at a wedding and on wood burned in the bridal smoke bath. It is an important ingredient in women's cosmetics such as *dilka* (which, at another stage of its manufacture, is smoked over fragrant woods), and is mixed with Nile water in the *mushāhara* bowl, where it acts to protect visitors against breathing unsavory odors upon entering the room of a newly circumcised girl or a woman recently delivered.

Breathing a complement of "cold" and smoky odors is crucial to well-being, especially in the context of a wedding. The woods for bridal incense are tossed with sugar and cooked in a pan, then sprinkled with "cold" scent and smoked perfumes; their fragrance is released by smouldering the amalgam in a brazier. In order to make local wedding scent (*ḥumra,* "redness") a woman combines the oils of clove, sandalwood, and mahaleb[20] (among others), then adds granulated musk, smoked sandalwood powder, and "cold" perfumes. Next she pours the concoction into a bottle, lights a cigarette, and blows tobacco smoke into the lot, shaking the bottle to make sure the smoke is well dispersed. Women attending a nuptial dance daub themselves generously with *ḥumra;* this is aesthetically pleasing and guards against bad smells. The "redness" of the *ḥumra* (and, perhaps, its specific blend of "cold" and smoky (heated) scents) serves constantly to remind the wearer of fertility; it reiterates her femininity.

Remedies, too, can be achieved through inhalation: the afflicted inclines over a lighted brazier containing herbal medications or bits of paper inscribed with passages from the Quran, in order to breathe the restorative smoke and fumes. Alternatively, she drinks the water used to rinse a Quranic inscription from a wooden tablet or china plate.

In all of the above, items linked with masculinity ("cold" perfumes, spiritual recitations) are mixed with those having feminine connotations (heat and smoke, water) and, taken into the body under appropriate conditions, have a positive effect on health. Just as a person's identity and status are related to what he or she ingests, so is one's constitution—social and physical—affected by his or her perceptions: visual, olfactory, and as noted earlier regarding the feminine associations of heat and pain, tactile. Postively valued perceptions enhance bodily integrity and balance. Negatively valued perceptions sensed directly or through the faculties of others violate bodily integrity, rendering one open to further violation in the form of spirit intrusion or other illness.

Again we arrive at the importance of body orifices which, like doorways, are points of entry, of transition between internal and external space. Like other forms of passage, the exchange of sensory messages between the integral human body and its external environment is a dangerous process requiring close control.

20. *Prunus mahaleb,* a small cherry whose kernels yield a fragrant oil.

Balance

An unstated directive in much of the above is the maintenance of body balance, the need to harmonize emotions, blood characteristics, temperatures, internal qualities, and external influences, all of which bespeaks a humoral vision of physical and social reality. For example, certain cosmetics are considered hot or cold, and their application adjusts the body's internal heat. DelVecchio Good (1980: 148–49) notes that in Iran, popular models derived from Galenic-Islamic medicine depict females as relatively colder than males: postpartum mothers are fed "hot" foods to strengthen their bodies, build up their blood, combat the "coldness" of parturition, and increase their bodily heat to ensure that the next child is a boy. Such ideas complement those surrounding infibulation in Hofriyat, which protects fecund blood and enhances the heat of the womb. As in Iran, there is the suggestion here of an implicit natural relationship between femininity and cold (and masculinity and heat) which various cosmetic and ritual procedures strive to calibrate. This would go some way toward explaining why in Hofriyat the birth of a daughter as a first child signals the failure of a woman's fertility and is grounds for divorce: she may be regarded as having insufficient innate or ritually generated heat in her womb to transform her husband's seed into a male child. Barclay describes a wedding practice among residents of Buurri which symbolically confirms this point and resonates with Hofriyati themes:

> In the late afternoon the groom takes a small pot [cf. a *gūlla*], places *kisra* dough in it, and puts it on a fire that is usually located outside the door of the house. . . . Before entering the house [sometime later] the groom takes a sword [a masculine object cf. an axhead] and breaks the pot containing the *kisra*. The next morning the contents will be served with milk. If the *kisra* is cooked well, it means the first child will be a boy. If not it will be a girl. (Barclay 1964: 256–57)

Heat, whether inherent in the blood itself or in the womb, is less a feminine characteristic than a requirement whose augmentation is necessary to fulfill a woman's transformative, procreative role.

Despite a concern for temperature in other domains, Hofriyati are virtually distinct among those who espouse equilibrium models of physiology in not attributing hot and cold characteristics to foods.[21] Rather, as I noted earlier, foods that energize or increase the blood are described as clean, enclosed, white (by implication, pure), and moist. All are positive attributes, whose negative counterparts are "poor" (*miskīn*) and "dry"

21. See Foster (1987) for an extensive discussion of hot and cold pathology in classical medicine and contemporary Latin America.

(*nāshif*). Clean foods are strengthening to either sex, but especially beneficial to women's fertility, while poor, dry foods are debilitating.

A second dimension of foods is not bivalent but relative: some are considered light, others heavy. Light foods such as rice, pasta, and eggs should be consumed by those whose blood is heavy (*tagīl*): those who tire easily, feel sluggish, and are prone to swellings. Heavy foods, such as meat, are eaten to counteract "light blood" (*dum khafīf*), a cause of dizziness. Like odors and assimilated perceptions, various types of ingested foods play a role in the maintenance or disruption of internal body balance—as well as social status, ethnic identity, individuality, and moral integrity. Relevant here is women's concern to improve the quality of their blood, control its production, and prevent its loss. For not to do so imperils their social goals and financial security.

Tying and Binding

Desire to maintain sociophysical integrity (expressing the implicit value of interiority) and acknowledgment of the ambiguity inherent in social and physical thresholds (expressing its necessary relativity) constitute an essential problematic of Hofriyati culture. This is played out, in part, in relations between the sexes, who in certain contexts occupy complementary positions on the continuum between dialectical extremes. Before considering the broader implications of this dynamic and its relationship to the *zār*, I explore the position of women as they themselves portray it. I begin by considering the metaphoric associations of tying and binding, and their relation to female fertility.

In chapter 1, I noted that women enjoy greater residential stability than men. They spend most of their lives in their parents' village homes and move to urban centers less frequently than their husbands. Over 60 percent of men between the ages of fifteen and forty-nine are absent from the village, working elsewhere for most of the year and leaving 42 percent of Hofriyati households to be managed solely by women.[22] Much as Hale (1985:6) recounts for Sudanese Nubians to the north, it is women in Hofriyat who reproduce village culture and are viewed as its "keepers." Women, then, comprise the stable core of village society and symbolize village identity.[23] This is one expression of their essential "fixity" in local thought.

22. These figures compare favorably with Sondra Hale's (1985:4) from farther north along the Nile in Nubian Sudan, where there is a male absentee rate of 50–60 percent, and more than 40 percent of households are headed by women. See also Constantinides (1982).

23. Cf. Cohen (1974:16). For an interesting example from another social context where the women of a relatively insular group symbolize its identity both to members and outsiders, see Okely (1975).

The idea of holding in place or binding is symbolically developed in Hofriyat. When a couple marries, the *faki* (religious practitioner) is said to tie a knot in a rope at the mosque which binds the two together. But the rope is controlled by the husband who may "tie" more knots in it as he takes other wives, or "loosen" a knot should he wish to divorce (*ṭallug*, meaning to loosen, set free). Women do not relish cowifery and cite the following adage when describing the preferred marital situation: *Aḥsan wāḥid marā fi-l-ḥubāl* ("Better one woman on the rope").[24] The rope stands for a man's marital career, symbolizing his ability to bind various women to him as wives—of which he may have up to four simultaneously and any number serially. He is in control of his "rope" and may alter it at will. Not so a woman, who feels the fixity of her position keenly, especially if she is unhappy in a marriage and would just as soon be set free. Under normal conditions a woman cannot sue for divorce; such is the prerogative of men.[25]

Concepts of binding and loosening appear in other contexts, among them, the performance of injurious magic (*ʿamal,* in which knots must be tied) and easement of its effects.[26] More germane to the present discussion, the animal sacrificed by a man upon his wife's delivery of a child is referred to as the *ḥulāla,* "the loosening." Until the birth he was forbidden to slaughter; following the birth he must. Thus if pregnancy, resulting from her husband's act, quickens a woman's blood, birth itself causes it to flow like that of the slaughtered beast, and frees her to become pregnant once more. Her husband's action and restraint regarding the blood of livestock parallel those having to do with the blood of human life. It is hardly surprising to learn that in certain contexts women are symbolically equated with livestock, nor that the slaughter of an animal may be seen to substitute for the sacrifice of their blood (chapter 9).

However initially prosaic it might appear, the link between binding and women's hair is highly significant (Boddy 1982*a*). As part of a bride's cosmetic preparation, her hair is woven into dozens of tight thin plaits

24. The word for rope is *ḥabil* (pronounced *ḥabl*); *ḥubāl* is one way of forming its plural. Yet my informants noted that *ḥubāl* is used here as a singular. Whether *ḥubāl* is more euphonic, or its use reflects the synthesizing tendencies of women's speech (*ḥabal* means "pregnancy"), I do not know.

25. The only grounds on which a woman might seek divorce is withdrawal of support, and then she must petition the religious judge (*qāḍī*) who considers the merits of her case. A man, however, need only proclaim "I divorce thee" three times before witnesses to make the act official.

26. Should someone wish to cast a spell on another he visits a practitioner of *ʿamal* (who is said to be a *ṣadīg shawaṭīn,* a "friend of devils"; see also Al-Safi [1970 : 23]) who, for a fee, knots (*ʿugda*) a string while murmuring appropriate incantations. The injurious knots (*ar-ribuṭ,* bonds or fetters) are then buried or thrown in the river; they are said to "bind" the intended victim (who is known as *am-marbūṭ,* "the bound") rendering him powerless before his assailant's nefarious intent. To undo such damage a victim enlists a religious *faki* who locates the knotted string and countermands the spell with a charm, thereby "loosening" the perpetrator's grasp. See also Nalder (1935 : 236) and Trimingham (1965 : 170).

(*mashaṭ*) resembling miniature wheat stocks less than half a centimeter wide. The plaits hug the contours of her head from crown to nape, then hang below in slim black cords.[27] A maiden might wear braids before marriage, but should not undertake this more elaborate coiffure until shortly before her wedding. The custom is an ancient one: temple reliefs at Meroë and Musawwarrat (near Shendi) depict Meroitic candaces whose hair is worn in a similar style.

Considerable importance is attached to hair. As was observed, Hofriyati differentiate between "impure" hair on the body—which married women must remove—and hair on the head—which they must dress and confine. Head hair cuttings are always collected then burned lest they be magically used against their owner. Sudden headache may be attributed to a person or animal trampling the trimmings of one's hair (also Nalder 1935 : 239). Moreover a woman's head hair is directly associated with her nubility: at menarche a girl must begin to cover her hair when in the company of men, particularly those to whom she is marriageable or must demonstrate respect. She continues this practice throughout her childbearing years. No other part of her body must be so carefully shielded from masculine view. Women told me that in the recent past when less clothing was worn than today, a woman otherwise perfectly naked would rush to conceal her hair if a man appeared. Except under certain conditions discussed below, exposure of a woman's hair to men, especially strangers and those outside her immediate family, is an embarrassment, an unbearable impropriety. She covers her head, they say, because she is ashamed (*khajlāna*) (cf. Delaney 1988 : 82).

As Christine Eickelman (1984 : 70) notes in her ethnography of an Omani village, *khajal* signifies propriety, constraint caused by the fear of behaving improperly. It is a propensity whose inculcation in Hofriyati girls begins dramatically and severely with circumcision. So ingrained is *khajal* in women's personalities and interactions that even I acquired a degree of it, feeling uncomfortably exposed if I neglected to wear my head scarf and being shocked by the "brazen" gypsies who wore none. Given these circumstances, the additional operation of plaiting a bride's hair—which, in contrast to everyday situations, is not covered during her wedding dance—publicly marks a loss of sexual innocence and the activation of her fertility. More than this, it represents the taming of her potency and binding of her reproductive potential to the groom. The procedure is described as *ḥārr:* "hot" or "painful"; the pain and constriction reiterate and affirm in her an appropriate feminine disposition.[28]

Weddings are the only occasions when girls who are reproductively

27. El-Tayib (1987 : 59–61) and Cloudsley (1983 : 31–33, 52) provide fuller descriptions of this procedure.

28. See Obeyesekere (1981) for an engaging discussion of hair in cultural symbolism where Leach's (1958) distinction between public and private symbols is taken to task. In

mature expose their hair in the presence of marriageable men, and married women appear in public with plaits undone. As wedding guests they perform the "dance from the neck," miming the strut of a courting pigeon with suitable languor and grace, backs well arched, arms extended, hair falling loosely over *tōbs* rearranged to form wing-like protrusions at their sides. Slowly and barefoot they advance toward the groom down a runway of fiber mats; each, on nearing, inclines her head and with a shake flings her loosened hair in his direction, brushing the groom's shoulder or his head. This is called "giving the *shabāl*" and is said to confer luck (*ḥuzz*) for a prosperous and fruitful marriage. Other men might now approach the dancer, inclining their shoulders toward her and snapping their fingers above their heads. This is called "asking for the *shabāl*" and compliments her charms. Should she wish to comply, the indifferent dancer flicks them her unbound hair with another quick toss, then resumes step. I have often seen mothers approach a dancing woman bearing infant sons in their arms, that the babies might also receive *shabāl*.

According to my informants, *shabāl* is comparable, on a secular level, to what *baraka* is on a spiritual one. *Baraka* "Allah's blessing," "holiness" is a miraculous force or power which one is endowed with or acquires by contagion.[29] Though *baraka* inheres in certain holy families, its beneficial effects are open to all and transmitted by contiguity. As Crapanzano explains,

> The moment the baraka has passed to the supplicant . . . it is no longer contagious. It ceases to be itself. The individual to whom the baraka has been passed obtains something—the state or potential state of good health, good fortune, business success, or fertility. A transformation analogous to the conversion of energy into matter, or semen into infant, has occurred. Baraka is thus a potentializing force which in the process of transference is actualized into that which is sought. (Crapanzano 1973: 120–21)

In Hofriyat, rubbing oneself with sand from the grave of a holy man or being spat upon by a powerful *faki* as he utters a passage from the Quran are two means for acquiring *baraka*'s effects, sought mainly by women from men of spiritual renown. Conversely, in giving the *shabāl*, reproductively mature women transfer the positive effects of *their* power onto young men by touching them with their loosened hair, their unleashed feminine potency. Each sex confers on the other the effects of what the other is thought to lack in his own potential, for the essence of each resides in a different combination of *ʿagl* and *nafs*. And each sex confers its effects

---

Hofriyat, plaited hair is a public symbol signifying a woman's status; it may also be a personal symbol invested, as I suggest, with an affective load.

29. See Crapanzano (1973), Geertz (1968), and Eickelman (1976) for extensive consideration of *baraka* in Morocco; its meanings there are similar to those in Sudan.

on the other in the context it symbolizes: men the eternal, the spiritual realm, and women the earthly, the social—whose paramount expression is the wedding.

Niḥna Bahāim *("We Are Cattle")*

Women see themselves as powerful, as valuable contributors to Hofriyati society; they are the repositories and reproducers of morality, the rightful loci of fertility. *Mushāhara* injunctions, female circumcision, the *shabāl,* all attest the importance of fertility to women and ultimately to society as a whole.[30] Yet women's power is a double-edged sword. If they bear primary responsibility for social procreation, they are also first to be held accountable for its mishaps: sterility, miscarriage, stillbirth, the amorality of *awlād ḥarām.* And if they are, in some respects, guardians and symbols of the salient value in Hofriyat—of interiority—they are highly susceptible to its violation. The ideas of closeness, consuming, and binding convene to illumine the metaphor by which women most often describe themselves and express the ambivalence of their position. "*Niḥna bahāim,*" they say, "We are cattle."

This statement, uttered in a variety of contexts, has several implications. First, women say they are livestock or cattle because, like village animals, they mate with close relatives and, should they fail to do so, are considered "she-goats" from the market by their husbands' kin. Animals, women say, are not very discriminating. Women's metaphoric self-image, while descriptive, is hyperbolic and not without a touch of humor.

Most families in Hofriyat own livestock. Prevalent are goats, kept mainly for their milk, but in some households the herd may be augmented by some sheep or a cow. When not grazing or scavenging, the animals are penned in small thorn corrals within the *ḥōsh* or just beyond its walls. Alternatively, they are tied to stakes in the house yard, given little room to move. Whenever my friends wished to impress on me the harshness of their lives, they invariably said, "We are livestock," noting that they live like their goats: pent up in tiny crowded rooms and *ḥōsh*s in the dust of the desert, tethered to men by the nuptial rope, forced to subsist on the poorest of foods (among which they include *kisra*).

Other meanings surface around the contradictory premises of gender complementarity and asymmetry. Domestic animals are valuable, expensive to acquire and maintain. If well nourished, they provide rich and plentiful milk, and reflect a family's prosperity. Similarly, women are socially valuable. As wives they are expensive to acquire (the costly wedding is financed by the groom) and to maintain. A man whose wife is obviously

30. See also Kennedy (1978*c*: 159).

well nourished acquires repute as a good provider, which enhances his esteem in the eyes of his peers.

Domestic animals consume fodder secured for them by human labor and convert it into meat and milk for the benefit of a man's family and village. Prodigiously fertile animals are extremely valuable and rarely slaughtered for meat. Likewise, women are consumers and transformers of food acquired by their husbands' labor, and reproducers. They are "kept" by men primarily for their reproductive abilities: if a women does not demonstrate fertility by becoming pregnant soon after her wedding, she stands a good chance of being divorced. And when undervalued by her husband, a woman complains of being "eaten," the ultimate fate of infertile livestock.[31]

In likening themselves to livestock, women also confess a lack of worldly and religious sophistication. The uneducated and theologically naive are described as "cattle people" (*nās bahāim*)—specifically, Sudanese pastoralists like the Nuer or Dinka, "pagans" who once could be enslaved. The term is applied by women to themselves not least because so few of them are literate. Finally, as women say, they follow custom and the wills of their husbands much as cattle follow each other in herds (see also Trimingham 1965 : 24).

The polysemous metaphor *niḥna bahāim* synthesizes the position women perceive themselves to occupy in the scheme of Hofriyat. They are the inner core of village life: fertile, enclosed, domesticated; bound by custom, husbands, and kin; threatened by violations of interiority and its attendant values. Like metaphors described in chapter 2, *niḥna bahāim* resonates with meanings that inform the concept "woman" and thus contributes to the construction of women's selfhood. Yet it also contains an implicit critique. It is, I submit, a feature of women's muted or subordinate discourse, a discourse anchored in the system of meanings that men and women share, but which contextualizes that system from women's perspective (see Messick 1987). In subsequent chapters, considerable attention is devoted to this issue with reference to the *zār.* More immediately, I will suggest that through such expressions, women exhibit a critical awareness of the contradictions in their lives.

It is in reference to a view of themselves as livestock—at once humorous and positive, passive and pessimistic—that women evaluate their experiences of husbands and nonvillagers, all of whom are symbolic outsiders to one or another degree. For women, men in Hofriyat epitomize relative exteriority: it is men who mediate between the world outside the *ḥōsh* and the feminine world within; and further, between the religious domain and

31. See O'Laughlin (1974) for an analysis of a similar metaphoric association between women and livestock among the Mbum of Chad. Hofriyati, unlike the Mbum, do not prohibit women from eating goat meat.

the earthly one, tamed and enclosed. Men, in other words, link the village to sources of power—economic, political, and spiritual—that lie beyond its physical and moral precinct. The power of the outside is ambivalent, as the poetic example of "clean" foods suggests. Clean foods are those that are white or, like tinned goods and certain fruits, enclosed and protected by natural or artificial casings. As I noted earlier, they are associated with foreigners whose skin is "white", in part because they are expensive or, like goat's milk, symbolic of wealth; in part because many were introduced by foreign colonial masters (Turkish, British, Egyptian) or are imported from economically dominant foreigners today. "Clean" foods are prized in Hofriyat. They represent not only the value of interiority (because white or enclosed) but also the power of the outside which, when harnessed and brought into the *ḥōsh* by men, positively contributes to the inherent generative power of women, their fertility. As such, foods that are "clean" convey the proper combination of complementary powers. Hofriyati men mediate political and spiritual power to women; Hofriyati women bestow the effects of generative and socially reproductive power onto men. Yet the current of these exchanges is unidirectional: movement directed to the inside from without is met, not by its opposite, but with containment. For however "other" village men might be to village women, they are nonetheless Hofriyati.

Ortner (1974), drawing on the insights of de Beauvoir (1974) and Lévi-Strauss (1969*a, b*), has attempted to account for the apparent universality of gender asymmetry in terms of women's ineluctable reproductive role, arguing that since women produce and initially socialize "raw" human beings, they are regarded as marginal creatures, symbolically linked to the wild world of nature in contrast to men, who are more fully grounded in the controlled and orderly world of culture. But for Hofriyati this would be an androcentric view. For them what is, on the secular level, controlled and orderly—hence eminently cultural—is physical and social reproduction, with which women are more closely identified than men. As women see it, they are politically subordinate to men not because they represent nature to be tamed, but because they are generatively, and in this respect culturally, superior: they are the essence of village society which must be shielded against the ambivalence and disorderliness of the outside world. But if women symbolize the earthly stability of village culture, men represent its pliancy and resilience, its negotiability in the face of external threat. Thus it is men who are poised between the outside and within, actively filtering and processing external influences, ensuring that they contribute to the Hofriyati system and do not destroy it.[32] And so it is men

32. For an interesting parallel from another African Islamic society, the Tuareg (who have, incidentally, a matrilineal social organization similar to that of pre-Arabized Hofriyat), see Knight (1985).

who, from women's perspective, are liminal beings: powerful and unpredictable, simultaneously "other" and "us".

Men, of course, might argue somewhat differently from the standpoint of Islam. For them, women are indeed de Beauvoir's "second sex" and Ortner's liminal beings. Men hold that women are unpredictable (and powerful) because, unlike men, they are naturally possessed of a greater proportion of *nafs*—life force—than *ʿagl*—the ability to transcend one's natural inclinations in order to follow the will of God. Women, then, are less perfectible than men in a spiritual sense; because more constrained by their "natural" behavior (however transcended by surgery and inculcated dispositions), they are religiously inferior.[33] The women I spoke to do not wholly acquiesce to this ascription, but are willing to acknowledge the spiritual leadership of (some) men. Importantly, local ideology is sufficiently unspecified to support a range of interpretations, allowing women scope to negotiate their position by pressing their social complementarity with men (cf. Altorki 1986; Wikan 1982).

In Hofriyat, women are the repositories of worldly value, and men, of religious potential. For women, "otherness" comprises all that is outside, embracing men, to an extent, as well as what is foreign and untamed; for men "otherness" is all that is not fully contained in their vision of Islam, and hence is relatively inclusive of women. Within the Hofriyati universe of meanings, each sex contextualizes the other; each taps a locus of power which the other cannot reach, each is symbolically dominant to its counterpart on a complementary plane. Each, in the process of engenderment, becomes empowered within specific contexts and denied power in others. The pervasiveness of both gender asymmetry and gender complementarity is basic to understanding the symbolism of the *zār*, the possession cult that engages our interest for the remainder of the book.

Implications of Interiority: Ambiguity, Contradiction, and Women's Perspective

The value of interiority informs a great many practices and attitudes in Hofriyat. Yet the considerable focus it commands can detract from the positive value of openness and exteriority in villagers' lives, of, for example, the benefits to be derived from exogamous unions or from cultivating relationships with outside groups. One feature of the *zār* is, we shall

33. See also Rosen (1978: 569 ff.) with reference to opposed gender conceptions in Morocco. As he notes, "women focus on the specifically *social* as opposed to *natural* relations between the sexes, and their conceptual orientation is, therefore, substantially different from that of the men" (p. 569). For complementary views of women's symbolic position in other Islamic societies, see Thayer (1983) and Vinogradov (1974).

see, its capacity to offset the determining tendency of cultural dispositions and imperatives: it cautions villagers, and women in particular, to keep cultural values in proper perspective, to acknowledge their inherent relativity. I have already explored the relativity of the Hofriyati ideational system, the indeterminacy of its external boundaries, the impossibility of complete enclosure. The hesitant demand for openness despite the value of containment is most tangibly expressed in ideas and practices concerning the human body.

Body orifices are threatening: potential entrées for possessive spirits and other maladies, possibly misappropriated in other ways. Yet physical apertures are inevitable, and so, exceedingly ambiguous. Hence villagers compromise: surgically reducing perhaps the most significant and ambiguous such opening, that through which new humans pass at birth, while valuing smallness of size in regard to others, and surrounding all with a variety of ritual precautions: activities and sayings to thwart the evil eye, *mushāhara* customs, and others. Such measures may not reduce the ambiguity of body orifices[34] so much as call attention to that which Hofriyati find so meaningful yet so paradoxical: the need to protect from violation both individual integrity and that of the village as a whole, and the practical impossibility of accomplishing either. Absolute closure of physical and social openings means, and in burial customs signifies, death for the individual and for society. Yet it also signifies purity and rebirth: in burial customs, closure prepares one to continue life on the spiritual plane. There the body will be reconstituted in perfect corporal form: uncorrupted, self-contained, needing no nourishment, experiencing neither entropy nor decay (cf. Delaney 1988). Earthly life, however, requires openings: doorways, mouths, vaginas, eyes, ears, marriages, indeterminacies in social structure. It is through such apertures that humans establish communication, that individuals are linked to one another and situated in the sensible world. Humans must, however grudgingly, admit their imperfectibility and their need for other humans—kin, nonkin, even other cultures. Only Allah is one unto himself, invariant perfection, complete and absolute in all regards. Only Allah is all: ultimate unity, ultimate containment, ultimate openness. Indeed, only Allah is beyond the dichotomies that plague and inform villagers' lives. Humans can hope to approximate the transcendent in but relative measure.

The idiom of enclosure proclaims the danger to Hofriyati of unmitigated, uncontrolled openness. Unregulated marriage, lack of restraint, lack of respect for the integrity of others, lack of dignity, promiscuous mating, all of these are pernicious and threatening—in a very material sense, as

34. As Radcliffe-Brown (1939) pointed out, ritual procedures likely precipitate anxiety over their proper performance as much as allay anxiety over what is beyond human control. See also Malinowski (1931, 1948).

Hofriyati know from past altercations with "foreigners" of various stripe. Such behaviors represent what is clearly external to the village and its emphasis on harmony, symmetry, and cooperation. Insofar as they are obvious violations of propriety, Hofriyati who commit them are likened to wild animals or cannibal-sorcerers, beings well beyond the rules and ideals of village life. But in less transparent contexts, propriety and impropriety appear as contingent qualities, their invocation subject to interpretation. The premise of interiority frames and informs behavior, it cannot determine it. Hofriyati are often faced with indefinite boundaries, with grey areas betwixt ideal right and undisputed wrong; and these provide sustenance not only for human action, but also for the actions of *zayran*.

Regarding this problem of indeterminacy, villagers maintain that human nature, imperfect in essence, is also variable in manifestation. Just as human bodies are inherently diverse with respect to orifice size and skin color, so are people acknowledged to have different "natures" (*ṭabīʿa*): personality quirks, eccentricities, habitual behaviors and preferences. It is accepted that despite shared ethics and dispositions, not all people react alike in a given circumstance. Further, a person is considered changeable; his or her responses to similar situations at different times may vary. And should someone's behavior fail to conform exactly to Hofriyati ideals, possibly to be judged improper, this is his or her entitlement and responsibility. If disputed, that person should not presume to force a construction on the event; at most she or he should publicly state a case in the effort to garner support. A person who attempts to impose his or her views on another punctures that other's integrity. In Hofriyat the onus for morally appropriate action—for maintaining one's family honor, preserving its reputation, and simply doing good—rests with the individual. This is similar to what Wikan (1977, 1982) describes for Oman. As she writes:

> It is up to every person to behave as correctly—i.e. as tactfully, politely, hospitably, morally and amicably—as possible in all the different enounters in which he engages, rather than to demand such things of others. To blame, to criticize, to sanction those who fall short of such ideals is to be tactless and leads to loss of esteem . . . it is not for me to judge or sanction them, unless the person has offended me in the particular relationship I have to him. (Wikan 1977: 311)

During my first months in Hofriyat I was struck by the lack of overt conflict among the women of my acquaintance. I thought that once my presence in their midst had become commonplace, discord would rise inevitably to the surface. But generally it did not. That tension and disagreement exist in Hofriyat is unquestionable; but for the most part such feelings are kept within. Rarely does hostility boil over to produce the sort of confrontation observed between ʿIsa and his brothers. Open displays of emotion, though they occur, are undignified, running counter to ideals which Hofriyati strive to maintain. Moreover, one must respect the integrity of others if one's own integrity is to be maintained: humans must be tolerant of each other. Still, this leaves an individual with the problem of how to express dissatisfaction without damaging his own esteem and the public self-image of those with whom he dissents. Junior men and women, especially, are curtailed by cultural sanctions from open dissent with close kin. Yet it is legitimate for men to defend their honor, even to the extent of physically fighting other distantly related men. Men are categorically permitted greater latitude than women in most social contexts, hence the question of how to express disagreement so as to effect a change in one's situation may be less problematic for males. Here the spirit idiom offers women a partial solution (Lewis 1971*a;* Morsy 1978; Gomm 1975), however unwittingly they employ it in this vein.

Hofriyati concerns for (1) tolerance of diversity in others' behavior and (2) maintenance of propriety conceal something of a paradox: one should be willing to accept indeterminacy in others' actions while seeking to minimize it in one's own. And although a person ought to cultivate self-control and dignity—qualities which make social interaction predictable—there also exists a subtle desire to distinguish oneself from others, particularly those to whom one is most closely linked. Underlying these conflicting interests is a view of the self as constituted not only ideally, but also relationally: it is virtually impossible for a villager to think of himself or herself except in relation to kin. More than this, the self is fragmented and multidimensional: individuals relate to each other not as whole entities, but in aspects of themselves, as the following incident illustrates. Selfhood, in short, is not individuated in Hofriyat, but ultimately inheres in relationships.

At tea one day in a neighboring village I met a beautifully dressed young woman, Nur, a divorcée living with her sister in their absentee brother's village house. The two had no other kin outside of Khartoum.

During a conversation about marriage Nur revealed that although she had no children she was in little haste to remarry. Her desires run counter to the Hofriyati norm, yet no one questioned her or scoffed. Those present accepted the eccentricity as part of her ṭabīʿa, *her "nature." Back in Hofriyat, however, I mentioned the encounter to one of my friends. "Yes," she said, "I know the woman. She is* maṭlūga *(literally, a "loose" woman), she exchanges her company for gifts."*

Her meaning was clear. But knowing how upstanding was my hostess of that afternoon (she was the faki's *bit* ʿamm *and sister-in-law), I refused to believe her. Nur had been warmly received when she entered the room; and though uninvited, she was not shunned or made to feel uncomfortable in any way. So I decided to consult someone else.*

My puzzlement deepened when the story was confirmed. Reasoning in a way which I soon realized had no foundation in Hofriyat, I asked why, if Nur's illicit activities were common knowledge, did other women associate with her so freely? Would their menfolk not object? Would these women not be suspect too? The answer was no, not so long as the women refrained from visiting Nur in her home. Nur's violations had never been proved conclusively, for her brother in Khartoum knew nothing of her behavior, and other villagers—none of whom are her kin—were unlikely to inform him. Significantly, Nur's alleged prostitution was a matter solely between her and her brother, her only living male relative, the only one empowered to defend the family's jeopardized honor. If in her dealings with others Nur observes proper decorum and does not give offense, there is no reason to shun her. Her supposed immorality is none of our concern, and is she not, after all, a most amiable and amusing woman?

This incident echoes those which Wikan (1977, 1982) recounts from Oman, and her conclusions are also applicable to Hofriyat. Here, as there, "the conceptualization of the person is subtle and differentiated. One act or activity is only one aspect of a person, and only one facet of a complex personality" (Wikan 1977:312). In Hofriyat this notion of a multifaceted personality is attributable in part to endogamy: people related to each other in multiple ways are continually activating some relationships and suppressing others, even within the same kinsman, while working their personal networks of friendship and support. Yet it also extends itself to the possession phenomenon, for some aspects of an individual's character may be attributed, not to caprice, even less to impropriety, but to the intervention of spirits in the life of their human host. Moreover, possession provides an individual with the means to interpret experiences that are incompatible with those enjoined or expected (see also Obeyesekere 1981), thus ultimately to defend the culturally constructed self. These issues are explored at greater length in chapters 4 through 6.

Human interaction in Hofriyat always takes place in the face of some uncertainty; relationships are never "closed": immutable or wholly determined. Individual desires often wrestle with kin and marital obligations, and significant tension exists between the respective worlds of women and men. When areas rife with potential ambiguity are manipulated, they become more apparent. When expectations and the actions of others fail to mesh or when practice, rules, and reality clash, people may find themselves in untenable positions, without obvious recourse. Importantly, should a situation like this go unredressed, the person who perceives himself or herself victimized might well fall ill (see also Constantinides 1977) and wish for death. A common diagnosis in such cases is possession.

More often than men—who have considerable room to maneuver in Hofriyat—it is women who find themselves in difficult or untenable situations and express their afflictions as illness; they also comprise the majority of those possessed. In Hofriyat, women are at a disadvantage. Subject to overt control by men, they are rarely free to articulate their interests in ambiguous contexts or express conflicting views. Further, the limits of acceptable behavior are wider for men, who may have up to four wives at once, divorce more readily, travel outside the village or visit within it at will, even behave licentiously on occasion without permanently injuring their reputations. Despite their positively acknowledged generative power or, indeed, because of it, women are more restricted than their husbands or brothers by rules and implicit obligations, and less able to manipulate them for their purposes. It is not surprising that women sometimes see themselves as the victims of husbands who subtly or blatantly manipulate ambiguities in the marital relationship to their own ends. Husbands, and men in general, are thought to be capricious and inclined toward selfishness, likening them to *zayran* in women's eyes.

The metaphoric image by which women describe their plight, *niḥna bahāim*—"we are cattle"—expresses the ambivalence of their position relative to men. Like domestic animals and unlike men, women are "edible": their assets and labors may be (mis)appropriated by their husbands; "salable": they may be married against their wills, even to outsiders, whence becoming she-goats from the *sūq*; "disposable and replaceable": as wives, they may be divorced without reason or recourse; "accumulable": a man but not a woman is entitled to be polygamous; and frequently "unindividualistic": women are exhorted to behave with restraint, to obey, and refrain from voicing opinions in male company. Yet women, again like domestic animals, are extremely valuable. Just as livestock are a prime reflection and repository of wealth for Hofriyati, so women give men the ultimate source of their supremacy in bearing them descendants. The one powerful bargaining card that women have, both individually and collectively, is their fertility. But since fertility (like husbands or *zayran*) is neither predictable nor always controllable, it is in essence a wild card, and may be of no help at all.

Here lies a major contradiction: women are collectively indispensable to society while individually dispensable to men. Though valued and protected by men as a class and society as a whole—as their abundant restrictions attest—Hofriyati women often feel undervalued by dilettante husbands who may be protractedly absent from the village or otherwise unmindful of their wives. A husband who neglects to uphold his end of the marital dynamic appears also to deny its implicit premise, gender complementarity.

At the root of gender complementarity in Hofriyat lies a need to balance opposing forces—generative power : spiritual power; female : male; stasis : motion; relative enclosure : relative openness; the village : the outside world. And it is precisely in terms of this demand for balance (which is not of necessity symmetrical) that women assert their social and cultural worth. Women do not, however subtly, compete with men for common goals, so much as negotiate the sexes' interdependence.[35] And much as Du Boulay (1986: 145) describes for rural Greece, women do not deny their ascribed inferiority; rather, they transcend it. As was seen in chapter 2, transcendence involves the use of "reason" to temper a prodigious *nafs:* it involves their strategic compliance.[36] In this culture which reduces womanhood to essences, women feel acutely the material need to demonstrate fertility and are understandably anxious for any progenitive mishap. Yet the female self in Hofriyat not only is essentialized, but also, remember, extremely vulnerable to other selves and outside forces beyond its control (see also Nelson 1971). When a woman's self-image and expectations clash with experiential realities, as often they must do, the result is a paradox. And when the paradox is realized subjectively it may lead her to claim she is possessed.

The stage is now set for a closer examination of the *zār* and its counterhegemonic potential. Chapter 4 describes possession in some detail and, since both topics are considered in greater depth later on, provides a gloss of *zār* ceremonials and spirit types. Chapter 5 investigates connections among the often equivocal marital situations of women, fertility, and spirit possession. And chapters 6 and 7 document case histories of the possession affliction in an effort to elucidate the richness and potential of the spirit idiom, its multiple facets and significances. Thus, part 2 of the book focuses on those whom the spirits afflict and their location in the Hofriyati world. It deals with relations among those who are implicated in a possession event, both human to human, and human to spirit. Relations among spirits and their potential meanings, by no means ignored at this point, are nonetheless reserved for separate treatment in part 3. There, *zayran* abstracted from the contexts of their appearance in Hofriyat are considered as constituting a system of meaning in their own right. It is only by effecting this shift of emphasis that we can begin to appreciate the dynamics of possession in Hofriyat; only by focusing on now one, now the other pole of the possession dialectic might we elucidate both the anthropology and the demonology of the spirit system (Crapanzano 1977*a*: 11).

35. Wikan makes similar observations for Muslim communities in Cairo (1980) and Sohar, Oman (1982). Apropos of the latter, she writes, "For many purposes wife and husband, indeed woman and man, regard each other as supplementary and interlinked rather than opposed: they are so basically different that they do not think of themselves as competing" (Wikan 1982: 227). In Hofriyat, competition does of course take place, as when a man uses his wife's property without her consent. But competition is both mystified and tempered by the marital dialectic.

36. See also Abu-Lughod (1986: 104–17) for a discussion of "voluntary deference" among Egyptian Bedouins. As she describes it, voluntary deference is the honorable mode of dependency, which, by being freely given, is an assertion of independence by the weak (women, younger men, and clients).

Part 2

Women, Men, and Spirits

4

Zār

July 20, 1976, 4:00 P.M. The door to my ḥōsh *bangs open. Asia ducks beneath the lintel, lifts the water container from her head, and pours its contents into my* zīr. *Her face is seamed with sweat.* "Allaaah!" *she exclaims, "the land is hot today!* Shufti, ya *Janice, I've heard they are drumming in Goz. Do you want to go?"*

Of course!—a zār *is on. But the walk in this heat is a long one, and my leg has been badly swollen for several days.*

"Sadig is borrowing camels from his cousin. You must ride."

Moments later I am teetering sidesaddle, following the equally inexpert Sadig along a trail that hems some withered fields of maize. My camel munches lazily at each low acacia, and I am soon covered in scratches from their thorns. Prodding seems only to anger the beast, and I fear a painful bite; it would have been faster to walk. Still beyond sight of Goz we are reached by the deep bass of drumming, fitful through the sultry air. The camels perk, raise their heads, start trotting toward the sound.

Goz is a newish settlement, an odd assortment of square thatched huts, thorn corrals, and a couple of half-completed mud-brick ḥōsh*s. The drumming comes from one of these. Ambulatory Hofriyati preceded my arrival; the* zār *has just begun. Ideally, a* zār *should take place in the room of a house, if capacious, but because of the heat, today's has been mounted in the yard.*

A litany of greetings over, I am seated near the dancing ground, an open area (mīdān) *bounded on three sides by palm-fiber ground mats. Here sit several dozen chanting women: the spirit possessed. Now and then one rises to her knees and begins to move her upper body in time with the sonorous beat. In the center of the* mīdān *stands the* shaykha—zār *practitioner or "priestess"—a forceful, brawny woman in an electric-pink pullover,* tōb *tied loosely at her waist. She is arguing with a woman just as brash as she, who, between expletives, puffs furiously on a cigarette. I learn that the* shaykha *speaks not to the woman but to her spirit, in an effort to diagnose the source of the woman's complaint. Observing from the side is a tall, very black, incongruously muscled figure clad in a* tōb, *large wristwatch, and hairnet—the* shaykha's *reputedly transvestite assistant from south of Shendi. In contrast, the* ʿayāna*—"sick woman" and focus* *of the ceremony—is frail, elderly. She rests quietly on a pillow next the musicians, facing the front of the* ḥōsh, *arms and legs curled tight against her white-*tōb*ed body.*

The shaykha *concludes her discussion, sits down, and starts to drum. Using only the tips of her fingers, she beats a large earthen* dallūka *stretched with goat hide, its whitened flanks boldly adorned with mauve geometric designs. Another* dallūka *responds in shifted accents, joined half a second later by the* nugarishan, *a tall brass mortar that rings, when struck, like a cowbell, only deeper. A fourth woman beats a complementary rhythm on an inverted aluminum washtub or* ṭisht. *The result is a complicated synocpation, its underlying pattern one long beat, three short. The sound is less soothing than cacophonous, yet endlessly repeated and accompanied by reiterative chants, the effect is indeed soporific. The chants, I learn, are called "threads"—*khuyūṭ *(a "thread," singular, is* khayṭ*)—and when sung they are said to be "pulled."*

The rhythm intensifies; the ʿayāna *rises to dance. Now visible over her* tōb *is a red sash attached to a reddish waist cloth in the style of a Sam Browne belt. She is possessed, my companions say, by* Khawāja *(Westerner) spirits: a doctor, lawyer, and military officer—all of these at once. Yet it is the lattermost she appears to manifest in dance. Her* tōb *is folded cowl-like over her head, obscuring her face; she flourishes a cane—hooked, as in vaudevillian burlesque. Her dance is a slow, rhythmic walk crisscrossing a chimeric square, feet first moving side to side, then forward and back. With a leap of the imagination she is an officer of the desert corps conducting drill. Every so often she bends rigidly at the hip and, cane pressed to her forehead, bobs her torso up and down. I am told that her spirits have requested the white* tōb, *cane, cigarettes, "European" belt, and yet to be purchased, a radio.*

The band takes up the chant of another zār. *The* ʿayāna *sits; the* shaykha *leaves her drum and starts to dance,* tōb *covering her head. Suddenly, the* tōb *is thrown off. She turns on her heel, goose-steps the length of the* mīdān, *stops before me, abruptly pulls herself to attention. She salutes me three or four times, stiffly, eyes glazed and staring, a grin playing wildly on her face. Her left hand grips a sword within its sheath; with her right she grasps my own with unusual strength and pumps it "Western style" in time to the drums. I am shaken by this treatment and by thoughts of her sword. The chant sounds like a military march: I recognize the British Pasha spirit,* Abu Rīsh, Ya Amīr ad-Daysh *("Owner of Feathers, O Commander of the Army"). The drums desist. At once my hand is released. The* shaykha*'s features assume a more dignified composure and she returns to the center of the* mīdān.

Evening falls. Women rise to dance—or "descend" (nazal), *as the* zār *step is called—throughout the night. Others respond to the spirits' chants from a kneeling position, bobbing up and down from the waist,* tōbs *covering their heads like so many Halloween ghosts. One who stands has mounted a* zār *in the past: she has "slaughtered"* (dabaḥat, *for* dhabaḥat) *for the spirits, thus confirming relations with those by which she is possessed. A woman who remains sitting or kneeling has yet to sacrifice; though acknowledged to be possessed, and perhaps even aware of the types of* zayran *that bother her, she remains somewhat uncertain of her spirits and limited to kneeling at their ceremonies until she undertakes a cure. Yet she is no less an adept for this.*

In the waning, eerie light I see a woman—spirit—performing a strange pantomime with a sword, crouching low, sweeping the flat of the weapon back and forth along the ground. She dashes through these postures with skill and grace; I am reminded of a hunter flushing game, or a soldier wary of enemies lying hidden in dense vegetation.

At the start of another chant a tall older woman dressed in red lights a cigarette. She struts down the mīdān, *smoking, walking stick held perpendicular to the ground at the end of an outstretched arm, pompous, indifferent, mandarinlike. Some chants later she reappears, transmogrified. Now she and the transvestite stage a sword fight closely resembling the men's dance of a nearby desert people. The combatants leap at each other with apparent abandon, landing within inches of the audience, their sharp unsheathed blades swooping dangerously from aloft. Spectators shrink in terror at their bravado. The two are possessed, I learn, by* zāyran *of the* ʿArab *(Nomad) species.*

Occasionally during the evening's drumming, the shaykha *dances around the* ʿayāna, *encircling her with her arms, coaxing a seemingly reluctant spirit to enter its host and fully reveal itself before the assembly. But the* ʿayāna *has not risen since her foray into the* mīdān *at the start. She sits, silently watching.*

I notice at the end of each chant that several who have "descended"—standing or kneeling—begin to scratch themselves, and hiccup and burp indiscriminantly. Zaineb tells me these reactions signify the spirit's departure from the body of its host, of a woman's leaving trance.

July 21, 3:00 P.M. Today I am early; I find the ʿayāna, shaykha, *and musicians sprawled on* angarībs *inside the house, some of them asleep. Last night's drumming ended just before dawn and everyone is weary. A small girl enters the room, carrying a tray of tea; somnolence and lethargy dissipate as we drink. I return to the yard where others have begun to assemble while those inside change clothes.*

The shaykha's tōb *is bright pink, like yesterday's sweater; I am told the color is associated with her principal spirit, an Ethiopian* (Ḥabish). *She puts some "bitter" incense*[1]*—unlike the "sweet" kind made for weddings—in a hand held brazier, lights it, and sprinkles it with Evening in Paris cologne. Soon the* ʿayāna *emerges from her room wearing a green shift belonging to the spirit* Sitti Khuḍara, *"Green Lady," atop her everyday clothes, and over that the white* tōb *and red "belt" as before. She inclines toward the incense, shrouding the censer with a shawl. After a few minutes the* shaykha *passes both brazier and cologne to women gathered around the* mīdān, *then sets about to drum. With the first few*

1. It is called *bakhūr taymān,* "incense of the twins," or *dowā,* "medicine."

beats the ʿayāna *begins to move, more confidently than before, first kneeling, then standing, one fist pressed to her head. Someone fetches her cane; several others start to "descend."*

The tall woman who earlier impressed me with her regal bearing dances today with an exaggerated swagger and, like the ʿayāna, *makes use of a cane. (Canes, like batons, fly whisks, and walking sticks, are symbols of authority in Sudan.) Now she is host to a colonial* Khawāja zār; *last night to an Ethiopian.*

A portly grey-haired lady wearing a red head scarf with crenelated border designs dances through a series of gestures; at one point she performs a convincing benediction. She is host to Gasīs Romay, *the Catholic priest. Several chants later she rises again and is handed a sword. At this point a man who had been watching from the sidelines—one of the* ʿayāna's *worried kin—leaps into the* mīdān *to challenge her, unarmed. She rushes toward him, brandishing the sword. He dodges her swings; she lunges more menacingly. At last the man is forced for fear of injury to vacate the* mīdān, *his cowardice rewarded by derisive jeers from female spectators. Victorious, the possessed resumes her dance, still wielding the sword.*

Another woman approaches, also entranced. She goes into the jabūdi, *a dance of nomad* (ʿArāb) *women similar to the sensuous "pigeon" step performed by Hofriyati, but quicker, its movements more pronounced. Toward the end of the chant the* jabūdi *dancer flicks her hair at the "swordsman," bestowing* shabāl.

The drumming shifts. The jabūdi *dancer hesitates, then calls for a white* tōb. *This she fastens shoulder to waist, Beja style, assuming the dress of an* ʿArab *male. She wraps a blue and green checked cloth over her head then around her neck and face in the manner of a Palestinian herdsman or a lorry driver traversing the desert. Now she is host to* Ḥoliba ʿArabīya*—"Automobile Gypsy"—a Beja spirit also of the* ʿArāb.

Another chant. Immediately, a young woman starts flailing about on the mats, out of control. She is guided to the center of the mīdān *and left to kneel at the* shaykha*'s feet, "descending." The music stops; she continues to move convulsively. The woman's white* tōb *slips off, revealing a green dress beneath—the outfit of* Sitti Khuḍara, *spirit daughter of a Holy Man* zār. *But this is not* Sitti Khuḍara*'s chant. Some other spirit has seized her. The entranced is censed; she falls to the ground, immobile. The* shaykha *knocks on her back saying,* "Dayri shinū?"*—"what do you want?" A whispered response. The woman is handed a purple* tōb. *Onlookers chorus,* "Maʿlish, maʿlish. Mā fī ʿawaja" *—"Too bad, too bad. There is no impediment." The chant is drummed again. Again the woman dances, then falls. I ask what is happening. Someone tells me the trancer is nauseous, a second that she is married (this is important, as she is young), a third that her spirit has requested black trousers. Mid this lack of consensus, drumming resumes; the woman is left where she is.*

Zaineb's mother-in-law is here; now out of trance, she seats herself beside me on the angarīb. *"The Zār is heating up," she says, "It's getting good!"*

Now a chant for a prostitute spirit: another dancer falls to the ground, entranced. The shaykha *covers her with a red and white* tōb: *her* zār *is an Ethiopian prostitute called* Lulīya *The* shaykha *knocks on the woman's back and asks the spirit what it wants.*

"Two short dresses and a transparent tōb*!"*

The audience howls with laughter.

Meanwhile, the young woman in purple dances on unrestrainedly, watched over by an older adept who, I am told, will prevent the possessed from hurting herself or others.

July 24, 5:30 P.M. Last day of the ceremony. The sacrificial ram is led into the mīdān, *and a red and gold cloth—a* garmosīs *or bridal shawl—is placed over its back and head. The musicians play a chant. Incense is freshly lit, and the brazier thrust beneath the shawl. The animal is forced to inhale the smoke, then led from the* mīdān *and slaughtered by the* ʿayāna*'s son. Blood spurting from its throat is collected in a bowl and placed before the drums. The* ʿayāna *crosses seven times over the carcass before it is dragged off to be butchered. With the others I now step forward to deposit a few piasters in the victim's congealing blood. Someone whispers an invitation to drink* araki *(liquor) . . . being* khawāja *I am expected to imbibe. The possessed anoint themselves with blood, some also take a sip; the* shaykha *daubs it on herself and the* ʿayāna*'s feet and arms. Drumming and chanting recommence. Still wearing her stigmata of the* zār, *the* ʿayāna *rises to dance.*

A woman "descends" with a prayer shawl round her neck, holding its fringed ends in her hands, rocking to and fro as she paces the mīdān. *The gesture echoes that of men at a* zikr, *a "remembrance" ceremony of the Islamic* (ṣūfī) *fraternities from whose membership women are excluded.*

Later another woman (Zaineb's cousin and sister-in-law) dances briskly wearing trousers of a European cut; she is possessed, I learn, by the Airplane Captain zār.

Later still, an older lady performs the local "pigeon dance," concluding with a shabāl *to the dancer in the Mediterranean head scarf. She has been seized by* Mūna, Sitt ash-Shabāl, *a southern prostitute* zār *given to mimicking village women when appearing in their midst.*

An unwed girl now rises, snatches up the bridal shawl, and flings it over her head. She shuffles forward, out of time with the chant. Onlookers gasp. This is the costume of Lulīya, *the Ethiopian prostitute fond of Hofriyati weddings whose thread was sung some time ago; it is unlikely that She*[2] *would return so soon, and uninvited. The audience tries to dissuade the girl without success. It is not right, they say, for an unmarried girl to dance so like a bride, in public. Has she*

2. I use an initial capital letter (e.g., He, She) when referring to a specific spirit in order to indicate its sex while distinguishing it from its human host.

no shame? Beside me a woman snaps, "That virgin is not possessed (mazūr). *She just wants a husband!"*

Night falls; a pressure lamp is placed on a low table near the musicians. The mīdān *is a pond of light shallowing to darkness at its sides. Dancers cast weird shadows on the sand; eyes in faces lit from below appear enormous, wild. Drums throb without flagging; redolent smoke of incense clouds the evening air. The atmosphere is tense, intoxicating, eerie.*

A piercing cry—a uniformed schoolgirl nine or ten years old has sprawled forward into the mīdān, *upheld on all four limbs, body jerking rapidly up and down from the shoulders. Immediately, she is led off by some older women, told it is not proper for a child to behave this way at a* zār. *But she does not stop. Outside the* mīdān *the women try to calm her. Now she is sobbing and has gone quite limp. When efforts to revive her fail she is dragged, resisting, back into the center. She balks at attempts to bring her to the* shaykha *and is desposited before the drums. The* shaykha *approaches; the girl cringes. The* shaykha *censes her, covers her with a white* tōb, *and asks, "What do you want? Who are you?" No response.*

Onlookers taunt the intrusive zār, *trying vainly to garner its sympathy: "Ah, her father is poor! Her mother is blind! Her brother is ill!" The* shaykha *sends for the girl's father. He is brought into the* mīdān *and made to give his daughter's spirit ten piasters (about twenty-five cents). Still there is no word from the* zār; *the girl remains limp, appearing deeply entranced.*

It is getting late. Smells of cooking waft through the mīdān, *and laughter from the kitchen. More drumming and dancing are called for. The* shaykha *requests certain threads to test for various species of* zayran, *hoping the presumptuous spirit will be drawn to identify itself. She blows into the schoolgirl's ears and behind her neck; she pulls at her limbs, whips her softly with a length of rope, beats her lightly with an iron spear. She censes her, rolls her head along the girl's body. She takes the girl in her arms and dances to and fro, blowing a whistle to the incessant beat. She leads the girl around the* mīdān *and is twice successful in getting her to move briefly of her own accord. At last the girl jogs back and forth through the open space, one arm pumping like the wheel of a locomotive, the other, raised and crooked at elbow, sounding an imagined alarm. The* shaykha *blows her pipe whistle in accompaniment. The troublesome spirit is identified:* Basha-t-ʿAdil, *the* Khawāja *railway engineer.*

Still the espisode continues. For over an hour the shaykha *tries every technique in her repertoire, aiming to convince the implacable* zār *to abandon its newfound host and refrain from bothering her again until she is a woman and married. Finally the* shaykha *guides the girl out of the* mīdān *and out of the* ḥōsh. *They cross the threshold, the* khashm al-bayt, *backwards, facing the assembly; they remain in the path for several minutes, then return as they had left, facing the* mīdān. *The girl, now calmed and weeping softly, is brought to sit near me—a human* khawāja*—but placed with her back to the ritual.*

Soon the sacrificial meal is served and proceedings brought to a close. It is almost 2:00 A.M. *The* ʿayāna *is now formally well, though tomorrow she must eat the head meat of the ram in a private ceremony followed by a procession to the Nile. Several people approach the* ʿayāna, *touch her right shoulder, and say* "Insha Allāh byinfʿik," *"God willing, it is benefiting you." In the company of my neighbors I return, exhausted, to Hofriyat.*

Zār *and* Zayran

Smoking, wanton dancing, flailing about, burping and hiccuping, drinking blood and alcohol, wearing male clothing, publicly threatening men with swords, speaking loudly lacking due regard for etiquette, these are hardly the behaviors of Hofriyati women for whom dignity and propriety are leading concerns. But in the context of a *zār* they are common and expected. The ceremony is rich in complex imagery and movement. Yet it has none of the solemn pageantry of a Mass, nor the predictable, repetitive manipulation of symbols which I, raised as a Catholic, might have found familiar. The tone of a *zār* resembles neither the subdued formality of a Muslim Friday prayer, nor the unorchestrated ceremoniousness of life cycle rites in Hofriyat. It is closer in character to *zikr*s of the Qadriya and Khatmiya *ṣūfī* orders in Sudan, but lacks their cohesion and transcendent focus. What is singular about a *zār* is its spontaneity, its imagination, whose basis nontheless is a comprehensive repertoire of symbols and spirit roles—a resource on which participants draw for inspiration. Moves are lightly choreographed—improvisations on well-known themes; "players" are interchangeable, costumes readily borrowed and exchanged. But during the performance, neither players' bodies nor their costumes belong to village women—they belong, instead, to *zayran*. *Zār* rituals are always fraught with tension and surprise, for at any moment a woman might be "seized" by a spirit that Hofriyati did not before know existed, or she did not know she had.

How is all of this to be understood? What is this phenomenon; who or what are these spirits which so dramatically appear in women's bodies? To tackle the question, we begin by looking briefly at the cult's origin, distribution, and place in the religious lives of Hofriyati.

Zār refers to a type of spirit, the illness such spirits can cause by possessing humans, and the rituals necessary to their pacification. The cult is found throughout the northern Sudan (Al Hadi 1987; Barclay 1964; Cloudsley 1983; Constantinides 1972, 1977, 1982; Trimingham 1965; Zenkovsky 1950) and variations of the same name appear in Egypt (Fakhouri 1968; Al-Guindi 1978; Kennedy 1967; Morsy 1978; Nelson 1971; Saunders 1977), Ethiopia (Leiris 1958; Messing 1958; Rodinson 1967; Young 1975), Somalia, where it is called *sar* (Lewis 1966, 1969, 1971*a, b,* 1983, 1986), Arabia (Trimingham 1965 : 258), and southern Iran (Modarressi 1968). Cloudsley (1983 : 75) writes of attending a *zār* in

Tamanrasset, a south Algerian market town, and speculates that the cult was spread throughout the Sahara and North Africa via caravaneers.[3] Crapanzano (1973, 1977*b,* 1980) notes that in Meknes, Morocco, where the Ḥamadsha brotherhood specializes in curing cases of possession by female *jinn,* members are especially devoted to the spirit *Lalla ʿAīsha Qandisha* who, according to legend, was brought to Morocco (along with trance) from the palace of the king of Sudan (1973 : 43). On this point it is intriguing to compare the epithet, *Qandisha,* to the term for "queen" or "queen mother" in ancient Meroë: *candace,* which Hofriyati pronounce *kandesa.*

Etymologically, most scholars consider the word *zār* to derive, not from Arabic, but from Persian (Frobenius 1913; Modarressi 1968) or more plausibly—given the long establishment of the cult in Gondar and vicinity[4]—Amharic (Barclay 1964; Kennedy 1967; Seligman 1914; Cerulli (in the Encyclopaedia of Islam) 1934 : 1217).[5] Popularly, however, it is assumed to be a corruption of the Arabic *zahar,* "he visited," while in Hofriyat it is often pronounced as *ẓahr,* from "he became visible, perceptible, or manifest." Both shifts are apposite in the possession context, where spirits become visible by entering the human realm via human bodies, temporarily displacing those bodies' human selves.

The origins of the cult are obscure; like its name, it is generally thought to have begun outside the Sudan (cf. Al Hadi 1987 : 95–96). According to Constantinides (1972 : 35, 1982), *zār* was well established in Sudan by the mid nineteenth century and, by the time of the Anglo-Egyptian reconquest at its end, had attracted such a wide following that it was seen as a threat to orthodox Islam and denounced by religious leaders as "innovation." Current learned opinion echoes this view; nonetheless, the cult is tolerated, and *zār* programs occasionally appear on Television Omdurman (Lewis 1986 : 102). Despite their negative public stance, religious clerics in Sudan subscribe to the foundation on which the *zār* rests, for *zayran* are considered to belong to the class of spirits known as *jinn,* whose existence the Quran substantiates.

In Africa, possession cults are common and not confined to peoples professing Islam. I have noted that *zār* itself is practiced in Christian Ethiopia (though beliefs here differ from those in Sudan), and John and Irene Hamer (1966) have written about a similar cult in the south of that country called *shatana* (from the Arabic for "devil"). In Chad there is the correlative *liban sheitan* (Constantinides 1972 : 25); among the Digo of the

3. In January 1988, Professor I. M. Lewis organized a conference on the *zār* in Khartoum. Delegates who spoke about the cult had observed it in Djibouti, Tunisia, Morocco, Saudi Arabia, Quwait, Qatar, United Arab Emirates, Iran, and West Africa, in addition to Sudan, Egypt, Ethiopia, and Somalia.

4. See Young (1975 : 571).

5. Al Hadi (1987 : 114, n. 6) discusses possible Ethiopian origins of the word.

south Kenya coast *shaitani* (Gomm 1975), and among Segeju Swahili speakers in Tanzania *shetani* (Gray 1969). *Masabe* spirit possession among the Tonga of Zambia (Colson 1969) shows marked resemblance to the Sudanese *zār,* as do *bori* in Nigeria and North Africa (Besmer 1983; Onwuejeogwu 1969; Tremearne 1914), *trumba* and *patros* in Mayotte, Comoro Islands (Lambek 1980, 1981), *saka* or *pepo* among the Wataita of Kenya (Harris 1957, 1978), *takuka* among the Ndembu of Zambia (Turner 1974: 250), *holey* (specifically, *hauka)* among the Songhay (Rouch 1960), and *jnun* curing activities of the earlier mentioned Ḥamadsha in Morocco (Crapanzano 1973, 1977*b,* 1980). These cults share a focus on relieving illness or other personal distress caused by intrusive spirits—often the spirit analogues of human foreigners.

Many of the cults are related historically, as their names suggest, though evidence for this is often indirect. In several, for example, possessive spirits or their invocations are referred to as "winds": *pepo* in Swahili, *iska* in Hausa, *riḥ/rowḥān* in Arabic. But in other cases, connections can be more firmly established: following the Ottoman conquest (1820–21), Sudanese and West African pilgrims in and en route to Mecca are known to have attended each others' spirit ceremonies (Constantinides 1972: 31). Indeed, until recently, two forms of the *zār* were practiced in the area of Hofriyat: *zār-bori,* sharing elements with *bori* in Nigeria, and *zār-tambūra.* The latter, once concerned with grave illness and malevolent spirits (Zenkovsky 1950), has now been subsumed by the former, and together they are known simply as *zār.*[6] Yet African possession cults are not all alike; however much interlinked and cross-fertilized, they vary significantly with local beliefs and social conditions.

The Possession Concept

In writing of spirit "possession" in Hofriyat, I am using indigenous terms. When someone is considered to be affected by a *zār,* people say of her, *inda riḥ, inda zār,* or *inda dastūr*[7]—"she has a spirit." Alternatively, they say she is *mazūr* or *madastīr*—"with spirit," possessed. *Zār* influence, being possessed of and by a spirit, is considered an affliction and expressed as illness. A spirit causes its novice host to suffer; however, initial misery should be surpassed by a more positive concern on the part of the spirit for

6. According to Al Hadi (1987), *zār bori* and *zār tambura* are still distinguished in Omdurman, though the latter has few followers.

7. This term literally means "statute" or "constitutional law," and colloquially, "permission" (Wehr 1976: 281). In northern Sudan, however, the term also refers to a door jamb (Constantinides 1977: 65–66, n. 6) or a bolt (Hillelson 1930*a*: 35). The reference to doorways is significant, and discussed later on.

its host's well-being as their relationship progresses. Once possessed, always possessed: *zayran* never wholly abandon those they have chosen as their hosts.

Someone diagnosed as *zār* possessed is liable to be affected by her spirit(s) at any time. *Zayran* are able to infiltrate the bodies of their hosts at will, a move which villagers say always coincides with the latter's entrancement. According to Hofriyati, possession trance (*ghaybīya* or *ghaybūba*) is a state induced by the spirit's forceful entry into the body, which displaces or shifts the person's human self to another perceptual plane. It is, as Bourguignon (1973 : 12–13) suggests, "a radical discontinuity of personal identity"; yet in contrast to her model, the distortion of perception this entails pertains not only to the self but to other entities as well. This point is clarified in chapter 10.

Still, trance is only one manifestation of possession in Hofriyat, for *zayran* affect their hosts in countless additional ways (see also Constantinides 1972, 1977; Cloudsley 1983 : 81). They are always near, or in local parlance "above" (*fōg*), their human hosts, whence they might influence people's perceptions and behaviors in the course of daily life. Further, despite the acknowledged powers of *zayran,* possession trance rarely occurs unpremeditatedly, outside of ritual contexts. Here, one is not diagnosed as possessed because she becomes entranced; rather, she becomes entranced because she is possessed. Schoolgirl mishaps notwithstanding, the possessed rarely enter trance spontaneously; this is something one must learn to do in the course of a curing ceremony in order to negotiate an appropriate relationship with instrusive *zayran*. As adepts put it, one must learn how not to resist a spirit's attempts to enter the human world through the medium of her body. The implicit link to ideas about sexual intercourse in Hofriyat is striking and reiterated in the fact that a woman should be married before she becomes possessed.

Thus trance is in no way aberrant; it is a practiced behavior which the possessed are expected to display under certain conditions. Although an integral part of possession therapy and relapse prophylaxis, it is not consistently evinced by the possessed during ceremonies, and when evinced, it is variable in apparent depth and duration from one episode or individual to the next. Since it is considered inappropriate to be entered by a spirit (or a husband) while menstruating, a woman at a *zār* signals *zayran* of her condition by tying a knot in her braids, so constraining the spirits' activity. Moreover, because it must conform to prescribed patterns of "spiritness," trance performance requires skill and considerable control. Thus it is not, as some would assert, a spontaneous neurological manifestation of nutritional deficiency which (at least originally) is accounted for after the fact as possession (e.g., Kehoe and Giletti 1981). Such models betray their foundation in a Western rationalism which derogates any mode of consciousness other than that of critical self-awareness. In the search for reductive biological explanations as to why trance should occur, trance itself is misconstrued, parted from its cultural context. Here an essential point is missed. For villagers the system of meaning—possession—is both logically and contextually prior to the behavior—trance—through which it finds expression (cf. Lambek 1981 : 7).

This is not to deny that biological factors might affect the proclivity to enter trance or the ease with which the behavior is learned. Some of the possessed initially experience difficulty in becoming lost from themselves and allowing their spirits to assume control; others do not. Here perhaps one's nutritional status plays a role. Still, it must be stressed that Hofriyati generally enter trance *after* having been diagnosed as possessed or, if undiagnosed, when attending a spirit ritual. And in either case, an individual's trance behavior is learned (cf. Bourguignon 1973 : 4–15, 1976 : 37 ff.), shaped by her knowledge of *zayran* and their provenance. It may be novel and unexpected, but must be consistent with villagers' understanding of spirits to be accepted as legitimate possession and not considered dissimulation or idiosyncratic madness. The few women who do enter trance spontaneously—apparently uninduced, in nonceremonial situations—are hardly neophytes. Rather, they are long-term adepts of the *zār* who, in the course of their possession careers, have become progressively more skilled at alternating modes of consciousness and allowing the spirits to exhibit themselves through their bodies (see also Besmer 1983 : 24).

According to Hofriyati, the fact that possession trance typically must be induced and is rare apart from public ritual has less to do with human ability or volition than with spirit caprice. Humans convoke *zayran* through ritual drumming and singing, and normally the spirits—for whom access to the human world is a principal motive for possession—are willing to oblige. Indeed, they regard such invitations as their due, in partial fulfillment of bargains struck with humans, and are likely to become disgruntled and dangerous when neglected or put off. If the possessed take care to mollify them, spirits ought to respond by confining their appearance to ritual contexts where they can frolic and be entertained. Yet none of this is certain. Spirits are willful, and for sport or revenge might "descend" into their hosts without benefit of prior summons. So despite the controlled nature of possession trance and spirit display, the startling possibility exists that at any moment a woman might not be who she usually is.

January 23, 1984. Samira and I have come this morning to Asur, a village I have never before visited several kilometers north of Hofriyat, and home to a well-known midwife I would like to meet. We make obligatory calls on Samira's distant kin who live here, drinking quantities of water and limūn, *a fresh limeade. As we leave the* ḥōsh *en route to the midwife's home, Samira's mother's cousin calls her back; I await her alone in the alley.*

A woman carrying a pail of water on her head rounds the corner. On coming face to face with me she stops abruptly, taken aback in fright. "Ya Khawājīya," *she says,* "*how are you? What do you want from me?*"

"*Peace to you,*" *I reply,* "*I want nothing. I am waiting for Samira who is inside.*"

As if on cue Samira exits the ḥōsh. *She greets the woman who has been staring at my feet, clad in Dr. Scholl's sandals—fashionable this year in Sudan (and, I later learn, a current request of* zayran).

"*This* khawājīya *has human feet!*" *she exlaims.* "*I thought she was a* zār*!*"[8]

In Hofriyat possession is a matter of fact. Here the reality of spirits and their powers goes unchallenged, even by villagers who have no firsthand experience of them and regardless of how hotly they dispute the proper therapy for possession affliction, discussed below. Clearly, Hofriyati, like the rest of us, face doubts concerning their beliefs from time to time. But cosmological mavericks they are not. Doubts, like beliefs, are grounded in a social context. *Zayran* are immanent in the world of Hofriyat; sceptic and zealot, both, are canopied by their existence.[9]

Further, possession is a holistic social reality. It penetrates all facets and levels of human life, resisting analytic reduction to a single component dimension, whether psychological, aesthetic, religious, social, or medical. Studies that focus on one of these to the virtual exclusion of others cannot but derogate the complexity with which such factors interweave. Works of this sort may be read most comfortably, perhaps, by members of Western cultures, but ultimately they distort and impoverish what they seek to understand.[10] Possession has numerous significances and countless implications: it defies simple explanation. It has no necessary cause, no necessary outcome. Its province is meaning, and it is best addressed in that light. Hence my concern to describe the potential range of its significance within the social and cultural context of Hofriyat.

Given this intention, a caveat is in order. Although I am interested in how possession, as an idiom of social discourse, may inform how individuals speak about themselves and others, the question of those individuals' specific deep motivations is not one that I feel competent to broach. To an informed reader, deep motivation might well be suggested in the cases of Umselima and her family (chapter 6). However, I do not, because I could

8. *Zayran* may transform themselves into human shape, but incompletely: their feet are always those of hooved animals such as camels or donkeys. See also Cloudsley (1983:74 n.); Crapanzano (1973:44).

9. Cf. Berger (1967). For an analytical consideration of this issue see Jean Pouillon, "Remarks on the Verb 'To Believe'" (1982).

10. On this point see also Crapanzano (1977*a*), Kapferer (1983), Lambek (forthcoming).

not, undertake the kind of psychodynamic analysis that Obeyesekere (1981) presents in his convincing study of Sri Lankan ascetics.

Perhaps this is not the disadvantage it might seem. *Zār* is first of all a cultural phenomenon, better still, a cultural resource appropriated by individuals under certain conditions. Viewed as such, it consists of symbols and associations available to be taken up and manipulated in hundreds of different ways. But if they are symbolic, spirits defy conventionalization: they are beings, actors, agents. They are inherently capricious, amoral, ambivalent, and by villagers' own accounts, incompletely understood. In possession of a human, one might modify its characteristics, or exhibit different sides of its personality in different women. Spirits' selfhood, too, is constituted in relationships with others. And because of this openness and manipulability, *zayran* are available to become, in Obeyesekere's (1981) terms, "personal symbols" (p. 45), those "that give expression to psychological travail" (p. 53, see also 1970: 105). Yet possession rites and individual experiences of *zayran* are public matters: they enhance villagers' knowledge of spirits and spirit associations and are a continual source of information about the parallel world for possessed and nonpossessed alike. And it is in terms of this information that specific individuals may be led to appropriate a particular spirit idiom. Public culture and individual psyche are complexly intermeshed.

My principal aim in parts 2 and 3 of this book is to depict the richness and complexity of the *zār* as a cultural resource, its capacity—worked out through the people it affects—to contextualize the prosaic, relatively taken-for-granted world and, in so doing, to reshape but also reproduce it. Possession in Hofriyat is a cultural idiom, an idiom (1) that is based on consensually validated, ritually confirmed information; (2) that is conceptually removed (since more explicit and less immediately invoked) from primary idioms (e.g., "interiority") intrinsic to routine practice; and (3) that is drawn upon collectively and individually by villagers to articulate certain problems and experiences of everyday life (cf. Crapanzano 1977*a;* Obeyesekere 1970, 1981). Articulation, as Crapanzano explains, is

> the act of . . . constructing an event to render it meaningful. The act of articulation is more than a passive representation of the event; it is in essence the creation of an event. It separates the event from the flow of experience . . . gives the event structure . . . relates it to other similarly constructed events, and evaluates the event along both idiosyncratic and (culturally) standardized lines. Once the experience is articulated, once it is rendered an event, it is cast within the world of meaning and may provide a basis for action. (Crapanzano 1977*a*: 10)

With these ideas in mind the two poles of the possession dialectic suggested at the close of chapter 3 can be better distinguished. In this and the next few chapters I consider the articulatory aspect of the *zār* by focusing on the contexts of possession incidence, while in subsequent chapters attention shifts to its semantic aspect. Admittedly, this distinction between context and meaning is artificial: a heuristic emphasis made for the sake of clarity. The subject of meaning can hardly be eliminated from the discussion of possession contexts; some of its features, however, are examined more intensively later on. Present throughout what follows is a dialogue—often, though not always, implicit—between the idioms of daily life and those of its extraordinary counterface, the *zār*.

The Possessed

In Hofriyat, as elsewhere in Sudan, possession activity is mainly though not exclusively the province of women.[11] Somewhat more than 40 percent of Hofriyati women ever married and over the age of fifteen (N = 129 [1977] and 135 [1984]) claim a *zār* affliction. Marital status is a significant factor in possession illness: spirits, villagers assert, rarely trouble themselves with the unwed—with women whose fertility has yet to be activated. Most affected are those between the ages of thirty-five and fifty-five, two-thirds of whom have spirits. This proportion is due to a cumulative effect: once possessed a woman is always possessed thereafter.

By contrast, only a handful of men from the entire village area are publicly acknowledged to be possessed. In Hofriyat itself only four men (about 5 percent of the resident adult male population) are considered adepts of the *zār;* three have undergone the requisite ceremonies, one when only thirteen years of age. Two men born in the village but now living elsewhere are known to have spirits, and I obtained information concerning ten others from the vicinity, five of whom were deceased prior to fieldwork. During my six-year absence from the village, only one man had become possessed in contrast to sixteen women (see table 5.1). In 1984, several male acquaintances privately declared themselves to be possessed and confessed admiration for the *zār,* but would not publicly seek to confirm their afflictions for fear of losing face.

Why is this the case? Why, assuming that possession is a public idiom for the articulation and interpretation of experience, should there exist a sexual disproprotion among those who acknowledge having spirits? An obvious approach is to ask whether the range of experience that possession constructs is more common to Hofriyati women than to men. This I think to be the case, mainly because possession is closely linked to fertility with which women are identified and for which they bear responsibility, a point

11. See Barclay (1964:196–206); Cloudsley (1983:67–87); Constantinides (1972, 1977); Trimingham (1965:174–77); Zenkovsky (1950).

more fully explored in chapter 5. I do not entirely agree with I. M. Lewis (1966, 1971*a*, 1983, 1986, chapter 2) on this issue, who, arguing from a sociological perspective, suggests that *zār* possession is a strategy which women use in an oblique attempt to redress the effects of their subordinate social status. Lewis holds that since spirits demand desiderata which husbands must provide if their wives are to regain well-being, possession can be seen as a measure of gender conflict: it is a strategic evocation of shared beliefs by women wishing to mitigate their subordination to men.

The perspective is illuminating, but presents a number of difficulties. First, it places unwarranted emphasis on the assumed intentionality of women and thus insidiously underestimates the factuality of spirits in the Sudanese world. Words like *strategy* imply volition, which may certainly be present and, if so, motivated by status considerations in some cases of possession but not, as later seen, in all. Moreover, Lewis's deprivation hypothesis appears to presume that women seek the same status held by men, which, since men have deprived them of it, was originally within their purview. Such assumptions fail to bear scrutiny in Hofriyat, where the social worlds of men and women are largely separate and distinct, a condition due not to happenstance or the prevailing wills of men, but to cultural design. Wilson's (1967) critique of the model tries to address this problem by shifting the locus of proposed status competition from intersex to intrasex relations and, so doing, is sympathetic to the Sudanese context. However, it shares with Lewis's theory the drawback of a conflict orientation to social interaction that is firmly rooted in Western premises of individualism,[12] whose validity in non-Western cultures must be open to debate (cf. Morsy 1978; Boddy 1988; Lambek forthcoming). Even granting that status may be a consideration in certain episodes of possession illness, the sociological argument cannot account for the *zār* in its entirety. It glosses over the issue of belief and is therefore unable to explain or interpret possession forms (for example, the characteristics of spirits, the nature and variety of possession symptoms) and processes (such as the reevaluation of one's past that acquiring a spirit entails). Such factors, however important to the possessed, are implicitly deemed incidental when the investigator's focus is competition.[13] The social status model is unidimensional, at once too general in application and too narrow in concern to deal adequately with the complexities of *zār*.

It is imperative to ask why so many Western scholars—among them

12. Although the fluctuating kinship networks of Hofriyati are individualistic, this is not to say that the individual is the focal social unit in Hofriyat. Hofriyati women and men are always subordinate to a range of collective interests: family, lineage, village, religious group, etc.

13. Lewis (1971*a*:30, 1983) certainly does not consider other factors unimportant, yet they do not figure in his analysis to the same extent as does the question of cross-sex competition.

Kehoe and Giletti (1981) earlier discussed—are committed to viewing possession as a consequence of women's deprivation rather than their privilege, or perhaps their inclination. Such explanations consistently mislocate the question of why women should be more susceptible to possession than men. Especially in his early work, Lewis (1971*a*:77), for example, suggests that joining a *zār* coterie enables women to express solidarity vis-à-vis men, who are seen as their oppressors. Men have Islam, which excludes women from active participation; hence women, who are socially peripheral, must resort to the equally peripheral cult of *zār* both to mitigate their subordination and to express religious fervor (Lewis 1971*a*: 66–99; see also Lewis 1986:23–50, 102–5). This is a classic but unhappily androcentric portrayal of women, who are forever seen as *re*acting to men rather than acting for themselves within a specific cultural context.

To avoid such pitfalls, we need to examine closely how the sexes in Hofriyat conceive of their interrelations both collectively (as in chapters 2 and 3) and individually. Judging from my informants, some women—by no means all or only those who are possessed—clearly feel subordinate to men, resent their positions, and are not consistently above vituperation. However, their feelings seem to derive less from their status as women than from the specific actions of individual men, notably husbands. And the problem these men pose is not that they deny women, as a class, an elevated social position, but that they sometimes—often inadvertently—thwart individual women's legitimate attempts to achieve it. The reverse can also be said for women (see chapter 5), who may frustrate the status aspirations of men. As depicted in earlier chapters, both sexes are active participants in the social life of Hofriyat, bisected as it is into gender-distinct yet partially overlapping spheres. If men are central and women peripheral with respect to Islam and external relations, women are central and men peripheral when it comes to physical, social, and cultural reproduction: the worldliness of village life. Although men and women are subject to different constraints, the actions of each bear consequence for those of the other.

Indeed, whatever consciousness women have of themselves as a group is hardly one of inferiority and wholescale subordination to men, but of complementarity. As villagers see it, the sexes are engaged—not in a war—but in a dialectical relationship of qualitatively disparate yet socially equivalent parts, each commanding certain resources but reliant on the other for fulfillment. They do not conceive of themselves as locked in a struggle between classes, hierarchically understood. While a Marxist critique might legitimately consider this to be a mystification of political realities, it cannot be ignored if we are truly concerned with the meaning of *zār* to women and men in Hofriyat. Political relations are mystified for both within the Hofriyati universe of meaning.

When properly situated in the framework of sexual complementarity, the question of why women as a category should be more likely than men to interpret certain experiences as possession expands to two: Why women? Why not men? As Kapferer (1983:98) astutely argues with respect to women's preponderance in Sri Lankan exorcisms, such questions cannot be resolved by focusing on the possessed's motives and intentions alone, independent of the cultural constructs which inform them. We need to consider the qualities that define the sexes in Hofriyat, the typifications each sex holds of the other, the components of gender identity (see also Nelson 1971). Only then might we have a basis for deciding whether a particular incidence of possession constitutes attempted cross-sex or intra-sex status manipulation, or something else—an expression of psychological or social disturbance (cf. Crapanzano 1973, 1977*b*, 1980; Obeyesekere 1970, 1981; Kapferer 1983, 1986), cross-sex communication (cf. Lambek 1980, 1981), religious experience (cf. Constantinides 1972, 1977; Lewis 1986), a form of play, dramatic allegory, or all of these and more. Its cultural underpinnings—idioms of the everyday world, prosaic conceptualizations of gender—empower possession as a form of social discourse.

Thus put, a focus on the articulatory potential of possession instead of on the status aspirations of individuals possessed changes the tenor of the analytic enterprise. It widens the interpretive net and does not attempt to simplify matters where simplicity belies the facts. Rather, it makes possible a variety of explanations at different levels of analysis and experience, all of them immanent in the *zār* as a system of meaning, all of them potentially relevant to any specific episode of possession.

Returning to Hofriyati gender constructs and the *zār,* both sexes allege that women are naturally more vulnerable to spirit attack as a function of their femininity.[14] Spirits are attracted to women—and married women in particular—for it is they who use henna, perfumes, soaps, and scented oils; wear gold jewelry and diaphanous wraps, all human finery which spirits are known to covet. The proclivities of *zayran* are symmetrical to those of Hofriyati women: both are regarded as consumers of goods provided by men.

Recall, too, that women are more constrained than men behaviorally. Moreover, their bodies are protected by a battery of physical and ritual defenses designed to reinforce the Hofriyati world at its most significant but potentially weakest point, the vaginal meatus, where alien others—non-Hofriyati humans and *zayran*—threaten to intrude. And such defenses and restrictions, if neglected, render women prone to spirit assault. *Zayran,* like other *jinn,* are likeliest to invade the human world when its

14. See also Kapferer (1983:100–110) for a similar view of the susceptibility of Sri Lankan women.

proper order is confounded and its defenses are down, as when a woman is opened while giving birth or, having delivered, sees the prepotent blood of circumcision, an uninfibulated gypsy, or someone who has looked upon a corpse. For spirits, ambivalence and ambiguity are windows of opportunity. But *zayran* can also create disorder, the very conditions which permit their penetration of the human world. And here they wield considerable power to disrupt human fertility, so closely identified with women. Further, women are thought more susceptible than men to emotional excess; they have greater contact with the impurities of daily life and a correspondingly greater need to avoid them, whether smelling bad odors, seeing blood and feces, becoming dusty and sweaty from domestic work. All of these situations draw *zayran*. In short, violations of interiority, the salient informative quality of Hofriyati culture, both signify and precipitate intrusion by *zayran*. And, as women—who embody this quality—are more prone to such violation than men, possession is a feminine susceptibility.

While many questions remain to be addressed, this goes some way toward explaining why women interpret certain experiences and illness episodes as possession. It also suggests why, in this sexually polarized community, men do not. But here more remains to be said. A common characterization of women which they do not completely share is that because they are wanting in *ʿagl*, they lack sufficient moral strength to uphold the tenets and ideals of Islam. According to local religious authorities it is reprehensible and abhorrent—though not, strictly speaking, *ḥarām* (forbidden)—for Muslims to traffic with spirits. They say that each individual has the responsibility to steer a proper course of spirit avoidance, something women find more difficult to do than men. Women's perceived inability to resist and so deny *zayran* access to earthly pleasures is put down to their inherent moral frailty, notwithstanding that they are more likely to encounter *jinn* than men. Just as the public identity of women accounts for their greater participation in the *zār*, so the public identity of men as pious Muslims accounts, in part, for their forbearance (see also Lambek 1981: 62–64).

The last is solely a masculine perspective. Women see no incompatibility between the *zār* and Islam: to them possession ritual is part of a general religious enterprise (cf. Constantinides 1972:98). Hofriyati culture therefore contains conflicting interpretations of the relationship between possession and Islam. These, in turn, have divergent implications for the handling of troublesome spirits.

Exorcism versus Accommodation

Where men hold the reputedly orthodox view that intrusive spirits can and must be dislodged from the body by force, women maintain that *zayran* cannot be got rid of at all.[15] Adepts insist that if one's illness is caused by a *zār,* no amount of Islamic or even Western medicine will effect a cure. Attempts to exorcise the spirit serve merely to exacerbate the patient's condition. Symptom remission alone can be achieved, and only if the afflicted agrees to hold a propitiatory ceremony on behalf of the as yet unnamed *zār.* During this ceremony, often held long after her initial illness has dissipated, the possessed enters into a contractual relationship with the spirit(s) responsible for her lapse from health. There, in response to drumming and singing chants associated with the various named *zayran,* she ideally enters trance: a spirit's chant is an invitation to "descend" (*nazal*) and enter the body of its host, where its identity can be affirmed and its demands revealed.[16] In return for certain offerings, acquisitions, and observances, the invasive spirit agrees to restore, and refrain from further jeopardizing, its host's well-being.

Henceforward, human host and possessive *zār* are joined in continuous but unequal partnership. The spirit remains above her (*fōg*), able to exert its influence or infiltrate her body at will. To some extent the possessed can rely on the spirit's compliance in maintaining her health, but only so long as she regularly attends the ceremonies of others, abstains from traditional mourning behavior, associates herself with clean and sweet-smelling things, and is not given over to strong emotion. A violation of these provisions renders her vulnerable to relapse. Yet the curing rite has opened communications between the two entities, and it is hoped that any future problems can be dealt with expeditiously. From the spirit's perspective, contracts with humans are infinitely renegotiable, so if the possessed wishes to allay further attack from her *zār,* she must take scrupulous care to mollify it. If all goes well, what begins as an uneasy truce between a willful spirit and its initially reluctant host might graduate to positive symbiosis as their relationship stabilizes and matures. Alleviating the symptoms of possession illness is a matter of establishing reciprocal obligations between spirit and host; their relationship should become, like that between partners in a marriage, one of complementarity, exchange, and mutual accommodation.

Although the majority of men denounce the propitiation of *zayran,* this is not because they deny that such spirits exist. In Hofriyat, *zayran* comprise a distinct class of *jinn,*[17] mischievous invisible beings which popu-

15. Interestingly, this is similar to the situations of men and women in a marriage: while men may divorce an unwanted wife at will, women must accommodate themselves to the marriage, however unhappy.

16. Spirits are hardly inanimate or genderless, as my use of the impersonal pronoun implies. But when not referring to specific spirits and possession episodes, I use the neuter form to avoid confusion between humans and *zayran.*

17. However, the classification of spirits varies somewhat from area to area in Sudan, and in some places (though not in Hofriyat or its environs) *zayran* and *jinn* are considered

late a world parallel to our own and contiguous with it but imperceptible to humans most of the time. Typical of their exceptional attributes, *jinn* can transform themselves into animals, assume human form (but incompletely so, for their feet are always hooved), or take possession of live human bodies at will. *Jinn* are mentioned in the Quran (Suras 6, 17, 18, 34, 37, 46, 55, 72, and 114); they are a constant if often low-key part of both men's and women's daily lives.

Further, should a man become ill there is a chance that the diagnosis will be possession regardless of its feminine associations. Men recognize the powers of *zayran* and acknowledge that even the most pious among them occasionally succumbs to spirit attack. But this is where their public support for the cult stops: most insist that, despite a practiced resistance, *zayran,* like other *jinn,* must eventually capitulate to the powerful exorcistic techniques of Islamic medicine. In the company of their fellows they decry as un-Islamic women's ceremonial attempts to assuage and socialize the spirits.

In face of such weighty opposition the *zār* cult thrives, and its rites are attended even by the most submissive and religious of wives. For women, *zār* falls squarely within the purview of Islam. And when arguing their position with men (something I witnessed only twice), women said that Allah expects the afflicted to seek respite from their suffering: clearly, it is better to be healthy than "broken" by spirits or overzealous efforts to dislodge them.[18] Perhaps men are right that involvement in the cult imperils one's prospect of a pleasurable afterlife, but then, is Allah not merciful?

Men, for their part, though publicly adamant that only exorcism is correct in the eyes of Islam, are privately not so intractable (cf. Barclay 1964:206; Constantinides 1982). Often hesitant, concerned, uncertain that Islamic medications will effect a cure or fearing reprisals of a powerful spirit if it is put off, most do not interfere when their womenfolk conduct propitiatory ceremonies, and provide money to meet the spirits' demands. Here perhaps, as Lewis (1971*a*:88) suggests, men tacitly recognize the contradiction between the formal ideology of male supremacy and the social (and cultural) importance of women. Intriguing, too, in light of the ethnographic situation in Hofriyat, is Lewis's more recent view that women's participation in the *zār* might offer men "the privilege of vicarious participation in what they ostensibly condemn as superstition and heresy.

different forms of spirit being. On this issue, see Constantinides (1972:102–4), and Trimingham (1965:171 ff.).

18. In 1920 the editors of *Sudan Notes and Records* (Anonymous 1920:245–59) report a case from El-Obeid, Kordofan, of a sixteen-year-old girl possessed by *dasatīr* (or *zayran*) who was murdered by a curer attempting to exorcise the intrusive *jinn* via beatings. The curer claimed in court to have beaten the spirits, not the girl. Exorcistic techniques like this are commonly performed by Islamic healers in recalcitrant cases of possession, especially by malevolent (black) *jinn,* discussed below.

Thus, if there is a dual spiritual economy [male and female], its two branches are interdependent and complementary" (Lewis 1986 : 106). It seems plausible that just as men's religious devotions count also for their womenfolk (1986 : 106), so women's *zār* devotions might count indirectly for their men. As noted earlier, several male informants confided in 1984 that they believe themselves incurably possessed by *zayran*. These men enjoy listening to spirit rituals from afar or watching *bi shubbāk* ("through a window"), but do not openly attend for fear of ridicule. Such peripheral and vicarious participation echoes that of women at a *zikr*—the "dervish" rite of Islamic fraternities whose membership is exclusively male.

Possession as Illness and as Text

In Hofriyat, possession usually begins as illness, whether spirit induced or spirit intensified. But not all sickness is linked with possession. Villagers consider a variety of ailments to result from natural causes, and only patients whose symptoms are stubborn or fairly generalized are led to suspect *zār* affliction. Persistent headache, nausea, anorexia, lassitude, apathy and depression, sleeplessness, anxiety (*ḥarrāg rūḥ*: "burning soul"), unspecified aches and pains, being easily saddened, fertility problems, all may be ascribed to *zayran*. Here we must also include symptoms resembling those of hysterical conversion disorders in the West: blindness or paralysis of one or more limbs without apparent organic cause, aphonia (see also Nelson 1971 : 203). Though many of these conditions are associated with possession, Hofriyati might also link them to sorcery (*ʿamal*) or the evil eye (*ʿayn ḥārra*), both of which increase susceptibility to spirit attack. Thus, deciding whether one's symptoms are signs of possession, of some other condition—or, indeed, of both—can be problematic for the sufferer.

Moreover, a woman might be inclined to resist a possession diagnosis. It is not necessarily good or desirable to have a spirit. Possession is a lifelong affliction which, however manageable, intensifies the already tangible constraints on her behavior. The rituals and daily observances essential to restore and maintain her health are both costly and time-consuming. Yet even assiduous fulfillment of the spirits' requests cannot guarantee her freedom from further attack. *Zayran* are inherently amoral; their behavior is predictable only in its caprice, despite occasional professions of Islam or well-intentioned bargains struck with humans. Further, since an individual may be host to several different spirits, achieving stability in her relationship with one *zār* does not preclude invasion by another. These factors combine to militate against ready acceptance of possession as the appropriate etiology of dysphoria. And unless a woman has a history of *zār* affliction or oneiric evidence that she is possessed, she must first look elsewhere for relief; not to do so is to risk being thought disingenuous.

Villagers generally approach any illness that is not completely and immediately disabling by testing various etiologic avenues, moving from an initial presumption of organic or natural causes and, eliminating these, through consideration of nonorganic ones. Someone who is sick first takes advice from family members, trying a selection of home remedies (like salt or henna poultices) and available patent medicines (such as aspirin, Contac-C, and Beecham's Powders). Should these prove ineffective, one should next seek a cure from Western medical practitioners. If doctors can find nothing wrong, or if something is wrong but fails to respond to treatment, then nonorganic factors are implicated. Now the individual visits a male religious practitioner, or *faki islām,* who performs an astrological divination.[19] He then consults religious texts and ancient Arabic manuals in an effort to diagnose the complaint. The *faki* specifies whether the prolonged illness is due to sorcery, the evil eye, or possession by *jinn,* then prepares restorative charms and potions. These he ministers to the patient over several visits, along with a liberal sprinkling of paternal or psychically inspired advice. If a *jinn* is implicated and the patient not gravely disturbed, he may perform a minor exorcism, which treatment *zayran* alone among the *jinn* are able to resist.

Hence failure of both Western and Islamic medicine reads as a positive indication that one is possessed by a *zār.* For men, who, as noted, disparage bargaining with spirits, this is where the diagnostic process ends: except in rare cases they do not seek further treatment for *zār* possession. But for women whose symptoms persist, the next step is to consult a (usually female) *zār* practitioner in order to verify the diagnosis and begin to accommodate the spirit responsible. Athough possession by *zayran* is now a foregone conclusion, it is only when the patient is convinced of her condition by others and assured of wide support for the diagnosis that she will accept it publicly and begin to organize a "cure."

Symptoms associated with possession might occur with any number of diseases, whether natural, imputable to human antagonists, or spirit inflicted. Yet most are expressly linked to situations which Hofriyati consider stressful (see also Morsy 1978). Regardless of sex, those in mourning, embroiled in domestic disputes, worried over the welfare of loved ones, or financially troubled might claim to suffer illness (Constantinides 1977). As noted in chapter 3, such somatic expressions of negative affect are culturally appropriate responses in Hofriyat (cf. Kleinman 1980), and consonant with the vectoral disposition of interiority.

Though most villagers somatize emotion, fewer acknowledge their illnesses to be possession. Yet those under stress are thought to be targets of spirit attack and for some, mainly women, an eventual diagnosis of possession is reached. Such admission signals a change of context more profound

19. In this the patient's mother's name is most significant.

than from normalcy to ordinary illness. In the village, illness is an experiential idiom for disorder and threatened selfhood. It is either precipitated by or symptomatic of violated propriety and, like *mushāhara* hemorrhage, originates outside the affected human body. Likewise, illness for the possessed originates not within her body (or self), but outside it. Indeed, the etiology of her dysphoria lies beyond her self's constitutive relationships, beyond even the village and the human realm. Possession illness represents a complete violation of integrity in all its forms: social, spatial, physical. Thus, when a woman acknowledges possession, her context shifts from one that is narrowly governed by the relative precept of interiority to a broader one, which places this orientation squarely in relation to its ultimate converse. The essential Hofriyati dialectic (interiority/exteriority) reiterated in possession takes a form more extreme than in routine, non-*zār* social situations like negotiating marriages. *Zayran* are paragons of otherness; as such the spirit context is one which contextualizes other, mundane contexts (cf. Bateson 1972:304). On these points, more will be said later on and in subsequent chapters. Here it should be noted that possession is an intrusion for which neither the sufferer nor her neighbors, kin, and affines are responsible. Relationships within the realm of the village are thus preserved unrent, despite the apparent source of a woman's difficulty.

An implication here is that successful negotiation of the possession context requires the patient to have or develop considerable cultural awareness. It is thus inapplicable to those who suffer severe psychological disturbance.[20] If the average *zār* patient must be characterized in Western psychological terms, one would have to say that at worst she is mildly neurotic (Constantinides 1977:65) and seeking adjustment to a difficult situation. Certainly, when one considers the character of its initial symptoms, their resistance to biomedicine, and their apparently self-punitive characteristics, it becomes tempting to think of possession as an idiom for the sorts of dysphoria that our culture labels as "neurosis." But this would be inaccurate. Not all who become possessed appear to be neurotic, and many who evince so-called neurotic symptoms are never diagnosed as possessed. Further, if possession is an idiom for certain kinds of illness, the reverse is also true: illness is an idiom for possession (cf. Jilek 1974:32; Kapferer 1983:87–89; Lambek 1981:53). Those who exhibit nondysphoric signs of possession, like having visions of spirits and spirit-related things, are automatically considered ill even if they seem perfectly healthy. This is not because such visions are abnormal in Hofriyat, where the existence of spirits (not only *zayran*) is an undisputed fact and seeing one rare, but not unusual. Rather, the possessed are ill because they are possessed.

Zār adepts in Hofriyat are not eccentric or deviant. Unlike Hausa *bori* enthusiasts (Besmer 1983:18–22), there is little obvious about their

20. See Lewis (1971*a*, chapter 7) for an exhaustive discussion of this issue.

everyday behavior to distinguish them from the nonpossessed. And in contrast to Messing's (1958:1125) observations on the *zār* in Ethiopia, Hofriyati maintain that *zayran* cannot cause psychological incapacitation. Nor can they cause illness to the point of death. Spirits, they argue, would hardly wish their hosts so debilitated that they could neither reveal nor supply the desiderata for which they were possessed. Those whose physical symptoms are severe suffer from natural illness or an affliction wrought by sorcery, the evil eye, or other *jinn*. *Zayran* might well contribute to grave malady if the situation promises gain, but they are never its principal agents. The seriously disturbed, on the other hand, are almost always possessed by malevolent "black" *jinn* or demons (*shawaṭīn*), who are not open to coercion and socialization in the manner of *zayran*. Treatment in such cases is violent exorcism; even women agree that any other therapy would be fruitless.

Possession by a *zār* clearly requires more control on the part of the possessed than those who are severely ill can muster (cf. Crapanzano 1977*a*:15; Lambek 1981:52). Acceptance of the diagnosis initiates a process of accommodation to the affliction, of learning how to be possessed. The recruit must achieve an ability to enter trance. And she must do so while remaining alert to her surroundings, for when her spirit descends she will have to be sensitive to cues from other spirits and the audience of human observers (Bourguignon 1976:41). Moreover, she must internalize the cultural constraints on idiosyncratic behavior during the trance episode (Lambek 1981:50–52). If, for example, a spirit has an aggressive nature—like the Arab swordsman encountered at the outset of this chapter—the possessed must learn to control its aggression, to channel it in acceptable ways so that no one is hurt when the spirit descends. *Zayran* may be unpredictable, but they are not usually malicious.

This leads to an important point: a spirit must make sense to those whom it encounters. And the sense that it makes is a product of human and spirit collaboration. Its enactment by the possessed must refer to the known corpus of spirits and spirit species whose characteristics, though not invariable, are sufficiently constant as to be easily recognized by adepts. The permutations of spirit behavior manifest in a particular host are consistent not with the personality of the possessed (if this happens it is, theoretically, adventitious), but with the personality of the spirit as it has revealed itself to other humans and the possessed herself on former occasions.

However much it resembles a dialogical situation, where a woman, as spirit, converses with her human audience, possession trance is better seen as the production of a text, as a "publication" available to interpretation (cf. Ricoeur 1976, 1979; Lambek 1981). More accurately, it is an idiosyncratic performance that is based on an implicit cultural text and also constructive of it (cf. Becker 1979; Geertz 1973; Kapferer 1983; Obeyesekere 1981). In trance, the possessed produces something, a spirit "text," which takes shape as an event. The text event is structured, bound by rules of production—the state of entrancement, the appropriate stage in ritual action, the known characteristics of spirits—much as works of literature are constructed according to genre. In possession, as in literature, textual meaning has an intentional dimension—what the author means to say—and a semantic one: a text has "sense," or internal coherence, and "reference," or ostensive and nonostensive meaning "in the world" (Ricoeur 1976). Further, though each performance of a possession text is grounded in past information (in past performances, hence other texts), each also takes place in a new context (in a different woman, at a different ceremony, in light of recent occurrences) from which it takes new meaning (Becker 1979: 213). This is in addition to any previously unknown characteristics of a spirit that its current manifestation might introduce.

The intentional meaning of a trance-enacted possession text is often opaque to its readers. As with other textual forms, the creator's motivation, her past, her reasons for producing the piece—in short, her subjectivity—may be overborne by the semantics of the production, remaining implicit and open to interpretation. But the intentional meaning of a possession event is more than usually problematic: here the apparent creator of the text is not, in fact, its author. It is not she who acts but the spirit, an alien existent. Whereas to Western observers the possessed's radical detachment from her performance recalls that of the author from his text in allegorical fiction, as of Swift from Gulliver's narrative, to villagers the situation is reversed: a woman does not act through her spirit, the spirit acts through her.

Still, throughout the performance the audience sees the same individual whom it saw prior to her entrancement. For readers of the event—including the possessed herself—to be convinced it is truly a spirit who engages them, the text performance must be virtually transparent: semantically autonomous, freed from apparent human input. The spirit makes keen use of signs that proclaim its identity. It swaggers, struts, is impolite, gives commands and refuses to answer when addressed, none of which are typical for Hofriyati humans, and women least of all. The spirit reveals characteristics—a gesture; a penchant for a certain food, color, or accoutrement—specific to its type and individual identity. *Zār* being in the human world has all the appearance of a well-staged burlesque; spirits' actions are both exaggerated and cliché. Their stereotypical behaviors direct attention to the semantic pole of meaning, thereby eliminating or suppressing any hint of human motivation.

Thus, what the possessed might wish to articulate through possession lies hidden behind the spirit text; it is not directly related to what she says or does while actively possessed. Her conscious or unconscious motivation must be framed metaphorically, to the extent she has scope to express it—for as we see later on, the possessed is not alone in determining the identities and symbolic associations of her spirits. In trance, cultural meaning is foregrounded—spirit intent and spirit semantics, the product and proof of spirit existence. It is this autonomy of the text from ostensible (here human) motivation which, as Ricoeur (1976 : 31) points out, "opens up the range of potential readers and, so to speak, creates the audience of the text." Opening the text to an indefinite number of readers correspondingly creates the opportunity for multiple readings and interpretations (ibid, p. 32), and here, I will argue, lies the aesthetic and therapeutic power of possession rites. The woman who can successfully enact such dramas becomes progressively familiar with the "roles" she might, as spirit, be called upon to play. But most important, she must be able to bracket her own very substantial concerns in deference to those of the *zār*.[21]

In contrast—and with license—we might regard the behavior of a gravely disturbed individual as focusing on human intent to the neglect of semantic (spirit) coherence and reference. Despite her claim to be *zār* possessed, if she cannot sustain the demand for cultural congruity she will fall by the wayside, classed as misdiagnosed. She is seen to engage in idiosyncratic fantasy, which patently the *zār* is not, or may be accused of "playing" with the spirits and thus provoking their wrath. Alternatively, *zayran*, who have few scruples, may have elected to tease the unfortunate, for to possess her fully would net them little in the way of human delights. Whatever therapeutic benefit the *zār* cult presents to one who is severely disabled, adepts insist she is *kazzaba*—a dissimulator—and does not have a *zār*. Instead, she is likely *majnūna*, possessed by a black *jinn* or demon, the hallmark of which is violent uncontrolled trance and antisocial (not foreignly social) behavior.

He Said, She Said

The identities of a woman and her possessive spirit are categorically distinct. Indeed, it is the task of the curer (*shaykha*) to establish and reaffirm this distinction for both the possessed and the public at large. Yet in practice the separation is not always apparent. An excerpt from Zaineb's possession narrative will help to illustrate my point.

On the fourth day of a wedding some years ago, two women who had grown tired of performing love songs began playfully to sing the chants of certain zayran. *The women had not intended to provoke the spirits, and were surprised when the latter descended into their hosts at the party. Some* zayran *were not amused at having been summoned out of context, and it was decided to hold an impromptu*

21. On this point Lambek (1981 : 52) remarks, "If the spirit expresses the unconscious, it also engages actively in the process of again repressing that unconscious, and it does so in an orderly, culturally established way." See also Bourguignon (1976).

ritual in order to appease them. Zaineb described what took place as spirit after spirit appeared in their midst. (Note that all possessive spirits here are male, and the possessed, female.)

> *My mother's brother's new wife, she began to cry. . . . Then she got up and she said, in a deep voice, "Unless you put on a ceremony for her!" she would not recover. . . . And then He said, "I want a dress like the dress of Zaineb there, and I want henna and incense!" . . . He also said He wanted a white ram. There was another, she was possessed by an Ethiopian* zār. . . . *When she descended* [entered trance] *she said, "You must make Him coffee right now!" They made Him coffee and she drank it . . . and they brought coffee and They drank it and she became quiet and she stopped* [came out of trance]. *Another woman said, "I want . . ." and they did it for her, for this* NyamNyam Kubaida [Azande cannibal spirit]. . . . *She said, "Bring Him meat, raw meat!" She would eat.*

Observe that goods and comestibles were to be obtained for the spirits, but to be worn, consumed, and used by the women they possess. The requests of *zayran* are to be enjoyed by them through the senses of their human hosts. Yet, if it is the spirit who desires, it is not always the spirit who speaks or is thought to speak. Zaineb remarks that her uncle's wife's spirit said, "I want . . .", but elsewhere that *she* said, in a deep (male) voice, "Unless you put on a ceremony for her!" Again, "she said, 'You must make coffee for Him. . . .' They made Him coffee and *she* drank it." Thus, although the identities of host and spirit are distinct and even here remain functionally independent, it appears that they coalesce in possession trance. Both host and spirit are present in the host's body to varying degrees. The host is said to perceive, speak, eat, and perform other activities witnessed by onlookers, yet it is the possessive *zār* who motivates such actions and often its voice which is heard. The personality of the host is submerged in deference to that of the *zār*; however, adepts insist that the host is still there. And her awareness is not diminished: rather, it is heightened in sympathy with the intrusive spirit's identity, for spirit and host exchange experiential domains. I return to this point later on.

The federation of spirit and host may be tacitly recognized, as when Zaineb notes that "they"—spirit and host—drank coffee. Indeed, some of my possessed informants periodically think of themselves as pluralities. On being asked, for example, whether she had mounted a ceremony of her own, Asia replied: "Never yet has this happened. But, if there is a *ḥafla zār* [literally, *zār* party, or ritual] going on in the area, we bathe, we put on perfume, we change into good clothes, and we go over to the ceremony. We descend and then we come back, I myself."

The apparent coalescence of distinct entities in a single human body provides ample possibility for confusion, and possession trance can be a highly ambiguous event. Just which entity is doing what is not always clear to the audience. Were it otherwise, and the spirit alone considered present,

Zaineb would have phrased her remarks rather differently. She would have said, "He said, 'Unless you put on a ceremony for her!'" But she did not. The ambiguity, the risk of confusion is, I think, essential to understanding what possession trance in Hofriyat is all about. For it is precisely this which, in light of the supposed autonomy of the performance, creates a paradox, suggesting a variety of interpretations and allowing both possessed and nonpossessed to make of the event what they wish. When the identities of human and spirit are brought into intimate and potentially perplexing association, they become mutual, transitive metaphors, each contextualizing the other in a negative or complementary sense as well as, perhaps, in a positive one. She is He; she is not He: both are equally descriptive.

So the interpretation of possession trance is never given in the event, despite the fact that certain demands for textual coherence must be met if the episode is to be considered genuine. This lack of precision, so common and so necessary to metaphor (Fernandez 1974), is the creative force of possession in Hofriyat, permitting both host and audience to experience several events simultaneously or, more accurately, to participate in the same event on several different levels at once. Combined with the semantic independence of the performance, it promises that no single message can be pointed to as having been sent by the possessed. Rather, the trance event comprehends a range of potential interpretations that is limited only by readers' imaginations, experience, and cultural expertise.

Diagnosis

The individual who does not suffer grave psychological disturbance and is capable of sustaining in her body the temporary confusion of entities detailed above, whose illness is not alleviated by Western or Islamic therapies, and who perhaps has oneiric evidence of spirit intrusion, still might resist a diagnosis of possession. Though friends and kin will encourage her to accept her plight, she may refuse, claiming a lack of funds to mount the requisite propitiation. Adepts agree that such reluctance will only intensify the spirit's attack until at last the patient concedes. And when she does, she must be more lavish than initially required in order to mollify the spirit(s) affronted by her obstinacy or that of her husband in refusing to sponsor a cure. One who rejects her possession may become convinced should her symptoms worsen or seem unduly prolonged. Here, suggestion feeds the cycle: social pressure to acknowledge the diagnosis could well be an added source of anxiety for one whose initial syndrome is stress related, hence a lodestone to *zayran*.

On the other hand, her resistance verifies that she is acting in good faith, that she does not seek to be possessed, but has become so against her will. Thus it obliquely validates the possession diagnosis. This is important, for if the *zār* is a means to articulate certain problems and experiences, the person who, consciously or not, wishes to utilize it can do so *only* in the context of undesirable, intractable illness. As was earlier suggested, illness is an idiom for possession, much as possession is an idiom for illness. She who dances at a *zār* but has not complained of spirit-related ailments risks being thought an imposter.

There is another side to this coin, which reveals the essential tautology of possession in Hofriyat. I mentioned earlier that various circumstances are thought to increase one's vulnerability to spirit attack. Several commonly mentioned are mourning, smelling foul odors, feeling tired and overworked, being fearful, worried, or anxious, eating "poor" foods rather than "clean" ones, being depressed and physically unwell, shedding vaginal blood. These are considered dangerous, even intolerable conditions and especially jeopardize the ideals and integrity of Hofriyati womanhood. Yet they are not unusual: they are conditions which everyone experiences from time to time. As women are frequently made vulnerable to spirit intrusion, the realization that they could become possessed might precipitate the very illness that is later attributed to *zayran*.

However, where illness and spirits are concerned, Hofriyati are not troubled by what to us would be causal enigmas. Here, cause and effect are not linear, but synchronous (cf. Ohnuki-Tierney 1984: 85). A breach of feminine ideals is either a sign of spirit intrusion or its harbinger: the condition is the same—possession. And *zayran,* remember, are capricious; they are equally apt to possess an already vulnerable woman as to create her vulnerability should they find the prospect of possessing her attractive. Certain circumstances are not caused by *zayran,* among them, death. And when one who is bereaved finds herself afflicted it is likely because in her distraction she has denied her spirits their due. But with other conditions the cause of the affliction is indistinguishable from its effects. If a woman complains of fatigue, her discomfort may be traced to a spirit desirous that she perform certain ritual "work"(*shoghul*) on its behalf, such as smoking a perfumed cigarette or bathing with scented soap. Yet, if her fatigue is not occasioned by a *zār,* it may yet have furnished an opportunity for spirit assault. *Zayran* "inflame" (*itḥarrag*) when their hosts are unwell or otherwise out of sorts. They wish the latter, through whom they experience the human world, to take good care of themselves. Paradoxically, they require their hosts to avoid conditions that provide spirits entry and that spirits themselves might inflict, over which humans have less than complete control.

Zayran are known to enjoy the business of possessing humans. They love cleanliness, beauty, enclosed female bodies, expensive human finery—in short, anything associated with the Hofriyati feminine ideal. *Zayran* are ambivalent in most regards, but single-minded in the pursuit of earthly pleasures. And if thwarted, they can be vindicitive. Regardless of prior contractual arrangements with human hosts, they rarely refrain from intruding into situations that promise them delight. In their hedonism as in other traits, women deem *zayran* to be like husbands, a comparison resumed in subsequent chapters.

When a woman is convinced she is possessed, the diagnosis should be confirmed publicly and formally before a cure is mobilized. She may have been warned in the course of religious therapy that she is bothered by a *rīḥ al-aḥmar,* a "red wind" or *zār.* Alternatively, she might enlist the aid of a *sitt al-ᶜilba*—"lady of the box," a reference to the tin which holds the spirits' incense. The *sitt al-ᶜilba* is a woman known to have prophetic dreams and usually an adept of the *zār.* During consultation she takes a bit of cloth that has been in contact with the patient's body, and a coin, some sweets, or perfume the latter has brought as gifts—items understood in the language of *zār* to be the "keys of dreams" (Constantinides 1977:68). On retiring for the night, the practitioner burns some spirit incense and, while fumigating the objects, chants a *zār* thread that collectively invokes the spirits. Having thus linked her client to the world of *zayran,* she places the objects beneath her pillow. When she wakes, she informs her client whether she dreamt of spirits and, if so, what they desire in return for her rehabilitation—a sacrificial animal of a certain color, a ceremony of a certain length, a specific piece of clothing or jewelry.

A woman's own dreams interpreted by those with knowledge of such matters might confirm a possession diagnosis or alert her to impending spirit attack. A dream of henna, smoke, whiskey, chairs, a man or woman who suggests she wear a certain type of *tōb,* or anything else associated with *zayran,* is a clear indication of possession.

Dream evidence is not the only kind which confirms a possession diagnosis. However rarely, it may happen that a woman becomes spontaneously entranced (*ghabiyāna,* "unconscious" or "absent") for the first time outside a possession ritual context. When this occurs, a *shaykha* is summoned—an adept who, over time, has cultivated mature, relatively controlled relationships with the several *zayran* by which she is possessed. The *shaykha,* whose title implies religious or political authority,[22] can appeal for her spirits' assistance when diagnosing an illness or coaxing a recalcitrant *zār* to reveal itself in her client's body. An aspiring *shaykha*—who might also practice as a *sitt al-ᶜilba*—learns her art by apprenticing with an established curer, often a close maternal kinswoman. The proclivity itself tends to be handed down in the maternal line: a woman whose mother or mother's sister is a *shaykha* is more likely than others to become one herself. During her apprenticeship she learns how to call the spirits,

22. In chapter 1 I noted that the political role of *shaykh* in Hofriyat is an achieved position with very limited power. However, the term is also applied to leaders of religious brotherhoods who are considered to have considerable *baraka,* or divine blessing.

bargain with them, recognize their characteristics and demands. But having done so, she does not proclaim herself a *shaykha;* others will attribute her this status as her reputation as a curer grows.

On arrival at the patient's home the *shaykha* censes the entranced while calling on the intrusive *zār* to manifest and identify itself. If successful, the *shaykha*—who is not in trance at this time—converses with the spirit in an attempt to discover its requests, important clues to its identity. Should the *zār* fail to speak, she at least hopes to discern its species by gauging its response to different types of fumigation: each spirit society has its own combination of incense "medicine" to which its members respond with increased physical activity.

Muteness on the part of a spirit is not unusual at first, especially if the patient is a novice. Even during public ceremonies a spirit's initial manifestation in a host is tentative and unlikely to be articulate. It grunts or screams, or speaks its own—foreign—language (*roṭāna* or "gibberish"). But as spirit and *shaykha* negotiate, the spirit should become increasingly communicative and start speaking to the *shaykha* in Arabic. It is during this process, which may take several hours or even days, that the patient begins to learn how to be possessed, how to conduct herself in trance. Like her illness, the spirit intruder assumes coherent shape and character as the *shaykha*'s questions are assimilated, her hints or suggestions—and those of other villagers—confirmed or modified. The spirit and its influence on the patient gain elemental concreteness in the dialogues between healer and *zār,* between healer, other Hofriyati, and unentranced human host. The patient, of course, has prior knowledge of *zayran,* their attributes and powers. Since childhood she has attended their rituals and among her kin are several who are possessed. Thus, both neophyte and *shaykha* are guided in negotiations with the spirit by a shared, though at this point unequal competence in the *zār.* A woman's subjective recognition that she is truly possessed emerges as a product of social discourse involving herself, curer, spirit, and ultimately the entire community. Gradually such conversations naturalize the spirit's existence within or "above" her body.

Should the *shaykha* initially fail to draw an afflicting spirit into dialogue, she may call for a *zār* test (*tajruba*), a trial drumming held indoors on three consecutive nights. The *ʿayāna* (patient, "sick woman") meets with the *shaykha* and other adepts, who together perform the repertoire of *zār* incantations or "threads" (*khuyūṭ*). The test is a miniature healing ceremony: incense is burnt, cologne and other spirit items are made available to the patient, spirits are invited to descend into their hosts one by one as their chants are played. The *shaykha* directs close attention to the patient, noting songs during which she appears uncomfortable and agitated, or her movements become impossibly quick.

Chances are good that the patient will now go into trance and her spirit identify itself by its chant. But should this fail to occur, *zār* possession is hardly ruled out. Perhaps the spirit declines to appear because the patient has not yet accepted her possession. Alternatively, it may not wish to place its cards on the table so soon: it might insinuate its presence but hold off bargaining until it receives assurances that a full-scale ceremony will be held and some of its demands will be met.

Clearly, once a *shaykha* has been summoned, possession is a foregone conclusion: the patient has little choice but eventually to acquiesce. More than this, it is deemed essential to her recovery that she become entirely convinced of her spirit's presence. The *shaykha*'s task is twofold: to awaken in the patient a subjectively felt recognition of the alien within, and to give assurances that the woman's personality and her spirit's are separate and distinct. They key to the healing process lies in building up the possessive *zār*'s identity and establishing this firmly in the minds of all concerned. The spirit should become manifest, publicly, coherently, as part of a woman's person that is not, so to speak, a part of her self. Though exogenous to her self, from now on it is linked inextricably to that self and becomes increasingly essential to its comprehension (cf. Young 1975 : 578). The process is a parallel socialization: just as the patient is gradually socialized to accept possession as the source of her affliction and to construe both past and future experiences in its light, so the *zār* is socialized, first to communicate with humans, then to contract a mutually beneficial agreement with the *shaykha,* who acts on the patient's behalf.

Importantly, the patient's acknowledgment of possession and her family's promise to mount a cure are often followed by a notable remission of her symptoms—if not their underlying cause. Thus her curing ceremony might take place, if at all, months or even years after the initial illness has abated. Public acceptance of one's possession is itself therapeutic, taking the urgency out of having to undergo a "cure" (Boddy 1988). It has what Tambiah (1977 : 124) refers to as a "performative effect": it shifts her illness to another (nonordinary) plane of discourse and, so doing, transforms it, effects a change of state. Those who accept that they are possessed are, in villagers' eyes, truly possessed; they are adepts of the *zār* whether or not they have been "cured."

Zār *as Antilanguage*

In becoming socialized to her possession, a woman begins to internalize an alternate reality to that of quotidian life. She becomes increasingly familiar, in an experiential sense, with the vocabulary of the *zār,* which is derived from that of daily life but constitutes a metaphoric variation on its themes. The language of the *zār* reflects what is, in essence, a counterreality, wherein salient social values and cultural orientations are played with, reassessed, weighted differently than in everyday life, opened up to other interpretations. This transformative process is described more thoroughly and concretely in subsequent chapters. Here I wish to point out that the *zār* world is in many respects like an "antisociety," and its language an "antilanguage" in the sense proposed by Halliday (1976).

An "anti-society," writes Halliday (1976 : 570), is a society, like that of a criminal underworld, "set up within another society as a conscious alternative to it." Following Gramsci (1971), and more specifically Williams (1977), an antisociety can be seen as counterhegemonic: it formulates an alternative view of the world in response to an elite's implicit domination of discourse, represented in Hofriyat by the ideology of Islam which legally and materially privileges men. The subaltern group which constitutes an antisociety is nonetheless constrained by the system of meanings it shares with society at large; yet it is concerned to articulate those meanings from its own, unprivileged, perspective (cf. Bakhtin (1981) on heterology; also Messick 1987).[23]

Halliday analyzes antisocieties in terms of Berger and Luckmann's (1966 : 152ff.) insights on the role of conversation in maintaining and creating an individual's subjective reality through continuous socialization. That subjective reality must be maintained through conversation implies that it can be transformed (ibid, p. 156). A transformation of one's subjective reality Berger and Luckmann (ibid., p. 157) term an "alternation", and this, to be successful, requires processes of resocialization, again involving conversation. Alternation to an antisociety requires an antilanguage—a distorted reflection of the language characteristic to the society from which it derives—to generate and maintain its alternative reality (Halliday 1976 : 573–74).

One of the most obvious forms of alternation is religious conversion which, on the face of things, one might think is what is happening when a woman becomes subjectively convinced she is possessed via conversations with curers and other Hofriyati. But this would be incorrect. The possessed does not experience the sort of large-scale transformation of her subjective reality that conversion implies, for she continues to function within the monistic world of Hofriyat, its meanings are still meaningful to her, she is no less a Muslim for being possessed by *jinn*. Rather, her subjective reality gains a dimension that allows her to contextualize what she formerly took for granted. She might well undergo what Bateson (1982 : 4) refers to as deuterolearning, a "learning about the self that results in a change in the self," enabling her to apprehend the broader context of the contexts which engulf her (Bateson 1972 : 159ff., 304 ff.) and of the dispositions she embodies. She might experience a subtle shift of conscious-

23. For a provocative example of a Western feminist antilanguage that attempts to recapture patriarchally suppressed etymological significances of English words in formulating a women's perspective, see Mary Daly's work, especially *The Wickedary* (1987). See also Luce Irigaray (1985).

ness. Here I think Halliday's observations on the different processes of resocialization are singularly helpful:

> It is a characteristic of an anti-language that it is not just an ordinary language which happens to be for certain individuals a language of resocializing. Its conditions of use are different from the types of alternation considered by Berger and Luckmann, such as forms of religious conversion. In such instances an individual takes over what for others is *the* reality; for him it involves a transformation, but the reality itself is not inherently of this order. It is *somebody's* ordinary, everyday, unmarked reality, and its language is *somebody's* "mother tongue." An anti-language, however, is nobody's "mother tongue"; it exists solely in the context of *re*socialization, and the reality it creates is inherently an alternate reality, one that is constructed precisely in order to function in alternation. It is the language of an anti-society. (Halliday 1976 : 575, emphasis in the original)

In subsequent pages we shall witness several dimensions along which the *zār* cult can be viewed as an antisociety, a counterhegemonic reality opposed to the everyday norm. As Halliday notes, it is not the distance between the two realities—quotidian and extraordinary—that is significant here, but the continual *tension* between them. Indeed, as the one is a metaphorical variant of the other, the distance between them may not be great. And an individual is unlikely to bridge it just once, as in successful religious conversion, but countless times, switching "back and forth between society and anti-society, with varying degrees of intermediate standing" (Halliday 1976 : 576).[24]

The *zār,* in this sense, is a muted expression of women's alternate reality (cf. Ardener 1975; Messick 1987). Though obliquely conveyed through the ascendant social paradigm (Islam)dominated by men, the *zār* contains a metaphorical transformation of quotidian reality that resituates it in light of women's special concerns. Yet women who are possessed still participate in the everyday world with other Hofriyati, still adhere to Muslim beliefs and are versed in the dominant masculine ideology, still share with men a view of themselves as symbols of local tradition. If the *zār* permits them to gain new perspective on their lives, it by no means wholly supplants the old. Yet the *zār* differs from the context of daily life in a critical sense: for if it recontextualizes quotidian reality, it must be located at a different hierarchic level than that which it speaks about (cf. Bateson 1972 : 274ff.; also Geertz 1973 : 443). Like other antilanguages, *zār* is a form of social discourse that is also *meta*cultural, and it is this which allows

24. However, in a recent article Cucchiari (1988) suggests that the actual experience of religious conversion is by no means instantaneous, despite idioms representing it as such. Instead, Sicilian converts he has studied undergo a gradual process of maturing and gaining insight into their selves and social contexts, or becoming (not yet being) full adherents to the faith. In this sense, conversion is a process similar to that which I describe for possession.

those possessed to view their world from, as it were, "without." Subsequent chapters are essentially devoted to examining the *zār*'s metacultural, counterhegemonic potential. The broadening of women's consciousness it encourages and obliquely expresses is addressed in chapters 9 and 10.

The "Cure"

Once she accepts her possession, a woman agrees to hold a *zār* ritual, the exact date of which remains undetermined until she has amassed sufficient funds. Her husband should be willing to contribute, but should he refuse, her sons and brothers might assist lest the cure be stymied.[25] The expenses of a rural *zār* may be in the neighborhood of £S 100 to £S 200, or between US $50 and US $100 in 1984, depending on the nature of the rite: if it is her first it must be longer and more elaborate than any she need mount in future. (Interestingly, this parallels the distinction between a woman's first wedding, as a virgin bride, and any later remarriage.) Whatever money is collected goes to buy incense and cologne for the ceremony, tea, cigarettes, liquor, and beer (at least before the imposition of *sharīʿa* law in 1983), a sacrificial animal, plus specific demands of the spirit to be appeased: new clothing, jewelry, household goods, or special foods for the afflicted to consume on its behalf. The cost of a *zār* is certainly high in relation to the resources of most Hofriyati, who subsist on remittances or uncertain income from farming. Yet it is not so high as in the cities where the cult is formally organized;[26] nor does it rival the expense of a wedding. As occurs at other village-wide events, those who attend can be expected to help defray costs by bringing sugar or some other small gift for the patient's household.

In the possession antilanguage, the patient during her ceremony is referred to as the "bride" (*ʿarūs*) of the *zār*, inviting comparison with the wedding. Throughout the event (which, odd numbers being propitious, lasts one, three, five, or seven days) she remains, like a virgin bride, in virtual seclusion, communicating with no one who is not directly involved in her cure. Unless her husband is also possessed—which is unlikely—she avoids him altogether. She must abstain from sex and do no physical work. Others cook for her, care for her children except those not yet weaned,[27] clean her house and supply it with cooking fuel and water. It is imperative

25. In the case of a divorced woman or, very rarely, one who has not yet married, brothers and fathers are the principal source of support for a *zār*.

26. I was told by Hofriyati migrants that a *zār* held in Khartoum might cost the equivalent of US $500 or more, representing three to five times the average monthly wage for Hofriyati in the city.

27. A baby nursed during his mother's spirit illness is also possessed by her afflicting *zār*; being intimately associated with her body, he is not yet an autonomous human, available to be possessed in his own right.

that apart from a trip to the Nile on the day after the sacrificial meal, she stay within the walls of her *ḥōsh,* and limit her activities for a further week after completion of the rite.

On each day of the ceremony, adepts gather at the patient's home or, less commonly, in that of the officiating *shaykha*. The time to start "beating the *zār*" varies with the weather, but things rarely get under way before late afternoon. The entertainment-*cum*-devotion-*cum*-therapy extends well into the night; women leave for a few moments now and then to pray, prepare their families' evening meals, or put young children to bed. Drumming and dancing may continue until dawn.

Although the ritual is meant to take place inside a room, if the night is hot or a crowd is expected it may be staged out of doors, yet still within the *ḥōsh*. All such curing ceremonies have the same basic form, but as each occasion is different there may be variations in the order of spirits summoned or other details of performance. What follows here is therefore a generalization.

When participants and musicians are assembled, the patient is led forth and seated on a mat. If this is her first *zār* she is dressed in white, as is a virgin bride; but her garment is usually a *jalabīya,* the long, loose shirt worn by men. Over it are placed two strips of red cloth forming an *X* across her chest; these are attached to a red sash at her waist, as described for the *ʿayāna* at the beginning of this chapter. *Zayran* are known as red winds or red *jinn,* as opposed to malevolent spirits whose color is black.

The patient faces east, the direction of Mecca, or—as happens more often in Hofriyat—she faces the *khashm al-bayt,* the "front" or men's door of the *ḥōsh*. Musicians, who are always adepts and never, in the village, professionals, are positioned to the left of the *ʿayāna* with their instruments: drums (*dallūkas*), a shallow aluminum washtub (*ṭisht*), brass mortar (*nugarishan*), and one or more empty jerry cans (*jarikāna*). The *shaykha* takes her place on the patient's right. Other attendants sit facing each other on mats laid in two rows adjoining that of the patient at right angles, with a space left between them to form the *mīdān,* the arena for spirit theatrics. Thus the party is arranged in the shape of a *U* whose opening is commonly oriented toward the principal door, an important symbol both in the everyday life of Hofriyat and the more esoteric context of possession.

When all humans are settled, a lighted censer is passed among the gathering; each woman fumigates her body orifices which, as noted earlier, are potential entrance points for spirits. The drumming begins. Blessings are first requested from the Prophet and several well-known Muslim saints (*walīs*). Next the *zayran* are marshaled by a chant addressed to them as a group. The spirits are now ready and waiting to enter the *mīdān;* the musicians begin to play the "threads" appropriate to each in turn, in order of its social group.

One by one, *zayran* descend, appear, and take their leave. The atmosphere is lively: a host responds to her spirits' chants by rocking to and fro or bobbing up and down from a kneeling position, moving ever more rapidly as she enters trance and the spirit takes control. If she has had her own ceremony she rises to her feet, allowing the *zār* to manifest its characteristics. A number of women may be possessed by the same spirit and will exhibit it simultaneously. A well-behaved spirit relinquishes its hosts' bodies when its chant is over and the rhythm shifts to that of another *zār*. But should it be tenacious and reluctant to quit, the *shaykha* attempts to draw it into conversation. She coaxes it to state its desires and bargains with it should these prove outrageous. Since an adept may be possessed by several different spirits, a woman is likely to be in and out of trance all night as her various spirits descend and manifest themselves for roughly twenty minutes each.

The *ʿayāna* or *ʿarūs* is expected to become entranced in this way at some point in the proceedings, and certainly before the final night of drumming. When her afflicting spirit (or spirits) descends into her as its chant is being sung, the cure can begin in earnest. Onlookers, kin, and curers, led to suspect the identity of the spirit because of diagnostic indications, now have their suspicions confirmed or, indeed, challenged. Should the patient respond in trance to more than one thread this need present no problem: hers is a case of multiple possession, more common than rare. Yet the spirit most strongly expressed in ritual trance is generally held responsible for her current illness and must be pacified.

Identifying the spirit antagonist is a crucial development, necessary to both the patient's recovery and further ritual action. Once labeled, the formerly diffuse and uncommunicative spirit is brought firmly within the realm of the choate. As the spirit's character is revealed and its identity verified, its presence is temporarily reduced to human proportions. Correspondingly, the patient's subjective experience—her problem or illness—is articulated: objectified and externalized. It, too, assumes a choateness that it formerly did not have. The spirit responsible for the affliction becomes accessible, open to dialogue with human curers and, through their mediation, the patient herself. For now it has been partially socialized, drawn into the Hofriyati world in a controlled, orderly manner far removed from the disruptive context where first it made its presence felt. The patient's trance experience is a sign that all parties in the matter of her illness—patient, curers, kin, and spirits—are open to communication. The *zār*'s newly revealed identity is like a password: it announces the code in terms of which meaningful negotiation can take place.

Through all of this the patient's illness undergoes further transformation, bringing to fruition the process begun when she publicly accepted the possession diagnosis. The illness, originally seeming to arise from within the possessed or her community, is now proved to derive from without. The patient's condition is considered to meliorate once she has internalized this fact (before or during her cure); however, recovery is not deemed complete until after the sacrificial meal on the final evening.

The intrusive *zār* requires the slaughter of a sheep or goat for the covenant with its host to be finalized. This animal must have colors and markings that accord with the spirit's type; for example, if the spirit is an Ethiopian, an animal with reddish wool should be provided since red is the color associated with that spirit group (cf. Besmer [1983 : 7] on the Hausa *bori*). The sacrificial animal is elaborately readied. First, it is washed and its head and back are stained with henna. Then it is led into the *mīdān* and, while held before the unentranced patient, draped with a *garmosīs,* the red and gold cloth whose primary function is to veil a bride at her wedding. A smoking censer is thrust beneath the cloth as adepts address a chant to all *zayran*. The performance is considered a success if the animal bobs its head up and down (as it tends to do in trying to break free) in the manner of a woman in trance. This reads as a sign that the spirit accepts the sacrificial transaction.

Afterward the animal is led out of the *mīdān* where it is killed by a man, frequently the only adult male permitted to attend the ceremony. In slaughtering the animal, the man takes a coin in his mouth to prevent him from saying "in the name of God" (*b'ism Allāh*) as he would normally do. The invocation is inappropriate to the *zār,* as it is feared that on hearing the name of Allah the spirits would flee the ceremony (see also Nelson 1971 : 200). Yet, given the significance of Islam, the act can also be considered counterhegemonic.

When the animal's throat has been slit, some of its blood is collected in a bowl. The patient steps over the carcass and blood-soaked earth seven times—a mystically significant number which figures in other ceremonial contexts (such as weddings) and in the wider system of Islam—then she resumes her place in the *mīdān*. The *shaykha* uses the victim's blood to anoint the patient's forehead, painful or troublesome areas of her body, and clothing. The bowl then passes to other adepts who anoint themselves in similar fashion, or take a sip—expressly forbidden by Islam—and place a piaster or two on top. In the course of such events the *zār* is both linked to and distinguished from Islam and other village ceremonies.

A sacrificial meal of meat, bread, rice, and spicy broth is prepared by the patient's female kin and neighbors, and all in attendance are invited to partake. The dish, called *fatta,* is the same as that served at a *karāma* ("generosity, favor, mercy": a public sacrificial meal held to thank Allah for good fortune[28]), providing yet another association with non-*zār* ceremonial contexts. Here, however, the bones and head of the animal are reserved for use in a ritual the following day, along with the blood-caked bowl. After dinner more chants are drummed as the party gradually disbands.

28. To indicate some reasons for a *karāma,* I attended one staged by the family of a man who survived a terrible traffic accident in Jiddah, another by a labor émigré whose wife's stolen gold was recovered, and a third for a woman who had come through difficult surgery.

Next morning the *shaykha*, patient, and several adepts meet again in the *ḥōsh* where the *zār* was held. Threads are drummed and the spirits invoked with incense. Then the *shaykha* performs the *fakka-t-ar-rās*, the "opening" or "disjointing of the head." The head of the sacrificial animal, which was boiled the night before, is brought out on a tray. As others hold the tray above the patient's head, the *shaykha* pulls apart the victim's jaws. The patient is now made to eat the "head meat"—especially the brain and sensory organs (though not, I am told, the eyes).

Following this comes a procession to the Nile with a basket containing the victim's bones, the blood-caked bowl, and some sweets. On arriving at the riverbank, the officiating *shaykha* and the "bride" of the *zār* wade into the water to wash their faces, arms, and legs. The contents of the basket are released into the river, and the bloody bowl is rinsed. All return to the patient's home.

There the patient changes clothing, perfumes herself, and moves to a room other than the one she has occupied throughout the drumming. Incense is lit, and her body orifices smoked a final time. The *zār* is now concluded; however, the patient is still in a vulnerable state and admonished to remain in semiseclusion, avoiding her husband for a further seven days. Her possession is now said to become "cool" (cf. Al Hadi 1987: 94).

Having acceded to her spirit's desires and staged a ritual, the woman hopes her future will be untroubled by *zayran*. Yet she is enjoined to vigilance: she must be continually attentive to her spirits, perform such daily "work" as they require, avoid dirt, and refrain from negative emotion. Failure to do so will provoke relapse. Possession, remember, cannot be cured, only managed. And its management is an ongoing process of spirit socialization and human accommodation, optimistically expressed as exchange. Just as humans are variable and imperfect and, for one or another reason might neglect the *zayran*, so *zayran*, inherently less reliable than humans, can never be socialized completely. Despite her diligence a woman might at any time be struck by possession illness merely because it is a spirit's whim. It is a comment on both human and spirit natures that relationships between individuals can be ambiguous and easily perverted through carelessness or self-seeking behavior.

The Cult

In the larger towns and cities of Sudan the *zār* is an organized cult, composed of a number of independent coteries. Structurally, these appear to be feminine counterparts of Islamic fraternities like the Qadriya and Khatmiya, and they often employ similar emblems, such as flags (see Barclay 1964; Constantinides 1972, 1977, 1982). Moroever, in Khartoum and Omdurman there are a number of full-time, professional *zār* practitioners—male (homosexuals and therefore sexually neutral) and female—who are well paid for their services and attract large followings of the possessed. Several maintain clinic-like establishments where patients can reside while undertaking therapy, and they exercise considerable authority over those to whom they minister. Some city *shaykhat* (plural) are entrepreneurs in the business of selling *zār* paraphernalia—clothing and accessories—with which the spirits demand that their hosts attire themselves upon "descent." In these regards, the city cult differs from the rural in Hofriyat. Yet in both, a *shaykha* learns her art by apprenticeship, and is more likely to take it up if preceded in the vocation by a maternal relative.

Rural *shaykhat,* like their urban sisters, are charismatic, yet notably less jealous and competitive in professional stance. They neither presume authority over their clientele nor object if other curers are called in to deal with a difficult case. Remuneration is minimal, scaled to what the *ʿayāna* feels she can afford. A *shaykha* who presides at a ceremony can expect to find £S 5–10 placed beneath the *ṭisht,* which she must share with those who help her drum. In addition she receives a few piasters from each adept who attends, and may be gifted further by a grateful patient if the ritual proves successful. All such donations are, however, voluntary; unlike city *shaykhat,* those in the village stipulate no set fees for their work.[29]

In Hofriyat the group of *zār* adepts is informally organized; the possessed are linked by kinship, common residence, ethnicity and mutual concern rather than shared allegiance to a curer. Their relationships are, in Gluckman's (1955 : 18–19) terms, multiplex: as opposed to city adepts, they interact in a plethora of day-to-day contexts distinct from the *zār.* In cities, cult membership is broadly based and, at least initially, consists in an aggregate of autonomous curer-client relationships; contacts among adepts are generally ephiphenomenal, however much they intensify after the adepts have joined a curer's group (Constantinides 1982). On the other hand, relationships among rural possessed always antecede their involvement with the *zār.* The informality of the rural cult is therefore inevitable and precludes local *shaykhat* from adopting a strictly professional attitude toward their patients. All adepts are intimately acquainted with each other's circumstances, financial resources, and domestic difficulties. While this state of affairs facilitates the diagnostic process, it might also hinder the resocialization "cure" by eliminating some of the healer's mystique.

Spirits

Up to now I have referred to *zayran* in general terms, noting that they are also called "winds" (*rīḥ, rowḥān*)—specifically, *red* winds (*rīḥ al-aḥmar*)—

29. The notable exception is the only male curer in the vicinity, considered in chapter 7.

and are considered to be a class of *jinn*. *Zayran* are essentially amoral, capricious, hedonistic, and self-indulgent. Significantly, by these qualities they exemplify what villagers are not, or ought not to be.

In like manner, *zayran* originate in locales exotic to that of the village. Not only are they nonhuman existents, they belong in addition to the spirit counterparts of non-Hofriyati ethnic groups. While these points will be dealt with in greater detail later on, it should be noted here that the *zār* world invisibly parallels the human. Differences among spirit societies roughly correspond to differences among human cultures. And every *zār* society contains several individually named spirits, each of which has some distinctive trait that marks it off from others of its type. Societies and, within societies, spirits themselves are distinguished by such considerations as style and color of dress, typical gestures and demeanor during trance descent, ceremonial demands, and illnesses most likely caused to humans. When invoked during a ritual, *zayran* appear sequentially as their threads are drummed in the following general (and not immutable) order: Holy Men (and women) (*Darāwīsh*); Ethiopians (*Ḥabish*); Westerners or Europeans—including North Americans, Hindus, and Chinese (*Khawājāt*); Pashas or Egyptian, Turkish, and British colonial officials (*Bashawāt*); desert nomads (*ʿArāb*); Syrian tinkers or gypsies (*Ḥalib*); West Africans, including western Sudanese (*Fallata*); southern Sudanese and black Africans (*ʿAbīd*, or *Khudām*) among whom may be counted witches and crocodiles, said to be Azande (*Sāḥar, Nyam Nyam*) from Juba in the Sudd (see map, p. 2).

Conclusion

In this chapter I have outlined salient features of the *zār* in Hofriyat, erecting a scaffold on which to construct further discussion of possession contexts, links between the discourses of daily life and possession, and the metacultural significance of *zār* as a system of knowledge. A number of subjects I have raised will soon be readdressed, expanded, and reworked, for an interpretation of possession in Hofriyat must be multidimensional, like the *zār* itself. When viewed from a single angle—social, psychological, medical, aesthetic—it appears flat, incomprehensible. As in the photographic image of a sculpture or other deeply textured work, its reality is reduced to a single phenomenal plane and intricate relationships among its constituent parts are distorted by a lack of depth and proportion. But by shifting our view among the *zār*'s dimensions, it may be possible to partially correct for this restriction, to construct a more holographic image which conveys some sense of the system's potential and complexity.

5

Possession, Marriage, and Fertility

If, as I have asserted, spirit possession in Hofriyat is an idiom for the articulation of a certain range of experience (cf. Crapanzano 1977*a*), what generalizations can be made about the experiences of those who publicly acknowledge themselves to be possessed? In chapter 4, I noted that between 42 percent (1977) and 47 percent (1984) of Hofriyati women who are or were ever married have succumbed to the affliction. Marital status is a significant factor here, for spirits, villagers assert, rarely trouble themselves with the unwed. The connection between women who have been espoused and the incidence of possession is explicitly stated by villagers themselves. I once asked a betrothed girl of fifteen if she had a spirit. "I think so," she replied, "but I won't really know until I'm married." Her companions concurred.

But the issue here is not the state of marriage itself: it is what marriage signifies. In the village there are several unwed women aged twenty-five or more, well beyond the average age for first marriage (fifteen to twenty). One of these, an invalid from birth, is exceptional in having been officially diagnosed as possessed and having drummed the *zār*. Four others, one an invalid of twenty-five, and three otherwise healthy women in their thirties or early forties, privately affirmed a spirit affliction, yet none wished to acknowledge this formally or undertake a cure because of the public implications.[1] A single woman is, they say, *khajlāna*, abashed or ashamed to admit she might have spirits. And this is because, properly, possession is associated with the loss of virginity. *Zār* is the province of women whose fertility has been activated, not merely of women who are married, for one may be widowed or divorced when initially diagnosed as possessed. Thus, a woman's first wedding does more than transfer her reproductive potential to an appropriate male or establish her social adulthood by giving her the means to exercise her generative powers; it also establishes her as legitimately possessible by spirits. Here again one sees an implicit link between the actions of husbands and *zayran*.

1. These five represent approximately 10 percent of women aged fifteen and over who have never been married, and 28 percent of that population aged twenty-five or more (N = 18).

Even if an unattached woman realizes the presence of *zayran* above her, she is confident they will not trouble her greatly until she is wed. Spirits know how little is to be gained by afflicting a virgin: one of their principal targets is fertility, regardless of what symptoms they cause. Given enforced premarital chastity, a single woman should neither comprehend nor suffer from threats to her reproductive ability. Seizing a virgin would therefore be counterproductive for a *zār*, netting it little in the way of earthly delights.

The association between activated female fertility and possession is also expressed negatively, in the case where a virgin (*fatā*) spontaneously goes into trance outside the *zār* ceremonial context. As was previously discussed, spirits are known to "play" with virgins who attend possession rituals, and encouraged by the rhythmic drumming, some of them do enter trance. But it sometimes happens that a virgin becomes entranced without such prompting, and when it does, the malady is not considered a portent of *zār* possession. On the assumption that the girl is otherwise mentally sound, thus not possessed by black *jinn*, her problem is diagnosed as a kind of "love sickness" (*maraḍ al-ḥubb*), something which also afflicts young men. Yet "love sickness" is imprecise, for it is not love the girl is said to crave, but sex. Knowing the premium that villagers place on fertility, I asked my friends if this was because the victim was anxious to become pregnant. No, they said, a desire for sexual intercourse itself is the cause of her illness. Its cure must be marriage, arranged as quickly—and quietly—as possible. The discriminations between virgin women, sexuality, and the *zār* verify and support an association of possession with activated fertility.

Zayran are held responsible for numerous fertility disorders. They are known to "hold" or "seize" (*masak*) the womb in order to prevent generative feminine blood from mixing with semen and forming a child. Alternatively, they might "loosen" (*ḥall*) a fetus so as to precipitate miscarriage. Again, in considering the *mushāhara* complex, I noted that *jinn*, and specifically *zayran*, are drawn to genital blood and body openings and may bring about unstaunchable hemorrhage and sterility.

Among the *zayran*, several spirits in particular are associated with reproductive abnormality. The Dervish spirit *ʿAbdalgadir al-Jaylani* is *zār* counterpart to the popular Baghdadi holy man (died A.D. 1166), who is a focus of appeal for barren women throughout the Muslim world. Hofriyati regularly invoke the powers of this human saint, the supplicant pledging to sacrifice a goat in his honor if her debility is assuaged. On the other hand, and in keeping with the amorality of *zayran*, the *zār* parallel of Jaylani is said to have considerable power to inflict as well as correct fertility problems: only the *zār* causes the problem it also amends.

Ethiopian *zayran* are especially linked to fertility disorders. Not only do they effect such symptoms in their human hosts, but the group itself includes several characters who exemplify aberrant fertility and perverse sexuality. The spirits *Banāt Jozay* are twins, but female, indicative of extremely potent fertility that has produced inappropriate results. *Lulīya Ḥabishīya* is an Ethiopian prostitute *zār* who poses as a virgin Hofriyati bride. And *Sulayman Ya Janna* is a male homosexual spirit from the Ethiopian border with Sudan[2] whose name, Sulayman O Veiled One, is a pun with feminine connotations: the similar sounding word *janā* (fruit or harvest) is a euphemism for offspring.

Characteristics of the Possessed

Given that the *zār* is closely linked with fertility, how do the women in Hofriyat who are possessed differ from those who are not? Are we to assume that between 53 and 58 percent of the female population never experiences fertility problems? The answer is not so obvious. Fertility is, as we shall see, a major concern of women who suffer from possession, but it is not the only one. And the context of fertility dysfunction appears to be a more significant factor than the fact of dysfunction itself. From an observational perspective it will soon become clear that stress and anxiety over fertility and all that its demonstration means within sexually asymmetric Hofriyat—material security, attaining and preserving a valued social status that gives one power over others in later life—are some of the most common experiences women articulate via the idiom of possession (cf. Morsy 1978).

But a caveat is in order: although data presented in the next few pages come closest to portraying what those of the "status deprivation" school (see Lewis 1966, 1971*a*, *b*, 1986; Gomm 1975; Morsy 1978; Wilson 1967) consider an appropriate approach to possession, they comprehend only one facet of the *zār*. Such information is epidemiological in nature: it should not be seized upon as the "objective" explanation for women's possession behavior; nor does it necessarily correspond to women's individual intentions in appropriating the spirit idiom. Fertility problems do figure in motivations for acknowledging possession, but only when situated in a context that has both cultural implications and personal (perhaps unconscious) significance for the possessed. In what follows, I briefly depart from an interpretive stance in order to consider in general terms the characteristics of possessed and nonpossessed women in Hofriyat. The next two chapters contextualize these figures with examples from life histories of the possessed.

Through census interviews conducted during two periods of field-

2. He is also classed as an *ʿArab*.

Table 5.1. Populations of Ever-Married Women in Hofriyat, 1977 and 1984

	Population Years				
	1977		1984		New Cases of
Status in 1984	Possessed (N = 54)	Other (N = 75)	Possessed (N = 63)	Other (N = 72)	Possession (N = 16)
Remained in Hofriyat (N = 95)	41	54	54	41	13
Deceased before 1984 (N = 14)	6	8	—	—	—
Moved away (N = 20)	7	13	—	—	—
Married between 1977 and 1984 (N = 29)	—	—	2	27	2
Former residents returned to village (N = 11)	—	—	7	4	1

work, I obtained reproductive and marital information concerning the 129 ever-married women whose principal residence in 1977 was Hofriyat, and updated this in selected areas with the histories of all 135 ever-married resident women in 1984, 40 of whom were not included in the earlier tabulation (table 5.1). The two populations therefore differ in composition by roughly 30 percent; later figures also reflect any changes in marital status, reproductive history, and possession affliction for the original population still living in Hofriyat on my return. However, they do not take into account economic distinctions, which are poorly developed in Hofriyat: there are few differences of wealth among villagers, and those that exist are weak and often transitory. Some families own a bit more land than others; some have a greater proportion of members working for wages outside the village. But any such distinctions fall within a range that makes it impossible to differentiate among the two populations of ever-married women on the basis of class.

Nonetheless, the results show some slight, but interesting contrasts between those who acknowledge possession and those who do not. For one thing, the first marriages of nonpossessed women tend to have been more stable than those of the possessed: only one in seven (1977) and one in nine (1984) nonpossessed women has been married more than once, where for the possessed this figure is more than one in three for both fieldwork years (table 5.2).

Moreover, at some point in their lives, possessed women are more likely than their nonpossessed sisters to have experienced divorce or separation involving withdrawal of financial support. Table 5.2 shows that

Table 5.2. Marital Histories of Possessed and Nonpossessed Women (percentage)

Events		Population Year 1977 Possessed (N = 54)	Other (N = 75)	1984 Possessed (N = 63)	Other (N = 72)
Divorces:	1	31.5	24.0	33.3	18.1
	2	7.4	0.0	6.4	1.4
	>2	0.0	1.3	0.0	0.0
Marriages:	1	68.5	85.3	71.4	88.9
	2	24.1	13.3	23.8	11.1
	>2	7.4	1.3	4.8	0.0
Cowifery		18.5	13.3	17.5	5.6

38.9 percent (1977) and 39.7 percent (1984) of the possessed have done so, while comparable figures for the remaining female population are 25.3 percent (1977) and 19.5 percent (1984). Further, when divorces are distributed respectively throughout the two populations, the possessed demonstrate a women : divorces ratio of 2.2 : 1 (1977 and 1984), producing crude rates of 46.3 percent of the population in 1977 (N=54), and 46.0 percent in 1984 (N=63). For the nonpossessed, these ratios are 3.6 : 1 (1977) and 4.8 : 1 (1984) yielding crude rates of 26.7 percent in 1977 (N=75) and 20.8 percent in 1984 (N=72). Discrepancies between these measures and the percentages of ever-divorced women (table 5.2) signify that a woman possessed is more likely than her counterparts not only to have undergone divorce, but also to have done so more than once.[3]

Now, the above figures do not reflect when divorce (or fertility mishap, discussed below) might have occurred in relation to the onset of possession or its public acknowledgment. Accurately sequencing such events is problematic for the investigator, since a woman who becomes possessed uses her knowledge of that affliction to reinterpret experiences in light of the spirits' influence. As happens when someone tests positive for allergies after suffering symptoms for several years, the past is illuminated by present information. Thus, a possessed woman will say she has been ill with the *zār* her entire adult life, regardless of when she or her kin first noted

3. For the possessed, the proportion of all *marriages* ending in divorce or permanent separation was 33.3 percent in 1977 (25 divorces for 75 marriages) and 34.5 percent in 1984 (29 divorces for 84 marriages); for the remaining female population these figures are (1977) 23.0 percent (20 divorces for 87 marriages) and (1984) 18.8 percent (15 divorces for 80 marriages). Despite the fact that more possessed women have experienced multiple divorce than have the nonpossessed, the overall numbers are low: my records show five in the 1977 ever-married female population (N = 129) and five in 1984 (N = 135). In both years, four of these five were possessed.

the problem. It is rarely possible to disengage other events from this salient fact.

Marriage, however, is a precondition for acknowledging possession; it occurs prior to a public diagnosis, if not the onset of spirit distress. And the two groups exhibit differences with regard to type of first marriage: nonpossessed women are more likely than their possessed sisters to have married traceable kin, and to have married within the village itself or a five-mile radius of it. A greater number of the nonpossessed are or have been wed to the preferred spouse, the *wad ʿamm ṭawālī* or actual father's brother's son, and their marriages tend on average to be with closer kinsmen than do those of the possessed (table 5.3). From this, one might speculate that closeness and preferability of prior relationship between husband and wife serve to mitigate the occurrence of *zār* or its public diagnosis. Although spouses who are close kin are perhaps as likely as others to be plagued by reproductive problems, previously established patterns of communication within the extended kin group, family pressures, moral obligations, and the like might lessen their perceived severity, provide alternate means by which they can be addressed, or necessitate their suppression lest they appear to compromise family honor. This is consistent also with the observation that between 90 percent (1977) and 94 percent (1984) of the first marriages of nonpossessed women are to men from the village area. By contrast, area endogamy characterizes 76 percent (1977) and 75 percent (1984) of first marriages for women who admit to being possessed.

Table 5.3. First Marriages of Possessed and Nonpossessed Women (percentage)

	Population Years			
	1977		1984	
Type of Marriage	Possessed (N = 54)	Other (N = 75)	Possessed (N = 63)	Other (N = 72)
Between traceable kin	72.2	86.7	71.4	80.6
Area endogamous	75.9	90.7	74.6	94.4
Village endogamous	51.9	66.7	52.4	75.0
Preferential marriage:				
1. Patrilateral // cousin	14.8	30.7	23.8	29.2
2. Other first cousin	16.7	13.3	15.9	15.3
3. Parents and/or grandparents are first cousins	22.2	24.0	22.2	20.8
4. *Garīb sai* ("just close") via lineage, distant matrilateral, or affinal ties	29.6	17.3	19.0	13.9
5. *Mush garīb* ("not close")	16.7	14.7	19.1	20.8

But all of the above, I should caution, are the tendencies of groups, not individuals: many possessed women are stably married to close kinsmen also born and raised in Hofriyat. Such trends are only valuable insofar as they indicate some of the constraints that might lead to a diagnosis of *zār* possession or its acceptance and public acknowledgment. And what can be seen is that when the collective marital history of nonpossessed women (including, of course, the yet to become possessed) is compared with that of the possessed, it more nearly approximates the ideal for marriage in Hofriyat as characterized by the qualities of enclosure and interiority earlier discussed. Conformity with or failure to meet Hofriyati ideals plays a significant role in the etiology of *zār* possession, both implicitly, as noted here, and explicitly, as discussed below.

Turning now to questions of fertility, table 5.4 demonstrates a degree of divergence between the possessed and the remainder of the married female population. For one thing, possessed women have been pregnant, on average, more often than the nonpossessed, a fact which at first seems to obfuscate women's association of the *zār* with fertility disorder. Comparison of the average ages of each group fails to resolve the issue: in 1977 the average ages of possessed and nonpossessed women were 47.8 and 48.1, respectively; in 1984 these figures were 37.6 and 35.0—in both years too close to explain why the possessed should have had more pregnancies. One explanation emerges when the groups are divided into cohorts (figure 5.1) rather than broadly averaged: possession is not likely to be diagnosed until a woman has been married for several years, sufficient time for fertility (or related) problems to develop and be interpreted as signs of possession. Younger cohorts demonstrate fewer cases of possession, but also fewer pregnancies since they have had shorter reproductive careers. This point is resumed later on.

Apart from relative age, the apparent contradiction fails to hold for another reason: possessed and nonpossessed differ inversely with respect to numbers of *failed* pregnancies, in other words, reproductive success. Reproductive success rates were calculated by totaling the number of pregnancies reported for each group (minus current gravidity), and comparing these figures with the number of pregnancies brought to term, excluding stillbirths and, adopting a Hofriyati view of effective fertility, children who died in early childhood (before the age of five). The rates, while proximate, show that possessed women have lost more children than those who are not possessed. Moreover, a higher percentage of possessed women married five years or more have never been pregnant at all.

Another slight but intriguing difference has to do with the sex of known conceptions and the gendered reproductive success rates for possessed and nonpossessed women in the two fieldwork years (table 5.5). The number of known conceptions of male and female offspring includes

Table 5.4. Reproductive Histories of Possessed and Nonpossessed Women

	Population Year			
	1977		1984	
Trait	Possessed (N = 54)	Other (N = 75)	Possessed (N = 63)	Other (N = 72)
Average no. of pregnancies per woman	5.13	4.16	5.27	4.21
Average no. of children surviving to age 5	4.13	3.60	4.19	3.46
Reproductive success rate	80.5%	86.5%	79.8%	84.1%
Rate difference between possessed and other	6.0%		4.3%	
Percentage women married five years or more and never pregnant	13.0%	5.3%	9.5%	2.8%

Table 5.5. Gendered Reproductive Success Rates for Possessed and Nonpossessed Women

	Population Year			
	1977		1984	
Trait	Possessed	Other	Possessed	Other
No. of known conceptions of males	122	142	158	140
Reproductive success rate for known males conceived (A)	75.4%	83.8%	78.5%	85.0%
Rate difference between possessed and other	8.4%		6.5%	
No. of known conceptions of females	154	170	166	148
Reproductive success rate for known females conceived (B)	85.1%	88.8%	84.3%	87.8%
Rate difference between possessed and other	3.7%		3.5%	

all live births, stillbirths, and miscarriages in the second and third trimesters where the sex of the fetus could be determined. In each year, the ratio of known males to females conceived is similar for possessed and nonpossessed: in 1977 the figures are 1:1.26 (possessed) and 1:1.20 (nonpossessed); in 1984, 1:1.05 (possessed) and 1:1.06 (nonpossessed). The major difference here is between years, that is, populations of resident women, not between those who have spirits and those who do not. Again this may be understood in terms of the relative youth of the 1984 population. However, despite the fact that possessed women apparently conceive as many male offspring as the nonpossessed, they have been less successful than their sisters in bringing these children to term and past the critical first years of life. The fact that the sex of a miscarried offspring is remembered, indeed noted beyond the confines of a woman's family, reflects the importance Hofriyati attach to gender, and specifically to producing male descendants. And this, I believe, is a critical issue addressed in the *zār:* not only do possessed women exhibit a lower reproductive success rate than other Hofriyati women, their success with female offspring is greater than with males, and the difference between these gendered rates is almost twice as great as the comparable difference for nonpossessed women (9.7 percent in 1977 and 5.8 percent in 1984 compared with 5.4 percent in 1977 and 2.8 percent in 1984, subtracting figures in row A from those in row B in table 5.5). Although attrition rates for XY conceptions are, in normal populations, greater than those for XX (Hutt 1972; Money and Tucker 1975), and both groups lose more males than females, the possessed lose a higher percentage of males than the nonpossessed.

At this point it is worth reiterating that in Hofriyat, marriage and fertility are closely linked. For both men and women the purpose of marriage is to produce descendants toward the advancement of one's social position. Though female children are certainly desired, it is deemed socially more necessary to have males. The loss of male offspring is therefore viewed with alarm by Hofriyati, the degree of alarm depending upon where the loss occurs in a woman's sequence of pregnancies and her husband's interpretation of the event or, perhaps, her fear of his—and his parent's—interpretation. Recall that women shoulder considerable responsibility for reproduction. Thus, for example, a woman who bears a daughter as her first child is at risk of divorce should her husband consider this an ominous start to their joint reproductive career, as many do. Her marriage is equally jeopardized if her first pregnancy ends in stillbirth. But it is also possible that either outcome may be read as proof of her fertility, and the couple will try again. Each pregnancy is a source of anxiety for a woman; each prolonged and undesired reproductive hiatus, a test of nerve. So too for her husband, but here there is a difference: for he retains the legal option to instigate divorce, remarriage, or polygyny that he might, as villagers say, "make good his expectation" (*ligā rugūbtu*) of descendants, and fulfill his mandate from Allah to procreate. Given her husband's powers, it is only when a woman has demonstrated the ability to produce and raise sons that she can hope to achieve security in her marriage.

Not unexpectedly then, fertility problems recognized by villagers are both physical and social in origin, going beyond apparent sterility, stillbirth, miscarriage, infant mortality, and early childhood death depicted in table 5.4. They include experiencing lengthy intervals between pregnan-

Table 5.6. Fertility and Marital Problems in Possessed and Nonpossessed Populations (percentage)

	Population Year			
	1977		1984	
Trait	Possessed (N = 54)	Other (N = 75)	Possessed (N = 63)	Other (N = 72)
No known problems	7.4	34.7	9.5	26.4
Fertility problems only	29.6	24.0	36.5	40.3
Marital problems only	9.3	20.0	8.0	15.3
Both fertility and marital problems	53.7	21.3	46.0	18.0

cies, bearing a daughter as the first child, and having daughters only or daughters who survive and sons who do not. Certain menstrual disorders, pelvic inflammations, and other potential complications of pharaonic circumcision are sometimes viewed as foreboding, but I was unable to collect full information on these problems for all women in both fieldwork years. Marital factors too may constitute threats to a woman's security and continued reproductive success: divorce, separation, withdrawal of financial support, cowifery, preliminary divorce where one's husband might return before the final severance, having a husband with a history of divorce or polygyny or whose previous wife died in childbirth, hearing rumors (*kalām*) from other women of one's pending divorce or cowifery—all are potential sources of distress. Relying on my informants to elucidate what was or was not potentially problematic in these regards, I obtained the following comparisons between possessed and nonpossessed populations (table 5.6). Significantly, it is rare for a possessed woman never to have experienced any problems of this sort, far rarer than for one who is not (or not yet) plagued by *zayran*. But most impressive is that one of every two possessed women has sustained both fertility and marital problems in the course of her life, whereas for the nonpossessed this figure is only one in five.

All of this begs the issue of relative age. Since conjugal difficulties and fertility problems are closely linked, both actually and potentially, the above figures need to address differences among the various stages of women's marital and reproductive careers. A newlywed who is her husband's first wife should exhibit no apparent trouble in either domain, whereas a longer married woman with several pregnancies to her credit might well have encountered some problem along the way. One might expect that of these two, the longer married woman is more likely to be possessed. And this is indeed the case. Figure 5.1 compares *zār*-possessed women by age cohort figured in ten-year increments beginning at age six-

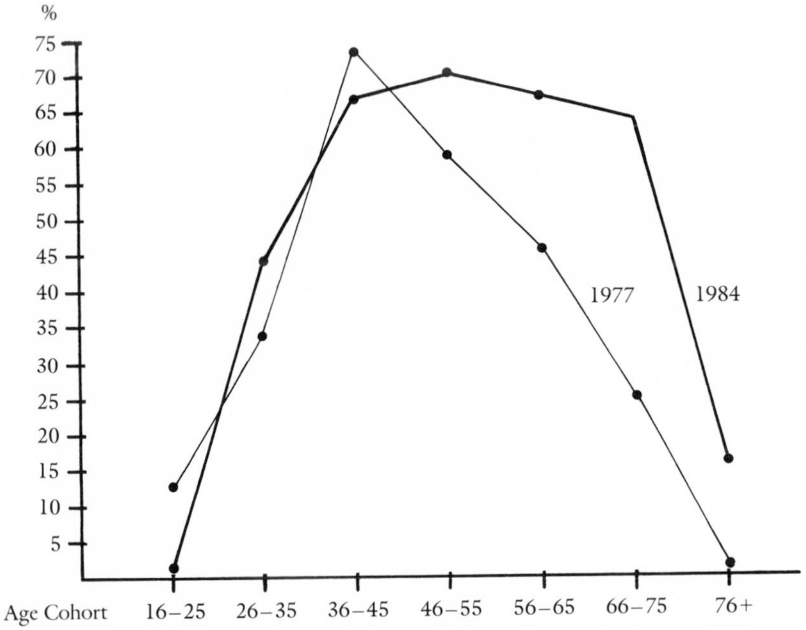

Fig. 5.1. Percentages of Women Possessed in 1977 and 1984, by age cohort

teen,[4] expressed in the percentage of each cohort that is possessed. In the youngest cohort of ever-married women, 13.8 percent were possessed in 1977, and none in 1984. Percentages rise steadily after age twenty-five, then begin to decline in cohorts of older women. This decline is steepest for 1977 and should be read in light of the fact that the *zār,* according to my informants, began to gain ground in the village sometime after 1920. For a woman under age forty-five in 1977, the possession complex was fairly well established prior to her birth, whereas for older women such was not the case. The implication here is that to the younger women, possession may have been a more "natural" idiom for interpreting experience than to women who learned it at some point in their lives. The curve for

4. In both fieldwork years there were no married women below this age, though two younger girls were married just before I left the field in 1984.

1984 reflects aging of this earlier population (once possessed, always possessed), attrition in the older age groups where fewer women acknowledged possession, and cases of the illness that developed between 1977 and 1984. Importantly, in 1984, two-thirds of all women between the ages of thirty-six and seventy-five claimed to have spirits; both years indicate a clear relationship between the stage of life a woman has reached and the probability that she will have become possessed.

Clever Virgins Make Good Grandmothers

Here I consider the developmental context of hazards that villagers allege can lead to possession illness. And again it is useful to turn for instruction to a tale about Fatna the Beautiful, the heroine first encountered in chapter 3. Fatna, recall, is the epitome of Hofriyati femininity, a lovely and resourceful woman who manages to escape dangerous or undesirable situations—including incest—sometimes by luck, other times by what appears to be her absurd naïveté, still others by courage and daring, skill and wit. Fatna is a rare mixture of youth and senescence: simultaneously ingenue and sage. Initially tossed on the winds of fate or victimized by some deceitful exploiter, she eventually seizes the moment and proves herself so perceptive, so cunning and capable, as to be a match for any man and the nemesis of many.

Fatna stories are recited to girls and young women by elders of their sex, and are always received with delight. They express, I suggest, essential truths about the predicament of being female in northern Sudan: women begin their adult lives as virgin brides, like Fatna, idealizations of femininity. With skill and luck they end their days respected *ḥabōbāt,* grandmothers, outrageously forthright old ladies renowned for their earthy wisdom and considerable ability as social manipulators. At the outset a woman is attributed high status, but however much an achievement this may be, it is symbolic or ritual status: it adheres to her less because of individual accomplishment than because she represents in her person significant cultural values; she is a cultural artifact, objectified, an idol. Toward the end of her life, she hopes to have parried this standing into social power by having borne and retained some control over several offspring, whose marriages she has helped arrange and whose children she governs with an eye to prospective betrothal. She seeks, then, to deobjectify herself, to assert her subjectivity. But the interim is fraught with danger. It is a complex process whereby women, in exercising their fertility, inevitably relinquish bridely status, becoming progressively "drier" and less fertile as they mature and attain this position of respect. Heroic Fatna exhibits qualities associated with both end points of this journey: she is at once object and subject, bridelike and grandmotherly. And to village women she is an impossible contradiction. Yet implicitly, it is Fatna whom most wish to emulate, for only by combining bridely qualities with those of fruitful motherhood can they expect to achieve social success. The key to this riddle is marriage.

A story called "Fatna and the Sultan's Son" provides a fulcrum for further discussion (see also Hurreiz 1977:83–85; F. C. T. Moore 1975: 117–20).

On the night her parents betroth her to her brother, Fatna escapes from her village with seven sisters (or girl friends) who now fear a similar fate. The girls wander about and have a variety of escapades until they meet an old man. Fatna tricks him into revealing (in some versions he volunteers) that an old man can be killed and his skin removed by inserting two acacia thorns into his head.[5] This she does, and promptly dons his skin. She then leads her companions to the river, and poses as their grandfather to the boatman who ferries them across. Later they are captured by the sultan's son and his caravaneers, and taken to the sultan's village.

The sultan's men each take a girl, leaving his son the "old man" who becomes his servant (or slave). But the son has trouble finding suitable work for the old man to do. He suggests herding cattle; the old man refuses. He suggests horses, then camels; excuses again. Finally, they agree on pigeons (in another version, geese). A mute slave is assigned to help him and report back to the sultan's son.

Every day Fatna drives her pigeons to the river so they can bathe. There she strips off her disguise and goes for a swim. In one version (Hurreiz 1977:85) she also dances and sings her own praise, "Oh what a beautiful gait [I have], just like the pigeon's movement! Oh what beautiful hair that is just like ostrich feathers!" On observing this the slave would run to his master and try to convey in gestures what he had seen, but without success. Several mute slaves fail in the attempt, each losing his life because he is thought to have gone mad. Finally the sultan's son surreptitiously follows the old man to the river, sees Fatna swim, and resolves to end the ruse.

He challenges the old man to a game of *sīja*[6]—not unlike chess—stipulating that the winner of the game shall skin the loser or, in some ver-

5. This episode begs a psychodynamic interpretation, given the practical association between acacia thorns and female circumcision, and the Freudian one between head and penis (cf. Obeyesekere 1981; Leach 1958).

6. *Sija* is played on a "board" of twenty-five places or depressions in the sand. Opponents have twelve pieces (stones or date pits) each. The point of the game is for each player to block all possible moves of his opponent's pieces by surrounding them in turn, thereby removing them from play. The game proceeds in this manner until one player checkmates the last of his opponent's men.

sions, open the loser's stomach. The version offered by Hurreiz is again instructive:

"'You want to kill me,' replied the old man.

'Then let it be a small scar,' said the son of Nimer [Nimir];[7] 'And I pledge to give you all the security that Allah grants.'" (Hurreiz 1977: 85).

They play one game and Fatna wins. She spares the sultan's son. She wins a second round, and spares him once again. But she loses the third round, whereupon the sultan's son flays her by removing the old man's wizened skin, exposes the radiant Fatna, and marries her at once.

Now, *pace* other potential readings of this myth, the image of beautiful, virginal Fatna emerging from the skin of an old man to become a bride captures an exaggerated reversal of the Hofriyati woman's reproductive career. In the real world, women are circumcised (compare the "small scar") and perceptibly virginal first. It is later that they are "opened up"; still later they become elderly and manlike in their powers to "herd" young girls ("pigeons") and manipulate the social environment. And while Fatna's problem, once she has assumed the guise of an old man, is how to reveal her true self to a mate she considers appropriate,[8] the Hofriyati woman, once married, must do the converse: she must work to achieve the position she deserves in old age. Cut off from her kin, Fatna challenges the sultan's son from an inferior position: he/she is a slave, and the son of Nimir a wealthy and powerful man; yet, when they engage in *sīja* it is as equals: man to man. For a Hofriyati woman, the opposite is true: she is part of a family, and together they engage her husband and his kin from a position of relative symmetry; yet on a personal level, hers is a situation of admitted gender imbalance. The antagonists of Fatna and the Hofriyati wife are in some respects more powerful than they, but power is fundamentally ambiguous (cf. Balandier 1970: 40), and it is the objective of each to turn this ambiguity to her advantage. In the process—the game or the marriage—they show that they, too, are powerful; and for both, the source of their power is internal.

Women enter first marriage at the peak of their purity and value. A bride's body is at once chaste and socially virginal (cf. Hayes 1975): prepared initially by circumcision, then by elaborate cosmetic procedures, she

7. The sultan in these stories is usually called Nimir (Nimer, Nimr, Nimair), meaning "Little Leopard." In Hofriyat the name contains an implicit reference to Mek Nimir, the last of the traditional rulers of Shendi who fled to the Ethiopian frontier after engineering the murder of Ismaʿil Pasha (1822) during the Turkish occupation. Jokingly, the character was sometimes also linked to then President Nimeiri (whose name has the same connotation).

8. Hurreiz's version is paradoxical in this regard, for in it the son of Nimir also has a sister Fatma (Fatna), whom he threatens at the outset to wed. It is left to the audience to puzzle whether Fatna initially escapes marriage with her brother, only to be reunited with him at the end of the tale.

has become a perfect vessel for reproducing moral human life. Her womb is enclosed, its generative moisture contained, protected, and all the more significant for having been empowered through marriage. She is the focus of village attention, coddled, displayed, idolized, protected by potent charms, virtually sanctified.

Paradoxically, however, the social status of a bride is low: she is a married woman with no children to her credit. And subsequent to her ritual defloration on the *layla-t-ad-dukhl,* "the night of entrance" that climaxes her wedding feast, she is somewhat tarnished as a cultural symbol. The fortieth day after her wedding dance marks the end of her bridal confinement, her liminality, during which she was pampered and permitted to do no work. From now on she may go abroad during daylight hours. Then, immediately prior to the next Ramadan (the fasting month), her family completes the economic transactions surrounding her wedding by sending food and new kitchen utensils to the mother of the groom. And at the *ʿĪd aṣ-Ṣaghīr,* the "small feast" marking the end of Ramadan, each woman married in the previous calendar round receives guests for the last time as an *ʿarūs,* a bride. From now on she is but a wife.

A woman's vulnerability is keenly felt once she steps down from the bridely pedestal and resumes daily life. For unless she is already pregnant, she has no capital, no weapon with which to deflect her husband's untoward behavior or his mother's abuse. Yet her ceremonial status is high despite its recent diminution. Now she must use this position judiciously to substantiate her marriage and establish her reproductive career. The recently married woman continues to perform the taxing cosmetic routines to which she was initiated as a bride: smoke bathing, hair removal, using henna, *dilka, koḥl,* making and using a variety of scents. The results of these procedures are considered alluring, erotic; whatever else, they indicate to a man that his wife is sexually receptive. In this way she seeks to maintain her husband's interest lest he be dissuaded by another beauty and the marriage precipitately dissolved. And this she does at some cost to herself, for the preparations are "hot" and painful, as is intercourse for the infibulated wife. But pain is symptomatic of activated femininity and, if pregnancy results, suitably prognostic.

Importantly, having a Hofriyati child is not something which occurs spontaneously and automatically, as a natural function of womanhood. A villager who merely wants offspring, women say, should find himself a wife among the uncircumcised peoples of southern Sudan: for such women, pregnancy is a simple matter and it is no trouble at all to bear child after child. Yet they do not produce quality offspring. Giving birth to moral beings is a more delicate task, and the province of Hofriyati wives. The fact that village women bear primary responsibility for appropriate reproduction is therefore viewed less as a burden thrust upon them by men than as a right which their achievement of gender entails.

But the exercise of that right can be an arduous feat, requiring subtlety no less than strategy in the face of formidable constraints. For as noted earlier, a woman's anxieties are not wholly allayed with the first signs of pregnancy. Even if she successfully carries a child to term, her first might well be female or die in infancy. The presence of any locally defined fertility dysfunction portends a difficult reproductive career and is considered suitable grounds for divorce. Should a newlywed woman divorce she might well remarry, but never again as a first wife imbued with the mystical aura of virgin bridehood.

The conclusion of her first pregnancy enormously depreciates a woman's purity and enclosedness. Her genital orifice must be surgically enlarged to permit the baby's birth; she is polluted by the malodorous "black" blood of childbirth, blood no longer potently reproductive. But immediately after the birth, she is reinfibulated, enclosed, made virginal again. Seven days later she is dressed as a bride and given gifts by her husband, as before. Then, after forty days of confinement she bathes fully and resumes the cosmetic routines of her sex. Such postpartum practices refurbish a woman's bridely qualities, but can never restore them completely.

If approximation to the bridal image progressively diminishes as a woman moves through her reproductive career, her social status increases so long as she also becomes a successful wife, the mother of daughters and sons. However, between her late twenties or early thirties and menopause there may come a time when the marriage she has worked so hard to establish seems headed toward divorce or cowifery, when the conjugal dialectic is threatened by entropy. Her perceptions are often well founded, for there exist a number of conditions to prompt such action on the part of husbands. Informants suggest that once an arranged marriage has fulfilled its purpose a man might wish to take a second, younger wife of his own choice. Or his first wife may be experiencing fertility problems at an advanced stage, and if his "expectation" is not yet satisfied he may want to try his luck elsewhere. Further, a woman whose husband works for lengthy periods outside the village may sense her reproductive career to be jeopardized both by his absence and the justifiable fear that another will have drawn his attention.

At the same time, a woman must be wary of having too many births in rapid succession. It is accepted that children have a greater chance of survival if pregnancy does not occur until after the previous child has been weaned. Should she become pregnant too soon after her last successful birth, and either the fetus or the child she is nursing die, then her procreative ability may be called into question.

It might also happen that a woman has successfully borne too many children. A large brood demands considerable time, decreasing that available for making herself attractive, or entertaining her husband and serving coffee to his friends. Moreover, if she relies on remittance income insufficient for her family's needs, she will likely cultivate a kitchen garden, make baskets, or sell cooked food in addition to her domestic duties. When spouses reside together, and even when they do not, a woman might well complain of being overworked: caught between the necessity of ministering to her children and catering to her husband's whims.

But men, too, are in a difficult position. In the eyes of the community it is important to have many descendants, to be known as the founder of a lineage section by the end of one's life, if not before. Yet at the same time it is a mark of a man's ability if he can support a wife who need do little else than make herself attractive and tend to his personal wants. In the last century, slavery provided the means for one wife to cope with both roles. Now polygyny supplies a partial solution: Hofriyati women claim that polygyny has increased since their grandparents' time[9] and that men who feel they can afford it usually avail themselves of this option.

In Hofriyat and its environs, cowives must be maintained in separate households and domiciled in different villages. But few men are wealthy enough to support equally and adequately two or more (a maximum of four under Islamic law) establishments at the same time. Thus polygyny may be short-lived, and divorce of the first wife, of she who has already given her husband descendants, becomes a real possibility. Depending upon a woman's age; the number, sex, and ages of her children; and the quality of her relations with natal family members, threat of divorce may be more or less worrisome at this point. If she has adult sons or if close male kin are alive and willing to support her, it is less difficult to bear. But without such support, divorce can be devastating, especially once she is beyond childbearing, hence unlikely to rewed.[10]

The possibility of becoming a cowife is equally problematic, for then the first wife, despite Quranic injunctions to the contrary, generally suffers financial neglect. And since husbands are notorious for evincing greatest enthusiasm toward more recent acquisitions, a woman whose husband takes a second wife realizes that her own childbearing career may become

9. Slavery was formally abolished with the Anglo-Egyptian Condominium at the end of the nineteenth century; however, it continued in practice for a number of years. Many former slaves remained attached to the households of their masters, rendering much the same service as before manumission. The eventual abolition of slavery and increased labor migration are conditions that informants hold responsible for the perceived increase in polygyny. It is extremely difficult to verify this perception from village genealogies, since it is not generally remembered whether an ancestor with two wives had been married serially or polygynously.

10. There were two such women in the village in 1977, both of whom lived in poverty and occasionally were reduced to begging meals from neighbors.

stymied. Moreover, she fears a pending increase in the number of her husband's children, for this proportionately reduces the inheritances of her own. A man's second marriage also extends the range of marital choice for his first wife's children to points and locations beyond her personal reckoning. This imperils her aspirations to play a major role in choosing spouses for her sons and daughters, and ultimately to achieve *habōba*-hood in her natal village (Boddy 1985).

Individual cases vary, but it is clear that marriage for Hofriyati women is a continuous negotiation in which husbands seem to have the upper hand. A woman's marital, hence reproductive, success depends on her ability to balance two elusive assets, fertility and bridely purity, to bargain these against the ubiquitous threat of divorce. However, to use the first she must progressively relinquish the latter. Smoke bathing, reinfibulation, and all the rest shore up her procreative potential but cannot in the end conserve it. For purity—idealized femininity—must be spent so that fertility can be demonstrated. Yet prevalent male attitudes demand both bridelike qualities and actual fertility in a wife. So the Hofriyati woman walks a tightrope in gale force winds: she must have children—not too few or too rarely lest her husband and others doubt her fertility, but not so many that she expends the source of her attractiveness and her husband loses interest.

As she matures, a woman comes to appreciate the extent to which she must rely on her children, and her children's fertility, to advance her social position.[11] She knows well what good she must make of her own reproductive years. In the harsh light of reality, marriage is revealed less as an end in itself than an unsteady means to use her fertility gift, to produce spouses both for her husband's kin, as required, and for her siblings' children and other personally relevant kin so as to consolidate her own support. But like husbands and marriages, fertility is not always predictable; it is minimally subject to human control. A woman can make herself sexually available to her husband or put off his attentions in a number of ways. Surreptitiously she can take the pill or receive birth control injections. But she cannot predetermine the sex of her child, nor prevent stillbirths and miscarriages; she cannot, under present conditions, forestall the sterility that might occur owing to complications of pharaonic circumcision. Despite its positive connotations, the irony of this practice is patent and grim.

All told, marriage in Hofriyat can be compared to a game of chess where women play with a full complement of pieces, each with its own limitation, while most of their husbands' pieces are queens, capable of unlimited maneuverability. By necessity, a woman plays the board defen-

11. And equally, her mother's position. A woman's mother is usually her ally and co-strategist in dealings with her husband.

sively, frequently having to control the uncontrollable in order to succeed. Yet even a lowly pawn can capture a powerful queen, or mate the king. If marriage is an inevitable and, all too often, a losing game, it is not without its rewards.

And so the story of Fatna the Beautiful outwitting the sultan's son has a special appeal for women in Hofriyat. The son sees Fatna as an old man, and his interest in her is minimal: he fails to realize that this dry, masculine external presence contains a beautiful virgin. Like the neglected first wife, she becomes a servant, one who helps with the herds—descendants—nothing more. Yet the old man is strange in his refusal to herd cattle, the metaphor for married women that stresses their contradictory position in Hofriyat. Instead, he insists on herding pigeons or geese. Here, perhaps, Fatna provides a clue to her real identity, for pigeons and water-linked birds represent the positive values of femininity, fertility, morality, and a host of other qualities symmetrical to those connected with males. But if her choice of occupation was intended as a hint, it is not taken up by the sultan's son. For him, reality lies in appearances: that men are overly concerned with what is external and superficial is understood. On the other hand, Fatna in the skin of an old man herding pigeons may be likened to the Hofriyati grandmother who, in her authoritarian role, sedulously guards the purity and fertility of her brood, upholding values essential to the maintenance of village morality.

Now Fatna, the image of feminine perfection, has disguised herself as a man. Yet it is clear from the outset, when she and her companions escape incestuous marriages, that they are in search of suitable mates. The other girls fail to conceal their identities and are taken against their wills by the sultan's men, presumably as concubines or slaves. For Fatna, things will be different: we know it is *she* who chooses the sultan's son, and not as master but as mate. To succeed, she must somehow reveal her feminine self while retaining her masculine advantage. So, she steps out of her male covering to go swimming in the Nile knowing she will be observed by the sultan's uncommunicative slaves. She reveals her true nature (note the association of femininity with wetness and the Nile) covertly, as women are enjoined to do, while maintaining the fiction that she does not seek to wed. She draws attention to her beauty and likens herself to birds, thereby establishing her real identity and moral worth. The conventional themes of containment, moisture, and birds guide listeners to the story's deeper significance.

Eventually, the sultan's son secretly observes Fatna swimming and, overconfident, perhaps, of his talents, determines to expose her. So he challenges her to a game where the winner shall skin the loser. Twice Fatna plays more skillfully than he, and twice she spares his life. But the third time she loses. Whether or not both parties play to the utmost of their abilities, and whether Fatna allows herself to be defeated in the end, are questions for the audience to ponder. The point is well stated nonetheless: it is only in losing to men that women can win; only in losing, and losing judiciously, that they can activate their fertility, pursue reproductive careers, and attain their social goals. Women who wield power must do so implicitly, leaving the appearance of power to men (Bourdieu 1977:41). Through strategic compliance, women might negotiate their subordination.

In relinquishing the guise of a witless elder, Fatna doubly reverses the chronology of life as lived by ordinary women in Hofriyat. For while Fatna cleverly uses her bogus identity as an aged male to achieve desirable bridehood, mortal women use their bridely status to achieve an authentic social position not unlike that of a male in old age. Lastly, for village women there is solace in the thought that even the redoubtable Fatna cannot sustain two competing definitions of herself for very long.

Spirits, Wives, and Husbands

These, then, are some of the parameters controlling women's lives. Women must exercise skill and strategic acumen if they are to maneuver through the indeterminacies of their conjugal relationships, control potentially disruptive situations, and mobilize support for their social goals. Like all villagers, but more often than their male counterparts, women are confronted by paradoxical demands and circumstances. And in response to these, they are more circumscribed than men by cultural constraints on their behavior. Moreover, there are limits to what can be negotiated.

Within Hofriyat, which is neither isolated nor self-sufficient but a part of wider political, economic, and religious systems, there exists no controlling, hegemonic group, only the fiction of one—men (cf. Rogers 1975). Whatever latitude and apparent control is granted to men, they are equally subject to cultural constraints and no freer than women to alter the fundamental conditions of their existence. It is Hofriyati culture which is, in this sense, hegemonic: power is vested less in agents of hegemony than in the practices whereby it produces its effects (Foucault 1980:97; cf. J. L. Comaroff 1986). Here, such practices are assimilated to Islam.

Throughout this book I have noted the strong identification that women are implicitly and materially "subjected"—in the Foucaultian sense (Foucault 1980:97)—to feel with their fertility. Hofriyati tolerance, even indulgence, of ambiguity and relativity in a range of social situations is matched only by an explicit intolerance of ambiguity where gender is concerned.[12] Male and female are mutually relative terms, yet each in itself is absolute. The objective intent of pharaonic circumcision and women's subsequent socialization is to create, emphatically and performatively (cf. Austin 1962), appropriate social reproducers, to realize persons—conformists, who, "in reproducing in word and deed the norms of a given traditional order, [manifest] the relations of that tradition" (Burridge 1979 : 5). And as subsequent possession narratives attest, women are often snared in the web of compelling images that discipline and so thoroughly shape their lives, for ideals cannot always be maintained. Yet materially and subjectively, they are ill disposed by this context to challenge their subordination in a self-conscious way.

When a woman's fertility mandate is impaired—for whatever reason—her self-image, social position, and ultimately general health are threatened. Women undergoing perceived marital and/or fertility crises tend to phrase their experiences as illness or, less directly, to colocate their difficulties with the onset of apparently unrelated physical symptoms. In thus complaining of illness or *zihuj* (boredom, apathy, depression) a woman avails herself of a culturally sanctioned medium for articulating her dysphoria.[13] Once this is done, she can act upon her problems where before she could not, by setting out to find a cure. The woman who claims to be ill yet does not appear diseased does not feign sickness: her pain is real and in the final diagnosis attributed to natural agents—*zayran*.

But clearly not all confessions of illness are spawned in this manner, and undoubtedly some that are get resolved before possession is suggested as the cause. Assigning *zār* as an appropriate etiology is first a process of eliminating other potential sources of illness, described in chapter 4, and also of taking into account the patient's social milieu. If a woman is at a stage of life which villagers recognize as problematic, and if other remedies have failed to cure her completely, then *zār* can be presumed. Throughout the forty case histories I collected in detail, the onset, acknowledgment, or relapse of possession ailments regularly coincided with the experience of reproductive disorder.

Hofriyati explicitly link fertility problems and possession illness, but more subtly and obliquely than I have here proposed. A woman who is anxious or depressed or whose situation vitiates the ideals and integrity of Hofriyati womanhood is considered a prime target for *zayran* seeking entry to the human world; should such a spirit descend on her, it makes her feel unwell. But, tautologically, *zayran* are able to create the very circumstances that make a woman anxious and prone to spirit assault. Their most

12. Al-Guindi (1987) suggests this is true throughout the Middle East and Muslim North Africa. The notable exception here appears to be Sohar, Oman (Wikan 1982).

13. Also Constantinides (1977 : 65); cf. Kleinman (1980); re possession, cf. Crapanzano (1977*a*); Firth (1967); Lambek (1981); Obeyesekere (1970).

common tactics, earlier described, are to "seize" or "hold" the womb, and "loosen" or "steal" progeny, bringing about sterility, miscarriage, stillbirth, amenorrhea, menorrhagia, or any number of problems affecting women's blood. The symbolism of the *zār* echoes this link between blood and possession illness, and obliquely expresses both the equivocal nature of human fertility and its extreme identification with Hofriyati women. But to pursue this point, something more must be said about the species of spirit to which *zayran* belong.

Hofriyati recognize three kinds of *jinn,* natural beings inhabiting the same physical space as humans, but invisible to them under normal conditions. Each type of *jinn* can possess human beings, but to different effect. The species and their respective characteristics are coded by color: white *jinn* (*jinn al-abiyaḍ*) are benign and principally Muslim. Possession by one is not serious—the basis for behavioral quirks and harmless eccentricities—and may in fact go unnoticed. White *jinn* are also known to work on behalf of Islamic holy men (*fugarā-t-islām*).

Black *jinn,* however, are malevolent, invariably pagan (yet capable of salvation), and bring grave disease or intractable mental illness that could well result in death. Possession by one is a dire matter, curable, if at all, only by violent exorcism. These beings are known to befriend powerful though unorthodox *faki*s, who thereby gain an ability to see into the invisible spirit world, find lost objects, foretell the future, and deal in black magic (*ʿamal*).

Lastly, there are *zayran:* red *jinn* or red winds (*rowḥān al-aḥmar*) which are pleasure seeking, capricious, and ambivalent. *Zayran* cause milder forms of illness which, though initially distressful, never result in death or severe emotional impairment. They are neither good nor evil but, like humans, something of both. Their color and amorality place them squarely between extremes. Red is associated with ambivalence, but also, of course, with blood. On the one hand, spirit recipients of ceremonial sacrifice are known, in the language of *zār,* as the "owners of blood," and blood is used therapeutically to anoint the *ʿayāna* and other adepts at a ceremony. A *shaykha* who performs a *zār* on another's behalf is thereafter related to that person "by blood" (cf. Cloudsley 1983 : 78). On the other hand, it is progenitive blood over which *zayran* exert control. Among the *zayran* are spirits doubly linked with red and its principal referents: Ethiopian (*Ḥabish*) spirits are both identified by that color, demanding red dresses for their hosts and reddish sacrificial beasts, and considered more guilty than other *zayran* of causing or taking advantage of their hosts' reproductive grief.

For its part, feminine blood stands in ambiguous relationship to fertility (cf. Constantinides 1977 : 80). Hofriyati women are quick to point out that while regular menses indicate continuous fertility, they also signify that a woman is not pregnant. Likewise, irregular or interrupted menstrual flow is symptomatic either of pregnancy or its opposite, sterility. Red, in the symbolism of weddings and women's crisis rites, signifies feminine blood; red and feminine blood connote ambiguity and ambivalence; and all potential meanings of these associations are bodied forth in ambivalent red spirits which control equivocal feminine blood. Through these associations the *zār* provides a suitable idiom for articulating and meaningfully constructing women's anxieties having to do with their fertility.

In holding *zayran* responsible for procreative mishap, whether real or feared, a woman asserts that her fertility is negotiable. Yet she bargains not, or not directly, with her husband in the mundane human world, but with *zayran,* capricious existents of a different earthly plane. If, having kept her part of the contract, negotiations with spirits fail, she cannot be held liable for consequences to her reproductive potential. Possession thus lifts from her shoulders a measure of the responsibility for social reproduction she is continually schooled to accept via the process of socialization. For it suggests that the identification of womanhood with procreation is more problematic than pharaonic circumcision and the imagery of womanhood attest. *Zār* illness contains an oblique admission that fertility, though socially regulated and vested in women, is not humanly governable, for beings more powerful than Hofriyati may intervene at will to obstruct its proper course.

Acceptance of a possession etiology for progenitive difficulty thus redirects query into a woman's apparent fate (*gadr*). It is not because fertility dysfunction is in her "nature," and not necessarily because it was foreordained by Allah, that she suffers. Possession, in fact, asserts the opposite: that she *is* fertile, for spirits have usurped this asset in a bid to attain their selfish ends. Thus it rationalizes the untoward event in a way which vehemently defends and absolves the socialized self. Here it is a conservative force. Yet at the same time it requires her husband to assume some procreative liability—though indirectly—for it is he who is called upon to provide desiderata that coax her spirit to relent. In this light, possession reads as a bid to transfer limited control of fertility from the wife to whom it is originally attributed, to the married couple and their kin, who together are encouraged to seek its restoration through a series of therapeutic transactions with offending *zayran.* While this is hardly revolutionary—it does not reform hegemonic constructs governing feminine selfhood—it might nonetheless ease a woman's predicament. But whether the bid is dispatched by spirits or, as we would prefer to think, the Hofriyati wife, it can only succeed if the acquiescence of her husband and kin is secured.

Still, this might take some doing. Recall that women and men publicly disagree about the classification of *zayran.* Hofriyati men, for the most part, place *zayran* with black *jinn* in a broader category, *shawaṭīn*—malevolent devils. To them, red *jinn* are just slightly less evil than black; they suggest that *zayran* bring illness because they enjoy meddling in the lives of gullible women, extorting from them the things they desire, appearing in the human realm, and being treated to lavish displays. But, men say, a woman needn't play along with *zayran* to achieve symptom relief, for red *jinn* can be exorcised like other *shawaṭīn,* and since they are less malignant than black *jinn,* usually this can be done without violence.

If men blur the distinction between red and black *jinn,* for women the lines are clearly drawn. As I noted earlier, the two precipitate different kinds of illness and respond distinctively to curing techniques. But more than this, they differ in appearance and behavior when taking human form or inhabiting their human hosts. Black *jinn* are ugly, *kᶜab,* colloquially, the "lowest of the low": horrific, filthy beings which, when visible to humans, have tangled hair and unkempt nails, go ragged or unclothed, and exude a foul smell. Those whom they possess soon acquire this image and are said to eat dust and human excrement: their behavior is both disgusting and dangerous; they are a serious threat to their own and others' lives.

Not so with *zayran,* who love cleanliness and beauty; desire gold, fine clothing, delicate perfumes; and demand a similar concern in their human hosts. When appearing in human form, they are always bathed, well dressed, and lovely to behold.[14] Moreover, unlike black *jinn, zayran* are refined gastronomists. They prefer that their hosts eat "clean" foods: those described as white, enclosed, expensive, often difficult to obtain, and thought to contribute to the fertility of Hofriyati women by increasing or strengthening their blood. Hosts of *zayran* may also be asked to consume foods associated with their spirits' ethnic groups or homelands; black *jinn* make no such socially intelligent requests. And a *zār* occasionally signifies its presence in a woman by drinking straight cologne (cf. Constantinides 1972:119; Lambek 1978), or demanding to smoke perfumed cigarettes. This use of scent is an extravagance which heightens the distinction between *zayran* and malodorous demons while distinguishing the former from their less indulgent human hosts. Lastly, possession by a *zār* is characterized by the relatively controlled, stereotypical gestures of its human

14. According to Leiris (1958:41), *zār* spirits in Gondar, Ethiopia, are thought most likely to possess beautiful women. Further, a myth about the origins of *zayran* attributed to Christian Ethiopia accounts for their inordinate concern with beauty and products of the human world (Messing 1958:1122; Fakhouri 1968:49). As Messing (1958:1122) writes, *zayran* are said to have been born in the Garden of Eden, as children of Eve: "One day the Creator came to visit and began to count the children. In apprehension, Eve hid the fifteen most beautiful and intelligent ones; as punishment they were condemned to remain always hidden, nighttime creatures. Consequently, they envy their uglier and weaker human siblings who are the children of light." A version of this story was recounted to me in Hofriyat, though it is not the only origin myth having currency among adepts.

host, whereas black *jinn* cause their hosts to relinquish bodily control, move recklessly and with abandon.

Indeed, according to local women, the chief difference between red and black *jinn* rests with this matter of control: black *jinn* are associated with asocial chaos, grave dysfunction, utter lack of control and death; *zayran* are social beings who bring milder, regulable ailments and cause their hosts to have controlled, even pleasant experiences when entranced. Black *jinn* want permanent custody of human bodies and must be driven out. *Zayran* rarely incorporate themselves and in ritual situations both enter and vacate their hosts on cue. For Hofriyati women as for heroic Fatna, the taking on of other selves reflects neither lack of inner strength nor loss of self-control; rather, it has much to do with preservation and enhancement of feminine ideals.

A husband's private attitude toward the *zār* possession of his wife is rarely so adamant as his official stance, particularly once the diagnosis has garnered kin support. If he seems intransigent, a woman's brothers generally intervene on her behalf, however reluctantly they themselves might accede to the illness in their wives. But accede most eventually do, for there is something to be gained by a man from his wife's acknowledgment of possession.

Aside from and because of its relation to fertility, the *zār* provides an idiom through which individuals whose communication is otherwise constrained might publicly comment on their relationship. It thus enables a couple to modify an overly polarized, increasingly schismogenetic marriage (see Bateson 1958), and forestall its disintegration in the face of negative gossip. On the one hand, *zayran* who attack a woman's fertility hold for ransom her husband's most valuable asset. They negotiate the release of their hostages, his unborn descendants, in return for certain demands, a curing ritual, and luxury items to be used by their host, his wife. In addition, they require her compliance via regular performance of the appropriate cosmetic procedures, in maintaining and revitalizing the bridely qualities that she diminishingly embodies. *Zayran,* remember, want their hosts to be clean and attractive. And here, they obliquely call upon a man to recognize his wife's value, implying that neither she nor her fertility should be taken for granted.

To restore his wife's *zār*-usurped fertility, a man must enter into an exchange relationship with her spirits; so doing, he implicitly renegotiates the relationship he has with his wife. As both Crapanzano (1977*b*) and Lambek (1980) note, possession provides an idiom through which spouses can communicate about and even resolve issues it might otherwise be inappropriate for them to discuss. And because most *zayran* are male as well as more powerful than humans, it permits such negotiation to take place in a context that need not entail loss of face for the husband who, to an outside observer, could be perceived as bending to his wife's requests.

Still, a woman's acknowledgment of possession might fail to yield favorable results. Like any course she pursues in Hofriyati, it is a gamble. For his wife's possession illness could intimate to her husband the existence of a fertility dysfunction of which he was unaware; thus it could backfire, and imperil the conjugal relationship. Here again, a woman must carefully weigh the risks involved in publicly admitting the diagnosis. And this is why she is reluctant to do so without assurances of support from family and friends, support which both temporarily neutralizes competition from other women and mitigates the unhappy reaction of her husband on discovering that his wife is possessed.

But possession might just as well and just as obliquely solidify a problematic marriage. For in attributing fertility disorder to spirits whose existence and powers are known and routinely validated, it obviates doubts concerning her own *and* her husband's abilities to reproduce. *Zār,* as shown more concretely in subsequent pages, changes the context of human relationships—rephrases them in a different, less quotidianly literal, and more productive register than that in which they must be played out when possession is not invoked. *Zār* alters the conditions of discourse: where before its invocation, interlocutors (husband and wife) speak past each other from positions of (gender) inequality, with its public assertion, their positions draw more proximate. For both, as human beings, are equally powerless before a transcendental third, the *zār,* which replaces gender discourse as the current locus of meaning (cf. Crapanzano 1980: 151). Like pharaonic circumcision before it, possession precipitates a context, enabling parties to change a previously accepted state of affairs.

And in this, possession positively reinforces husband's and wife's public self-images. Earlier, I hinted that the myth of Fatna and the sultan's son was open to a number of equally plausible interpretations. If you are female, you might wish to think that Fatna, knowing the sultan's son had discovered her ruse, legitimately won the first two games, thereby placing him at a disadvantage, provoking him to realize her ability and value; then, that she deliberately lost the third round so as to acquire a worthy—and proven manipulable—mate. But if you are a male, quite the opposite rendition is appropriate: you can consider the sultan's son deliberately to have lost the first two games, gambling correctly that the "old man," whom he knew to be a life-giving woman, would not cause his death. In doing so, he was granting her some lead: temporarily allowing her to feel powerful before showing his real strength, then defeating her in the last match, gaining her final submission in marriage. These competing interpretations, which in no way exhaust the myth's potential readings, demonstrate that its power lies in its capacity to say something truthful about conjugal relationships in Hofriyat: it illuminates their essential ambiguity. And it does so eloquently, without damaging the self-image of either sex or the images each popularly holds of the other. So, too, with *zār*. Clearly, it can act as a counterhegemonic process enabling wives to negotiate their subordination, but for all that, it is infinitely subtle. Possession does not obviate the disparities and uncertainties in a marriage so much as provide new light by which they may be read. Gender complementarity is in no way elided, but reinforced and enhanced when people requalify the human factor in fertility control. For neither sex need see itself capitulating to the other: the delicate balance of powers is preserved and stated anew.

There is another level to the Fatna tale, and it is one I return to in forthcoming discussions of the *zār*. In Hofriyat, gender relations, and notably marriage, constitute a rhetorical prototype for relationships between villagers and non-Hofriyati others. Recall that the ideal dynamic between husband and wife is one in which she remains within the village, bearing children and preserving morality, while he mediates politically and economically between the *ḥōsh* and the outside world. The universe of the inside is feminine, that of the outside, masculine. When beautiful Fatna disguises herself to gain advantage of a powerful male outsider, the implications are not lost to her admirers. For the heroine of the story is both a woman and that which she represents: the village and its people, local praxis, local morality. The sultan's son, for his part, personifies a range of external forces prevailing on the village at different times: he is conqueror and colonizer, politician, soldier, religious legalist, wealthy foreigner. And the lessons of their interaction apply as readily to the broader context as to its gendered allegory: the statement Hofriyati women make about how to negotiate their subordination with men and assert gender complementarity reads also as a statement about how to negotiate with powerful outsiders while avoiding wholesale surrender and loss of cultural identity.[15] And when approached from a masculine perspective, the story of how to gain the compliance of women suggests how those in authority should deal with Hofriyati, who are less powerful than they. Gender relations in Hofriyat capture a consciousness of history in the dynamic interplay of their contrast (cf. Comaroff and Comaroff 1987). But the reverse is true as well: villagers' consciousness of their history and the import of foreign encounters constructs local praxis and informs appropriate dispositions of gender, specifically, women's seclusion. The larger context is integral to the local just as male is integral to female. And read at either of its levels,

15. The irony of my own position is neatly stated in the narrative, for I, too, was seeking in the negotiation of fieldwork to unveil Hofriyati womanhood.

"Fatna and the Sultan's Son" owns that power rests equally with the perceptibly powerless as with the ascendant regime.

All of this is relevant to the *zār,* for *zayran* are powerful outsiders par excellence. The addition of *zār* to a marital relationship reverses the vector of the allegory detailed above: now relations between Hofriyati and alien others help to contextualize relations between husbands and wives. *Zār* is a kind of metalanguage: acknowledgment of her possession by both husband and wife shifts their relationship into another, more powerful mode, reencoding, as it were, the frequently disparate, frequently inaudible messages they might wish to exchange in a manner which makes their decipherment both possible and secure. What *zār* does—though this is hardly the conscious intent of those who, by means of it, articulate distress—is open the potentially destructive ambiguity in a marriage to interpretations which, if taken up in the appropriate circumstance, might turn it in positive directions. Ambiguity is not resolved, merely diverted along a path that has increased creative potential, the promise of fresh interpretation. Paradox remains, despite the adoption of a spirit idiom through which it can be brought to light. Possession has, then, aesthetic implications (cf. Lambek 1978, 1981; Leiris 1958; Kapferer 1983), and these I believe supply a measure of its therapeutic force (Boddy 1988). Like a literary text, it "speaks of a possible world and of a possible way of orienting oneself within it" (Ricoeur 1976 : 88). Should Hofriyati husbands choose to appropriate the possession texts elucidated by their wives, their relationships may be enriched by the addition of new horizons of meaning, new pathways for fruitful communication and, of course, new arenas for the generation of conflict. The next two chapters illustrate these and earlier points with excerpts from several possession histories.

6

Zaineb and Umselima

Possession as a Family Idiom

> I am inclined to agree with Wilhelm Dilthey . . . that *meaning* . . . arises in *memory,* in *cognition* of the *past,* and is concerned with negotiation about the "fit" between past and present. . . .
>
> —Victor Turner, *From Ritual to Theatre*

One of my principal informants in Hofriyat is Zaineb, whom I introduced in chapter 1. Of all the women I met in Hofriyat, it was Zaineb who seemed to comprehend what I was about from the start. We became, within the often formidable restraints of research, confidantes and friends. It is my conceit that we shared an ethnographic curiosity, and I was privileged to have her guidance as I wound my way mentally and physically through the labyrinth of Hofriyat. I realize now that my presence in the village altered her awareness of herself, confirming intuited potentials of womanhood not within her grasp, and this, if it has caused her distress, I regret. Without Zaineb my first period of fieldwork could well have been sterile and unrewarding. Her family and its appendages, scattered between Khartoum and Hofriyat, befriended me and at every juncture smoothed my way. From all of them I learned what it means to have brothers and sisters in northern Sudan.

Zaineb is an exceptionally perceptive woman who, like many Hofriyati, has a keen sense of humor verging sometimes on the wry. In 1976 she was in her mid thirties, mother of seven children ranging in ages from two to sixteen. Zaineb is possessed by several different *zayran;* during my first field trip she experienced an illness that was partly attributed to possession. This chapter explores her illness in the context of her family background, for it was Zaineb's story that alerted me to how possession can operate as a family affliction. *Zār,* villagers say, runs in families; though strictly speaking neither inherited nor hereditary, the proclivity to attract *zayran* and even the affliction itself may be transmitted between kin, yet only in the maternal line. Moreover, a particular spirit is considered more likely to possess a woman if it has also seized her mother or some other maternal kinswoman, typically her mother's mother or mother's sister. Though still an affliction, possession under these conditions is not without positive effects. For when the idiom is shared by family members, the fact that they have spirits adds further dimension to established roles and relationships, thickening them in ways other than those determined by kinship.

Zaineb's story therefore begins before her birth, with her mother, Umselima, and the chronicle which she and her sisters and daughters related over several months in 1976. Admittedly, this account is the written product of my elicitation and, at minimum, therefore doubly constructed (cf. Crapanzano 1977*a*, 1980). That said, women who are possessed in Hofriyat (and I daresay those who are not) frequently indite personal narratives in the genre employed by Umselima, and these stories (*ḥikāyat*) or anecdotes (*giṣaṣ*) circulate widely among groups of visiting women. Perhaps because Umselima was a popular *shaykha* of the *zār,* her possession experiences are more generally known than most, for they have served to establish the credibility of her vocation. And perhaps because she is older, they also provide a retrospective direction to her life that the stories of much younger women lack.

The events of Umselima's story are, in fact, extraordinarily well integrated; and in this can be discerned an implicit function for possession as an idiom: it enables the possessed to construct and continually reconstruct her experiences in a personally meaningful way (Crapanzano 1977*a*, 1980; Obeyesekere 1970, 1981). Hofriyati women typically speak about their lives as if describing the desert: prolonged expanses—"just living; eating and drinking only"—punctuated by oases of discrete events—important weddings, changes of residence, divorces, pregnancies, the births and deaths of kin. For those who are possessed, repeated *zār* experiences bind these events into comprehensive wholes, into patterns displaying greatest coherence for women in their senior years. Presumably, then, as she ages, a woman periodically reinterprets her past in light of her current relations with *zayran*. For Umselima, the pattern was complete; when I met her she had just returned from the *ḥaj* and had abrogated her role as *shaykha* so as to be reconciled with mainstream Islam in preparation for her death.

In what follows, informants' narratives, passages of which consist of translated tape-recorded statements, are periodically interrupted by discursive passages in which I attempt to make cultural sense of what I have been told.

Umselima

At first glance, Umselima seemed a delicate woman, small of frame, thin, her fine-boned features declaring faded beauty, now a quiet elegance. Her skin a cracked and burnished vellum; her eyes dark, clouded with age, and spoked by fine taut lines; her cheeks hollowed with hardship, each rent by three long scars—her tribal marks; her hands long, slim, painfully arthritic. But fragile she was not. Her energy was boundless. Umselima was always going somewhere, to visit a friend, fetch some recalcitrant goats, retrieve an errant child. And every Friday, shod in cracked plastic slippers, grey hair primly braided, dressed impeccably in white, she would march off under a tattered black umbrella toward Malkab and noontime prayers at the mosque.

Malkab, a neighboring hamlet, is her birthplace and still her sisters' home. Umselima was born third in a family of five. Her parents were matrilateral parallel cousins, *awlād khālāt,* their marriage "immediately close" (*garīb ṭawālī*) in local terms. Although it had been fruitful, a major source of tension existed, for their second child was to be their only son.

When she was young, Umselima would accompany her father and his mother to their *wadī* plantation each year at the start of the rainy season, camping there for three to five months while her father cultivated the family's subsistence crop of *dura.* Umselima's job was to help her *ḥabōba* keep house in their hut, called a *raqūba,* loosely built of mats, rushes, and poles. Mohammed, her brother and senior by two or three years, remained in Malkab to take religious instruction from the local *faki,* while their older sister, Sittalbenat, was left at home to assist with the younger children.

At eight or nine, Umselima was circumcised, an operation Sittalbenat had undergone some years before. Umselima volunteered only that this had been a painful experience and for "a long time" after she was unable to urinate.

When Umselima was ten, her mother, pregnant again, endured a difficult labor and gave birth to twins, a girl and a boy, both stillborn. Immediately, her father went north to Dongola in search of new lands to farm and "his expectation"—another wife to give him descendants. Before departing, he betrothed Sittalbenat, then fifteen, to an older unrelated acquaintance in Omdurman; despite her protestations she was quickly wed and removed from the village. His father and elder sister gone, Mohammed soon left to seek his fortunes in Khartoum; there he married a stranger without apprising his family or asking his father's permission. Umselima was left with her mother and two younger sisters in Malkab. And it was in the wake of these events that she had her first experience with beings she would later identify as *zayran.* She was then twelve or thirteen.

> It was summer and at night. There was a full moon; it was bright as in daytime. I was walking back to my uncle's house where I was sleeping, for he [her *khāl,* mother's brother] was away in Khartoum and I was keeping his wife and her daughters company. I was alone, coming back after seeing a

> *ṭabl*[1] of the Qadriya brotherhood (*ṭarīga*). All the men in my family belong to the Qadriya.
>
> My *khāl*'s people had a *ḥōsh,* not like us, we had no *ḥōsh*. There were few *ḥōsh*s back then, and few people, not like now. My *khāl*'s people were better off and they had walls around their house.
>
> When I reached their *ḥōsh* I saw three boys standing near the wall wearing caps and wedding costumes, *jalabīyas* and beads—little Europeans (*Khawājāt*). I asked, "Who's that? Who's that?" I called some names of boys who lived nearby; I called to the son of my uncle, his hame is Ali. No one answered. I ran inside, I was afraid. During the night I drank water every five minutes. I did not sleep, not a bit. The next night my mother walked with me for I refused to go alone. But I told no one that I had seen those boys against the wall. I became ill immediately; my health declined from that moment.

When this occurred Umselima was no stranger to the *zār;* she knew quite a lot about spirits, and had witnessed possession ceremonies in Malkab and neighboring villages from an early age. Her mother, Neʿma, was possessed by Ethiopian *zayran*, consonant with her fertility problems. And although *shaykhat* in those days strictly forbade the attendance of unwed girls at a *zār,* Umselima and her sisters used to observe as best they could, peering over *ḥōsh* walls when a ceremony was held within, or spying through open windows. Umselima told me that whenever she stood outside a "place of the *zār,*" just the smell of the spirits' incense would, in her words, "*mutkayifi,*" make her feel cheerful and well.

Umselima's first spirit vision coincides with tumultuous family events which cannot have failed to impress her. At the time, she is twelve or thirteen years old, fast approaching the age of marriage. Her sister has been wed precipitately to a much older man in the city; neither the bride nor her mother and brother were consulted. Her father has gone off in search of another wife after Neʿma produced stillborn twins. Her only brother, who could be relied on to support and protect her and to prevail on their father to select for her an appropriate spouse, has departed for Khartoum where he, too, marries in haste. Umselima's world is crumbling—her close male kin have abandoned her. Returning to her maternal uncle's *ḥōsh* late at night and alone after attending a ceremony of the religious fraternity to which her father and brother belong, with its quick, rhythmic drumming and trance-inducing incantations, Umselima witnesses an apparition.

Several points suggest themselves in this encounter which Umselima reveals to no one at the time. The boys are light skinned and wear caps,

1. A religious ceremony that involves singing and drumming songs in praise of Allah. It is usually held to commemorate the deathday of a saint, a wedding, or male circumcision.

identifying them as *Khawājāt,* Westerners or Europeans, yet they are dressed in clothing worn by village bridegrooms. Mohammed has gone to Khartoum which—because it is the locus of Western influence in Sudan, is considered the "home of *khawājāt*" (human Westerners) by many rural Sudanese—and he has just married. The *Khawāja* boys insinuate her brother, who straddles both cultures as they seem to do. And Mohammed, himself still a boy, behaves like a European in marrying an unrelated woman of his choice. Lastly, Sittalbenat's situation echoes that of her brother from a feminine perspective.

Again, Umselima sees the boys when she is walking outdoors alone at night, something women are exhorted not to do. Since she has no chaperone, Umselima is conducting herself like Western women and prostitutes are reputed to behave. What is more, she walks through open spaces which *jinn* are known to frequent. The three boys are leaning against a wall of one of the few *ḥōsh*s in her village, indicative of her uncle's wealth and concern for his wife and daughters. This family's situation describes the inverse of her own: she and her mother and sisters live in an unprotected, "open house" (*bayt fātiḥ*), and one with no male residents to afford them protection. All of these circumstances are breaches of feminine ideals and cultural practice. They render her vulnerable to attack by *zayran* or signify spirits' ingress of the human realm. It is fitting that Umselima's vision take place against the outside wall of a *ḥōsh,* a contemporary architectural symbol of interiority, expression of the boundary between the family and the outside world.

That night, out of fear, Umselima drinks a considerable quantity of water, which links this event to her circumcision and, as revealed below, to her second possession attack. After circumcision she retains water inordinately; following her vision she consumes it. Both episodes are idiomatic, involving body orifices and boundaries; both are therefore "legible" to Umselima and her associates.

In Dongola Umselima's father soon found out about Mohammed's marriage. He was livid. He went to Khartoum, fought bitterly with his son, and forced him to divorce. Mohammed, said Umselima, was devastated, for the marriage had been a love match. Their father arranged a second marriage for him to Neʿma's brother's daughter, who lived in the *ḥōsh* Umselima was visiting before her vision. (Was this another meaning of the vision? Was there a previous arrangement which Mohammed had spurned?) His bride was maternally related to the local *faki,* Mohammed's former teacher. Mohammed's employment remained in Khartoum, but he returned frequently to Malkab for holidays. His wife soon gave birth to a baby girl.

When she was thirteen or fourteen, Umselima's father married her to a Hofriyati farmer twice her age, the son of her mother's maternal half brother. Though he lived with his parents nearby, Umselima was left to reside with her mother and unmarried sisters for several years after the wedding. Her husband paid her visits now and then, whenever he was not at his family's *wadī* plantation or tending his fields in the floodplain where he had built himself a *raqūba*. Sometimes, Umselima would go to stay with him in his hut near the Nile, always returning to Malkab after the winter harvest.

Sittalbenat, meanwhile, had also come back to Malkab, but permanently. She had borne a daughter by her elderly husband, then a son who died in infancy. At this her husband repudiated her, but kept their daughter to be raised by his kin in the city. Soon after returning home, she rewed and immediately acknowledged herself to be possessed.

Around 1928, when Umselima was fifteen or sixteen years old, she conceived and bore a son. Sometime later, she had a daughter, and shortly thereafter experienced her second vision.

> I saw the *zayran* again after I had given birth to two children. I had a son who died after four years, and I had just given birth to a girl, maybe a fortnight before. I was lying in a hut like the nomads still use, on an *angarīb,* and again I saw the Westerners, standing in the *raqūba*. Again I was afraid. I said to my mother, "I do not wish to stay in the *raqūba,* I want to lie outside. Help me move my *angarīb* outside." Still I did not tell her what I had seen. I told no one. Again that night, when I was lying out of doors, they appeared to me. I was fearful and I became ill.
>
> About two weeks later, a month after I had given birth, my illness worsened. For three days I was unable to urinate, I could not eat, and I had a fever and strong sickness. Then I went to a *faki islām*. The *faki* said, "Never have you been ill [from organic causes]. You have a red spirit, that is all!" My baby was still living then. The *faki* told me I had a red spirit—a *zār*—and he said that I had seen him myself. I said, "No! No!" I denied this.
>
> Then Mohammed my brother, he was visiting from Khartoum, he went to Kabushiya and bought perfume, incense, a white *tōb*. He said, "We must do a *zār* for Umselima." I said, "No! No! I do not want this. I do not have a *zār*." Then they said there was a *zār* party happening in another quarter of the village. My people said, "We must take her there, at night." [As her forty-day confinement had not ended, she could not be abroad in daylight.] Reluctantly, I agreed to go. Then I bathed and dressed in a *tōb,* and they burned some incense for me. For three days I had not urinated. Someone carried my baby, and they led me to the house of the *zār*. As soon as we arrived outside, I felt the need to urinate. Immediately, I crouched on the ground and I urinated maybe a quarter of an hour and still it had not stopped. When it was finished, I said, "I can stay to see anything. I am empty, I have become well."
>
> When I entered the *zār* the *shaykha* brought perfume and incense. She

censed me and I descended [*nizalta*]. I descended a little and then I said, "Enough!" But I was happy. I stayed to the end. I became well immediately, but I said, "It is finished. I do not want a ceremony."

Subsequent to this, Umselima's infant daughter died. Then for several years [1933 to 1938], she says she "sat empty," unable to conceive.

In her second vision, the themes of openness and closure return, but in a slightly different context. The boys now show themselves inside her hut, described as being "like the nomads still use." The nomads' peripatetic lifestyle is the antithesis of villagers', yet not for Umselima, who still shifts residence between her mother's house and her husband's. When Umselima moves outside—which, having so recently given birth, she should not do—so do the *Khawājāt*. She fails to escape them: *zayran* are able to move through walls and barriers; they cannot be kept out or kept in. Again she falls ill, and again tells no one of her vision. Even when the *faki* confirms that she is possessed and suggests she has seen "her *zār*," she denies it. Significantly, soon after this vision her baby dies: Umselima implicitly (and later explicitly) associates the deaths of her children with the intervention of *zayran*. Her reluctance to acknowledge their presence and refusal to grant them a ceremony merely intensify the spirits' effect, and for the next several years she "sits empty." This phrase links her childlessness to her second possession illness, when, following postpartum reinfibulation, she retains urine for three days, and only obtains relief (emptiness, in a positive sense) when she inhales spirit incense and approaches the place where a *zār* is being held. It also links her second *zār* experience to the first, and to her circumcision. For Umselima, marriageability, childbirth, the deaths of her children, pregnancy and its absence are all bound up with her visions of *zayran*. Her reproductive problems are, like the events preceding her initial apparition, violations of feminine ideals that precipitate or signify possession.

One last point: Umselima recovers from a retention illness after her brother demonstrates support, an event that reverses her drinking quantities of water in the wake of his, and their father's, abandonment. Still, she has yet to inform her husband of the affliction, as she must do in order to negotiate a positive relationship with her spirits.

During the period when Umselima "sat empty," her two younger sisters married and moved away from Malkab. Sadiya wed a member of her father's subtribe, a distant relation. But Nyla, the youngest, married the preferred *wad ʿamm ṭawālī*.

Sittalbenat suffered no more procreative difficulties, producing for her second husband sons and daughters in rapid succession. While she had earlier acknowledged herself to be possessed, she did not feel the affliction serious enough to warrant a full-scale ritual, and kept her spirits appeased by attending the cures of others.

But for Mohammed, things were not going well at all. Though his second wife had borne a daughter soon after they were wed, she seemed unable to conceive again. Like Umselima, she "sat empty." So, as his father had done, Mohammed left his Malkabi family behind and went north to Dongola. There he took his third wife, a kinswoman of his stepmother.

In the late 1930s, Umselima became pregnant and gave birth to a daughter, Leyla, her eldest surviving child. Soon after, she bore a son, who did poorly from the start. It was then that her vision recurred.

> My husband had built a house for me in Hofriyat and I had just moved there with Leyla and the baby. Again, at night I went into the house for a moment and when I came out I saw the same boys as before. Right away I called my husband. I told him what I had seen. I said, "I am in the habit of (*mitʿauwada*) seeing such and such and such." Immediately he called *nās* [people, the people of] Sosan and Bozeyna [an apprentice *shaykha* and her assistant] and they put on a big ceremony for me. It lasted three days. I was happy. It was finished and I became well. Much later when I felt pain in my arms, pain in my head, we had a seven-day ceremony and slaughtered a white ram.

Shortly after this, Umselima's baby son died. But she soon became pregnant again and gave birth to a healthy boy, Osman. She was then between twenty-eight and thirty years old. She said she had become interested in the *zār* and was learning about the spirits with an eye to becoming a curer herself.

Following Osman, Umselima lost two more babies, a girl, then a boy, both of whom died within a week of their births. Umselima was *ḥaznāna,* stricken with grief. She recalled a dream she had after the death of this latest son. She saw a woman, fat, beautiful, and light skinned, sitting on an *angarīb* surrounded by children; Umselima's baby boy was on her knee. When she awoke, Umselima found she was weeping.

When Umselima has her third vision of the *Khawāja zayran,* she is extremely vulnerable. She has a history of children dying in infancy, and, after a reproductive hiatus of several years, has ominously produced first a daughter, then a sickly son. Her husband has just moved her into a house of their own. While this suggests to all that their marriage is well established, it also removes Umselima from the supportive environment of her natal family and puts her under closer scrutiny of his kin in Hofriyat. Then and there she suffers her third and decisive *zār* experience, finally admitting to her husband what she has seen. He is highly supportive and arranges her cure, after which, though their baby dies, Umselima regains her vigor and *goes on to produce a healthy son.* The couple's implicit exchange of messages here revitalized, possibly saved, their marriage, shifting what ordinarily would be considered interpersonal tension to an alternate mode of discourse where conversation is less determined by quotidian male supremacy and less ambiguous than when wives normally address their husbands (or not ambiguous in quite the same way), and where the factor of human responsibility—female or male—is greatly reduced. Moreover, the timing of Umselima's subsequent reproductive success both ratifies the source of her earlier troubles and establishes that the culpable *zayran* are now positively disposed to negotiation so long as she and her husband openly admit her affliction and agree to her spirits' demands.

Although Umselima suffers two more infant fatalities, she does not mention being bothered by her *Khawāja zayran* at these times. But she does have a vivid dream; it must have been very disturbing, for in recounting it, her voice was choked with emotion. The woman who holds Umselima's son is fat, healthy—all that Umselima is not. And the woman is a manifestation of a *zār;* despite their ethnic characteristics, female *zayran* always appear to women as idealized versions of themselves. This is also, then, a manifestation of Umselima as she wishes to be, of an Umselima who need not work hard helping her husband in the fields because he has only one son, who is too young to assist; of an Umselima fat, pampered, and healthy in the ideal image of womanhood; of an Umselima boundlessly fertile.

Unselima is also possessed by two female spirits of the *Khudām* (servant) or *ʿAbīd* (slave) *zār* society and, though she is not sure when these first came "above" her, they had made their presence known by the time of her dream. *Khudām zayran* are spirit parallels of southern Sudanese tribespeople, and the two which possess Umselima, *Baharanil* (River Nile) and *Jata,* are prostitutes—inversions of moral fertility. Yet *Jata* wears clothes that a local bride might have worn in the past: white satin dress with the traditional thong skirt of maidenhood (*rahaṭ*) over top. Like her *Khawāja* boys, *Jata* is a paradox: she belongs to another culture and is inherently a paragon of "openness," yet she covers (and attempts to disguise) herself in local wedding clothes. The disparity between appearances and what they conceal echoes Fatna's antics in her "courtship" of the sultan's son.

Possession by southern Sudanese spirits resonates with Umselima's history: like their human counterparts, they live in thatched huts and are known to move with the seasons. The specific spirits above her are prostitutes and servants, the first suggesting a lack of feminine control over fertility and of masculine control over the behavior of female kin, the second, a life of hard work and little ease. On the other hand, Umselima says that, like her mother, she is strongly affected by Ethiopian *zayran,* linked with problematic fertility.

Until this time, Umselima and her children had been living in her husband's house in Hofriyat. It was a house in the open, built without a *ḥōsh.* But, said Umselima, even peasant farmers were then beginning to read the Quran. They were becoming increasingly concerned to surround their houses with walled enclosures, something which, though always desirable, only the well-off had been able to do in the past. So she and her children were moved to an unoccupied *ḥōsh* in Hofriyat owned by her husband's half brother, a *faki islām* then residing in Khartoum.

Meanwhile, Umselima's siblings were getting on with their lives. Sittalbenat now had two sons and three daughters. After a lengthy hiatus, her spirits were again beginning to "burn" (*itḥarrig*), and she had taken to mollifying them by drumming *zār* threads with other possessed women for a day or two now and then.

Mohammed's third wife had died, childless, in Dongola. At once he was given her sister's daughter to wed (a kind of leapfrog sororal marriage that emphasizes the cognatic quality of kinship in northern Sudan). His new wife bore a son, next a daughter, then lost two babies in quick succession and died in childbirth.

Sadiya, who had been living with her merchant husband in Khartoum, moved with him to Shendi. But she returned to Malkab with each pregnancy. Her first child was a daughter, as was her second, who died in infancy. Then Sadiya bore a son, Hamid. While carrying him she fell ill and, failing to respond to Western or Islamic medications, was diagnosed as possessed. When Sadiya suffered from *nazīf*—hemorrhage—at Hamid's birth, thus confirming her spirit affliction, a seven-day cure was held; the spirits responsible were found to be *Khawājāt.* Sadiya recovered and, as she says, "Allah be praised, I have never suffered *zār* illness again!" (Her spirits have not since "inflamed.")

Nyla and her husband, a shopkeeper, lived in Kassala near the Ethiopian border. They had two healthy children, a boy and a girl.

. . . *and Zaineb*

In the mid 1940s, Umselima bore Zaineb and three years later became pregnant again. In her seventh month her husband suffered a heart attack and died. Deep in mourning, Umselima gave birth, prematurely, to a healthy boy. In remembrance, he was given his father's name, Hassan.

Following her husband's death Umselima and the four children were supported by Mohammed, and by her husband's paternal half brother in whose *ḥosh* they dwelt. The latter was achieving notoriety as a religious leader in Khartoum; the two families drew very close. Leyla and Osman were circumcised with the eldest daughter and son of this man, their *ʿamm* and benefactor.

Mohammed had returned to Malkab after the death of his fourth wife, and married there again. His bride was the daughter of his mother's mother's, and his father's mother's, brother's son: Mohammed's parents were *awlād khālāt*—matrilateral parallel cousins (figure 6.1). Though technically Mohammed and this woman were *awlād ʿamm,* Umselima and Zaineb emphasized maternal links in speaking of this marriage.

When Zaineb was seven, her cousin Hamid, Sadiya's son, fell seriously ill and was treated with traditional medicines to no avail. Now, as he had been born in the midst of his mother's most significant possession attack, Hamid was born possessed. His mother's *zayran* were above him as well, for so they had been in the womb. Thus when his current illness was attributed to spirits, the diagnosis was readily accepted.

Sadiya made preparations to hold a ceremony for him in Malkab. Umselima, whose favorable reputation with the *zār* had been growing steadily under the tutelage of a noted curer in Shendi, would officiate as *shaykha.* Sadiya and Umselima were very close, and Sadiya gave her sister this opportunity to better establish her practice. Umselima's daughters attended the ceremony with her, as they had done since they were small.

When Hamid was diagnosed as possessed, he was said to be *maqfūl,* "closed." His symptoms, like Umselima's, were those of body closure, a common indication of *zār*. Hamid was found sitting straight up in a chair (also symbolic of the *zār;* Constantinides 1977), hands tensely clenched, arms folded hard against his shoulders, legs drawn close to his chest. He could not open his mouth to eat or speak, and was locked in this position for several days. Umselima recalls,

> They spread the *zār* in Malkab. They put henna on him and a mattress on the ground. When we drummed *ʿArab* threads, Hamid stood up. He could not stand up before. He said, "I want a whip, and *ʿArab* sandals, and an *ʿArab tōb*" [a man's garment worn criss-crossing the chest, as among the Beja]. We put on a seven-day *zār* and his condition improved.
>
> But one day during the drumming, Sosan and I were late in arriving from Hofriyat. The women of Malkab wanted to start the *zār* without us, but Hamid prevented them. He sat on the *dallūka* and would not allow anyone near it until the people of Hofriyat had come.

Evident here is the gist of a rivalry between Malkab and Hofriyat, significant to Zaineb's affliction, considered below.

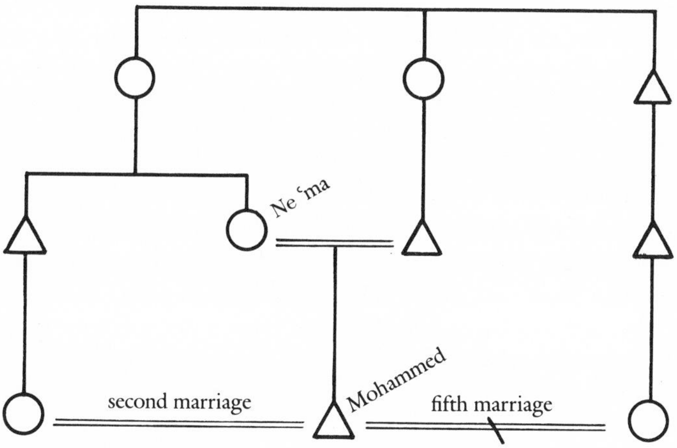

Fig. 6.1. Mohammed's Second and Fifth Marriages

Hamid's *ʿArab zayran,* counterparts of nomadic Muslim Sudanese, were provided a whip and long pantaloons. But the *Khawājāt* whom he had acquired in the womb had also to be appeased, and were given socks, shoes, and a watch. Not only did Hamid recover from his illness, never again to be plagued by *zayran,* but he was suddenly able to play the tambourine (*riq*), an instrument of the *ʿArāb.*

Not long after Hamid's successful seven-day *zār,* Umselima rewed. The marriage was a leviratic union entered into reluctantly and doomed from the start. The man was a full brother of the *faki islām* in Khartoum, thus another of her first husband's paternal half brothers and *ʿamm* to her children. He had been married several times before: none of his wives conceived while married to him, though all had borne children with other husbands. So, Umselima said, she was unenthusiastic. Nor did she need the marriage from a financial standpoint, for Mohammed and the *faki* were supporting them adequately and without apparent hardship. The couple did not cohabit. Umselima continued in Hofriyat, while her husband remained in Omdurman. The marriage designed to confirm existing obligations lasted but a year. Umselima claims responsibility for securing her divorce:

I told him, "Do as you like. I do not want you! I do not desire this marriage."

Having obtained her freedom, Umselima continued to pursue a career as *shaykha* of the *zār*. For several years now she and another apprentice *shaykha,* Sosan, had been attending local ceremonies and learning the techniques of speaking with *zayran*. Umselima's possessive spirits were very cooperative, and through them she became adept at diagnosing the identities of patients' *zār* intruders. When an older *shaykha* died and her partner retired, Umselima and Sosan jointly assumed their practice. Their fame as curers soon exceeded the village area.

By then it was 1952 or 1953: Zaineb was eight years old, and Umselima newly divorced. Mohammed's fifth wife had not conceived after four or five years of marriage, so he divorced her on grounds of infertility and married in the north yet again. Then Nyla (their youngest sister), seven months pregnant and accompanied by her two children, boarded a train in Kassala en route to Malkab for delivery. But the baby arrived while she was in transit, prematurely. By the time Nyla landed in Malkab with her infant son, she was sick from the *zār*. A seven-day cure was held for her as soon as possible, Umselima and Sosan officiating. She appeared to recover, but decided to remain in Malkab for an extended visit.

Nyla's ceremony had just concluded when, in Hofriyat, Zaineb's cousin (*bit ʿamm*) suffered a tragic accident attributed to the action of a *zār*. Following her hospital convalescence, a curing rite was held for her in Hofriyat, after which she could walk again, though not without some difficulty. Umselima officiated at her ceremony and Zaineb, again, attended.

Around this time Umselima suffered the relapse of *zār* sickness that earlier she described as causing "pain in my arms, pain in my head." Zaineb was eight or nine at the time, newly circumcised, still lying on an *angarīb* recuperating from the operation when her mother drummed the *zār* as a patient for the second time. Umselima's spirits demanded a white ram, provided by Mohammed who, she said, "loved the *zār*."

Umselima implies it was because of the *zār* that she obtained her divorce. The status of a widow or divorcée would release her from certain obligations and limitations by which married women are bound, freeing her to pursue her own interests (Boddy 1985)—to become a full-fledged *shaykha*. Umselima, sure of Mohammed's support and his admiration for the *zār*, says, "I did not wish to marry again." Once when we were at a wedding together she turned to me and said, "The *zār*, I love the *zār*, and I love *zār* parties more than weddings." Again note the juxtaposition and opposition of *zār* and wedding themes in Umselima's discourse.

Umselima says she became possessed about this time by *Ḥakīm Basha*, "Doctor Pasha," an Egyptian doctor *zār* of the nineteenth century (sometimes held to be Turkish or European) who has more recently taken on the traits of a modern medical practitioner, complete with lab coat and stethoscope. That the spirit articulates her curing vocation seems patent. *Ḥakīm Basha* in physical possession of His host divines illnesses and recommends appropriate therapies. Umselima's apparent abilities in this regard are, however, not confined to *Ḥakīm Basha*'s presence: she is endowed by her entire pantheon of *zayran* with remarkable diagnostic abilities even for illnesses not inflicted by spirits. In this, her role is considered similar to that of a medical doctor.

Umselima is also possessed by *Shaykh Mohammed* of the *Darāwīsh*, or dervish species of *zayran*.[2] She does not recall when this *zār* first made its presence felt, but it appears to be a recent addition to her group; it may articulate her growing rapprochement with Islam. But the spirit is said to belong to the Qadriya fraternity, of which her brother is a member. And, although I precede myself, her brother happens to be possessed by a Qadriya *zār* as well. The fact that brother and sister share a spirit society or, perhaps, that a single group participates in them both, may (eliding other significances) effect a realignment of family relationships in the idiom of possession, discussed below. Of course, their father belonged to the Qadriya too; significantly, after his departure for Dongola, he is dropped from Umselima's narrative completely. Though he frequently returned to the village, she does not even mention his death.

Umselima's story contains several suggestions of how she has articulated her experiences—or from our perspective if not from hers, her selfhood (Boddy 1988)—in terms of *zayran*. As Crapanzano (1977*b*:142) notes, for those whose fundamental assumptions about the nature of reality include the possibility of possession, "the locus of the individual's selfhood appears to be differently oriented and the dimensions of individuality appear to be differently determined for him than for the Westerner." In Hofriyat (and neighboring Malkab) it seems that experiences and feelings excepted from the culturally prescribed feminine self-image or out of keeping with the vector of interiority are more likely than others to be attributed to the influence of *zayran* or linked to the onset of possession illness. Such experiences would include reproductive problems and anxieties, lack of male protection, even, perhaps, religious fervor more readily associated with Hofriyati males.

It must be remembered, however, that Umselima is not the only one responsible for deciphering the identities and characteristics of her spirits. These must be discovered in the course of therapy, in negotiations between the *shaykha,* normally well informed by the patient's kin about her life situation, and afflicting *zayran*. As the community of adherents aids the patient in naming spirits responsible for her malady, so also do they aid her in achieving the appropriate orientation of her selfhood—and not a bounded, individuated selfhood such as we in the West might articulate, but one firmly embedded in the lives of human and spirit others.

The spirit idiom according to which Umselima articulates certain ex-

2. The name is not that of her brother since I have used pseudonyms throughout.

periences casts a mantle of coherence over the story of her life. When we spoke, Umselima was in her early sixties and had obviously recontextualized the experiences of her youth in light of events that happened later. One example of this is the recurrence throughout her narrative of the number 3. Umselima sees three *Khawāja* boys on three separate occasions: once before marriage, again after giving birth to a girl having recently lost a boy, and again after giving birth to an ailing son. She lost, in all, three sons. Did a vision foretell each of these deaths? Do the three *Khawāja* boys retrospectively represent her three lost sons? After holding a three-day curing ceremony, she becomes pregnant and gives birth to a healthy boy. Further, her initial tentative acknowledgment of possession following her second vision was preceded by an inability to eat or urinate for three days. Thus for three days Umselima's body is "closed," its essential orifices blocked, her symptoms those of *excessive* interiority, diametrically opposed to the excessive openness of events (among them, giving birth) that precipitate her vision. For Umselima, the number 3 provides one of several threads that stitch together events already cut from the fabric of her experience and constructed to the pattern of the *zār*.

Later in the year of Umselima's seven-day cure, Zaineb's older sister Leyla married a distant paternal cousin of their father, and shortly confessed to a spirit affliction. After Leyla's wedding, Nyla returned to Kassala with her infant son, but following their arrival he sickened and died. When Nyla left, Umselima's mother, Neʿma, who had been living all this time with Sittalbenat in Malkab, came to live with Umselima in Hofriyat.

Following her move to Hofriyat, Neʿma's *zayran* began to "burn." Umselima with Mohammed's help put on a ceremony for her in Umselima's *ḥōsh*. But she was getting old and her sight had failed; doctors at the eye clinic in Khartoum could do nothing to restore it. Nor it seems could the *zār*.

Around 1955 Leyla gave birth to a son at Umselima's home in Hofriyat. At his naming ceremony, Sittalbenat, now approaching fifty, revealed that periodically drumming the *zār* and attending others' rituals had ceased to do her any good. Her illness, she felt, was intensifying, and she was determined to have a proper seven-day cure. She asked her husband for funds to mount it, but he wavered. First he agreed, then, as Sittalbenat says, "The anger rose in him and he refused. Came his half brother by the same mother and killed the anger. His brother said the *zār* is good. He said, 'I have spread the *zār* [spread mats and a spirit feast] for each of my wives.'"

Sittalbenat's husband finally agreed to finance her cure. This too was attended by Zaineb, now eleven or twelve years old. A year later, at about the same age as Umselima when first she saw the *Khawāja* boys, Zaineb had a vision.

> I had a strong fever. Many people in the village were sick. It was during the winter and everyone was sleeping indoors. I became *ghabiyāna* [entranced, absent, delirious], a great sickness. I saw a distant dream. Where clothing hung on the wall, the wall was open. I saw some *Ḥalib* people, some gypsies. I was very frightened and I said to Leyla, "See the *Ḥalib* people!" And Leyla said, "There are no gypsies on the wall, only clothes." When next I attended a *zār* party with my mother I found I was possessed by a *Ḥalib* spirit. I began to cry and I descended. Even now, whenever I have a fever, whenever I am ill, this dream returns.

Despite their differences, Zaineb's description echoes Umselima's story thematically: she speaks of being inside, enclosed by walls, and of an opening in a wall. The opening leads to a group of foreigners, Syrian gypsy spirits whose human counterparts are variously antithetical to the Hofriyati version of humanity and antagonistic to village women in a weakened state. Again, *zār* has to do with that which is "other," inconsistent with ordinary, everyday, prescriptive Hofriyatiness.

But the vision may have a more subtle significance. For *Ḥalib zayran* possess Umselima's sister, Sittalbenat, and Zaineb has just been betrothed to Sittalbenat's son, Abdelrahim. The dream might, then, articulate anxiety or simply expectation surrounding her upcoming marriage, and since marriages are regarded as openings or passageways between families, perhaps it is her marriage that is meant by the gap in the wall.

A few months after Zaineb's illness, Sittalbenat's eldest son married Mohammed's daughter by his second (first Malkabi) wife. But within a year the couple were divorced. This was surely a poor omen for Zaineb, who that same year married Abdelrahim. She was thirteen or fourteen years old. And two weeks after their wedding came a tragic event: Neʿma, her *ḥabōba* and Abdelrahim's, took sick and died. Zaineb had to surrender the privileges of bridehood to go into mourning.

Mohammed, who had just divorced his sixth wife for failing to conceive, returned for his mother's funeral. He had always admonished his kinswomen not to mourn in the traditional manner, wearing rough garments and flinging dust on their heads. Such behaviors give offence to *zayran,* and Mohammed, a champion of the cult, now insisted the women bathe, use oils and cologne, wear their most colorful *tōbs,* and fine-plait their hair to avoid provoking the spirits' wrath.

After the funeral, Mohammed stayed on in Malkab with his second wife, whom he had not divorced and occasionally visited. And there he became ill. He consulted a Western-style doctor, he consulted a *faki,* to no avail. Then Umselima, established as a *shaykha,* suggested he drum the *zār.* He agreed. The ceremony was held in Umselima's *ḥōsh* so as to elude the ire of his wife's uncle (*khāl*), the *faki,* who promised to sever all connection with his niece if they drummed in her house.

Mohammed's *zār* lasted seven days and was well attended by both women and men, the last, fellow members of the Qadriya fraternity. When the spirits' threads were drummed, Mohammed did not actively descend in response. Instead he sat quietly on an *angarīb*—usual, said Umselima, for men who are possessed. The spirits afflicting him belonged only to the *Darāwīsh,* Holy Men: *zayran* which, on entering the bodies of their hosts—a transition otherwise marked by the host's energetic, unrestrained movement—prompt them to assume a serene and dignified manner. As Mohammed's Malkabi daughter says, "He [it is unclear if she means Mohammed or the spirit] gave out cigarettes to those present and he smoked, and everyone was made happy by him. He conversed pleasantly with the men who had come to observe."

Mohammed provided a large white ram for the sacrificial meal and soon regained his health. He remarried (his seventh) in Malkab; his new wife conceived shortly thereafter.

Mohammed has long approved of the *zār* and is said to "love the spirits." He is quick to provide funds for his sisters' and mother's rites, but does not suffer from possession himself until later in his life. Though little is known about his northern wives, his Malkabi wives are possessed; no one doubts he would have leapt to their support if any had needed a cure.[3]

Mohammed succumbs to possession attack in his late fifties. His mother has just died and he has just repudiated yet another wife for failing to conceive. His father is still alive and, presumably, has attended his mother's funeral, for his parents were not divorced. It seems likely, given his personal history, that Mohammed was under considerable strain at this time.

According to Umselima, Mohammed's spirits had been above him for several years but remained calm out of respect for his defense of the cult. Now his spirits were angered because Mohammed had been struck by the evil eye, and this because he was an energetic man and financially successful. As a saying goes, "The evil eye brings the *zār*" (*al-ʿayn bitjīb az-zār*).

The *zār* groups likely to possess men, disregarding cases of in utero transference, are *Darāwīsh* and *ʿArāb*. Both exemplify masculine ideals in the extreme. Human Darāwīsh are, of course, mendicants, religious scholars, and fervently pious men; and *ʿArāb* are nomadic Arabs known for their immoderate displays of masculine valor such as competitive whipping and self-mutilation. In the Hofriyat area, spirits who possess men are always male themselves,[4] and may aid in their victims' construction of a

3. See pp. 217–18 for a description of his seventh wife's first possession.

4. This contrasts with Morocco, where men become possessed by she-demons (Crapanzano 1977*b*, 1980). It may not even hold for all of the northern Sudan, for coteries in

felicitous masculine identity. This I think to be true for Mohammed in at least two respects.

On the one hand, Mohammed and his father belong to the Qadriya order, as does the spirit causing Mohammed's illness. Mohammed's spirit, by all indications of its character, is *ʿAbdalgadir al-Jaylani, zār* parallel of the founder of this brotherhood. But whatever Umselima and her sisters think to be the case, Mohammed himself remains mute about his spirit's nature. He does not descend during the ritual nor move in rhythm to the drums; he does not, it seems, enter trance, or if he does, his spirit does not speak. Its identity has to be gleaned from its (his) actions. The ambiguity here may be intentional, for it enables Mohammed to acknowledge his affliction and benefit from this act without jeopardizing his masculinity by appearing to lose self-control.

Now Mohammed's cure takes place when his mother has just died and his father is an old man (he died five years later). Conceivably, Mohammed's illness has something to do with his earlier parental difficulties. As often happens in Sudan with the sons of polygynous men, he may have felt resentful that his father rewed *fōg ūmhu,* "above his mother"—a resentment suggested by his subsequent defiance. At the same time Mohammed closely identifies with his father: both occupy positions of prominence within the local Qadriya, and Mohammed, in his own search for descendants, follows his father's footsteps north. However, where his father is successful in his marriage to a Dongolese, siring five sons and three daughters there, Mohammed suffers only setbacks. What he is thinking and feeling we cannot tell, but his acknowledgment of possession and the presumed identity of his spirit may have enabled him to articulate certain ambivalences he harbored with regard to his identity. The fact of possession associates him with his mother and full sisters, all of whom are possessed, while the form his possession assumes links him to his father and patrilateral kin.

The second respect in which Mohammed's possession might figure in the construction or reconstruction of his identity has to do with the powers of the *zār Jaylani* to obstruct and facilitate female fertility. When he becomes unwell, Mohammed has been married six times, with only two daughters and a son to show for it. Four of his wives have failed to conceive, one bore a daughter then conceived no more, another suffered stillbirths and died in childbed. Given this history it is possible that Mohammed has come to view the fertility problems of his wives in terms of his own experience, phrased in the dual idiom of the Qadriya and the *zār.* Does his problem in acquiring descendants stem from a *zār* affliction of his own, brought on in the wake of contamination by the evil eye? Have

---

Khartoum and Omdurman frequently contain male homosexuals who cross-dress during rituals.

zayran been attempting to attract his attention through the various reproductive disorders of his wives, and has he foolishly disregarded them? Should he have kept his first wife? Like his sister Umselima, Mohammed may have found in the *zār* an interpretive framework, a context which gave his life meaning and coherence. For why should a man like himself, financially successful, energetic, able to provide for more than one wife with comparative ease, be so often defeated in attempting to achieve his "expectation"? Why should he fail where his father succeeded so well? One or two wives might have problems producing children, but surely not five or six! In accepting his *zār* affliction, Mohammed may have eluded confrontation with a deficiency far graver, perhaps, in the eyes of his peers: his own reproductive inadequacy. And the cure appears to have ameliorated this situation, for his seventh wife soon bore him a healthy son.

We have now arrived at a turning point in the story. Zaineb is fifteen and newly married. Soon she will become pregnant and, after the birth of her daughter, acknowledge a possession affliction. But before moving on, I pause to consider the possession afflictions of Zaineb's maternal aunts, Sittalbenat and Sadiya. The first is her mother-in-law, the second, her mother's ally.

Sittalbenat

Sittalbenat is a portly woman possessed by spirits from several *zār* societies, the majority signifying power and vested authority. Two are *Ḥabish* (Ethiopian): *Romani, Ya Wazīr Galla,* "Roman, Vizier of the Galla," is a spirit personifying the Italian presence in Ethiopia before the Second World War; *Mohammed Saᶜdabi* is a *zār* of the Saᶜdab tribe, to which Mek Nimir, last lord of Shendi, belonged, and whose members took refuge in Ethiopia following the murder of Ismaᶜil Pasha in 1822. Importantly, Sittalbenat and her siblings are themselves Saᶜdab. Sittalbenat also hosts at least two *Khawājāt: Dondo Ya Rundu,* a wealthy Westerner, and *Mistayr Brinso,* "Mister Prince," an archaeologist. Above her too are *Fallata* (western Sudanese and West African Muslims), nomadic *ᶜArāb,* and a number of *Ḥalib zayran.*

Sittalbenat describes her relationship with *zayran* thus: "Should a person say bad words to me, and I become angry, I become entranced immediately" [a spirit assumes control of her body]. Now this woman has a reputation for being irascible. She is, from my experience of her, forever shouting at some small child about to commit some folly, continually ordering her daughters, nieces, and grandchildren about. But still she is a

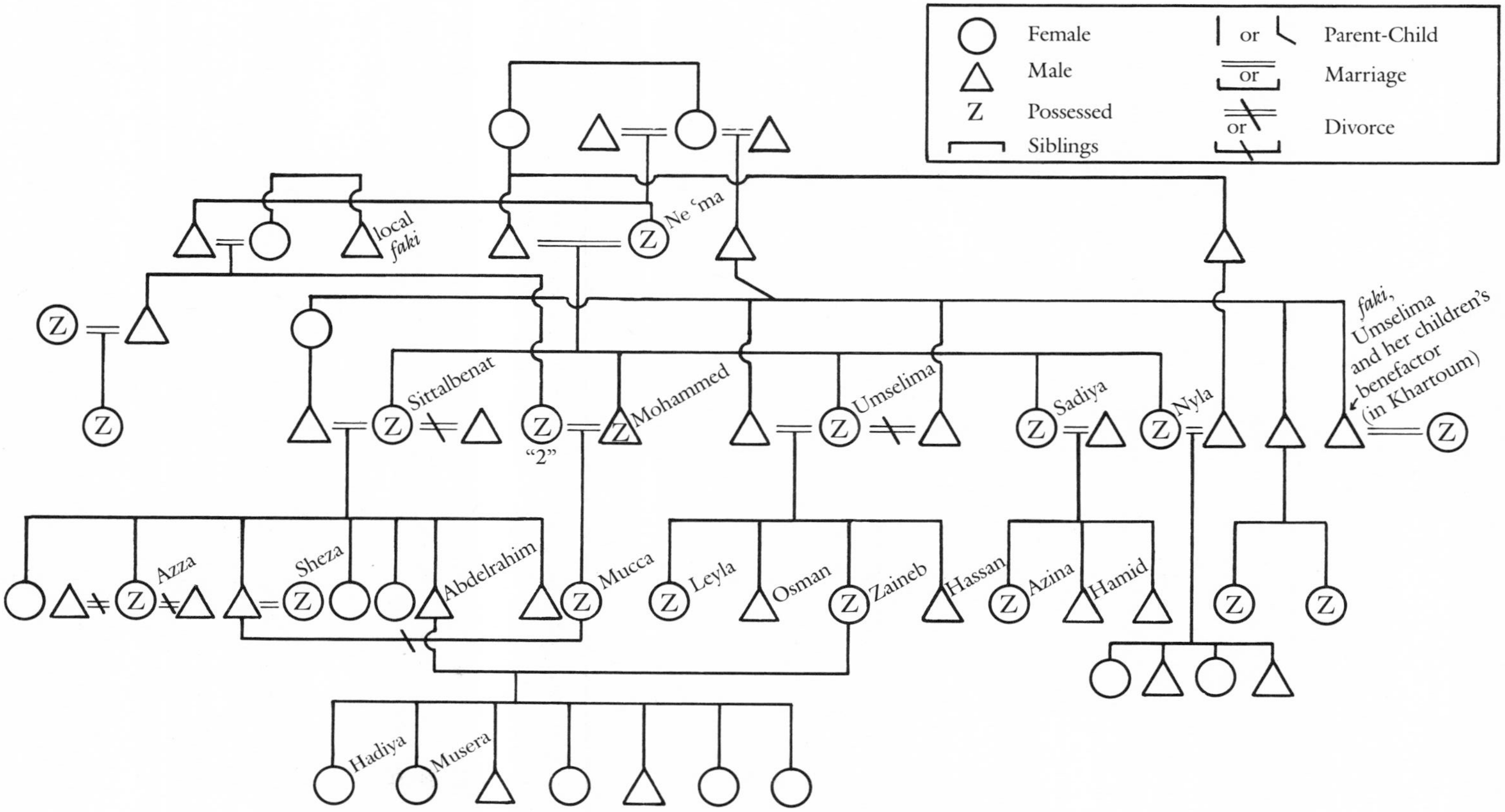

Fig. 6.2. Zaineb's Extended Family (expansion of fig. 6.3)

pleasant, even jolly woman, fond of leisurely conversation and certainly no stranger to a joke. So when she becomes truly angry (which, given the cultural constraints on expressing emotion, she ought not to do), her *zayran* intervene at once to alter the context of the situation and refocus responsibility for her untoward behavior. By removing her anger from the realm of human intent, possession salvages her relationships before she can go too far.

Sittalbenat is possessed principally by male *zayran,* and most of these, as I said, occupy positions of wealth and power. The females in her pantheon are typically poor, or give that impression while concealing great wealth, and all have forceful personalities. Perhaps, then, her affliction has more to do with overall social status—her identity as a female member of a once powerful ruling elite—than with fertility, however much reproductive disorder may have precipitated her initial possession illness. *Zār* may enable Sittalbenat to articulate a desire for power, an ability to control the lives of others, or authority, the right to do so. But the overt manifestation and legitimate, public use of power is the province of men. Here again, *zār* may be associated with feelings and assertions of identity, but in contrast to her brother's, Sittalbenat's assertions do not conform to those prescriptive for her sex.

It is interesting that Sittalbenat shares few spirits with her sister Umselima. Their only common *zayran* are adult *Khawājāt.* This point is pertinent to Zaineb's affliction, considered below.

Sadiya

The illness she sustained in 1943 when pregnant with Hamid was Sadiya's second and only major possession attack. Her first brush with *zayran* came when she was living in Shendi with her husband and two young daughters. When one of her daughters died, Sadiya became sick and was diagnosed as possessed. But her husband obtained the objects her spirits had showed her in her dreams and she recovered. The loss of an infant son following Hamid was not ascribed to spirits, nor did they inflame and cause her further distress. Sadiya says the spirits have been "good with her" because her husband has always complied with their demands. To them she attributes her skills as a poet and raconteuse for which she, and her daughter Azina, have earned renown.

Sadiya's spirits belong to the *Ḥabish,* resonant with her reproductive career, and to the *Fallata, Khawāja,* and *Ḥalib* societies. *Zayran* of the last group also possess Sittalbenat and Zaineb but no other family member. Interestingly, too, Sadiya is possessed by the same *Khawāja* boys that possess Umselima; these spirits may have been passed from elder to younger (who are of course maternal kin) and articulate their shared childhood experiences, for the sisters were born two years apart and have a close and supportive relationship. Not only this, but they have similar personalities and resemble each other physically: they are often mistaken for twins.

Sadiya is forever doing some small thing to please her spirits. Once when I visited her, she was applying henna to the soles of her feet in what seemed an odd design: the heel and ball of each foot was fully coated, but the instep, which women generally cover with the paste, was being dyed incompletely in three broad stripes. When I asked the meaning of this, she replied that her *Khawāja* boys wanted the bottoms of her feet to bear the imprint that sneakers—*Khawāja* shoes—leave on the sand. While Sadiya, like Umselima, has made the *ḥaj* and no longer attends curing rituals, she remains faithfully devoted to the *zār*. More than once I heard her rise to defend *zayran* accused of being malevolent devils by men, and with Umselima she wistfully says she would rather attend a *zār* than a wedding any day.

Zaineb, Married

After Zaineb's wedding she continued to live with her mother in Hofriyat. Her husband, Abdelrahim, a farmer and son of Sittalbenat, continued to live with his parents in Malkab. Genealogically, their marriage is considered "immediately close" and highly appropriate: not only are they matrilateral parallel cousins, but Abdelrahim's father is also the son of Zaineb's paternal aunt. The union thus consolidates both patrilateral and matrilateral links between the couple's natal families. Despite this, Umselima and her son-in-law did not get along from the start.

Zaineb had her first child when she was seventeen—a daughter whom she called Hadiya (meaning "gift"). There were plans afoot to move her to Sittalbenat's house in Malkab after the birth; at her daughter's *sīmaya*—the naming ceremony held when a baby is seven days old—Zaineb was told she would depart imminently, following her confinement. She says she did not wish to leave Hofriyat. She felt unwell: "I became ill from the *zār* on the day of Hadiya's *sīmaya*. I have been afflicted ever since. My *Ḥalib* spirits inflamed."

Soon after Zaineb's move to Malkab, her sister Leyla was divorced. Leyla had borne a son, then a daughter, only to find herself pregnant three months later—too soon, she said, after her daughter's birth. When the baby, a boy, was delivered stillborn, her husband set her aside in favor of another woman. Leyla and her children had recently moved to her husband's *ḥōsh* in Hofriyat; now they returned to Umselima. The breakup was bitter: her husband "abandoned them," leaving his son and daughter to be

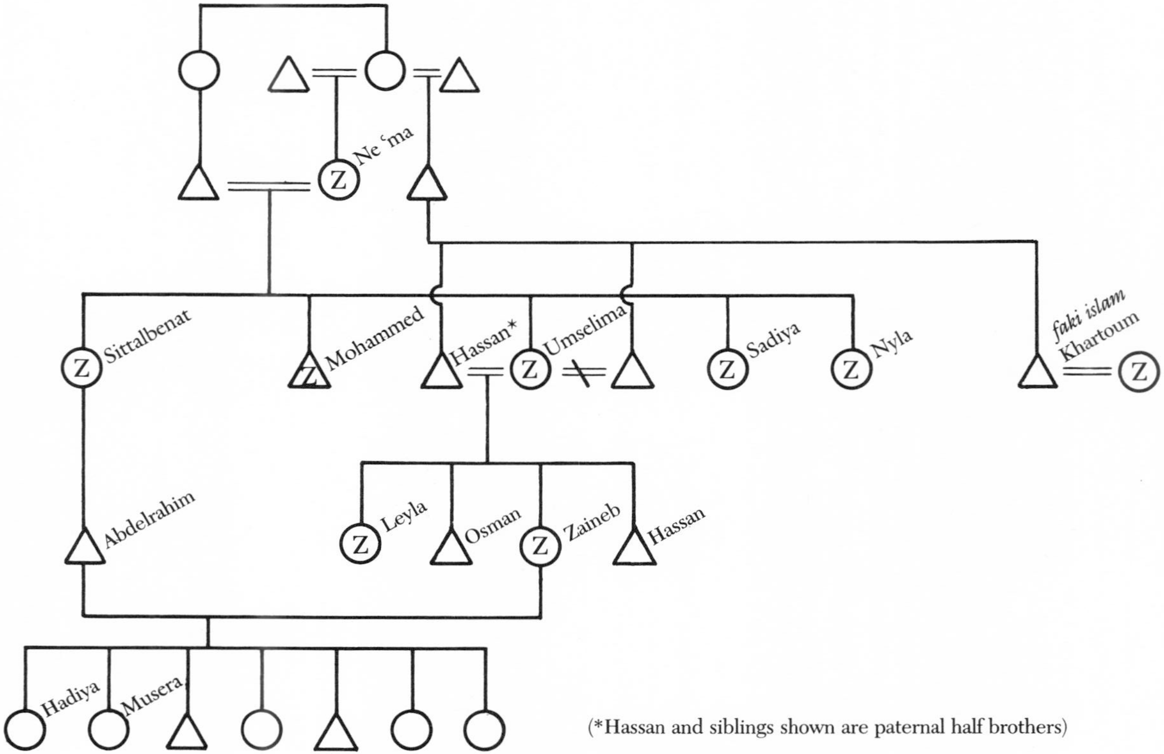

(*Hassan and siblings shown are paternal half brothers)

Fig. 6.3. Umselima's and Zaineb's Immediate Families

supported by Leyla's family from then on. Leyla has never rewed and avows no desire to do so, preferring relative liberty as a divorcée to the restrictions of matrimony. Her *zayran,* she says, ceased to distress her from the moment of her divorce.

A year later, Zaineb, still living in Malkab, became pregnant again. These were difficult times. Up to then, Abdelrahim had made a good living farming with his father. Jointly, they owned a *wadī* plantation and rented some irrigation land above the floodplain. On a neighboring tract farmed by others, they operated a *sagīya* (waterwheel), receiving in payment a substantial share of the crop they watered. But in the early 1960s the Nile in this area had begun to change course, moving westward in its floodplain and away from fields on the eastern shore. By 1962 the well of Abdelrahim's *sagīya* was dry, too far from the river to be any use. All along the eastern bank, irrigation farming declined—orchards withered, fields of baked black earth cracked apart—while alluvial farming burgeoned.[5] Some farmers banded together or formed family cooperatives to purchase diesel pumps powerful enough to pipe water the greater distance. Others sought work in the city. Shortly after the birth of their second child Musera, another daughter, Abdelrahim departed for Khartoum. When her brother Osman was also compelled to leave, Zaineb's situation bore an uncanny resemblance to that of Umselima years before.

Zaineb said she was very ill following Musera's delivery, and attributed her trouble to the influence of a *Ḥabish zār.* When next she attended a ritual with Umselima, she responded vigorously to *Ḥabish* threads. She descended a little, too, to the thread summoning *Rundu,* the wealthy European which, like gypsy *zayran,* is also above her mother-in-law.

Then Zaineb and her family attended a wedding in Hofriyat. Mohammed was there with his second wife, and also the seventh whom he had wed not long before.

> We were sitting over there, in the acacia grove. There came the sound of a beautiful *dallūka,* and that put an end to drumming for the wedding! There were many people sitting in the shade of the grove. Then Leyla and Mucca [Mohammed's Malkabi daughter; both are divorcées], they began to sing the thread, "*Dondo ya Rundu, ya Khawāja ʿindu; Dondo ya Rundu, ya Khawāja ʿindu*" [*Dondo* oh/you Rundu, oh Westerner who has/owns]. They were just joking, that is. Only the new wife of my *khāl* Mohammed, immediately she rose up and began to descend, and then another one got up to descend. All of those sitting were descending. So Leyla and Mucca went and took the *dallūka* to drum in the grove.
>
> Came the groom, "Who are you [to take the wedding drum]?"

5. This is a boon only to those who can afford to rent floodland from its owners on the west bank. For an explanation of alluvium ownership see chapter 1, note 27.

"*Lā, berri, berri!* [protestations of innocence]," said the people in the grove. "*We* did not do it."

Then this one, my *khāl*'s new wife, she became ill straightaway. She began to cry and to descend, she did this for a long time. And she was just a girl! She had never given birth or anything! Then she got up. She said, "Unless you put on a ceremony for her!" [That is, she would not stop, would not recover. Zaineb spoke this in a deep voice, imitating masculine tones.]

Right away Umselima's people, *shaykhat* and musicians, they got up and spread the *zār* right there at the wedding! And He said, "I want a dress like the dress of Zaineb there, and I want henna and incense." They censed her and Umselima's people put on a ceremony that lasted seven days, just over there, in the acacia grove.[6] And they brought a ram. He [*Dondo*] said He wanted a white ram. They brought it and slaughtered it; they put on a sacrificial meal. It continued until we went back there to our village.

Sittalbenat, she wanted to die that first day in the grove. Her spirits burned. The others brought her perfume and incense . . . she began descending immediately! She had great dizziness. They brought her a white *tōb* to wear and a beautiful dress and she became well. There was no need to sacrifice a ram for her spirits then, because she had sacrificed at a seven-day *zār* in the past.

There was another one, she was possessed by a *Ḥabish zār: Dodo, ya Jabal Nado* [Dodo oh/you Mount Nado, an Ethiopian spirit of a mountain on which coffee is grown].[7] When she descended during the thread for *Jabal Nado,* she said, "You must make Him coffee right now!" They made Him coffee and she drank it and I forget what else they made for another of her threads.[8] She descended, and this before the ceremony had really begun; and they brought coffee and They drank and she became quiet and she stopped.

But my *khāl*'s wife, she refused to stop. She said, "Not unless there is a [genuine] *zār* ceremony."

And another woman said, "I want," and they did it for her, for this *Nyam Nyam Kubaida* [Azande cannibal *zār*]. She said, "Bring Him meat, raw meat." She would eat. And she took spoonfuls of meat right from the fire—Oh! [Zaineb demonstrated with a hiss]—right there in the grove, I saw it myself! She blew on the fire—uh, huh—to make it grow, and took meat flaming—it was not yet cooked—and put it in her mouth and her mouth was fine. We all said she had burned herself, but no! When again she took meat from the fire too soon, there was nothing wrong!

6. Mounting a *zār* outside the confines of a *ḥōsh* is extremely unusual, done in this case to appease spirits inadvertently summoned at that spot.

7. To say "spirit of a mountain" here is suitably ambiguous. It is not specified whether the spirit is the *zār* parallel of the mountain itself, or of one of its inhabitants.

8. Spirits, like their summoning chants, are also referred to as "threads"—which enter the body. See Cloudsley (1983:83).

A few months after this event, Osman was betrothed to the daughter of Umselima's half brother's son in Dongola. Zaineb, Leyla, Hassan, and Umselima traveled north with the groom for the wedding. They went by train, then by steamer along the navigable reaches of the Nile. The trip is one of Zaineb's most treasured memories. She would often speak of the cool breezes coming off the water as they sailed, of the steep riverbanks in the north and, in Dongola, of her grandfather's orchard where the dates grew thick and sweet. Dongola remains for Zaineb a symbol of opulence, joy, of relative freedom from the concerns of everyday life, not least, from her husband's and in-laws' control. When first she told me of this voyage she quoted a well worn adage, *nisībha naṣibaha*[9]—"her in-laws are her misfortune."

Meanwhile, Abdelrahim had found work in Khartoum, but it was not to last. After two years he returned to Malkab to resume farming. He built a *ḥōsh* next to that of his parents, but below the mound formed by years of continuous occupation and perilously close to the floodplain. Zaineb and he had lived there less than a year when again she became pregnant. Just before confinement, she returned to her mother in Hofriyat for delivery. Twenty days after the birth of their son, while Zaineb and her children were with Umselima, Abdelrahim again quit the village for Khartoum. Their house in Malkab was unfinished.

Since then, Abdelrahim has returned home only for visits. He has a respectable job, but it is not overly remunerative and requires him to travel a great deal. He is based in Khartoum but for many years preferred that his family remain in Malkab under the watchful eye of his parents.

Zaineb, for her part, was not altogether happy with the arrangement. True, she admitted having a fascination for city life; yet a desire to live in Khartoum did not fuel her reluctance, for she felt it was better to raise her children in the *balad,* "village" or (closer to its actual meaning) "homeland," away from the distractions and expense of an urban milieu. The difficulty lay with her place of residence near Sittalbenat in Malkab. Zaineb much preferred life in Hofriyat, with Umselima and Leyla, now alone in Umselima's well-appointed *ḥōsh,* far more comfortable than her own. She had not wanted to return to Malkab after the birth of her son, but was forced to comply. Zaineb was homesick for Hofriyat and the friends of her youth.

Over the next eight years, Zaineb lived dutifully in her unfinished *ḥōsh* in Malkab, and had four more children: another daughter, then a son, and two more daughters. She traveled occasionally, to neighboring villages for ceremonies of all kinds and twice to Khartoum for weddings; to Hofriyat for confinement and delivery; to *zār* rituals with her mother wherever the latter was called in as *shaykha.* One cure overseen by Umselima was held in

9. For the derivation, see Hillelson (1930*a*: 193).

Zaineb's *ḥōsh;* the patient was Azza, a twice-divorced daughter of Sittalbenat who had never conceived due to the wiles of *zayran*.

In 1971, archaeological excavations resumed in the vicinity: the first had ended in 1914,[10] around the time of Umselima's birth, the last in 1925.[11] The new expedition was a joint venture of the University of Khartoum and the University of Calgary, Canada. Crews of both Sudanese and (human) *khawājāt* returned each winter for the next five years, the last of which brought me to Hofriyat.

Zaineb recalled having been intrigued to see two European women at one of the last *zār* ceremonies Umselima oversaw, in 1974. That year, too, she gave birth to a daughter, and immediately fell very ill. After confinement she remained in Hofriyat, letting Umselima and Leyla care for her and help with the children. Her condition proved biomedically treatable but pertinacious; she was still receiving therapy when I met her early in 1976. Soon after we met, her full recovery was proved to be stymied by a *zār*.

Zaineb's earlier vision of *Ḥalib zayran* and her claim to be possessed by Ethiopian spirits reverberate idiomatically with events in her life to which they are temporally linked. The illness brought by Zaineb's Ethiopian spirits—usurpers of fertility—occurs when she has borne two daughters and no sons, an ominous start to her marriage. Though she does not undertake a cure at this time, she publicly acknowledges the spirits' presence by descending to their chants. Shortly thereafter, her eldest son is born, and she suffers no further bouts of spirit sickness until her health deteriorates with the birth of her seventh child.

Now Zaineb has faithfully attended *zārs* from an early age, learned about the spirits from her mother, discussed signs of possession and the spirits' probable demands, closely observed Umselima's technique. No one could deny that possession ran in her family, and many thought that Zaineb herself would become a *shaykha* and assume her mother's practice. Several times during the first six months of our acquaintance she voiced a desire to do so. Because Umselima and her colleague Sosan had both made pilgrimages in 1975 and subsequently retired from active practice, there was, in the year I arrived, a lacuna in personnel locally available to diagnose and treat *zār* illness. The situation was widely lamented by women in the area, for whom "the good old days" were only a year before. Others who, in 1976, openly aspired to *shaykha*hood were considered less capable in their dealings with spirits than Umselima and her people had been.

10. The Liverpool University expedition led by Professor Garstang, who excavated remains of the ancient city of Meroë, 1910–14.

11. The Harvard expedition under Professor Reisner, who excavated Meroitic cemeteries in the desert east of Hofriyat and Malkab between 1922 and 1925.

Sosan had no daughters, Leyla had no taste for it, but Zaineb was another matter. She was bright, a natural leader, curious about the outside world. Certainly, when I met her she was in the process of establishing, cautiously, her credibility with the *zār,* and of negotiating, albeit obliquely, a change in her situation that would permit a measure of release from her husband's control. But for reasons discussed below, she soon drew back from conceding her ambition publicly. The outcome was not to be felicitous, despite the suitability of her succession in the eyes of the *zayran.*

I first met Zaineb at a women's tea party in Hofriyat to which I and a member of the excavation had been invited. At once her wit and confidence were apparent. Every day thereafter, I would leave the dig site for the village hoping to deepen my contact with villagers and ultimately obtain their permission to do research. I had gone to Sudan wanting to study possession in a rural context, but did not immediately say so to Hofriyati, for if it turned out that *zār* was a sensitive subject, I was ready to shift my focus to something which was not—kinship, or whatever else seemed to matter. But I need not have worried. Soon after I arrived at the site the mother of a man employed on the dig fell ill and was diagnosed as possessed; he decided to sponsor her cure, which the archaeologists and I were invited to attend. It was held some distance from Hofriyat.

When next I appeared in Hofriyat after an absence of several days, I met Zaineb in the street. She asked where I had been. When I told her, she was regretful: had she known about the *zār,* she too would have gone, and stayed for the duration. Soon the entire village was apprised of my outing and possession received top billing wherever I went. I was overwhelmed, unable at this stage to take it all in. Women told me the names of their spirits, demonstrated their gestures, sang their chants, drummed their rhythms. They were just as keen to talk about *zār* as to let me in on their beauty secrets or fine-braid my hair. They asked if I was possessed. "How can she be sure?" Zaineb would say from somewhere in back of the room, "She isn't married yet. Besides, she's a *khawājīya*—a *naṣranīya* [Christian]—maybe her people don't know about the *zār.*"

One day Zaineb and her friends led me to the *ḥōsh* where she and Umselima had lived during Umselima's early days as a *shaykha.* In the corner of a room beneath some dusty sheets we found a beautiful *dallūka,* Umselima's, which Zaineb set about to play. Other women had brought different instruments of the *zār;* they spent the afternoon drumming the threads of *zayran.*

A few days later Zaineb said that she and Asha, who also aspired to *shaykha*hood, were holding a *zār* over the next three nights, not for the purpose of curing but, as she said, "just to comfort ourselves." Observing her those evenings, I could not help but notice how much at home she was behind her mother's drum. But had not the presence of human *khawājāt* in their midst influenced the women's decision to stage this impromptu rite?

In some ways I became a means, an opportunity, for Zaineb and also, perhaps, for Asha, to promote their interests in the *zār* at a crucial point in the history of the local cult. But Zaineb's interest went further than that. She was eager to learn as much as she could about my homeland and the ways of Western women. I think she may have seen in me the potential for a life-style different from her own and in some ways preferable to it, for she often remarked approvingly on my apparent freedom from male control. My presence and obvious interest in the *zār,* her personal dissatisfaction, physical ailment, and deep schooling in the idiom of possession, combined that year, propelling her, through the desires of possessive *zayran,* toward a studied defiance of her husband's authority: when he pressed her to return to Malkab, both she and the *zayran* above her insisted she remain with her mother—and me—in Hofriyat. What follows is an outline of this process as it took place.

In June of 1976 I accompanied Zaineb to Khartoum for her bimonthly hospital checkup. There we stayed with Osman and his wife, for though Zaineb's husband expected to be in town during our sojourn, it would have been unseemly to stay with him since he shared a *ḥōsh* with several other men, migrant workers like himself.

Zaineb's hospital visit was inconclusive and upsetting. The doctor gave her some pills which only made her feel worse.

A few days later we went to Omdurman to visit Zaineb's kin—the family of her *ʿamm,* the wealthy *faki* who had supported her family after her father's death. We were having a pleasant time when, in mid afternoon, Osman called to say that Abdelrahim was in town but would soon be leaving for the east. If Zaineb wanted to see him, she would have to come right now. She left me with her cousins and rushed to catch the bus for Khartoum and Osman's house to confront her husband. She wanted to know why last month's expense money had not yet arrived. How were she and the children supposed to live? The new school year was starting and uniforms had to be made. . . .

Two hours later Zaineb returned, dejected. She had failed to convince Abdelrahim to give her the funds for school clothes. He has only two sons, he said, the girls needn't go to school, and Zaineb could manage the boys' clothes on her housekeeping money. But he had yet to give her even that. And she had learned from Osman's wife that Abdelrahim had not worked all that week. He knew his wife was in town, but waited until he was leaving to get in touch with her. Things did not look good.

That night Osman's neighbor, Selua, a childless woman in her late forties, invited us over to watch TV—one of the few sets in the area. We saw an old James Garner detective film, English with Arabic subtitles.

I was given the role of translating the improbable sound track for my friends, who could not read, and fielding their myriad questions: "Why do you dress in so little clothing in North America? You told us it was cold!" (It was a sixties' film.) "Where is the powdered ice [snow] you spoke of? We see only palms!" When it came to the love scene, the women covered their faces with their *tōbs*, and Selua switched off the set.

We began to discuss the *zār*, for Selua belonged to an organized cult, and Zaineb was keen to see her spirits' wardrobe. Selua produced a trunk containing several beautiful costumes and a quantity of spirit jewlery. She showed us two gold bracelets belonging to *Lulīya Ḥabishīya,* an Ethiopian prostitute *zār,* then mentioned that she herself owned a lovely bracelet which she had lost. She had lent it to a bride to wear at her wedding, but after the feast the bracelet was not returned and the bride's kin claimed no knowledge of its whereabouts. So Selua enlisted a *faki ṣadīg shawaṭīn,* a powerful curer-magician and confidant of demons, to find her gold. The *faki* pledged to return her bracelet within two months for £S 25 (then about US $63.00); if he failed, he would return her money in full.

Zaineb remarked that he must truly be a strong *faki* if he could afford to make such promises. Too much was wrong with her own life, she said, for it to be mere coincidence. She really ought to consult Selua's *faki.* Selua agreed to take us there next morning.

The *faki*'s *ḥōsh* consisted of an "office" and a waiting room with facing rows of high-backed chairs. After Zaineb described her symptoms, he asked her for a coin, performed several sand divinations, consulted a well-worn tome containing astrological markings, and asked her mother's name.[12] Following a spectacular display involving the coin, an inverted bowl, some green feathers, and a small explosion, he delivered his diagnosis. She had been ensorcelled by a woman who wished to alienate her from Abdelrahim's affections. The *faki* described Zaineb's cure, a packet of specially mixed incense, and told her the treatment—if she wanted it—would cost £S 5: £S 3 for the ingredients, £S 2 for his fee.

Zaineb complained she was poor, her husband gave her little money, she had seven children to feed. The *faki* dropped his price to £S 4, and told us to come back for the medicine tomorrow.

Zaineb was no happier when we left the *faki*'s office than when we had entered, for she saw no way to obtain the money for her cure. She said she was ashamed to approach her brothers, and obviously there was no point in asking her husband. We made our way through a maze of streets to the rented house where her brother Hassan lived with his family; we were expected there for lunch.

12. Because motherhood is indisputable, one's mother's name is the surest identification for divinatory purposes.

Midway through the meal, Abdelrahim walked in, unexpectedly; it seems his departure had been delayed. He was clearly taken aback to see Zaineb there; the lunch had been arranged without his knowledge. At first Zaineb looked nervous, then, made bold perhaps by the presence of her younger brother and wanting him to realize the extent of her misfortune, she again asked her husband for her monthly allowance and reiterated the need for new school clothes. There followed much discussion, but no resolution. When Zaineb and I rose to leave, I realized how astutely she had played the situation, calculatedly raising a sensitive issue in the presence of her brother's "guest," for that is what I was, whatever kin terms we might use. Now in an effort to recoup their damaged pride, Hassan and Abdelrahim insisted we return to Osman's by taxi and argued heatedly over who would pay the fare. Hassan won, and we drove away from a much-abashed Abdelrahim. Zaineb was quietly fuming: she had won the point, but it was a small victory and Abdelrahim, she knew, would not let the matter rest.

Late that night he showed up at Osman's door. He and Zaineb withdrew to the *dīwān* and could be heard arguing loudly for a quarter of an hour. The topic was money. Abdelrahim, who earlier in the day had taken a defensive stance, now berated Zaineb for making unreasonable demands. Under no circumstance was their eldest daughter—at the top of her class in junior secondary school—to return to classes at the end of the summer break. "Hadiya is sixteen," he said, "too old to be running around between villages. She must now stay home until she is married." With this the dispute was ended. Before Abdelrahim left he gave Osman £S 5 toward a new *tōb* for Hadiya (that Zaineb also might wear): weddings were coming up and it was important that their daughter look her best to prospective suitors.

But Zaineb was not appeased. Hadiya had no desire for marriage at this point; she wanted to finish school and become a teacher, aspirations which Zaineb firmly supported. Besides, material for a *tōb* costs far more than £S 5—Osman would have to contribute at least twice that if they were to buy anything at all. And still no explanation for the missing allowance money. Abdelrahim, she said, is frequently neglectful in this regard and, though he earns £S 40 a month, the most he ever sends her is £S 15! Where was the money going? Unless, as she suspects, to another woman. But since she had no money with which to take the *fakī*'s cure and undo the spell which binds him in this woman's power, Zaineb saw no way out.

For several days she debated whether to ask Osman for the £S 4 she needed. She was embarrassed, she said, because he had already been so generous. The day of our return to Hofriyat she had all but despaired of obtaining the *fakī*'s medicine, when I offered her the funds. I had been intending to do so for some time, but took sick with a high fever and was unable to speak to her alone for several days (no one else knew of the *fakī*'s diagnosis and Zaineb had wanted to keep it that way for now). Our relationship was cemented by exchanges of all sorts, and the offer would not be out of place. I was also, of course, curious about the remedy and its effects.

At first she refused; but I insisted, pointing out that this would be her last opportunity to get the medicine until August, when she expected to return to Khartoum. A few hours before we were due to board the train, Zaineb slipped away unnoticed. She returned a short time later, motioned me into the *dīwān,* and closed the door. Cupped in her hand was a furry black capsule the size of an egg. It was a package wrapped in goatskin which, as she untied it, was shown to conceal a fragment of white cloth bound with thread. Inside the cloth was powdered incense and some sand. The *faki* had instructed her to undo the thread—so undoing the *ʿamal* or spell—then to wash the cloth in the incense and put the washings down the latrine. The cloth was to be placed somewhere in her house in Malkab. The woman who sought to disrupt her marriage, she explained, had constructed the nefarious object from a piece of Abdelrahim's clothing. The *faki* had retrieved it from where it lay hidden and also prescribed medicinal incense to banish Zaineb's symptoms.

Two weeks after our return, Zaineb's illness was as oppressive as ever though she had scrupulously followed the *faki*'s instructions. She was still in Hofriyat with Umselima when word arrived that Abdelrahim soon planned to visit Malkab, and expected to find her living there with his house cleaned and ready. It had not been lived in for almost three years. Zaineb was still smarting from their confrontation in Khartoum and said she wished he would stay away.

Umselima's Dongolese half sister was visiting at the time, and suggested that Zaineb's illness showed all the signs of possession. Umselima concurred: she had been saying that for a week. After all, neither Western medicine nor a *faki*'s cure had been of help, a sure indication *zayran* were involved. Zaineb hesitantly assented.

Four days later, Zaineb was back in Malkab and cleaning house. She felt feverish. Again she saw the *Ḥalib zayran* which had first appeared to her as a child.

Abdelrahim still had not arrived by early August, almost a month later. He sent a message through Sittalbenat that he would be back for Ramadan, due to begin in a few weeks time. Zaineb's condition had worsened steadily after her return to Malkab. She kept having a dream she attributed to *zayran*: she dreamed that a strange man approached her. He grabbed her roughly by the neck (something spirits commonly do) and pushed her head up and down by turns, forcing her to enact the mannerisms of a woman in possession trance, descending. He told her he wanted a seven-day ceremony and a tall white ram. Zaineb said she argued with the man, to no avail. The *zār* warned that her illness would not abate until she had suitably entertained him and his comrades (other *zayran*) for seven days.

Around this time I went to see Zaineb in the company of Samiya, an older, semiprofessional *shaykha* from Malkab and Zaineb's friend. We discussed how to raise the money for Zaineb's *zār*. Samiya insisted the funds must come from Zaineb's close male kin, preferably her husband, but failing him, her brothers. She also told me Umselima and Abdelrahim had had "words"—a heated argument. Abdelrahim dislikes Hofriyat and its people (his in-laws) and wants Zaineb to remain in Malkab—even though her house has no latrine and they must use Sittalbenat's next door. Zaineb's house, she said, is inconvenient, and Sittalbenat is angry much of the time.

Zaineb, for her part, had disregarded her husband's command and allowed Hadiya to return to boarding school in the nearby town. Her next eldest, Musera, was living with Umselima in Hofriyat, for the old woman had adopted her years ago. This left Zaineb little help around the house. With her illness, her husband's impending visit, and her deficient house, she was truly miserable.

Two days later I visited again and found Hadiya home from school. She had begun to return every evening in order to care for her mother. That day she had brought ingredients for henna, and Zaineb was preparing to appease the *zayran* by staining her hands and feet with an appropriate design. Hadiya had also purchased some white bread and *ṭāmīya,* fried chick-pea patties, clean food to mollify spirits. Leyla and several of their Malkabi relations visited; we discussed local curing techniques while Zaineb applied her henna. In the course of conversation a *tajruba, zār* test, was suggested for the next three nights to determine if Zaineb's current malaise was spirit induced.[13] When Leyla and I left at sunset, Zaineb seemed much improved.

Next evening we returned with several of Zaineb's Hofriyati friends. Umselima's *dallūka* was set in a corner of Zaineb's house, and the room soon filled with women. The drumming began, slowly at first, then gaining speed as more and more woman arrived to join in. When they began the thread "Wilād Mama"—for a powerful *Ḥabish zār,* vizier of all *zayran*—Zaineb, until then sitting quietly with eyes downcast, began to tremble. Soon her trembling intensified. She shook as though someone indeed held her neck and pushed her to and fro as she had dreamed. She started to descend. She continued to descend until all the Ethiopian threads had been drummed. Several times she fell, apparently exhausted, to the mat,

13. There was no doubt that Zaineb was possessed and, though she had not yet sacrificed for her spirits, an adept of the *zār*. What was open to debate was the etiology of this particular illness episode.

then was held by her cousin Mucca and fanned until she recovered. A number of *Wilād Mama* chants were tried, and Zaineb responded vigorously to each. Now and then I caught a glimpse of Abdelrahim's father standing on a sand dune next the house, observing through the window; he shrank back on detecting my gaze.

The roster of spirits played on. Zaineb descended to a thread for the Ethiopian twins and some *Khawāja* chants—British pasha *zayran*—as well. But during the last, Azina, Sadiya's daughter and also an aspiring *shaykha,* responded more strongly than she. After drumming till 1 : 00 A.M., the group began to disband, the consensus: Zaineb was well and truly afflicted.

The following night Azina arrived with a suitcase full of spirit clothes, given her by her husband when she had undertaken a cure some years before in Medani. Leyla brought coins, perfume, and some cigarettes which Zaineb distributed among the guests.

Zaineb's demeanor was markedly subdued from that of the former evening. She descended less frequently, looking pained and distracted through many threads to which she had earlier responded with energy. She did descend for *Ḥakīm Basha,* the doctor spirit above Umselima; indeed, the spirits whose threads had so provoked her the night before all plague her mother as well. Tonight, however, was different; Zaineb grew increasingly peripheral to the action. Something seemed to restrain her. And she looked most distressed, least able to move, when the threads for her *Ḥalib zayran* were drummed. These, remember, are not above Umselima, but above Sittalbenat and Sadiya—Zaineb's mother-in-law, and Azina's mother. And this evening Azina's *Khawāja zayran* stole the show, entertaining all with their dramatic burlesque. At one point there appeared in our midst *Dodomayo,* a drunken Greek *zār,* who called for the setup of two straight-backed chairs in the center of the *mīdān*. That done, He made toward me unsteadily, took my hand in His and, raising His arms above our heads, trotted me around the *mīdān* as His bride. The remainder of the chant we spent sitting on the chairs being admired by our "wedding guests." It was unsettling to be used as a ceremonial prop by a *zār,* especially one of such insalubrious character.

The ceremony had started rather late, and as it was exceptionally warm, the mats were spread outdoors within the *ḥōsh*. I was early, and sat visiting Zaineb for an hour or so before others began to arrive. She was feeling quite unwell, but had donned her newest dress and finest *tōb* in the hope that this would help. Several women popped their heads through the door, but Zaineb complained they were the first to do so that day. Privately, she alleged that the women of Malkab were less friendly than those of Hofriyat.

Samiya was among the first to arrive. She took one look at Zaineb and declared that drumming only in the evenings was doing her more harm than good. Zaineb was merely socializing with her spirits, she said. By making her worse, they were letting her know they require a proper ceremony, one that begins in the late afternoon, leaves off while the sun sets, and resumes at night. The hiatus is to avoid calling up *shawaṭīn,* known to be active at dusk. Samiya added that the next day we would drum in the afternoon, "so the illness does not become heavy"—does not build up so much during the day that drumming at night is insufficient to bring relief.

Zaineb remarked that Umselima, on learning the results of the first night's test, had come to see her that day from Hofriyat. She said she would personally ask her sons and Abdelrahim for the money to stage a seven-day cure: "My mother said to me, 'You have had *zayran* above you since you were small.' Since the day of Hadiya's naming I have been ill."

The last night of the *tajruba,* drumming was held indoors, and more than sixty women from Malkab and Hofriyat attended. Despite this show of support, Zaineb was more lethargic than before. Her condition appeared to have worsened.

Three days later, she still had not improved. I took some eggs and cheese—clean food—and went to Malkab to spend the day with her. She was weak; Hadiya and I had to persuade her to eat. She said she got sharp pains in her knees and then felt feverish, symptoms she ascribed to a *Khawāja zār* telling her it wanted *banṭalōn*—a pair of trousers. It was decided Zaineb should keep her doctor's appointment in the third week of August, returning to Malkab in time for Ramadan and her husband's visit. Then, funds permitting, she would drum the *zār,* but not immediately. She would have to wait until after the feast that marks the close of Ramadan, for during the fast *zayran* are prevented by Allah from manifesting themselves, and curers' boxes containing mixtures of spirit incense must remain closed.

There was a good deal of talk that day about Zaineb's place of residence. One of her cousins, a shopkeeper in Hofriyat, had publicly encouraged her return to Hofriyat. Other visitors, Sadiya, Abdelrahim's sister, his brother's wife Sheza, said they had voiced similar concerns to Sittalbenat. Then, just after noon, several Hofriyati men including the local *shaykh* stopped in after Friday prayers at the mosque. They told Zaineb that living in Malkab obviously did not benefit her, that her home was in Hofriyat. When, they asked, did she plan to return? "Ask my in-laws!" said Zaineb sharply, whereupon they rose and went next door to do precisely that.

A few hours later Sittalbenat stalked in, livid, her face a storm cloud waiting to erupt. Immediately, she berated Zaineb over some washing Hadiya was supposed to have done earlier in the week, "if she hadn't been off at school!" When Zaineb's sons began to quarrel, she upbraided her crossly, "Your children are short of manners!" When Samiya arrived to make the coffee demanded by Zaineb's *Ḥabish zār,* Sittalbenat was rude, neglecting to greet her and patently ignoring Samiya's cordial overtures.

The coffee drinking over, Samiya quickly departed. Tension in the air was palpable. Now Abdelrahim's father, having concluded discussion with the delegation from Hofriyat, entered the room, sat down, and fixed his gaze to the floor. Normally a friendly man, today he greeted no one and, worse, failed to inquire about Zaineb's health. After a strained half hour, he left with his wife without having spoken a word.

Then Abdelrahim's brother's wife returned, a jovial woman who often commiserated with Zaineb about life "in their affines' pocket." She joked that Abdelrahim had sent word of his desire to take another wife. "He wants a divorcée," she laughed, "because they come cheap! He will send you and the children back to Umselima and put his new wife in your house!"

Though said in jest, it had an ugly ring of truth and Zaineb was obviously distressed. She seemed unsure of the direction matters were heading—I knew she did not want to be divorced from Abdelrahim, for whatever else, she needed his support. Yet she desperately wanted to live with Umselima. As her sister-in-law rose to leave, I asked Zaineb if her husband would mind her moving back to Hofriyat. She said no, because if he came for Ramadan he too could stay with Umselima, whose *ḥōsh* was quite large. Knowing the relationship between Umselima and her nephew, I thought it unlikely that Abdelrahim would agree, but Zaineb offered it as a compromise which her husband, being a reasonable man, should accept. Though others were openly critical of his harshness and neglect, Zaineb refused to speak ill of him, preferring to let Abdelrahim's actions speak for themselves.

She went on to tell us that Abdelrahim had sent a curt reply to a letter from Hadiya reiterating her request for school clothes. The message was clear: he had sent material in colors and lengths appropriate only to the uniforms of his sons. His daughters were not expected to return to school.

Here, Abdelrahim's attitude ran against the current of thought, at least among men in Hofriyat. For various reasons, most were keen to have their daughters finish junior secondary school before they wed, at seventeen or eighteen.[14] Now, for Zaineb the education of all her offspring was a priority, but she was determined that her daughters should not be illiterate and unaware, as she described herself. The children of her family's benefactor (her *ʿamm*) had all received an education; indeed, the kinswoman we visited in Omdurman held a teaching position at a prominent girl's

14. Some said this was so that their daughters would attract educated husbands, others that it was a sin to waste the minds of women. Sudan has an established record of educating women, viz. the efforts early in this century of Babikir Bedri and family to promote schooling for girls. Generally, though, women's educational opportunities are fewer than men's.

school, and her daughters had been to university. Not least, my presence must have been a constant reminder of educational opportunities Zaineb never had. But her husband was unsympathetic: he seemed oblivious to the admonitions of his peers and resolved to thwart his wife's ambitions.

Soon another problem materialized to increase Zaineb's dysphoria: the annual flood had begun and the level of the Nile was rising hourly. Zaineb's *ḥōsh* in Malkab was near the floodplain, and she feared for her family's safety should the river overrun its course, as it had in the past. Zaineb owned that she sickened each year when the flood began and she was in Malkab; she longed to be back on higher ground in Hofriyat.

A week later Abdelrahim arrived. He was now fully apprised of developments that had taken place in his absence and clearly displeased; he barely spoke to his wife. Zaineb was due in Khartoum for a checkup five days hence. Abdelrahim decided she should go, but with Sittalbenat as chaperone. Hadiya was taken out of school to keep her father's house.

As I had to renew my visa, the three of us traveled to the city together. When we were about to board the bus, Abdelrahim handed his mother some money with which to buy food on the trip. He gave nothing to Zaineb and still had not addressed her when the bus rattled off.

Later, with Sittalbenat temporarily out of earshot, I asked Zaineb what was going on. She replied that it seemed she could not longer be trusted with money. It was bad enough that Abdelrahim always sent her household allowance through his parents, who would mete it out bit by sparing bit. Now she could have no funds at all. She was being treated like a recalcitrant child and it rankled.

Still, I could not help thinking that, short of divorce, this may have been the sole parry Abdelrahim had left. For Zaineb, a well-liked, extremely capable woman, had effectively mobilized support for her ventures in the oblique but irrefutable idiom of illness. And significant support came from local men whom her husband would now have to face.

Two days before the start of Ramadan, I saw Zaineb in Khartoum. She and Sittalbenat had been joined there by Umselima, and together we attended a *zār* held to honor the spirits before closing their incense tins for the duration of the fast. But Zaineb did not stay long. She told me she did not wish to anger her *zayran* by attending the rites of others before holding a cure of her own. Her brothers had been approached by Umselima for the money to stage a seven-day ceremony; she was confident they would comply.

By mid September the crisis had diffused. Zaineb had returned from Khartoum and was living in her mother's *ḥōsh*. Abdelrahim was with his parents in Malkab, though he frequently visited at Umselima's. Happily, he had given permission for his wife to remain in Hofriyat, on the understanding that in future she would return to Malkab for any holidays he might take. Zaineb's cure had been put off until November, when she intended to drum with Khalda, another recently afflicted woman in Hofriyat. Zaineb's health and outlook were much improved.

At the end of November Zaineb returned to Malkab for the *ʿĪd al-Aḍḥa,* or great feast. Now plans for her *zār* were in abeyance until after the *ʿĪd.* Hadiya was back in school and relations with Zaineb's affines were far smoother than before. Importantly, they were compelled to negotiate when the weight of public pressure, informally marshaled by a formally powerless woman, was brought to bear on those in positions of authority—husband, brothers, mother, in-laws—to recognize her demands as legitimate. When I left the field the following March, her *zār* had yet to be held.

Zaineb and Khalda did hold their *zār* two months after my departure, and it was said to have been a great success. Then in September 1977, I received a letter from Zaineb, written by Hassan, telling me that Hadiya had died, suddenly, of a severe illness. She was just seventeen.

Feeling helpless and inadequate, I sent condolences, but heard nothing more. Though an occasional greeting would arrive from other Hofriyati, there were no further letters from Zaineb.

When I returned to the village late in 1983, I learned that Zaineb had been very ill following Hadiya's death. Two months later she became pregnant, but her medical condition had worsened under the strain and she had to be hospitalized. She left Hofriyat—and Malkab—as soon as possible after that; Abdelrahim rented a *ḥōsh* in Khartoum which they shared with two other families from the area. Zaineb gave birth prematurely to a baby girl and was hospitalized again, immediately, with *nazīf*—hemorrhage. Her baby survived a few weeks.

Umselima died in 1981. Zaineb went home to Hofriyat for the funeral, but has not been back there since.

Shortly before I returned, Zaineb was hospitalized once more; she had been pregnant, but the baby died in her womb weeks before his birth. Again she suffered *nazīf* and this time was transfused. Moreover, she continues to receive medical treatment for her chronic condition. I found her weak, verging on despondence but for an occasional flash of spirit. "When *zayran* got hold of me," she said, "they would not let me go. They bled me dry. I guess they didn't know about transfusions!"

Zaineb still mourns Hadiya—deeply, her family says, but silently. I was advised not to mention her name.

Discussion

Considering the cases recounted in this chapter it is clear that possession means something slightly different to each individual who claims the affliction. In women, and also perhaps in men, the association of *zār* with problematic fertility is patent; however, no two members of Zaineb's family seem to experience possession illness in exactly the same ways, or precisely the same sets of circumstance.

Yet there is an undercurrent of similarity, and a number of common themes can be detected in the accounts. For instance, though problematic *zayran* vary from person to person, the demand for a white ram in sacrifice is called for by several: by Umselima, Mohammed, their mother, Mohammed's seventh wife, and Zaineb. In Mohammed's case, spirit and sacrifice are matched: white is the main color association of *Darwīsh zayran*. But for the rest, variously afflicted by *Ḥabish* and *Khawāja zayran* when a cure is required, the call for a white ram is, though not unheard of, somewhat extraordinary. Thus, the usual color assocation of Zaineb's *Ḥabish* spirit is red, and *Ḥabish zayran* typically demand sacrificial animals that have reddish wool. Yet this is not what the spirit demands in her dream. The similarity among their spirits' ritual requests serves, however unwittingly, to link Zaineb's possession experiences with those of certain matrilateral kin.

Umselima considered herself strongly possessed by Ethiopian spirits; in her own words, she was *milyāna* (full) of *Ḥabish*. Her principal spirit of this group, *Wilād Mama,* is that which especially troubles Zaineb in the summer of 1976. Here, several points may be significant: Zaineb first learns she is affected by *Ḥabish zayran* in circumstances where their intervention is generally known to take place, following the birth of her second daughter, Musera. Later, the *Ḥabish* inflame when she has borne her seventh child, a fifth daughter, and fails to recover after delivery. Again, attribution of her illness to *Ḥabish zayran* is apposite: the illness is linked to childbirth. Yet in both cases, something more may be hinted, for given its timing, her initial brush with Ethiopian spirits could well articulate the tenuous position she holds in her affines' household, and her affines are increasingly implicated in the relapse she suffers in 1976. Moreover, on both occasions, possession by *Ḥabish zayran* indirectly reiterates Zaineb's alignment with her mother: on the one hand, it is telling that Musera was later adopted by Umselima; on the other, Zaineb acknowledges possession by *Wilād Mama,* her mother's most powerful spirit, when she wishes to live with Umselima despite her affines' protestations. The relations intensified among uterine kin in the idiom of the *zār* are counterhegemonic: a shadowy yet practical challenge to agnatic ideology, recalling vernacular genealogies of maternal aunts in chapter 2.

On the *Wilād Mama* connection, something more can be said, for *Wilād Mama* is the "vizier of all *zayran,*" the spirit which must be summoned first at a ceremony and requested to marshal fellow *zayran* in preparation for descent. It also acts as a spokesman for the entire pantheon, receiving the blood of sacrificial victims on the others' behalf. Thus, threads addressed to *Wilād Mama* are addressed to all *zayran*. Possession by this spirit—or spirits, for *Wilād Mama* is often considered a plurality—is beneficial if not mandatory for aspirant *shaykhat*. Further, it emerges from Zaineb's *zār* test that the spirit *Ḥakīm Basha* is above her, as it is above Umselima. This *zār,* remember, is thought to confer the ability to diagnose illnesses and prescribe suitable remedies. Zaineb's acknowledgment of these spirits might obliquely express a desire to assume her mother's role.

Yet here it seems she is not without a rival: her cousin Azina also claims both spirits and has publicly stated that she is learning *zār*-related diagnostic techniques. Azina has already undergone a full-scale cure, another requisite of *shaykha*hood. And at her test, Zaineb frequently appears to be "upstaged" by the fine-tuned antics of her cousin's *zayran*. Both women could legitimately assume Umselima's relinquished practice because as matrilateral parallel cousins they are "sisters" and Umselima's maternal kin. But Zaineb is not favorably positioned to convince others of her calling, for until she recuperates she cannot claim to be on exemplary terms with *zayran*. For that she will need some luck and, at minimum, her husband's or brothers' support.

Zaineb is possessed by *Ḥalib* or gypsy spirits which also plague her mother-in-law Sittalbenat (and once potential mother-in-law, Sadiya). It may well be that *Ḥalib* represent for Zaineb her affinal relations: these spirits first appeared to her at the time of her betrothal to Sittalbenat's son, and she was made ill by them after learning of her imminent domicile with Sittalbenat in Malkab following Musera's birth. But the spirits enable her, perhaps, to impart a more subtle message, for female gypsies are characterized by their forthright behavior, their boldness in speaking to men. This, plus their mobile life-style and relative freedom from male control may crystallize something that Zaineb desires or sees in herself, but that her marriage, indeed her entire upbringing, has precluded. I state this too broadly, perhaps, for it is not, from Zaineb's perspective, her self which initiates such desires: these are effected by *zayran*.

There is another side to the *Ḥalib,* and it resonates with Zaineb's improprietous relationship with her husband. *Ḥalib zayran* are notorious confidence artists, forever relieving hapless others of their money by some trick or dissemblance, delivering touching appeals to passersby for alms ("in the name of Allah!") one minute, gloating as they top up their coffers the next. If we consider Zaineb's ongoing financial war with her husband (which, given the prescribed matrimonial dynamic, should never have taken place), overtly expressed in repeated attempts to wrest from Abdelrahim her household allowance and their children's uniforms, other potential meanings of her possession by *Ḥalib zayran* are suggested, bearing again on relations with affinal kin.

Remember, however, that Zaineb's affines are also her close matrilateral kin. In light of this, her *zār* dream and responses during the test assume additional relevance, for in demanding a white ram and revealing itself to be *Wilād Mama*—a *Ḥabish* that does not afflict Sittalbenat—the *zār* not only affirms Zaineb's relationship with her mother, it also separates both from her mother-in-law. The possession context thus permits Zaineb to distinguish publicly between facets of her dual relationship with Sittalbenat. It allows her to demonstrate an existing or desirable alignment of matrilateral kin whose divergence is obscured by a convoluted genealogy. Thus might the *zār* "open up" the dense, compacted relationships created by "close" or endogamous marriage. And in doing so, it operates against the quotidian vector of interiority, of overlapping obligations and identities. However intelligible to human others or however wittingly sent, revelation of a *zār*'s identity and demands is a message encoding information about the human interrelationships of its host. In this capacity, *zār* is an ingenious comment on the existence of ambiguity in human affairs.

First, and notwithstanding the fact that *zayran* are by nature paragons of ambivalence and caprice, possession may augment the ambiguity normally present in human interaction. For villagers often confuse (intentionally?) host and spirit behavior when observing episodes of possession trance (chapter 4). And in daily life, certain of an individual's responses, behaviors, and psychological and physical states may be attributed to extrahuman effects. In either case, just which entity one is dealing with, woman or spirit-influenced woman, is not always clear.

Yet, paradoxically, for those who have learned how to read the indigenous possession texts, *zār* may amplify coherence in human relations. Knowledge about one's own and others' possessive spirits provides an implicit social psychology, its textbook typifications making—or seeming to make—everyday interaction more predictable, clarifying perceptions and expectations of others' responses while absolving them of responsibility for inappropriate behavior. Or, as may be the case with Zaineb's maternal kin, whole groups of possessed persons, multiplexly related in the human world, may perceive realigned relationships among themselves in the spirit domain (Boddy 1982*a*). For sisters, to have no common possessive *zayran* might nuance distinction between them in a human context where they are otherwise regarded as social and physical equivalents, potential proxies in each other's marriages. Under such conditions, *zār* is at the service of individuality in an unindividuated world. Conversely, for people possessed by the same spirit, mutual affliction might contribute to their relationship, strengthening bonds or perhaps creating them where before there were none. To themselves and others, they become a social type distinct from what they were before.

Still, just as it clarifies, possession also obfuscates. For an individual usually acknowledges possession by more than one *zār,* and these do not reveal their presence all at once. Each time a woman discovers above her a spirit she did not know she had, her kin ties are repositioned. Each spirit acquisition adds another coat of meaning to the human relationships in which she participates; each progressively resituates dimensions of her selfhood constituted in relations with her kin. The metadiscursive aspect of possession, its ability to qualify interpersonal communication, unfolds layer upon successive layer as the extent of a woman's affliction is gradually revealed over the course of her life.

But older women rarely remember the exact progress of their afflictions. The social context of a spirit's first manifestation may be retrospectively unimportant, for the spirit was probably always there. Until the moment of its appearance, it had no reason to inflame or perhaps saw no advantage in it. So, stated from her perspective, a woman's awareness of her spirits increases over time, provoking a recontextualization of past experiences and present relationships; the sequence of spirit acquisition need not be precisely recalled, for it is the present situation that is, and has been, real and true. For those who are possessed, human relationships are ongoingly revealed through their own and others' association with the *zār. Zār,* then, functions in the human world as integument: it creates nongenealogical relationships and binds genealogical ones into continuously changing patterns of alignment; through it, ascribed social identifications and contrasts may be evaluated and commented upon, subtly, indirectly.

In a related vein, Crapanzano (1977*a*) has suggested that possession effects a refinement of the possessed's definition of self via negative metaphor: what is *not* an aspect of one's self is thereby distinguished from what *is*. To the normal dialectics of self and other are added two further dimensions, that of the extrahuman self and of the extrahuman self of the other. The village woman possessed has both a "Hofriyati" or "human self," qualities and dispositions consistent with the ideal feminine self-image to which she is continuously socialized, and what could be called a "*zār* self" (or, as I later suggest, a "nonself"), incorporating qualities and dispositions inconsistent with the Hofriyati self, or consistent but extreme: virtually unattainable by the former and thus considered abnormal. For villagers the human self is the true self. The *zār* self comprises what the woman sometimes manifests herself to be, but her self is not, and is therefore credited to spirits. Now like all individuals, the possessed receives and transmits information regarding her identity, her selfhood, dialogically.

But when doing so, she may interact in one or both of her "selves," and not only with the Hofriyati selves of others, but, perhaps, with their respective *zār* selves as well. Dialogue is potentially thickened in a variety of ways, for any apparently simple conversation may disguise a multidimensional enterprise—like Fatna's game with the sultan's son.

This raises an important point: once the idiom of possession has been invoked, people are freer to communicate in ways antithetic to the harmony-preserving tactics of everyday discourse. Close kin, spouses, affines, might indirectly discuss issues which otherwise could not be broached without injuring their relationship. And this is possible because of the potential for obfuscation inherent in the possession idiom: the distinction between human self and *zār* self is not rigidly drawn, even during possession trance. Responsibility can be assigned to *zayran,* to humans, to both. It is this latent confusion, the necessarily obscure and oblique nature of nonascriptive, nonquotidian discourse, that permits vitally important messages of a sort not normally countenanced to be transmitted without permanent rupture to the social fabric. Here is one way that possession turns ambiguity and paradox to creative use: Zaineb, without automatically damaging her marriage, might publicly voice dissatisfaction with her husband's behavior or, through her timely acknowledgment of a spirit illness, inform him of negative gossip about which he was unaware.

In 1976 Zaineb maneuvered through a personal crisis by invoking the possession idiom. From the start, the outcome was less than certain. She was understandably wary of the reactions of others—in-laws, husband, brothers, the community at large—to her various attempts to change her undesirable situation, reactions which, when they have come, have given her pause and led her to consider alternate paths. Zaineb was feeling her way, slowly, toward a more comfortable position in her world. But that position, when she grasped it, could not be sustained, and she has had to move on. Her desire to pursue a curing vocation is dormant and may never be resumed.

For the negotiation of Zaineb's illness has been at least as complex as the negotiation of her cure. She is physically unwell and still undergoing biomedical therapy; she was the victim of a ruinous spell cast by an envious woman; she is possessed. Her malady is multifaceted, each facet complicating the others, exacerbating her symptoms. Appreciation for the intercurrent aspects of her condition emerged gradually, over the course of a year, in just the order that villagers heed when attempting to locate the etiology of an ailment. Zaineb continued to work on the biomedical component of her illness while receiving treatment for ensorcellment, but when I left she had yet to drum the *zār.* Indeed, there occurred a perceptible slackening of momentum in her press for a spirit cure. Why, if a cure was deemed necessary to restore her health and crucial to becoming a *shaykha,* was she apparently reluctant to undertake it?

The answer, I think, is that she was wary of damaging the fragile credibility with the *zār* she had taken such pains to establish. *Zayran* forbid their hosts to consult biomedical practitioners and are known to intensify a woman's symptoms should she disobey. It is clear they would not quietly endure her taking pills while she also undertook to appease them with a ritual. This would be an egregious defiance of their authority. So Zaineb realized that though she risked angering her spirits, the non-*zār* component of her illness had to be resolved before she drummed her cure. If she drummed too soon and her condition failed to improve, doubts would spark as to her good relations with *zayran*. Her ambition to become a *shaykha* could be curtailed. It is another paradox of her position that Zaineb was tactically forced to wait until she had recovered before she could undertake a cure. By the following spring her health had improved sufficiently to let the ceremony proceed; however, a few months later she suffered a virulent relapse of both spirit and biomedical ailments at the time of her daughter's death.[15] Unhappily, to date she has recovered from neither.

For Zaineb, like Umselima and others encountered in this chapter, an association with *zayran* provides an ever expanding backdrop against which to make sense of the twists and turns in her life: childhood illness, betrothal, marital difficulties, anxiety surrounding pregnancy and childbirth, removal from the comfortable world of her mother's home, even, perhaps, a beloved daughter's death. But the reverse is also true: events in her life provide clues about developments in her relations with *zayran*. To those who experience possession, spirit world and human are delicately intertwined.

15. A number of women I spoke to linked the onset of a spirit illness to the death of an adult daughter, usually in childbirth.

7

Hosts and Spirits

In previous chapters I proposed that in Hofriyat and its environs possession is a form of social discourse shaped by the political relations of gender, and quotidian gender ideals and dispositions. I have also suggested that implicitly and metaphorically, the discourse is informed by villagers' concept of ethnicity and resistance to external domination. These two levels of the *zār* are mutually significant; but while the latter is reserved for discussion in chapter 8, succeeding pages broaden exploration of possession's articulatory potential by considering additional spirit narratives and incidents. The purpose here is to elucidate the spirit-host relationship: how spirits figure in the lives of the possessed, how the possessed speak about *zayran* above them; and so to delve more deeply into the antilanguage of the *zār:* its vocabulary, symbolism, symptoms, and diagnostic contexts.

Motherhood and Matrilineality

Sosan

Sosan is the elderly Hofriyati *shaykha* who formerly practiced with Umselima. Even before she had reached menarche, she was wed to her classificatory *wad ʿamm;* her first possession experience occurred a few years later, when she and her two young sons were living in her mother's *ḥōsh:*

> I fell ill when the father of my sons left Hofriyat and went to the area of the dam at Jabal Auwliya [on the White Nile south of Khartoum]. My husband left his sons, and they were beautiful, they have yellow [light] skin. He bought some land near the Jabal and married an ʿArab woman, *sākit* [silently, "for no reason"]. She was no relation to him at all! I became ill and I did not know anything. I was absent, entranced.
>
> I lay on a mat inside the sleeping room and a beautiful woman appeared before me. She was as tall as the center support post and she wore a lovely *tōb,* of plain crepe, and yellow, and she had yellow skin. She spoke to me

from above, but at first I could not hear; she informed me of what is above me, she tied me to her [cf. the notion of "threads"]. She told me of the spirits by which I am possessed, and they are many. . . . [Sosan listed several *Darāwīsh* and *Ḥabish zayran,* plus *Ḥakīm bi-Dūr,* a *Khawāja* doctor]. The yellow lady told me to have a curing ceremony. I did this and sacrificed a two-toned[1] ram as she instructed. Um al-Abbas, the *sitt al-ʿilba* from Shendi, came to officiate. My husband sent money for the ritual and for the special demands of my *zayran,* gold jewelry for *Sitti Khuḍara* [daughter of a *Darwīsh*], a gold *khatim* that protects from illness [signet ring of the *mushāhara* complex], *tōbs*, red clothes, and a red hat for the *Ḥabish.*

After drumming the *zār* I became its *shaykha.* Umselima and I went with the *shaykha* from Shendi and her male partner, a former slave and a homosexual, and I learned the threads and how to cense people and how to talk with spirits. . . .

Later, I had just become pregnant for the third time, and Umselima and I were called to drum the *zār* for an old man, Maowi. He was a little crazy, his mind was slow. He used to attend *zār* parties often, and he would dress like a *Khawāja,* wearing trousers, hat, and a suit coat. Or he would dress and behave like a nomadic *ʿArab,* forever drawing his sword. Maowi had taken ill, and since all other methods of curing him had failed, they decided as the last [resort] to drum the *zār.* But he was not weak. He dressed as an *ʿArab* and continued to draw his sword throughout the ceremony.

I was pregnant. A woman came up to me during the ritual. She told me the old man, Maowi, said he had heard my thoughts: that my baby was illegitimate [*ḥarām*]. I said to her, "I am legitimately pregnant." I denied his claim. The man said, "The child you carry will not prosper."

A short while later I gave birth to a son. Immediately after his naming, my baby died. The *dasatīr* [synonym for *zayran*] of Maowi took him, they took my son. The woman who heard Maowi say this saw his *zayran* making off with my baby's spirit [*rūḥ*].

Faiza

Faiza is in her late fifties, and married to her mother's matrilateral parallel cousin. Her initial possession illness occurred at the miscarriage of her first pregnancy, a baby girl. Her affliction returned at the end of her next pregnancy when she bore a son. At this time her father, who could "read the books," examined her and advised her to drum the *zār,* which she did with her husband's support.

1. *Ābrag,* literally, "shiny" or "glittery," like lightning (*burāg*); this is also the name of the animal on which the Prophet Mohammed was transported to Jerusalem, then ascended the seven heavens.

Faiza said that when a *zār* attacks her it grasps her by the legs and neck. It holds her head and prevents her from sleeping. And like Sosan, a possessive spirit has also seized her offspring:

> The *zār* stole my first daughter, and he stole two other daughters as well. And one day I had a dream. I saw my neighbor, Rabiʿa, sleeping on the ground. She was four months pregnant. I saw a *jinni,* one, a *zār.* And I saw Rabiʿa lose her boy child. At dawn when I awoke I told Rabiʿa what I had dreamed. And Rabiʿa said that during the night something had come down on her head. He was trying to make her abort. So she lay on the ground and slept that way, as I had seen, but just before sunrise she miscarried.

Faiza bore seven sons in addition to the three daughters she lost. Then, when her youngest son ʿAwad was four months old, Faiza's brother died:

> I was full of grief. I was shattered [*maksūra*], and I must have had *ḍuʿf* [weakness, specifically, a disease where the blood becomes thin or light]. I went to bed, and the baby at my breast, ʿAwad, he became ill. He had vomiting and diarrhea. My father said the reason for his illness was *zār.* He said, "The *zār* is inflamed because of the sorrow." My father said, "Above her is a *zār* and it has gone astray and descended on her baby."
>
> We obtained a light crepe shirt for ʿAwad, and good powdered perfume, and sweet soap, and a bit of clear *araki,* and when we had done this he became well. Even now, whenever ʿAwad is home, everything must be immaculately clean or his *zār* will inflame.

Howari

Like Faiza, Howari is perhaps sixty years old. She is the second of her husband's wives, the first having died in childbirth before Howari wed.

> I had *zayran* early, even before I had given birth. I had been married for a long while and I had not conceived and I became ill. It was the *zār.* I consulted a *sitt al-ʿilba.* She said that red spirits were above me. I had a *zār* party and I learned that among my spirits are many which are also above my mother and older sister. My sister and I received spirits from our mother, like an inheritance.
>
> I have had three more *zār* parties since my first, one following the birth of my first child, Nada, a girl; another after I lost a baby boy to the *zār* in miscarriage, and the fourth not so long ago, after Nada died in childbirth.
>
> When I am made ill by the *zār,* I go silent and my body becomes rigid. My arms and legs fold in close to my body. And my breasts swell and become very painful. If I put dirt on my head on hearing news of a death, a fever comes immediately. My spirits demand cleanliness. I must bathe with

> Lux soap, use incense and henna, because these things bring coolness and are pleasing to the spirits.

The narratives above strike a number of chords with those of Umselima's kin; both groups resonate with motifs evoking feminine ideals and praxis. Sosan's apparition is a beautiful woman of light complexion, and her spirits demand gold associated with the prevention of uterine hemorrhage, *mushāhara* illness; Faiza's *zār* afflicts her when she suffers from grief and thin blood (also linked to *mushāhara*), and the spirit is mollified by cleanliness and perfume; Howari's possession symptoms involve closure of body orifices and can be coaxed to relent when she bathes, censes herself, and uses henna.

Moreover, in all three cases plus that of Rabiᶜa, *zayran* are linked with problematic fertility. Not only do they prevent conception or bring uncontrollable bleeding, they go so far as to interfere with a pregnancy, whatever its stage of advance. *Zayran* provoke miscarriages; they bring sickness and death to the infants of women they possess; they steal their husbands' "expectations." Though *zayran* do not cause their hosts to suffer incapacitating illness or death, they do bring grave misfortune to the fruits of those women's bodies, the newly formed products of their blood. For it is blood that *zayran* control, and blood that they pursue.

The perils of motherhood are aptly suggested by one of Howari's symptoms, for whenever the *zayran* above her inflame, she suffers painful swelling of her breasts. The relationship of Howari's affliction to maternity is more transparent than most, figuring in each episode severe enough to warrant a cure: failure to conceive after years of marriage, the birth of a daughter as her first child, the loss of a son "to the *zār*" in miscarriage, the death of her adult daughter in childbed. But the link is no less present in Sosan's case, or in Faiza's, or those considered in chapter 6.

One point emerges more clearly from the last two narratives—that *zār* is linked to a particular form of matrilineality. This is only fitting, given the logic of the *zār*, for to spirits, maternity and matrilineality are not readily distinguished. Recall that Umselima's *zayran* are also above her daughter Zaineb, and her sister Sadiya's daughter Azina; moreover, Umselima shares her *Khawāja* boy spirits with Sadiya and these were transmitted to Sadiya's son Hamid because they descended on his mother just before his birth. Similarly, the spirits above Howari and her sister were above their mother as well, and came upon them "like an inheritance," yet long before their mother's death. More than inheritance, these bonds resemble the alignments of descent, and not without reason, for a principal target of *zayran* is uterine blood, and the spirits are wont to follow its flow. Sisters of the same mother share uterine blood; so then, do their daughters and, indeed, their sons. As they share blood, so might they share spirits.

Here, the case of ʿAwad is instructive. Unlike Hamid who was possessed in utero, ʿAwad is afflicted while at his mother's breast. The possession nevertheless occurs as he takes into his body a vital feminine fluid. And milk, like blood, is a fluid over which *zayran* exert control, for spirit threats to its availability are a major concern of the *mushāhara* complex earlier discussed. Importantly, though a man can be possessed, he cannot pass the affliction to his sons, since the sons' flesh and blood originate in their mother, not in him. From the moment a son is born, then weaned and wholly detached from his mother's body, he gradually loses his association with femininity and becomes less likely to be seized, intentionally or inadvertently, by her *zayran*.

The possession idiom thus implies a principle of matrilineal descent. And as was previously suggested, this is significant because it stands in sharp distinction to the overt patrilineal ideology that governs quotidian praxis. Here the *zār*'s counterhegemonic potential is obvious; yet it is also more subtle, for its lineal focus expresses gender complementarity and emphasizes the centrality of gender constructs to the Hofriyati discourse of contrast. And here again the relation between male and female echoes that between Islam and the *zār*. An agnatic organizing principle applies also to Islam, since *baraka*, Allah's favor or blessing, can be passed in its agentative form from father to son, occasionally to collateral male agnates, and also to daughters. Hofriyati maintain that a woman cannot transmit *baraka* to her children, just as a man cannot pass possession by alien spirits to his sons.

Still, like agnation in village social organization, uterinity is a relative principle in the domain of the *zār*. For maternal kin may be possessed by entirely different spirits or spirit types, and it is this which allows Zaineb to emphasize the affinal tie and underplay the matrilateral one in relations with Sittalbenat.

Amna and Sekina: The Spirit of Negotiation

In chapter 6 I noted that distant kin or unrelated individuals possessed by the same *zār* might perceive in this an opportunity to develop a bond between them where none existed before. Their common possession might enhance communication, even contribute to a mitigation of conflict where, under normal conditions, restraint and latent hostility would rule the day. Witness the following:

In 1974 Hessain divorced his first wife, Sekina, who was his classificatory *bit ʿamm*. A month later he wed Amna; it was her first marriage. Amna's father was not in favor, for Hessain, he said, had already set aside one woman, could he not be expected to do the same again? But Hessain is a matrilateral kinsman of Amna's mother, and it was she who promoted the match. After the wedding, Amna continued to live with her parents while Hessain worked in Khartoum. In January 1976 she delivered a baby girl.

Six months later, Hessain remarried Sekina. According to villagers, Hessain's sons had pressured him to return (*raja*ᶜ) because they wanted to work outside the village and feared leaving their mother unattended. But Sekina had another story. Hessain, she said, had missed her terribly, and suffered considerable remorse on realizing his mistake. She avowed they rewed on his initiative, not his sons'.

Now the problem was that Hessain could not afford two wives unless one continued to live with her parents. But Amna could not hope to stay with her family indefinitely, for they had a small *ḥōsh* and eight other children at home; moreover, Amna's sister Khalda was there with four of her children: she had just begun confinement after childbirth and her husband did not want her to return to Khartoum at its end. To make matters worse, a July wedding was planned for another sister, Nemad, and there would be little room for guests in a *ḥōsh* brimming with married daughters and their children. Amna had expected to join her husband in Khartoum, where he promised to rent her a house.

But Sekina revealed that she, not her cowife, would soon be off with Hessain to Khartoum. To Amna this seemed unfair, since years ago Hessain had built a house for Sekina in Malkab. But she closed it at the time of their divorce, claiming it belonged to her sons, and moved in with her mother. From then on, Hessain's house had gone unoccupied.

In July, with Hessain returned to Hofriyat for Nemad's wedding, the conflict between his wives escalated. Though disappointed not to be chosen for Khartoum, Amna said she would be content if she could live in Hessain's Malkabi house. But Sekina rejected this immediately, and Hessain would say no more. Amna then refused to speak to her husband or his other wife.

Sekina, for her part, made quite a show of her coup. She reopened Hessain's house, and invited residents of both villages to greet her there and offer congratulations on her marriage. Hessain's mother was so pleased by the event that she slaughtered a goat in thanksgiving, though Hofriyati said she pretended to be saddened by it all in Amna's presence.

At a funeral in Malkab a few weeks later, Sekina confirmed her plans to reclose the house in Malkab and rent another with Hessain in Khartoum. Amna, she said, would have to go on living with her parents.

But Amna's parents were not amused by these developments. And Hessain was two months behind in his payment of expenses for Amna and her daughter. All feared Amna's divorce was imminent.

In early August Amna wrote to Hessain, formally requesting the Malkabi house when Sekina joined him in Khartoum. The letter caused considerable stir among Sekina's kin. A delegation headed by a mutual kinsman of all three spouses arrived to discuss matters with Amna's parents, but left without resolving the issue.

So Amna took matters into her own hands and paid Sekina a visit at the disputed house. The visit was inconclusive. Later Sekina's kin bruited that Amna had come for no reason at all—the subtext: she had come on a nefarious mission. Sekina's mother circulated a rumor that Amna had visited a *faki ṣadīg shawaṭīn* prior to her "friendly" visit, to obtain some magical sand designed to bring misfortune. This she accused her of spreading in Sekina's *ḥōsh* so that when Sekina stepped on it she would fall violently ill.

A few days later, Amna and Sekina independently attended Zaineb's *zār* test in Malkab. And there, both descended to the thread for *Maray,* a beautiful Ethiopian prostitute *zār.* Sekina maintained that *Maray* has been above her for some time; in fact it was this *zār* for whom she slaughtered a ram years ago at her seven-day cure. Amna, on the other hand, was newly married and had but recently acknowledged a possession affliction. She did not know of *Maray*'s presence above her until that night.

When Amna descended to the thread for *Maray* she became entranced. The spirit entered her body. When she continued to descend even after the drumming had stopped, Samiya the *shaykha* coaxed *Maray* to relent. She placed her arms on Amna's shoulders and asked the spirit, "What do you want?" No reply, save Amna's continued bobbing up and down. Samiya called for the thread to be redrummed. And again *Maray* responded with Amna's quick rhythmic movements. When the drumming ceased Samiya asked *Maray* once more, "What do you want?" A small voice answered from under the *tōb* that covered Amna's face, "*Rundu* wants." *Maray* thus indicated Her willingness to depart Amna's body and Her desire for the ceremony to continue with the chant for *Rundu,* a wealthy male European *zār* impatient to enter the *mīdān.* Drumming promptly resumed with the appropriate thread. Amna again began to descend, then, in mid chant, rose and left the room. She was perspiring heavily and looked vague and disoriented.

Moments later Sekina also went outside. Then I observed them speaking in hushed tones in the doorway. Sekina warned Amna of the rumor her mother had begun and apologized, saying she would quash the story if she could, for she knew it to be false. Then Amna asked about the house in Malkab, and Sekina agreed to leave that decision to Hessain. They spoke amicably a short while longer, then each resumed her place in the *mīdān.*

A functional interpretation of the above might suggest that Zaineb's *zār* test provided Amna and Sekina with neutral ground and legitimate cause to meet and discuss their problems. On one level this was, of course, the case. But an anthropological interpretation faithful to the actors' view of the situation would have to include the spirits in that equation. And when this is done, at least two additional layers of potential significance must be taken into account.

Amna's departure from the room probably signaled *Maray*'s exit from her body, for the transition from spirit to human presence is often marked in such a way. But this is by no means certain. And whatever the case, *Maray* continued to hover near Amna and exert Her influence, for spirits, once summoned to a ritual, do not entirely withdraw from the *mīdān* until its end.

Now Sekina, too, is host to this spirit and is therefore under Her influence when she joins Amna at the door. The two women have more in common than a single husband; they are host to the same spirit. It might well be that Amna, wittingly or not, becomes possessed by *Maray* precisely because this spirit possesses her cowife. For *Maray* is already bound by an exchange agreement with Hessain, mediated by Sekina who has sacrificed on Her behalf. Since *Maray*'s claim is the same regardless which wife She affects, Amna could anticipate possession by *Maray* as a consequence of marriage to Hessain, and may have deployed Her to diffuse an explosive situation. Cowives' common interest in the spirit provided them a pathway for communication that temporarily overrode conflicting interests in their man.

But this is still too simple, for it fails to consider the subtle role the spirit Herself might play. Surely, *Maray*—a capricious, amoral *zār*—has Her own interests at heart in choosing to possess Amna. For two wives make far better leverage: adding Amna to Her list of human hosts tightens Her indirect hold on Hessain. So it is also in *Maray*'s interest to preserve both marriages, which means averting Amna's divorce. Hence *Maray* might have precipitated the cowives' meeting in a conciliatory atmosphere which She controls. Conflict between women in the human domain may be balanced by the interest of their mutual *zār* in the spirit realm.

Both Amna and Sekina were aware of *Maray*'s stake in their dispute, for both were versed in the idiom of possession from an early age. But here again the potential for confusion characteristic of communication between the possessed becomes apparent. Significantly, not only do Amna and Sekina meet under the influence of *Maray,* so that just who negotiates with whom is not entirely explicit, but their conversation takes place in the doorway: on liminal ground between the quotidian human world outside and that of the *zār* revealed in the *mīdān*. Thus even the context of their interaction is indeterminate, and each participant, each observer, has occasion to derive several different readings from the event. Some of these might later provide the basis for consultation and negotiation. For "Sekina" was able to soften her stance without denying it publicly, without losing face. And "Amna" was able to press her claim to their husband's house.

An apparently mundane confrontation between cowives is thickened enormously when it takes place in the idiom of *zār*. And still there are levels of meaning I have not plumbed, linked to the potential import of *Maray*'s identity as an Ethiopian and a prostitute, to the associative auras of these concepts in the human world, to their meanings in the personal lives of the protagonists. But whatever else can be said for such encounters, and though the ambiance of mutuality in this one could not be sustained [Amna was divorced eight months later], Amna and Sekina were briefly able to mitigate tensions in their relationship through the protective ambiguity of possession. When I returned to the village, the two were on friendly terms: Amna remarried Hessain in 1982 and had just given birth to a second daughter when I saw her in 1984. Tellingly, she was living in Hessain's Malkabi house; Sekina was living with their husband in Khartoum.

Contexts of Attack

Several narratives here and in the previous chapter suggest contexts other than procreation where spirits might afflict their hosts. Sittalbenat's *zayran* do not stand for her anger; Sosan's initial illness occurs, like Amna's possession by *Maray,* when she reluctantly acquires a cowife; a *zār* mistakes the baby at Faiza's breast for her when she is grief stricken at the loss of her brother; Howari's spirits inflame when she mourns for her daughter. All these situations compromise or violate the Hofriyati image of femininity. Becoming a cowife is problematic financially, fragmenting the complementarity between husband and wife; acquiring a cowife who produces more heirs for her husband means that a woman's aspirations for her own children suffer grave reverse. The death of a loved one signifies loss of support, provokes emotional excess, and calls for a woman to loosen and rub dirt into her hair, wear rough mourning clothes, and refrain from bathing for several days. However commonly such things occur, they are "other" than what Hofriyati women ought to be. As such, they precipitate intervention by extrahuman beings, *zayran*. Again, Zaineb's initial spirit vision happens when she is physically unwell, delirious, not herself. And Umselima's first apparition takes place when she and her brother have behaved in ways that villagers deem unsuitable. Subsequent possession attacks coincide with bouts of anger, unhappiness, fright, anxiety, depression, frustration with kin: feelings which fail to mesh with prevalent ideals of enclosedness—dignity, reserve, emotional control.

Asia

Asia had borne her first child, a daughter, by her *wad ʿamm,* and she was about to be moved to her husband's mother's *ḥōsh* when a dispute arose between her parents and affines. Her husband's parents insisted she live in the same room as her mother-in-law, despite the wisdom that "a house that shelters three men cannot hold two women." The dispute culminated with her divorce.

Two years later, Asia remarried. Her second husband, Ahmed, had earlier divorced his first wife for failing to conceive, but she had since re-wed and borne sons. Because of this, Ahmed was reputed to be impotent, or at best sterile. People in the area therefore began to ridicule Asia, and also her parents for allowing the wedding to take place. Their severest critic was Asia's ex-mother-in-law.

> They said of me, "Now she will never give birth, at all, at all!" [i.e., she will not even bear daughters now]. But I became pregnant not two years after the wedding. Then they said, "Ahmed has not taken that girl there." They claimed my child was illegitimate, that is.
>
> My mother said, "By the Prophet! Can you not give it up?" The people said I had done wrong, but I had not. And they did not give it up even after my son was born.
>
> When my son was seven months old, Ahmed moved me to his *ḥōsh* in Hofriyat. We had a "removal" party in Malkab before I left my mother. After the party they brought me here to Hofriyat. The moment I crossed the threshold into Ahmed's house, I became ill. . . . The *faki* said my illness was caused by a red spirit, a *zār.*

Asia's affliction, like Zaineb's, or that of Miriam soon to be discussed, is linked to a change of residence, indeed, a change of villages following marriage. Though the distance may not be great—less than a kilometer separates Malkab from Hofriyat—at such times a bride surrenders the protection and everyday support of close kin to venture unaided into a neighboring and potentially hostile village. Understandably, she is apprehensive of this shift in her social position. But Asia is also the focus of negative gossip. She is tacitly and wrongly accused of wanton behavior, of violating local ideals, a further and more serious violation of integrity than removal from her natal village could be. Such conditions of openness increase her susceptibility to *zayran.*

Note here, too, the suggestion of liminality in the onset of Asia's illness: "the moment I crossed the threshold . . . I became ill." Doorways and other thresholds constitute a major motif in the narratives and actions of the possessed, and are indications of the idiom's antilinguistic potential.

The inside, the enclosed, is marked in the language of daily life; what is outside, in between, or able to move between, is marked in the language of possession.

Bedriya

> My first illness from the *zār* came when I was very young, even before I was married. I was at a wedding and dancing [the pigeon dance] with other girls to the beat of the *dallūka*. One Sudani [stranger] man came close to me; he snapped his fingers, asking for the *shabāl*. But he stank so terribly from sweat that I fainted immediately.
>
> My family brought me home and censed me and perfumed me. And I awoke and I descended, there, in the belly of the house! I dreamed I saw three young girls say they wanted pretty wraps and plaited hair. I dreamed this song:
>
> What needs have I?
> We want henna, incense,
> A bottle of perfume on which there appears the face of a man,
> A *tōb* of plain crepe with no design.
> We are an ancient illness in the books of knowledge,
> Tell us noble persons that you fear the *dastūr*
> *Wilād Mama!*
>
> Thus did I learn I was possessed by a *zār*.

The wedding ceremony in Hofriyat is an implicit statement of propriety, of ideals which inform village life. As observed throughout, its principal symbol is the bride, whose ritually prepared body exhibits qualities of purity, whiteness, smoothness, cleanliness, imperviousness, and enclosedness. Perspiration violates these positive conditions and is considered abhorrent, but especially so if sensed at a wedding. Thus Bedriya's experience is counter to what Hofriyati might reasonably expect on such an occasion: it is literally non-Hofriyati and as such renders her vulnerable to spirit attack. Significantly, *Wilād Mama* demands her to refurbish the feminine qualities in herself that have suffered depletion through her negative experience.

Miriam

When Miriam, the local midwife, attended *zār* rituals as a child, her mother's spirits descended on her "like an inheritance." Her initial *zār* illness occurred shortly after her first wedding, when her husband brought her to live with him in Khartoum. Then, after four years of marriage she was divorced for failing to conceive.

A few years later she married again. This time she conceived, but the son she bore died at birth in a nearby hospital. At this point her spirits inflamed and made her unwell. Then, when the doctors told her she would never again become pregnant, her second husband set her aside.

In 1968 Miriam, divorced and childless, obtained support from the village area council to undertake government training in midwifery. Just after she had returned to the village following completion of the course, her sister died in childbirth, a tragedy that Miriam, despite her training, was powerless to prevent. Now Miriam lives with her mother and cares for her sister's child. She is the only licensed midwife in the area and for some distance into the desert beyond. Not only does she assist at births, she currently performs all the female circumcisions in Hofriyat and Malkab.

During my first fieldwork period, Miriam suffered a relapse of *zār* illness and made preparations to stage a cure.

> I was unhappy, tired, tired from "birthing," and the *zār* inflamed. The *zayran* inflame whenever I see or smell the black blood of childbirth, especially the blood that comes when a woman has difficulty in delivery. The *zār* inflames when it sees blood all the time and experiences the screaming and the confusion of a birth or circumcision.

Frequently, Miriam has to deliver a stillborn child or one who dies soon after birth. This causes her sadness which, she says, also provokes her *zayran*. The spirit responsible for her malady in 1976 was *Lulīya Ḥabishīya*, an Ethiopian prostitute and usurper of fertility not known to be above her until then.

Not only is *Lulīya Ḥabishīya* a prostitute *zār*, she is Ethiopian and uncircumcised, and during rituals mocks the Hofriyati bridal dance. She has considerable power to seize or "tie up" Hofriyati women's fertility, yet all the while exemplifies its opposite: inappropriate sexuality and inadequately socialized femininity. Now *Lulīya* afflicted Miriam at the height of the circumcision season, at a time when she was extremely busy operating on young girls. To complicate matters, during those weeks several women had also gone into labor. None was an easy birth: there was one breach delivery involving hemorrhage, one case in which the baby was stillborn, another where neither mother nor child survived. These were instances of fertility gone awry, and implicated *zayran*. Further, Miriam was being exposed to different types of blood on a regular basis and thus, in view of the *mushāhara* complex, was exceedingly vulnerable to spirit attack.

For blood, remember, is ambiguous in Hofriyat; depending on its context it may have positive or negative significance. And blood from different domains of productive and reproductive experience should not be brought into conjunction lest their inappropriate mixing cause *nazīf*, uncontrollable hemorrhage. Miriam's position is clearly ambiguous, not only experientially but also socially, for it is through shedding others' blood that she derives her livelihood.

The evident paradox of her life is aptly expressed by possessive *zayran* who inflame when exposed to black, postproductive blood associated with problematic childbirth. For this is consonant with her unfortunate procreative history and may tacitly concede a recognition that the circumcision she performs and has undergone herself is detrimental to women's health and fertility. Possibly, then, *Lulīya Ḥabishīya,* cynical caricature of sacred femininity, is for Miriam a personal symbol (cf. Obeyesekere 1981) that objectifies and articulates her subjective contradiction.

But for all that, the symbol's context is idiomatic: just as Bedriya is afflicted upon detecting human sweat at a wedding, so Miriam's spirits inflame when she sees and smells malodorous black blood of problematic birth and witnesses the emotional excesses of others at these times. Spirits, however capricious, afflict women whose experiences contravene interiority ideals, but are especially virulent at moments, ritual or otherwise, when those ideals are acted out, made obvious, and therefore exposed and endangered. Finally, Miriam's experience, like Asia's, like Amna's and Sekina's, involves a threshold. In Miriam's case the boundary is not a doorway, a *khashm al-bayt,* but its associative counterpart, the female genital orifice.

Bakheita

Bakheita, twice married and childless, had returned to Hofriyat from Khartoum where she was living with her husband, in order to attend a wedding. She was alone, preparing herself for the wedding dance when the ceiling of her room collapsed. Bakheita was found pinned beneath the heavy roof beam, her right hip and back severely damaged.

After trying a number of local bone setters and herbalists without success, her family took her to hospital in Khartoum. There she lay, "patient number 10" for six months and ten days. The *khawāja* doctors elected to operate, but there was a risk that the procedure could kill her or leave her worse off than before. Her relatives decided against it, and returned her to Hofriyat. By this time, her second husband had divorced her.

On arriving in the village, Bakheita's kin consulted a *faki,* who divined the ceiling collapse to be the result of a red *jinn* clumsily descending on her. So a *zār* cure was drummed on her behalf. Until then she had been unable to walk:

> They did a *zār* for me and I walked! I stood up tall, I arose to descend while standing erect. And I made requests. I asked for liquor and a cap and a khaki suit and a walking cane like those used by Europeans. I am possessed by Westerners, the Christians. No other spirit species is above me.

As was the case for Faiza's baby (and Seraitti not yet discussed), a *zār* causes Bakheita's injury by descending on her from above. Then, having achieved its purpose and obtained its requests, it makes her well, though not restored to her former state of health. The spirit's force and its caprice are equally evident here, but so is its idiomatic intervention. For like Bedriya's, Bakheita's possession attack takes place on the occasion of a wedding. At such times, young women are deemed especially vulnerable to *zayran,* for it is then that they make themselves beautiful by emphasizing and accentuating their bridely traits, whether by preparing themselves cosmetically or performing the pigeon dance. *Zayran,* who are great aesthetes, are powerfully attracted and seize the occasion to descend. Thus, exposure or demonstration of her positive qualities—enabling others to sense them—renders a woman open to attack, as does her own sensory experience if it is negative or untoward.

In Bakheita's case, *zār* explains an unfortunate coincidence of events that might otherwise be explained by witchcraft (cf. Evans-Pritchard 1976). Instead of attributing calamity to the psychic malice of covillagers, Hofriyati cast blame outside their society, thereby preserving its harmony and integrity. The explanation is nonetheless personal, for the perpetrator is a sentient being; yet it is also an alien existent. Still, witchcraft is a reality within the confines of Hofriyat, for villagers readily attribute certain ailments and adversities to the unwitting eye of the envious. But the circumstances of Bakheita's accident match criteria for attack by the evil eye less well than they match those for possession: the fact that something fell upon her from above, especially in the context of a wedding, is a clear indication that a *zār* was involved.

Asha

Asha's husband has three other wives and has been married eight times in all. Though an amiable man, he is considered profligate by his peers, for he habitually divorces and financially neglects his wives. When he began spending most of his time and money with another wife, Asha became openly angry. Then she had a dream: she dreamed of henna and *dallūka* music, signifying the *zār,* and when she awoke she discovered that a painful sore had arisen on the finger where she wore her wedding ring. The sore was hot (*ḥārr*), she said, and came "on its own"—not because she injured herself; it came because the spirits "inflamed with my anger."

Among women who already acknowledge possession, *zayran* are held responsible for a variety of strange events. Here the spirits explain the cooccurrence of Asha's anger and the appearance of a sore, both of which are linked to her husband's indecorous behavior. Yet, as is the case for Bedriya and others who are possessed, the *zār* not only expresses alienation from local values, but also buttresses a woman's Hofriyati self, in Asha's case, by physically chastising her expression of anger. Asha's spirits caused her to experience pain, which she describes as "hot": the episode resonates with those events of routine life, like baking *kisra,* that subtly reinforce appropriate feminine dispositions. Moreover, spirits require their hosts to control their emotions, especially strong emotions like anger and grief that are unseemly for women to display.

Spirits and Selves

All this returns us to the nature of womanhood in Hofriyat, and the issue of feminine self-image.[2] Remember that for villagers, who have a keen sense of who they are and how they differ from outsiders (cf. Kennedy 1978*a*), it is not only fertility but cultural identity that is vested in women's selves. In local thought the body is a microcosm of village society (cf. Douglas 1966, 1973). Like village boundaries, body orifices are ambiguous, however necessary and inevitable. They are prone to a litany of dangers—spirit intrusion not least—and regulated by complex ritual procedures. The most ambiguous and problematic boundary is the vaginal meatus, for it is through women's bodies and uterine blood that village society can be renewed appropriately, from within, or inappropriately opened up to potentially destructive influences from without. This boundary is defended by pharaonic circumcision.

Through her circumcision a woman's body is transformed into a living vessel of her culture's moral values, and she is henceforward exhorted to conduct herself accordingly. This, plus the entire system of knowledge and praxis through which femininity is realized and maintained, strongly supports the identification of the woman with her role—social and symbolic—in Hofriyati culture. The highly directed process of forging female persons physically, socially, subjectively, takes place despite the relativity of the Hofriyati moral world and despite villagers' recognition of human diversity—or, more plausibly, because of them. And here is my point: so tangibly socialized are women to this view of themselves that, for many, to experience the world otherwise is to experience it, quite literally, as a non-Hofriyati. Women's experiences of otherness are an implicit effect of hegemony. The central problem which possession addresses, in hundreds of idiosyncratic, counterhegemonic ways, is the cultural overdetermination of women's selfhood.

Drawing from Burridge's argument in *Someone, No One: An Essay*

2. The argument in this section first appeared in *American Ethnologist* 15(1):4–27 (Boddy 1988).

on Individuality (1979) and, in a parallel vein, from Kegan's (1982) constructive-developmental psychology, the self as a theoretical construct provisionally can be thought of not as an entity, but as a creative energy or process which actively engages the world, integrating the human biological organism with its physical and sociocultural environments, continually moving, becoming, maturing, making and organizing meaning (Burridge 1979:5 ff., 21; Kegan 1982:2–15; cf. Elster 1986). Burridge writes,

> The fact of integration—some sort of coherence or coordination of the parts or constituents of being—does not detach the integrative energy or self from its constituents, but still makes it more than the sum of the parts and, in that sense, conceptually and empirically distinct. (Burridge 1979:5)

In Burridge's terms, a self which is integrating in conformity with others manifests or realizes the "person," and it is female persons that daily practice strives to reproduce in Hofriyat. There the extreme identification of women with the cultural image of womanhood precipitates a compression of the subjective self into a normative set of roles and statuses, an entity in whom experience is continuously subordinated to cultural categories (ibid., p. 28), a publicly confirmed social representation (La Fontaine 1985*b*:124).

What the Hofriyati woman does not become, or is not at this stage given scope to become, is an "individual":

> Becoming aware of a gap between the person's reproductions and the truth of things by seizing on or being seized by particularly significant events, the self is moved to a transcendence of the traditional categories, to a reintegration of the event in a new rationalization assigning new meaning and relevance. In this transcendence and reintegration, manifest in the new realization, the self realizes the individual. (Burridge 1979:7)

Burridge (p. 5) suggests that most people oscillate between these two integrative moments, yet the quotidian context actively conspires against such movement and the realization of "individuality" in the Hofriyati woman's case. It effectively denies her the possibility to grow in self-awareness, to mature, to reflect on the categories of early socialization in which her selfhood is enmeshed. It is thus I consider her selfhood to be culturally overdetermined.

Why *over*determined? Because, paradoxically, the moral self-image that women are enjoined to assume cannot always be sustained by experience. The essential ambiguity of morality, the contrast between what is and what ought to be, poses problems that their continuous socialization eventually fails to overcome: how to deal conceptually and actively with infertility or other significant contraventions of femininity.

Yet when possession is invoked, another level of Hofriyati reality comes into play. The context shifts from that of the commonsense world governed by idioms of containment to a broader one which situates this orientation in relation to its converse: dysphoria for the possessed originates not within the self and its constituents, but outside them, indeed, outside the human world of Hofriyat. This, on the one hand, rationalizes the event in a way which vehemently defends the socialized self, for the self's experience is again subordinated to "natural" categories—*zayran*—however extraordinary they may seem. So, from an observer's perspective, *zayran* symbolize and render concrete a woman's experiences of the world which conflict with her consensually validated view of what that experience should be like.

With acceptance of a possession diagnosis comes disassociation of certain experiences from her Hofriyati self. And this both supports her objective self-image and plants the seeds of her subjective modification. First, by shifting the context of her experience from one of internal contradiction to external confrontation, of self or self-and-village-other to self-and-alien-spirit, there comes the promise of a negotiated resolution that does not question the felicity of indubitable truths. But more than this, *zayran* are representatives of non-Hofriyati cultures, and by virture of their extraordinariness, of their failure to conform with local norms and rules even as they intervene in the course of village life, possession allows for the possibility of ambiguity and otherness otherwise lacking in the continuous socialization of women in Hofriyat. The context of the possessed's quotidian situation is now widened to incorporate the actions of beings from an alien yet parallel world. Both the entropy of well-being and the location of its source in possession open up pathways for self-renewal, permitting a limited and, in this context, functional dissonance between person and self. In such cases, illness itself may be therapeutic.

What I am describing is, I think, rather different from what appears to happen in the case of emotional disorders common to Western cultures. If the self is truly a social construct and individual selves are constructed (cf. Berger and Luckmann 1966) or integrated (Burridge 1979) in the course of social interaction, the constituents and parameters of selfhood can be expected to vary from society to society. So, while parallels can be found between hysterical neurosis and Hofriyati possession—in that both conditions involve dissociation and may present initially as somatic complaints—these may be more obvious than real (cf. Ward 1982:416). The two "illnesses" are gounded in disparate cultural contexts, based on rather different conceptualizations of the self. At the risk of simplification, perhaps one could characterize certain neuroses in Western cultures, where self is conceived as a bounded, individuated entity (cf. Geertz 1983:59), as an overdetermination of selfhood whose symptoms are excessive subjectivity—a weakening of the ability to take the role of the "other" relative to one's self. In Hofriyat, where the essential feminine self is highly idealized, the problem seems to be one of objectification: self is firmly identified with village "other," and identity is emotionally realized in cultural symbolism to the point where any event perceived to negate that tenuous equation negates the woman's self. Thus, the most striking similarities occur between the normative process of curing or accommodating possession illness (disengaging the self from its context) and the aberrant one of developing a neurosis—resulting in many an unfortunate lay observation that adepts are chronic hysterics. Despite thorough disassociation of the untoward event from the Hofriyati woman's self, she does not, like the textbook hysteric, unconsciously deny her experiences of otherness so much as embrace them, while consciously recognizing them as aspects of her being over which she has limited if potentially increasing control.

When we see spirits as symbolic of symptoms (cf. Obeyesekere 1981: 34–35), and symptoms as idiomatic of spirit intrusion (cf. Kapferer 1983: 87; Lambek 1981 : 53), we do not stray far from Hofriyati logic. But if we view spirits and symptoms as dissociated facets of the possessed woman's self, as our own psychology might direct us to do (cf. LaBarre 1975 : 41; Bourguignon 1979 : 286), we violate villagers' reality. We tacitly (perhaps inadvertently) dismiss *zayran* as facts of Hofriyati existence and mistakenly employ an individualistic and compartmentalized concept of the self which has no basis in village culture. This, in turn, leads to an individualistic orientation to illness which, because it rarely addresses social context, misses the point of most illness in Hofriyat, including possession. Moreover, even the assumption that spirits represent projections of intolerable feelings is, as Crapanzano (1977*a*: 12) notes, a debatable one: spirits, like the illnesses they cause, originate outside the human self, not within it. And, unlike Western psychotherapy which encourages the patient to accept and integrate previously dissociated feelings as part of herself, *zār* therapy works by convincing her to recognize them as separated from herself in the first place. Clearly, any attempt to merge such feelings and experiences with the Hofriyati woman's self—which I have described as idealized and relational, but is, after all, her self—would be ethnopsychiatrically inappropriate. It could only deny her the validity of that self and potentially do more harm than good.

Again from an observer's perspective, one way to make sense of all this by reference to the concept of framing. Following Elster (1986 : 27), the Hofriyati woman's disconcerting experience is "reframed" by a diagnosis of possession in such a way that the precipitating behavior or event—for example, infertility—becomes compatible with her self-image: she is fertile, for spirits have seen fit to usurp this most valuable asset. And she generalizes: future untoward experiences do not undermine the equation of womanhood with fertility and all the rest; they signify the actions of *zayran,* who, unlike humans (except, perhaps, husbands relative to their wives), are invariably capricious and unpredictable. But for this there is a remedy. Thus, although dissociation may be psychologically adaptive for both Western neurotics and Hofriyati possessed, only for the former may it be symptomatic of pathology. For Hofriyati it is therapeutic. Most of those who acknowledge possession are competent, mentally healthy women who have responded in a culturally appropriate way to a stressful situation (cf. Crapanzano 1977*a*: 14).

When a village woman who feels unwell but has identified no organic or mystical source for her complaint accepts that she is possessed, she can begin to recover. Her possessive spirit or spirits, soon to be revealed, gradually take shape as a part of her being which is not, so to speak, a part of her person, her Hofriyati self. And it is during possession trance that the identity and characteristics of this nonkin, non-Hofriyati, nonhuman, but above all nonself existent are publicly established, both for the woman and those who observe her. Once established, this veritable nonself is linked, inextricably, to her self; it is not, however, integrated with her person, a situation that possession rituals stress and seek to maintain. Though rarely manifest in her body, the spirit constituents of her nonself are in constant attendance, influencing her decisions and perceptions to the point where some women speak of themselves as if they are pluralities, substituting "we" (*niḥna*) for "I" (*āna*). Furthermore, since a spirit might possess any number of Hofriyati simultaneously, a woman's nonself, like her self, is unlikely to be individualistic, for possession by a common spirit binds her to other Hofriyati selves and *zār* nonselves in ways other than those specified by kinship, providing new ways to think about human relationships.

The felt presence of an ever expandable, multiple nonself enhances, by opposition, a woman's sense of personhood, continuously affirming the integrity of what once might have been problematic. Though exogenous to her Hofriyati self, it is and becomes increasingly essential to that self's comprehension (cf. Young 1975: 578). Conversely, however, a woman's sense of self provides a negative ground by which to apprehend the parameters of her spirits. These two aspects of her being are maintained in contraposition throughout her life, neither reducing to its opposite, each becoming enriched in sympathy with the other, shifting, expanding, or contracting as their mutual situation changes over time.

And in this way, possession enables (yet does not compel) a woman to evolve: to reintegrate and recontextualize her experiences from a broadened perspective (cf. Kegan 1982). *Zayran* posit alternative sets of moral discriminations that are realized and displayed through her body and others' during trance. As is detailed later on, the observation and enactment of such episodes provides the possibility, by no means the assurance, that the integrating self will be "seized with a contrary or critical perception" (Burridge 1979:28) and empowered to alter her conditioning, to transcend the categories which have constrained her, recognize them for what they are: cultural constructs, not immutable truths. The paradox of Hofriyati possession is that it defends the person while also enabling the self: it is at once a self-enhancing and self-maintaining condition.

Male Possession: ʿUmer

Assuming that what I have written is pertinent to understanding possession among Hofriyati women, might it not also hold for men who publicly acknowledge themselves to have spirits? In Mohammed's case, perhaps: a spirit affliction clearly defended his self-image as a virile male capable of fathering sons. But given the small number of cases (and the fact that most men known to have been possessed were deceased prior to my fieldwork), I fear my data are too fragmentary to make any substantive generalizations. Since the following narrative suggests a rather different relationship between host and spirit than is typical for women possessed, I include it for comparison.

ʿUmer's mother was possessed from an early age. Just before his parents wed, his father also claimed a spirit affliction. ʿUmer's father was a friend to Umselima's brother, Mohammed: the two were possessed by the same *Darwīsh zār* and would often converse about spirits.

ʿUmer's family had come to Hofriyat from the north in 1930, just prior to his birth. Though the family owned irrigation and *wadī* fields elsewhere, its members had to rent land in order to cultivate near the village. While their standard of living did not differ greatly from that of other farming families, when based solely on tenant farming, as at first, it was somewhat less secure.

Yet ʿUmer's father's brother married a woman from an adjacent village, a nonrelative whose father owned some land. Since she had no siblings, she inherited much of this land when her father died, which ʿUmer's *ʿamm* continued to farm. After a youthful career trucking local onions to the Ethiopian frontier, ʿUmer contracted to marry the daughter of this *ʿamm*. He was then twenty-five years old. After the wedding he went to live with his wife in her mother's house, and began to work with his *ʿamm*.

Then one day shortly after his wife disclosed she was pregnant, ʿUmer was suddenly taken ill. His hands and arms folded inward to his chest; he could not move them. When his father- and brothers-in-law went off to their fields, he walked to Kabushiya, entranced, his body inhabited by a *zār*. In Kabushiya he sought a male curer reputed also to be possessed. The curer fumigated him with different types of incense to no effect; but when he tried the mixture for ʿ*Arab* spirits, immediately ʿUmer began to speak in a strange tongue. Someone in Kabushiya recognized the language as Hadendowi, the language of eastern Sudanese nomads. Soon after realizing he was possessed, ʿUmer drummed the *zār* at his mother-in-law's home; Umselima and Sosan oversaw his cure.

During the ceremony it was discovered that ʿUmer in trance was able to diagnose all manner of complaints among participants. After the ritual his reputation as a curer spread, and women began consulting him in droves. ʿUmer treated their illnesses and infertilities with great success, and free of charge.

One night a few months later, *zayran* appeared to him in a dream and demanded he begin to charge twenty-five piasters per consultation. Since then his fees have escalated steadily, always in association with an instructive message from his *zār*. ʿUmer is presently middle aged, a widely respected curer (people come from miles away to ask his advice), and by far the wealthiest man in the district. He has invested his earnings in farmland acquired through outright purchase and by a system called *rahan,* mortgage, in which he holds and uses land in exchange for an "interest-free" loan to the owner.[3] At the time of my last fieldwork ʿUmer had been married six times and built *ḥōsh*s for each of his wives in three villages. At present he has four wives including a new one in Dongola who recently bore him twins, and runs a very profitable onion warehouse and trucking business with his several sons.

The context of ʿUmer's possession illness is instructive: here is a man without heritable resources who has grown up in a milieu where *zār* possession is an unquestioned reality, for both his parents are possessed. He marries the ideal spouse, goes to live with his wife, and helps to farm her mother's land. This arrangement is not unusual for a newly married couple, but if the husband does not emigrate it is generally considered temporary. Though women seek to prolong it, by masculine standards it ought to terminate shortly after the birth of the first or second child, and the couple return to the husband's family (chapter 1).

Just after his wife announces her pregnancy, ʿUmer falls ill. That the revelation provokes both stress and joy can be imagined, for it heralds his imminent return to Hofriyat and resumption of tenant farming. But by now it is 1960 or 1961, and the Nile has begun its westward swing away

3. Theoretically, the owner or his heirs might redeem the land at some future date by repaying the lessee the original amount minus the owner's share of any crops produced. But villagers assert that such a transaction, also known as *damana,* frequently results in the permanent transfer of rights, for it may involve successive payments over a long period of time, resulting in a debt so large it can never be repaid. When this happens, the mortagee might sue for title. *Damana* is expressly forbidden by Islam as usurious.

from fields on the eastern bank: Hofriyati farming is in decline. Land in his in-laws' village is affected less severely, and if the land belonged to his *ʿamm,* it would be appropriate for him to continue farming there. Instead, it belongs to his wife's mother, who is otherwise unrelated to him. Consider ʿUmer's position: he is without resources of his own, forced to rely on those of his wife through his wife's mother. The ideal and honorable masculine practice is thereby reversed, and unless he emigrates or finds another line of work, ʿUmer will be unable to fulfill the social expectations of his sex.

Now ʿUmer's diagnosis is apparently self or spirit selected. Rather than consult Western or Islamic doctors, he goes immediately to a curer familiar with the *zār*. And in Kabushiya his affliction is publicly confirmed. It is important, I think, that all this takes place in a forum dominated by males—the market town of Kabushiya—for male acceptance is mandatory if ʿUmer's acknowledgment of possession is not to damage his reputation and masculine self-image.

But who in this case does what? While a cynical non-Hofriyati observer might think that ʿUmer consciously saw in the *zār* an opportunity to alleviate his troubles, it should be borne in mind that it is not ʿUmer who consults the curer, but a male Hadendowa *zār*. The spirit speaks through him in His own language—knowledge of which ʿUmer himself disavows—thereby verifying His existence and establishing ʿUmer's credibility as His host. Through the graces of this spirit, ʿUmer reverses his situation and goes on to attain the enviable and respected position he currently holds. The *zār,* Himself a paragon of masculine values, has enabled ʿUmer to fulfill the ideal role for villagers of his sex, more obviously than even Mohammed's spirit has done. It should not be assumed that ʿUmer's initial illness was in any way dissimulative: its context fits criteria for illness in Hofriyat, and for ʿUmer as for other villagers, possession is a fact of life. ʿUmer's cultivation of his relationship with the *zār* may well have been self-serving, yet this too is not unusual, for in any case of possession, both host and spirit intend to gain from their relationship.

When ʿUmer became ill he was, like many who acknowledge a spirit affliction, in something of a double bind. He turned from a situation overtly detrimental to his masculine self-image and sought refuge in another, more ambiguous one: possession. This, because of the taken-for-grantedness of *zayran* and ambivalent attitude of men toward the cult, he has bent to his advantage. In accepting his possession, ʿUmer veered from the path of orthodox Islam but, paradoxically, in doing so has fulfilled some of the highest expectations of his culture. And not all this success can be attributed to his spirit: since acknowledging possession, ʿUmer has learned much that there is to know about magic and divination from ancient Arabic treatises on these subjects, and has trained with herbalists in Kassala, the home of his Hadendowa *zār*. Moreover, once established as a curer, he became increasingly active in the Khatmiya religious brotherhood, thus assuming a more traditional stance toward Islam. Unlike most female adepts, ʿUmer has suffered only one bout of possession illness, followed by the development of a mature, controlled relationship with his *zār*. He is possessed only by the *Hadendowi* Who never inflames, is never capricious in His dealings, and continues to augment ʿUmer's abilities.

I was told that the pattern of ʿUmer's possession, if not his success, is common for local men who suffer the affliction; phrasing analytically: a single spirit steps into a man's life at a crucial moment, rescues his problematic self-image, and confers a lifelong benefit. That this is discrepant with the trajectory of women's possession is patent and reflects, I think, the different constraints surrounding women and men in Hofriyat: not only are men able to manipulate their social environments more readily than women, but women's self-image is more highly determined, more liable to become problematic and require reinforcement, which spirits continuously provide. And women's experiences are by their very nature more likely to invite the ingress of spirits or be read as signs of spirit involvement. However much *zayran* may figure in the lives of men possessed, they are for women in constant attendance, forming an implicit resource of otherness that contextualizes their daily lives.

Zār *as Antilanguage, Counterdiscourse: Saraitti*

Here I consider one last possession narrative which echoes the stories of other women but more explicitly raises the issue of the *zār* as an antilanguage or metacultural discourse.

> When I was a little girl, before I was circumcised, I climbed a tree. And I fell from it; I fell because of a *zār*, because a *zār* descended on me there in the tree. I fell on my arm and it became swollen. I had a fever and I was delirious. They called Umselima and she censed me and learned it was a *zār*.

Saraitti was the only issue of her parent's marriage. When she was very young her father took a second wife, then divorced her mother, who later rewed. Saraitti grew up in her stepfather's house. Her mother never conceived by him and he died when Saraitti was sixteen. In a continuation of the alliance between their families, Saraitti was immediately married to her stepfather's brother, a man more than twice her age.

Though they were married for many years, Saraitti never once became pregnant. Still, she lived with her husband until his death, in her late forties. Because he had not set her aside for failing to conceive, it was widely believed that her husband was impotent, and both knew the reproductive adversity to be his fault.[4] Yet the couple's public front left the situation ambiguous, for confirmation of his debility was never voiced. Moreover, Saraitti, whose self-image was at stake, was doubly muted: even had she wanted to, she could not unilaterally divorce in order to rewed. She was clearly in a bind. Saraitti has suffered repeated attacks of possession illness, which Hofriyati women link to the blockage or stagnation of her potential fertility. It may be because of her husband that Saraitti has no children, yet *zayran* are implicated too, for they have seized her womb and usurped its reproductive blood. Certainly, the couple's procreative quietude is not her fault; still, if *zayran* are involved, nor need it be her husband's.

Saraitti has had five *zār* ceremonies, the first occurring soon after her wedding. But always, it seems, she is ill. In the past, whenever her spirits would burn and make demands, these inevitably were met. "When I was ill, and delirious, my doorman spent his money on our requests. *Bowābi* bought them for us."

Note here that Saraitti uses the *zār* term for her husband whose conventional meaning is doorman or doorkeeper, *bowāb*. Moreover, like Asia and others, Saraitti possessed speaks of herself as a plurality, a corporate entity comprised of Hofriyati self and *zār* nonselves. Yet her husband is *her* doorman, not theirs: it is he who opens or closes the passage between parallel worlds through which Saraitti and her spirits might pass.

Occasionally, Saraitti's spirits provide funds for their own requests by stealing them from other humans. Saraitti said that she would often find money on the ground or under her mattress where *zayran* had left it as a gift. But ever since the time she used this to buy herself new kitchen utensils rather than meet their demand for gold, the spirits have observed a moratorium on this practice.

Still, *zayran* have given her a valuable, if less tangible gift. When she is entranced, when, as villagers say, she "changes herself," Saraitti says, "You can ask me anything!" *Zayran* speak through her, in whatever language they choose. Saraitti can locate lost objects and diagnose illnesses. Her dreams are so instructive that she practices as a *sitt al-ᶜilba*, a lady of the incense box who reveals the identities of her clients' possessive *zayran*.

Once when Saraitti was ill, her family took her to the hospital lying on an *angarīb*. A doctor entered the room to examine her, but soon withdrew in fear. For when he approached, the *zār* inhabiting her body began to speak. It introduced itself as a spirit and began to diagnose another

4. Since Saraitti's mother failed to conceive while married to Saraitti's husband's brother, it is rumored that impotence or sterility plagues all the men in that family.

woman on the ward whose case had baffled him till then. The patient suffered persistent nausea and Saraitti, through her *zār,* correctly informed the doctor that the problem was a stomach tumor.

Yet Saraitti's *zayran* are not always benevolent:

> Once my right arm died [became paralyzed] and so I could not eat! When at last I had to eat to stay alive, the *zār* forced me to use my left [unclean] hand, though Allah was displeased. The *zār* said to me, "It is not as *you* wish. It is as *I* wish!" And another time my right leg died until I bought socks and shoes for my *Khawāja zayran.*

Like many adepts, Saraitti's symptoms always involve some form of immobility: paralysis or an inability to open her mouth to speak or eat. And when she cannot open her mouth, this means that one of her spirits desires her to consume a special type of food. Once for over a year she could eat nothing but *bilīla,* boiled whole grain, and drink nothing but water. She was permitted "no meat, no *kisra,* no *molah* (sauce)." The spirit, a powerful Egyptian *zār* called Sitt agh-Ghwayshat (Lady of the Bracelets), treated Saraitti like a slave until Saraitti obtained for the spirit Her special requests: apples, cherries, fish, sausages, and figs.

On the other hand, Saraitti's Shilluk *zār,* a member of the slave spirit society from southern Sudan, wishes her regularly to consume *bilīla,* its national food, not as punishment for the human, but to satisfy Herself. Saraitti's possessive spirits frequently conflict: most spirits demand "clean foods," but some *Khudām* (southerners) and *Fallata* (West Africans) desire "poor" foods on occasion. When she gives in to one group, the other sometimes inflames. Here the ambiguities of possession replicate those of women's daily lives.

Once when Saraitti heard news of a death and threw dust on her head in the traditional manner, she immediately went into trance. She lay immobile on an *angarīb* for seven days, and for seven days she did not eat. Her kinsmen entered the room where she lay and instructed the women to bring her food and water. Saraitti shot bolt upright and said in a very deep voice, "Eating is not possible, I am *zār*!," whereupon the men ran from the room in fright. They called Umselima, who censed Saraitti and said to the spirit, "*Maʿalish, maʿalish, dayr shinnu? Inta minu*?" [Too bad, it is of little consequence, what do you (masculine) want? Who are you (masculine)?] The spirit responded in gibberish (*roṭāna*), a foreign language no one understood. Then they fetched one of the female schoolteachers from Kabushiya. She listened to the spirit and revealed that Saraitti was speaking English. The spirit said, "I want biscuits and plain tea [no sugar]. I am a *Khawāja* and I demand a seven-day ritual!"

Another time when Saraitti was ill and unable to speak, villagers could not discover what was wrong. A *shaykha* from a neighboring village happened to be visiting relatives in Hofriyat. She heard about Saraitti, who had neither eaten nor uttered a word for three days. She told Saraitti's kin, "If it refuses to speak, it is the Azande cannibal sorcerer *zār*!" She visited Saraitti and censed her, asking the spirit, "Who are you? What do you want?" Saraitti's spirit spoke to the *shaykha* and they became friends. The spirit said, "I am a *zār,* I am a sorcerer," opening wide Saraitti's eyes and drawing in her mouth. The spirit growled and said, "I want raw meat, I am *Bayakuba*!" So her kinsmen brought her raw meat and she ate a quarter of a kilo of it then drank some water and some tea and she recovered.

Saraitti's possession narrative consists of a succession of anecdotes, each recalling a significant encounter with *zayran,* or between her *zayran* and other humans. And in many of these she, through her spirits, succeeds in frightening men or impressing them with "her" abilities. In Hofriyat, Saraitti is a beacon of women's empowerment in the idiom of the *zār,* and the episodes in her life are virtually mytholoized. The following compares Saraitti's description of a *zār* experience with one about her told by another village woman.

> SARAITTI: Once when I was in Omdurman visiting kin I became ill. I had a vision: five *zayran* appeared to me when I was alone. They told me *Birono,* one of my *Ḥabish zayran,* wanted a special ebony walking stick. I had to find the stick before I could recover. The spirits told me I could find the stick in such and such a store. I went there, I bought the stick for £S3, and I became well immediately.
>
> ZERGA: The first time Saraitti went to Khartoum she became ill. She said, "I do not want a doctor, I have a *zār* and He wants an ebony walking stick of special shape and design, like so and so and so." Her relatives said, "We do not know where to find such an unusual walking stick." But Saraitti said, "I know where!" She said there was one like it in a certain shop in Khartoum. But how could she know where to find such a shop, as this was her first time in the city? She said, "The *zār* knows where to go." So Saraitti and her stepsister's son climbed into a taxi. And Saraitti gave detailed directions to the shop. But it was not Saraitti herself who spoke, it was the *zār*. The *zār* guided them to a tiny shop in a remote corner of the city. Saraitti's nephew became embarrassed then. The store before them did not look the sort to sell walking sticks. He said to himself, "How do I go in there and ask for such a thing? How do I explain that my *khālta*'s spirit wants a specific type of walking stick?" The spirit heard his thoughts. Immediately, Saraitti entered the shop and spoke to the merchant herself. She said, "I want a walking stick of ebony with such and such a design and a gold top . . . and I know you have one like it." The merchant said no, he did not sell walking sticks. When she insisted, he said, "Well, yes, a long time ago I had three walking sticks like the one you describe. I sold two of them but the

> third got away from me. I have not seen it around my shop for some time, though I have searched for it everywhere." Saraitti replied, "I know it is here in this store!" He invited her to look, but warned that he had looked before and it was not there. He suspected it had been stolen. Saraitti searched and within a short while she found the walking stick, and it was exactly as she had described. When she went to pay for it the owner of the store was so surprised she had found it, and so awed by the power of her *zār* that he refused to take any money for it and gave her the walking stick as a gift.

Zayran are more powerful than humans and a woman actively possessed or influenced by a *zār* can outwit men, reversing the tables of everyday life where men hold most of the cards. Note also that throughout Saraitti's narrative there are hints of possession's antilanguage, better construed as a counteridiom or context since not all of its meanings are lexically coded. Those that are, are obvious: husbands of the possessed are their doormen, women made ill by spirits are brides of the *zār,* spirits who require a cure are the owners of blood, certain objects are keys unlocking dreams about possessive *zayran*. Doors, blood, brides: all resound with the idioms of daily life yet differ from them in important ways, for they refer, not to enclosedness and the value of the inside, but to their opposite, to the external parallel universe contiguous with the human, or to verges between the two realities by which spirits intrude into our own. Their meanings are derived from those of everyday parlance, but vary from them metaphorically. Importantly, by using symbols whose auras embrace hegemonic values, the possessed reproduce the quotidian system even as they transform it. Here, *zār* demonstrates the fundamental ambiguity of all subordinate discourses: they do not express an explicit class consciousness; they are neither revolutionary nor alternatively hegemonic; instead, they are *counter*hegemonic, rephrasing consensually accepted realities from the perspective of the oppressed (cf. Comaroff 1985; Messick 1987).

Throughout possession narratives here and in the foregoing chapter, there have been repeated references to liminal points and situations: concern for doorways, orifices of the female body, ambiguous feminine blood. In Saraitti's case, for example, both the symptoms of her illness and the remedial requests of possessive *zayran* involve an essential orifice, her mouth. Recall that the front door of the *ḥōsh* is its mouth, which also refers to a man's descendants and, by extension, his wife's genital meatus. Certain wedding payments are made to "open the mouth" of the bride, encouraging her to communicate with her husband as a married woman. Recall, too, that mouths and vaginas are potential entrées for spirits. Saraitti's spirits prevent her from talking; only when the invasive *zār* has been contacted does she speak, in a language other than her own. Saraitti possessed is no longer Saraitti the Hofriyati woman, she is other than her self. Still, in Saraitti's fits of silence there is a logic comprehensible in either discourse: the noisiest and most confusing human occasions are childbirths, but at the moment of parturition all is hushed. Even the mother stifles her cry as the baby is born. The silence of birth is metaphorically reversed in the silence of possession, which articulates Saraitti's silenced fertility. Experiencing her body, her everyday world, in a way other than that prescribed for her sex, Saraitti experiences it as a non-Hofriyati. She appropriates the diets of her spirits and, in the idiom of incorporation, temporarily becomes a member of those societies to which they belong. And she speaks French, she says, with her spirit from Chad, Zande with *Bayakuba,* English with *Rundu,* Pasha *Beshir,* and Mister Prince the archaeologist, Tigré with the Ethiopians. In Saraitti can be seen a subtly differentiated self whose facets are revealed as much in interactions with alien existents as in those with other humans. The dissonance between lived reality and objective self-image is drastic and complete: Saraitti more than any woman I know resides in the counterworld of *zār*.

The values of other everyday items like perfumes, cosmetics, cattle, foods are altered slightly in the context of the *zār*. And undoubtedly, there are terms and references which I was unable to discover or, indeed, to understand. Some of the messages that can be formulated in possession's oblique vocabulary are given fuller consideration in chapters 8 and 9, the first in discussing spirits' natures, the second in comparing the wedding to the ceremony of the *zār*. Yet hints of their direction can be gleaned from women's narratives and the lexicon itself.

The capriciousness of *zayran* is evident throughout the possession accounts of women, less so in those of men. Sometimes Saraitti's spirits give her money and other means to obtain their desires, sometimes they bring grave suffering and near starvation. Saraitti's *zayran* impose numerous restrictions on her behavior, many of them concerning food: her spirits demand delicacies that are expensive and difficult to obtain in Sudan, let alone Hofriyat. What is more, her spirits disagree among themselves. Some want this food, others abhor it and want that. When she appeases one lot, she inevitably affronts another: whatever she does, she cannot win. Characteristics such as these are typical of spirits regardless of whom they possess, and in this, women say, they are like husbands. Sometimes you get a good one who treats you well and never neglects to provide you with expense money, sometimes you get a bad one who never sends a pound. Often a good one will have a change of heart and, occasionally, for no reason at all, a bad one behaves rather well. As with husbands, so with *zayran*.

If spirits are like husbands, hosts are like brides and referred to as brides of the *zār*. Moreover, spirits, like husbands, demand that their female hosts conduct themselves as brides: eat clean foods, associate themselves with clean and sweet-smelling things, bathe with scented soaps, apply henna regularly, perfume themselves, wear clean and untorn *tōbs*, keep their hair neatly plaited, refrain from strong emotion. They must, in other words, approximate as closely as possible the ideals of femininity embodied in the bride. Here, too, it should be recalled that the onset of possession illness frequently occurs on or about the occasion of a wedding.

At a different level, the symptoms of possession illness are generally linked to stasis and closure: whether, like Howari, Hamid, and ᶜUmer, this involves the folding of limbs against the body, or the possesseds' inability to move, open their mouths, urinate, or conceive. Others fall ill on sensing the inappropriate discharge of bodily fluids, either sweat or various forms of blood. And not to be forgotten is the link between fertility, blood, and uterinity. In all such regards, the possession idiom constitutes a metastatement on Hofriyati daily life. The contextualizing, counterdiscursive potential of the *zār* is explored in the final section of this book.

Part 3

Allegories of the Spirit World

8
The Parallel Universe

Meaning always involves retrospection and reflexivity, a past, a history.
—Victor Turner, *From Ritual to Theatre*

There is a mystery here . . . and it is not one that I understand: without this sting of otherness, of—even—the vicious, without the terrible energies of the underside of health, sanity, sense, then nothing works or *can* work. I tell you that goodness—what we in our ordinary daylight selves call goodness: the ordinary, the decent—these are nothing without the hidden powers that pour forth continually from their shadow sides.
—Doris Lessing, *Marriages between Zones Three, Four, and Five*

We are the children of Mama, born of the wind . . .
As we advance by kind, O Lord, our felicitations!
They have spread our display, they have lined up our chairs.
Those who mock us . . . transform consciousness in our midst.
—Opening thread of a *zār*

This chapter is about spirits apart from specific contexts of possession, about *zār* as a system of meaning in its own right. Its pages map the alien world that parallels the human, and consider potential significances to be derived from women's experiences of that world. But more than this, in discussing the traits of *zayran,* their ethnic identities, their temporality, it adumbrates villagers' consciousness of their history, a history of domination from without met by resistance—in the guise of flexibility and accommodation, negotiation and mollification—from within. As it is in women's bodies that the mores of Hofriyati culture are inscribed, so to women's bodies we must look for villagers' statements on how the external world impinges on their own. The story of Fatna and the sultan's son suggests that gender complementarity contains an implicit message about the asymmetric complementarity between Hofriyati and their dominators, about the ambiguities of power and its various types. In the context of possession too, the apparently powerless and subordinate gender represents the apparent powerlessness and subordination of the community in wider perspective. The *zār* is as much a treatise on ethnicity—on what O'Brien

(1986 : 906) describes as Sudanese villagers' creative response "to the challenges of colonial capitalist encroachment"—as a treatise on the local discourse of gender. An indigenous metaphoric text, it is available to be read in either light.

The *zār* is at once a verbalized, dreamed, and ritually enacted cultural text to which people refer and on which they draw in understanding and evaluating experience, and a metaphoric construction on quotidian reality, a metacommentary which, in calling attention to both the idiom of interiority and the ideology of Islam, obliquely illuminates their significances yet refrains from enforcing specific conclusions about them. In this respect, *zār* functions like satirical allegory in Western literature, a point resumed later on. For present purposes it is important to reiterate the existential autonomy of the text, qua text, from human authorship.

The manifestation of a particular spirit in or above a particular human being is simultaneously meaningful in at least two ways (cf. Basso 1979; Crapanzano 1977*a*). First, the event contains personal and social meanings, expressive of the possessed's position or identity; these comprised my focus in part 2. Beyond this, however, the possession event contains cultural or textual meanings, derived from the broader possession text out of which social and personal meanings may be construed, but existing independently of them. If the supposed intention of the possessed is to articulate aspects of her being that are exotic to her self, that of the spirit is merely to present its self in the human world, to intervene in the life of its host and thereby attain its desires. A spirit manifestation must reverberate with spirit meaning if its host's experience—the expression of her alienation in dream, trance, or vision—is to be judged authentic. It must be suffused by what Obeyesekere (1981 : 100–101), writing of demonic possession among Sinhalese ascetics, calls the "myth model," a social and cultural template through which individual experience is filtered and correspondingly produced, a system of knowledge that both informs the possessed's behavior and renders it widely intelligible. Obeyesekere characterizes the relationship between personal and cultural meanings thus:

> The personal (not private) experiences of the patient are readily intelligible through the myth model; and the myth model is revitalized and rendered real by the personal behaviour of the patient. Spirit attack is both a personal experience and a cultural performance. The myth model is, as Geertz [1973 : 93 ff.] puts it, a model of and for reality; but, unlike Geertz, I include under the term "reality" the personal reality of afflicted individuals. (Obeyesekere 1981 : 101)

I remarked above that cultural—spirit—meanings exist independently of the social and personal meanings that are constructed from them, and this is entirely accurate from villagers' point of view. But from an analytical perspective it is hardly the case, as Obeyesekere notes. For cultural meanings are recreated with every spirit performance, thereby contributing to the reservoir of knowledge about the spirit domain on which others in future might draw. Villagers' knowledge of spirits derives in part from a body of shared understandings concerning the nature of the universe and how it operates, a cosmology and cosmogony legitimated and extended by Islam. Yet it also comes from personal experiences of the possessed with their *zayran;* this is demonstrated knowledge, a continual source of verification and elaboration for postulates about the spirit world. Equally, of course, the system of cultural knowledge, both given and demonstrated, shapes Hofriyati's experiences of *zayran*. Knowledge and experience reciprocally nourish and modify each other: neither is created of whole cloth; each is a product of their dynamic tension at any one point in time. Adepts' understanding of *zayran* expands when a familiar spirit reveals new characteristics and demands, possibly contracts when another once popular *zār* now fails to appear at village rites. Yet the entire process is subsumed by a wider dialectic. Knowledge and experience of the spirit world together keep pace with knowledge and historical experience of the human, interpreted in the ideologically dominant discourse of Islam (cf. Lewis 1986:107).

Still, for Hofriyati, the spirit world is not continuously created by them, but continuously revealed. Hence a possession performance or text event is far more than what its ostensible author might wish to convey by it. It stands alone as a manifest truth having a certain autonomy of meaning. As Ricoeur asks,

> What is indeed to be understood—and consequently appropriated—in a text? Not the hidden intention of the author, which is supposed to be hidden behind the text. . . . What has to be appropriated is the meaning of the text itself, conceived in a dynamic way as the direction of thought opened up by the text. In other words, what has to be appropriated is nothing other than the power of disclosing a world that constitutes the reference of the text. . . . If we readers may be said to coincide with anything, it is not the inner life of another ego [the author, an alien being], but the disclosure of a possible way of looking at things, which is the genuine referential power of the text. (Ricoeur 1976:92)

Even if we acknowledge the author to be a spirit whose motives are patently understood, the text's meaning is nonetheless autonomous, and it is this dimension of the text's significance that is most readily available to be appropriated by its audience—among whom we must count the human performer herself. My concern in what follows is to suggest directions of thought potentially opened up by the *zār* in light of its relationship to quotidian reality and villagers' shared past. For although I maintain that Hofriyati who are possessed or merely attend spirit performances may be subjectively transformed by the experience of otherness that the context affords, I cannot predict specifically how or when this might occur. Women say they "see things differently" during and after a *zār*, but do not describe the meanings they consider a spirit to express or they themselves have appropriated. The relative ineffability of their experiences brings to mind Isadora Duncan's riposte when asked to explain her dance: "If I could tell you what it meant, there would be no point in dancing it" (Royce 1977 : 155).

Spirit Nature, Spirit World

Recall from chapter 5 that *zayran* are a type of *jinn*, specifically, red *jinn* who are capricious and amoral, bring milder forms of illness (generally those involving blood), love cleanliness, beauty, and human finery, cause their hosts to have relatively controlled and, given practice, pleasurable experiences when in trance. These traits distinguish them from black *jinn* or devils (*shawaṭīn*) in the minds of village women, though not always village men. Where black *jinn* are associated with what is unequivocally negative, antithetical to human life as Hofriyati ideally conceive it (filth, lack of control, grave disease), and white *jinn* are unequivocally benign, the associations of red *jinn* imply ambiguity and ambivalence.

Despite such differences, all three types of *jinn* share certain traits. They are nominally governed by the prophet Sulayman (Solomon; Trimingham 1965 : 172) whose abode is the ancient ruined city of Meroë near Hofriyat. In composition they are massive amorphous beings with great fiery bodies (cf. Constantinides 1972 : 103). *Zayran* are said to have been created of smokeless fire, like other *jinn* (Sura 55 : 14), and of wind. Additional attributes of all three include the ability to transform themselves into certain animals, typically snakes, hyenas, and crocodiles (cf. Nalder 1935 : 227–30; Trimingham 1965 : 171). While normally invisible to humans they can appear at will in human form. They fly great distances in very little time; are most active at night; lurk in rubbish heaps, cemeteries, ruined *ḥōsh*s, latrines, and body cavities. Not only can they enter a human body through its orifices and play havoc with its health according to type, *jinn* are also able to move unimpeded (yet occasionally with difficulty) through ceilings and walls: they cannot be shut out or kept in.

Characteristics of *zayran* outlined above, together with others earlier described, suggest that these spirits occupy an ambivalent position relative to the humans they possess. In their love of beauty, desire for precious goods, and craving for diversion, red *jinn* are not unlike their human hosts. Yet certain qualitative differences exist, for here *zayran* exaggerate human ideals and transcend the practical constraints of village life. Inexorably they demand more of their hosts than the latter are able to give: rarely does a *zār* consider the financial burden its desires for finery and lavish display might place on the possessed and her kin. Further, a woman's spirit inflames when she works so hard that she neglects to perform the traditional beautification regimen or inadvertently sullies its effects. Physical labor, inevitable but hardly prestigious in the human world, is regarded wholly askance by *zayran,* especially so if it diminishes their hosts' purity and enclosedness. In this sense spirits represent a positive exaggeration and tacit enforcement of Hofriyati values.

Yet in other respects, *zayran* contrast strikingly with humans. Behavior in Hofriyat is ideally regulated by custom and a strict moral code; it ought to be predictable but, as women attest of their husbands, it frequently is not. *Zayran,* however, are the quintessence of amorality and equivocation. Their behavior is predictable only in its caprice, even among spirits who profess Islam or when, like husbands, they are drawn into contractual relationships with human hosts. Indeed, the contrast is sharpest when qualities of *zayran* are juxtaposed to those of local women.

So, behavioral traits of *zayran* both surpass and invert those of humans: in some regards, *zayran* are antitheses of Hofriyati; in others, they are their caricatures. And the ambivalence extends to existential concerns. Quite apart from their enormity and fiery aspect, *zayran* unlike humans, live exceedingly long lives and are able to cover great distances with amazing speed. But if the coordinates of their existence are broader than those of humans, *zayran* are nonetheless bound by time and limited by space. They are not eternal: they are born, eventually they die. *Zayran* are male or female; children, adults, or elderly. They marry and reproduce; are related by kinship; live in organized societies; engage in occupations; practice religions; reside in homelands—specific locations in the invisible parallel world. Indeed, to think of them as "spirits" in the Western sense of the term is hardly accurate, for while less constrained than humans, *zayran* are not above the laws of nature. Spatially, temporally, and, in a general sense, socially, differences between humans and *zayran* are relative ones.

However, in certain respects *zayran* and humans are complementary beings. According to the Hofriyati version of Galenic-Islamic cosmology, air, earth, fire, and water are the basic constituents of the natural world. Whereas Adam, the original human, was molded by Allah from moistened clay (Sura 55:13)—earth plus water—*zayran* were created of fire and wind. Humans have perceptible form, are visible, and diurnal "children of the light," while *zayran* are formless, invisible (to humans most of the time), and nocturnal. *Zayran* are sapient, natural beings: they comprise the existential complement to humanity in a holistic quadripartite creation. Each form of being is the essence of otherness to its counterpart; each contextualizes its converse, here digitally, there analogously. The complementarity between humans and *zayran* echoes that between women and men in Hofriyat.

Significantly, *zayran* acknowledge no physical boundaries. Unlike humans they are formless in their own universe—not composed into bodies of specific shape and limited size whose regular inhabitants experience the world through potentially dangerous orifices. While *zayran* can move through walls and ceilings at their whim, humans must pass through doors when intent on entering rooms or other enclosures. A *zār* is able to invade a human's body whenever it feels so inclined, yet a human wishing to initiate relationship with another is constrained by her substantiveness and strict moral code to communicate that desire in less immediate ways. *Zayran,* then, are personifications of openness anatomically, kinetically, morally. And it is here that their contrast with humans, and especially Hofriyati women, is most acute.

The relationship between human and spirit existence forms a complicated tapestry of exaggerated similarity and contrast. On one level, spirits hyperbolize Hofriyati, disporting with villagers' ideals and the praxis of their daily lives in the dramatic caricature of spirit behavior and spirit demands. But on another, *zayran* provide a foil for humanity as a whole, casting its diagnostic traits into photographic relief. One who takes up the issue is thus confronted by a riddle, to wit: how might those who are so entirely "other" to humanity be, in certain of their attributes, more human than Hofriyati themselves? The question is, of course, rhetorical, and one cannot presume the woman who faces it will be led to any particular resolution, only that she is given pause to consider the assumptions which tacitly guide her behavior day by day.

Like humans, *zayran* are social beings. And in this regard too they are like and unlike Hofriyati. I noted briefly in chapter 4 that the genus *zār* embraces several kinds of spirit. There are said to be seven *zār* societies, but in practice, classification is flexible and more than seven may be distinguished.[1] Since the *zār* world parallels the human, differences between spirit species generally correspond to those between human cultures. In turn, every society includes a number of individually named spirits, each of whom has some distinctive trait that marks it off from its compatriots. Like the parent category, *jinn,* each society of red spirits is typically associated with a color, mainly white, red, and black, whose quotidian significations are preserved and expanded in the possession context. During a ritual the several *zār* societies are distinguished by drum rhythm and variations in the mixtures of incense burned to summon them.

The roster of spirits presented below follows the general order in which their threads are chanted and drummed during a seven-day cure: *zayran* are invoked sequentially by "pulling the threads one by one" (cf.

1. Constantinides (1977:71) suggests that since seven is a significant number in popular Islam, its application here may serve to link the *zār* to the wider system of belief and other local customs. However, putting things this way assumes a peripherality for the *zār* with which I disagree. Since seven is idiomatic in the human world, logically it is also idiomatic in the parallel world of *zayran.*

Constantinides 1972). But the reader would be misled if left to think that all known spirits descend at every ritual, that each slice of drama I describe below is automatically replayed whenever spirits are invoked. Sometimes when a thread is drummed, no one present is host to the relevant *zār*. On other occasions, though its hosts are present, the spirit summoned fails to manifest; this may be due to the *zār*'s caprice or its host's suggestion, for if she is menstruating a woman will tie a knot in her braids to warn *zayran* of her condition and ask them not to enter her that day. Then again, a woman may be seized by a spirit she did know she had, one which, because it is not yet socialized in her, causes her to move with less gestural finesse than would an established host. There is no such thing as a "typical" *zār* ritual: no two are alike with respect to the spirits who choose to descend or the dramatic elaboration achieved by a particular *zār* when manifest in the *mīdān*. A *zār* rite is always something of a surprise; its salient events, and the thoughts these might provoke among its witnesses, can never be foretold.

Darāwīsh

As noted in chapter 5, these are the *zār* parallels of well-known founders of Islamic fraternities represented in Sudan, many of whom lived in Baghdad or Cairo during the twelfth and thirteenth centuries A.D. Most, like the spirit counterpart of ʿAbdalgadir al-Jaylani, are locally associated with disorders of female fertility and their cure. *Sayidi Bedawi* (Our Lord Bedawi) is the *zār* parallel of Sayid Ahmed al-Bedawi (deceased 1276), founder of an offshoot of Jaylani's Qadriya order, whose shrine is at Tanta in northern Egypt and of whom it is said, "he . . . was especially notable for securing the fecundity of women" (Willis 1921 : 181). In this group are also found *Shaykh Ḥamid*, the spirit analogue of a local holy man long deceased (Hamid Abu ʿAṣa, sixteenth century A.D.),[2] and a spirit called *Shaykh Mohammed* associated with the Khatmiya brotherhood founded by Shaykh Mohammed Osman al-Mirghani (deceased 1853).[3]

Female *Darāwīsh* are the daughters of these spirits, and represent morally appropriate fertility. For example, the inherent attributes of *al-Jaylani's* daughter, *Sitti Khuḍara,* Green Lady, are those of idealized Hofriyati womanhood: She is pious, graceful, supremely dignified, and when appearing in human form, richly dressed and bejeweled, light of skin, beautiful beyond measure. Green, Her color and that of the dress Her hosts are required to obtain, evokes fecundity and abundance. Outwardly She is the acme of Hofriyati feminine ideals. Befitting Her lofty station,

2. See Hasan (1967 : 178).
3. Not to be confused with *Shaykh Mohammed Saʿdabi* of the *Ḥabish zayran*.

Sitti Khuḍara, like Her father and His comrades, commands deference from the humans She encounters in Hofriyati *mīdāns*.

Yet in social respects, *Sitti Khuḍara* breaks with Hofriyati praxis and ideals. For She is married to *Birono,* an Ethiopian *zār* and a Christian. Her marriage is therefore trebly exogamous: where kin, culture, and religious endogamy is proper human practice, *Sitti Khuḍara*'s spouse is an unrelated foreigner and, most surprisingly, non-Muslim. Further, Hofriyati sometimes classify *Sitti Khuḍara* Herself as *Ḥabish,* an indication that the pedigree of a female *zār* might shift on marriage to that of Her husband. This runs counter to the custom of Hofriyati humans, who stress lifelong natal affiliation for female members regardless of marital status.

Sitti Khuḍara is a shining example of a *zār* who is both "other" than Hofriyati and more Hofriyati than ordinary village women. She is the embodiment of interiority ideals with regard to comportment, appearance, faith, and fecundity, yet of exteriority with respect to marital and jural practice, and of course, Her ontology. This spirit is a paradox which calls attention to significant tensions in the experience of Hofriyati: the dilemma of relativity, the shifting boundaries between the inside and without. And like all powerful symbols, She signifies neither one side of the opposition nor the other, but different facets of both at the same time, at once illuminating the essential dialectic of Hofriyati society—and in a narrower sense, of Hofriyati marriage—and providing its mediation.

Bedawi's daughter is *Bedawīya,* while *Shaykh Mohammed*'s daughter is *Saida Zaineb*—*zār* parallel of Mirghani's Sudanese great granddaughter. Their characteristics are similar to those of *Sitti Khuḍara.* Moreover, all have inherited their fathers' *baraka* and exemplify female religious power. Yet religious power can translate into secular power, as it has with the highly placed Mirghani family (whose history is closely bound up with that of Egyptian influence in Sudan [Holt and Daly 1979: 147–48]), and as the thread for *Saida Zaineb* suggests:

> Saida Zaineb,
> Guardswoman of Egypt,
> Saida Zaineb,
> Holding sway in the palace.

In keeping with their holiness and purity, *Darwīsh* spirits generally demand white rams in sacrifice. Females among them request white dresses or green, males similarly colored *jalabīyas* with white prayer shawls, skullcaps, and turbans, plus prayer beads and forked walking sticks commonly used by mendicant religious scholars. In active possession of their hosts, these spirits behave in a calm and dignified manner: one might cause its host to remain peacefully seated throughout its thread, another might call on her to finger prayer beads or sway gently back and forth like participants in a *zikr,* the remembrance ceremony of Muslim religious fraternities in which praises are drummed and recited to Allah.

Here is another paradox: male *Darwīsh zayran* cause women whose bodies they temporarily inhabit to exhibit qualities and behaviors normally associated with elders in a religion these women profess but, by reason of their sex, are curtailed from participating in fully. A number of key issues surface as a result of this drama. First, and most apparent, women are seen to behave as men—and not just ordinary men, but the *zār* personifications of masculine ideals. When masculine qualities are portrayed by women—like Shakespeare's Portia or Rosalind—they are more perspicuous than when portrayed by men, since the contrast between the vehicle and what it communicates is that much more acute (cf. Lambek 1978:400). Female hosts thus provide a striking foil against which to depict masculine ideals, so that during the rite the ideas of maleness and masculine piety are presented as issues in themselves, as distinct from humans who might exhibit such qualities in the everyday world. But if a spirit's masculine qualities jar with the physical reality of its female host, the reverse of course, will pertain when the host is male; for Umselima's brother, *zār* portrayal of masculine ideals resonates positively and supportively with his masculine self-image.

Still, women comprise an overwhelming majority of the possessed, and when they are inhabited by a male *Darwīsh* (singular), the ideas He embodies are wrenched from their ordinary, commonsense constructions and granted a degree of play. This is but compounded by the ambiguity of possession trance, by the uncertainty of the audience concerning which entity, human or intrusive spirit, performs successive actions in their midst. Since would-be readers of the event are provided no clear instruction as to how it should be interpreted, those confronted by seemingly incongruous entities within a single physical presence are left to form their own conclusions, to derive whatever messages befit their own experience and textual expertise.

For example, a woman observing a male *Darwīsh zār* might be led to contrast His demeanor to that of a contumacious kinsman. Another, at a more general level, might be provoked to consider the very notion of gender, the inventory of social discriminations imposed on Hofriyati humans by the fact of their sexual identity. Yet another might be prompted to think about the relationship between women and Islam, which by women's account has become increasingly restrictive and problematic over the last forty years. Not that any of these are de facto messages of the event, they are but potential readings—directions of thought, to use Ricoeur's phrase—that the enacted text opens up for contemplation. They are immanent in the possession text, yet latent until appropriated by one or more individuals. But if latent, they are nonetheless informative of possession as an idiom of social discourse.

The second major issue that arises when *Darwīsh zayran* are invoked has less to do with masculine ideals than with the broader question of Islam, and through this, the relationship between the *zār* and orthodox religion. Indeed, it is in the forum of the *zār* that Hofriyati women feel free to broach the subject of Islam, of which they consider the cult a legitimate part. To them, *zār* is by no means "peripheral," in the sense Lewis (1971*b*: 214) suggests when arguing that because the spirits "strike their victims haphazardly and mischieviously without direct reference to moral infringements and misdemeanours," they play no role in maintaining public morality. According to Lewis, morality is the concern only of the "main morality cult," Islam, conceived as masculine, public, visible, liturgical, and textual. His rendering of Islam appears to be based on an implicit distinction between public (hence important) and domestic (insignificant) domains common to an androcentric Western anthropology and resonant with apparent ethnographic realities in Sudan. Yet women deny this assertion. For them Islam is not divorced from the total social reality they live: it *is* their way of life, and as such embraces local gender ideals, domestic ritual, pharaonic circumcision, *mushāhara* practices, and all the rest, plus, of course, *zayran* who, however wittingly, do enforce local morality idiomatically coded as enclosure. Spirits are hardly oblivious to their hosts' misconduct: violations of interiority and infringements of integrity precipitate disorder, illness, and spirit intrusion. Possession narratives in earlier chapters endlessly reiterate this point. So, in saying that the *zār* is part of Islam, adepts assert, quite rightly, that it has to do with essential values and moral tenets of their culture.

Moreover, even if the *zār* is not officially part of Islam, as most Muslim clerics avow, its context is nonetheless Islamic, for *zayran* are a type of *jinn*. And the possession idiom is laced with symbols—like tying and the number seven—that demonstrate its contiguity with the wider system. Further, Constantinides (1972: 324) sees a remarkable similarity between Sudanese Muslim fraternities (*ṭarīgat*) and organized coteries of the possessed in Khartoum and Omdurman, suggesting that the latter are modeled on the former. In the city a *shaykha* commands honor from adepts much as a *ṭarīga shaykh* does from his following. And public *zār* ceremonies periodically organized by individual *shaykhat* greatly resemble in their format the public *zikr*s of the *ṭarīgat;* both use a common set of ceremonial props including flags, and both direct prayers to Allah and the Prophet. Even in Hofriyat, where virtually all *zār* rites are private ones held for the purpose of curing, a ceremony opens with greetings to Allah and requests for the Prophet's blessing. Then, following a general invocation to all *zayran,* the first spirits summoned are *zār* parallels of Muslim holy men and founders of religious orders. In Hofriyat, as in Khartoum, "most of those women who participate in the cult genuinely believe that it is a part of Islam" (Constantinides 1972: 14).

Yet despite such linkages, *zār* and Islam occupy separate behavioral niches: women attending a *zār* leave the *mīdān* in order to pray; Sosan and Umselima quit their practice as *shaykhat* after going on the *ḥaj;* no drumming can take place during the observances of Ramadan. *Zār* is thus distinguished from and respectful of villagers' religious obligations. *Zayran,* remember, belong to the natural world, and like other sentient creatures may or may not profess Islam. Muslim spirits pray, give alms, fast during Ramadan, and make the pilgrimage to Mecca. The *zār* and orthodox Islam are not competing religious ideologies, but different facets of a single conceptual system. The salient distinction between them is that between *dunyā*—matters of earthly, natural existence—and those of God and the afterlife (*ākhra*); between contingent and ultimate causes. Though women and *zayran* take care to distinguish the two, what men regard as un-Islamic about the cult is its apparent preoccupation with worldly concerns.

Seen reflexively, *zār* is less a comment upon Islam per se than upon the wider social and cultural reality—the world of everyday life—in which Islam participates. The *zār* illuminates potential deficiencies in Hofriyati culture, implicitly cautioning via dramatic contradiction against too strict an enforcement of ideals, such as endogamy and gender segregation, that are buttressed and legitimated by doctrinal Islam. And *zār* rituals in Hofriyat, if modeled after anything, are modeled less on the *zikr* than on the wedding, though in complex and often inverse fashion (chapter 9). For it is the wedding that celebrates the totality of life as it ought to be, that extols the value of relative containment, of limited, morally restricted openness within the Muslim context of village society. And it is women's attainment of a constrained and bridely selfhood that sparks their involvement in the *zār*.

Darwīsh zayran personify village ideals in the extreme: they represent attributes to which women aspire but which are largely inaccessible to them, either because women are precluded owing to their sex (i.e., piety, learnedness, supreme dignity and forbearance, leadership) or because the ideals are, like controlled fertility and exemption from physical labor, beyond women's powers to command. As such the manifestation of a *Darwīsh zār* in a female villager is another paradox, one that illumines the paradox of femininity in Hofriyat: though a woman is, by physical definition, exemplary, she is virtually excepted from achieving the political recognition associated with this state such as pious men might acquire and the spirit claims through her body during trance. The paradox is complete when aspects of village morality are epitomized by alien existents whose foreignness is apparent in their patently non-Hofriyati marital and jural arrangements. From all of this, it emerges that *zār* indeed has to do with the exclusion of women "from full participation in the men's world of Islam" (Lewis 1971*b*:214), but more subtly and complexly than one might initially suspect.

Subsequent pages in this chapter document the range of treatment that Islam, as a subject for consideration, receives in the *zār*. In the possession idiom, Islam appears in several guises, not only that which simultaneously expresses and counterpoints local ideals. While *Darwīsh zayran* are respected Muslim elders and their daughters (note: never their wives), *Fallata zayran* are impoverished West African Muslims, zealous but undignified, whose lives are dedicated to accomplishing the pilgrimage to Mecca; and *ʿArab zayran* are pastoral nomads and militant Muslims, analogues of humans who fought in the holy war of the Sudanese Mahdi at the end of the nineteenth century. Beyond this, there are societies of *zayran* whose members profess various forms of Christianity, and others regarded as "pagan." Here the *zār* acknowledges that Islam, though foremost in importance, is hardly the sole religion practiced in the parallel planes of the natural world.

In this lies an important point: *zār* species contrast with each other as well as with Hofriyati humans. The spirit domain must be seen as a system of relations in which each element derives its significance both from its place in the whole and from its relations to other like elements (cf. Dumont 1972:71; Lambek 1978; Langer 1942:56). In part, therefore, the meaning of a particular spirit consists in the scope of its suggested references to other spirits or spirit societies along specific lines: the different facets of Isam, the difference between religious and secular authority, moral versus immoral sexuality, and so on. If we or indeed Hofriyati are but patient and persistent enough to trace the system through to the limits of our respective spirit competences, the result would be a complex network of relations, a virtually inexhaustible pool of ideas reflecting upon spirit—and of course, human—existence.

Ḥabish: *Ethiopians*

This group includes *zār* parallels of Ethiopian Christians, plus some Arabic-speaking Muslims who reside on the Ethiopian frontier. With the possible exception of the *Khawājāt* (Westerners), *Ḥabish* spirits are the most popular *zār* society in Hofriyat, embracing more than twenty-five named individuals.

Listed as *Ḥabish* and invoked as a solitary spirit is *Wilād Mama,* Children of Mother, vizier of the *zayran*. The spirit is often referred to as a plurality, and the "mother" to whom the name refers is sometimes said to be male. Although the blurring of singular/plural, male/female identities is provocative, its origin may well be prosaic, resulting from the merging of two spirits which elsewhere are distinct. In Khartoum, for example, Constantinides (1972:331) notes the existence of *Wazīr Mama,* a male spirit and emissary of *Mama,* who, like *Wilād Mama,* is the representative or overseer of all *zayran* Still, a Hofriyati woman entered by *Wilād Mama* makes gestures of mothering an infant as His thread is drummed. The spirit is a powerful male, who therefore acts like a female. As in the case of *Darāwīsh* but in a radically different mode, gender identity and its implications for behavior are rendered ambiguous here, and the ambiguity is offered to participants as food for thought.

Male *Ḥabish* spirits exemplify political power and legitimate, heritable authority. They include *Birono,* a king and husband to *Sitti Khuḍara; Shamharush,* a petty prince; *Yo,* a court official; *Bishir Tadir,* a dark-skinned nobleman; *Sulṭan al-Ḥabish,* the king of Ethiopia who wears red, sits on a horse, and is likely the spirit analogue of Haile Selassie who was exiled in Khartoum during the Italian occupation of Ethiopia in the late 1930s. There is also an Ethiopian priest, and *Shaykh Mohammed Saᶜdabi,* counterpart of the lord of Shendi who fled to Ethiopia in 1822. *Galay Galay* is chief of the Galla tribe and requires a spear for its host to carry; *Romani, Ya Wazīr Galla* (Roman, Vizier of the Galla) is a spirit representing the Italian presence in Ethiopia from 1936 to 1951.[4] *Sulṭan ar-Rīḥ* and *Sulṭan al-Aḥmar* (Sultan of the Wind, Red Sultan) are alternate names for a spirit said to be king of the *zayran.* Few women in Hofriyat are possessed by this *zār:* His political functions appear to have been arrogated by *Wilād Mama,* revealing that even spirits' fortunes can suffer a reverse. Other male *Ḥabish* are *Sulṭan Maraᶜiy* (Sultan of the Grazing Land); *ᶜOwdalay,* an Ethiopian servant; *Amelio,* an Italian emir or count; and *Ḥabishi Nakhadar,* about whom little is known. All demand red *jalabīyas*, red shawls, and fezes, and dance in their hosts' bodies in a proud, stately manner. Several request ebony or ivory walking sticks in particular designs; all invariably smoke cigarettes.

Remaining *Ḥabish zayran* popular during my fieldwork are female. They request red dresses and head scarves to be worn in Ethiopian (East African) style. All are prostitutes or at the very least salacious, and dance provocatively in Hofriyati *mīdāns*. They smoke, imbibe any form of liquor available, make copious use of perfume, even to the point of drinking it. Several such spirits are known, some vaguely, others in greater detail.

Dodo, Sitt aj-Jabana (*Dodo,* Lady of Coffee) is a *zār* who demands that coffee be prepared whenever She descends at a ritual. She further requires that Her host obtain a gold Abyssinian crucifix to wear on Sundays, during a special coffee-drinking service staged on her spirit's behalf. But *Dodo* is equally the name of a male spirit, *Dodo, Ya Jabal Nado* (*Dodo,* O Mount Nado), a hill in Ethiopia on which coffee is grown. Here again gender ambiguity surfaces as an issue.

Ḥamāma-t-al-Bahr, Pigeon of the River, is a *zār* considered as beau-

4. Constantinides (1972: 331) notes a *Ḥabish zār* named "Roma" (Rome) which "is said to be a *place* which brings all the Ethiopians together—i.e., the spirit of the Italian conquest?"

tiful and graceful as water birds. In Her host She either gestures as though swimming in the Nile or performs the languorous Hofriyati pigeon dance. Though classed as *Ḥabish,* Her thread is often drummed—whether for effect or comic relief—near the end of the ritual in tandem with that of the sorcerer spirit *at-Tumsaḥ* (Crocodile). The logic of this relation becomes apparent later on; for now it is important to note that given Her association with pigeons and the Nile, *Ḥamāma-t-al-Bahr* suggests Hofriyati womanhood. Feminine qualities are depicted in a context at once appropriate—a Hofriyati woman's body—and antithetical to that in which they usually appear—a foreign prostitute and alien being.

Maray is a beautiful Ethiopian noblewoman whose wantonness is patent; *Sitt am-Mandīl* (Lady of the Hankerchief) is extremely flirtatious, as is the prostitute *zār Lulīya.* The case of *Lulīya* is interesting, for villagers' considerable knowledge of Her character extends the covert message about Hofriyati femininity glimpsed with *Ḥamāma-t-al-Bahr. Lulīya*'s demands are for wedding incense, agate beads, a golden nose plug, silver earrings, and a silk *firka garmosīs,* the red and gold ceremonial veil—accoutrements of a Hofriyati bride. When She descends, a red bridal mat is spread, and *Lulīya* in the body of Her host begins to dance in the manner of a bride.

A wedding in the village is a protracted affair. Its climax comes near dawn of the third morning when, after a long night of women's pigeon dancing and bestowing the *shabāl,* the bride is led out from seclusion, a *garmosīs* draped over her head, concealing all of her body but her legs. She is positioned on a bridal mat in the center of the courtyard, where she stands, barefoot and immobile, until her husband steps onto the mat and removes the shawl. Now unveiled, she is seen in all her finery and her family's gold, with elaborately hennaed hands covering her face in a gesture of timidity. Gently, the groom releases her arms and she begins the exacting bridal dance: eyes tightly shut, arms extended, back arched, feet moving in tiny mincing steps that barely leave the mat. Toward the end of each song she breaks off her dance and shyly recovers her face, then recommences with the groom's signal, as before, repeating the sequence until she has had enough and her kinswomen lead her away. At no time ought the bride to have seen her husband or the gathering for whom her dance was the focus of rapt attention and long anticipation.

In the *zār mīdān,* when the silken veil is removed, *Lulīya*'s host's hands cover Her face; when these are pulled away She starts to dance, though with less inhibition than the bride and with obvious pretense at shyness. *Lulīya* dramatizes explicitly the *zār*'s implicit, subtle parody of the wedding (discussed in chapter 9), thus reinforcing participants' intuited conclusions in this regard or cultivating an initial awareness of the link. When *Lulīya* presents Herself in the *mīdān,* a *zār* ritual becomes a mock wedding in substance as well as in form.

But what is really happening here? On one level, a wanton, uncircumcised, nominally Christian alien presumes to dance as a chaste, circumcised, Muslim village woman. In the attempt, *Lulīya* tries bravely to suppress Her libertine disposition, but overcompensates, exaggerating the controlled steps of a bride to the point where simulated Hofriyati drama becomes a spirit farce. *Lulīya* is not by nature bashful; Her timidity must be feigned. The spirit's real personality shows through the façade She erects with the aid of Her host, illuminating enacted Hofriyati behaviors against a background of patently non-Hofriyati traits.

Yet this is not all. For what the audience actually observes is a normally restrained, circumcised Hofriyati matron in the role of a wanton, uncircumcised alien, who in turn "plays" a village maiden who is the epitome of purity and restraint. Here in observing the "other," Hofriyati see the other looking at them; while in looking at the woman entranced, they see themselves looking at the other looking at them. The multiple reflection is dramatically sustained . . . then suddenly shatters as *Lulīya* peeks furtively over the hands of Her host, giving Herself away to the uproarious laughter of Her human audience.

The event is an elaborate joke, a forcing together of several normally disparate levels of reality into a few densely packed moments in which so much is stated, so much more implied. It is, in Koestler's (1975 : 35–36) terms, a truly creative act, "a double minded, transitory state of unstable equilibrium where the balance of both emotion and thought is disturbed." The episode jolts the commonsense attitudes of those who witness it, calling taken-for-granted values and meanings to conscious attention, raising for consideration the issues of sexuality and fertility; motherhood, licentiousness, virginity, and the dense associative auras that surround these ideas in Hofriyat. No matter how often the joke is told, *Lulīya* always gets a laugh. But it is really Hofriyati womanhood that gets the laugh, at its embodiments' expense.

Still, participants cannot fail to note that however refined the attempt, wanton, uncircumcised aliens cannot ultimately pass for village women: invariably they give themselves away. The integrity of Hofriyati values is preserved in the very moment of their subversion, since only human villagers might genuinely and successfully embody them. Here the implication for expressing village identity through women's bodies is clear.

Female *Ḥabish* are associated with exaggerated and unsocialized sexuality: a prostitute, though she acts like a bride, is nonetheless incapable of producing moral children. Instructive too is the spirit or spirits (again the notion that one can be many appears) *Banāt Jozay, at-Tōmāt Rongay:* Paired Girls, the Splendid Twins. *Banāt Jozay* is a further reminder that *Ḥabish zayran* are especially linked with fertility disorders: twin girls personify potent reproduction gone awry. *Banāt Jozay* is an ambiguous symbol mediating between the extremes of desirable offspring: single girls and twin boys, and thus suggests a problem of meaning that villagers are not always given to acknowledge, namely, that procreative priorities are less clear-cut in practice than in the ideal.

As with *Banāt Jozay, Lulīya,* or *Ḥamāma-t-al-Bahr, Ḥabish* spirits dramatize ambiguity and paradox whenever they enter the *mīdān.* Recall that they constitute the red society of red *jinn* and are multiply linked with ambiguity and feminine blood. Like all *zayran,* but more explicitly than most, Ethiopian spirits are liminal beings which, as Turner (1977:69) suggests, "have the pedagogical function of stimulating the [participants'] powers of analysis and revealing to them the building blocks from which their hitherto taken-for-granted world has been constructed." Moreover, the antics of female *Ḥabish*—their brilliantly enacted double and triple entendres—contain an oblique suggestion that in such ambiguity resides women's power.

Secular power is a theme explored by all *Ḥabish zayran*—power not only of sexuality and dissimulation, but of masculine political endeavor. And the latter is itself transformed into something to think about when overtly powerless women become kings and princes strutting proudly with heads held high; eyes not downcast in modesty (real or mock), but level, haughty, glancing with disdain at anyone encountered. Gender, specifically gender complementarity as it exists in Hofriyat, is thus raised as an issue not only in the contrast between Hofriyati women and their male spirits, but also in the differences between female and male *Ḥabish.* Further, the might of *Ḥabish zayran* is neither Muslim nor otherworldly, but Christian and mundane. This contrasts strikingly with traits of female and male *Darāwīsh,* providing further ideational provocation.

ʿArāb

These are Muslim nomads, *zār* parallels of tribes who inhabit the Red Sea Hills and the deserts of Sudan. Some *ʿArab zayran* are alternately classed with the Ethiopians, and vice versa: the distinction between the two is not at all clear, much as the political boundary between the countries has long been ethnically artificial.[5]

In Hofriyat there are only two females among the *ʿArab zayran: Hassina ʿArabīya* and *Luli Hassīna,* both of whom are Beja.[6] Given their names, and their common requests for soured camel's milk, Hadendowa bridal jewelry, and *samn*—rancid clarified butter—to smear on their hair, they are likely derivations of the same *zār.* In contrast to the *Ḥabishīyat, ʿArab* brides are legitimate, not prostitutes who burlesque villagers' prac-

5. During the sixteenth century, for example, the Ottoman province of Habish (Abyssinia) was established on the Red Sea coast. It included Suakin, now within Sudan, and Massawa, currently within the boundaries of Ethiopia.

6. The term Beja is an ethnic category identifying several eastern Sudanese tribes, including Hadendowa, ʿAbabda, and Beni ʿAmir.

tice. They behave demurely when in active possession of their hosts, even more demurely than a Hofriyati bride. Hadendowa bride *zayran* refuse to speak at all, and to drink they must be "watered" by their husbands "like cattle." Here insinuated is the ambivalent self-metaphor of village women, "we are cattle," plus local wedding practices such as "opening the mouth": both establish reference to Hofriyati quotidian reality. Female Hadendowa *zayran* behave in Their hosts as if traveling in a camel *howda,* the large canopied seat that transports women, children, and the family's household goods from place to place. Or, They perform the *jabūdi,* similar to the Hofriyati pigeon dance but more animated and sensuous. Again, a number of issues ramify in these dramas: the Hadendowa female *zār* is in some ways more restricted—relative to Her husband—than the Hofriyati wife; Her peripatetic life-style, on the other hand, contrasts with the sedentary one of local women, just as the dance She performs is less constrained, and the "perfumes" She uses are unseemly.

Male *ʿArāb,* too, are mainly Beja: Hadendowa, ʿAbabda, or Beni ʿAmer, though other ethnic identities may be represented. Each spirit desires wide-legged pants and an oversized shirt, and most request some sort of weapon. *Sulayman al-Bedawi* (Sulayman the Bedouin) is a Hadendowa bridegroom, husband of *Hassīna,* who demands scented *jirtig* paste for His host's hair; while the Hadendowa *Ahmed al-Bashīr* is *shaykh* of all *ʿArab zayran* and requests a silk *tōb* and a whip. *Ḥoliba ʿArabīya,* "Nomadic" Gypsy or "Automobile" Gypsy is a lorry driver who requests a checked headcloth and long-toothed comb to wear in his frizzy hair; His name is a pun: the term *ʿarabīya* means either "automobile" or "female nomad," so it also contains a hint of gender ambiguity. Among remaining Beja, *Jamali* is an aggressive nomad who demands both sword and whip, plus a Beja *tōb* worn loosely crisscrossing the chest;[7] *Mohammed Bikeyfu,* "beloved of power," is a fierce and rather dangerous *zār,* the spirit parallel of one of Kipling's "fuzzy-wuzzy" warriors fighting on behalf of Osman Digna, Khalifa Abdallahi's eastern ally during the latter years of the Mahdiya. *Bikeyfu*'s demand is for a sword which its host must draw, brandish menacingly, and resheath throughout His chant. Here a third dimension of power is revealed: in contrast to the *Ḥabish* and *Darāwīsh,* male *ʿArab zayran* exemplify aggression and brute force.

Another *ʿArab* notable for His belligerence is *Bernowi,* a Taʿishi Baggara *zār* from Kordofan far south of Hofriyat and west of the Nile, who demands that His host carry a spear.[8] *Bernowi* is spirit analogue of the

7. See Holt and Daly (1979) for photographs of Beja in appropriate dress.

8. In Constantinides' (1972: 342) list of spirits, "Barnawi" is a spear-carrying West African Muslim *zār* from Bornu. If this spirit originated with the urban cult, His ethnic identification appears to have altered in the context of local historical reality. The pattern is not uncommon: spirits' names are borrowed and often encompass more than one *zār* in the same or another spirit society.

"highest in command in the Khalifa's army." Human Baggara were the principal supporters of Khalifa Abadallahi, the Mahdi's successor after his death in 1885; under him these Arabic-speaking cattle herders dominated Sudan. Villagers call "Baggara" the members of an expedition sent by the Khalifa in 1889 officially against Egypt but effectively against the disaffected riverain Jaʿaliyīn. And Hofriyati hold the Baggara responsible for the tremendous privations suffered by the village in these troubled times (chapter 1). Thus, when the Baggara warrior *zār* descends, Hofriyati see far more than a woman manifesting traditionally masculine behaviors, or a villager exhibiting the salient traits of an alien ethnic group. What they see is the *zār* counterpart of their historical enemy, who appears, ambivalently summoned, in their midst. The woman "invaded" by *Bernowi* displays physical traits of Hofriyati identity and behavioral traits of Hofriyati's most dreaded adversary at one and the same time, expressing in the contrast a consciousness of village history, and since *Bernowi* is amenable to negotiation, of how conflict can and should be overcome. The distinction between two sides in a lengthy and uneven quarrel is drawn, only to be temporarily mediated in the ambiguity of possession trance.

There are less odious figures than *Bernowi* among the *ʿArāb,* specifically, two child spirits, *Wad al-ʿArāb* (son of the ʿArabs), a schoolboy who wants a grown up's *tōb,* and *ʿAli Ababa* (whose name evokes the hero of popular Arab folktales),[9] a tiny lost boy *zār* who wears a nomad's *tōb* and cries for His father, whining, "They stole my camel and I am little, and my guardian has gone and left me alone!" When either of these spirits descends, an intriguing drama ensues: an ordinarily sedate, dignified adult woman suddenly takes on the behaviors of a wheedling, frightened, undisciplined child. The humor in the situation is patent: *ʿAli Ababa* runs around the *mīdān*—as a Hofriyati woman would not—searching for His father and His purloined camel under *angarībs* and in other impossible places, wailing brokenheartedly, tripping, or just staring at onlookers with pathetically rounded eyes. Here again, but in a context different from that noted before, the spirit's host displays actions and feelings which her culture repeatedly enjoins her to restrain—clumsiness, indecorousness, tempestuous emotion. Thus "she" behaves as she might have done before her socialization to femininity. This suggestion is reinforced by the allusion to a "camel," for the word *jamal* is a euphemism for "clitoris," which the woman indeed has lost. The spirit's behavior therefore contains a backhanded reference to female circumcision.[10] The three-way contrast (spirit/

9. Or perhaps it refers to the Beja chief ʿAli Baba who was defeated in A.D. 854 by an Arab military expedition launched to support immigrant Arab miners in the Nubian Desert. ʿAli Baba was taken to Baghdad as a tributary ruler and eventually returned home with gifts (Holt and Daly 1979: 16–17).

10. Constantinides (1972: 339) records a thread in urban Sudan for a *female ʿArab* spirit which goes, "When I was young, my camel was stolen." As she suggests, "the whole line alludes to female circumcision," here less obliquely than in Hofriyat.

adult woman/newly circumcised girl) is deepened in that *ʿAli Ababa* is male, belongs to another culture, and is existentially alien. When the spirit and human entities are juxtaposed during trance, the effect is bizarre, unexpected, and in a serious way, comical.

A similarly convoluted drama ensues whenever the *ʿArab Sulayman Ya Janna* enters the *mīdān*. *Sulayman* is an adult unwed male homosexual whose name is a complex pun: *Janna* means "one who is veiled or concealed," hence womanlike, and calls up the following supernumerary meanings: one who is possessed (*jinna*), paradise (*al-janna*), harvest or fruit (*janā*)—in colloquial parlance, offspring. The pun and its context evoke the opposed ideas of, on the one hand, femininity, containment, and reproduction, and on the other, male sexual pleasure as will be enjoyed in the afterlife. All of this underscores the essence of *Sulayman*'s character in the eyes of Hofriyati women: His misplaced fertility and problematic sexuality.

Sulayman requires His host to chew tobacco, drink *marīsa*—a thick native beer—and wear a man's *jalabīya,* apropos of both ʿArab and Hofriyati men. But in the *mīdān Sulayman* behaves like a local woman. He fusses constantly with His *jalabīya,* trying with limited success to wear it like a woman's *tōb,* the length of cloth she wraps around her body and pins tenuously in place by holding her left arm close against her chest. *Sulayman* struts simpering around the *mīdān,* impatiently tucking up whatever loose material He can gather from His *jalabīya-tōb* and stuffing it under His host's left arm, all the while holding the hem of His garment lest it drag. The spectacle is ludicrous: here a habitual gesture performed by women dozens of times each day—for *tōb*s are notoriously recalcitrant—is performed by a local woman in masculine clothing, who is, in reality, a male playing the role of a woman.

The structure of this episode reveals the paradox of *Sulayman* and other complex spirit manifestations; here William James's "law of dissociation" is instructive. According to James, if two parts of an object, *a* and *b,* regularly occur together, the placement of one of these, *a,* in a novel combination *ax* leads to the discrimination of *a, b,* and *x* from one another. "What is associated now with one thing and now with another, tends to become dissociated from either and to grow into an object of abstract contemplation by the mind" (James 1918:506). In the case at hand, when feminine gestures normally associated with feminine dress are portrayed in relation to masculine dress, all three traits are wrenched from their ordinary contexts, thus heightening awareness of the qualities to which they refer. The discipline implicit in the *tōb:* the requirement that a girl begin to wear it when she reaches marriageable age, the fact that it is a portable enclosure which women take care to arrange for maximum coverage before exiting the *ḥōsh,* now appears in an uncanny light, less as a taken-for-granted certainty of the quotidian world. Gender distinctions hegemonically entrenched in villagers' reality are at once emphasized and shown to be problematic, for if femininity is contrasted with masculinity, the foil is sabotaged by the spirit's ambivalent sexuality. The effect is a palimpsest of sexual meanings, a double dissociation. It is more than a comic discourse on the ambiguities of gender and sexuality, for in raising these as issues in themselves, it points to the somewhat subversive observation (in Hofriyat) that gender is not a determinable attribute but a cultural construct whose parameters can be modified. Yet at the same time, it demonstrates the necessity of heterosexuality to spirit—human—reproduction, for *Sulayman* (an *ʿArab* who ought to epitomize masculinity, but does not) is childless. A division between female and male is shown to be imperative, while the essence of their contrast, mutable.

In sum, *ʿArab* spirits evoke issues of discipline and physical restraint in their several forms: that of warfare and domination, youth and adulthood, gendered selves and sexuality.

Khawājāt: *Europeans or Westerners*

Alternately, these spirits are referred to as *Naṣarīn*—Christians, Nazarenes—though the category embraces a heterogeneous mix of personalities, not all of them Christian. *Khawājāt* have light skin, and the males among them, moustaches that They twist continually when appearing in human form. They demand "clean" Western foods associated with the power of the outside world: bottled beverages, expensive fruits, tinned goods, biscuits and white bread. Like other *zayran* they also demand perfume and cigarettes.

Khawāja zayran have considerable wealth, and thus portray a fourth dimension of power. If the woman undergoing cure for possession by *Khawājāt* has sufficient funds, a ritual sequence known as *mayz* will likely be held. Though none was staged during the rites that I attended, my informants had participated in several *mayz* in the past and were able to describe them in some detail. *Mayz* is likely a corruption of the English word "mess," referring to a group of people who take meals together, the meal eaten by such a group, and the place where it is eaten. The *zār* sequence derives either from the practice of the British army present in Sudan during the Anglo-Egyptian Condominium until independence in 1956 (cf. Constantinides 1972 : 201) or from the Turkish custom of *mezze*, the provision of cocktail snacks before a principal meal. At a *zār* the mess consists of a long dining table laid with a tablecloth and European-style metal cutlery, furnished with foods pleasing to *Khawājāt*. These range from individually wrapped packets of tea biscuits and Danish cheese, to olives, tinned sausages and fish, cherries, apples, oranges, bananas, guavas, jam, *towst* or French bread, bottled beer, sherry, Pepsi, and single shot vials of whiskey, brandy, or other liquor. Straight-backed chairs are placed round the table, and the hosts of *Khawājāt* invited to seat themselves and partake of the meal. Alternatively, the table might be set for a *bufay*—served buffet style. Constantinides' (1972 : 202) description of the *mayz* at an urban *zār* is intriguing: "All dance around the table, swaggering, speaking 'English' or 'Greek', pretending to drink from the bottles and generally exemplifying their image of Europeans. A typical exchange, in Arabic, between two 'Europeans' swaggering around arm in arm: 'C'mon, let's go to Church', 'Naa, let's go to the bar'."

Commercial alcoholic beverages were widely available in Sudan until the declaration of *sharīʿa* law in September 1983. When I arrived in the village a few months after that, several women possessed by *Khawājāt* expressed hope that I had smuggled them a supply of whiskey from home, as their spirits took unkindly to prohibition. In Hofriyat, if liquor can be procured, it is actually consumed by *Khawāja zayran,* via their human hosts.

Among the *Khawājāt* are *Mistayr Brinso,* Mister Prince the archaeologist who requires khaki pants and shirt, pith helmet, black shoes, socks, and spectacles; *Dodomayo,*[11] an Athenian fond of wine and overly fond of women; *Daidan,* an Englishman who requires a good mattress; affluent *Dondo Ya Rundu* who chain-smokes Benson and Hedges, drinks whiskey, and spends much of the day reclining on a bed or riding in a taxi. *Dondo*'s wife *Sitt Mama,* Lady Mother, is a Copt who loves eating pigeons and desires that Her hosts cap their incisors with gold. These traits are suggestive, given the metaphoric associations of gold, consuming, and pigeons, and the fact that a principal target of *zayran* is the demonstration of Hofriyati femininity.

Dona Bey is a male *Khawāja zār* whose second name is an Ottoman honorific. Yet *Dona Bey* is an American doctor and big game hunter who drinks prodigious amounts of whiskey and beer, wears a khaki suit, and carries an elephant gun. He is portrayed as fierce, though His prey are hardly becoming, for *Dona Bey* chases neither lions nor elephants but little animals called *saʿīd,* miniature antelope known to English speakers as dik-dik.[12] *Saʿīd* are occasionally captured in the desert east of Hofriyat and kept by villagers as pets. They are said to be lovely, having smooth blonde fur and large dark eyes. The term *saʿīd* metaphorically describes village maidens who are lithe, pale, and pretty: predictably, *Dona Bey* is a lascivious character.

Several ideas are potential in the character of *Dona Bey* and His ap-

11. Most *Khawāja* names, like those of non-Arab *Ḥabish zayran,* seem to be meaningless in Arabic, for they are, of course, foreign. It is possible, however, that they have earlier origins.

12. Antelope of the genera *Madoqua* and *Rhynchotragus* commonly found in East Africa.

pearance in Hofriyati *mīdāns*. To begin with, *Dona Bey* is a farcical spirit, chasing dainty little dik-dik with a weapon designed to bring down animals a hunded times their size. As such He insinuates Western technological overkill, the use of complex and possibly dangerous equipment to achieve ends better served by simpler, indigenous means. Villagers, after all, capture dik-dik with nets and stealth, and capture them alive; the American doctor *zār* destroys what He obtains and so gains nothing. Such messages are conspicuous to Hofriyati, as dubious recipients of a stalled canal scheme designed to increase their arable land whose half-completed ditch now merely impedes access to existing fields and provides new breeding ground for malarial mosquitoes. Villagers are also witness to a failed oil pipeline in the desert, and are just as subject to the vagaries of global politics and besieged by imported foreign goods as any African people can be. Women, who are in favor of bringing electricity and running water to their homes and acquiring such comforts as refrigerators and televisions, are thus tacitly warned by the *zār* that such technology could destroy the very life they seek to enhance. The warning extends to their use of Western medicine, a poignant implication of *Dona Bey*'s professional status as a physician.

But *Dona Bey* is more than a caricature of Euro-American technology, for He is a skilled and learned male, a wealthy and powerful curer and figure of respect. Yet the spirit's behavior—in stalking harmless little animals and Hofriyati girls—is not the sort to garner esteem. In this a number of ideas present themselves: that positive masculine traits such as erudition may be housed simultaneously with negative ones like lust, bellicosity, and at the very least, bad manners and poor judgment; that no matter how powerful, educated, or apparently benevolent, a foreign male cannot be trusted with village women. The hegemony of masculine science is here situated within a display of unprincipled action. Such messages harbor practical significance for Hofriyati's experiences of Westerners, and not only Western doctors, but archaeologists and anthropologists as well.

Still, *Dona Bey* portrays Himself in the body of a local woman, so creating another paradox: if the hunter in one sense "becomes" His prey, the reverse is also true, the Hofriyati woman "becomes" a *Khawāja* male who chases Hofriyati women. The other is equally within her as without. And here again a potential enemy is dealt with neither by denying His existence nor disclaiming His power, but by acknowledging them, by inviting Him into villagers' midst in a controlled if evanescent manner.

There are, in addition to doctors and archaeologists, several *Khawājāt* who represent occupations and vocations. *Miriam al-Azraq*, Miriam the Black (or Dark Blue), is the *zār* parallel of the Virgin Mary; Her thread goes, *shallat ʿIsa fi-l-kanīsa*, "She carried Jesus in the church," and She requires Her host to obtain a black dress and head shawl like those worn by

Catholic nuns. *Gasīs Romay* is a Roman Catholic priest, and *Gasīs Gom bi Ṭiyara* is a priest from a monastery, a Coptic monk who "takes off in an airplane." There is also a *Khawāja* lawyer and an airplane captain *zār*. The popularity of the last redoubled in the early 1970s after a plane landed in the desert east of Hofriyat and disgorged scantily clad *khawāja* models for a photo layout in *Vogue*.

Bamba Beya, "boy of the ancient monuments," is a "Turk" vacationing at the pyramids close to Hofriyat whose human counterpart may have been the adventurer Cailliaud, who, in 1821, rode upriver in the vanguard of the Ottoman invasion force; or it may have been Burckhardt or, much later, Budge (chapter 1). *Wad an-Naṣara, Ya Mama Miya!* is an Italian Christian *zār*; like *Dona Bey* He is a hunter, except that His victims are, significantly, water fowl. *Azīza*, Lady of the Bracelets, is a wealthy Egyptian Copt; *Hindīya* is a female East Indian *zār* who visits Shendi, drinks a Pepsi, and commands that Her hosts wear their *tōbs* like saris. *Hashīra* is the pithy *zār* parallel of a late Victorian Englishwoman, depicted as looking disdainfully out the window of Her railway carriage as it crosses the Nile on the bridge (apt symbol of the colonial encounter) between Khartoum North and Khartoum, well above the heads of Sudanese working on the banks below. *Jamama* is a female Chinese *zār* who demands a long high-necked dress of floral silk with slits up the sides, and is portrayed as walking through a garden of figs (*tīn*) with Her husband, *Arḍ as-Sīn* (Land of China)—said to live in England and own China (cf. Constantinides 1972:157). And briefly, there was a female Canadian *zār*, *Sitt an-Nisa*, "Lady of the Women," about whom more will be said later on.

Bashawāt: *The Pashas*

These are "big *Khawājāt*," powerful, authoritarian *Khawāja* males who command considerable deference in the *mīdān*. They are either *zār* analogues of military officers, doctors, and bureaucrats of the Ottoman administration who entered Sudan sometime after 1821, or twentieth-century government figures, and sometimes both at once. The pashas are alternately known as Turks—synonymous with "malevolent conquerors" in Hofriyat, hence another enemy group. However, the category is not wholly inimical, for villagers think well of the British among them, just as they allied with human British during the Anglo-Egyptian reconquest and fondly remember certain British colonial officials who once oversaw the area. Conquerors, then, are not all alike.

Here one finds the *zār* counterparts of well-known historical figures: in Khartoum and Omdurman (Constantinides 1972:338) these include *al-Wardi Karoma* (Lord Cromer) and *Gordel* (General Charles Gordon), though neither now appears in Hofriyat. Historical pashas in the village are several: *Nimir al-Khalā,* Leopard of the Desert, also known as *Nimir Kindo, Babūr al-Khalā* (Leopard Kindo, Steamboat of the Desert, is *zār* leader of an army contingent that sailed up the Nile sometime in the nineteenth century. The figure likely represents Sir Samuel Baker (cf. Constantinides 1972:95; Holt and Daly 1979:76), the man whom the Khedive Ismaʿil initially hired to suppress the southern Sudanese slave trade and whom Gordon succeeded.[13] *Basha Basha* is the *zār* parallel of Gordon's and Baker's nemesis, a merchant-prince engaged in the capture and transport to Shendi market of numerous southern Sudanese whom He chains together in long lines for the forced march downstream (possibly Zubayr Pasha; cf. Holt and Daly [1979:77]). *Birulu,* Lord of the Chains, is another spirit slaver. *Basha Birdon,* who "lands wearing a European suit and a fez," is more problematic in origin, but possibly represents Sir Richard Burton (1821–90), who traveled widely in the Arab world and made the pilgrimage to Mecca in 1853. And another *Basha zār, Basha Korday* is intriguing: though little is known about this spirit except that He has a moustache and wears khaki breeches, the name is strikingly similar to that of Sir Alexander Korda, the renowned film-maker, or his brother Zoltan who respectively produced and directed *The Four Feathers* (1939), lengthy sequences of which were filmed in Egypt and Sudan.[14]

The more "generic" *Bashawāt* include *Ḥakīm Basha,* Doctor Pasha, first encountered in chapter 6 in His dual manifestation: a turn-of-the-century practitioner of Islamic medicine who requests a white *jalabīya,* long topcoat, fez, and walking stick; and a modern biomedically trained doctor who desires a white lab coat and trousers, stethoscope, and tongue depressors.[15] When *Ḥakīm Basha* enters the *mīdān,* participants approach Him for advice about their health. Another modern doctor *zār, Ḥakīm bi Dūr,* Doctor by Turns, presides over a waiting room of patients seated in long rows of chairs or a hospital ward of beds lined up against the wall. *Basha-t-ʿAdil* is another powerful, multifaceted European: He is a civilian secretary in the Sudan Political Service of the Anglo-Egyptian Condominium who builds railways, travels by train, and has several employees; and He is a locomotive engineer, poised with arm raised to sound His train's alarm. *Basha-t-ʿAdil* requires a whistle, a peaked cap, and European-style men's suit. A popular comical *Basha* is *Beshir,* an English emissary who

13. Constantinides (1972:334) notes another *zār* called "Nimr al-Khala" who is a southern Sudanese and requests a leopard skin. In Hofriyat there is also a West African spirit called *Nimir al-Kondo,* a French-speaking merchant from Chad, and a *zār* Nuer of the Leopard Skin who is otherwise nameless.

14. Constantinides (1972:332), again describing the urban cult, mentions an Ethiopian spirit called "el-Kordi," who is said to have a fine moustache which He twirls.

15. The male nursing assistant for the Hofriyat area in 1984 confessed to being possessed by this *zār,* and could often be seen visiting in the area with stethoscope slung round his neck and blood pressure cuff in tow.

finds desert travel discomfiting, carries a handkerchief with which to mop His perpetually sweaty brow, and wears a towel slung over His shoulder ready at a moment's notice to plunge into the Nile. Lastly, there is *Abu Rīsh, Ya Amīr ad-Daysh,* Owner of Feathers, O Emir of the Army, a military officer who requires a khaki uniform complete with wide belt and epaulets, plus a topilike hat adorned with feathers. *Abu Rīsh*'s costume, then, is a cross between the uniform of a contemporary Sudanese officer and the parade uniform of a British soldier in the nineteenth century.

Basha zayran are spirit exemplars of the power of martial conquest and colonial rule, which in certain respects continues through the 1980s and whose military aspect was clearly evident during the regime of Colonel Nimieri. Thus a potential statement contained, for example, in the hybrid outfit of *Basha Abu Rīsh* may be something like "plus ça change. . . ." *Khawāja* and *Basha zayran* have to do with foreign, as opposed to indigenous domination, whether this be military, political, economic, technological, or religious and educational (viz. the Christian clergy), and whether or not those who perform such roles are ethnically European, Chinese, East Indian, Lebanese, Greek,[16] Turkish, Egyptian, or even Sudanese.

Sittat *and* Banāt: *Ladies and Daughters*

In Hofriyat, female *zayran* are occasionally drummed as a separate spirit society, one defined by gender rather than ethnic affiliation. They are summoned by a chant to "the ladies who come from Sinkat," a town in the Red Sea Hills west of Suakin. The only spirits indigenous to this category, whose threads are not usually drummed with those of their male ethnic counterparts, are *Sitt Amuna* and *Sekīna,* daughters to the Sultan of the Red Sea based at Suakin, and *Salma,* Daughter of the River. *Salma* likely represents a *mālayka-t-al-bahr* or "angel of the river," a benevolent Nile being whose existence, well known from Sudanese folklore, antedates the development of the *zār* possession complex there (Crowfoot 1919).

In Upper Egypt, river angels are known to seek incarnation in certain women and men who are thus gifted by their presence. There, *mālaykat-al-bahr* are the focus of *zār* curing rites, yet in a different sense than in Hofriyat, for during seances they actively possess only a *shaykha* and through her mediumship benevolently diagnose illnesses, prescribe remedies, and solve the personal problems of women who attend. Women also privately attempt to secure aid from these beings by throwing bits of candy, sugar, perfume, or henna into the river (Al-Guindi 1978 : 104–8).

16. There are vibrant Greek and Lebanese communities in Khartoum and most of the larger towns; members of these groups represent a large proportion of the merchants and business people in Sudan. In Khartoum the *Khawājāt/Bashawāt* spirits include Jews as well as Christians and Hindus.

In Hofriyat, however, knowledge about *mālaykat-al-bahr* is not highly elaborated: they are said to be extremely tall women who live beneath the river and have long flowing hair and tails like those of fish; as benevolent river beings per se, they are occasionally visited and asked for aid. But they are also regarded as capricious *zayran* who possess unwitting Hofriyati (cf. also Constantinides 1972: 160). Whether the Sudanese Daughters of the River represent *mālaykat-al-bahr* themselves, or *zār* parallels of *mālaykat-al-bahr*, is uncertain. River angels figure tentatively into the sequence of events in a *zār* ritual, discussed in the following chapter.

What is interesting, I think, about the society of daughter *zayran* is that its ambiguous existence crystallizes a pertinent dilemma: whether women are to be regarded generically, segregated from men and forming a virtually distinct society with its own culture and language, or seen as participants in the same society as their husbands and male kin. Are women a collectivity joined tenuously to a counterpart collectivity of men, or are they closely linked individually to individual men? Both are true, and each has different implications for gender complementarity and negotiation. Each has its drawbacks and its strengths, and can be used to advantage in different contexts. That solidarity comes of collective subordination is at least hinted in the *zār*. And this generic/solidarity dimension of womankind is always present, if latent, in possession rites: even when female *zayran* are not drummed as a separate category, it is appropriate to invoke them only after their male consociates have been invited to enter the *mīdān*. Gender segregation is preserved in the parallel domain, for spirits demand the observance of proper Hofriyati form, however much they play with its significances.

Ḥalib: *Tinkers, Gypsies*

These are the *zār* parallels of itinerant tinkers and petty traders whose homeland is said to be Syria (specifically, Aleppo, Ḥalib in Arabic). But as Al-Shahi (1972) points out, their origins may be less exotic. Permanent if not settled populations of Ḥalib live in the area around Karima some distance north of Hofriyat, and have done so since the turn of the century. They claim relationship to the Jaᶜāfra tribe, and to have come from Upper Egypt (Al-Shahi 1972: 92; also, MacMichael 1967, vol.: 1, p.142).

Ḥalib women make a living peddling kitchen utensils, clothing, perfumes, and ointments in return for grain or money, while their menfolk sharpen and repair farm tools and fashion leather goods. They wander in small groups from village to village along the Nile and camp to camp in the desert (in *zār* threads, "from tree to tree"), spending but a day or two in any location before moving on. It is thus that human Ḥalib are considered social outcasts by Hofriyati (and other settled groups in Sudan, cf. Al-Shahi [1972:97]), for though they are Muslim, they subscribe to a moral code and standard of behavior that is at variance with villagers'. Ḥalib women, for example, can in no way be considered shy or retiring. They are shameless by local canons, assuming welcome in any courtyard they choose to enter, initiating conversations with unrelated men, being prone to speak freely on the most sensitive topics in mixed company. They are forceful, earthy, aggressive women whose behavior shocked my own acculturated sensibilities as much as those of my friends. Earlier, I noted that they are feared for the reputed power of their glance to cause vaginal hemorrhage (*nazīf*), and must be prevented from making visual contact with vulnerable Hofriyati—brides, newly circumcised girls, women recently delivered. Should a Ḥalibīya enter the *ḥōsh* of a woman in confinement, her kin immediately shut the door to her room or usher her safely inside so as to preserve the boundary between Hofriyatiness and that which is dangerously other, between the domains of the inside and the morally alien outside world.

Attributes of human Ḥalib also describe their spirit analogues. Along with *Ḥabish* and male *Darāwīsh, Ḥalib zayran* are especially implicated in reproductive disorder. Their numbers include *Munīra, Ḥalibīya-t-ag-Gūffa* (Munira, *Ḥalibīya* of the Basket), who demands a green dress, blue *tōb,* and peddler's basket; *Abu Munīra,* her father;[17] plus *Naḥali* (Skinny One), and *Barow Nayyar* (Luminous Scraps), both males. Not all *Ḥalib* spirits have names; a woman will sometimes claim to be possessed by a "nameless" *Ḥalib.*

When a Hofriyati woman is inhabited by a female *Ḥalib zār* during possession trance, she assumes a range of aggressive mannerisms and attitudes for which *Ḥalibīyat* are known. The spirit places a peddler's basket on Her host's head and circulates among the assembly begging most persuasively, "For the love of Allah, give me a penny. C'mon, I'm hungry. In God's name, give me some bread!" Yet, as I noted in chapter 6, both human and spirit tinkers are considered reasonably well-to-do. *Ḥalib zayran* are charlatans, said to dress poorly in order to elicit sympathy and large donations of cash. And like their human counterparts, they bargain hard in dealing with Hofriyati. The harlequinade of a *Ḥalibīya zār* is highly amusing, but at the same time intimidating and somewhat frightening for women who know they are the butts of a ploy, but whose upbringing admonishes them to be tolerant, hospitable, and accommodating, particularly to those more powerful than they. Women do not wish to refuse the spirit and thus give offense, for if nothing else they dread Her recrimina-

17. Whereas Hofriyati daughters are known by their father's names (teknonomy is practiced occasionally for mothers, more rarely still for fathers), here the situation is reversed.

tions. Yet equally, they do not want to be taken advantage of or be seen succumbing to Her dissemblance. The event is unsettling in the extreme. Hofriyati laugh to see their kinswoman behave in so unusual and un-Hofriyati a manner, but are made uncomfortable by her performance, forced as they are to participate in a confrontation of incompatible values. Much as Goffman (1974 : 38) observes of circus goers (commenting on Bergson [1950]), when Hofriyati laugh at one whose behavior is improper in its most minute detail, they are all the while assessing their own behavior, their ideals, and finding them no laughing matter (see also Basso 1979).

Fallata: *West Africans*

These are the *zār* counterparts of West African Muslims who came to Sudan after the reconquest. Because of the country's sparse population, the colonial regime encouraged immigration of peasants from former Fulani states (O'Brien [1986 : 900]; Fallata is Kanuri for Fulani). According to Hofriyati Fallata (human and spirit) are working their way through Sudan intent on making the pilgrimage to Mecca. They are occasionally referred to as Takarīn, "those from Takrur," an allusion to their supposed homeland in Senegal (Al-Naqar 1971 : 98) and birthplace of the Fulani *jihad.* According to O'Brien (1986 : 901), the name Takari (Takarīn) was self-applied by Fallata seeking to rid themselves of a negative stereotype attributed to them by dominant Arabs, and to identify with fundamentalist, ascetic Islam. Though the term Fallata properly refers to West Africans, Hofriyati occasionally include in this category *zayran* from Darfur in western Sudan. Further, *Fallata* holy men spirits are sometimes classed with the *Darāwīsh.*

Fallata spirit society includes *Sarikin Borno,* the Sarkin of Bornu who requests a striped *jalabīya* and is also considered a *Darāwīsh*; and *Nimir al-Kondo,* Leopard of Kondo, an itinerant merchant from Chad who speaks French, wears a fez, and requires a navy blue vest to wear over His long white shirt. *Nimir's* human counterpart can be seen twice weekly at Kabushiya *sūq* selling everything from Chinese razors to Bazooka bubblegum. Here too are the *Fallatīyat,* unnamed spirit analogues of young Darfuri market women who hawk peanuts and perfume in nearby towns and whose morality village women suspect. Not only are *Fallatīyat* considered "loose" (*maṭlūgāt*), they are reputed to be adept at performing black magic which they use or sell for use against local women. *Fallatīyat* demand brightly patterned *tōbs* of homespun cloth plus *zumām,* gold rings worn through a perforation in one nostril.

Remaining *Fallata* are peasant pilgrims proper: *Meriam,* a female *zār* and shameless, who demands a flat mortar for grinding grain and a deep one for pounding spices to sell in the market; *Abu Bukari* who travels by camel and "relies on Allah" to supply Him with food; *Tekonday* who comes from Nigeria, but now resides in Darfur. All three spirits are humble and impoverished, wear ragged clothes, request plain boiled grain and water and, when manifest in their hosts, perform gestures of begging—though in truly pathetic fashion, not dissimulatively like *Ḥalib zayran*.

It hardly needs to be said that for Hofriyati women, both begging and peddling in public are undignified behaviors that go hard against their upbringing. To observe one of their own acting in this way is thus to focus attention by way of negative metaphor on values that *are* deemed appropriate: possession here again demonstrates its potential to stimulate thought about one's own culture in relation to the negatively valued diagnostic traits of other societies. Yet at the same time, *Fallata zayran* are engaged in a truly noble enterprise, the *ḥaj*, one of the five pillars of the faith which all Muslims are enjoined to undertake should they find the means. So if They clearly affront Hofriyati ideals in some regards, when it comes to following the dictates of Islam They are more zealous certainly than village women. Since *Fallata* females humble Themselves by working publicly to earn Their passage to Mecca, They outdo Their human hosts, most of whom will never make the *ḥaj* because of financial want or intervening secular priorities. And prominent among the latter is the need to stage curing rites for possession. When women regard the antics of *Fallata zayran* with sardonic eye, the paradox of Hofriyati womanhood receives further refinement.

Khudām, ʿAbīd, *or* Zurūg: *Servants, Slaves, or Blacks*

As the threads of *zayran* are drummed society by society during a rite, there occurs an incremental progression from relatively controlled behaviors and less severe forms of illness to less restrained behaviors and more grievous disease. And this is accompanied by drum rhythms that range from light (*khafīf*) to heavy (*ṭagīl*). The former is appropriate to the *Darāwīsh,* whose color association is white; the latter, to the black *ʿAbīd,* spirit parallels of southern tribesmen who in the recent past were enslaved by Arab Sudanese. Among the Blacks are found representatives of most of the better known southern tribes: Nuer, Dinka, Shilluk, Nuba; but the group also includes spirits from "pagan" western Sudanese tribes that were forced into submission by Muslim slavers.

ʿAbīd zayran generally require black clothing, often in scanty proportions, or animal hides, including for the Nuer *zār* an elaborately decorated leopard skin. Male *ʿAbīd* require spears, ebony walking sticks, and clay pipes; and females demand mortar stones for grinding millet or corn.

All are credited with a formidable talent for performing injurious magic and are thought to cause the more serious or prolonged of *zār*-inflicted ailments.

Popular among the *ʿAbīd* are *Dinkawi,* Herdsman of Cattle, who requests cow's milk for His host to drink; *Maryjan,* an elderly male slave who walks bent over from a life of hard work; *Farigallah,* literally, "separated God," an elderly female Nuba whose name refers to Her pagan beliefs, and *Aṭ-Ṭayr al-Akhḍar,* The Green Bird, a male servant whose thread goes:

> The Green Bird
> Between the town quarters you visit
> Mecca and Medina, ZamZam [the sacred well]—
> Destined for possession[18]
> On the day of resurrection.

The pagan slave accompanies His Arabian owner to the Muslim holy land, but the effects of this "*ḥaj*" are lost on Him.

There are two female prostitute *zayran* among the Blacks: *Jata,* Lady of the *Rahaṭ*—the thong skirt worn in the past by girls—and *Mūna,* Lady of the *Shabāl*—referring to the flick of the hair gesture performed by dancing women at weddings that confers luck on the men who request it. Much like *Lulīya,* the Ethiopian prostitute who tries to pass Herself off as a local bride, when *Jata* and *Mūna* arrive in the *mīdān* They behave like young Hofriyati women. They are, of course, anything but. They are pagan, uncircumcised, and "black," flirtatious and concupiscent, strangers to the moral code that rightly guides village maidens. Once more, the effect of their presence in the bodies of their hosts is that of a triple exposure—a palimpsest of signification—here layered with the images of Hofriyati maidenhood, foreign prostitution, Hofriyati matronhood, and complicated by the human/spirit dialectic. The *rahaṭ* was a garment associated with nubile girls and abandoned at marriage: the groom is said to *guṭaʿa ar-rahaṭ,* break or cut the *rahaṭ* (now wedding veil) of his bride to indicate her loss of virginity, though intercourse has not yet occurred.[19] The *shabāl,* while performed by women of any age, is most appropriately enacted by the "pigeons going to market": unwed women who display themselves to prospective suitors at others' marriage dances. Once again the Hofriyati wedding is educed in the *zār mīdān.*

And again multiple dimensions of contrast expose a number of directions for thought to take. At the most obvious levels, messages could be derived from the antithesis of human host—a married Hofriyati—and

18. There is a pun here on "heaven"—*jinna* ("possessed," "possession"), *al-janna* ("paradise").

19. The *rahaṭ* is similar in this respect to the beaded girdle of Gisu women (Uganda). La Fontaine (1985*a*: 138) writes, "to break a woman's beads was considered rape, even if intercourse did not take place."

spirit—a southern prostitute, the first a circumcised woman who uses her sexuality for the benefit of society in bearing legitimate children, the second an uncircumcised alien existent, a non-Hofriyati pagan who uses Her sexuality inappropriately and immorally, for personal gain. Elements of the one mingle with aspects of the other in the body of the woman entranced, effecting a potential exchange of significance such that concepts like morality, profit, prostitution can be seen in radically altered light. Or one might wish to pursue the relationship between human host and spirit impersonation: between married, sexually active village woman and unmarried, "sexually inactive" village girl. But the comparison cannot be sustained, for things are not what they seem. And this refraction brings the deepest contrast to the fore: between the spirit and Her role; of immoral, uncircumcised, concupiscent alien, member of a formerly enslaved ethnic group—whose human analogues now operate in local brothels, pocketing villagers' hard-earned cash—with moral, circumcised, appropriately socialized, yet still virginal village girls. While the spirit is openness demonified, the role She attempts to play is closure or interiority personified. The opposition is mediated by the human host who, in a concrete way, is both of these at once and, no less concretely, is neither. The episode's imaginative convolution forces to consciousness ideas central to Hofriyati identity alongside obverse qualities in an elaborate, three-dimensional puzzle—who is what and to what degree?—that evaporates from the *mīdān* as quickly as it was constituted, when the drumming stops.

Sāḥar: *Cannibal Sorcerers*

All sorcerer *zayran* are Azande, whose homeland is beyond that of the *ʿAbīd,* in Sudanese Equatoria and northeastern Zaire. They include *Bayakuba as-Sāḥar Juba: Bayakuba* the Sorcerer of Juba (a town in the extreme south), who loves dates; *Nyam Nyam Kubaida, Nyam Nyam* (Zande) the Severe Afflicter, who demands to eat raw liver (*kibda*);[20] and *at-Tumsāḥ,* The Crocodile, a Zande sorcerer in His animal form.

Crocodiles occasionally travel downstream, from the south, with the annual inundation, and their advent near villagers' farmlands is greatly feared. Every villager has a story about a *tumsāḥ* which terrified some farmer or snatched and devoured a hapless child who strayed too near the river. Its fondness for human flesh makes the crocodile an apt vehicle for Zande sorcerers: all *Sāḥar zayran,* like their human counterparts, are reputed to be cannibals. When a sorcerer spirit assumes control of His host during a rite, she suddenly leaps up and starts biting at fellow adepts who scatter in alarm. As a substitute for human flesh, *Sāḥar* spirits reluctantly

20. *Kubaida* and *kibda* are derived from the same root.

settle for raw meat, of which the possessed might consume half a kilo at a sitting.

Sāḥar zayran also demand that their hosts go naked: one seized by a sorcerer attempts to fling off all her clothes, though ultimately she is prevented from doing so by fellow adepts out of trance. *At-Tumsāḥ,* however, requires that His host don rags and that in addition to nipping at members of the audience, she crawl on her belly as His thread is being drummed. The descent of these spirits is dreaded by those who attend a spirit rite: while *Sāḥar* possess few Hofriyati and may not appear in their *mīdāns* for years at a stretch (like crocodiles in the river), there is always a chance that one will manifest Himself unexpectedly, in a participant who had not till then suspected her affliction.

Sāḥar represent the darkest side of spirit—indeed human—existence, the power of malevolence and antisocial conduct. In the local idiom of incorporation, they symbolize the violation of others' material and personal integrity: life as villagers most wish it not to be, but as in many ways it really is, its underside a mass of petty jealousies, rivalries, betrayals. Women drum the sorcerers' threads with trepidation. And yet there is a fascination here, in tempting fate, in confronting what is most parlous and alarming, most horrific, most alien and antithetical to themselves. Or perhaps it is a need, for the values and ideals of daily life are implicitly revitalized in the apical contrast of village women and *Sāḥar zayran.* Participants and possessed emerge from their encounter wiser, perhaps, but usually unscathed.

I noted earlier that the female Ethiopian *zār,* Pigeon of the River, is occasionally summoned in concert with *at-Tumsāḥ* at the end of the rite. Informants maintain that this is because of their mutual link with the Nile. But Pigeon of the River, however alien Her origin, is a metaphor for Hofriyati womanhood: Her name elicits the tentacular associations of purity, moisture, the benevolent Nile that weave the context of female fertility. Recall too that the charges of Fatna the Beautiful in her old man's guise were "pigeons of the river." That fertility is an issue here is reinforced by the spirit's identity as Ethiopian, whose color is red and who is attributed power over feminine blood. The Crocodile *zār* is, on the other hand, male, and a consumer of human flesh. He is also linked to the Nile, but in its malevolent aspect. The ritual juxtaposition of these spirits metaphorically displays the marital dynamic gone awry, via an elaborate spirit burlesque, forcing together myriad dimensions and levels of signification: domestic/wild, consumed/consumer (reversing the gender appropriate directions), female/male, purity/impurity, red/black, benevolence/evil, reproducer/cannibal, spirit/animal/human, Ethiopian/Zande/Hofriyati, to say nothing of links between the individual possessors and possessed (i.e., prostitute/married villager, in the case of *Ḥamāma-t-al-Bahr*). The range of potential readings is virtually limitless, each turning back on itself and suggesting yet another, leading the woman imaginatively engaged by the episode, or even the very idea of it, toward increasingly provocative, subversive interpretations. And this at the very moment that local values are reinforced.

A *zār* ritual builds gradually, carrying its participants along through successive allusions and confrontations, to its finale in the summons of *Sāḥar zayran,* most alien spirits of all. When Their threads have been drummed, the *shaykha* announces, "*Khallaṣ, wiṣilna!*" "At last, we have arrived!"

Possession: The Rhetoric and the Paradox

The *shaykha*'s summation begs some lines from Eliot's *Four Quartets:*

> We shall not cease from exploration
> And the end of all our exploring
> Will be to arrive where we started
> And know the place for the first time.

The process of the *zār* is a journey to self-awareness, a voyage through space and time within a continuous present aptly represented by the *mīdān,* the room beyond the looking glass where otherness appears within the world of Hofriyat. What renders itself so succinctly in the *mīdān* is a moment in the living history of the village, in the formation of the present through ceaseless interaction between indigenously rooted concepts and a range of foreign powers. The pantheon of *zayran* chronicles the external world's dynamic impingement on village reality since Mohammed ʿAli's conquest of Sudan in 1821 and possibly even before, via early Christian missionaries; Abyssinian trade; the establishment of Islamic brotherhoods and schools; contact with Ethiopian princes, prostitutes, southern slaves, "Syrian" gypsies, West African pilgrim peasants, Turkish officials, British and Egyptian colonial administrators and military personnel, Beja and Baggara Mahdist *mujahidīn,* Euro-American medicine and technology, East Indian, Lebanese, and Greek merchants, Chinese construction workers, Western archaeologists, airplane captains, lorry drivers, railway engineers, Zande sorcerers, even crocodiles. All have left their mark. All have entered into the poetics of contrast (Comaroff and Comaroff 1987 : 205)—a poetics not of duality but of relativity; a poetics, too, of gender—by which Hofriyati women engage the shifting border with the outside world in the act of constructing themselves.

But the *zār* goes beyond quotidian contexts of gender and foreign encounter to bring the process of self construction to conscious attention. It is metacultural, in the sense that Comaroff and Comaroff distinguish between culture and consciousness:

> Consciousness is best understood as the active process—sometimes implicit, sometimes explicit—in which human actors deploy historically salient cultural categories to construct their self-awareness. Its modes . . . may be subtle and diverse; and it is as crucial to explore the forms in which a people choose to speak and act as it is to examine the content of their messages. (Comaroff and Comaroff 1987:205)

The *zār* is such a process, and importantly, one which makes this level of awareness accessible to women whose selfhood is opaqued by its cultural overdetermination. *Zār,* or as Hofriyati women are knowingly fond of pronouncing it, *ẓahr,* meaning to make visible or manifest, makes visible in the *mīdān* what is implicit and unformed—muted, to use Ardener's (1975) evocative word—in the daily experience of womanhood and, by its extension as a trope, in the experience of being rural Sudanese. It is an implicit expression of gender but also, incipiently, of class. And an evaluation of the world is tacit in its portrayal. Yet no single conclusion can be forced from what is exposed, for here the actors are not humans but spirits, whose ontological status and amorality distinguish them from the women whose bodies they assume. The possessed and their audience need take no responsibility for their growth in self-awareness, indeed, need not even grow. In its ambiguous relation to its authorship, consciousness is no less muted than experience.

More than history, perhaps, the spirit world comprises an ethnography from which (at least for Hofriyati) history cannot be disengaged. Spirit societies are identified by a variety of traits combined in the way that resembles Lévi-Strauss's *bricolage:*

> The characteristic feature of mythical thought, as of "bricolage" on the practical plane, is that it builds up structured sets, not directly with other structured sets but by using the remains and debris of events . . . fossilized evidence of the history of an individual or a society. . . . Mythical thought, that "bricoleur," builds up structures by fitting together events, or rather the remains of events. (Lévi-Strauss 1966:21–22)

Yet however seemingly "mythic" their construction, *zayran* are by no means the "fossilized" evidence of history, for spirits are living, sentient beings with a history of their own. The roster of spirits described above is hardly static. Individual *zayran* become established in the village at particular moments, whether by indigenous appearance, as when a previously unknown *zār* is discovered in visions and dreams, or by importation, as when the thread of a *zār* formerly unknown to exist is heard elsewhere then added to the repertoire of chants at Hofriyati rites. A certain spirit may become fashionable for a time, but its popularity might also wane as it seizes fewer and fewer hosts and other, "newer" spirits appear in Hofriyati *mīdāns*.

A prime example of this is the *ʿArab* spirit *al-Quraishi* who comes from Mecca, is a member of the Prophet's tribe, and requires a Saudi four-cornered headdress. During my first period of fieldwork, few women were possessed by this *zār,* but when I returned in 1983 their numbers had increased. The expansion of *al-Quraishi*'s presence over Hofriyati women is coincident with the dramatic growth of Saudi (and the Gulf states') influence in Sudan, evident by the glut of Arabian banks in Khartoum, but experienced closer to home in the rise of labor emigration among Hofriyati men: by 1984, twenty-two of some five-hundred residents, or roughly 20 percent of the adult male workforce, had at some time been employed on the peninsula, compared with only one case in 1977. Taking into account men born in the village but currently residing in the city, it emerges that not one Hofriyati family has gone unscathed. The *zār* is inexhaustibly sensitive to the realities of everyday life.

Knowledge of the specific behaviors and characteristics *zayran* is, like all ethnography perhaps, somewhat arcane. It is information to which the possessed have greater access than others, acquired as it is by attending rituals and paying attention to the actions of spirits manifest in their hosts, through one's own and others' visions and dreams, in diagnostic consultation and informal discussions with adepts at home and abroad, and by learning the spirits' threads: in short, by spirit participant-observation. A particular spirit's qualities, typical gestures and demands, subtleties of dramatic performance are more elaborated, better known, if it possesses several women who attend the same *zār* rites. Each host brings something unique to the text she elucidates in trance. For a spirit reveals different aspects of itself in various women, and when joined with the experiences of others similarly possessed, these deepen the understanding of all. Spirits' traits are constructed out of locally salient categories, gender, for example, or color, in negotiation with images culled from foreign encounters in the human world. Human reality, because it visibly parallels that of *zayran,* provides continuously updated intelligence of the invisible world's texture and dimensions. And yet the spirit world is far more than a literal record of human types or past events: it is richly symbolic, speaking with understated eloquence to the issues of everyday life.

Zayran, recall, differ from humans substantially and existentially: the two are complementary forms of being in a holistic but eminently natural creation. If *zayran* are essentially other in respect of humans generally, the *zār* world is other in respect of Hofriyat: villagers know of no *zayran* that match themselves. The parallel world contains no parallels of Arabic-speaking sedentary rural Sudanese. The most it has in its regard are spirits who play at being Hofriyati but for one or another reason fail to pass. All *zayran* belong to other cultures in the spirit universe; all are analogues of other forms of human being. And significantly, qualities, behaviors, and social arrangements considered abnormal, undignified, antisocial, or immoral if undertaken by Hofriyati—and especially Hofriyati women—are seen to be perfectly normal and acceptable elsewhere: begging, belligerence, promiscuity, swaggering, lying, exogamy, shamelessness. At the same time, certain qualities, behaviors, and conditions considered ideal by village standards but rarely attainable—and especially beyond the reach of women—are typical and expected for some *zayran:* wealth, holiness, supreme dignity, political power, controlled fertility. The *zār* world inverts that of the village both positively and negatively: ontologically, existentially, and sociologically. If *zayran* can be thought of as non-Hofriyati, Hofriyati can be conceptualized as non-*zayran*. Each form of being contextualizes the other, as do women and men on the human plane.

From this perspective, possession is an aesthetic genre—a means to perceive new and rewarding or possibly unsettling significances in what was formerly taken for granted, a way to learn about oneself—which operates via negative metaphor. As a metacultural, secondary text it speaks about the village in selective portrayals of what it is not. Here, Basso's (1979:41ff.) discussion of Apache secondary texts—joking sequences modeled on unjoking activity in which Apache assume the roles of "Whitemen"—is relevant to understanding the *zār*. For as Basso suggests, the construction of secondary texts is based on principles of contrast and distortion: *zayran* are simultaneously other than Hofriyati, and either caricature their cherished traits or personify these to exaggerated degree, hence distorting them and intensifying the initial disparity. But *zār* performances, like Apache "Whiteman" jokes, provoke a serious response: "Whereas contrast and distortion constitute the main principles for constructing secondary texts, comparison and censure appear to constitute the major principles for interpreting them" (Basso 1979:56).

Apaches, in constructing their models of the "Whiteman," expect that these will be judged and found not only different but defective when compared with the models they have of themselves (ibid.). And clearly this is also the case for women observing the antics of *zayran*. Villagers' models of non-Hofriyati cultures, garnered from encounters with alien others, are inevitably assessed and found wanting. Prostitution is no more acceptable to a woman possessed by *Lulīya Ḥabishīya* than to one who is not. And even She insists her hosts follow assiduously the prescriptives of femininity in Hofriyat: refrain from strong emotion, behave with dignity and restraint, remain clean, well dressed, and perfumed. The *zār* positively reinforces villagers' self-image by exemplifying its obverse and sanctioning village praxis.

Yet not all that spirits do is wrongly guided. Some *zār* qualities are certainly desirable to Hofriyati: political power, economic leverage, and holiness among them. Here the *zār* contains a subtle criticism of a world order in which villagers are disadvantaged in relation to other cultures and, mindful of the trope involved, in which village women are disadvantaged in relation to village men. In such an evaluation the analogy between ethnic relations and gender protectively obscures a latent consciousness of women's political reality. Ritual enactment of the spirit world is thus more complex than a "rite of reversal" in the sense originally described by Gluckman: "a protest against the established order" which functions, in fact, "to preserve and strengthen" that order (Gluckman 1965 : 109), and which "is effective only so long as there is no querying of the order within which the ritual of protest is set" (ibid., p.130). Rather, expressions of cultural inversion in the *zār* embody an analysis both critical and reinforcing, destructive and reproductive at the same time.

If this sounds contradictory it is only because in the counterdiscourse of the *zār* there is and can be no insistence on interpretation. It is an example of what Messick (1987) has recently termed "subordinate discourse"—which, like Halliday's (1976) concept of antilanguage, is "a form of expression characterized by its power relation to a dominant ideology with which it coexists" (Messick 1987 : 217), and where "the whole of the 'said' . . . escape[s] not only observers," such as men, but "speakers"—the possessed—as well (ibid., p. 211). In fact, since spirits are taken-for-granted aspects of human existence, spirit texts can be read at face value, and frequently are, with neither personal meanings (cf. Obeyesekere 1981) nor subversive messages necessarily derived.

This wide potential of the *zār* may be credited perhaps to its particular combination of liminal elements with what Turner has termed the liminoid. Both evoke moments of "release from normal constraints" that make possible the deconstruction of commonsense constructions "into cultural units which may then be reconstructed in novel ways" (Turner 1977 : 68). But liminality, as in a rite of passage, is socially required (Turner 1982 : 42): one enters it in order to emerge an altered social person. Liminality is ritual "work." On the other hand, liminoid or "liminal-like" phenomena are not obligatory: like theater-going in the West, engaging in a liminoid experience involves both choice and play, or "leisure" (ibid., p. 42–43). Possession is liminoid in the sense that it is to some degree a matter of optional appropriation: not all women articulate experience in the spirit idiom or attend possession cures. Moreover, the optative nature of possession extends—again to a degree—to the specific identities of spirits through whom women articulate travail. The focus on choice and articulation recalls Obeyesekere's (1981 : 36–45) criteria for "personal symbols," symbols drawn by individuals from the public repertoire of myth models and invested with experiential significance; symbols whose meanings, like those of ambiguous spirits, are manipulable, available to be used, again and again—by individual women. In Turner's (1982 : 54) parlance, possession is liminoid because its symbols are more nearly "personal-psychological" than "objective-social."

Spirits, however, are actually both: liminal and liminoid. As liminal beings or symbols representing exogamous unions or non-Islamic faiths, they are "ultimately eufunctional even when seemingly 'inversive'" (ibid.). And as liminoid symbols appropriated by specific women in particular situations, they may embody "social critiques or even revolutionary manifestos . . . exposing the injustices, inefficiencies, and immoralities of the mainstream economic and political structures" (ibid., pp. 54–55). In its supportive and subversive modes the *zār* reflects women's double consciousness: their commitment to mainstream values and their awareness, however implicit, of their oppression. Possession's power is analogous to that of a satirical allegory in the West, where two lines of thought are joined within a single text and it is entirely up to the reader first to distinguish, then to decide, or not decide, between them. The comparison with allegory is a useful one, and resumed in chapter 10.

Zār, when viewed as an aesthetic genre, seems designed to open thought, to free it from limitations of prior associations, to pose challenging problems, and encourage reflection on the everyday. Symbolic inversion (cf. Babcock 1978) or negative metaphor (cf. Crapanzano 1977*a*) is its essence: during possession rites women become men; villagers become Ethiopian, British, Chinese; the powerless and impoverished become powerful and affluent. Essentially irreversible processes—genderization, aging—become reversible; established categories are undermined. Hierarchical orderings are telescoped and undone when Islamic holy men and pagan prostitutes possess the same Hofriyati woman. The external world is internalized, appearing in villagers' homes and through their bodies. The paradox of possession, the merging or juxtapositioning of opposing qualities and mutually exclusive entities, plays with human understanding, directs villagers' attention to the relativity of their categories and the limits of "common sense," is obliquely critical of all that is absolute (cf. Babcock 1978: 16–17; Colie 1966: 7–10; Douglas 1966).

The possession paradox is an immanent signification, it is saturated with potential meaning. Those led to the *zār* by untoward experience, a challenge to the taken-for-grantedness of daily life are, in its paradox, asked to face that challenge, to explore the taken-for-granted and its alternatives, to examine the dimensions of selfhood from every perceptible angle. Possession provokes those it claims to think about themselves via their inverse spirit counterparts. For paradox, Babcock (1978: 17) notes, "is at once self-critical and creative, 'at once its own subject and its own object, turning endlessly in upon itself,' one inversion leading to the making of another, into the infinite regress of self regard."

Lulīya Ḥabishīya, Sulayman Ya Janna, Dona Bey, indeed all *zayran* manifest in Hofriyati *mīdāns,* are in one way or another paradoxical entities from the standpoint of local reality. The dramas they enact through their hosts are thus doubly paradoxical: they are enactments of paradox dramatized in a paradox, in the manifestation of a spirit in its human alter. Such episodes are provocative, not so much in a ruminative, sit-down-and-think-it-out sort of way, as in the sense that behind their laughter, their terror, or surprise, participants are made to feel just slightly uneasy. One who attends is left with a vague sensation that something important has happened, that she has seen more than she has observed. Perhaps the messages potential in a slice of *zār* theatrics do not occur to villagers immediately, but lie dormant until taken up as circumstances warrant later on. The appropriation of meaning is a matter of individual disposition, as villagers' possession histories attest. Unlike the gender socialization process earlier described, the direction of thought opened up by a possession episode extends as far as a woman wishes to follow it; it is virtually inexhaustible, each interpretation leading to other interpretations, fresh insights, altered perspectives. In Burridge's (1979 : 5) terms, the *zār* makes it possible for female "persons" to attain "individuality": to have the opportunity and capacity to move from person to individual, between integrative and disintegrative moments.

> Because the self is capable of moving toward an integration of now one and then the other, the interplay between person and individual can yield either a dilemma—indicative of a self in disintegrative mode—or an apperception of own being in relation to traditional or alternative categories. Without this interplay and apperception, sociology and social or cultural anthropology would not be possible. (Burridge 1979 : 6)

This raises an important point: in learning about the *zār* world, women learn not only about themselves and their spirits, but about those spirits' human counterparts. In the *zār*, external influences on the village are rehearsed and assessed, and the historically relevant schedule of alternate realities tentatively incorporated within the very beings who see themselves as its antithesis. In this capacity, the *zār* may be an exercise in survival, preparing women for encounters where they might otherwise experience cognitive stress (cf. Peckham 1967; Sutton-Smith 1972). For as Sutton-Smith (1972 : 18–19, cited by Turner [1982 : 52]) suggests, liminoid or "antistructural" genres like *zār* "not only make tolerable the system as it exists, they keep members in a more flexible state with respect to the system, and, therefore, with respect to possible change."

But much as it habituates women to the possibility of change from without, the *zār* is a mechanism for addressing the problems of change and ambiguity arising from within. Lest we forget, possession in Hofriyat has to do with human illness, of the sort villagers associate less with the potential stress of a foreign encounter than with present anxieties, concerning, among other things, human fertility, ambiguous residence priorities, wayward and uncompromising husbands, dilemmas of personal integrity versus kin group obligation. It is here that the *zār* provides a vehicle for ordering and articulating untoward experiences of the everyday world.

A *zār* rite instructs not only by implication, by making local values and behaviors conspicuous by their absence from the trance performances of the possessed, and not only by means of the contrasts such performances set up, but also more directly in the behaviors of alien spirits trying to pass as Hofriyati in whose bodies they appear. Women see themselves clearly caricatured in the vaudevillian antics of prostitute *zayran*. For these spirits make a joke of the most earnest and dignified or feminine endeavors—the dances performed by brides and other women at local weddings. *Zayran* poke fun at those who thus display themselves as the legitimate embodiments of local values, who flaunt their personified enclosedness. Spirits whose morality is twice doubtful—as *zayran* they are amoral and as prostitutes, immoral—thus exhort resolutely moral women not to take themselves too seriously, hinting that they and the constructs which order their lives can hardly be one and the same, that the essential "bride" is neither a woman nor her *zār,* but the enduring image of an ideal, housed temporarily in her body. Perhaps more than other possession dramas, episodes of reversed inversion caution against the reification of conceptual categories and intellectually shatter overdetermined boundaries which, as much as excessive ambiguity, can be obstacles to understanding (Hamnett 1967: 387).

In considering possession as an aesthetic form, I depart from Hofriyati's views on the spirit world. For spirits are not—or not only—ritual symbols but living beings who intervene actively and often subtly in the lives of their hosts. They are not set apart from the everyday world, as I have heuristically located them, but are key performers in the most mundane social interactions. If art, and therefore "good to think," *zayran* are art with vehemence and vivacity and unsettling caprice.

Yet looking at possession aesthetically, I feel one comes closest to comprehending what the *zār* says to Hofriyati women, and what Hofriyati women say to themselves and others through the *zār*. Repeated "readings" of the metacultural texts enacted in the *mīdān* enable a woman to glimpse various dimensions of her subjectivity, of her Hofriyati self and her ever expandable *zār* nonself, growing "slowly more familiar [with them] in a way which opens [her] subjectivity to [her]self" (Geertz 1973: 451). And this, I think, is the therapeutic import of possession: all the implicit functions and significances of the *zār* seem to work, gradually and cumulatively, toward developing in the possessed a mature, considered perspective of herself and her life situation. A woman's first possession acknowledgment in a sense consummates her transition to adulthood, thence, perhaps, to individuality. For such transition is neither achieved in her precocious circumcision, nor completed in her wedding to which the *zār* is imaginatively linked. In contrast to the traumatic, disposition-cultivating experiences of these earlier rites, a woman's experiences of *zayran* orient her toward an awareness of nonprescriptive realities. They move her from a monological (monolithic) world where other voices—alien cultures, feminine perspectives—are disclaimed, exist only "in absentia," to a polyphonous world where others may speak, may enter into dialogue with her Hofriyati self (cf. Bakhtin, cited by Todorov (1984, pp. 76–80)). Here the *zār* as an aesthetic genre resembles the novel as described by Bakhtin (1981 : 186), where social heteroglossia, the existence of multiple expressive worlds, is not muted but incorporated into the "text" itself, effectively decentering hegemonic truths. And given the promise of a cure, a woman is admonished that to experience such openness, however dangerous, might yet be advantageous. Continued participation in the *zār* works to strengthen and replenish her intellectual and emotional maturity, providing nourishment for what Langer (1942 : 46) calls the "constant process of ideation." Possession in Hofriyat, to use the *zār*'s own parlance, "opens the door" to true adulthood for those who, because they are secluded and treated as jural minors, might otherwise find their desires stymied, their creativity blocked. So if a "rite of protest," possession is more than a contained rebellion against an established social order (cf. Gluckman 1965; Lewis 1971*a*); it is also rebellion of the human mind against the fetters of cultural constructs. *Zār* texts, in obliquely suggesting fresh interpretations for quotidian truths—in their essentially aesthetic task—help to develop adepts' consciousness of themselves, so providing them the possibility of more felicitous outcomes in their encounters with others, whoever those others might be.

9

Two Ceremonies

An Apology for the Devil: It must be remembered that we have only heard one side of the case. God has written all the books.

—Samuel Butler, *Note Books*

Though it is true to say that the dominant power group at any given time will dominate the intertextual production of meaning, this is not to suggest that the opposition has been reduced to total silence. The power struggle *intersects* in the sign.

—Toril Moi, *Sexual/Textual Politics*

Chapter 8 plumbed the shadow world of *zār* by focusing on the nature and identities of *zayran* manifest during rituals, and the messages Hofriyati might take from these events. One last piece remains to be added to the picture in order to grasp the full import of the *zār* as an allegorical genre or, in more obvious political terms, a form of antilanguage, subordinate discourse, or counterhegemonic process. It is necessary to consider the ritual itself: the context in which the parallel, external universe appears, contained, within the village. As it was in earlier pages, the double consciousness of village women is apparent here as well; so too is the subtle push toward self-awareness that the *zār* supplies by its protective, productive ambiguity.

I have suggested that possession can be seen as a kind of secondary text, a nuanced construction on hegemonic village reality. As such it is neither wholly derived from, nor fully dependent on, the quotidian discourse of enclosure that governs women's lives and is aptly crystallized in the wedding. True, there are significant correspondences and contrasts between them, such that appreciation of meanings potential in the *zār* presupposes familiarity with the context of everyday life. Both levels of discourse are built of common elements, since a shared symbolic code expresses their different "saids." Both play upon motifs of containment, marriage, fertility, doorways, orifices, brides; spirits and their characteristics are complex transformations of quotidian themes, kaleidoscopic mutations—negative and hyperpositive—of their key symbolic elements and associative auras. But once a woman has appropriated the possession idiom, a reverse dynamic is also implied: for her, each discourse imaginatively illuminates its counterpart.

If the Hofriyati wedding is—from women's perspective—a concentrated representation of hegemonic social values, and the *zār* rite a concentrated expression of adepts' broader, even counterhegemonic view, it is fitting that the ceremonies be compared. And the cue comes from women themselves: Sadiya, Umselima, and others who acknowledge possession avow they would rather attend a *zār* than a wedding; at one cure I witnessed, the *ʿayāna* berated her guests repeatedly because they had not prepared themselves as carefully as they would for a nuptial dance. The *ʿayāna* is herself referred to as the bride of the *zār*, or of the *mīdān,* and the onset of many a possession illness occurs in the context of a recent or continuing wedding. Not least, spirits are said to behave like husbands. Comparison of the *zār* and the wedding seems warranted on several counts.

Before going further, however, the point should be made that although these ceremonies are linked, a possessed woman is by no means thought to marry her possessive *zār*. The possession lexicon does imply that the *zār* is a kind of wedding, but a metaphoric one, by extending the trope that structurally equates the relationship between wife and husband with that between villager and foreign power. The relationship established at a *zār* between human host and alien spirit is similar to that established at a wedding because of its contractual character. Beyond this, their contracts are alike: much as the wedding establishes a husband's claim to the body of his wife, the *zār* rite establishes a spirit's claim to the body of its host; a husband physically reproduces himself through a woman's fertility, the spirit uses a woman's fertility to produce itself in the human world.

In short, two equally valid linked approaches are taken by villagers in comparing the *zār* to the Hofriyati wedding. On the one hand, wedding terms provide a figurative lexicon for the covenant between spirit and host. On the other, the wedding is a cultural performance, a statement of key cultural values as embodied in the bride, and the *zār* has something to say about those values. It is wedding terminology that points to the latter connection, orienting the newly possessed toward the allegorical nature of the *zār*.

The Wedding

There is a family resemblance among wedding customs throughout the main Nile region in Sudan. The ceremony in Hofriyat is similar to what Zenkovsky (1945) and Cloudsley (1983) describe for Omdurman and Khartoum, and Barclay (1964) describes for Buurri, but compares more closely with two discussed by Crowfoot (1922) for the Dongolese and

Jaʿaliyīn, respectively. The hybrid nature of the wedding in Hofriyat can be attributed to the village's residential profile, comprising as it does both Shendi district Jaʿaliyīn and Jawabra, who migrated upstream from Dongola in the seventeenth and early eighteenth centuries (chapter 1).

In the past, wedding festivities took seven days to complete, and newlyweds observed restrictions thereafter for a total of forty days. Now that so many men employed outside the village have less time for lengthy nuptials, and the expense of putting up hundreds of guests has grown, significant events have been compressed into three days. Despite this, the wedding is a costly affair, requiring between £S 500 and £S 600 (US $1,250–$1,500) in 1977 and, because of the recent escalation in wedding expenses (chapter 3), even more than the equivalent amounts in 1984. Practices described below pertain to the wedding of a virgin bride and bachelor groom: for although individuals may wed several times in their lives, only once is one truly an *ʿarūs* (bride), or *ʿarīs* (groom). Only once is a man obliged to fund such an elaborate marriage feast.

When a man wishes to marry, or better, when he is financially able to stage a wedding—though not necessarily yet to support a wife—he consults his mother, who provides him a roster of suitable candidates from which to choose a bride (chapter 1). Owing to sexual segregation and women's relative seclusion from men, his mother has access to knowledge which her son is not privileged to share: information about the identities and characters of eligible young women whom she has long been observing with just this day in mind. Preferably, her choices are close kin; realistically, they are the daughters of those with whom she wishes to initiate or intensify a relationship, to her own or her family's benefit. Needless to say, candidates' reputations must be above reproach.

Having made "his" choice, the groom selects a kinsman to act as his *wazīr* (spokesman, official), and plead his suit before relatives of the intended bride. If an agreement is reached (which may or may not involve the bride's consent), and the amount of *mahr*[1] is set, the groom's proxy gives the bride's people between £S 5 and £S 10 to *fataḥ-t-akh-khashm*, "open the mouth." Sometime later, at a meal sponsored by the bride's kin and attended by the groom and his *wazīr* (bride and groom avoiding each other), the groom publicly hands over the *mahr*. This is called *as-sadd al-māl*, the settlement of money, the term *sadd*, "payment of debt," having connotations of damming or blocking an opening. In addition, he presents his prospective wife with gifts of jewelry, clothing, and perfume. These are tokens of the *shayla* to follow and collectively represent *aw-waḍʿa*

1. A bridewealth payment which, because it is ideally retained by the bride's father for her support in the event of divorce or may be used by him to provide her with household furnishings, is similar in its use to a dowry. See also chapter 3.

ash-shubka, "the placing of the net" or "snare."[2] A propitious date is now set for signing the marriage contract and staging the wedding proper; though these events need not coincide, both ought to take place in an astrological phase favorable to begetting children.

Between a month and two weeks before the wedding itself, the groom delivers the *shayla* ("load" or "burden") to the home of his bride. As noted in chapter 3, the *shayla* comprises great quantities of flour, rice, onions, expensive spices, cooking oil, dried vegetables, fruit drink powder, cooking pots and utensils, animals to be fattened for butchering, and sundry necessities for the wedding supper, plus a *tōb* for the bride's mother and each of her unmarried sisters, and, not least, perfumes, cosmetics, aromatic woods, jewelry, and multiple sets of clothing for the bride herself. Because she "goes into marriage naked" and is forbidden to wear the clothes of her maidenhood once she is wed, the bride receives a trousseau, no part of which may be worn until the night she performs her wedding dance. The groom's gift of clothing to his bride inaugurates the essential dynamic between husband and wife; her first public appearance in this attire signifies her shift in status and incorporation into village society as a married woman. Until such time as they may be used, the clothing and cosmetics of the *shayla* are on display in the home of the bride. Villagers come to witness the evidence that a new social unit is being forged, to note the prestige it claims, and to view its productive potential.

The wedding night is immediately preceded by the *layla-t-al-ḥinnā,* the "night of the henna," when the principals are invested with *jirtig* jewelry and cosmetics designed to protect the vulnerable from harm. In Hofriyat, this ceremony mainly concerns the groom and his kin, but parallel events, though smaller in scale, take place in the home of the bride. Guests are first served dinner. When dishes are cleared away, the groom's aunts, bearing aloft a tray holding *jirtig* apparatus, proceed through an expectant throng to where the groom is seated in the middle of his parents' *ḥōsh.* A brazier of wedding incense is lit and placed on the ground nearby. The groom's hands and feet are now stained with henna by an older kinswoman, after which he is invested with the *jirtig* ornaments—the red tassel bracelet and strings of beads originally worn at his circumcision. Next, the top of his head is coated with a paste of fragrant oils and on this is placed a layer of *darīra:* powdered sandalwood and fenugreek. A band of blue or green cloth is then tied around the head to keep the mixture in place and a *hilāl* ("new moon"), a coin or crescent of gold, is fixed to that part of the band which covers the forehead. When this has been done, the groom and his guests are doused with cologne, to the shriek of women's

2. The root from which *shubka* (net) is derived connotes intertwining and entanglement, hence "engagement."

ululations. A dancing party follows. During it the groom's father or the *wazīr* collects small gifts of money (*nuqṭa*) from male guests, carefully recording the particulars for amplified repayment at appropriate events.

Elsewhere in the village, preparation of the bride is well advanced by this date. About a week before the wedding she begins by taking her first smoke baths and systematically removing the hair from her body. The last few days are spent with women specialists who apply henna in intricate designs to her hands, feet, and ankles and plait her hair in the traditional manner. On the henna night, her own vizier or *wazīra* and other female friends massage her skin with *dilka,* a smoked paste of *dura* flour and aromatic oils. She too receives a *jirtig* charm, but it differs from those of the groom and those that she herself wore when newly circumcised. The Hofriyati bride wears neither *harīra* (the red tassel bracelet) nor beads (*sūksūk*), but a piece of gold jewelry—a pendant or ring made from a coin on which there appears "the face of person."[3] It is the same charm worn by postparturient women and expectant mothers from the seventh month of pregnancy which figures prominently in the *mushāhara* complex. Specifically, it is thought to protect against excessive loss of blood and thus to guard a woman's fertility.

Before the couple separately don their respective *jirtig* charms, these are first dipped in milk and some sprouted grain called *zurīʿa* (cf. Crowfoot 1922 : 5), from the word Hofriyati use to describe their offspring. This is done to "brighten their days" and "make their union fruitful": the association of white with purity and green with fertility is obvious; so too are the associations of fluids with women's work and female procreative contributions, and grain with men's farming and semen or "seed."

While the groom enjoys a night of music and dancing with his guests, the bride is spirited away from her parents' *ḥōsh* by her sisters, *wazīra,* and other friends, and hidden in the home of a neighbor, or, better yet, an unoccupied house in the village. Her location is to be kept secret, but rarely is, until late the following night.

Dusk next evening begins the *layla-t-ad-dukhl,* the "night of the entrance," the most important eve of the wedding. Festivities get under way at the home of the groom where friends, family, and the *banāt*—unmarried girls of the village—dressed in their finest clothes, the men wearing silk *jalabīyas*, the women vivid diaphanous *tōbs*, gather to form a procession (*sayra*). Slowly and with considerable fanfare, drums beating, ululations piercing the air, they make their way to the home of the bride or the *ḥōsh* where, because it is more commodious than her parents', the night's entertainment will be held. Upon arriving at the *khashm al-bayt,* the front door and men's entrance to the *ḥōsh,* a mock struggle takes place

3. Preferably a Maria Theresa dollar, at one time used as currency in Sudan.

with the bride's kinsmen who attempt to prevent the groom and his entourage from passing over the threshold.

Eventually, they gain admittance. At this point, males and females separate: they are taken to different areas or *ḥōsh*s out of each others' sight, and fed an elaborate lamb supper. The meal ends sometime between eleven o'clock and midnight. While married women wash up and put younger children to bed, men spread the long dancing mats, light pressure lanterns, and set *angarīb*s and chairs around the open space. The band begins to play. Mixed festivities recommence, though men and women are careful to remain on opposite sides of the wedding *mīdān* when not actually dancing. As on the night before, young women and older female kin wishing to honor the groom perform the "dance of the neck" or "pigeon dance," and bestow the *shabāl*.

When the dancing is well under way the groom, attended by his *wazīr,* slips off to where the bride is hidden. She awaits him, seated on a "red" (multicolored) wedding mat (*birish al-aḥmar*) atop an *angarīb,* head and upper body concealed beneath her *garmosīs,* the red and gold silk wedding cloth. The groom now performs *ag-guṭaʿa ar-rahaṭ,* "the cutting of the *rahaṭ,*"[4] which in earlier times involved pulling seven leather thongs from the bride's maiden skirt and tossing these to her friends who had not yet wed, so they might soon find husbands. Now that Hofriyati brides no longer wear the *rahaṭ,* whether over their wedding dresses (as Cloudsley [1983: 58] writes is the case in Omdurman), or beneath them (as Barclay [1964: 254] describes for Buurri), this ceremony consists in pulling a few threads from the *garmosīs* and disposing of them in the same way. On breaking strings from the *rahaṭ* (or threads from the *garmosīs*) Barclay (1964: 260) remarks, "the groom may be regarded as symbolically breaking the hymen. . . ."

Having completed this rite, the groom returns to the celebration where he is greeted with ululations: the wedding is formally consummated. Dancing continues until the early hours of the morning. Then, when everyone is thoroughly exhausted and has just about given up waiting, the bride appears in all her finery.

Before the bride and her companions stealthily make their way to the dance, the *wazīra* passes a lighted brazier of wedding incense beneath the bride's skirts. Friends then carry the red mat on which the bride was seated and lead her to the party, concealed beneath the *garmosīs.* Once she is inside the wedding *ḥōsh,* her mat is spread on the ground in the center of the

4. Barclay (1964: 255) notes, "According to Herzog [Rolf Herzog, "Der Rahat, eine fast verschwundere Madchentracht im Otsudan," *Baessler Archiv,* n.s. 4, 1956] the Arab women of pre-Islamic times wore a *rahaṭ* before marriage, during menstruation, and during any period of stay in a sanctuary. The dress diffused to East Africa with the Arab immigrations of the seventh century, where its use was restricted to the unmarried."

gathering. The music stops. Guests tightly encircle the mat. In the soft glow of lanterns the bride now appears, barefoot, her upper body sheathed in the glittering silk. The groom approaches and takes a position facing her on the mat. Her friends commence to sing love songs, keeping time on the *dallūka;* the *wazīra* removes the *garmosīs,* and the bride stands revealed.

She wears a shimmering wedding dress[5] and all her family's gold; her hands and feet are hennaed in elegant designs. As was noted earlier, the bride's hands cover her face until the groom, on separating them, initiates her wedding dance, the "dance of the buttocks" (*ragīṣ bi ṣuluba*), for which she has been coached these past few nights by friends. As the girls sing to the beat of their *dallūka,* the bride moves her arms and hands in stylized gestures appropriate to the meaning of each song. Her eyes remain tightly shut; when necessary the *wazīra* gently intervenes to prevent her bare feet from leaving the mat and touching ground. Periodically, the bride appears to swoon and her hands revert to her face; immediately, she is caught by the groom or the *wazīra* who flings the *garmosīs* over her head. Another song: the groom once more removes the wedding veil and releases his bride's arms; she dances. The covering and re-revelation of the bride continue until the girls have completed their repertoire and the bride, who is under terrific tension throughout this display, is thoroughly wearied. She is led from the wedding party, veiled as before, and taken to her parents' *ḥōsh.* Soon the gathering disbands. The groom also retires to his bride's parents' *ḥōsh,* though tonight the couple remain apart.

The following day begins the *layla-t-ag-gayla,* the "night of the staying," when bride and groom spend their first night together. It begins with a morning party (*ṣubḥīya*) at the bride's house. After guests have been fed a late breakfast, the bride's girlfriends reassemble in the *ḥōsh* to drum and sing. Women get up to dance, but informally, since the sexes are separated most of the day. The bride is now out of hiding and unveiled, wearing her next best dress and most beautiful (usually white) *tōb* from the *shayla.* Accompanied by the *wazīra* and one or two kinswomen, she remains within the bridal chamber, seated on an *angarīb* spread with the bridal mat on which she danced last night. Her *garmosīs* is folded beside her. Thus she receives numerous women visitors; now and then a group of men enter to offer congratulations. Most brides are embarrassed—*khajlāna,* shy and reticent, ashamed—by attention from adult males, particularly if they are not relatives. During such visits, the bride speaks rarely and fastens her eyes on the ground.

On this day the bride is a paragon of obedience: she must reperform her dance on command. Whenever a guest so desires, the mat is placed on the ground, and she is led forth, head and body shrouded by the *garmosīs.*

5. The type and significance of this dress are treated below.

Her dance is the same step, slow, rhythmic, controlled, with the exception that if the groom is not present, the *wazīra* acts his part. As on the night before, the bride's person and her performance make visible—manifest and concrete—key cultural values, those whose meaningfulness is undisputed by Hofriyati whatever their significance for particular individuals or gender groups.

Just before sunset, the groom, his friends, village girls and boys, and young women guests assemble just outside the village for a procession to the Nile.[6] When they reach the river, the groom wades into the water to wash his face and arms. Other men follow suit. Before leaving, they might also cut palm fronds with which to decorate the newlyweds' room.[7] On returning to his bride's home, the groom sees that a ram has been sacrificed before the *khashm al-bayt*. He must step over the pool of its blood in order to enter the *ḥōsh* (cf. also Crowfoot 1922 : 7).

After supper and a final night of dancing, the groom retires to the marriage chamber to find his bride veiled in her *garmosīs* sitting on her mat on an *angarīb*. He gives her a present—some money—in order to "open the mouth" (*fataḥ-t-akh-khashm*) (cf. Crowfoot 1922 : 8). Until this point, and even afterward, the bride has maintained silence in her husband's presence. A cord[8] has been tied around the bride's waist which next the groom must try to remove. The bride, for her part, should struggle bravely to prevent his success, for it is shameful to surrender easily. The couple remain together until morning—ostensibly consummating their marriage, but as noted in chapter 2, physical consummation often happens much later.

If the groom is free to remain in the village, dancing may continue for several evenings, though the celebrations are much reduced. Then, on the seventh day of the wedding, a ceremony called *al-asbūᶜ*, "the seventh" or "week," takes place. In it the groom sacrifices a ram referred to as the *ḥulāla*, "loosening," on behalf of the young women who taught the bride to dance and provided her musical accompaniment.

Occasionally the couple now leaves on a honeymoon trip to Khartoum or Kassala. Regardless of what transpires, the bride is under further

6. I was told that in weddings a generation ago, bride and groom were brought together just before sunrise and sunset each day after the *layla-t-ad-dukhl* for a ceremony known as *hadāna*, "stillness." The couple was seated cross-legged and side by side on a bridal mat, the bride's *garmosīs* stretched over them, covering their upper bodies. They were made to stay that way, in total silence, until the sun had either risen or set. As Crowfoot (1922 : 7) notes, "Sunrise and sunset are known as the *ḥamārain*—the two reds, and the people think that spirits are particularly active at these periods."

7. Informants say that until recently the bride's *angarīb* was always decorated with a bower of palm fronds. The custom has not completely lapsed, though I did not witness it in the dozen or so weddings I attended.

8. In some areas this is a beaded belt. See Cloudsley (1983 : 45–47), who notes that in Omdurman the beads are left on for the first few nights the bride spends with her husband. As far as I know, this is not done in Hofriyat.

restriction until forty days after the *layla-t-ad-dukhl*. During this period she is permitted neither to do domestic work nor be abroad while the sun shines. When she departs the *ḥōsh* at dusk to pay funeral condolences or visit an ailing relative, she wears the black visiting *tōb* of a married woman, not the brightly colored *tōb* of a bride.

Wedding Dresses, Wedding Feasts

When I began attending Hofriyati weddings, brides invariably wore white to perform their dance—beaded and elaborately sequined knee-length dresses imported from Cairo or Jiddah. But by 1984 the bridal outfit had changed, and the wedding dress could be white, white with splashes of black, or red. This reflected more than a simple variation in style for, given the significance of the wedding dress as that part of the bride's appearance properly controlled by her husband and indicative of his productive and defensive potential, it also insinuated certain pressures villagers were experiencing from the world outside of Hofriyat, as mediated by men to those within. The white and white with black dresses are products of Egyptian influence; the red, of Saudi Arabian. Most striking, where before there was one wedding night, or "night of entrance," now, funds permitting, there are two. In the first the bride wears a white (white and black) dress, or rented Western-style wedding gown complete with veil or Lady Di hat over a Victorian upswept wig.[9] Her make-up and nail polish are distinctly Western, and the entire effect is like something from *Modern Bride* magazine. In the second ceremony, which generally takes place the next day, though the order, I am told, can be reversed, the bride dons a red-spangled shift, her hair is braided in traditional *mashaṭ* elongated with black wool thread and adorned with a cap of linked golden discs. She wears other "traditional" jewelry, including the recently revived *rushma*, a gold chain extending from right nostril to right ear; plus *koḥl* around her eyes and locally concocted wedding perfume. This second costume is referred to as the *ṭugm baladi*—the indigenous, rural, or traditional outfit, though little originates locally save the bride's cosmetics. Her dress and jewelry are both imported from Saudi Arabia and said to be what a traditional Saudi bride might wear.

The bridal costume of 1984 captured an existential dilemma that villagers then confronted—and, I am assured, they continue to deal with today—whose consideration furnishes insight into the role of the wedding as a cultural performance. The problem has arisen mainly because of men's

9. Or her own hair may be coiffed in this fashion. If so, the following night she wears a braided wig.

expanded employment opportunities in the Arabian peninsula. Numerous nonresident Hofriyati whose remittances go to support village households have also worked in Arabia, to the point where nearly every household has at sometime or other provided at least one overseas émigré. The men use kin sponsorship to obtain work visas and jobs in Arabian cities where they are employed as taxi drivers, construction workers, office messengers, bank tellers, and clerks and, according to informants, are paid 4–10 times the going wage for these jobs at home. They return to the village on month-long annual vacations, valises brimming with lavish gifts of clothing, French perfume, and manufactured household goods; minds and hearts suffused by a heightened sense of Islamic idealism.

The influence of men's Arabian sojourns on the lives of village women and nonmigrant men has been considerable. Quite apart from the acquisition of labor-saving devices such as pressure cookers and mechanical grinders, whose benefits women extol, this influence is being felt in three areas that reflect on women's status in different and sometimes conflicting ways. If the first place, increased awareness of the tenets of fundamentalist Islam has prompted a few men to demand that the practice of pharaonic circumcision cease in favor of the less drastic and, in their view, religiously approved "*sunna*" operation.[10] Not surprisingly, this proposition has met with resistance by the majority of women, for whom pharaonic circumcision is a principal component of selfhood and central to an implicit gender complementarity. As I noted in earlier chapters, it is only partially correct to view the operation and the context it reproduces as vehicles of women's subordination; circumcision and its social implications are strategically used by women as bargaining tools with which to negotiate subaltern status and enforce their complementarity with men. Most view circumcision less as a source of oppression (after all, none has experienced adulthood intact) than one of fulfillment,[11] however difficult this is for Western readers, imbued with Western notions of sexuality and self-realization, to comprehend. And women saw men's attempts to regulate their activities as trespass on women's preserve. When I left the field at the end of April 1984, no change had occurred in the way female circumcisions were performed. But there was considerable debate of the issue among women, and a tacit condemnation of the suggested innovation.

A second arena in which men's Arabian labor experience has had an impact on village life is in the politics of wedding negotiations. Not only

10. Properly, this entails removal of the prepuce of the clitoris without infibulation; popularly, however, the term refers to anything from this to the intermediate operation (*ṭahūr wasiṭ*) in which all so-called inner flesh is excised but the labia majora are left largely intact, followed by infibulation.

11. For a similar view of women in rural Greece, see Dubisch (1986:28), and Caraveli (1986) in the same volume.

has the wedding ceremony become more elaborate and the quantum values of the *shayla* jumped dramatically, but migrants' independent incomes have prompted some of them to ignore kinship ideals and circumvent their parents' desires when deciding whom to wed. In two instances during the winter of 1984, men in their late twenties, acting on their own, selected children—distant cousins—as their brides. Neither girl had reached puberty; both were taken out of school and, at the ages of ten and eleven, respectively, were married. Women in the village and a good many men were horrified. Things had been improving, they said, until now: daughters had been able to stay in school until their late teens, and only then would their fathers entertain proposals of marriage. Moreover, girls would usually be consulted as to their preferences,[12] a privilege the child brides had been denied. Yet both unions were deemed legal under *sharīᶜa* law and sanctioned by the local *faki*.

The two men who had worked in Saudi Arabia wanted young brides, for, said informants, had not the Prophet married the nine-year-old daughter of his companion Abu Bakr? And is it not better to marry one's daughter before she becomes reproductively mature (that is, potentially disruptive), or to have a wife whose earliest procreative years are not wasted in school, learning what she does not need to know? Still, these are not the views of most Hofriyati and one must ask why, in the face of peer opposition, the fathers of these girls acquiesced. The answer, it seems, rests with the productive abilities of the migrants: the men whose daughters were wed that winter had been offered an alliance they dared not refuse. A married couple's productive and reproductive reciprocity should be seen not only in terms of its own dynamic, described in chapters 3 and 5, but also in terms of its potential as a strategic resource for kin who sponsor and stand to gain from the match.

A third influence stemming from villagers' involvement with Arabia is television. There are now three battery-powered television sets in Hofriyat—two black and white, one color—whose presence has quite transformed village nightlife. Most weekday evenings a large crowd gathers in the courtyard of one of the three households to watch the latest episode of an Egyptian drama (*timsīlīya*) broadcast from Omdurman.[13] Strict decorum is observed: men sit to one side of the set, women to the other. While waiting for the broadcast to begin there is a good deal of animated conversation—mainly segregated gossip about forthcoming weddings. Following the play comes the news and, once weekly, a "foreign film"—at the time of my fieldwork it was *C.Hi.P.s* with Arabic subtitles. But few people stay beyond the end of the drama: at eight o'clock the men's and

12. See chapter 1, note 37.

13. Because they run on car batteries which must periodically be recharged, rarely is more than one set operational on a given evening.

women's groups disband, noisily debating implications of the latest twist for the outcome of the plot.

The stories themselves are variable in length: some go on for several weeks, others are completed within a few episodes. Yet, though characters and plots change regularly, the formula remains the same. And so do the actors, whose offscreen lives have become matters of local concern.[14] In these respects, Egyptian video plays are like American daytime soap operas, and like them, they deal with themes of problematic kinship, marital intrigue, and thwarted ambition, often absorbing current issues within traditional frameworks where they are, in a sense, naturalized. One story, for example, depicted a young couple who worked in the same engineering firm, who fell in love and wished to marry. As it happened they were also patrilateral parallel cousins and as such preferred spouses. The theme of traditional marriage was thus depicted in association with cross-sex work relationships, and one message taken by my friends was that the two are not incompatible. The fact that the protagonists overcame opposition from the woman's father, who wished her to marry a wealthy but polygynous client, coincidentally reaffirmed villagers' scale of values which ranks kin marriage over all other kinds.

The impact of these television dramas can be seen in an increased use of Egyptian dialect words in everyday speech,[15] in a concern to acquire the material goods displayed in Egyptian households and TV advertisements (so reinforcing the labor emigration of village men), and more subtly, in ideas about fertility and the ideal relationship between spouses. A few young people I spoke to said they had sought companionship in their marriages and, like Egyptian couples on TV, were presently sharing a bedroom. Neither behavior was deemed possible or desirable during my first period of fieldwork, when sexual segregation was observed at home as well as in public. Cohabitation of this sort was something done by *khawājāt,* not by Hofriyati. Moreover, three young men of my acquaintance now stress the need to practice birth control in order to have fewer, better-cared-for children, a sentiment I had heard in 1977 only from women, and then only in private. All of this represents a shift of attitudes: earlier emphasis on gender solidarity and the concern for founding a descent group is, for some Hofriyati, apparently giving way to marital solidarity and an intensification of nuclear family relationships. While it is undeniable that economic factors are playing the major role here, video dramas legitimize the process and show it to be congruent with accepted values. Yet the irony

14. They are tremendously popular not only in Sudan, but, of course, in Egypt where they are written about extensively in fan magazines. And on two visits to Cairo I saw huge billboards along the highway that advertised upcoming stories, caricatures of the actors in costume and facial expression.

15. Like the studied use of *eh* for "thing," as opposed to the local word *shī;* the pronunciation *ʾawah* for *gawah* (coffee) and *galabīya* for *jalabīya.*

remains: televisions purchased with money earned in fundamentalist Saudi Arabia and the Islamic principalities of the Gulf are contributing to the diffusion and appropriation of ideas which villagers have long considered un-Islamic.

Hofriyati are currently caught in a predicament: whether to adopt the values of the West as filtered through an Egyptian lens or to intensify their commitment to Islam (and dependence on Arabia) by purifying their practice and eliminating Western elements. The problem is, in essence, hardly new: how to negotiate and choose among powerful external influences so that villagers might obtain the proffered advantages while maintaining their distinctiveness, might retain autonomy despite acknowledged subaltern status. It is Fatna's dilemma replayed. And like the outcome of Fatna's game of *sīja* with the sultan's son, the dilemma is conceptually resolved in a wedding. The dual wedding of the 1980s displays publicly and visually the external pressures being exerted on village society as a whole, and displays them on the body of that society's exemplar, the icon of Hofriyatiness that is the bride. The wedding is more than a poetic expression of male and female roles—of the wife, fertile, silent, and immobile "inside"; of the husband, productive, who crosses thresholds and overcomes obstacles to reach her from without. In the dance of the bride, the juxtaposition of her dress with her infibulated, ritually prepared body, it is also a condensed performance of the distinction between the foreign world (now Arabia and Egypt) and that of the village, expressed metaphorically in the salient precepts of gender.

But this is not all. Nor, perhaps, is the bride's altered costume the most illuminating change. For in association with the two wedding dances there are now two wedding feasts. When the bride wears her Western dress, guests are treated to a *ḥafla koktayl,* a cocktail party, in which each participant is given his or her own plate of food and an individual bottle of soft drink or glass of lemonade. Here, men and women eat in the same room, or even side by side. But when the bride wears her *baladi* dress, the feast is a traditional communal one where guests are sexually segregated in different courtyards and sit in groups, each surrounding a tray. They eat *kisra* with their hands, dipping it into sauces and stews in common bowls. And when water is passed, all at a table drink from the same cup. Like the bride's dress, these two feasts exemplify contrasting influences, but here something more is being said. As the bride's "Saudi" dress is considered a "traditional" one, and suitably accompanied by a "traditional" feast, local custom once again is identified with Islam. So the new wedding expresses, and perhaps attempts to reconcile, the conflicting values of economic individualism and community life; of the "Western" capitalist world and the local world of kinship and Islam; of sexual mixing, and sexual segregation and complementarity. It is a conflict that strikes at the very heart of Hofriyati life. And it is fitting that its venue of consciousness should be the wedding, the moment when key cultural values are displayed, affirmed, negotiated perhaps, and modified, in the local poetics of contrast.

Formal Correspondences

One issue must be raised before proceeding to a detailed comparison of the wedding with the *zār:* the extent to which the wedding is a template for all crisis rites in Hofriyat (cf. Kennedy 1978*c*). Clearly, this is the case for secular rites of passage such as circumcision and childbirth, orchestrated by women. Death, however, is a spiritual transition rather than a social one, hence the responsibility of men and formal Islam.

Wedding terminology is used to describe the status of a boy precociously about to become a "man" through circumcision: the neophyte is alternately referred to as a "bride" or "groom," indicative, perhaps, of a mildly androgynous identity which persists until the operation has been successfully performed. Likewise, a girl is a "bride" on her circumcision day, as is a newly delivered mother.

Moreover, all secular crisis ceremonies exhibit the three stages of status transition described by Van Gennep (1960), and best exemplified by events surrounding the bride: (1) separation, when the bride is hidden away; (2) margin and transition, marked in several ways—when she removes the clothes of her youth and dresses in wedding garb, when the groom pulls the threads from her *garmosīs,* when she dances in a highly restrained manner before the audience whom she is forbidden to see, when she is coaxed to "open her mouth," in short, when she is being ritually socialized to womanhood; and (3) reaggregation, when she is taken back to her parents' *ḥōsh,* greeted the following morning by villagers, and gradually reincorporated into routine daily life. Similar stages, though never so elaborate as this, characterize male and female circumcision ceremonies and the events surrounding childbirth. The wedding is the quintessential rite of passage in Hofriyat. But there is more to it than a simple equation between neophyte and "bride." For regardless of biological sex, persons undergoing a formal change of status and referred to as "brides" have all undergone genital surgery and shed "feminine" blood, as brides themselves must do. The basis for comparing other crisis rites with the wedding lies in the physical experiences of those undergoing transition. Since the *zār* rite not only establishes a contract, but is also a cure marking a woman's formal passage to health from a state of illness linked closely to feminine blood, it is entirely appropriate that it be seen as a kind of wedding.

As is true of rites of passage cross-culturally, there is considerable emphasis on rebirth and renewal in the Hofrityai wedding, and much use of liminal symbolism. Quite apart from the bride's liminal status and her newborn's inability to see or speak, both color associations and events concerning thresholds bespeak ambiguity and transition, and resonate with those of the *zār*. The bride's mat and her *garmosīs* are polychrome, but, like wedding perfume (*ḥumra,* chapter 3), referred to as "red," symbolizing blood and fertility but also ambivalence and caprice. The *garmosīs* is particularly intriguing for, being both red and brilliant gold, it simultaneously expresses paramount gender complementary values: the inherent fertility of women and the productive wealth of men. Likewise, it points to both the bride's ambiguous social position and her culturally exalted status. In earlier times when newlyweds kept the *hadāna,* silence at sundown and sunrise,[16] these transitions between night and day were tellingly known as "the two reds" (*ḥamārayn*). Considerable attention is devoted to transitions and thresholds throughout the wedding: for example, the groom's struggle with his prospective wife's kin before her family's *khashm al-bayt* or "mouth of the house," his stepping over the blood of a ram on the threshold of the room the pair will later occupy, convincing his bride to open her mouth, removing the rope around her waist, and of course, breaching the physical defenses of her chastity: the "mouth of the house of childbirth." Thresholds and blood are inextricably linked.

As for rebirth and renewal, protective *jirtig* charms are dipped in milk and newly sprouted grain—recalling the reproductive contributions of females and males to their offspring, present here in suitably activated form. For forty days following the night of entrance, the couple are said to be green (*akhḍar*), after which they become *yābis,* dry or firmly planted (cf. Crowfoot 1922 : 26). The transition between moist (green) and dry is resonant with the process of maturation, at least for women, who begin their adult lives as vessels of life-giving fluid that is progressively expended as they age. It also recalls the distinction between brides (moist) and prostitutes (dry), which would seem a contradiction. But although they share an idiom, the contexts differ: two implications of dryness are at work. Where it is a positive thing for newlyweds to become "drier" and more firmly planted, for their relationship to mature, a woman's misuse of her reproductive potential through immoral behavior automatically results in the moral sterility of her issue.

As was noted in earlier chapters, the *zār* rite, too, makes extensive reference to symbols of transition, and one might ask whether similarity between the ceremonies is merely that of rites of passage within the same symbolic universe. Perhaps the liminal symbolism in each has no more than positional meaning (cf. Turner 1969*a* : 12), bearing relation to other symbols and events within the rite, but not to aspects of Hofriyati life as a

16. See note 6, this chapter.

whole. Do the ceremonies therefore share only a formal relationship, and not, as I have suggested, a substantive one? This I think is doubtful, for in the possession context as in the discourse of everyday life, doorways and orifices, fluids and grain, blood and substance, gold, all have significance beyond the specific roles they play in the wedding or spirit cure. Shortly, I hope to demonstrate a substantive link between the two, one in which the *zār* reworks certain meanings of the wedding in parodical fashion. It is, I submit, one task of the cermemonies' formal correspondences to develop a consciousness of that link in the minds of the possessed.

Several other associations are available to aid in developing an awareness of the *zār* as a comment on the wedding and, by extension, on quotidian transition rites for which it serves as model. For example, the two ceremonies take place over seven days, and when shortened for expediency, both are shortened to three. Moreover, the bride of a wedding is secluded: she must avoid seeing her prospective husband before the ceremony and on the wedding day itself. For the duration of the wedding she remains within the walls of a *ḥōsh*—with the occasional exception of her dance[17]—and is forbidden to perform her usual domestic tasks; these restrictions are repeated with every childbirth. Similarly, the bride of the *zār mīdān* must avoid seeing her husband during the rite, remain within the walls of her *ḥōsh* or a kinswoman's where the *zār* is held, and refrain from domestic work.

The bride of a wedding wears a white, white and black, or red dress and has purified her body by completing the cosmetic procedures of married women. But during the wedding she must neither bathe herself entirely, all at once, nor wash her hair or clothes. Throughout the festivities, she sits or reclines on her red bridal mat; her *garmosīs* is within reach and may be worn over her head to express *khajal,* embarrassment or shame. Like requirements apply to a postparturient woman, who is re-presented to her husband as a bride. For her part, the bride of a *zār* wears a white robe and red sash, particularly if this is her first spirit cure. She too prepares for the rite by performing the matron's beautification regimen, is forbidden to bathe her entire body or wash her clothing for the duration of the rite, reclines on a red bridal mat, and keeps near her a *garmosīs*.

Before her wedding a bride receives from her husband-to-be gifts of clothing, perfume, scented soap, and jewelry in fulfillment of the marriage negotiations. Similar gifts are forthcoming at the birth of a child. In both cases, the goods she receives become her personal property. During a *zār* the patient, on behalf of possessive *zayran* with whom she covenants, receives gifts of clothing, perfume, scented soap, gold and silver jewelry

17. Sometimes, if the wedding gathering is large and no *ḥōsh* suitable to accommodate the mixed festivities exists, dancing takes place in a village *mīdān*—a square or open area surrounded by the outside walls of courtyards.

from her husband or close kinsmen. These are owned exclusively by the spirit and used by the woman, who is proxy for the spirit's pleasure.

The bride of the wedding dances on a mat in the center of a ceremonial *mīdān*, a ritual space. She performs to love songs sung by women accompanied on a *dallūka*. Her dance consists partly of mimetic gestures appropriate to the principal character of each song. Likewise in the *zār*, the possessed "bride" manifests her spirit while standing, usually, on a plain mat in the center of the *zār mīdān*. She moves to "threads" sung by female adepts who keep rhythm on one or more *dallūkas*. Her "dance" consists in performing the behaviors of her spirit, indeed, in being the spirit for a limited period of time. No transition rites other than these are characterized by the formal staging of a performance in a *mīdān*.[18]

Such obvious structural parallels between the *zār* rite and the wedding pave the way for consideration of their more esoteric aspects. In succeeding pages it can be seen that the *zār* provides a subtle, at times trenchant, comment on the wedding: the directions of thought it suggests, if taken up by adepts as they may or may not be, are clearly provocative. Following my procedure for outlining the discourse of daily life in chapters 2 and 3, further comparison of the ceremonies is focused around the significant processes and themes that occur in each. These, in their various manifestations, play on the issues and associations of closing, opening, and fertility.

Opening, Closing

Recall that when the wedding arrangements are made, a man's *wazīr* gives a monetary gift to the kinsmen of his bride known as the "opening of the mouth," *fataḥ-t-akh-khashm*. Given Hofriyati symbolism, the gift represents the initiation of an alliance: the "opening" of one *khashm al-bayt* to another, or of mouths to communicate. Similarly, when a woman is diagnosed as possessed, she receives a preliminary censing, in private, known as the *fataḥ-t-al-ᶜilba*, the "opening of the [incense] box" (cf. also Constantinides 1972: 181–82), which requires a token payment—perhaps fifty piasters—to the *shaykha* or *sitt al-ᶜilba* who controls the box. Like the wedding payment, this marks the positive beginning of a relationship, here between possessive spirit and human host. Moreover, the censing the patient receives involves her essential orifices: nostrils, mouth, vaginal open-

18. Occasionally a *zikr* of one of the Islamic fraternities may be held to celebrate a boy's recent circumcision or the *sīmaya* (naming ceremony) of a male baby. However, this is not a fundamental part of the ceremony, but an embellishment. In fact, it may occur several days after the precipitant event and is not the focus of the ceremony as is the dance of the bride or the trance performance of the possessed.

ing, through which incense mixtures of several spirit societies are taken into her body. The patient's response, or rather, her spirit's, enables the *shaykha* to diagnose the offender's type, its ethnic identity. The practice is resonant with wedding payments and customs concerning the bride's body orifices, specifically, her mouth and vaginal meatus: the purpose of the wedding, after all, is to establish a new conjugal unit and activate the bride's fertility under appropriate circumstances. On the night of staying, the bride must be coaxed to open her "mouths"—resulting both in speech and the consummation of her marriage. The spirit must be coaxed to reveal itself in its host, resulting in speech and the establishment of a lifelong relationship with a chosen human being.

A *zār* rite is precipitated by illness whose specific symptoms often have to do with bodily closure: the patient's hands and arms may be folded inward and her legs drawn up against her chest in fetal position; she may suffer blockage of the reproductive and/or urinary tracts, paralysis, an inability to open her mouth to speak or eat, aphonia, even blindness. Likewise, the bride of a wedding suffers the constraints of a newborn: she enters marriage naked, remains sightless during her dance, immobile in seclusion, and speechless before her husband. Moreover, her genital orifice is closed. Both bride and *ʿayāna* suffer from bodily closure, but in radically different ways: the one valued and appropriate, the other morbid, inappropriate. Their respective rituals are devoted to altering these conditions: the wedding, to opening the bride's body in a controlled and restricted manner (aptly expressed by the *sadd al-māl,* the transference of wedding wealth which literally "blocks a gap or opening"); the *zār,* to reopening the *ʿayāna*'s body and establishing the conditions for normal functioning. But the *zār* does more than this, for it encourages the spirit to become manifest in the patient in a controlled and articulate manner. The *zār* rite parallels and extends statements made in the wedding about the prior and subsequent condition of the bride and, by extension, of village society, suggesting, on the one hand, that closure is in fact a morbid estate, while affirming on the other that openness must be controlled.

Tying, Loosening, Cutting, and Pulling Threads

This theme pervades both ceremonies. To begin with, when a man signs his marriage contract, he is said to be "tying a knot" in his "rope" at the mosque: as was noted in chapter 3, the groom binds the woman to himself when he legitimately appropriates her fertility. Similarly, he presents his bride with a preliminary gift of finery referred to as "the setting of the snare." The woman is a creature—like *Dona Bey*'s *saʿīd*—to be caught, baited, and bound by the wealth of the groom. For its part, a spirit often makes known its intent toward a woman by confiscating her procreative ability: it is said to "seize," "hold," or "tie up," the woman's womb until its demands for human finery are met. The idiom is the same, but directions of transfer are reversed, as are the consequences of the act. In the wedding a contractual relationship results in the birth of children; in the *zār,* a contractual relationship is initiated by preventing conception.

On the "night of staying," when the marriage is formally consummated, the groom struggles to untie a cord or band of cloth knotted around his bride's waist. The rite is known as the *ḥal al-ḥizāna:* the "loosening of the belt." Then, on the wedding's seventh day, the groom slaughters a ram for his wife's girlhood friends who helped prepare her for her dance. The ceremony is referred to as the *ḥulāla,* the "loosening." An animal sacrifice by the same name is offered by a man immediately following the birth of his child. Here, *loosening* signifies for both partners a change in social-*cum*-reproductive status: old relationships are loosened as they are rewrought. More specifically, however, what is loosened is the woman's fertility: freed from girlhood by marriage or unbound by childbirth. The *ḥulāla* marking the birth of a man's child ends the prohibition against shedding blood during his wife's pregnancy at the moment when her own blood is released. In a similar but obverse vein, a woman whose fertility has been usurped by a *zār* can expect her spirit to release or loosen its hold on her womb once she has sacrificed a ram on its behalf, whereupon her body, like that of the formally deflowered bride or parturient woman, again becomes potent and fertile.

In Hofriyat when the groom "cuts the *rahaṭ*" of his bride, initiating their intimate personal relationship, he in fact pulls several threads from her wedding veil, the *garmosīs.* When adepts summon spirits to their midst by drumming the chants of various named *zayran,* they are said to pull (*jarr*) or drum (*dugg*) those spirits' threads (*khuyūṭ*). *Thread* is also a synonym for *spirit* (Cloudsley 1983 : 83; Constantinides 1972 : 178). In the wedding, the bride sits passively, completely veiled; she is timid and reluctant, and does not speak. In the séance, adepts pulling the spirits' threads summon them to descend into the *mīdān* through the bodies of their hosts. The bride of the *zār* sits veiled beneath her *tōb* anticipating the advent of her spirit.

The events are clearly similar, though partially reversed: where pulling threads at a wedding foreshadows the groom's physical penetration of his reticent, infibulated bride, pulling threads at a *zār* explicitly invites a possessive spirit to enter a "bride's" body and make itself manifest. The bride of the wedding is reluctant, passive and relatively closed; the bride of the *zār* is acquiescent, active, and as a married woman, relatively "open."

As Constantinides (1972 : 222) points out, thread imagery in the *zār* "extends itself into one of tying," and thus rounds back on the wedding theme. On the one hand, *zayran* are thought of as being tied in the sky, with the ritual operating to untie or loosen them (ibid., pp. 223–24), and pull them into the *mīdān*. On the other, the *shaykha* and bride of the *zār* are seen as "tied to the *zār*" (ibid., p. 224; see also Sosan, chapter 7). Here it must be remembered that *zayran,* women say, are like husbands.

The themes of tying, binding, and loosening circulate throughout the *zār,* their contexts sometimes running parallel to those in the wedding, sometimes intertwining and opposing. As an example of the latter, when a menstruating woman attends a *zār,* she alerts her spirits *not* to enter her body by tying a knot in her braided hair.[19] As a *zār* rite unfolds, it does so in a complicated weaving of point–counterpoint using the wedding as its base, its reference; this is similar to what was observed for individual spirits whose characteristics both confirm Hofriyati values and subvert them at the same time.

Incense and Inhalation

Just before the bride of a wedding is led forth to perform her dance, an incense burner is passed beneath her dress. Similarly, before drumming at a *zār* ritual begins, the patient is fumigated: an incense burner is put before every body orifice and passed between her legs. The censer is then passed to other adepts, who do likewise.

But the incense mixtures used in these contexts differ, and the nature of their difference dispels any obvious correspondence between the two events. *Bakhūr az-zār, zār* incense, consists of bits of brownish red wood[20] and yellowish mastic resin, a kind of myrrh,[21] with bottled cologne sprinkled over all. This is the basic incense of the *zār* to which other items and perfumes are added according to the identity of the spirit society invoked. For example, frankincense (*kandur*) is added to the brazier when *Khawāja* spirits are summoned (Constantinides 1972 : 158), and local wedding incense is added for *Ḥabish* prostitute *zayran*. Importantly, *zār* incense is meant to be inhaled.

Wedding incense is composed of sandalwood (*ṣandal*), *shaff* (a pale yellow acacia wood), and *kilayt* (a light brown wood with pronounced striations), all said to come from "Africa" to the south and available in the *sūq*. First, the latter two are broken into pieces and set aside. Next the sandalwood is meticulously slivered and saturated with essence of clove. To the leftover clove marinade are added some powdered *ṣandal* and *dufra*

19. Recall too that in the wedding a woman uncovers and/or loosens her hair before performing the pigeon dance.

20. *ʿUda,* a nonspecific term.

21. *Lubān mistīka, Pistacia lentiscus.*

(said to be the tips of crocodile claws); then all three woods are mixed in a wok and the liquid poured over top. Sugar is now added and the combination heated through. When cool, it is sprinkled with cologne and smoked perfumes. Wedding incense is *ḥilū,* sweet, and not to be inhaled. Its purpose is to make fragrant and to purify, to drive away evil spirits attracted by noxious odors.

There is thus a significant contrast between *zār* incense, designed to be inhaled or taken in through other body orifices and intended to attract *zayran,* and uninhalable wedding incense intended to repulse potentially intrusive spirits. Here as elsewhere the difference in treatment received by the two "brides" is between boosting feminine defenses and resisting penetration by alien others in the wedding, and defusing those defenses, thereby encouraging penetration in the *zār.*

Performance

When the bride's *garmosīs* is lifted she begins to perform her wedding dance, eyes closed, led when necessary by her *wazīra* and the groom. With her hands she illustrates in mime the lyrics of each song her friends perform. Though secretly the bride has undergone a week of training for this day, the danger always exists that at the moment of truth she will make a mistake, enact the wrong gesture, miss a beat—that her dance will not be *samiḥ,* beautiful and well executed. Tension, then, is high.

Much as revelation of the bride climaxes the wedding, revelation of the afflicting spirit's identity is the most suspenseful event at a *zār.* Although there will have been indications in the patient's dreams, proclivities, symptoms, and in her responses to certain combinations of incense, drum rhythms, and the *shaykha*'s diagnostic queries, nothing is known for sure until the spirit manifests through her body. In these few anxious moments, adepts assess the validity of prior diagnoses and evaluate the fit between the spirit's performance and the clues it provided during earlier negotiations. In a parallel vein, when the bride dances, she is seen for the first time as a woman, fully prepared and elaborately adorned. For days afterward there is animated discussion among members of the audience as to whether she justifies the claims her family made for her in negotiations with the groom's *wazīr.*

When a spirit decides to manifest itself to those assembled at a *zār,* its host rises to dance. Here too there are correspondences with the wedding. Like the *wazīra* of the bride, the *shaykha* guides the entranced patient, confining her movement to the long dancing mat, for the soles of her feet, like those of the virgin bride, ought not to touch bare earth. Sometimes confinement to the mat is impossible, but should the patient stray, her spirit is offered shoes and kept within the *mīdān.* In contrast to the movements and meaningful gestures of the bride, those of a spirit are considerably freer, less restrained. Yet they must conform to an external text, as do the bride's: the intrusive spirit performs gestures appropriate to its identity, some of which are mentioned in its song. *Khawājāt* smoke innumerable cigarettes or feign doing so if none are available; Ethiopian priests give benediction; *Ḥalibīyat* hawk their wares; *Fallata* beg for grain. But unlike the bride, a spirit is neither shy nor reticent. Its host's face is no longer covered by her *tōb* as it was prior to invasion. For the *zār* wishes to see, to experience the Hofriyati world, and it does so through the eyes of its host. Hence *Lulīya*'s inability to remain blinded to the proceedings when She mockingly performs the wedding dance.

The matter of costumes needs to be addressed. When the bride dances, she wears a dress provided by her husband, which in ways earlier discussed represents his involvement with the world outside of Hofriyat. Similarly, when her spirit descends, a bride of the *zār* dons clothes appropriate to her spirit's identity, and invariably these reflect the nature of the world beyond the village. I should be clear that not all Hofriyati women can afford the elaborate costumes of their spirits: spirit paraphernalia may be borrowed for the occasion, or one part of an outfit—a cane perhaps—will serve to indicate the spirit's presence. A *zār* ritual is dramatic and colorful, yet much of its richness is mimetic: a spirit creates an inpression of itself that must be completed in the imagination, according to participants' knowledge of what that spirit is like. And spirits' costumes, real or imagined, are less limited than those of Hofriyati brides to villagers' actual experiences of other cultures. Here the *zār* ranges further afield than contemporary village men, and reaches deeper into the past.

Both the bride of the *zār* and the bride of the wedding play dramatic roles that are the centerpieces of their respective rituals: each portrays the essence of her discourse. The possessed's performance is an enactment of otherness, of non-Hofriyati reality, of exteriority and openness in the extreme; that of the virgin bride, of enclosedness and self-control, of interiority at its most humanly intense. Yet at the same time, both women *are* the roles they play: the possessed temporarily *is* her intrusive *zār;* the virgin bride is, and is encouraged to think of herself as, the objective exemplar of Hofriyatiness. Ostensible parallels such as these knit together the *zār* and the wedding: the rituals share a network of associations drawn from a common symbolic code. But they conceal disparate meanings. They are related as a language to its antilanguage.

Sacrifice, Blood, and Thresholds

This brings us to some of the more trenchant though nonetheless implicit comments of the *zār* about realities of life in Hofriyat. On the last day of the cure, after the afflicting spirit has revealed its identity and temporarily become manifest in its host, the sacrificial animal necessary to appease it is led forth. The ram's coat must be of a color that corresponds to the spirit's ethnic group, the color symbolically expressing skin tone, appropriate dress, or a salient quality of the society in question. The ram's head, sometimes its back and hooves, have been stained with henna. Over its head is now placed the patient's *garmosīs*. A brazier containing *zār* incense is thrust beneath the cloth while participants sing the thread for *Wilād Mama,* vizier of all *zayran* who accepts the sacrifice on the spirit's behalf. The animal is held in place throughout the chant, and as it strains to free itself its head bobs up and down in the manner of a woman entering trance. The ram is said to be "descending" as the afflicting spirit enters its body. With this, the sheep is slaughtered.

Here an association between the sacrificial victim and the bride of a wedding (and domestic animals and village women, generally) is strongly intimated in the use of the *garmosīs,* henna, incense, and drummed "dance." Yet *zār* meanings are equally patent, for the incense is an inhalable kind that entices *jinn,* and the song to which the animal responds is a "thread" that is being "pulled" (suggestive again of the wedding), inviting the alien to enter the animal's body. Moreover, the ram itself is at once proxy for an icon of enclosure, the "bride," and linked to a foreign society. In all of this, two distinct lines of thought interweave, that of the wedding providing a line of bearing around which the double entrendre of the *zār* revolves.

The parodical nature of the *zār* becomes clearer if one considers the issues of sacrifice and blood. When *Wilād Mama*'s chant has ended, the sacrificial animal is taken to the edge of the *mīdān* where its throat is slit and its spurting blood collected in a bowl. Then the patient steps seven times over the body of her proxy and any of its blood that has spilt on the ground. This act echoes that of pilgrims newly returned from Mecca before reentering their homes, and of the groom newly returned from the Nile who steps over a pool of sheep's blood on the threshold of his bride's *ḥōsh*. The bride of the *zār* is also newly returned: as later discussed, a woman in trance is inwardly transported to the parallel world of *zayran;* out of trance, at the end of the rite, she reverts to the human realm of Hofriyat. Moreover, all three sacrifices take place before thresholds: the *khashm al-bayt* in the case of pilgrims and the groom, the border of the *zār mīdān* in the case of a woman possessed. The two sorts of thresholds are thus metaphorically linked: the former, a potent symbol in Hofriyat of the relationships between woman and man, family and society, the village and the outside world; the latter, the boundary between the place where the alien universe—trebly other and external to Hofriyat—is summoned to appear, and the village core which temporarily contains it, the space within the confines of a *ḥōsh*. Yet the *zār* subverts the clear separation and asymmetric complementarity of inner and outer domains represented by the threshold in the discourse of daily life. For now the alien is within. The possessed's polysemous term for her husband in the language of the *zār*—*bowābi*, "my doorman"—implicitly expresses her consciousness of the burlesque and is entirely apt.

The sacrifice of a ram is modeled on Allah's redemption of Ishmael at the moment he was to be killed by his father, Abraham, on Allah's command.[22] Shedding the animal's blood thus bears connotations of a covenant: between returning pilgrims and God, between bride and groom in a wedding, between spirit and host in the *zār*. Stepping over the animal's body or blood at a threshold suggests a return to mundane reality from a context that is sacred or somehow set apart, and marks the liminality of those enjoined to perform it. *ʿAyāna*, groom, pilgrim, all are initiates undergoing a permanent change of status, and all are symbolically reborn in the covenant blood of the threshold: the figurative vaginal meatus.

Yet the bride of the wedding does not overstep this blood; instead, like the sacrificial victim, she sheds it. When the groom crosses blood on entering the *ḥōsh* of his bride, it is blood shed on *his* behalf: blood spilt next the *khashm al-bayt* foreshadows the vaginal blood she sheds at consummation and childbirth that he might obtain descendants. Like the bachelor groom, the bride of the *zār mīdān* is required to perform the crossover rite just once, however many cures she undertakes. And the blood she steps over is that which was shed on her behalf, that her own blood, the blood of human fertility, might be spared, redeemed from intrusive *zayran*. In the *zār* it is the "bride" who is spared; in the marriage, it is she who is sacrificed.

During a *zār*, blood of the sacrificial victim is used to anoint the patient and other adepts; most, despite religious prohibition, take a sip of it as well. Now the sacrificial animal not only substitutes for the bride of the *zār*,[23] it is also, I noted, an effigy for the bride of a wedding; hence its blood simultaneously represents, in different ways, the blood of both. While the blood of a virgin bride will be shed as a result of her wedding, and it is feminine reproductive blood over which *zayran* wield such con-

22. Or, in its Judeo-Christian equivalent, the sparing of Isaac. As the forbears of Hofriyati were Christian, the model has deep historical precedence.

23. This relationship was graphically illustrated by one of my informants. Her spirit communicated His demand for a ceremony through a dream in which He held a knife to her throat, threatening to slaughter her in the prescribed manner. Here she was substitute for a sheep which would substitute for herself. Constantinides (1972:228–29) gives the following interpretation of the role of the sacrificial victim: "The sheep is alternatively viewed as an obstacle in the patient's path from illness to normality over which she can now step, or as a repository of the illness itself, a patient-substitute, and in leaping over it she leaps away from the illness." In this chapter I have not stressed the medical context of the *zār*, as my emphasis is on its relationship to wedding imagery.

trol, during possession treatment the blood of the bridal proxy is therapeutically incorporated by the very women who suffer blood loss due to others' (husbands', spirits') command of their bodies. Figuratively, the *zār* reverses the inevitable consequence of a wedding and, given the significance of incorporation, provides women an active role in the restoration and maintenance of their fertility, their very lives.

Reproduction, Fertility, and Opening the Head

On the day after the sacrificial culmination of a *zār,* adepts gather in the patient's home for the *fakka-t-ar-rās,* the "opening of the head." Threads are drummed, incense is lit. Now the *shaykha* enters the *mīdān* bearing the boiled head of the sacrificial victim on a tray. While the tray is held in place above the head of the patient, the *shaykha* pulls apart the animal's jaws, opening the head in which the afflicting spirit was briefly housed. Then the patient is fed the "head meat," becoming one with her proxy in more than a figurative sense. Both host and spirit have partaken of the sacrifice: the spirit has received the offering of blood, symbolizing that of the patient herself, while the host consumes the animal parts most closely associated with her possessive *zār.* Their sharing of the victim (specifically, the victim's "feminine" parts: its flesh and blood) confirms their contractual relationship, a relationship forged in blood. Its focus on a third, a mediating entity, serves also to emphasize the separation of spirit and host, who were earlier resident in the same human body. It formally states that the possessed has successfully discriminated between the identities of the afflicting spirit and her Hofriyati self, which constitutes the basis of her cure.

The "opening of the head" through the animal's jaws recalls a number of events associated with the wedding, notably the payments to "open the [bride's] mouth," the "loosening of the [bride's] belt," and the groom's symbolically resonant struggle to enter through the *khashm al-bayt* of the bride's *ḥōsh.* In both ceremonies, the contractual relationship between two individuals is achieved in the symbolic or actual opening of a body orifice. Yet in the *zār* the mouth of the sacrificial victim is not merely opened, but completely pulled apart: here total physical separation of spirit and host is crucial to their contract by which the host's well-being is restored. In the wedding, however, openings are highly restricted and controlled; moreover, its purpose is to cement a social contract by the physical *union* of husband and wife. Emphasis in the wedding is on overcoming social and physical distances: the groom struggles against a succession of obstacles to achieve his wife, to establish a new social unit and the couple's close if unequal interdependence. Emphasis in the *zār* is on overcoming proximity: the ritual creates and maintains distance, separating spirit and host, assuring both of relative autonomy in their continuous relationship. *Zār* executes a mode of alliance other than that which the wedding—in all its meanings—condones.

Recall that at dusk on the "night of the staying," following the formal consummation of marriage the evening before, the groom and his *wazīr* lead guests in a procession to the river, where the groom ritually cleanses himself before returning to the village. Similarly, after the inversive "opening of the head" at the end of *zār,* patient and *shaykha* lead adepts in a procession to the Nile where, like the wedding party, they wade in to wash their faces and arms. Again brides of the *zār* become symbolic grooms. But more than this, they cast into the river the cleaned bones of the sacrificial victim and the remains of the blood collected at its death.

If, as I suggest, the *zār* is a construction on themes at play in the wedding, paralleling that ceremony but presenting its significances from a feminine perspective, what sense can be made of the last event, of throwing the sacrificial remains into the Nile? Friends described it as a beautiful and enjoyable part of the ceremony, but did not pursue the matter further. However, one potential interpretation has to do with memory or myth of an ancient practice: several villagers remarked that it was customary "long before Islam" periodically to sacrifice a virgin to the angels of the Nile by drowning her in the river. And a woman who met her end in such a way was referred to as a bride. Remember that the sacrificial sheep both substitutes for the bride of the *mīdān* and symbolizes the bride of a wedding. Perhaps there is some sense that the spirits of the river, who are, after all, constituent of the *zār* farther north, in Egyptian Nubia, must be rendered their due. It is not entirely far-fetched that the Nile—feminine, fluid, source of fertility—should receive the sacrificial substitute of a human "bride" seeking remedy for problematic fertility.

Still, the parts of the victim disposed of in the Nile are its bones and blood, resonant with the male and female contributions to the body of a child. This extends to the complementary domestic responsibilities of men to provide grain, and women water. On the henna night, bride and groom are invested with protective *jirtig* ornaments that have been dipped first into milk and then into sprouted grain, stressing the couple's productive and reproductive complementarity. Fittingly, in the context of the wedding these contributions have undergone a generative transformation: they have been made potent, moist, activated for nurturance and growth. But in the *zār,* the opposite obtains: the symbolic male and female contributions have been rendered impotent, deactivated; the victim's bones are disjointed and cleaned of all flesh, its blood is dried and caked in a bowl. When the desiccated bone and fluid elements of human reproduction are thrown into the Nile, what meanings might Hofriyati derive from the event?

Given the aged association of the Nile with fertility together with previously established links between fluids and femininity, it is worth noting that Nile water, though consumed by all whenever possible, is obtained especially for pregnant women, for it is considered particularly beneficial to a fetus. Moreover, Zenkovsky (1949 : 40) notes that in Omdurman, a measure taken to encourage conception is to pour Nile water over a woman seated in a *ṭisht,* a flat aluminum basin used also as an instrument for drumming the *zār.* Later, when the woman is toweled and dressed, "she presses a cupful of the same water to her womb under her clothes" (ibid. p. 40). Disposal of the victim's bones and dried blood in the river could thus represent conception, which afflicting spirits invariably threaten to prevent. On the other hand, it might equally signify the reverse, for the "bride's" animal proxy has been killed and disassembled, its ineffectual male and female parts inexorably segregated in the cool, disjunctive current of the Nile. Indeed, it may represent both of these at once, the bittersweet cycle of birth and death, the capricious process of human reproduction for which Hofriyati women assume such thorough liability. And here the ceremony expresses, perhaps, a claim to spirituality that men's control of funerals quietly denies: it extols women's power not only over the birth that brings life, but also (since one must be born before one can die) over the birth that is death.

However it may be read, the association between the *zār* and the wedding is once again apparent, in that it is the purpose of the wedding to create the appropriate conditions for human reproduction, to produce moral persons meriting Allah's reward in the afterlife. The finale of the *zār*—opening the victim's head, consuming its flesh, disposing of its bones and blood in the river—at once signifies, reverses, and ridicules the expected outcome of a wedding: consummation and conception.

And so Sadiya's and Umselima's seemingly bland, transparent statements must now be viewed in a different light: to "love the *zār* more than the wedding" is tacit endorsement of possession's capacity to effect a subjective transformation in the possessed, to make the hidden visible, to "*ẓahr.*" Even if the whole of the *zār*'s satirical, pungent "said" escapes the consciousness of its speakers, this does not invalidate its richness and complexity. For its immanent feminist significances are ever present, recreated with every ritual performance, available to be appropriated by individuals in their reflective moments, or perhaps simply appreciated, implicitly, mutedly—aesthetically.

10

Arrivals: Allegory and Otherness

We next went to the school of languages, where three professors sat in consultation upon improving that of their own country.

The first project was to shorten discourse by cutting polysyllables into one, and leaving out verbs and participles, because in reality all things imaginable are but nouns.

The other project was a scheme for entirely abolishing all words whatsoever; and this was urged as a great advantage in point of health as well as brevity. For, it is plain, that every word we speak is in some degree a diminution of our lungs by corrosion, and consequently contributes to the shortening of our lives.

—Jonathan Swift, "A Voyage to Laputa," *Gulliver's Travels*

In several ways the *zār* rite is a parody, an imaginative construction on the discourse of everyday life. In convention, the *zār* is a ludic portrayal of the Hofriyati wedding[1] and the values it extols. In content, it conjures a menagerie of alien life forms which both caricature and subvert village praxis and the socially appropriate dispositions (Bourdieu's [1979:78] "habitus") of local women and men. Numerous idiomatic links between the wedding and the *zār* combine to cultivate (not ensure) participants' awareness of the *zār*'s allegorical nature, revealed gradually through its extraordinary imagery and verbal puns. For the *zār* not only follows the wedding format in its sequence of ritual acts, it also presents symbols and practices associated with the wedding in unusual contexts, wrenching them from their quotidian significances and repositioning them in startling, often illuminating ways. In this process, the *zār* provides an appropriate ambiance for the invocation of equivocal spirit personalities and, more importantly, for their appropriation by village women. Through its imaginative relationship between content and context, the ritual process itself contributes to the pool of meanings inherent in spirit manifestations.

For instance, the *garmosīs* which veils the exemplary bride at her wedding, and covers women in childbirth and girls at their circumcisions is, in

1. According to Barclay (1964), Constantinides (1972), and Lewis (1986:102), *zār* rituals in the Khartoum area resemble more closely the remembrance ceremonies (*zikrs*) of Islamic fraternities (*ṭarīgat*). In the Hofriyati *zār*, reference to *ṭarīga* symbolism exists but is underplayed.

the *zār,* placed over the head of the sacrificial animal prior to its slaughter. The act is not unlike feminists' crowning of a sheep on the boardwalk of Atlantic City during the 1968 Miss America pageant, and immediately calls up women's self-description—"We are cattle"—with its fan of implications. The *zār* rite deftly reminds the possessed of the fate of all brides. Some of its "messages" are trenchant, acerbic: if sheep are substitute brides, are brides regarded as substitute "sheep"?[2] Others are poignant: where the contract between spirit and bride of the *mīdān* is established through a sacrificial sheep which substitutes for and symbolizes the woman, it is equally true that the contract between a man and his wife in the wedding often results in the unmitigated sacrifice of herself in childbirth. These and other issues raised contribute in turn to meanings immanent in manifestations of, among others, *ʿArab* pastoralist *zayran,* southern Sudanese slaves and cattle keepers, and Ethiopian prostitutes such as *Lulīya,* who demands a *garmosīs.* And the reverse is also true: non-Hofriyati nonhuman beings appearing in the context of a—albeit satirical—wedding, provoke consideration of that ceremony's normal significances.

Thus the *zār* provides opportunity for reversing or adjusting messages appropriated and reproduced by villagers in the marriage rite. The meaning of fumigation is a case in point: in the wedding, uninhalable, unabsorbable incense is passed beneath the bride's dress before she dances in order to parry evil spirits drawn to her vaginal meatus. In the *zār,* inhalable, medicinal incense is passed beneath the "bride's" dress before drumming begins in order to encourage spirits to enter her body. Where the wedding extols the virtue of enclosure, the *zār* underscores the benefit of openness.

But the *zār* says none of this explicitly. Its reference to symbols and events in the wedding is oblique: rather than assault the intelligence, its counterpoint merely tantalizes, suggests a vector of thought as might a work of satirical allegory in Western literature. The *zār* forces neither favorable nor negative conclusions about the Hofriyati wedding and the hegemonic discourse it encodes. Instead it hints, and hints ambiguously. The wedding and its attendant significations are transformed into subjects for reflection, and it is up to participants themselves to assign or derive meaning as and where they will.

2. As Griselda El-Tayib (1987:46–47) notes, *rahaṭs* (no longer worn by Hofriyati maidens, now merely keepsakes locked away in women's metal chests) were always made by women from the skins of domestic animals slaughtered in the ritual way. Unlike *rahaṭs* for everyday use (which were left their natural color), those worn by brides in Hofriyat and elsewhere (ibid., p. 47) were dyed red or dark purple, and referred to as "red." That the skins of domestic animals were worn as clothing affirms the metaphor "we are cattle," while the wedding *rahaṭ*'s color resonates with the theme of blood expressed in the *garmosīs,* the wedding mat, local wedding perfume (*ḥumra,* "redness") and so on. The relation between brides and sheep is obvious.

Comparison with the genre of post-Renaissance satirical allegory is apropos, and warrants further attention. Like the *zār*—here conceived as an unwritten, indigenous text that unfolds anew with every ritual performance—the allegorical writings of, among others, Swift, the second Samuel Butler, Kafka, and Orwell sustain disparate levels of meaning, the one explicit, the other implied, that correspond in the pattern of relationship among their constituent elements (cf. Leyburn 1956 : 6). The structural resemblance between the account as "read" and the underlying reality it satirizes, like that between the *zār* and the wedding in Hofriyat, enables the work's deeper and potentially more contentious significances to lie hidden within the text. Since the surface level of the text exists to illuminate something else, there must, according to Leyburn (1956 : 6), "be likeness enough to make the reader feel that the use of one to stand for the other is legitimate, and also to guarantee that the elect will perceive the hidden meaning." The sense of the work and its representation should not converge, lest the metaphor be lost, nor be too remote, lest dramatic tension evaporate; instead, they should intersect along a common line of bearing (ibid., p. 12). Allegory is an elaborate, protracted metaphor where relationship between lines of thought is supported at both levels of meaning and whose truth resides in their conjunction (cf. Van Dyke 1985; Quilligan 1979).

Van Dyke (1985 : 42) suggests that with allegory, "the reader's task is not simply to identify the components but also to understand the nature of the synthesis—the common denominator, the residual incongruities, the shiftings of balance—by following the signs that constitute and develop the relationship." Although an analyst seeks, as I have done, to identify levels of reference in the text, this is not, she notes, equivalent to reading. And for readers, too, it is but a preliminary stage that prepares one to understand what *can be* said (ibid., p. 43). Reading is an intensely personal process, internal, virtually ineffable. And it must also be distinguished from interpretation, the act of seeking a more authentic text behind the apparent one. For as Todorov (1977) suggests, "reading" does not involve replacing one text by another so much as perceiving the relation between the two.

The *zār*, to provoke a subtle restructuring of women's perceptions—to fulfill its therapeutic mandate—uses the wedding as its foil, its allegorical "pretext" (Quilligan 1979): this accounts for the appearance in the *zār* of marriage symbolism, which sustains the ceremonies' imaginative relationship. And the wedding is, of course, a felicitious choice, since, apart from its other significances, it represents the quintessential moment in every woman's life when her culturally appropriate dispositions are reinforced and she is publicly established as a cultural artifact. Its clear invocation of her self-image as exemplar of Hofriyati values, plus the physical trauma it inevitably occasions for the infibulated bride, subjectively confirms her generative and transformative import to Hofriyati society. The wedding—both as model for transitions at circumcision and childbirth and as celebration of a marriage—is the principal purveyor of a gender identity which, because it is not tenable in real life situations, has precipitated her disenchantment. If she is to be restored to health, the messages of the wedding, its "calls to order from the group" (Bourdieu 1977 : 15), must be modified. But modified delicately, because as a member of the village community she is at once committed to its values just as she is, in another sense, their victim. The *zār* in Hofriyat is a muted expression of adult women's consciousness; but at the same time, I submit, it can only work this way *because* of its mutedness. It is counterhegemonic: it places an alternative construction on lived experience without denying the validity of culturally salient categories. And in this it expresses the sensitivity of women's double consciousness, and their emergent awareness of the contradictions that govern their lives. The didactic purpose of *zār,* like that of other allegorical texts, is achieved by indirection or not at all.

Thus possession's method is an adroitly crafted ambiguity. Controversial realities are embedded in overt text performance, and each gains from association with the other. Possession ritual, viewed as an allegorical genre, is designed to compel the imagination; in making an adjustment between the apparent meaning of the rite and its multiple connotations, a participant leaps to the significance of the *zār* and is initiated to its course. This is, and given its potential subversiveness, must be, a personal, subjective, transformation. But because of that it may be therapeutic. For if discovery occurs through a participant's own intellectual effort, if, in other words, she restructures the *zār* text by reflecting in her own imagination the creative process it embodies, thus renewing the inner consciousness of the work (cf. Honig 1966 : 29), then her consciousness of her own position in Hofriyati society may grow.

Still, initiation to an allegorical text, like initiation to the *zār,* is not always efficacious. Discovery, like health, is not an inevitable outcome. Witness the Irish bishop who, when asked what he thought of *Gulliver's Travels,* said in all honesty, "I don't believe a word of it!" And whenever I read aloud passages of Miner's *Body Ritual among the Nacirema* (1956) to an introductory class, there are always a few who fail to catch on. Hidden meanings are always and only potential in an allegorical text. Readers are shown a direction of thought, not explicitly told what to think. And as anyone who has had to explain the *Nacirema* knows, the impact of the work is appreciably dulled by its exposition. So too with *zār:* the possessed must participate imaginatively for its double communication to be successful, for its underlying messages to be emotionally assimilated and perhaps effect a change of outlook. Whatever a woman's conclusions here might be, witnessing the *zār*'s parallax commentary on the nature of her reality cannot but reaffirm the meaningfulness (if not the meaning) of village culture. For one who is led to acknowledge possession because she suffers severe disenchantment with her life, *zār* offers the possibility of a fresh interpretation for her experience.

Both possession and quotidian discourses share a symbolic code and draw upon a common fund of themes. Yet the discourse of daily life is hegemonic, and must be considered prior to its counterpart in the experience of village women. Although a maiden (*bint*) might think herself possessed, rarely will she admit the affliction until she is married and a "woman" (*marā*); it is only after she has celebrated her wedding that she might undertake a cure on her own behalf. And this, I think, is the point: only after she had been a bride of the wedding might she fully grasp the range of meanings potential in becoming a bride of the *zār*. Although a woman is intimately familiar with the *zār* before her wedding, having attended rituals with kinswomen from an early age, her consciousness of womanhood is incomplete. It is only in the context of full feminine consciousness—sexually active, reproductive—that the allegorical messages of the *zār* can have their sharpest impact.

I have emphasized that the *zār* says nothing explicit about hegemonic values and significances; rather it focuses attention upon them and shows them in unconventional light. Yet there is an overriding message to be derived from possession ritual. Where the wedding celebrates the value of enclosure, symbolically in the body and constrained dance of the bride, and socially in the contractual union of close kin, the *zār* takes a broader perspective. Where the wedding reiterates, through the repeated difficulties experienced by the groom in gaining access to his bride, that openings of the human body and village society are dangerous and must be controlled, the *zār* acquiesces, but moves beyond also to show the reverse. On the one hand, *zayran* admire the ideals of Hofriyati womanhood and enjoin their hosts to revitalize their bridely qualities by bathing with perfumed soaps, eating clean foods, and all the rest. On the other, the *zār* demonstrates the possibility of establishing a contractual relationship between human villagers and alien existents, who not only are nonhuman, but also culturally foreign. Although such relationships can have negative consequences and require continuous negotiation, the *zār* stipulates that benefits can be derived from them as well. Illness and disability can be assuaged—even, perhaps, poverty and subordination.

In earlier chapters I noted that women most often claim to be possessed who are in something of a double bind, where identity or social position is jeopardized. Such women are thus brought face to face with the limitations of hegemonic constructs for which they, paradoxically, provide ultimate expression. Transition rites of the mundane, secular world—

pharaonic circumcision and the wedding—promote their socialization to a culturally overdetermined self-image and fail to encourage the achievement of mature awareness. *Zār* provides occasion to redress this lack by stressing that which lies beyond village society. It orients participants to the possibility of otherness; its antilinguistic, parodic elements create an atmosphere for the directed experience of trance, discussed below. Participation in the *zār* cultivates positive appreciation for the existential as opposed to the ideal, and for ambiguity—in gender constructs, personal relationships, cultural typifications—that can be manipulated by women as well as men to their advantage.

In short, the *zār* emphasizes the importance of openness in a way that directly challenges the cautious, controlled significance of this value as it surfaces in the wedding. Focus in the *zār* is on openings and doorways that lead into an alternate reality: one opens the incense tin to discover which spirits plague her; coins and incense given the diviner are "keys of dreams" that enable her to unlock the door between the human world and the parallel world of *zayran*. As in the wedding, thresholds figure prominently in the *zār,* but their contexts differ significantly: during a *zār* the patient sits facing the door of the *ḥōsh,* confronting, rather than sheltering in, its attendant significances; the slaughter of the sacrificial animal takes place at the limits of the *mīdān,* on the border between the temporarily manifest world of *zayran* and inside, humanly social space. Persons who fail to come out of trance on cue are led out of the *mīdān,* through the doorway of the *ḥōsh* and back again, in an effort to coax the spirit to leave. The term *dastūr,* a synonym for *zār* spirit, colloquially means "permission" and is shouted upon entering a latrine so as to appease resident *jinn.* Yet it also popularly signifies "door jamb" or "bolt" (see Constantinides 1977:65–66 n. 6; Hillelson 1930*a*:35). Moreover, the first spirit to manifest itself when a patient is diagnosed as possessed is said to stand "locking up the door." Once it has appeared, then other *zayran* above her can reveal themselves and disclose their demands (cf. Constantinides 1977:67). In the discourse of possession, doors and other openings link principals not, as they do in the wedding, to other households in the village, but to the world of entities, cultures, and ideas beyond the physical and conceptual precinct of Hofriyat. Thus does the possessed consider her husband a "doorman" in the parlance of the *zār,* for clearly, he is the point of articulation between the planes of her experience: between quotidian realities and alien existence; between commitment and oppression. He actively controls the "doors" that enable a woman to transcend herself: through childbirth, and the possession ritual he is requested to finance.

I mentioned that another issue dealt with in the *zār* is ambiguity. *Zayran* themselves are capricious and ambivalent, evincing simultaneously a penchant for good and, if not exactly evil, then depravity. They are, in fact, amoral, for however ideally restricted by contract, they are erratic in the extreme. That lubricity is their salient trait is captured in another synonym: a *zār* is referred to as a *rīḥ al-āḥmar,* or red wind. A wind, of course, is changeable; and red, in Hofriyat, is the color of ambivalence and marginality especially where feminine blood is concerned. Conceptually, the latter is expressed in the *mushāhara* complex and the notion of *ḥamārayn* ("two reds": sunset and sunrise); materially, in the bridal mat, *garmosīs, ḥumra,* also the *ḥuqq,* a red wooden container for storing *jirtig* perfumes that protect villagers undergoing status transition.[3] Yet if equivocation, ambiguity, and liminality are issues evoked in the *zār,* they are hardly depicted as negative qualities, merely unavoidable. Where, in the discourse of everyday life, openings are dangerous and therefore begrudged, in the *zār* they are revealed to be manageable, and not through minimization but through public acknowledgment and contractual agreement. Where, to use Bourdieu's (1977 : 79) terminology, the "objective intention" of the "habitus" is to restrict openings—in female bodies, families, the village as a whole—so as to attenuate their threat, the extraordinary context of the *zār* implicitly recognizes the futility of such an enterprise and obliquely suggests that villagers cultivate them. Doors, orifices, and other apertures open into a world which clearly presents hazards to the unwitting traveler but which, the *zār* asserts, is knowable and can be dealt with advantageously if one can obtain the compliance of its inhabitants. The logic of possession posits the feasibility of negotiation between Hofriyati, particularly women, and beings which not only are amoral and both culturally and linguistically foreign, but also more powerful than they themselves. Surely at least this is an optimistic message for the woman in conflict with an unyielding "other," her spouse.

Moreover, during *zār* rituals the alien world regularly appears within the very heart of Hofriyat, the family compound, yet no grave alteration in village values and ideals results. Patent here are implications for villagers' dealings with intrusive foreign nationals who have colonized, controlled, or otherwise disrupted them in the past. So too are suggestions for Hofriyati taking employment outside the village, journeying within and beyond the country, or coping with government officials, development workers, and prying anthropologists.

Zār comments on the discourse of enclosure by stressing the nuances of its relativity. It warns that individuals are more complex than their self-

3. Constantinides (1972 : 231) mentions that in the vicinity of Khartoum a *zār* patient wears on her wrist a handkerchief that has been dipped in the blood of the sacrificial animal. This object suggests the *harīra,* the red tasseled bracelet that is part of the *jirtig* donned by the groom on the henna night. In Khartoum and Omdurman the bride of the wedding wears a *harīra* as well (see Cloudsley 1983 : 56), unlike women in Hofriyat who wear it only at their circumcisions. The link between the *zār* and the wedding is clearly not confined to Hofriyat.

idealizations propose. It encourages Hofriyati women to ponder the taken-for-granted world and realize its essential paradox: that despite their drawbacks, indeterminacies in social structure, body orifices, indeed all links to the external world—and their attendant ambiguities—must be maintained if village society is to persist and flourish, and avoid the centripetal collapse that a reification of its values threatens to produce (cf. chapter 3). This is, perhaps, the distilled therapeutic message of the *zār:* it "says" something fundamental about humans and their cultural constructs—that the latter must always be inadequate and the former can only abide by them in relative measure. It admonishes people to remain aware of what happens beyond the village and, paraphrasing its own metaphor, urges them to modulate when up against shifting winds. If villagers remain vigilant when dealing with alien others, the benefits of encounter might well outweigh anticipated harm—if they are but willing to assume the risk. For above all, the logic of possession stipulates that exchange and communication between Hofriyati and other existents is possible without assimilation, without permanent absorption into an alternate reality, and so without jeopardy to the integrity of village culture.

Subordination and Consciousness

Allegory, it is said, is a natural mirror of ideology (Fletcher 1964: 368), and not surprisingly has been of greatest literary import in the West during periods of political conservatism and rigidly hierarchical social organization. The *zār* cult flourishes in Sudan under similar conditions. There, gender hierarchy is marked; however much villagers assert gender complementarity, it is undeniable that women's behavior is more rigorously controlled than men's. Moreover, women are under considerable pressure to conform to the rather specific ideals of their sex—to be chaste and modest, conduct themselves with dignity, marry a "close" kinsman, produce an appropriate complement of offspring. Despite their exhaulted value in Hofriyati society—or possibly because of it—they are jural minors all their lives and subject to notable constraints throughout their reproductive years. And this situation, if the fundamentalist repercussions of men's Arabian labor experience and the recent (1983) declaration of *sharīʿa* law are any indication, is currently intensifying. Here perhaps, is a partial explanation for the rise observed between 1977 and 1984 in the percentage of the female population acknowledging possession (chapter 5). As the constraints of Islam—or of hegemonic constructs locally conceived of as "Islam" but embracing a range of concerns not strictly associated with a properly religious lifestyle—gather strength and threaten to undermine women's position, so it may be that women's resistance, or at least their awareness of the threat, is registered in increased acknowledgment of possession. I am by no means convinced of a direct correspondence, or even that the increase in cult participation reflects other than a demographic shift (figure 5.1), but it is a possibility.

Nonetheless, as parts 2 and 3 of the book have variously tried to document, the *zār* is intimately, and subtly, connected with women's resistance to subordination. This link is less perhaps an instrumental one, as Lewis (1971*a*) earlier suggested, than it is a matter of perception. *Zār,* I propose, is a medium for the cultivation of women's consciousness. To pursue this suggestion requires consideration of women as actors in their world.

At the level of everyday, "natural" reality, women actively negotiate their ascribed subaltern status. And they do so not by denying validity to those constructs which support it, such as their greater amount of sexual magnetism than men's, but, instead, by transcending them (cf. Du Boulay 1986 on women in rural Greece). For Hofriyati women, pharaonic circumcision, modesty, chastity, the maintenance of integrity in all its forms are means whereby the limitations of ascribed inferiority are overcome. Through women's behavior and appropriate dispositions—by their conformity—the social good, order, and morality triumph over self-interest and potential chaos. They use, perhaps unconsciously, perhaps strategically, what we in the West might prefer to consider instruments of their oppression as means to assert their value both collectively, through the ceremonies they organize and stage, and individually, in the context of their marriages, so insisting on their dynamic complementarity with men. This in itself is a means of resisting and setting limits to domination: women publicly demand that their value be socially recognized not by competing with men in a common arena, but by artfully emphasizing their difference from men and using this as a positive source of self-worth.[4] Women are moral exemplars, beings in whom reason has checked the admittedly disruptive effects of sexuality, "keepers of tradition" whose domain is the village, whose concerns are the earthly concerns expressed in crisis rites. But above all, Hofriyati women are mothers, generative, transformative, those entrusted with reproducing village society physically and socially, thereby maintaining and replenishing its moral worth, its symbolic capital.

4. Rogers (1975:732), writing of rural France, suggests that in peasant societies women's selective compliance by behaving in ways that affirm their subordinate status helps to maintain a "myth" of male dominance which disguises gender relations that are more nearly balanced. This is especially true where men and women experience approximately equal dependence on one another socially, politically, and/or economically. To some extent this model holds for Hofriyat; however, men's dependence on women is partially mitigated by the ease with which they can divorce. The central contradiction that women are collectively indispensable but individually dispensable to men renders any assertion of nonhierarchical gender relations fragile at best.

These are aspects of womanhood which men clearly acknowledge and, given the exigencies of labor emigration, just as clearly appreciate, however much their perspective on gender relations varies from that of women.[5] Both genders in Hofriyat occupy common ground that is centered on the bride and immured in her vast associative aura. But if the relevancy of this symbol goes unquestioned, its meaning is an arena of continuous implicit negotiation. Women's strategies, such as their support for pharaonic circumcision, their individual attempts to determine where they reside or whom their sons and daughters marry, their management of their fertility, represent efforts to (re)interpret ideological imperatives and have political ends (cf. Altorki 1986: 160). For as much as women are committed to their cultural system, they are tacitly aware that it oppresses them. The process outlined earlier by which women become social persons is one in which women are active participants, not passive pawns. Yet their attempts to live up to this self-image are fraught with difficulty and may, as we have seen, precipitate illness.

It is here that possession may enter the picture and, if all goes well, amplify a woman's double consciousness to the point where she is able to see her life, her society, her gender, from an altered perspective and heightened sense of awareness. The *zār* provides a second line to the negotiation process, allowing those it claims—or are successfully guided by its allegorical course—the possibility of dealing with others from a position of expanded consciousness. The *zār* at once cultivates, reflexively, a deepened commitment to local values, and fosters recognition of the arbitrary nature of hegemonic constructs. These it presents from a perspective broadened to include alternate ways of life and reformulated in light of women's singular experience. The discourse of possession does not deny the meaningfulness of cultural constructs so much as reorient their strategic value and provide through ritual an opportunity to contemplate them *as such*. It is left to individual women to take up the suggested directions of thought, to question such constructs, if and when they will.

Perhaps it is unsurprising that those women who, while probing my cultural practices, volunteered that their own—such as pharaonic circumcision, endogamy—were neither ineluctable nor universally appropriate, yet morally significant for *them*, were all possessed. That my very presence in the village provoked their reflection is certain. But as the descriptions of spirits attest, the *zār* provides the context, the vehicle through which "spectacles of the other" are dealt with intellectually and actively engaged. During my first visit, for example, one of the possessed received in a spirit

5. Chapters 2 and 3 suggested there are some differences along these lines, but also a great deal of overlap, as evidenced in men's recitation of male and female genealogies when attempting to convey a complete picture of the village social order, i.e., how it is enduringly structured through descent lines of men and integrated through sibling links among women.

dream a song addressed to a foreign archaeologist working nearby. Part of it went like this, "Oh Mr. ______, he has hired young boys to wash his old broken pottery. Why does he not hire women? We, who wash dishes every day, for free—dishes we do not break. Boys cannot do women's work as well as women. Why does he not hire us, we who are poor and need the cash?" Here the conventional idea that "women's work" is an attribute of women jars with the unorthodox demand that they be hired to perform it by a foreign male. The song was extremely popular in the village for several months, and prompted considerable debate among my friends. Though nothing practical came of it, the poet's construction of the apparent injustice, to say nothing of her boldness in publicly articulating a demand for redress, was overtly (and perhaps subjectively) attributed to her spirits' influence.

From this, two implications arise: first, that women's negotiation of their ideological subordination in the context of daily life is undoubtedly affected, reciprocally, by their participation in the *zār*. In other words, it is impossible to separate levels of resistance except heuristically, for in reality strategic compliance and the perception of alternate arrangements creatively interpenetrate. Second, it may be through the *zār* that Hofriyati women will come to address the growing external and perceptibly masculine demand that pharaonic circumcision cease, and achieve alternate understandings of the operation which, in turn, may transform both feminine self-image and local practice in unpredictable ways. For women, possession actively mediates the historical dialectic of acquiescence and resistance, of determined social persons and self-determining actors.

Participation in the *zār* fosters women's increased awareness of their identity as a group, where emphasis in the quotidian context is more particularistic, focusing on individual women's relationships with individual women and men. And importantly, in the process, the *zār* induces participants to see their society—the *nās al-balad* or "country folk"—in categorical terms. Here, gender consciousness spawns, or is itself spawned by, an incipient consciousness of class, an emotional and intellectual realization of the village's conflictual status relative to the surrounding world. From this perspective, *zār* operates to maintain the integrity of villagers' identity as villagers, despite its avowed counterhegemonic tendencies.

It is intriguing that in Hofriyat, women and not, for the most part, men, should embody villagers' historical consciousness. That they do may, I think, be attributable to their dual subordination as women and rural Sudanese. Men, who are dominant within the village because jurally senior to women within Islam, are virtually powerless in respect to the state or other external pressures. Their dominance is, if not illusory (cf. Rogers 1975), at least ambiguous and incomplete. Because they share privileges with elites and more powerful men both in Sudanese society and general

Muslim contexts, their relative disadvantage in state and global terms is, in a sense, mystified. Through migration and, in a more limited way, through agricultural work, men seem to engage the outside world on their own terms and withdraw from it at will. Moreover, they mediate between the village and its surrounds, and as such are less firmly *of* the village than are its womenfolk. All these circumstances militate against their conceiving of themselves as a subaltern class.

For women, jural minority and economic dependency lead them to identify village men with more powerful "others" to some extent, while conditions of rural impoverishment, not wholly relieved by men's involvement in the outside world, identify men with their families in the village. The position of Hofriyati men is, from women's perspective, anomalous, in between. And just as the village is symbolically feminine in relation to powers beyond its walls, whether Western technology, Arabian bankers, or mythical sultan's sons, so are women—and especially women's bodies—appropriate to express, via possession, the historical consciousness of villagers' interactions with the ambivalent, masculine, outside world. So, too, are women more likely to feel their relative disadvantage as rural Sudanese.

Consciousness and Trance

If the *zār* is a medium for cultivating a woman's personal and cultural self-awareness,[6] how might such a *prise de conscience* be brought about? The allegorical nature of *zār* rituals clearly contributes to such an awakening (cf. Honig 1966). So do spirit performance "texts" which, in subtly suggesting fresh interpretations for everyday realities, in their essentially aesthetic task, help to develop adepts' consciousness of themselves. But an equally important factor here is trance, experienced as well as observed. And possession trance occurs in an ambiance clearly other than that of everyday life.

During propitiatory rites, *zayran,* marshaled by drums and attracted by ascending incense, remain "above," waiting their turns to enter the *mīdān* through the bodies of their hosts. Though *zayran* transcend the boundaries between human and spirit worlds in series, all of them are immanent in ritual time and space. For a brief period the patient's room or courtyard becomes the parallel universe, that which is normally invisible to humans and external to Hofriyat. Invariably, the ritual for onlookers and adepts alike is an excursion into the unknown and unexpected, and in this

6. By excluding men from this discussion I do not mean to imply that the *zār* does not also operate for them in this way. In fact its allegorical qualities may be what attracts adult men who confess an admiration for the cult. Unfortunately, I have too few cases to make generalizations about their involvement.

quality too, it is resonant with Western satirical allegory, whose fundamental narrative form is that of an exotic journey, quest, or transformation: "some form of controlled or directed process" (Clifford 1974: 15). During a *zār*, women who, in their ordinary lives, strive to maintain an aura of self-restraint and dignity, suddenly take on bizarre mannerisms, dancing animatedly, even wildly, in an already hot and overcrowded room or congested courtyard, a place made double eerie by the faint glow of oil lamps and heady scent of incense. A *zār* is always something of a surprise for those who attend. Women whose spirits demand their presence approach with a mixture of trepidation and excitement: spirits are powerful, often frightening, yet the rite on the whole is a pleasurable event. Still, one can never foresee when she might be seized by a *zār* that she did not know she had. And spirits, when they descend, may be startlingly innovative in their gestures or demands (see Lambek 1981, 1978; Crapanzano 1977*a*: 16). Some spirits fail to show up when summoned by their chants, for reasons known best to themselves; others choose not to depart their hosts immediately the drumming stops. The actual events of a ritual can never be determined in advance.

But this is not to suggest that trance itself is an unknown or unstructured experience, for nothing could be further from the truth. Setting aside concerns about the authenticity of trance, were it amenable to measurement, it is important to note that Hofriyati employ various methods conducive to developing altered states of consciousness in those who participate (cf. Kiev 1968; Ludwig 1968; Neher 1962; Prince 1964, 1968; Sargant 1957): for example, focusing attention via persistent rhythmic drumming; hyperventilating, including the hyperventilated intake of tobacco smoke; consuming alcohol when available, inducing dizziness by quick up and down movements of the head and torso from a kneeling position, called *nizūl*, "descent." Moreover, from an early age, future adepts and other villagers learn to expect and in some cases cultivate alterations of perception in themselves, for dreams and visions are accorded positive import and prognostic value. Hofriyati, then, are not burdened by those inhibitions which, given an empirical tradition that attaches significance to conscious rationality while disparaging other modes of ideation, seem to prevent members of Western cultures from experiencing trance as readily or willingly as villagers seem to do. At some *zār* rituals I became apprehensive lest I succumb to trance and lose self-control. But Hofriyati do not share my fear. For them, trance, once induced, is tamed if initially uncontrolled by developing the entranced's consciousness of the spirit by which she is possessed. Hofriyati not only are disposed to experience trance, but to experience it in a directed and orderly way.

Questions as to the authenticity or simulation of possession trance, assuming the entranced remains faithful to the possession text, are essentially meaningless to Hofriyati (cf. Middleton [1969: 225]). The reality of trance, which we might wish to define in biomedical terms, is for them perhaps more a social reality than a physical one. Just as possession is real for the possessed (Crapanzano 1977*b*: 141), so trance is real for the possessed in the context of a ritual, whatever her physiological indications to a foreign observer. She is involved, deeply or not, in experiencing and being experienced by an alien form of existence. Hers is a transcendent excursion into otherness.

For importantly, it is through possession trance that her non-self existent becomes subjectively real to the possessed, or "introjected" (cf. Crapanzano 1977*a*: 13), and the culturally overdetermined self may be felicitously repositioned, perhaps transcended. The experience of trance and its observation in others is the locus of possession's creativity, for in trance a woman becomes, legitimately if temporarily, non-Hofriyati. And in doing so she is indirectly cautioned that she and the symbolic constructs that define her sex are separate and distinct, however much the latter inform her image of self. Trance provides her the possibility of insight, yet it does so obliquely, without demanding she take responsibility for her conclusions.

To begin with the notion of introjection, or the patient's subjective realization of a spirit's attachment and influence, the self of the possessed is not merely absent or repressed during trance in deference to that of the spirit, but, according to Hofriyati, actively engaged. I asked several women what happens to them when *zayran* enter their bodies; the answers I received are remarkably similar, confirming that trance is, to some extent, experienced according to a public model of what it ought to be like, and reinforcing the notion that active possession is neither frightening nor uncontrolled. Though she may be unaware of what her *zār* is doing while manifest to others, she is, villagers say, still aware, for when she and her spirit coalesce in her body they exchange experiential domains. As Asia says,

> When it descends into you, you "go the limit" until the drumming stops, and then the person stops. When the drums are beating, beating, you hear nothing, you hear from far away, you feel far away. You have left the *mīdān,* the place of the *zār.* And you see, you have a vision. You see through the eyes of the European. Or you see through the eyes of the West African, whichever spirit it is. You see then as a European sees—you see other Europeans, radios, Pepsis, televisions, refrigerators, automobiles, a table set with food. You forget who you are, your village, your family, you know nothing from your life. You see with the eyes of the spirit until the drumming stops.

Asia's description is echoed by other adepts too numerous to mention. Saraitti, for example, told me that were she to see me at a *zār* ritual when possessed by her *Khawāja* spirit she would see me not in the village, surrounded by goats, sand, and dark-skinned Hofriyati, but in Canada, my own country, surrounded by things with which I am familiar, behaving as it is appropriate for *khawājīyat* to behave among their own: drinking liquor, smoking, going to the cinema with unrelated men.

Among other peoples, descriptions like these are, to my knowledge, rare: adepts in most possession cults have, or are supposed to have, no memory of the event.[7] But in Hofriyat such reports are common. They indicate that the entranced is indeed, as Crapanzano (1977*a*: 9) suggests, "lost from her socially constructed self." Yet, equally, they suggest that the experience does not involve a "depossession" of self, the temporary absence to herself of the entranced's soul or essence, which de Heusch (1962) has argued is the necessary complement to spirit intrusion. Instead, trance for Hofriyati, though controlled by the spirit and regulated by human drumming, is a participatory act. While the spirit fords boundaries between the visible and invisible worlds to become manifest in its host's gestures and audible through her voice, she herself is transported to another domain. She transcends the visible world and "sees with the eyes of the spirit" into the normally invisible parallel universe.[8] Given the efficacy of "seeing" in Hofriyat, the possessed is now internally transformed. And she has, less a mystical experience, than an eminently social one. For that brief period, she forgets who she is, her village and family; she "knows nothing from her life." In having such a vision or, to keep faith with villagers' description, in briefly stepping outside of Hofriyat and into another world, a woman also briefly divests her self of its personhood, of its normative contents and constraints. And in proportion to her subjective experience of otherness, her everyday reality is made to appear as one of many—less naturalized, less unquestionable, indeed, less subjectively real.[9]

In more than a figurative or vicarious sense, host and spirit now participate in each other's essence. Yet the construction of their relationship is similar to that of a literary metaphor, for metaphor, like possession, consists in a predication (cf. Fernandez 1974; Ricoeur 1976: 50). Possession, however, is a mutual predication. Borrowing Fernandez's (1974) phrasing, the spirit, named or soon to be named and having certain known characteristics, is predicated upon an inchoate human subject, she who is led to possession by dysphoria and disillusionment. And as a result, the possessed's inchoate feelings are structured and objectified (Crapanzano 1977*a*: 16). But the human host, visible, named, having a social identity known to observers, is reciprocally predicated on an inchoate spirit, who

7. See, for examples, Lambek (1978, 1981); Leiris (1958).

8. As Wallace (1959) has so ably demonstrated, how one experiences an altered state of consciousness is strongly influenced by cultural meanings and expectations.

9. See also Kapferer (1983: 201).

gains concreteness for possessed and audience alike. Formless in its own universe, and variably diffuse in the minds of adepts, it enters the known human world through the visible body of its material host. Two worlds coalesce in the temporary trance experience of the possessed, each entity becoming the other while ultimately remaining itself. Spirit and human do not unite, but gain identity by briefly becoming what they are not. When the drumming stops, the possessed returns to herself, exhausted, a little dazed, but as villagers say, feeling well.

The experience of trance is, I have noted, a cultural one.[10] Spirits are recognized entities; their social milieus are known, if incompletely understood. Yet despite this cultural patterning or, in fact, because of it, trance is a liminal excursion. By the possessed's own admission, the experience is one of temporary isolation, of alienation from her Hofriyati world.

There is, I think, a subtle difference between this situation and what Kapferer (1983, 1986) suggests takes place during the complex Sinhalese exorcism ceremony, which it is instructive to explore. There the demonic victim comes to the ritual already in "an existential state of solitude in the world" (Kapferer 1986: 185), and it is the purpose of the ceremony to reintegrate her with society. This is accomplished in the structure of the performance where "the culturally understood subjective world of the patient finds external form" (ibid., p. 199): the demonic, in all its chaos and terror, becomes temporarily manifest and dominant in the human world. Having drawn the victim's family and friends—nonpossessed participants—to experience what is construed to be the subjective state of the possessed, and thus linked their perceptions, the ritual then proceeds, via a subsequent comedic episode, to reassert cultural order and bring both patient and audience back into the world of shared understandings (ibid., p. 201).

In Hofriyat it is not so much that shared understandings are precipitately undermined by a woman's untoward experience, but that the rigidity of these understandings and her emotional identification with them may *prevent* them from being undermined, prevent her from being able to appreciate the distinction between ideals and the exigencies of concrete situations. If anything, she is too firmly grounded in her world. In villagers' view, spirits are attempting to subvert the order of that world but she resists their influence—as she is exhorted to do. Yet as curers and adepts rightly observe, it is only when she lets them in, when she loosens her hold on her reality and enters an "existential state of solitude," that she can begin to recover.

And recovery entails participation in *zār* ritual: the experience and

10. The substance of remaining pages in this section appeared first in *American Ethnologist* 15 (1) (Boddy 1988).

observation of trance, exposure to its allegorical direction. Like other such ritual moments, the occasion is rife with ambiguities and potential ambivalences: the qualities of spirits when juxtaposed to those of humans give play to the imagination. The aesthetic power of the *zār* rests with its capacity to thrust into proximity disparate ideas and diverse realities (cf. Geertz 1973:444; Bateson 1972:203 ff.; Turner 1977:68), to wrest concepts from their everyday constructions and juxtapose them in novel and sometimes highly surprising and informative ways, yet always to keep them apart. The dialectic of self and other, of Hofriyati women and foreign *zayran,* is one from which no true synthesis can emerge. Human and spirit contextualize each other, maintain each other in contraposition. During possession dramas, two levels of meaning—quotidian and extraordinary—oscillate and nourish one another, enabling the ritual to accumulate the weight of allegory with each spirit manifestation, challenging would-be readers to derive their own inferences and create their own solutions. It is during such episodes that, as Burridge (1979:145) argues, the would-be individual "perceives a hidden message and accepts the invitation to explore." Possession trance encourages reflection, a limited dismantling of the taken-for-granted world, enabling the possessed, in its aftermath, to see her life in a very different light. It affords the participant an opportunity to mature, to grow, as Turner (1982:114) says, through antistructure to grasp not only her context, but the context of her context (cf. Bateson 1972). Possession is as much a cultural aesthetic: a means to perceive new and rewarding or possibly disturbing significances in what was tacitly accepted as given, as it is therapy: a means to correct faulty perceptions, to cure.

Many who consider possession trance and ritual to be legitimate psychotherapy nonetheless disclaim their capacity to promote insightful reflection among the possessed (Bourguignon 1979:290–91; Kennedy 1967:191; Prince 1964:115). Such "folk" therapies are generally considered to be effective in repatterning idiosyncratic conflicts and defenses in culturally appropriate ways, and furnishing a corrective emotional experience, the sanctioned release of negative affect (Bourguignon 1979:274; Devereaux 1980:17–18; Kennedy 1967:189; Kleinman 1980:169–70). Here the patient's condition may be remedied, not cured, though her acknowledged vulnerability to relapse may be mitigated if she is incorporated into a cult providing group support for a healthful reorientation (Bourguignon 1979:291; Kennedy 1967:191–92; Lewis 1971*a;* Messing 1958:1125). Yet, despite the success of "folk" psychotherapies in securing symptom remission, and regardless of how culturally appropriate such techniques may be, they are often dismissed as lacking when compared with Western psychoanalysis (Kiev, 1964; e.g., Derret 1979:291; Ozturk 1964:362). And they are judged deficient because apparently unable to provide the patient an opportunity for mature reflection which constitutes the basis for a psychiatric cure (Devereaux 1980: 17–18).

Such views do little justice to the richness of the possession experience. In Hofriyat the context of possession carries within it the potential for insightful self-examination, however differently conceived from that of Western psychoanalysis. For what constitutes insight into the self—and the society in which it is located—is surely described by the cultural construction of an individual's selfhood. In cases of neurosis in Western cultures, psychotherapy provides a context in which the patient can learn to objectivate himself through conversation, to gain distance from an exaggerated "I." In Hofriyat possession trance provides a context in which the patient is encouraged to achieve distance from her cultural context, the source of her overobjectification. Both therapies aim at replenishing the culturally specific constitution of the self by exploring and transcending former pitfalls: as individuals acquire insight into the process of self construction, healthy, more appropriate dispositions of selfhood are suggested.

In the *zār,* dialogue takes place between a woman and her spirit(s)—her nonself—internally, through visions and dreams, and externally, via the reports of fellow villagers about her spirit's actions during trance (cf. Lambek 1980). Through such oblique discussion the possessed might work through her problems to achieve a greater understanding of herself and her society (Crapanzano 1977*a*: 26). She is now given occasion to effect a degree of detachment from the gender constructs that have so completely shaped her being and, in the process, to establish a firmer basis in consciousness for negotiating her subordination. Possession, like anthropology, is a reflexive discourse: through it Hofriyati women might step outside their world and gain perspective on their lives.

Trance is a significant factor in this process, whether experienced or observed. It has been defined as a temporary, subjectively felt change in an individual's reality orientation accompanied by a fading to abeyance of reflective, critical awareness (Deikman 1969: 45; Ludwig 1968; Shor 1969: 246; Van der Walde 1968). If we accept this view, the woman who sees into the spirit world during trance is in a state of heightened receptivity; she becomes, like the Ndembu initiand, a virtual tabula rasa (Turner 1969*b*: 103). If her trance is deep enough and involving enough, she is thus presented with pure experience, vivid, unedited, emotionally real, and not just once, but several times as throughout the ritual she takes on a sequence of other selves. It may not be during trance that she deepens her understanding of herself but afterward, in remembering her trance experiences (cf. Kapferer 1986: 198) as she is expected to do. Such insights as are gleaned come indirectly, through witnessing several dimensions of what her self is not. Yet none of this is certain. The therapeutic efficacy of possession trance resists objective measurement, as does any aesthetic experience. For some who say they "see things differently," this may signal a real change in outlook, somatic disposition, and emotional balance. For others, it may not.

When discussing the therapeutics of possession trance, its potential effect on an unentranced audience (adepts and observers) is rarely considered. But possession trance is only part experience; it is also part performance (Leiris 1958). When *zayran* manifest themselves in the bodies of their hosts, a catalog of otherness springs to life. The spirits behave in ways appropriate to their respective ethnic groups, social roles, religions, and sex. They may be wanton and undignified, take on superior airs, beg piteously, dance about wildly, speak in brash tones or coy ones, exhibit any conduct fitting to their type. Spirits may be kings or slaves, prostitutes, nuns, male homosexuals, merchants, Coptic priests, fierce tribal warriors. When a spirit's chant is sung and all whom it possesses ideally enter trance, it manifests itself in each simultaneously, sometimes presenting different aspects of its character, but always interacting with the audience in strange and sometimes terrifying ways.

To observe possession trance in another is to witness a paradox: a woman who is not who she is—not human, not Hofriyati, not even, in most cases, female. Although the identities of the possessed and her intrusive *zār* are distinct, and it is the aim of the ceremony to cultivate awareness of their distinction in the possessed, for observers this separation of entities is not always easy to maintain. During trance the two are brought into intimate and often perplexing association, and as noted in chapter 4, those describing the episode often refer to the woman and her spirit interchangeably. Yet this risk of confusion, this ambiguity, is I think key to the aesthetics and the therapeutics of *zār* in Hofriyat. Just as when one sees a play, the interpretation of a trance event is never wholly given in the event but must, in part, be constructed anew by each observer, who brings to the moment her own past experiences, present concerns, and critical awareness. But unlike the audience at a play, the Hofriyati observer of possession trance is utterly committed to the literal reality of what she sees. And what she sees is someone at once essential to her own construction of self and a symbol of it, who is also her own sheer antithesis. This thorough paradox, taken with the various properties of the entranced and her spirit, their individual traits and biographies, and the relations of parody, travesty, and inversion among elements of the display, makes possible any number of readings, destructuring naturalized associations and temporarily freeing ideation from its moorings in the everyday world. In the course of a ceremony the possessed alternately observes and experiences trance; thus, for an entire evening she is given to see herself and those around her as in a hall of mirrors, the proportions of her selfhood shifting from moment to moment, context to context, now familiar, now alien, now frightening, now bizarre. In the course of her long association with the *zār* there are many such occasions, each affording her the possibility of new insights, refined understandings, and continued growth.

Zār (as both possession and performance) is a powerful medium for unchaining thought from the fetters of hegemonic cultural constructs and, to paraphrase Ricoeur (1976), for opening it up in different and possibly illuminating directions. In the possession (meta)context, of which trance is an integral part, the self becomes a pure issue: a subject for contemplation, negotiation, and, perhaps, felicitous regeneration. If possession ultimately cannot assuage women's chronic subordination, it clearly works to cultivate awareness, feminist consciousness, in the possessed. To rephrase an old adage: woman's reach should exceed her grasp, or what's a "meta" for?

Ethnography through the Looking Glass: A Womb with a View

At the same time, culture itself becomes available for contemplation in the *zār*. Not only are particular spirits and humans mutually predicated on each other, but the entire universe of other societies and alien existents is negatively predicated on Hofriyati praxis, giving the latter an implied objectivity and significance rarely apparent to those who live it day by day. And as an aesthetic genre the *zār*, like satirical allegory in Western literature, permits a great deal to be implied which might be too inappropriate, heretical, or politically dangerous to express overtly. Ricoeur (1976:47) describes the literary text as "that use of discourse where several things are specified at the same time and where the reader is not required to choose among them. It is the positive and productive use of ambiguity." This is even truer in the case of allegory, where the relationship between the author and the meaning of her text is more than usually opaque: by choosing her method she automatically disclaims responsibility for readers' inferences. It is also true in the case of the *zār*, where human "authors" disavow authorship entirely: whatever is said is said by spirits, whose existence is a matter of fact. In both "genres," worlds peopled by alien beings—disproportionate humans, spirits, foreigners, animals—counterpoint the lived-in worlds of the works' intended audiences. The practices of these alien societies exaggerate, invert, travesty, and distort the authors' own, which are implied in the texts by their absence or, when present, injected to provide moments of contrast for the exotic and arcane. Indeed, such texts could pass as ethnographies. And ethnographies most certainly they are, but ethnographies by reflection. Swift, Butler, the women of Hofriyat, all use other cultures as means to speak about their own.

For their part, Western satirical allegories have much of the flavor of anthropology's classic texts, and in some ways adumbrate the current trend toward self-conscious, experimental ethnography first critiqued by Marcus and Cushman in 1982.[11] A number are written as accounts of journeys to distant lands, as the travel memoirs of those who have lived for extensive periods in societies quite different from their own—for example, Butler's *Erewhon* and Swift's *Gulliver's Travels*. Like many anthropological monographs, they are written with an extravagance of realistic detail (maps supplied) that lends credibility to the imaginary lands they depict. Gulliver, sounding like the exemplary meticulous fieldworker, tells us that his descriptions of Lilliputians are based on the nine months and thirteen days he spent among them, and so sets out the limitations of his work. He conscientiously places himself in the narrative, revealing his many indiscretions while learning to conform to his hosts' standards of conduct, and writing with a naive literalness about the hazards he faced, how he coped, what he ate, indeed, how he eliminated. He does not wholly refrain from judging the peoples he visits, yet his attitude toward them—his "voice" or, of course, Swift's—is mainly that of a scientifically detached participant-observer; his account has the factual tone of explorer's reports to the Royal Society. But for all this, Gulliver is not unaffected by his informants. Like the ethnographer who immerses herself in an alien culture, or like Hofriyati who journey to other cultures during trance, he experiences his most severe culture shock on returning home.

Irish bishops notwithstanding, Swift's work is not about other societies. He clearly did not intend his readers to believe that Lilliputians and Brobdingnagians existed. Instead, it is auto-ethnographical. And, although *zayran* exist unquestionably for Hofriyati, the result in that case is much the same.

Anthropological monographs, while they declare themselves to be about the cultures they depict, can be read in a similar light. To say that our ethnographies are fictions, as to say that *zayran* are not real, is clearly to overstate the case: we hardly construct from whole cloth. Yet surely, since we write at a physical and cultural remove from our subjects, we portray highly processed visions of their worlds. What we have to say about other cultures is doubly filtered, first, in the course of observation, then through the writer's memory and the constraints of her medium. The outcome is a kind of allegory based—like that of the *zār*—on actual observations of human foreigners, but—as in Hofriyat—put together so as to meet the demands for cultural coherence which the "author" shares with her audience. In either case the product is a negotiated one, which in turn acts as a foil for more culture-bound readers' lives. But despite our best intentions—whether explicit or, as in the *zār,* covert—the meanings readers may take from our works cannot be determined in advance . . .just as *Animal Farm*

11. See also Marcus and Fischer (1986) and Clifford and Marcus (1986).

might yield a different significance to contemporary animal rights activists than to those who lived through the events of Stalinist Russia.[12]

The analogy I am suggesting between the anthropological enterprise and the *zār* extends beyond their common allegorical qualities. The two systems allegorize each other. Like possession, the doing of anthropological fieldwork is a participatory act, one involving the literal predication of an investigator on initially inchoate others. The investigator, named and socially situated, having a known ethnic or national identity, predicates her humanity on a group of alien beings in the conviction that by becoming the other, however temporarily, she will achieve an understanding of and accommodation to their lives. Just as the *zār* rite provides villagers with the possibility of learning what it means to be non-Hofriyati, fieldwork, rite of passage that it is for aspiring adepts, provides the investigator with the possibility of becoming lost from her socially constructed self and, in the process, of learning what it means to be the other.

In "seeing through the eyes of the spirits," my friends in the village were accomplishing, to their satisfaction, what I labored for in living among them, a reciprocal understanding of the world through *their* eyes. While our assumptions and theoretical paradigms were often at odds, we both firmly believed in the reality—the possibility—of our ventures. Together we brought to our respective field situations a load of cultural biases that surely obscured our visions. Our separate endeavors were coincidentally intellectual and affective; we would come away from them feeling that we had learned something not only about others, but also about ourselves.

Both fieldwork and possession are, in a special sense, forms of aesthetic perception. Both stem from what are basically gnostic traditions, rooted in the conviction that knowledge is achieved through transcendence of the self in the other. But more than this, perhaps, both rest on a tacit acknowledgment that what is attained is self-knowledge as much as it is knowledge of an alien reality.

However temporally limited, the anthropological experience, like possession, is continuously interactive, an ongoing reciprocal predication. Just as the spirits of transient non-Hofriyati remain in the village, leaving something of their essence encapsulated in the *zār,* so the spirits of our informants remain with us long after we have returned from the field. Their voices haunt our memories, inform our daily lives. Much like Hofriyati, an ethnographer exorcises these possessive others, or at least (and in my own case, I hope) symbolically placates them, in writing her ethnographic articles and monographs.[13] We, too, transform our experiences of otherness into cultural texts.

12. More seriously, perhaps, one is reminded of the New York publisher who turned down Orwell's book with the remark, "Americans aren't interested in animal stories."

13. For a lively discussion along similar lines, see Lewis (1986 : 6 ff.).

Yet the corresponding influence of us as other to our informants should not be underestimated. As I was preparing to leave the field, Saraitti, a *sitt al-ʿilba,* was consulted by a woman who suspected she was possessed. That night in a diagnostic dream, Saraitti saw her female Egyptian spirit, a Christian *Khawājīya,* fly away to Canada and return to the village in the company of a *Khawājīya zār* called *Sitt an-Nisa,* Lady of the Women, who carried metal with which to make musical instruments for the *zār.* The development was, for me, provocative. So, I thought, if something of my informants' essence remains with me, then something of mine remains with them, in the form of a female *Khawāja* spirit whose unflatteringly inquisitive mannerisms I recognized too clearly as my own, and, just as I was renowned for clanging from *ḥōsh* to *ḥōsh* weighed down with camera, tape recorder, and a mess of house keys each the size of a spoon, a spirit linked with metal, exemplar of Western materialism. It was, in fact, only after the conception of *Sitt an-Nisa* that I realized the extent to which the *zār,* whatever else it does, provides a path to knowledge through experiential reciprocity: provoking an anthropological *prise de conscience* through "spirit" and human participant observation. Possession and ethnographic inquiry clearly intersect.

But everyday life in the village goes on, foreigners come and go, and just as clearly, the ethnographer must not *over*estimate her influence as enduring other to her informants. On returning to Hofriyat six years later, it was a humbling experience to learn that *Sitt an-Nisa* was no longer around and had never, in fact, become firmly established. Saraitti's patient's *zār* soon turned out to be a manifestation of the Coptic spirit *Sitt agh-Ghwayshat,* Lady of the Bracelets. The reasons for *Sitt an-Nisa*'s demise are likely manifold, but I have no doubt that my departure from the village contributed to a perception that whatever external influences I may have exerted were no longer culturally relevant. While *Gordel,* spirit analogue of the British General Gordon, has taken leave of Hofriyati *mīdāns*, *Bernowi,* the Baggara soldier *zār* of the Mahdi's Islamic regime, continues to appear. Still, I am grateful for the insight *Sitt an-Nisa* afforded me, however short-lived Her existence.

In his *Moroccan Dialogues* (1982) Dwyer cautions that the reflexive effect of Western ethnographies may be to strengthen our own institutions and cultural constructs, not—as with satire or the *zār*[14]—to deconstruct and critically examine them. And this, because the questions we put to our informants are implicitly dictated by *our* concerns, not theirs. Fair enough: we may never come to know another culture as it is actually lived by its participants. Yet this need not invalidate the enterprise, only its more extreme claims to scientific "truth." When read, in part, as allegory, eth-

14. Though, as noted throughout this discussion, the *zār* and, for that matter, satirical allegory support cultural practice as much as they criticize it.

nographies contain a wealth of potential messages about the culture they silently imply: some critical, others clearly supportive. Their power, like that of other allegorical genres, lies in their capacity to contextualize the world from which they spring (Clifford 1986). And this is a distinctly human preoccupation: all cultures and times have their ethnographers and their ethnographic "texts." For as Boon suggests,

> A "culture" can materialize only in counterdistinction to another culture. . . . Before any culture can be experienced *as a culture* displacement from it must be possible; and . . . there is no place outside it to be except in other cultures or in their fragments and potentialities. (Boon [1982 : ix]; emphasis in the original)

If—*pace* Eliot—we can learn less about other cultures than we had hoped from our intensive explorations of them, there may be some consolation that the point all along has been to learn about our own. And the achievement of self-awareness may be necessary for learning to inhabit a world of selves and others more felicitously, however powerful, capricious, or amoral they might seem. Whatever else ethnography is and has been, perhaps it, like the *zār*, is a form of subordinate discourse whose elusive, yet allusive "said" confers the possibility of expanded consciousness, even therapeutic realignment.

References
Index

References

Abdalla, Raqiya Haji Dualeh
1982 *Sisters in Affliction: Circumcision and Infibulation of Women in Africa.* London: Zed Press.

Abu-Lughod, Lila
1986 *Veiled Sentiments: Honor and Poetry in a Bedouin Society.* Berkeley: University of California Press.

Adams, William Y.
1967 Continuity and Change in Nubian Cultural History. *Sudan Notes and Records* 48 (1 and 2): 1–32.
1984 *Nubia: Corridor to Africa.* London: Allen Lane.

Al-Guindi, Fadwa
1978 The Angels of the Nile: A Theme in Nubian Ritual. In *Nubian Ceremonial Life,* edited by John Kennedy, pp. 104–113. Berkeley: University of California Press.
1987 Female Circumcision in Historical and Cultural Perspective. Paper presented at the symposium, Clitoridectomy and Infibulation ("Female Circumcision") in Africa, Yale University, April 25.

Al Hadi al Nagar, Samia
1987 Women and Spirit Possession in Omdurman. In *The Sudanese Woman,* edited by Susan Kenyon, pp. 92–115. Khartoum: University of Khartoum Graduate College Publications no. 19.

Al-Naqar, ʿUmar
1971 The Historical Background to "the Sudan Road." In *Sudan in Africa,* edited by Y. F. Hasan, pp. 98–108. Khartoum: Khartoum University Press.

Al-Safi, Ahmed
1970 *Native Medicine in the Sudan: Sources, Conception, and Methods.* Khartoum: Khartoum University Press.

Al-Shahi, Ahmed S.
1972 Proverbs and Social Values in a Northern Sudanese Village. In *Essays in Sudan Ethnography,* edited by Ian Cunnison and Wendy James, pp. 87–104. New York: Humanities Press.

Altorki, Soraya
1980 Milk Kinship in Arab Society: An Unexplored Problem in the Ethnography of Marriage. *Ethnology* 19: 233–44.

1986 *Women in Saudi Arabia: Ideology and Behavior among the Elite*. New York: Columbia University Press.

Ammar, Hamed

1954 *Growing Up in an Egyptian Village*. London: Routledge and Kegan Paul.

Anonymous

1920 Two Murder Trials in Kordofan. *Sudan Notes and Records* 3(4): 245–59.

Ardener, Edwin

1975 Belief and the Problem of Women and the "Problem" Revisited. In *Perceiving Women,* edited by Shirley Ardener, pp. 1–28. London: J. M. Dent.

Area Handbook: Republic of the Sudan

1960 Washington, D.C.: Superintendent of Documents, U.S. Government Printing Office.

Arkell, A. J.

1961 *A History of the Sudan from the Earliest Times to 1821*. 2d ed. London: Athlone Press.

Asad, Talal

1986 The Concept of Cultural Translation in British Social Anthropology. In *Writing Culture: The Poetics and Politics of Ethnography,* edited by James Clifford and George E. Marcus., pp. 141–64. Berkeley: University of California Press.

Assaad, Marie Bassili

1980 Female Circumcision in Egypt: Social Implications, Current Research, and Prospects for Change. *Studies in Family Planning* 11(1): 3–16.

Austin, J. L.

1962 *How to Do Things with Words*. Oxford: Clarendon Press.

Ayoub, Millicent

1959 Parallel Cousin Marriage and Endogamy: A Study in Sociometry. *Southwestern Journal of Anthropology* 15: 266–75.

Babcock, Barbara

1978 Introduction to *The Reversible World: Symbolic Inversion in Art and Society,* edited by Barbara Babcock, pp. 13–36. Ithaca, N.Y.: Cornell University Press.

Bakhtin, Mikhail

1981 *The Dialogic Imagination*. Edited by Michael Holquist, translated by Caryl Emerson and Michael Holquist. Austin: University of Texas Press.

Balandier, George

1970 *Political Anthropology*. New York: Random House.

Barclay, Harold

1964 *Buurri al-Lamaab: A Suburban Village in Sudan*. Ithaca, N.Y.: Cornell University Press.

Barth, Fredrik

1954 Father's Brother's Daughter Marriage in Kurdistan. *Southwestern Journal of Anthropology* 10: 164–71.

1969 Introduction to *Ethnic Groups and Boundaries: Social Organization of Cultural Differences,* edited by Fredrik Barth. Boston: Little, Brown and Co.

1973 Descent and Marriage Reconsidered. In *The Character of Kinship,* edited by J. Goody, pp. 3–19. Cambridge: Cambridge University Press.

Basso, Keith

1979 *Portraits of "the Whiteman": Linguistic Play and Cultural Symbols among the Western Apache.* New York: Cambridge University Press.

Bates, Daniel, and Amal Rassam (Vinogradov)

1983 *Peoples and Cultures of the Middle East.* Englewood Cliffs, N.J.: Prentice-Hall.

Bateson, Gregory

1958 *Naven.* Stanford, Calif.: Stanford University Press.

1972 *Steps to an Ecology of Mind.* New York: Ballantine.

1982 Difference, Double Description, and the Interactive Designation of Self. In *Studies in Symbolism and Cultural Communication,* Publications in Anthropology no. 14, edited by F. Allan Hanson, pp. 3–8. Lawrence: University of Kansas.

Becker, A. L.

1979 Text-Building, Epistemology, and Aesthetics in Javanese Shadow Theatre. In *The Imagination of Reality: Essays in Southeast Asian Symbolic Systems,* edited by A. L. Becker and A. Yengoyen, pp. 211–43. Norwood, N.J.: Ablex.

Bell, Diane

1984 *Daughters of the Dreaming.* Winchester, Mass.: Allen and Unwin.

Berger, Peter L.

1967 *The Sacred Canopy: Elements of a Sociological Theory of Religion.* Garden City, N.Y.: Doubleday.

Berger, Peter L., and Thomas Luckmann

1966 *The Social Construction of Reality.* Garden City, N.Y.: Doubleday.

Bergson, Henri

1950 *Le Rire: Essai sur la signification du comique.* Paris: Presses Universitaires de France.

Besmer, Fremont E.

1983 *Horses, Musicians, and Gods: The Hausa Cult of Possession-Trance.* South Hadley, Mass.: Bergin and Garvey.

Bledsoe, Carolyn

1980 *Women and Marriage in Kpelle Society.* Stanford, Calif.: Stanford University Press.

1984 The Political Use of Sande Ideology and Symbolism. *American Ethnologist* 11(3):455–72.

Boddy, Janice

1982*a* Parallel Worlds: Humans, Spirits, and *Zār* Possession in Rural Northern Sudan. Ph.D. dissertation, University of British Columbia.

1982*b* Womb as Oasis: The Symbolic Context of Pharaonic Circumcision in Rural Northern Sudan. *American Ethnologist* 9(4):682–98.

1985 Bucking the Agnatic System: Status and Strategies in Rural Northern Sudan. In *In Her Prime: A New View of Middle-Aged Women,* edited by Judith K. Brown and Virginia Kerns, pp. 101–116. South Hadley, Mass.: Bergin and Garvey.

1988 Spirits and Selves in Northern Sudan: The Cultural Therapeutics of Possession and Trance. *American Ethnologist* 15(1):4–27.

Boon, James A.

1982 *Other Tribes, Other Scribes.* New York: Cambridge University Press.

Bourdieu, Pierre

1977 *Outline of a Theory of Practice.* Translated by Richard Nice. London: Cambridge University Press.

1979 Symbolic Power. *Critique of Anthropology* 4(13 and 14):77–85.

Bourguignon, Erika

1966 World Distribution and Patterns of Possession States. In *Trance and Possession States,* edited by Raymond Prince, pp. 3–34. Montreal: R. M. Bucke Memorial Society.

1973 Introduction: A Framework for the Comparative Study of Altered States of Consciousness. In *Religion, Altered States of Consciousness, and Social Change,* edited by Erika Bourguignon, pp. 3–35. Columbus: Ohio State University Press.

1976 *Possession.* San Francisco: Chandler and Sharp.

1979 *Psychological Anthropology.* New York: Holt, Rinehart and Winston.

Brown, Judith K.

1970 A Note on the Division of Labor by Sex. *American Anthropologist* 72:1073–78.

Bruce, James

1813 *Travels to Discover the Source of the Nile.* Vols. 1–7. 1790. Reprint. Edinburgh: George Ramsay.

Buckley, Thomas

1988 Menstruation and the Power of Yurok Women. In *Blood Magic: The Anthropology of Menstruation,* edited by Thomas Buckley and Alma Gottlieb, pp. 187–209. Berkeley: University of California Press.

Buckley, Thomas, and Alma Gottlieb, eds.

1988 *Blood Magic: The Anthropology of Menstruation.* Berkeley: University of California Press.

Budge, E. A. Wallis

1907 *The Egyptian Sudan, Its History and Monuments.* Vols. 1 and 2. London: Kegan Paul.

Burckhardt, John Lewis

1922 *Travels in Nubia.* 1819. Reprint. London: John Murray.

Burridge, Kenelm O. L.

1979 *Someone, No One: An Essay on Individuality.* Princeton, N.J.: Princeton University Press.

Butler, Samuel

1935 *Erewhon.* 1872. Reprint. Harmondsworth: Penguin.

Cailliaud, Frederic

1826 *Voyage à Meroe 1819–1822.* Vols. 1–4. Paris: L'Imprimerie royale.

Caraveli, Anna

1986 The Bitter Wounding: The Lament as Social Protest in Rural Greece. In *Gender and Power in Rural Greece,* edited by J. Dubisch, pp. 169–94. Princeton, N.J.: Princeton University Press.

Cerulli, Enrico

1934 *Encyclopaedia of Islam,* s.v. Zar.

Chodorow, Nancy

1974 Family Structure and Feminine Personality. In *Woman, Culture and Society,* edited by Michelle Z. Rosaldo and Louise Lamphere, pp. 43–99. Stanford, Calif.: Stanford University Press.

1978 *The Reproduction of Mothering.* Berkeley: University of California Press.

Clifford, Gay

1974 *The Transformations of Allegory.* London: Routledge and Kegan Paul.

Clifford, James

1986 On Ethnographic Allegory. In *Writing Culture: The Poetics and Politics of Ethnography,* edited by J. Clifford and G. Marcus, pp. 98–121. Berkeley: University of California Press.

Clifford, James, and George Marcus, eds.

1986 *Writing Culture: The Poetics and Politics of Ethnography.* Berkeley: University of California Press.

Cloudsley, Ann

1983 *Women of Omdurman: Life, Love, and the Cult of Virginity.* London: Ethnographica.

Cohen, Abner

1974 *Two Dimensional Man: An Essay on the Anthropology of Power and Symbolism in Complex Society.* London: Routledge and Kegan Paul.

Colie, Elizabeth

1966 *Paradoxia Epidemica: The Renaissance Tradition of Paradox.* Princeton, N.J.: Princeton University Press.

Colson, Elizabeth

1969 Spirit Possession among the Tonga of Zambia. In *Spirit Mediumship and Society in Africa,* edited by J. Beattie and J. Middleton, pp. 69–103. London: Routledge and Kegan Paul.

Collier, Jane, and Michelle Z. Rosaldo

1981 Politics and Gender in Simple Societies. In *Sexual Meanings: The Cultural Construction of Gender and Sexuality,* edited by Sherry B. Ortner and Harriet Whitehead, pp. 275–329. New York: Cambridge University Press.

Comaroff, Jean

1985 *Body of Power, Spirit of Resistance: The Culture and History of a South African People.* Chicago: University of Chicago Press.

Comaroff, John L.

1986 One-Party Democracy, Two-Party Autocracy: A Transcultural Discourse in Political Philosophy. Unpublished manuscript, University of Chicago.

Comaroff, John L., and Jean Comaroff

1981 The Management of Marriage in a Tswana Chiefdom. In *Essays on Af-*

rican Marriage in Southern Africa, edited by E. J. Krige and J. L. Comaroff, pp. 29–49. Cape Town: Juta.

1987 The Madman and the Migrant: Work and Labor in the Historical Consciousness of a South African People. *American Ethnologist* 14(2): 191–209.

Comaroff, John L., and Simon Roberts

1981 *Rules and Processes: The Cultural Logic of Dispute in an African Context.* Chicago: University of Chicago Press.

Constantinides, Pamela

1972 Sickness and the Spirits: A Study of the "Zaar" Spirit Possession Cult in the Northern Sudan. Ph.D. dissertation, University of London.

1977 "Ill at Ease and Sick at Heart": Symbolic Behavior in a Sudanese Healing Cult. In *Symbols and Sentiments,* edited by loan M. Lewis, pp. 61–83. New York: Academic Press.

1982 Women's Spirit Possession and Urban Adaptation in the Muslim Northern Sudan. In *Women United, Women Divided: Comparative Studies of Ten Contemporary Cultures,* edited by P. Caplan and D. Bujra, pp. 185–205. Bloomington: Indiana University Press.

Crapanzano, Vincent

1973 *The Hamadsha: A Study in Moroccan Ethnopsychiatry.* Berkeley: University of California Press.

1977*a* Introduction to *Case Studies of Spirit Possession,* edited by Vincent Crapanzano and Vivian Garrison, pp. 1–39. New York: John Wiley.

1977*b* Mohammed and Dawia: Possession in Morocco. In *Case Studies of Spirit Possession,* edited by Vincent Crapanzano and Vivian Garrison, pp. 141–76. New York: John Wiley.

1980 *Tuhami: Portrait of a Moroccan.* Chicago: University of Chicago Press.

Crowfoot, J. W.

1919 Angels of the Nile. *Sudan Notes and Records* 2(3): 183–97.

1922 Wedding Customs in the Northern Sudan. *Sudan Notes and Records* 5(1): 1–28.

Cucchiari, Salvatore

1988 "Adapted for Heaven": Conversion and Culture in Western Sicily. *American Ethnologist* 15(3): 417–41.

Cunnison, Ian.

1966 *Baggara Arabs: Power and the Lineage in a Sudanese Nomad Tribe.* Oxford: Clarendon Press.

Daly, Mary

1987 *The Wickedary.* Boston: Beacon.

Das, Veena

1973 The Structure of Marriage Preferences: An Account from Pakistani Fiction. *Man,* n.s. 8(1): 30–45.

de Beauvoir, Simone

1974 *The Second Sex.* 1953. Reprint of English edition translated by H. M. Parshley. (First published in French in 1949.) New York: Random House.

de Heusch, Luc
1962 *Cultes de possession et religions initiatiques de salut en Afrique*. Brussels: Annales du Centre d'Etudes des Religions.

Deikman, Arthur J.
1969 Deautomization and the Mystic Experience. In *Altered States of Consciousness,* edited by Charles T. Tart, pp. 25–46. New York: Anchor Books.

Delaney, Carol
1988 Mortal Flow: Menstruation in Turkish Village Society. In *Blood Magic: The Anthropology of Menstruation,* edited by Thomas Buckley and Alma Gottlieb, pp. 75–93. Berkeley: University of California Press.

DelVecchio Good, Mary-Jo
1980 Of Blood and Badies: The Relationship of Popular Islamic Physiology to Fertility. *Social Science and Medicine* 14(B) : 147–56.

Derret, J. Duncan
1979 Spirit Possession and the Gerasene Demoniac. *Man,* n.s. 14(2): 286–93.

Devereaux, George
1980 *Basic Problems of Ethnopsychiatry.* Translated by Basia Miller Gulati and George Devereaux. Chicago: University of Chicago Press.

Douglas, Mary
1966 *Purity and Danger: An Analysis of Concepts of Pollution and Taboo.* London: Routledge and Kegan Paul.
1973 *Natural Symbols.* Harmondsworth: Penguin.

Dubisch, Jill
1986*a* Introduction to *Gender and Power in Rural Greece,* edited by Jill Dubisch, pp. 3–41. Princeton, N.J.: Princeton University Press.
1986*b* Culture Enters through the Kitchen: Women, Food, and Social Boundaries in Rural Greece. In *Gender and Power in Rural Greece,* edited by Jill Dubisch, pp. 195–214. Princeton, N.J.: Princeton University Press.

Dubisch, Jill, ed.
1986 *Gender and Power in Rural Greece.* Princeton, N.J.: Princeton University Press.

Du Boulay, Juliet
1986 Women—Images of Their Nature and Destiny in Rural Greece. In *Gender and Power in Rural Greece,* edited by Jill Dubisch, pp. 139–68. Princeton, N.J.: Princeton University Press.

Dumont, Louis
1972 *Homo Hierarchicus: The Caste System and Its Implications.* Paperback ed. London: Paladin.

Dwyer, Daisy
1978 *Images and Self-Images: Male and Female in Morocco.* New York: Columbia University Press.

Dwyer, Kevin
1982 *Moroccan Dialogues: Anthropology in Question*. Balitmore, Md.: Johns Hopkins University Press.

Eickelman, Christine
1984 *Women and Community in Oman*. New York: New York University Press.

Eickelman, Dale F.
1976 *Moroccan Islam: Tradition and Society in a Pilgrimage Center*. Austin: University of Texas Press.
1981 *The Middle East: An Anthropological Approach*. Englewood Cliffs, N.J.: Prentice-Hall.

El Dareer, Asma
1982 *Woman, Why Do You Weep? Circumcision and Its Consequences*. London: Zed Press.

El Saadawi, Nowal
1977 *Woman and Psychological Conflict*. Cairo: al-muᶜassasa al-ᶜArabiya lil-dirassat wa'l-nashr.

El Tayib, Abdalla
1955 The Changing Customs of the Riverain Sudan. *Sudan Notes and Records* 26(2):146–58.

El-Tayib, D. Griselda
1987 Women's Dress in the Northern Sudan. In *The Sudanese Woman*, edited by Susan Kenyon, pp. 40–66. Khartoum: Graduate College Publications no. 19, University of Khartoum.

Elster, Jon
1986 Introduction to *The Multiple Self*, edited by Jon Elster, pp. 1–34. Cambridge: Cambridge University Press.

Evans-Pritchard, E. E.
1976 *Witchcraft, Oracles and Magic among the Azande*. 1937. Reprint. London: Oxford University Press.

Fakhouri, Hani
1968 Zar Cult in an Egyptian Village. *Anthropological Quarterly* 41(1):49–56.

Farb, Peter, and George Armelagos
1980 *Consuming Passions: The Anthropology of Eating*. New York: Washington Square Press.

Fernandez, James
1974 The Mission of Metaphor in Expressive Culture. *Current Anthropology* 15:119–46.
1980 Edification by Puzzlement. In *Exploration in African Systems of Thought*, edited by I. Karp and C. S. Bird, pp. 44–59. Bloomington: Indiana University Press.
1982 The Dark at the Bottom of the Stairs: The Inchoate in Symbolic Inquiry and Some Strategies for Coping with it. In *On Symbols in Anthropology: Essays in Honor of Harry Hoijer 1980*, edited by Jacques Maquet, pp. 13–43. Malibu, Calif.: Udena Publications.
1985 Macrothought. *American Ethnologist* 12(4):749–57.

Firth, Raymond
1967 *Tikopia Ritual and Belief.* Boston: Beacon.
Fletcher, Angus
1964 *Allegory: The Theory of a Symbolic Mode.* Ithaca, N.Y.: Cornell University Press.
Foster, George
1987 On the Origin of Humoral Medicine in Latin America. *Medical Anthropology Quarterly,* n.s. 1(4):355–93.
Foucault, Michel
1972 *The Archaeology of Knowledge.* 1969. Translated by A. M. Sheridan. London: Tavistock.
1980 *Power/Knowledge: Selected Interviews and Other Writings.* Edited by C. Gordon. Translated by C. Gordon, L. Marshall, J. Mepham, and K. Soper. New York: Pantheon.
Friedl, Ernestine
1975 *Women and Men: An Anthropologist's View.* New York: Holt, Rinehart and Winston.
Frobenius, L.
1913 *The Voice of Africa.* Vol. 2. London: Hutchinson.
Gassim, Awn al-Sharif
1965 Some Aspects of Sudanese Colloquial Arabic. *Sudan Notes and Records* 46(1 and 2):40–49.
Geertz, Clifford
1968 *Islam Observed: Religious Development in Morocco and Indonesia.* Chicago: University of Chicago Press.
1973 *The Interpretation of Cultures.* New York: Basic Books.
1983 *Local Knowledge: Further Essays in Interpretive Anthropology.* New York: Basic Books.
Geertz, Clifford, H. Geertz, and L. Rosen, eds.
1979 *Meaning and Order in Moroccan Society: Three Essays in Cultural Analysis.* New York: Cambridge University Press.
Geertz, Hildred
1979 The Meanings of Family Ties. In *Meaning and Order in Moroccan Society: Three Essays in Cultural Analysis,* edited by C. Geertz, H. Geertz, and L. Rosen, pp. 315–91. New York: Cambridge University Press.
Ghalioungui, Paul
1963 *Magic and Medicinal Science in Ancient Egypt.* London: Hodder and Stoughton.
Gilbert, John P., and Eugene A. Hammel
1966 Computer Simulation and Analysis of Problems in Kinship and Social Structure. *American Anthropologist* 68(1):71–93.
Gilligan, Carol
1982 *In a Different Voice: Psychological Theory and Women's Development.* Cambridge, Mass.: Harvard University Press.
Gluckman, Max
1955 *The Judicial Process among the Barotse.* Manchester, England: Manchester University Press.
1965 *Custom and Conflict in Africa.* Glencoe, Ill.: Free Press.

Goffman, Erving
1974 *Frame Analysis: An Essay on the Organization of Experience*. New York: Harper and Row.

Goldberg, Harvey
1967 FBD Marriage and Demography among Tripolitanian Jews in Israel. *Southwestern Journal of Anthropology* 23:176–91.

Gomm, Roger
1975 Bargaining from Weakness: Spirit Possession on the South Kenya Coast. *Man,* n.s. 10:530–43.

Goody, J.
1980 Thought and Writing. In *Soviet and Western Anthropology,* edited by E. Gellner. New York: Columbia University Press.

Gramsci, Antonio
1971 *Selections from the Prison Notebooks*. Edited and translated by Quintin Hoare and Geoffrey Nowell Smith. New York: International Publishers.

Gray, Robert F.
1969 The Shetani Cult among the Segeju of Tanzania. In *Spirit Mediumship and Society in Africa,* edited by J. Beattie and J. Middleton, pp. 171–87. London: Routledge and Kegan Paul.

Gruenbaum, Ellen
1982 The Movement against Clitoridectomy and Infibulation in the Sudan: Public Health Policy and the Women's Movement. *Medical Anthropology Newsletter* 13(2):4–12.

Hale, Sondra
1985 Women, Work, and Islam: Sudanese Women in Crisis. Paper presented at the Annual Meeting of the American Anthropological Association, 3–8 December. Washington, D.C.

Halliday, M. A. K.
1976 Anti-Languages. *American Anthropologist* 78:570–84.

Hamer, John, and Irene Hamer
1966 Spirit Possession and Its Socio-Psychological Implications among the Sidamo of Southwest Ethiopia. *Ethnology* 5:392–408.

Hamnett, Ian
1967 Ambiguity, Classification, and Change: The Function of Riddles. *Man,* n.s. 2:379–92.

Harris, Grace
1957 Possession "Hysteria" in a Kenyan Tribe. *American Anthropologist* 59:1046–66.
1978 *Casting Out Anger: Religion among the Taita of Kenya*. London: Cambridge University Press.

Hasan, Yusuf Fadl
1967 *The Arabs and the Sudan from the Seventh to the Early Sixteenth Century*. Khartoum: Khartoum University Press.

Haycock, Brian G.
1971 The Place of the Napatan-Meroitic Culture in the History of the Sudan and Africa. In *Sudan in Africa,* edited by Yusuf F. Hasan. Khartoum: Khartoum University Press.

1972 Mediæval Nubia in the Perspective of Sudanese History. *Sudan Notes and Records* 53 (1 and 2): 18–35.

Hayes, Rose Oldfield
1975 Female Genital Mutilation, Fertility Control, Women's Roles, and the Patrilineage in Modern Sudan: A Functional Analysis. *American Ethnologist* 2: 617–33.

Hilal, Jamil
1972 Father's Brother's Daughter Marriage in Arab Communities: A Problem for Sociological Explanation. *Mid East Forum* 46(2): 73–84.

Hillelson, S.
1930*a* *Sudan Arabic, English-Arabic Vocabulary.* 2d ed. London: Sudan Government.
1930*b* Nubian Origins. *Sudan Notes and Records* 13(1): 137–48.

Hills-Young, Elaine
1940 Charms and Customs Associated with Childbirth. *Sudan Notes and Records* 23(2): 331–35.

Holt, P. M., and M. W. Daly
1979 *The History of the Sudan from the Coming of Islam to the Present Day.* London: Weidenfeld and Nicolson.

Holy, Ladislav
1988 Gender and Ritual in an Islamic Society: The Berti of Darfur. *Man,* n.s. 23: 469–87.

Honig, Edwin
1966 *Dark Conceit: The Making of Allegory.* New York: Oxford University Press.

Huelsman, Ben R.
1976 An Anthropological View of Clitoral and Other Female Genital Mutilations. In *The Clitoris,* edited by T. P. Lowery and T. S. Lowery, pp. 111–61. St. Louis, Mo.: Warren H. Green.

Hurreiz, Sayyid H.
1977 *Jaʿaliyyin Folktales: An Interplay of African, Arabian and Islamic Elements.* Bloomington: Research Center for Language and Semiotic Studies, Indiana University.

Hutt, C.
1972 *Males and Females.* London: Penguin.

Irigaray, Luce
1985 *This Sex Which Is Not One.* Translated by Catherine Porter. Ithaca, N.Y.: Cornell University Press.

Isbell, Billie Jean
1985 *To Defend Ourselves: Ecology and Ritual in an Andean Village.* Prospect Heights, Ill.: Waveland Press.

James, Wendy
1988 *The Listening Ebony: Moral Knowledge, Religion, and Power among the Uduk of Sudan.* Oxford: Clarendon Press.

James, William
1918 *Principles of Psychology.* Vol. I. 1890. Reprint. New York: H. Holt.

Jilek, Wolfgang G.
1974 *Salish Indian Mental Health and Culture Change*. Toronto: Holt, Rinehart and Winston.

Kapferer, Bruce
1983 *A Celebration of Demons: Exorcism and the Aesthetics of Healing in Sri Lanka*. Bloomington: Indiana University Press.
1986 Performance and the Structure of Meaning and Experience. In *The Anthropology of Experience,* edited by V. W. Turner and E. M. Bruner, pp. 188–206. Chicago: University of Illinois Press.

Kegan, Robert
1982 *The Evolving Self: Problem and Process in Human Development*. Cambridge, Mass.: Harvard University Press.

Kehoe, Alice B., and Dody H. Giletti
1981 Women's Preponderance in Possession Cults: The Calcium Deficiency Hypothesis Extended. *American Anthropologist* 83(3):549–61.

Kennedy, John G.
1967 Nubian Zar Ceremonies as Psychotherapy. *Human Organization* 26(4):186–94.
1978*a* Nubia: History and Religious Background. In *Nubian Ceremonial Life,* edited by John Kennedy, pp. 1–18. Berkeley: University of California Press.
1978*b* Mushahara: A Nubian Concept of Supernatural Danger and the Theory of Taboo. In *Nubian Ceremonial Life,* edited by John Kennedy, pp. 125–50. Berkeley: University of California Press.
1978*c* Circumcision and Excision Ceremonies. In *Nubian Ceremonial Life,* edited by John Kennedy, pp. 151–70. Berkeley: University of California Press.

Keyser, James M. B.
1974 The Middle Eastern Case: Is There a Marriage Rule? *Ethnology* 13(3): 293–309.

Khuri, Fuad I.
1970 Parallel Cousin Marriage Reconsidered: A Middle Eastern Practice That Nullifies the Effects of Marriage on the Intensity of Family Relationships. *Man,* n.s. 5(4):597–618.

Kiev, Ari
1964 The Study of Folk Psychiatry. In *Magic Faith and Healing,* edited by A. Kiev, pp. 3–35. New York: Free Press (Macmillan).
1968 The Psychotherapeutic Value of Spirit Possession in Haiti. In *Trance and Possession States,* edited by R. Prince, pp. 143–48. Montreal: R. M. Bucke Memorial Society.

Kirwan, L. P.
1937 A Contemporary Account of the Conversion of the Sudan to Christianity. *Sudan Notes and Records* 20(2):289–95.

Kleinman, Arthur
1980 *Patients and Healers in the Context of Culture*. Berkeley: University of California Press.

Knight, James

1985 Gender and Twareg Ideologies of Production and Reproduction. Paper presented at the Annual Meeting of the American Anthropological Association, 3–8 December, Washington, D.C.

Koestler, Arthur

1975 *The Act of Creation.* 1964. Reprint. London: Pan.

Kronenberg, A., and W. Kronenberg

1965 Parallel Cousin Marriage in Mediæval and Modern Nubia, Part 1. *Kush* 13:241–60.

La Barre, Weston

1975 Anthropological Perspectives on Hallucination and Hallucinogens. In *Hallucination: Behavior, Experience and Theory,* edited by R. K. Segal and L. J. West. New York: John Wiley.

La Fontaine, J. S.

1985*a* *Initiation: Ritual Drama and Secret Knowledge around the World.* London: Penguin.

1985*b* Person and Individual: Some Anthropological Reflections. In *The Category of the Person,* edited by M. Carrithers, S. Collins, and S. Lukes, pp. 123–40. Cambridge: Cambridge University Press.

Lambek, Michael

1978 *Human Spirits: Possession and Trance among the Malagasy Speakers of Mayotte.* Ph.D. dissertation, University of Michigan. Ann Arbor: University Microfilms.

1980 Spirits and Spouses: Possession as a System of Communication among the Malagasy Speakers of Mayotte. *American Ethnologist* 7(2):318–31.

1981 *Human Spirits: A Cultural Account of Trance in Mayotte.* New York: Cambridge University Press.

Forthcoming From Disease to Discourse: Remarks on the Conceptualization of Trance and Spirit Possession. In *Altered States of Consciousness and Mental Health: A Cross-Cultural Perspective,* edited by Colleen Ward. Sage.

Langer, Suzanne K.

1942 *Philosophy in a New Key: A Study in the Symbolism of Reason, Rite, and Art.* New York: Mentor.

Leach, Edmund R.

1958 Magical Hair. *Journal of the Royal Anthropological Institute.* 88:147–64.

Leacock, Eleanor

1981 *Myths of Male Dominance.* New York: Monthly Review Press.

Leiris, Michel

1958 *La Possession et ses aspects théâtraux chez les Ethiopiens de Gondar.* L'Homme: Cahiers d'ethnologie, de géographie et de linguistique. Paris: Plon.

Lévi-Strauss, Claude

1966 *The Savage Mind.* Chicago: University of Chicago Press.

1969*a* *The Elementary Structures of Kinship.* Edited by R. Needham. Translated by J. H. Bell and J. R. Von Sturmer. Boston: Beacon.

1969*b* *The Raw and the Cooked.* Translated by J. Weightman and D. Weightman. New York: Harper and Row.

Lewis, Ioan M.

1966 Spirit Possession and Deprivation Cults. *Man,* n.s. 1(3):307–329.

1969 Spirit Possession in Northern Somaliland. In *Spirit Mediumship and Society in Africa,* edited by J. Beattie and J. Middleton, pp. 188–219. London: Routledge and Kegan Paul.

1971*a* *Ecstatic Religion: An Anthropological Study of Spirit Possession and Shamanism.* Baltimore, Md.: Penguin Books.

1971*b* Spirit Possession in North-East Africa. In *Sudan in Africa,* edited by Yusuf F. Hasan, pp. 212–27. Khartoum: Khartoum University Press.

1983 Spirit Possession and Biological Reductionism: A Rejoinder to Kehoe and Giletti. *American Anthropologist* 81(2):416–17.

1986 *Religion in Context: Cults and Charisma.* Cambridge: Cambridge University Press.

Leyburn, Ellen Douglass

1956 *Satiric Allegory: Mirror of Man.* New Haven, Conn.: Yale University Press.

Ludwig, Arnold M.

1968 Altered States of Consciousness. In *Trance and Possession States,* edited by R. Prince, pp. 69–96. Montreal: R. M. Bucke Memorial Society.

MacMichael, Harold A.

1967 *A History of the Arabs in the Sudan.* 1922. Vols. 1 and 2. 2d ed. London: Frank Cass.

Malinowski, Bronislaw

1931 *Encyclopedia of the Social Sciences,* s.v. culture.

1948 *Magic, Science and Religion, and Other Essays.* Boston: Beacon Press.

Marcus, George, and Dick Cushman

1982 Ethnographies as Texts. *Annual Review of Anthropology* 11:25–69.

Marcus, George, and Michael Fischer

1986 *Anthropology as Cultural Critique.* Chicago: University of Chicago Press.

Meeker, Michael E.

1976 Meaning and Society in the Near East: Examples from the Black Sea Turks and the Levantine Arabs. *International Journal of Middle East Studies* 7(2):243–70 and 7(3):383–422.

Messick, Brinkley

1987 Subordinate Discourse: Women, Weaving, and Gender Relations in North Africa. *American Ethnologist* 14(2):210–25.

Messing, Simon D.

1958 Group Therapy and Social Status in the Zar Cult of Ethiopia. *American Anthropologist* 60(6):1120–26.

Middelton, John

1969 Spirit Possession among the Lugbara. In *Spirit Mediumship and Society in Africa,* edited by J. Beattie and J. Middleton, pp. 220–31. London: Routledge and Kegan Paul.

Miner, Horace
1956 Body Ritual among the Nacirema. *American Anthropologist* 58: 503–7.
Ministry of Information and Culture, Government of Sudan
n.d. *Facts about the Sudan*. Khartoum: External Information and International Relations Administration.
Modarressi, Tahgi
1968 The Zar Cult in South Iran. In *Trance and Possession States,* edited by Raymond Prince, pp. 149–55. Montreal: R. M. Bucke Memorial Society.
Mohammed Kheir, Hag Hamid
1987 Women and Politics in Medieval Sudanese History. In *The Sudanese Woman,* Graduate School Publications no. 19, edited by Susan Kenyon, pp. 8–39. Khartoum: University of Khartoum.
Moi, Toril
1985 *Sexual/Textual Politics: Feminist Literary Theory*. London: Methuen.
Money, John, and Patricia Tucker
1975 *Sexual Signatures: On Being a Man or a Woman*. Toronto: Little, Brown.
Moore, F. C. T.
1975 An Approach to the Analysis of Folktales from Central and Northern Sudan. In *Directions in Sudanese Linguistics and Folklore,* edited by S. H. Hurreiz and H. Bell. Khartoum: Khartoum University Press.
Moore, Sally Falk
1975 Epilogue: Uncertainties in Situations, Indeterminacies in Culture. In *Symbol and Politics in Communal Ideology,* edited by S. F. Moore and Barbara Myerhoff. Ithaca, N.Y.: Cornell University Press.
Morsy, Soheir
1978 Sex Roles, Power, and Illness in an Egyptian Village. *American Ethnologist* 5:137–50.
Murphy, Robert, and Leonard Kasdan
1959 The Structure of Parallel Cousin Marriage. *American Anthropologist* 61:17–29.
1967 Agnation and Endogamy: Some Further Considerations. *Southwestern Journal of Anthropology* 23:1–13.
Mustafa, Zaki
1971 *The Common Law in the Sudan*. Oxford: Clarendon Press.
Nalder, L. F.
1935 Folklore and Fable in the Sudan. In *The Anglo-Egyptian Sudan from Within,* edited by J. A. de C. Hamilton. London: Faber and Faber.
Neher, Andrew
1962 A Psychological Explanation of Unusual Behavior in Ceremonies Involving Drums. *Human Biology* 4:151–60.
Nelson, Cynthia
1971 Self, Spirit Possession, and World-View: An Illustration from Egypt. *International Journal of Psychiatry* 17:194–209.

Nordström, H.
1972 Neolithic and A Group Sites. Report. Scandinavian Joint Expedition to Sudanese Nubia Publications 3, no. 1.

Obeyesekere, Gananath
1970 The Idiom of Possession. *Social Science and Medicine* 4:97–111.
1981 *Medusa's Hair: An Essay on Personal Symbols and Religious Experience.* Chicago: University of Chicago Press.

O'Brien, Jay
1986 Toward a Reconstitution of Ethnicity: Capitalist Expansion and Cultural Dynamics in Sudan. *American Anthropologist* 88(4):898–907.

Ohnuki-Tierney, Emiko
1984 *Illness and Culture in Contemporary Japan: An Anthropological View.* London: Cambridge University Press.

Okely, Judith
1975 Gypsy Women: Models in Conflict. In *Perceiving Women,* edited by Shirley Ardener, pp. 55–86. London: J. M. Dent.

O'Laughlin, Bridget
1974 Mediation of Contradiction: Why Mbum Women Do Not Eat Chicken. In *Woman, Culture, and Society,* edited by Michelle Z. Rosaldo and Louise Lamphere, pp. 301–20. Stanford, Calif.: Stanford University Press.

Onwuejeogwu, Michael
1969 The Cult of the Bori Spirits among the Hausa. In *Man in Africa,* edited by Mary Douglas and Phyllis Kaberry, pp. 279–305. London: Tavistock.

Ortner, Sherry
1973 On Key Symbols. *American Anthropologist* 75:1338–46.
1974 Is Female to Male as Nature Is to Culture? In *Woman, Culture and Society,* edited by Michelle Z. Rosaldo and Louise Lamphere, pp. 67–87. Stanford, Calif.: Stanford University Press.

Ortner, Sherry B., and Harriet Whitehead
1981 Introduction: Accounting for Sexual Meanings. In *Sexual Meanings: The Cultural Construction of Gender and Sexuality,* edited by Sherry B. Ortner and Harriet Whitehead, pp. 1–27. New York: Cambridge University Press.

Orwell, George
1951 *Animal Farm.* 1945. Reprint. Harmondsworth: Penguin.

Ozturk, Orhan M.
1964 Folk Treatment of Mental Illness in Turkey. In *Magic, Faith and Healing,* edited by A. Kiev, pp. 343–63. New York: Free Press.

Patai, Raphael
1965 The Structure of Endogamous Unilineal Descent Groups. *Southwestern Journal of Anthropology* 21:325–50.

Peckham, Morse
1967 *Man's Rage for Chaos: Biology, Behavior and the Arts.* New York: Schocken.

Peters, Emyrs
1972 Shifts in Power in a Lebanese Village. In *Rural Politics and Social Change in the Middle East,* edited by R. Antoun and I. Harik. Bloomington: Indiana University Press.

Pouillon, Jean
1982 Remarks on the Verb "to Believe." In *Between Belief and Transgression,* edited by M. Izard and P. Smith, pp. 1–8. Chicago: University of Chicago Press.

Prince, Raymond
1964 Indigenous Yoruba Psychiatry. In *Magic, Faith and Healing,* edited by A. Kiev, pp. 84–120. New York: Free Press.
1968 Can the EEG Be Used in the Study of Possession States? In *Trance and Possession States,* edited by R. Prince, pp. 121–37. Montreal: R. M. Bucke Memorial Society.

Quilligan, Maureen
1979 *The Language of Allegory: Defining the Genre.* Ithaca, N.Y.: Cornell University Press.

Radcliffe-Brown, A. R.
1939 *Taboo.* The Frazer Lecture. London: Cambridge University Press.

Rehfisch, F.
1967 Omdurman during the Mahdiya. (A translated and edited version of a manuscript by G. Rosignoli.) *Sudan Notes and Records* 48(1 and 2):33–61.

Reisner, G. A.
1922 The Pyramids of Meroe and the Candaces of Ethiopia. *Sudan Notes and Records* 5(4):173–96.

Richards, Audrey
1982 *Chisungu: A Girl's Initiation Ceremony among the Bemba of Zambia.* 1956. Reprint with an introduction by J. S. La Fontaine. London: Tavistock.

Ricoeur, Paul
1976 *Interpretation Theory: Discourse and the Surplus of Meaning.* Fort Worth: Texas Christian University Press.
1979 The Model of the Text: Meaningful Action Considered as Text. In *Interpretive Social Science,* edited by P. Rabinow and W. M. Sullivan, pp. 73–101. Berkeley: University of California Press.

Robinson, E. A.
1925 Nimr, the Last King of Shendi. *Sudan Notes and Records* 8(1): 105–118.

Rodinson, Maxime
1967 *Magie, medicine et possession à Gondar.* Paris: Mouton.

Rogers, Susan
1975 Female Forms of Power and the Myth of Male Dominance. *American Ethnologist* 2:727–56.

Rosaldo, Michelle Z.
1974 Woman, Culture, and Society: A Theoretical Overview. In *Woman,*

Culture and Society, edited by Michelle Z. Rosaldo and Louise Lamphere, pp. 17–42. Stanford, Calif.: Stanford University Press.

1980 The Use and Abuse of Anthropology: Reflections on Feminism and Cross-cultural Understanding. *Signs* 5(3): 389–417.

Rosen, Lawrence

1978 The Negotiation of Reality: Male-Female Relations in Sefrou, Morocco. In *Women in the Muslim World,* edited by Lois Beck and Nikki Keddie. Cambridge, Mass.: Harvard University Press.

1982 *Bargaining for Reality.* Chicago: University of Chicago Press.

Rouch, Jean

1960 *La Religion et la magie Songhay.* Paris: Presses Universitaires de France.

Royce, Anya Peterson

1977 *The Anthropology of Dance.* Bloomington: Indiana University Press.

Sacks, Karen

1976 State Bias and Women's Status. *American Anthropologist* 78: 565–69.

1982 *Sisters and Wives: The Past and Future of Sexual Equality.* 1979. Reprint. Urbana: University of Illinois Press.

Sanderson, Lilian Passmore

1981 *Against the Mutilation of Women.* London: Ithaca Press.

Sargent, William

1957 *Battle for Mind.* Garden City, N.Y.: Doubleday.

Saunders, Lucie Wood

1977 Variants in Zar Experience in an Egyptian Village. In *Case Studies in Spirit Possession,* edited by Vincent Crapanzano and Vivian Garrison, pp. 177–91. New York: John Wiley.

Schutz, Alfred

1962 *The Collected Papers.* Vol. 1. *The Problem of Reality.* The Hague: Martinus Nijoff.

Seligman, B. S.

1914 On the Origin of Egyptian Zar. *Folklore* 25: 300–323.

Shinnie, Peter L.

1967 *Meroe: A Civilization of the Sudan.* New York: Praeger.

Shor, Ronand E.

1969 Hypnosis and the Concept of Generalized Reality Orientation. In *Altered States of Consciousness,* edited by Charles T. Tart, pp. 239–67. New York: Anchor Books.

Sider, Gerald M.

1980 The Ties That Bind: Culture and Agriculture, Property and Propriety in the Newfoundland Village Fishery. *Social History* 5(1): 1–39.

Simoons, Frederick J.

1976 Food habits as Influenced by Human Culture: Approaches in Anthropology and Geography. In *Appetite and Food Intake,* edited by Trevor Silverstone, pp. 313–29. Berlin, W. Germany: Dahlem Konferenzen.

Singer, Milton

1955 The Cultural Pattern of Indian Civilization. *Far East Quarterly* 15: 23–36.

1958 The Great Tradition in a Metropolitan Center: Madras. In *Traditional*

India: Structure and Change, edited by M. Singer, pp. 140–82. Philadelphia: American Folklore Society.

Solway, Jacqueline
n.d. Affines and Spouses, Friends and Lovers: The Passing of Polygyny in Botswana. Unpublished manuscript, University of Toronto.

Spaulding, Jay L.
1972 The Funj: A Reconsideration. *Journal of African History* 13(1):39–53.

Strathern, Marilyn
1981 Culture in a Netbag: The Manufacture of a Subdiscipline in Anthropology. *Man,* n.s. 16:665–88.
1985 Kinship and Economy: Constitutive Orders of a Provisional Kind. *American Ethnologist* 12(2):191–209.
1987 An Awkward Relationship: The Case of Feminism and Anthropology. *Signs* 12(2):276–92.

Sutton-Smith, Brian
1972 Games of Order and Disorder. Paper presented at the Forms of Symbolic Inversion Symposium, annual meeting of the American Anthropological Association, Toronto.

Swift, Jonathan
1967 *Gulliver's Travels.* 1726. Reprint. Harmondsworth: Penguin Books.

Tambiah, S. J.
1977 The Cosmological and Performative Significance of a Thai Cult of Healing through Meditation. *Culture, Medicine and Psychiatry* 1: 97–132.

Tapper, Nancy, and Richard Tapper
1987 The Birth of the Prophet: Ritual and Gender in Turkish Islam. *Man,* n.s. 22(1):69–92.

Thayer, James Steel
1983 Nature, Culture, and the Supernatural among the Susu. *American Ethnologist* 10(1):116–32.

Todorov, Tzvetan
1977 *The Poetics of Prose.* Translated by Richard Howard. Ithaca, N.Y.: Cornell University Press.
1984 *Mikhail Bakhtin: The Dialogical Principle.* Translated by Wlad Godzich. Minneapolis: University of Minnesota Press.

Tremearne, A. J. N.
1914 *The Ban of the Bori: Demons and Demon-Dancing in West and North Africa.* London: Heath, Cranton and Ouseley.

Trigger, Bruce
1965 *History and Settlement in Lower Nubia.* Publications in Anthropology no. 69. New Haven, Conn.: Yale University.

Trimingham, J. Spencer
1965 *Islam in the Sudan.* 1949. Reprint. London: Oxford University Press.

Turner, Victor
1967 *The Forest of Symbols: Aspects of Ndembu Ritual.* Ithaca, N.Y.: Cornell University Press.
1969*a* Introduction to *Forms of Symbolic Action: Proceedings of the 1969 An-*

nual Spring Meeting of the American Ethnological Society, edited by Robert F. Spencer, pp. 3–25. Seattle: University of Washington Press.
1969*b* *The Ritual Process.* Chicago: Aldine.
1974 *Dramas, Fields and Metaphors: Symbolic Action in Human Societies.* Ithaca, N.Y.: Cornell University Press.
1977 Process, System, and Symbol: A New Anthropological Synthesis. *Daedalus* 106(3):61–80.
1982 *From Ritual to Theatre: The Human Seriousness of Play.* New York: Performing Arts Journal Publications.

Van der Walde, Peter H.
1968 Trance States and Ego Psychology. In *Trance and Possession States,* edited by R. Prince, pp. 57–68. Montreal: R. M Bucke Memorial Society.

Van Dyke, Carolynn
1985 *The Fiction of Truth: Structures of Meaning in Narrative and Dramatic Allegory.* Ithaca, N.Y.: Cornell University Press.

Van Gennep, Arnold
1960 *The Rites of Passage.* 1909. Reprint. Chicago: University of Chicago Press.

Vantini, Giovanni
1981 *Christianity in the Sudan.* Bologna, Italy: EMI Press.

Vinogradov, Amal (Rassam)
1974 French Colonialism as Reflected in the Male-Female Interaction in Morocco. *Transactions of the New York Academy of Sciences,* 36:192–99.

Wallace, Anthony
1959 Cultural Determinants of Response to Hallucinatory Experiences. *A.M.A. Archives of General Psychiatry* 1:58–69.

Ward, Colleen
1982 A Transcultural Perspective on Women and Madness: The Case of the Mystical Affliction. *Women's International Journal Forum* 5(5): 411–18.

Wehr, Hans
1976 *A Dictionary of Modern Written Arabic.* 3d ed. Edited by J. Milton Cowan. Ithaca, N.Y.: Spoken Language Services.

Whyte, Martin
1978 *The Status of Women in Preindustrial Societies.* Princeton, N.J.: Princeton University Press.

Wikan, Unni
1977 Man Becomes Woman: Transsexualism in Oman as a Key to Gender Roles. *Man,* n.s. 12(2):304–319.
1980 *Life among the Poor in Cairo.* Translated by Ann Henning. London: Tavistock.
1982 *Behind the Veil in Arabia: Women in Oman.* Baltimore, Md.: Johns Hopkins University Press.

Williams, Raymond
1977 *Marxism and Literature.* London: Oxford University Press.

Willis, C. Armine

1921 Religious Confraternities of the Sudan. *Sudan Notes and Records* 4(4):175–94.

Wilson, Peter

1967 Status Ambiguity and Spirit Possession. *Man,* n.s. 2:366–78.

Young, Allan

1975 Why Amhara Get Kureynya: Sickness and Possession in an Ethiopian Zar Cult. *American Ethnologist* 2(3):567–84.

Yousif Bedri, Balghis

1987 Food and Differential Roles in the Fetiehab Household. In *The Sudanese Woman,* Graduate College Publications no. 19, edited by Susan Kenyon, pp. 67–91. Khartoum: University of Khartoum.

Zenkovsky, Sophie

1945 Marriage Customs in Omdurman. *Sudan Notes and Records* 26(2):241–55.

1949 Customs of the Women of Omdurman, Part 2. *Sudan Notes and Records* 30(1):39–46.

1950 Zar and Tambura as Practised by the Women of Omdurman. *Sudan Notes and Records* 31(1):65–81.

Index

New Directions in Anthropological Writing
History, Poetics, Cultural Criticism

George E. Marcus, Rice University
James Clifford, University of California, Santa Cruz
General Editors

Nationalism and the Politics of Culture in Quebec
Richard Handler

The Pastoral Son and the Spirit of Patriarchy:
Religion, Society, and Person among East African Stock Keepers
Michael E. Meeker

Belonging in America: Reading Between the Lines
Constance Perin

Himalayan Dialogue:
Tibetan Lamas and Gurung Shamans in Nepal
Stan Royal Mumford

Wombs and Alien Spirits:
Women, Men, and the *Zār* Cult in Northern Sudan
Janice Boddy

People as Subject, People as Object:
Selfhood and Peoplehood in Contemporary Israel
Virginia R. Dominguez

Sharing the Dance:
Contact Improvisation and American Culture
Cynthia J. Novack

Debating Muslims:
Cultural Dialogues in Postmodernity and Tradition
Michael M. J. Fischer and Mehdi Abedi

Power and Performance: Ethnographic Explorations
through Proverbial Wisdom and Theater in Shaba, Zaire
Johannes Fabian

Dialogue at the Margins:
Whorf, Bakhtin, and Linguistic Relativity
Emily A. Schultz

Magical Arrows: The Maori, the Greeks, and
the Folklore of the Universe
Gregory Schrempp